What's Fair

Ethics for Negotiators

Edited by

Carrie Menkel-Meadow
Georgetown University Law Center

Michael Wheeler
Harvard Business School

 A Publication of the Program on Negotiation
at Harvard Law School

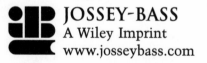 JOSSEY-BASS
A Wiley Imprint
www.josseybass.com

Published by Jossey-Bass
A Wiley Imprint
989 Market Street, San Francisco, CA 94103-1741   www.josseybass.com

Jossey-Bass books and products are available through most bookstores.
To contact Jossey-Bass directly call our Customer Care Department within the
U.S. at 800-956-7739, outside the U.S. at 317-572-3986, or fax 317-572-4002.

Jossey-Bass also publishes its books in a variety of electronic formats. Some
content that appears in print may not be available in electronic books.

Library of Congress Cataloging-in-Publication Data
What's fair : ethics for negotiators / edited by Carrie-Menkel Meadow,
Michael Wheeler.— 1st ed.
p. cm.
Includes bibliographical references and index.
ISBN 0-7879-6916-8 (alk. paper)
1. Negotiation—United States. 2. Negotiation—Moral and ethical
aspects. I. Menkel-Meadow, Carrie. II. Wheeler, Michael, 1943-
KF9084.Z9W493 2004
174'.4—dc22
2003024914

Printed in the United States of America
FIRST EDITION
HB Printing   10 9 8 7 6 5 4 3 2 1

CONTENTS

To our inspiring friend and colleague Larry Susskind
whose teaching, writing, and practice all continue
to advance the greater good

PREFACE

This is a book about how we should treat each other when we work with others to accomplish something. As two scholars, teachers, and practitioners of negotiation for close to two lifetimes of work, we came to this project because we felt that the issues of how people should deal with each other in negotiation were treated implicitly or secondarily in our major texts too often. As those texts and other writings about negotiation have proliferated in the past two decades, we noticed that often simplified oppositions of "principled" "problem-solving" or "integrative" bargaining to "competitive," "distributional," or "zero-sum" negotiating assumed similarly oppositional ethical precepts. Cooperation and trust, in search of joint gain, often assumes openness and sharing of information, equality of power or relationships between the parties, and goodwill on both sides. Competitive negotiations require hardball tactics and suspicion when dealing with parties on the other side, assumed to be taking advantage of us. Although both of us are clearly members of the "joint gain," problem-solving association of negotiation academics, we undertook this project because, as with most other things that academics look at, we saw the complexities of the ethics issues when we asked ourselves, our students, and real-world negotiators, What's fair in negotiation?

In working with the many wonderful people who have made this book a reality, we learned that it is not true, as in love and war, that all's fair (and really, we do not think all's fair in love and war, either). We decided to compile this book about what is fair in negotiation because we know that so many wise and savvy people have reflected on these questions in many different contexts and have explored the many diverse dimensions of answers to profound ethical dilemmas that we face every day. And because we are both teachers of negotiation in theory and practice, we were committed to focusing on what happens to negotiation ethics as they are actually practiced, not only how they are thought about by moral philosophers who negotiate mostly with their academic peers. We have learned (and selected from) the writings, teachings, and practices of moral philosophers, legal ethicists, corporate and business negotiators, public interest lawyers, and others who serve as agents for the subordinated and from the founding generation of modern negotiation theorists.

We begin with two pieces of our own to set the stage for what has concerned us about assessing what's fair and just in negotiation: the big questions about what duties are owed to others; their sources in personal, religious, familial, role, and professional morality and ethics; and the practice of ethics in actual negotiations. We hope that the chapters in this book orient readers and negotiation practitioners to what we call a moral realist's negotiation compass: knowing what questions to ask of self and others, searching out directions (yes, even you men out there) from those who have gone before, and then applying some basic principles—of the relation of means to ends and relations to relationships, distributive fairness, and just resource allocation—to real negotiation situations. We follow with an overview of orienting ethical frameworks developed by several of the major leaders in modern negotiation theory. We then treat five of the major issues, as we see them, in negotiation ethics, as others have written about them: issues about truth telling, candor, and deception in negotiation; tactics and strategic behavioral choices; relationships with others (opponents, adversaries, partners, counterparts); relationships of agents and principals (and role morality) in negotiation; and the social influences on negotiators (antecedent to) and social impacts (consequences and effects) of negotiation outcomes. In each part of this book, we provide an introduction to suggest some questions and orient readers to what is a diverse, provocative, and sometimes conflicting collection of readings on particular ethical dilemmas. We have sought to demonstrate that while we are searching for some universal principles in negotiation ethics, situations, contexts, and variations in negotiation structures (dyadic or multiparty, direct or representational) and cultures make universal generalizations difficult. Yet just because universal abstractions are often falsified in the realities of practice does not mean that we should either avoid ethical deliberation or leave it all to situational or relativist ethics. Many of the authors represented here (including ourselves) suggest that it is time for negotiation theory and practice to be more explicit about the ethical and moral assumptions or foundations on which both descriptive and prescriptive advice is presented. What's fair in negotiation depends in large measure on what we are trying to accomplish with other people: using them, aiding them, or collaborating with them to improve the situations we are all in from before the negotiation began.

Several rules of thumb guided us in selecting the chapters. First, our focus was on the negotiation process generally. For the most part, that meant that we have not included material that deals with substantive ethical issues that arise in specific negotiation contexts, such as in the representation of children's interests in divorce cases. Likewise, we left for another day a considerable amount of material on the ethical responsibilities of mediators, arbitrators, and other third parties. Finally, we did our best to include perspectives from a range of disciplines and practices.

We encountered some challenges in putting this collection together. There was a good news–bad news aspect to the fact that there has been a lot of thoughtful writing about negotiation ethics. Although the book expanded beyond our original expectations, we could not include everything that we would have liked, and many of the selections that are included had to be trimmed in the name of overall economy. Interested readers will certainly find additional useful concepts and illustrations in the original material that we have had to condense. The Bibliography suggests additional resources. Finally, other than our own essays and Larry Susskind's contribution (Chapter Thirty-One), all of the material in the book was written at different times for different purposes. We hope that the categories and sequence that we have created provide a useful structure for exploring negotiation ethics, but most of the chapters are too interesting and too complex to roost obediently in our pigeonholes. Readers are encouraged to let their own curiosity lead them wherever it may.

ACKNOWLEDGMENTS

We owe a large debt (some of which we have paid off in copyright permission payments; the rest will come as intellectual tribute) to all of the individual scholars and practitioners (and their publishers) who have agreed to share their thinking and words in this book.

If it is possible, we owe an even greater debt to those with whom we have created a working relationship in completing this project: Bill Breslin, Mary Alice Wood, and Rachel Campanga, who helped us compile and assemble the growing corpus of materials on this important topic; the research assistance of James Bond and Jaimie Kent; and the advice and commentary of many of our colleagues at the Program on Negotiation at Harvard Law School, the Harvard Business School Ethics and Law working group, and many of our students in law and business school courses and professional training programs who have helped us see, clarify, and examine the issues presented here.

We are grateful that Alan Rinzler, our editor at Jossey-Bass, was enthusiastic about our project and patient in seeing it through. We are delighted as well that this book continues the fruitful collaboration between Jossey-Bass and the Program on Negotiation.

The biggest debt by far is owed to Dana Nelson, research associate at the Harvard Business School, whose labors, both creative and organizational, are the glue that tie the pages of this book together. We thank her for all she did and hope that she found some value in the relationship she had with us.

Finally, of course, we both thank our families who allowed incursions into "quality," as well as "quantity," time in our relationships in order to allow us to complete this project. We remind them that it could have been worse: this is, after all, an edited, not authored, book. And what is somewhat of a departure for formal acknowledgments, we would like to publicly thank and acknowledge each other: the "negotiations" that resulted in this book have been a model of what good working relationships can be. We hope you think so too.

July 2003
Washington, D.C.
Carrie Menkel-Meadow

July 2003
Boston, Massachusetts
Michael Wheeler

Introduction

What's Fair in Negotiation?
What Is Ethics in Negotiation?

Carrie Menkel-Meadow

What do we owe other human beings when we negotiate for something that we or our clients want? How should we behave toward our "adversaries"—opponents, partners, clients, friends, family members, strangers, third parties, and future generations—when we know what we do affects them, beneficially, adversely, or unpredictably? How do we think about the other people we interact with in negotiations? Are they just means to our ends or people like us, deserving of respect or aid (depending on whether they are our "equals" or more or less enabled than ourselves)? How do we conceive of our goals when we approach others to help us accomplish together what we cannot do alone?

Perhaps after the question, "What should I do?" in negotiation (seeking strategic or behavioral advice), the next most frequently asked question is, "What may I do?" (seeking advice, permission, or approval for particular goals, strategies, and tactics that comprise both the conceptualizations and behaviors of the human strategic interaction that we call negotiation).

This book presents some answers to these questions, culled from a voluminous and growing literature on what we think is "good," "ethical," or "moral" behavior in negotiation, all of these things not being equal. Ranging from strategic advice that urges negotiators to take advantage of the other side in order to maximize individual gain, to longer philosophical disquisitions on the deontological (Kantian) versus consequentialist and utilitarian justifications for moral action, taking account of how negotiation actions affect not only the negotiators but those affected by a negotiation, including the rest of society, writers about negotiation ethics know that they are creating what one philosopher, Simon Blackburn (2001), has called an "ethical climate." Many have suggested that negotiation, practiced in different contexts, creates its own ethical climate, where expectations are that negotiators (whether principals or agents) are seeking to maximize their own gain and are "using" the other parties, as means, not ends in themselves, to achieve their own goals.

SOME ORIENTING ISSUES: THE RELATIONSHIPS OF ENDS TO MEANS

The past two decades of work on negotiation, in theory development and practice, has broadened our conceptions of what negotiation can be, as well as what is: we have learned to "seek joint gains," "expand the pie," "create solutions to problems" or "create value," and make "wise, robust, and efficient" agreements (Fisher, Ury, and Patton, 1991; Menkel-Meadow, 1984; Lax and Sebenius, 1986; Raiffa, 2002). Negotiation ethics are therefore as variable and changing as our theories, empirical and laboratory studies, and practices are revealing ever more complexity to our enterprise. Negotiation theorists have aspirations about making "better" human agreements at levels of dyadic contract formation or dispute resolution, multilateral peace and international cooperation, commercial and trade agreements, as well as in everyday human negotiations in family and work life (Kolb and Williams, 2003). These aspirations and newer approaches to negotiation raise questions about the relationship of goals and ends sought in negotiation to the behaviors chosen to meet those goals. Behaviors alone are neither good nor bad, effective or ineffective; we must also focus on the goals sought to be achieved by a particular negotiator and whether negotiators focus exclusively on themselves (or their principals, if they are agents) or whether they consider what effects their actions and outcomes will have on others outside the immediate negotiation activity. So the ethical climate of negotiation consists of more than behavior. It includes goals and ends sought, the context in which the negotiation is located, the relationship of parties and negotiators to each other, and, most controversial, the effects of the negotiated agreement, if there is one, on the parties themselves and on others outside the negotiation process.

LAYERS AND LEVELS OF ANALYSIS: THE ACTORS IN NEGOTIATION

"What's fair?" in negotiation is a complex and multifaceted question, asking us to consider negotiation ethics on many different levels simultaneously. First, there are the concerns of the individual negotiator: What do I aspire to? How do I judge my own goals and behavior? What may I do? How will others judge me (my counterpart in a two-party negotiation, others in a multilateral negotiation, those with whom I might do business in the future, those who will learn of and judge my behavior or results in any negotiation that might become more public than the involved parties)? How do I calibrate my actions to those of the others with whom I am dealing? (Should I have a relative ethics that is sensitive, responsive, or malleable to the context, circumstances, customs, or personalities of the situation at hand?) What limits are there on my goals and behavior, set from within (the "mirror" test—how do I appear to myself at the end of the day?) or without, either informally (the "videotape test"—what would my mother, teacher, spouse, child, or clergyperson think of me if they could watch this?) or formally (rules, laws, ethics standards, religious or moral principles to which I must or choose to adhere)? With what sensibility should I approach each negotiation I undertake?

For those who negotiate as agents, there is the added dimension of what duty is owed a client or principal. When do agent and principal goals properly align? When are they different (incentive structures like contingent billing arrangements or long-term dealings in the particular field may separate agents from principals in their goals), and how are differences to be reconciled (Mnookin and Susskind, 1999)? When do legal rules, like the creation of fiduciary relationships, define the limits and obligations of negotiator-principal interactions?

Third, there is the question of duty, responsibility, or relationship to the Other (call him or her "counterpart," "opponent," "adversary," "partner," "boss" or "subordinate," spouse or lover, child or parent). Even the labeling of the other actors in a negotiation has moral or ethical weight. To name a relationship is to invoke thousands of years of thinking and writing on duties and obligations owed: fealty, loyalty, candor, obeisance, caretaking, skepticism, and other predetermined stances or assumptions that affect how we approach the Other. Do we follow some version of the Golden Rule and treat others as we would hope to be treated by them (a norm of aspirational reciprocity), or does the Golden Rule tarnish a bit on application in particular contexts? Don't competitive sellers and purchasers expect to be treated strategically or with lack of full candor in bargaining for price in exotic souks (Lubet, 1996) or contested mergers and acquisitions (Freund, 1992)? And once we choose an ethical sensibility, to what extent do we change our approach and behaviors when others act on us, demonstrating the strategically, as well as biologically, robust "cooperative" program of tit for tat ("reciprocate, retaliate, but forgive"; Axelrod, 1984).

When we expand the Other to include, more realistically in modern negotiations, multiple Others (agents and principals in both dyadic and multiparty negotiations), we are then faced with the complexity of dynamic and sequential negotiation ethics. How firm is a commitment to hold to a coalition or interest-based or strategically based subgroup? How many participants in a multiparty setting must agree for a negotiated result to have legitimacy? What duties do the parties have to each other to provide adequate voice, participation, and involvement in agreements with mixed resources, mixed interests, and power imbalances? Adding more than two parties almost always adds dimensions of the ethics of transparency, privacy, conspiracy, publicity, defections, and betrayals that are not present in the same way in dyadic negotiations. How do multiparty negotiators police themselves and others? Withdrawal or withholding by one will not (as in dyadic negotiations) terminate the proceedings.

If negotiations are successfully concluded, meaning some agreement is reached, what are the ethical implications of follow-through, promise keeping or breaking, implementation, and enforcement? What is left to trust, and what must be formally drafted for, with clear enforcement, penalty, and incentive structures specified? How are the actors from within the negotiation to judge if they have done well and created a fair agreement? Do they measure themselves by client or self-satisfaction? By distributional effects (how are considerations of equity or distributional fairness made by parties to a negotiation)? By the robustness or longevity of the agreement? How do we judge our negotiated American constitutional agreement (Lansky, 2000), with its Civil War, scores of amendments, interpretive contests, but stable and lasting power, both symbolic and real?

THE EFFECTS OR OUTCOMES OF NEGOTIATIONS

How do those outside a negotiation judge its ethical externalities, or social effects? Has a particular negotiation done more good than harm? For those inside the negotiation? Those affected by it: employees, shareholders, vendors and clients, consumers, the public? And to what extent must any negotiation be morally accountable for impacts on third parties (children in a divorce, customers in a labor-management negotiation, similarly situated claimants as in mass torts, employees in an acquisition) and for its intergenerational effects (future generations in environmental disputes)? What efforts can third parties, like mediators, make to ensure accountability to those both inside and outside a particular negotiation? Are third parties, like mediators, ever morally responsible for the outcomes they preside over (Bernard and Garth, 2002; Susskind, 1981)?

At a level of ethical policy and social effects of negotiation, one can think of such macroethical issues (as distinguished from the still-important microethical concerns of particular individual ethical behavioral choices) as what the practice of plea bargaining does to our criminal justice system and the enforcement of society's ultimate moral rules and sanctions; what settlements secretly arrived at, and protected with confidentiality agreements, in our civil justice system do to civil law enforcement and knowledge of human wrongs and corrected remedies; and whether a culture of negotiation is itself ultimately a social good in promoting reasoned, as well as preference-driven, deliberation and mutual fair dealing or whether it promotes an assumption of self-interested, unprincipled compromise or self-aggrandizement. As modern political theorists and philosophers have recently noted, the very use of negotiation processes is itself an ethical and moral question (Hampshire, 2000; Elster, 1995; Forester, 2001; Pennock and Chapman, 1979).

CONTEXT IN NEGOTIATION ETHICS

Ultimately, whether there are any universal principles of negotiation ethics or whether ethics in negotiation must be related to specific negotiation cultures, whether professional (law and business), functional (horse trading and souk bargaining or political and institutional deal making), role based (family, friend, agent-principal, diplomatic or commercial, long-term or one-shot relationship), or social grouping (national "culture"; Avruch, 1998; Acuff, 1997), religion, gender, or socioeconomic status, remains an intriguing, if unanswerable, question, hanging like an uninvited moral philosopher or clergyperson above the table at any negotiation session. The selections in this book move through many layers of generalizations and assertions (some supported with empirical data, most not) about what constitutes fair or morally defensible conduct in negotiations in specific contexts.

What is clear through the contextual variety of situations in which questions of what's fair in negotiations comes up is that negotiation ethics issues arise at both process and outcome levels. As the different actors in negotiation approach each negotiation, they must ask not just what they may do behaviorally and processually; they must also consider what goals to set for themselves as they begin, how those goals change when dynamic interaction and more information become available during a particular negotiation, what relationships, if any, they create (or destroy), and how a final settlement or agreement is to be morally, as well as instrumentally, assessed at its conclusion. Negotiation ethics are contextually complex, but they are also temporally dynamic. What looked fair today may look different tomorrow.

Is what's fair in negotiation negotiable itself, depending on the context of the matter or the relationships of the parties? Are one-shot litigation settlement negotiations or one-off company or material goods purchases (cars, houses, washing machines) closer to each other in internal morality than to repeat player litigation (class actions, employee-employer, supplier-customer) or venture capital transactions? Is dispute resolution negotiation, regardless of parties' relationships or numbers, necessarily more adversarial or competitive than transactional deal-creating negotiations, or are these distinctions more illusory in practice (when deal makers try to grab advantage in contract clause drafting and risk allocations)? Do entities (companies, organizations, unions, governmental agencies, universities) and clients have ethical reputations of their own that they value when choosing agent negotiators or when shifting leadership (Wolgast, 1992; Nash, 1993; Paine, 2003)? Do friends, family members, and others who know each other expect different conduct than when dealing with strangers (Bazerman and Neale, 1995)?

The negotiator's understanding of what ethical principles or precepts may apply to him, to help him (and us) evaluate and morally judge what we and he does, are quite varied, as the chapters in this book demonstrate. Whether from personalistic, familial, religious, or early moral teachings, there are principles of right human conduct (the Ten Commandments, the Golden Rule of doing unto others as you would have them do unto you) that we are taught should apply to everyone always (Kantian imperatives). These may be modified by more specialized teachings and learning in professional norms (for lawyers, the Model Rules of Professional Conduct in formal rules and, more important, the behavioral norms and expectations of specific practice settings) or in special contexts, such as anonymous commercial dealings (Caveat emptor!). Wise negotiators learn that often (not always) instrumental, pragmatic, or market ethics (your reputation for truth telling, value creation, and follow through, which enhances trust and market value; Norton, 1989; Gilson and Mnookin, 1994, 1995) may conform to more aspirational ethics (to do the right or fair thing). Finally, there are formal rules and laws (notably the law of fraud and misrepresentation; Shell, 1991), which can void a deal or subject a negotiator to legal penalties and even professional discipline and sanctions.

EVALUATING ETHICAL CLAIMS

There are many ethical issues in negotiation, though many treatments of the subject focus almost exclusively on questions of deception, truth telling, and candor in negotiation. This book presents a wider variety of ethical issues and dilemmas, treated by a broad spectrum of scholars and practitioners working from many different conceptual frameworks and practical settings. As each negotiation ethics issue is presented here, it may be useful to ask the following questions:

1. What are the author's underlying assumptions about the purpose of the negotiation discussed?

2. What implicit or explicit norms of value or behavior does the author rely on?

3. What data or empirical support does any author present for claims made about how negotiations are conducted in a particular setting or culture? Are such data sets (or their absence, in the form of assertions or claims) persuasive to you?

4. To what extent are claims made about what is permissible, prohibited, or advisable in negotiations dependent on the context of the negotiations? Is all fair in arms-length business negotiation, with fewer tactics being fair in family or international diplomatic negotiations? What distinguishes one context from another?

5. Should negotiation ethics track what is (empirical realities or customary expectations), or should they aspire to what should be (aspirational) fair to both those engaged in or outside of the particular negotiation?

6. What is the best way to socialize or educate negotiators about both good and best practices in negotiation?

7. How can negotiation ethics best be effectuated (expressed, monitored, enforced, sanctioned, made accountable) when there is little agreement on universal or foundational principles to be applied and negotiation is practiced in so many different contexts, but most often in confidential, nontransparent settings?

We hope that by presenting many different perspectives on what is fair or appropriate or advantageous in negotiation, we will be offering something of a moral realist's compass—some clarifying markers and directions, with points along the way illuminated by those who have gone before—but ultimately, it is you, the traveler, who has to decide where you are going. As editors of this book, we have our own points of view: if there is no true north for all destinations, there are certainly better ways to get from one point to another. We do believe that analytic rigor, practical and philosophical deliberation, and humanistic concern for our fellow negotiators should produce better negotiations, in terms of quality solutions to negotiated problems and to better relationships between parties and future generations. A central theme of this book is to present multiple voices that consider whether changing theories, norms, and approaches to negotiation (from distributional strategies to integrative ones) have changed the underlying ethical climate with which negotiators now approach each other, especially after several decades of scholarly, pedagogic, and practical attention to negotiation, particularly in business and law schools.

THE CORE ISSUES

This book explores a number of the key issues confronting all negotiators, most often presented by several different treatments of those issues. We begin with an overview of several different statements of what some core values might be in conducting fair negotiations. Some of the key negotiation theory founders of the modern generation—Roger Fisher, Howard Raiffa, David Lax, and James

Sebenius—suggest that every negotiation presents the negotiator's dilemma: whether to act as you would want others to act toward you (with candor, in search of a good joint solution for both parties) or as you might expect them to act in a world of assumed scarce resources and competition (with lack of full disclosure and with the intention of taking advantage of you).

Whether termed an issue of what candor is required or expected or what misrepresentations might be permissible in custom, or actionable at law, or simply whether to approach the other side with trust or suspicion, this is what Howard Raiffa has labeled the "social dilemma game"—only it is not a game. In virtually every negotiation, the initial ethical orientation to oneself and to the Other can be quite serious, with iterative consequences for all players. Whether termed a behavioral question of cooperate or defect, claiming or creating value, or being open and trusting or skeptical and closed, this behavioral choice is really a proxy for a much bigger question of what one hopes to accomplish in a negotiation for the self (or client), for the Other, and for the long-term consequences of both the negotiated agreement and the relationships of all affected parties. Although in "the long run, we will all be dead," said John Maynard Keynes, the long run in negotiation is often longer than the short run of a particular deal. Thus, most modern treatments of negotiation ethics ask us to consider from the outset not just this deal or this lawsuit settlement, but also the possible long-term effects of the agreement itself and the reputation of the negotiators.

Instrumental ethics (making a good, enforceable, and lasting deal) here can be coextensive with aspirational ethics. In Howard Raiffa's terms, "All of us are engaged in a grandiose, many person, social dilemma game where each of us has to decide how much we should act to benefit others. . . . We have to calculate, at least informally, the dynamic linkages between our actions now and the later actions of others. If we are more ethical, it makes it easier for others to be more ethical" (1982, pp. 354–355).

Deciding whether to behave ethically toward others implicates at least five common issues, which we explore in separate parts of this book: (1) what duty we owe to others to tell the truth, or something like the truth, in our negotiated dealings with them; (2) what tactics and behaviors we choose when interacting with others; (3) what the duties and responsibilities are with respect to our relationships with clients and principals in negotiation (agent-principal issues); (4) what relationships we seek to create with the Others in our negotiation activity; (5) the social influences and distributional fairness of outcomes and of negotiated agreements on the parties themselves; and the social impact of negotiation agreements on others who are, or might be, affected by the negotiation result.

These ethical issues are significant for both those inside the negotiation, who must make choices about what to do and how to evaluate their own behavior and that of others, and for those who stand outside and seek to evaluate or judge both negotiation behaviors and outcomes. Some will be more concerned with process issues: How do individuals treat each other? Are they honest, candid, and well meaning? Do they take advantage of power or informational asymmetries to maximize gain? Do they threaten force or coerce concessions or gains in monetary or other ways? Have all necessary parties participated? Is the agreement likely to be complied with? Others will be more concerned with the outcomes or effects of negotiation. Have resources been fairly or optimally allocated? Is there "waste" left under or over the table? Are absent parties (children, future generations) considered fairly? What are both the short-term and long-term effects of negotiated agreements on parties and others?

The chapters in this book span a full range of approaches to these issues, from James J. White who argues, from his assumptions of the empirical reality of legal negotiations and commercial sales, that the negotiator's job is like that of the poker player—"To conceal one's true position, to mislead an opponent about one's true settling point, is the essence of negotiation" (1980, pp. 926–927); to philosopher Sissela Bok (1978), who argues for more transparent behavior in both public and private negotiations; to legal commentators like Richard Shell (1999) and Alan Strudler (1995), who remind us that the degree of candor in a negotiation is one of the few things regulated by law (fraud and misrepresentation law, in both contracts and torts). We present advice from those who suggest that difficult adversarial negotiations with more powerful parties might justify tactics otherwise thought problematic in other contexts (Meltsner and Schrag, 1974; Freund, 1992), a claim of justified retaliatory, reactive, or protective tactics, sometimes supported by game theorists and other social scientists (Axelrod, 1984). The old adage of "when in Rome, do as the Romans" (Weiss, 1994a, 1994b) implies a kind of morality of reciprocity, common in treatments of negotiation norms that can serve not only to justify mirroring tactics or cultural conformity but in some cases has been argued to justify the paying of bribes in negotiation (when not otherwise declared unlawful by the Foreign Corrupt Practices Act; Acuff, 1997). While some commentators distinguish between statements made about fact or opinion or material representations about value or quality and merely ancillary matters to a commercial negotiation about price, there is little expectation in modern negotiation writings that parties will be totally honest about what they are really willing to pay or settle for, at least as an initial offer.

What can be said for those who enter into negotiations without knowing the culture or unwritten rules or norms? Should there be an obligation on the part of more knowledgeable negotiators to socialize, instruct, or serve those on the other side of the table? The cultures of American business and law seem to deny such obligations with their expectations of adversarial practice in which each side is master of his or her own fate or negotiation agent. There is little formal duty to take care of the other side, either informationally or substantively.

Some authors represented in this book are interested in what we can learn about the claimed empirical effectiveness of particular tactics or truth-telling variations. Is it really more efficient to have two sides attempt to maximize their gain while dividing whatever "surplus value" exists within the zone of possible agreement? And what happens to strategic considerations of candor and truth telling when there are alternative sources of information (whether publicly or privately available), especially when there are more than two parties to a negotiation?

More analytic and thoughtful (and, dare one say, academic) treatments of issues about tactics and candor in negotiation are concerned with the conditions under which negotiators are more or less likely to be candid or use more collaborative or joint-gain-seeking activity (Cramton and Dees, 1993). Thus, the empirical and instrumental are used to test the aspirational in different contexts and with different sets of negotiators. Are women more likely to be honest or seek joint gain (Menkel-Meadow, 2000; Kolb and Williams, 2003)? Do friends and those who trust each other fail to exploit opportunities for substantive gain and more efficient outcomes (Bazerman and Neale, 1995)? Does one act of lying or discovered deception ruin one's reputation and "marketability" for trust in future deals (Norton, 1989; Gilson and Mnookin, 1994)? Can the use of other tactics (more probing and more direct questioning) reduce the dangers of dissembling and deception in others (Schweitzer and Croson, 1999)? To what extent can the instrumental (better skills) correct for bad manners or ethics by others?

Clashes of tactical advice presented here (and in the popular negotiation literature reviewed by Michael Wheeler in this book) not only reveal contrasting philosophies of the purposes of negotiation, but present interesting opportunities for challenges to different worldviews. Whether it is necessary for two negotiators to share the same frameworks or orientations to negotiation remains one of the field's million-dollar questions, but knowledge here surely is power. To the extent that a "tactic perceived is no tactic" (Cohen, 1980, p. 138), description of and revelation of particular tactics allows even those of different negotiation religions to attend each other's churches (or at least seek a neutral ground). Good preparation, probing questions, seeking other sources of information: all of these instrumental skills of negotiation can often expose or correct for those who seek to gain advantage from less-than-forthcoming practices.

If changed norms or improved skills do not level the ethical playing field, then at least in the realm of commercial and legal negotiations, there are some limits. Regulation of negotiation occurs at several different legal levels, and no negotiator should leave home without some knowledge of how formal rules, regulations, and sanctions may affect them. The law of fraud and misrepresentation in the state law of contracts and fraud may make some negotiation conduct actionable in several ways. Negotiated agreements may be declared void for such reasons as intentional, reckless, or negligent misrepresentation, and misrepresentation (as defined by state law) may encompass not only false statements but misstatements, failures to correct misunderstandings, and even, in some cases, silences and omissions. Mistakes, whether mutual or bilateral, may also be grounds for voiding a contract (the result of most negotiations).

Contracts procured by outright fraud, coercion, and unconscionability can lead not only to voiding of a negotiated agreement but also to punitive and restitutionary damages. Modern corporate law also regulates what negotiators can say to each other when selling stock, whole companies, or even negotiating employment contracts and other deals in publicly traded companies. Recent corporate scandals involving misrepresentations of company value in both public and private settings are beginning to spawn another generation of corporate and professional laws, regulations, and legal common law decisions, calling for not only greater candor in internal and public dealings but greater sanctions when candor and public trust norms are violated.

Although the law provides some outside limits on what negotiators can do, legal philosophers have long noted the line of separation between positive law and morality (Fuller, 1964; Hart, 1961), and negotiation is no exception. What Oliver Wendell Holmes's "bad man" can get away with under the law does not hold a candle to what a "bad" or immoral negotiator can still do without fear of legal sanction, in large measure because so much of what negotiators do, they do in private, where no one can see them. Efforts to peer into and assess, whether by common morality or more formal legal sanction, the negotiation behaviors and outcomes consummated in private have been controversial and are continuing. For some negotiators, professional regulations attempt some minimal control of particular tactics and obligations for candor and fairness. The lawyer's Model Rules of Professional Conduct, for example, provides, "A Lawyer shall not, in the course of representing a client, make a false statement of material fact or law to a third person; or fail to disclose a material fact to a third person when disclosure is necessary to avoid assisting a criminal or fraudulent act by a client (unless disclosure is prohibited by Model Rule 1.6, the client confidentiality rule)" (American Bar Association, 2003, Rule 4.1). However, commentary to this rule makes it clear that certain statements in negotiation, which are merely "opinions" (such as of value) and are not "fact," are not subject to this rule. According to the Comment, there are "generally accepted conventions in negotiation" in which no one really expects the truth will be told and several specific kinds of statements made in negotiation are exempt from the rule. Lawyer negotiators need not tell the truth about "estimates of price or value placed on the subject of a transaction," a party's intention as to an acceptable settlement of a claim or value, and the existence of an undisclosed principal (say, Donald Trump or Harvard University in real estate negotiations). Thus, what the professional rule seems to "give" or require, the Comment to the rule taketh away. The Comment further recognizes that negotiators may "puff" or exaggerate about value, and this too is within the tolerable limits of the law. Efforts made twice in recent years (1983 and 2000) to toughen up the lawyers' rules of ethics to require candor and fairness to other parties (including a proposal to limit a lawyer's ability to negotiate a substantively "unconscionable" agreement; Schwartz, 1978) have been defeated in formal recognition of a professional culture that deals with regularity in expected deception.

Other legal jurisdictions, like the United Kingdom, are just beginning to review these issues; solicitors there have a duty of good faith and frankness when dealing with other solicitors (see Rules 17.01 and 19.01 of the Law Society's *Guide to the Professional Conduct of Solicitors,* 1999). For example, courts have voided an agreement or ruled on legal proceedings as a sanction for bad and "misleading" behavior in a negotiation (see *Ernest and Young* v. *Butte Mining,* PLC, 1 WLR 1605, 1996), in which one lawyer deliberately misled another lawyer about a procedural matter in order to take advantage of that lawyer and dismiss the case; O'Dair, 2001.

Although some other professionals have internal ethics rules (real estate brokers, accountants, doctors), there are vast numbers of professional negotiators, including most daily business negotiators, who are entirely unregulated. Although professional discipline for violating a lawyer's duty of candor in negotiation is virtually nil, there is still some regulation through voiding of contracts and some legal scrutiny of a small class of legally settled cases, such as class actions. In other professions, scrutiny of negotiation behavior is virtually nonexistent (with the exception of some specialized consumer protection laws and similar specialized areas of regulation, such as residential real estate and securities sales). While lawyers may be heard to complain that subjecting them to overly "restrictive" ethical mandates (such as candor and fair dealing) will cause them to lose business in the multidisciplinary professional tournament of business getting, there is barely a whisper that perhaps stronger ethical mandates might themselves be a marketable advantage in the competition for getting and keeping clients.

Related to the issue of the private location of most negotiations is the more recent development of privacy and confidentiality agreements negotiated for in lawsuit settlements. If an assessment of the fairness and justness of a particular outcome is part of the ethics of negotiation, then failure to make public or disclose settlements of publicly filed lawsuits impedes such inquiries and has recently drawn the attention of legal commentators who suggest that it is morally unacceptable for settlement agreements to be privatized, especially when public issues such as health, safety, and social welfare are at stake (Luban, 1995).

Such concerns about the privatization of negotiated agreements are relatively new since for most of our social, economic, and legal history, most negotiations, both litigational and transactional, have been conducted in private. There is some evidence that more legal cases are settled (less than 3 percent of all civil cases filed in federal courts are currently completed with a public trial), but settlements of lawsuits have long accounted for a great majority of publicly filed lawsuits. With the advent of Sunshine Laws and the Freedom of Information

Act at both federal and state levels, at least governmental negotiations probably have more transparency than ever before. With new negotiation processes involving multiple parties, such as negotiated rule-making (Harter, 1982) and consensus-building forums (Susskind, McKearnan, and Thomas-Larmer, 1999) in which multiple stakeholders meet together to negotiate governmental allocations, environmental issues, and complex federal and state regulations, there is probably more public access to those kinds of negotiations. There are, however, complex legal issues about the conflicts presented when assurances of confidentiality are made in mediated settings that may conflict with public accessibility laws (Pou, 1998). However, where, as in the American legal system, so much is decided by common law lawsuits, the increased private settlement of class actions and individual lawsuits about product liability, consumer rights, securities fraud, and civil rights has caused those who care about outcome measures of justice to be concerned about the social impact of increasingly private negotiations.

Like the general public, clients of lawyers, brokers, and other agents may also not know all that has been done (or not done) on their behalf. The use of agents to negotiate on behalf of principals has long been justified on grounds of efficiency, superior knowledge, and stress reduction for the principals. However, with different incentive structures (in payment, negotiation reputation, repeat player possibilities), agents may not always be working in the best interest of their clients, and this has led to serious questioning of the separate ethics duties and responsibilities that agents (some as formal fiduciaries) may have to their clients. Where principals may not even be present at negotiations, as in many legal negotiations, assessment of the behavior of lawyer negotiators on behalf of their client-principals may be difficult to view for both process and outcome assessment.

The claim that specified roles allow for role-specific morality has also been claimed for professionals engaged in work on behalf of others. Whether as lawyers, brokers, or business negotiators, the claim has been long articulated that agents may do for others what they might not be able to do for themselves. If soldiers can kill in war, which other humans cannot do without impunity under most conditions, then lawyers and business agents are permitted, in common understandings of role morality, to be slightly more rapacious, aggressive, or deceptive in trying to extract gain for their clients. In this book, we present an excerpt of Arthur Applbaum's discussion of adversarial role morality, featuring the ultimate role moralist, M. Henri Sanson, executioner, who survived the many regime changes of the French Revolution because of his complete commitment to craft, and not political or social values. Sanson represents the ultimate in role morality: he was a professionally sanctioned killer who performed with such skill that those who were sentenced to death often requested his services. Applbaum attempts the philosopher's defense of a role so well played (and all in the name of laws passed by the various regimes of the French Revolution) that the role player is not to be judged for what he does (killing, which is sanctioned by the law, like the lawyer's "puffing") as is the ordinary citizen, but judged simply by the quality of his craft. Is the negotiator to be judged by a craft well exercised (maximizing interests of the client, finding creative solutions), by standards of the craft or profession alone, or, unlike executioners, for both what they do and how they do their work as ordinary citizens? Applbaum likens the role performed by Sanson (a profession well executed, so to speak) to that of lawyers whose professional job is to "try to induce others to believe in the truth of propositions or in the validity of arguments that they themselves do not believe" (Applbaum, 1999, p. 42).

If role morality or the quality of performance in role is to be a measure of what is good or well done as a negotiator, then perhaps the person for whom the work is performed should be its judge. The work of agents raises questions about whether client satisfaction is enough of a moral standard by which negotiators should evaluate what they do and whether the rest of us can be satisfied with the role morality justification.

Role morality neglects consideration of a category of ethical concerns that concludes this book. Client satisfaction and efficient and effective role performance assess the ethics of negotiation from one side only. Modern considerations of ethics in negotiation go beyond the achievement of client goals and the behavioral choices of individual negotiators. We are interested in evaluating whether outcomes have been good for the parties—fair in a distributional sense and often fair in a procedural sense as well. Some empirical work suggests that the norm of reciprocity is not only a procedural one, of alternating and more or less equal concession patterns, but that negotiators do move toward a reciprocal sense of what is fair in distributions of surplus, though not in all situations and not with perfect equity (Bazerman and Neale, 1995; Thompson, 2000). Determining whether an outcome of a negotiation is fair or good for the parties includes evaluations of prior and postnegotiation endowments, whether the negotiation has made the parties better or worse off than they would have been without the negotiation, and whether all relevant issues between them have been considered.

Beyond considerations of fairness are issues of implementation, follow-through, and commitment to any agreements and, where relevant, continuing relationships of the parties. Should we judge a negotiator by how well he behaves as a promise keeper and trustworthy implementer of what has been agreed to? Reputations for following through on commitments and promises may be as significant as what negotiators do in the process of reaching agreement. Often implementation and resolution of postagreement disputes or issues may be even more visible than the actual negotiations themselves, and thus they may be subject to scrutiny of others besides the principal actors or beneficiaries to the negotiation.

Beyond the immediate parties, many now believe that in considering the morality of a negotiation, concerns for those outside the negotiation (future generations, others affected, especially those who could not participate) require us to consider the effects on third parties—whether intentional, as when negotiators make representations of value that are relied on by others, such as investors who are not the negotiator's immediate client (Langevoort, 1999), or nonintentional, as in environmental decisions affecting the nonpresent or future generations (Susskind, 1981).

Negotiated outcomes, whether public or private, have social effects on the parties immediately present in the negotiation, of course, but others are affected as well, such as employees, other customers, other claimants, and other family members. To what extent negotiators should feel morally responsible for those affected by their work is at present a difficult question that has not been much studied. Political and social movements seek to make international organizations (like the World Bank, the International Monetary Fund, the United Nations) morally responsible for investment and debt negotiations and social and relief action that affect huge populations; environmentalists seek to make developers responsible to whole communities when they are negotiating with single sellers of land or with governmental agencies. Mediators seek to involve insurers in simple two-party negotiations about liability. Modern negotiation theory has begun to take account of the multilateral nature of most negotiations. Whether structured as dyadic negotiations between plaintiffs and defendants or buyers and sellers, so many negotiations now implicate or affect other parties that questions of inclusion at the process level and fairness at the justice level are woven into many disputes and transactions we negotiate about. How should we take account of the externalities, or effects of negotiated outcomes on those who are not present? What are the social effects of individually arrived at negotiated solutions to commercial sales, property deals, settled lawsuits, and negotiated rule making?

Some would go even further and claim that negotiation itself, as a process, should be considered on moral grounds. When is it appropriate to negotiate or settle matters between the parties (with their consent), and when should matters be ruled on publicly, by an authoritative agent or government official, where the stakes are significant for the larger public outside the dispute (Luban, 1995; Menkel-Meadow, 1995)? Does negotiation suggest an ideology or ethics of compromise with lack of principled outcomes? Philosophers and others have argued that compromise is not necessarily unethical, especially when compromise itself is a moral commitment to peace, continued relations with others, or achievement of a more "precise justice" or presents an opportunity to attempt to satisfy the good of the greatest number, the utilitarian defense of negotiation (Pennock and Chapman, 1979; Machiavelli, 1961; Menkel-Meadow, 1995). Here we offer no definitive answers to these questions. The questions are raised because they present issues of systematic ethics or macroethics and justice in the negotiation process, and we think they deserve further study and elaboration.

WHY NEGOTIATION ETHICS MATTER

To the extent that we continue to have competing theories about the goals of negotiation (individual gain maximization, joint gain, or peaceful coexistence, with or without agreed-to foundational principles) and competing practices about how those goals might be achieved (economic efficiency, distributional strategies, property and legal entitlement claims, integrative and creative solution-seeking collaborative methods, moral-desert claims), with little empirical or phenomenological accounts of how negotiations are actually conducted in different contexts (outside of social psychology laboratories), it will be difficult to develop any metatheory of negotiation ethics.

Every attempt to construct a metanarrative or analysis of how negotiation is conducted at a very abstract level is immediately resisted by different accounts (see Fisher and Ury, 1981; White, 1984; Cohen, 1980). So it goes with attempts to construct a metaethics of negotiation. It is bad to lie or deceive others (Bok, 1978; Hazard, 1981), but it is impossible to regulate private behavior or use unenforceable professional regulations or law to change common everyday expectations and negotiation culture (White, 1980). Adversarialists or professional role theorists tend to see negotiation as inherently distributional, competitive, and economically wealth maximizing, justifying a wide range of behaviors that puts each negotiator firmly on his or her own two legs, with little responsibility for anyone else. Those who see negotiation as an opportunity for mutual gains, learning, and human coordination to solve human problems see trust, nonstrategic communication, and sharing or creation (not division) of resources as animating principles. Can these different worldviews about negotiation coexist, and if they do coexist, how do we choose our goals and actions in negotiations?

Our assumptions and starting points can become self-fulfilling prophecies. As Sissela Bok (1978) noted when she began her study of lying and moral choice in public and private life, the expectation of "telling little white lies" accumulates and in turn lowers our expectations of each other and the system as a whole. So when we come to expect that generally accepted conventions of negotiation allow us to puff, dissemble, and exaggerate our preferences and needs, our expectations soon are experienced as requirements or defenses to how others are likely to behave. They become self-rationalizing and reflexive rather than reflective, and most often they call forward reactive and mirroring behaviors from others. It becomes dangerous to tell the truth or express what your client or principal really wants because you will be taken advantage of.

Some of us who study, teach, and practice negotiation have recognized that exaggerations and failures to disclose information or to take the needs and preferences of the other side really seriously do not produce efficient solutions but often produce economic and social waste with incomplete information, falsely expressed preferences, and weak split-the-difference compromises. Suboptimal arrangements or monetary proxies for a host of other terms, needs, and issues are the result of suboptimal disclosure, strategic deception, and boilerplate solutions. Those of us who believe this (or have watched it happen time and time again in real-world negotiations, as well as in classrooms and laboratories) prefer to engage in a thought experiment that we hope these readings will illuminate: Suppose we really did treat everyone as we hoped, not expected, to be treated (how about a "Golden Rule of Candor" in negotiation? Menkel-Meadow, 1990)? What if we really did consider how what we do in negotiations has the power to affect the lives of our clients, the other parties across the table, and others who might be affected by what we do together? What incentives would we need to make these hopes a reality?

It is often said that we cannot require truth in negotiation because then the other side would not do its due diligence and proper investigation or that superior skill at negotiation and information management would no longer determine outcomes. Imagine that what is fair in negotiations might turn on the merits rather than on the strategic skill or energy of the negotiator! Some years ago, a savvy real estate broker suggested to me that regardless of what ethical and disciplinary authorities do, eventually all middle persons or brokers would likely have to become more ethical, or at least more information disclosing, as increased information (pricing; past deals; availability of products, land, and services; more pictures; more endorsements and public complaints; not to mention more legal documents and boilerplate clauses and do-it-yourself deals) becomes available to all comers and principals on the Internet (perhaps that is too optimistic about the "truth" available on the Internet) and clients would feel more empowered to represent themselves. What value-added will agents, lawyers, and businesspeople bring to negotiations in such a world? If skilled negotiators cannot offer something in addition to strategic information manipulation, what can they offer?

Consider how much more efficient and just, as well as fair, negotiations might be if the presumptive expectations about information and the purposes of negotiation were reversed from current assumptions and expectations. Clients and negotiators might say what they really wanted, needed, or expected and would be required to produce information to support such needs and claims. As Howard Raiffa (1996) and other negotiation analysts have pointed out, we already do this in negotiations with people we already trust (spouses, colleagues, partners, friends, children, some relatives, and some business associates, even with some "intimate adversaries," like trusted superiors at work or in long-term contractual relationships like management and labor (Walton, Cutcher-Gershenfeld, and McKersie, 1994; Follett, 1995), or with those with whom we are required to behave honorably (fiduciaries and accountants), with people whose help we need (doctors), or who interact with us frequently enough to know when we are telling the truth ("repeat players"). Consider that we might actually be able to begin to specify degrees of trust or relationships that might alter the conventional expectations about what we owe to other people by beginning with those to whom we owe the most and altering our negotiation practices to reflect increasing levels of trust and collaboration, rather than assumptions of arm-distant unfair dealing—family members, fiduciaries; continuing relations; legally created relations of good faith and fair dealing (regulated industries, banks, securities, truth-in-lending, residential real estate sales); special relations of parties (doctors-patients, lawyers-clients); care-dependent, special needs parties (unable to develop own information sources, poorly resourced, "incompetent" negotiators)—and only then to more distant relations of open market transactions, communal governmental issues, organizational and intergroup relations, and finally to disputes, lawsuits, and distrusted domestic and international adversaries. Most of our understandings of ethical norms in negotiation begin at the bottom of this list, assuming adversary distrust. And what does adversary distrust produce? More of the same. Perhaps reversing expectations of trust and care might also beget more of the same (Axelrod, 1984).

We are not suggesting that completely open, information sharing, trusting, and joint-solution-seeking behavior will be appropriate or fair in all settings. Trust must be earned or well established and demonstrated. (This is why I always counsel negotiators to ask questions of their counterparts they already know the answer to. This is a competitive tactic in the service of testing and establishing trust for strategic collaboration.) Trust is hard won and easily lost. And trusting relationships are not the only measure of fairness in negotiation, at either the process or outcome level. Some suggest that law and legal endowments should be the measure of fairness or justness of negotiated outcomes (Luban, 1995; Condlin, 1985). We believe that fairness or justness in negotiation processes has many measures, but they are more varied and complex than only legal legitimacy, economic efficiency, or single-party maximization.

This book offers different treatments or nuggets of writings, teachings, meditations, and speculations on what is ethical, moral, or fair in negotiation because we think there are many ways to think about and assess what is fair in both process and outcome measures. We think that more analysis, reasoning, and even feeling about the subject will cause us to make better behavioral choices in negotiations and suggest broader criteria by which to measure whether we have accomplished good outcomes. We close by suggesting some questions to think about in contemplating the fairness of negotiations suggested by some of the readings that follow and our own thinking:

1. Is the structure of a particular negotiation fair? (Are all relevant parties included? Are the physical space and time appropriate for the negotiation? Are there significant structural imbalances between the parties that might impair the process: economics, information, or quality of representatives, for example?)

2. Are rules of process and proceeding clear to all? (Are issues for the agenda transparent to all? Do all of the parties understand the rules of the game being played? Has one party controlled the development of the rules or the agenda in an unfair way?)

3. Do the parties understand their respective purposes and goals? (Does it matter if the parties do not share distributive or integrative problem-solving orientations to the negotiation? Is one party trying to create a long-term relationship while the other is not?)

4. Do the parties have a fair shot at achieving a mutually satisfactory solution, or is one party "unfairly" positioned to take advantage of the other side?

5. Do the parties share expected criteria for assessing outcomes? (Must outcomes track legal endowments or entitlements? Can a party agree to an outcome he or she knows might cause substantial injustice to another party?)

6. To what extent should the justice of negotiated outcomes be measured by principles outside the parties' own criteria: equity, equality, need, social welfare, precedential value, likelihood of enforcement, and effects on others?

7. Should we assess the fairness of a negotiated outcome after we see what it actually achieves or accomplishes for the parties? For others? (Should all negotiated agreements be available for public scrutiny and assessment? When should the parties' agreements for confidentiality and secrecy be honored?)

To ask these questions of each negotiation we are engaged in or asked to evaluate is to probe the various dimensions of the difficult question of what's fair in negotiation. We hope the chapters that follow explore some of these questions. Some will provide provocative and clarifying answers; others might pose more questions.

Stuart Hampshire, the social philosopher, recently suggested that since we will never agree "on the substantive good," we can at least agree on the process by which a civilized society decides how it will act to decide the good, by "hearing the other side *(audi alteram partem)*" (Hampshire, 2000). This approach sees justice as procedural and implicates even private negotiations in considerations of what is fair process. Negotiators, whether they operate dyadically in private to make contracts, create business ventures, or buy or sell land and goods, or settle lawsuits or operate in larger groups of politicians, diplomats, lawmakers, and citizens to make decisions, combine to form the ethical climate of negotiation activity. To the extent that we are all morally responsible for the system of negotiation that we create by our individual behaviors, might we not create a better ethical climate by at least asking these questions of ourselves and others and aiming to produce negotiation processes and outcomes that seem fair to those who participate in them? Perhaps if we could do this, then, in the words of one modern ethicist, we might "live so that we can look other people, even outsiders [as well as ourselves] in the eye" (Blackburn, 2001, p. 128).

References

Acuff, F. L. *How to Negotiate Anything with Anyone Anywhere in the World.* New York: AMACON, 1997.

American Bar Association. *Model Rules of Professional Conduct.* Chicago: ABA Press, 2003.

Applbaum, A. *Ethics for Adversaries: The Morality of Roles in Public and Professional Life.* Princeton, N.J.: Princeton University Press, 1999.

Avruch, K. *Culture and Conflict Resolution.* Washington, D.C.: U.S. Institute of Peace Press, 1998.

Axelrod, R. *The Evolution of Cooperation.* New York: Basic Books, 1984.

Bazerman, M., and Neale, M. "The Role of Fairness Considerations and Relationships in a Judgmental Perspective of Negotiation." In K. Arrow and others, *Barriers to Conflict Resolution.* New York: Norton, 1995.

Bazerman, M. H., and Neale, M. A. *Negotiating Rationally.* New York: Free Press, 1992.

Bernard, P., and Garth, B. (eds.). *Dispute Resolution Ethics: A Comprehensive Guide.* Washington, D.C.: American Bar Association, 2002.

Blackburn, S. *Being Good: A Short Introduction to Ethics.* New York: Oxford University Press, 2001.

Bok, S. *Lying: Moral Choices in Public and Private Life.* New York: Pantheon Books, 1978.

Butte Mining PLC v. *Smith,* 76 F.3d 287 (9th Cir. 1996).

Cohen, H. *You Can Negotiate Anything.* Secaucus, N.J.: Lyle Stuart, 1980.

Condlin, R. "Cases on Both Sides: Patterns of Argument in Legal Dispute Resolution." *Maryland Law Review,* 1985, *51,* 1–104.

Cramton, P. C., and Dees, J. G. "Promoting Honesty in Negotiation: An Exercise in Practical Ethics." *Business Ethics Quarterly,* 1993, *3,* 359–394.

Elster, J. "Strategic Uses of Argument." In K. Arrow and others (eds.), *Barriers to Conflict Resolution.* New York: Norton, 1995.

Fisher, R., and Ury, W. *Getting to Yes: Negotiating Agreement Without Giving In.* Boston: Houghton Mifflin, 1981.

Fisher, R., Ury, W., and Patton, B. *Getting to Yes: Negotiating Agreement Without Giving In.* (2nd ed.). New York: Penguin Books, 1991.

Follett, M. P. *Prophet of Management: A Celebration of Writings from the 1920s.* (P. Graham, ed.). Boston: Harvard Business School Press, 1995.

Forester, J. *The Deliberative Practitioner: Encouraging Participatory Planning Processes.* Cambridge, Mass.: MIT Press, 2001.

Freund, J. C. *Smart Negotiating: How to Make Good Deals in the Real World.* New York: Simon & Schuster, 1992.

Fuller, L. *The Morality of Law.* New Haven, Conn.: Yale University Press, 1964.

Gilson, R., and Mnookin, R. H. "Disputing Through Agents: Cooperation and Conflict Between Lawyers in Litigation." *Columbia Law Review,* 1994, *94,* 509–566.

Gilson, R., and Mnookin, R. H. "Foreword: Business Lawyers and Value Creation for Clients." *Oregon Law Review,* 1995, *74,* 1–14.

Hampshire, S. *Justice Is Conflict.* Princeton, N.J.: Princeton University Press, 2000.

Hart, H.L.A. *The Concept of Law.* New York: Oxford University Press, 1961.

Harter, P. "Negotiating Regulations: A Cure for the Malaise." *Georgetown Law Journal,* 1982, *71,* 1–118.

Hazard, G. "The Lawyer's Obligation to Be Trustworthy When Dealing with Opposing Parties." *South Carolina Law Review,* 1981, *33,* 181–196.

Kolb, D., and Williams, J. *Everyday Negotiations.* San Francisco: Jossey-Bass, 2003.

Langevoort, D. "Half-Truths: Protecting Mistaken Inferences by Investors and Others." *Stanford Law Review,* 1999, *52,* 87–125.

Lansky, D. "Proceeding to a Constitution: A Multi-Party Negotiation Analysis of the Constitutional Convention of 1789." *Harvard Negotiation Law Review,* 2000, *5,* 279–338.

Law Society. *The Guide to the Professional Conduct of Solicitors.* (8th ed.). London: Law Society, 1999.

Lax, D., and Sebenius, J. *The Manager as Negotiator: Bargaining for Cooperation and Competitive Gain.* New York: Free Press, 1986.

Luban, D. "Settlements and the Erosion of the Public Realm." *Georgetown Law Journal,* 1995, *83,* 2619–2662.

Lubet, S. "Notes on the Bedouin Horse Trade or Why Won't the Market Clear, Daddy?" *Texas Law Review,* 1996, *74,* 1039–1057.

Machiavelli, N. *The Prince.* (George Bull, trans.). New York: Penguin, 1961. (Originally published 1640.)

Meltsner, M., and Schrag, P. "Negotiation." In *Public Interest Advocacy: Materials for Clinical Legal Education.* Boston: Little, Brown, 1974.

Menkel-Meadow, C. "Toward Another View of Legal Negotiation: The Structure of Problem Solving." *UCLA Law Review,* 1984, *31,* 754–842.

Menkel-Meadow, C. "Lying to Clients for Economic Gain or Paternalistic Judgment: A Proposal for a Golden Rule of Candor." *University of Pennsylvania Law Review,* 1990, *138,* 761–783.

Menkel-Meadow, C. "Whose Dispute Is It Anyway? A Philosophical and Democratic Defense of Settlement (in Some Cases)." *Georgetown Law Journal*, 1995, *83*, 2663–2696.

Menkel-Meadow, C. "Teaching About Gender and Negotiation: Sex, Truths and Video-Tape." *Negotiation Journal*, 2000, *16*(1), 357–375.

Mnookin, R. H., and Susskind, L. E. *Negotiating on Behalf of Others: Advice to Lawyers, Business Executives, Sports Agents, Diplomats, Politicians and Everybody Else.* Thousand Oaks, Calif.: Sage, 1999.

Nash, L. *Good Intentions Aside: A Manager's Guide to Resolving Ethical Problems.* Boston: Harvard Business School Press, 1993.

Norton, E. H. "Bargaining and the Ethics of Process." *New York University Law Review,* 1989, *64,* 494–539.

O'Dair, R. *Legal Ethics: Text and Materials.* London: Butterworths, 2001.

Paine, L. *Value Shift: Why Companies Must Merge Social and Financial Imperatives to Achieve Superior Performance.* New York: McGraw-Hill, 2003.

Pennock, J. R., and Chapman, J. (eds.). *Compromise in Ethics, Law and Politics.* New York: New York University Press, 1979.

Pou, C. "Gandhi Meets Elliot Ness: 5th Cir. Ruling Raises Concerns About Confidentiality in Federal Agency ADR." *Dispute Resolution Magazine,* Winter 1998, pp. 9–19.

Raiffa, H. *The Art and Science of Negotiation: How to Resolve Conflicts and Get the Best Out of Bargaining.* Cambridge, Mass.: Belknap Press, 1982.

Raiffa, H. *Lectures on Negotiation Analysis.* Cambridge, Mass.: Program on Negotiation Books, Harvard Law School, 1996.

Raiffa, H. *Negotiation Analysis: The Science and Art of Collaborative Decision Making.* Cambridge, Mass.: Belknap Press, 2002.

Schwartz, M. "The Professionalism and Accountability of Lawyers." *California Law Review,* 1978, *66,* 669–697.

Schweitzer, M. E., and Croson, R. "Curtailing Deception: The Impact of Direct Questions on Lies and Omissions." *International Journal of Conflict Resolution,* 1999, *10,* 225–248.

Shell, R. "When Is It Legal to Lie in Negotiations?" *Sloan Management Review,* Spring 1991, pp. 93–101.

Shell, R. *Bargaining for Advantage: Negotiating Strategies for Reasonable People.* New York: Penguin Books, 1999.

Strudler, A. "On the Ethics of Deception in Negotiation." *Business Ethics Quarterly,* 1995, *5*(4), 805–822.

Susskind, L. "Environmental Mediation and the Accountability Problem." *Vermont Law Review,* 1981, *6,* 85–117.

Susskind, L., McKearnan, S., and Thomas-Larmer, J. *The Consensus Building Handbook: A Comprehensive Guide to Reaching Agreement.* Thousand Oaks, Calif.: Sage, 1999.

Thompson, L. *The Mind and Heart of the Negotiator.* (2nd ed.). Upper Saddle River, N.J.: Prentice-Hall, 2000.

Walton, R. E., Cutcher-Gershenfeld, J., and McKersie, R. *Strategic Negotiations: A Theory of Change in Labor-Management Relations.* Ithaca, N.Y.: Cornell University Press, 1994.

Weiss, S. E. "Negotiating with the Romans—Part 1." *Sloan Management Review,* 1994a, *35*(3), 51–61.

Weiss, S. E. "Negotiating with the Romans—Part 2." *Sloan Management Review,* 1994b, *35*(3), 85–99.

White, J. J. "Machiavelli and the Bar: Ethical Limitations on Lying in Negotiation." *American Bar Foundation Research Journal,* 1980, *1980*(4), 926–938.

White, J. J. "The Pros and Cons of Getting to Yes." *Journal of Legal Education,* 1984, *34*, 115–124.

Wolgast, E. *Ethics of an Artificial Person: Lost Responsibility in Professions and Organizations.* Stanford: Calif.: Stanford University Press, 1992.

Swimming with Saints/Praying with Sharks

Michael Wheeler

The two best-selling negotiation books—*You Can Negotiate Anything* (1982) by Herb Cohen and *Getting to Yes* by Roger Fisher and William Ury (Fisher, Ury, and Patton, 1991)—were published within a few months of each other in the early 1980s.[1] Both are still in print and influential today.

More than anything else written in the field, these books have both reflected and shaped popular attitudes about negotiation. They have also marked the territory for scores of other authors who have followed since. Cohen's book is regarded as the standard field manual for hard bargainers and *Getting to Yes* the bible for so-called principled problem solvers.

Neither book neatly matches its reputation, however. There are ambiguities and inconsistencies in each of them. It actually is Cohen, not Fisher and Ury, who uses the phrase "win-win negotiation," just as he is the one who invokes Jesus Christ and Socrates as "ethical negotiators." He notes that both men "deliberately used many of the collaborative techniques I will teach you through this book" (Cohen, 1982, p. 20).

Readers have been split, however, on whether Cohen delivers on that promise. At least one reviewer commended his book for its high ethical standards: "Cohen has taken a subject that is normally associated in the public's eye with a sleazy purveying of snake oil and shown it to be a needed methodology that can be practiced not only with a clear conscience, but with honor" (George, 1981, p. 1158). Another reviewer had a very different reaction, noting that although Cohen "preaches the gospel of bargaining so that everybody wins," that optimistic message is "nearly lost in a book laced with enough manipulative ploys to make Niccolo Machiavelli nervous" (Press, Glass, and Foote, 1981, p. 86).

Getting to Yes has drawn fire from exactly the opposite direction. Some readers found the book sanctimonious in spite of the authors' disavowal that it "is not a sermon on the morality of right and wrong; it is a book on how to do well in negotiation" (Fisher, Ury, and Patton, 1991, p. 154).[2] One reviewer friendly to its overall approach admitted being put off by "a certain take-it-or-leave-it righteousness in the new religion" (Menkel-Meadow, 1983, p. 919). Other critics have been harsher. One panned the book as "condescending" (Goldhirsh Group, 1982, p. 140), and another felt it was written as though "there were one and only one definition of appropriate negotiating behavior handed down by the authors" (White, 1984, p. 117).

Swimming in ethical waters is perilous business: it is open season on both sharks and saints, though sometimes it is hard to know precisely what the fuss is about. Readers often have a visceral reaction to the stance of the book but do not specify what constitutes a manipulative ploy or when pleas for ethical conduct slip over into self-righteousness. Given the continuing impact of these classic texts on negotiation theory and practice, it is worth reexamining their ethical implications. Although neither book purports to define negotiation ethics comprehensively, their prescriptions and examples reveal implicit attitudes about what negotiators owe one another in respect to candor, fairness, and the use of pressure tactics.

The first part of this brief essay examines a seemingly simple negotiation that Cohen describes in *You Can Negotiate Anything* and uses it as an ethical litmus test. Some readers may regard aspects of his approach as wholly acceptable, while others may have their doubts, just as two of Cohen's reviewers had markedly different reactions. A case that teeters on the edge should tell us more about ethical boundaries than conduct everyone agrees is egregious. The next part of the essay explores the same case through the lens of *Getting to Yes* to illuminate what it is about the book that strikes some people as preachy. The piece concludes by examining self-interest in negotiation, a notion that is important to both books.

GAMESMANSHIP

Herb Cohen's *You Can Negotiate Anything* is constructed around a series of vignettes, many from his everyday personal experience. In one he tells a story of chatting up an owner of a small appliance store, spending time with the fellow, commiserating with him about how big shopping malls were crushing mom-and-pop businesses like his. Only after twenty-five minutes of seeming small talk did the author get around to dickering over a VCR: "I don't know what these things cost," he said. "In fact, I haven't the faintest idea. I'll trust you when it comes to a fair price" (p. 174).

But when the store owner started to write out the sales slip, Cohen emphasized that he would be relying on the owner's honesty: "I want you to make a reasonable profit, John . . . but, of course, I want to get a reasonable deal myself" (p. 175).

A moment later, Cohen casually asked if the remote control was part of the package. He hinted that if the price were fair, he would buy another set in a few months, though added: "But, John, if I should find out that my trust was misplaced, this disappointment will prevent me from giving you any additional business" (p. 175).

Throughout all this, the owner was scribbling down numbers, crossing them out, and recalculating the price. Cohen blandly inquired if, instead of taking a credit card for the purchase, the owner would find it "more convenient" to accept cash. Most certainly, was the eager answer, after which Cohen said, "You'll install this for me, right?" (p. 176).

The deal was made, and the owner even threw in a stand that Cohen had not thought to ask for. True to his word, he bought a second VCR two months later, and by his account has since developed a "close, trusting relationship" with the store owner.

Cohen relates the story to illustrate the importance of trust building in negotiation. Some people may see his approach as manipulative, while others may see it as perfectly normal business behavior. Three aspects of this transaction deserve attention. First is whether the way Cohen used the casual relationship to get a better price should give us any qualms. Second is his use of ethical norms of trust and fairness as psychological leverage. Third is the sly cash deal that avoided taxes for both parties.

Cohen may be on strongest ground in respect to how he crafted a relationship with the store owner in order to get a sweeter deal, though there is a slight whiff of deception in the exchange. It is doubtful Cohen would have spent any time with the store owner if he did not want something in return. Had he been talking instead to a Wal-Mart sales clerk on the outskirts of town, his patter about the local business environment might have been very different.

Cohen understands that small talk often is anything but that. Here it establishes that "mutual trust is the mainspring of collaborative Win-Win negotiations" (p. 164). There is certainly empirical support for that proposition. Experiments confirm that negotiators who schmooze for just a few minutes are more likely to reach agreement—and more creative agreements at that—than those who just plunge into the substance of the transaction. Glad-handing salespeople know this well when they heartily shake your hand and offer you a cup of coffee (Cialdini, 1993). Seen in this light, Cohen was only engaging in a familiar dance, though he was striving to lead rather than follow. By shooting the breeze, he was hoping the owner would drop his defenses and treat him differently from customers who just barge right up to the counter.

Where should the line be drawn, however? Most of us properly take relationships into account when we negotiate. We bend over to be fair to people we like and do not haggle when we sell an old car to a cousin or the teenager next door. If we are dealing with a stranger or car salesman, by contrast, we may leave it to the other to determine if the price we put on the table is fair.

Perhaps the issue turns on the difference between taking into account an existing relationship and ingratiating ourselves for the sole purpose of securing personal advantage. When we give or get a break negotiating with a friend or family member, after all, the deal is incidental to the relationship, not the other way around. Those relationships are mutually developed and enjoyed for their own sake, not as bargaining chips. At some point, the idea of friendship, even simple civility, loses something if it is practiced for selfish ends. That may be a quaint position to take, of course, in a day and age when networking is celebrated as the key to professional advancement.

Intent and impact are important factors in thinking about negotiation and relationships. Two hypotheticals may define ends of a spectrum. Consider two strangers who happen into conversation while waiting at a bus stop and discover that one of them is selling a VCR and the other is looking to buy one. Contrast them with a suitor who falsely swears love in order to win the heiress's heart and fortune. In the first case, neither party enters the relationship intending to manipulate the other; in the latter, the gold digger dupes his fiancée into surrendering real value in return for a worthless relationship.

Cohen's banter with the store owner is innocent compared to the cad's behavior, though his intent is no less result oriented. He may be absolved because the owner in his story was not deeply invested in the relationship. This kind of behavior still may have some social cost in the aggregate if it contributes to a general sense that smiles conceal hidden agendas and that someone who extends a hand is reaching for your wallet. Using relationships with others as means to private ends may make us devalue simple acts of kindness on the part of others.

Cohen may be on less defensible ground in regard to the second issue, specifically his cheerful account of invoking ethical norms of honesty and trust to coax the owner into making repeated concessions. While lauding collaboration in the abstract, he treats ethics in practice as just another tool for gaining leverage. Cohen observes that people reared in Western traditions like to think of themselves as fair, and then concludes, "That's why, if you *lay morality on people* in an unqualified way, it may often work" (p. 80, emphasis added).

Cohen's technique was almost subliminal. He methodically dealt out potent words like *fair, reasonable,* and *trust,* and the store owner responded each time by cutting his price or tossing something else into the package. This velvety patter was followed by a steely threat to sever the relationship if it turned out that the owner had not been fair.

Car salesmen do much the same thing, of course, cooing stock phrases about "earning your trust" and "treating you fairly," but then warning you that another customer will snap up the vehicle if you do not buy it right now. Cohen himself notes that the common practice of sticking a price tag on an item is simply a technique that retailers use to confer a kind of legitimacy on what often should be regarded as only a first offer in negotiation.

Cohen's deliberate use of words with an ethical aura thus might be excused as fighting fire with fire, though there is a cynical tone to his phrase "laying on morality" that debases the very notions that he invokes. Fairness and trust become part of the lexicon of spin, much like "new and improved" from decades ago. In his conversation with the store owner, his language seems hollow, as he does not offer a standard of fairness or invite his counterpart to propose criteria that might be mutually acceptable.

Using ethical language as rhetoric to promote self-interest may make us jaded when it comes to reading other people's motivations. Cohen himself seems prone to this. He remarks, for example, that "Mahatma Gandhi is generally revered as a practitioner of nonviolence, but his tactical means were just a variation on the old guilt ploy" (p. 137). Well, that's one way of looking at it. Another would be that Gandhi's nonviolent tactics were ends in their own right, a way of respecting values regardless of their practical consequences. Gandhi's reputation can survive this jaundiced view of his motivations. It is Cohen's loss not being able to recognize virtue when he sees it.

An instrumental view of ethics can lead any of us to easy rationalizations, citing certain principles when they justify our behavior and finding some convenient way of ignoring them when they do not. To be sure, many of our choices involve balancing different considerations and sometimes choosing between "right and right," as Joseph Badaracco (1997) has put it. Depending on the context, the scales might tip one way or the other in different cases. Relativism in that sense, however, seems quite distinct from the kind of bootstrapping that Cohen describes.

Cohen is most vulnerable to criticism in regard to the third issue: his ingenuous question about whether the owner would prefer cash. Here the breach seems clear even if the practice is common. The owner jumped on the suggestion, of course, as cash would not show up on the company's books. The government cannot tax income it does not see, nor can any partners claim their share of the profit. A cash deal may also save the buyer sales tax.

It is no defense to say that tax compliance is the store's responsibility, not the customer's. Making it a cash deal expanded the pie for both parties at the corresponding expense of other stakeholders not at the table. Cohen first floated the cash idea with the innocent air of offering to do the other guy a favor, but as soon as the owner seized on the proposal, Cohen tacked on a stipulation that the dealer include installation. In addition to the substantive quid pro quo, this minitransaction tightened the bond between Cohen and the store owner. Nothing had to be said directly about skirting the tax laws. With a wink and a nod, they were a couple of old sharpies who understood how the game is played.[3]

Ethical norms sometimes require more than compliance with the law, but can they ever encompass less? If not, then we had better creep down the interstate at 55 mph while the rest of the traffic whizzes by at 70. Speeders can say, of course, that they comply with the unwritten law that adds a grace factor to the posted limit. Is that any different from people who justify the "convenience" of cash deals by citing the enormous underground, off-the-books economy? The cases are different, however, because pushing the speed limit is a visible act—one that is implicitly condoned by the troopers parked at the side of the road. By contrast, the very purpose of a cash transaction is to evade detection by the authorities.[4]

Cohen describes the petty dodge without comment or apology, nor does he reflect on how he uses relationship building or "lays on morality" for bargaining advantage. The choices he makes are unexamined. Whatever justification is implicit in the fact that a deal was reached between a willing seller and a willing buyer, neither of whom was under duress. Cohen got his bargain only because the price worked for the store owner too. If the parties are satisfied and the outcome is legitimate, maybe that ends the ethical analysis. Apparently that was enough for Cohen.

CHANGING THE GAME

Getting to Yes (Fisher, Ury, and Patton, 1991) does not deal with gray areas where strict legal requirements may require one thing but common practice another. Unlike *You Can Negotiate Anything*, however, none of its examples involve skirting the law. The book does treat at length the other two highlighted dimensions of the VCR story: cultivating relationships to get a better bargain and using principles, including the norm of fairness, as a method for winning agreement. Predictably, the *Getting to Yes* approach would result in different conduct in some important respects, though in other ways there are some surprising parallels to Cohen's recommendations.

Getting to Yes is ambiguous when it comes to relationship issues.[5] One of the book's central themes is the importance of "separating the people from the problem." That precept is an aspect of the rational problem-solving orientation of the book. It also supports the notion of maintaining a consistent negotiation strategy that is not contingent on the good or bad habits of others. Fisher, Ury, and Patton also push the issue of trust aside, maintaining that no one at the bargaining table should be expected to make leaps of faith. Instead, rational assessment of interests and identification of objective criteria should generate solutions that each side sees as superior to stalemate. If so, it becomes in everyone's individual interest to embrace the deal and make it work.

Getting to Yes is not utterly depersonalized, however. It grants the inevitability of emotion in many negotiations, for example, and emphasizes the importance of good communication. Of particular relevance here is its advice on developing a relationship before the actual negotiating begins. "The more quickly you can turn a stranger into someone you know, the easier the negotiation is likely to be. You have less difficulty understanding where they are coming from. You have a foundation of trust to build upon in a difficult negotiation" (p. 37).

Standing on its own, this sounds very much like how Cohen engaged the store owner before he got down to negotiating for the VCR. Indeed, the authors approvingly cite Benjamin Franklin's technique of asking an adversary if he might borrow a particular book. That adversary would be flattered and left with "the comfortable feeling of knowing that Franklin owed him a favor" (p. 37). If Cohen's approach verges on being manipulative, he is in august company.

In many respects, however, Fisher, Ury, and Patton seek a much deeper sense of relationship than Cohen seems to contemplate. Much of the advice that they offer is directed toward the individuals, but they are fundamentally interested in the attitudes and behavior of all participants noting, "A more effective way for the parties to think of themselves is as partners in a hardheaded, side-by-side search for a fair agreement advantageous to each" (p. 37). Collaboration can be facilitated if discourse is shifted from a positional contest of wills to a mutual exploration of underlying interests.

Fisher, Ury, and Patton concede that in one time, single-issue transactions with strangers, "simple haggling over positions may work fine" (p. 152), but they regard those cases as exceptional and less important. In negotiations with valued customers, suppliers, and colleagues, the authors urge looking beyond mere dollars-and-cents issues and giving weight to relational considerations. Indeed, a properly conducted process should yield wise, enduring, and efficient agreements that enhance the parties' relationship.

Even in cases like the VCR purchase where important relationships are not at stake, the authors would see opportunity for mutual gain, just as Cohen himself implicitly did. *Getting to Yes* diverges from *You Can Negotiate Anything,* however, with respect to how that potential is first identified and then distributed. Fisher, Ury, and Patton instruct negotiators to "insist on using objective criteria" and not of risking relationships by issuing ultimatums. Instead, "the more you bring standards of fairness, efficiency, or scientific merit to bear on your particular problem, the more likely you are to produce a final package that is wise and efficient" (p. 83). Searching for appropriate precedent and norms allows negotiators to learn from others' experience and generates agreements that are more likely to be seen as legitimate by the parties themselves and others. Fairness thus is not something one party uses to dignify his or her demands. Instead, it is an area for mutual inquiry and exploration.

The authors grant that "you will usually find more than one objective criterion available as a basis for agreement" (p. 85). Parties may argue for one principle over another as a way of bootstrapping a favorable result. "Ideally, to assure a wise agreement, objective criteria should be not only independent of will but also legitimate and practical" (p. 85). Thus, a home buyer who is insisting on certain warranties should be open to offering the same assurances for another property he or she happens to be selling. Essentially this captures the Rawlsian notion of identifying the appropriate principle without knowing one's stake or role in a transaction. Fisher, Ury, and Patton note that objective criteria are relevant to both outcomes and process, citing as an example of the latter the age-old solution of having one person cut the cake and the other choose the piece.[6]

In the first edition of the book, the authors maintained that one standard usually will prove more persuasive than others by being "more directly on point, more widely accepted, and more immediately relevant in terms of time, place, and circumstance" (p. 154). In the supplement to the revised edition of *Getting to Yes,* the authors backed off somewhat from that claim:

> In most negotiations there will be no one "right" or "fairest" answer; people will advance different standards by which to judge what is fair. Yet using external standards improves on haggling in three ways: An outcome informed even by conflicting standards of fairness and community practice is likely to be wiser than an arbitrary result. Using standards reduces the costs of "backing down"— it is easier to agree to follow a principle or independent standard than to give in to the other side's positional demand. And finally, unlike arbitrary positions, some standards are more persuasive than others [p. 153].

Fisher, Ury, and Patton further asserted that consensus on a single fairness standard is not essential for success:

> Criteria are just one tool that may help the parties find an agreement better for both than no agreement. Using external standards often helps narrow the range of disagreement and may help extend the area of potential agreement. When standards have been refined to the point that it is difficult to argue persuasively that one standard is more applicable than another, the parties can explore trade-offs or resort to fair procedures to settle remaining differences. They can flip a coin, use an arbitrator, or even split the difference [p. 154].

Their argument for fairness thus oscillates between being idealistic and prag-matic. At points, they make a practical case for objective criteria generally and for fairness in particular, contending that debates over principle are likely to be less explosive than contests of will. In other places, there seems to be an under-lying notion that there really are objective truths to which all decent people must subscribe. Objectivity is a hard sell in this postmodern era, when such claims are taken as privileging certain positions at the expense of others and, still worse, doing so in a way that brooks no argument.

Seen in either light, this concern about objective criteria and fairness would likely lead a faithful *Getting to Yes* practitioner to conduct the VCR negotiation somewhat differently. For one thing, a mutual discussion of fairness standards would be required. The conversation might consider whether an owner of a small store is obliged to match the price of a wholesale discounter or can legit-imately ask for somewhat more in return for personal service and attention. A buyer who had initially built the relationship by professing sympathy for the hard times being expressed by Main Street businesses might have trouble resist-ing that principle; hence, the price that Cohen paid for the equipment and all the add-ons might seem unfair.

In some cases, then, the *Getting to Yes* negotiator might end up paying more than would a classic hard bargainer. To this possibility, the authors respond:

> If you want more than you can justify as fair and find that you are regularly able to persuade others to give it to you, you may not find some of the suggestions in this book all that useful. But the negotiators we meet more often fear getting *less* than they should in a negotiation, or damaging a relationship if they press firmly for what they do deserve. The ideas in this book are meant to show you how to get what you are entitled to while still getting along with the other side [p. 155].

How people negotiate thus affects the substance of the deal and the ongoing relationship of the people who reach it. Trade-offs often have to be made between dollars in hand today and long-term payoffs, monetary and otherwise. Fisher, Ury, and Patton appealed to enlightened self-interest, warning negotia-tors that whatever short-term gains might be won through deception and dirty tricks are often small compared to strained relationships and a tarnished repu-tation. Being fair and principled thus pays off personally in the long run.

If you have the chance to get more than your fair share, they ask, Should you take it? Not without careful thought, they warn. "More is at stake than just a choice about your moral self-definition. (That too probably deserves careful thought, but advising in that realm is not our purpose here)" (p. 155). Before seizing a windfall, they counsel a full reckoning of costs and benefits: how unfair the outcome is, whether the deal really will stand up, its impact on your reputation, and how it will sit on your conscience.[7]

FAIRNESS AND SELF-INTEREST

It is understandable why its authors tried to cast *Getting to Yes* in these prag-matic terms. It is hard enough to sell good manners today, let alone ask people to sacrifice for the greater good. If we take Fisher, Ury, and Patton at their word, however, they really are making a utilitarian argument, not a moral one. Rather than declaring certain things right or wrong, they simply warn that what goes around often comes around.

They thus give self-interest primacy, just as Cohen does, although they emphasize a broader sweep of interests, especially in regard to relational issues and long-run impacts. They grant that positional bargaining sometimes may work in one time single transactions with strangers but essentially relegate hag-gling to unimportant cases. In negotiations with valued customers, suppliers, and colleagues, the authors would give priority to relational considerations, but the utilitarian formula is the same. The weights given to specific factors simply vary according to the situation. Cohen would not disagree.

The language also can be read, however, as invoking social welfare more broadly. The authors' disavowals about moralizing notwithstanding, their own values seem to peek through at times. In a footnote, for example, they allow that "we do think that, in addition to providing a good all-around method for getting what you want in a negotiation, principled negotiation can help make the world a better place. It promotes understanding among people, whether they be parent and child, worker and manager, or Arab and Israeli" (Fisher, Ury, and Patton, 1991, pp. 154–155).

Focusing on interests fosters creativity, which in turn promotes economic effi-ciency and mutual gain. "Relying on standards of fairness and seeking to meet the interest of *both* sides helps produce agreements that are durable, set good precedents, and build lasting relationships" (Fisher, Ury, and Patton, 1991, p. 155). In addition to reducing the cost of conflict, negotiators "may find that using this approach serves values of caring and justice in a way that is personally satisfying" (p. 155).

The last assertion is provocative. The fairness standards the authors invoke—legal precedents, business norms, and the like—may not themselves be just. Workers whose pension funds have been raided may not have a viable legal claim for their losses. Divorce laws may have gender bias when it comes to divi-sion of property and child custody. Inventors who do not secure the right kind of patent protection may not reap the fruits of their genius.

Getting to Yes does not purport to change the larger game. Success at the bar-gaining table is measured by how well the outcome compares to the practical nonagreement alternatives. It is nonetheless meant to help people better play the hands that they are dealt. In this respect, it is an optimistic book, one that earnestly aspires to reduce the individual and social costs of conflict and to increase the value of exchange.

By contrast, the underlying assumptions of *You Can Negotiate Anything* seem pessimistic. Cohen (1982) sets up his VCR story, for example, by noting that "after spending an entire week in an exasperating negotiation overseas, I didn't relish the thought of facing off with a department store clerk or a local shop owner" (p. 172). It is a revealing comment. Even the self-proclaimed "world's best negotiator" apparently dreaded a routine encounter, imagining it as "facing off," a metaphor that recalls gunslingers in the old West.

In an earlier personal anecdote, Cohen described how he knocked down the price of a refrigerator that listed for $489.95. He made three separate trips to the store, first alone, next with his wife, and finally with his mother-in-law, each time displaying enough interest to command the salesman's attention while never being quite ready to make a deal. Finally, after getting the salesman to "waste" (Cohen's word) six hours of time with this hemming and hawing, he finally emptied his pockets and offered $450—all he supposedly had with him—to make the deal. He said he would walk out of the store if it was not good enough. "Will the salesman follow you? Yes. He has an investment in the situation, and he wants some return on the effort he has expended" (p. 36).

Short-circuiting this arduous process by just offering $450 up front would have failed, Cohen says. His success depended on creating what behavioral economists call a sunk cost trap for the salesman. That required a lot of work on Cohen's own part and a high tolerance for tedium. It also seems to require an attitude of "do unto others before they do unto you." The world often is a hostile place, but bringing that attitude to every encounter can only make it more so. The preemptive steps that we take to defend ourselves can easily be read as aggressive by others. Unless they practice forbearance more than we do ourselves, escalation can easily ensue.

Even when things do not blow up, something may be lost, and we may not even know it. Toward the end of his book, Cohen notes, "By now you must realize that I do not share the cynical view that people are inescapably greedy or evil" (p. 163). Then a few pages later, he goes on to tell a story about pulling up in a cab in front of a New York hotel. A crowd was pressed around a police barricade and was gaping upward. According to the doorman, someone on the eleventh floor was threatening to jump. "Gee, that's too bad," Cohen said. As he entered, he was "upset at the thought of a fellow human being tumbling to the sidewalk" (p. 227).

The story then takes an unexpected twist. This is not a tale of how a gifted negotiator raced to the elevator and talked a desperate man off the ledge or about how he deftly enlisted volunteers to hold a rescue net. Instead, Cohen strode directly to the front desk, where his mood quickly changed. The clerk acknowledged that Cohen did have a guaranteed reservation, but unfortunately no rooms were available. The clerk offered to call other hotels. Cohen describes what happened next:

"'Hold it!' I snapped. 'You *do* have a room! You know that guy on the eleventh floor? The one who's causing all that commotion outside. *He's checking out!'*

The windup? The guy didn't jump. The police corralled him but checked him into a different facility for psychiatric examination. I got his vacant room" (p. 227).

It is true that Cohen had no role in pushing the stranger into despair, nor was he rooting for the man to jump. His dogged self-centeredness simply led him to construe another person's disaster as his own good luck. Somebody would eventually get that empty room. Why not him?

What is missing in Cohen's account is self-awareness. It is not the outcome so much that is unseemly but the haste with which it was reached. It required a marked attitude on his part: within a minute, the "fellow human being" perched on the ledge became the "one who's causing all the commotion." That less sympathetic characterization suited Cohen's need for a room. Apparently he slept well that night, though the clerk who had to deal with his insistence had one more experience of hard-boiled life in the city. And, who knows, maybe the family of the poor soul on the ledge was distressed to learn that someone had commandeered their father or husband's room even before he left it. All this in the name of self-interest.

Notes

1. The original Fisher-Ury edition was published in 1981. Commentary in this essay is based on the later revision, which Bruce Patton joined as a coauthor, as it includes an epilogue with several pages on fairness in negotiation.

2. They also say, "We do not suggest that you should be good for the sake of being good (nor do we discourage it)" (Fisher, Ury, and Patton, 1991, p. 154).

3. One wonders how the store owner might feel about that relationship after reading Cohen's description in the book.

4. By this reasoning, using an illegal radar detector to evade police is unethical.

5. All three authors of the second edition went on to write their own books on negotiating better relationships (Ury, 1991; Fisher and Brown, 1989; Stone, Heen, and Patton, 2000).

6. As it happens, Cohen cites this example too.

7. Cohen, incidentally, makes this same point, warning readers against making sharp choices that they will come to regret.

References

Badaracco, J. L., Jr. *Defining Moments: When Managers Must Choose Between Right and Right*. Boston: Harvard Business School Press, 1997.

Cialdini, R. B. *Influence: The Psychology of Persuasion.* (Rev. ed.). New York: Morrow, 1993.

Cohen, H. *You Can Negotiate Anything.* New York: Bantam Books, 1982. (Originally published 1980.)

Fisher, R., and Brown, S. *Getting Together: Building Relationships as We Negotiate.* New York: Penguin Books, 1989.

Fisher, R., Ury, W., and Patton, B. *Getting to Yes: Negotiating Agreement Without Giving In.* (2nd ed.). New York: Penguin Books, 1991.

George, E. S. "Review: *You Can Negotiate Anything.*" *American Bar Association Journal,* 1981, *67,* 1154–1158.

Goldhirsh Group, "Getting to Yes." *LexisNexis™ Academic,* 1982, p. 140.

Menkel-Meadow, C. "Legal Negotiation: A Study of Strategy in Search of a Theory." *American Bar Foundation Research Journal,* 1983, *4,* 905–937.

Press, A., Glass, C., and Foote, D. "Winning by Negotiation." *Newsweek,* Oct. 26, 1981, p. 86.

Stone, D., Heen, S., and Patton, B. *Difficult Conversations: How to Discuss What Matters Most.* New York: Penguin Books, 2000.

Ury, W. *Getting Past No: Negotiating Your Way from Confrontation to Cooperation.* New York: Bantam, 1991.

White, J. J. "The Pros and Cons of 'Getting to Yes.'" *Journal of Legal Education,* 1984, *34,* 115–124.

PART ONE

OVERVIEW

"Reading about ethics," Mason Cooley (1988) says, "is about as likely to improve one's behavior as reading about sports is to make one into an athlete." The only germ of truth in Cooley's wisecrack is that good intentions alone do not get us very far. Beyond that, analogizing ethics to sports misses the point.

Our ethical fitness cannot be built by pumping iron or running wind sprints. It depends instead on our intellectual and emotional capacity, starting with our ability to recognize difficult questions of right and wrong. These are not always easy to spot, particularly when they surface in the heat of negotiation and are entangled with high-stakes substantive issues. Moreover, we have to make ethical judgments while we are also trying to advocate our own interests, understand those of counterparts, manage feelings, and, oh yes, conjure up some sort of practical solution. Small wonder that people sometimes slip up.

Doing the right thing is more likely if we can anticipate potential issues before they arise and thus have well-reasoned principles to guide our response. Reading about the experiences of others sharpens our ethical vision. Comparing different frameworks and practices allows us to deepen our own values. You are therefore invited to read on, Cooley's jibe notwithstanding.

Most chapters later in this book explore specific ethical problems in negotiation, such as the issue of deception or possible conflicts of interest between principals and agents, to name just two examples. By contrast, the chapters in Part One represent broader perspectives on ethical decision making and introduce themes that are developed throughout the book.

In Chapter One, David Lax and James Sebenius succinctly identify three areas of ethical concern—tactical moves to influence others' perceptions, distributional fairness, and impacts on unrepresented stakeholders—and then offer practical tests for drawing the bounds of responsible behavior. They also distinguish between ethical concerns that are instrumental and those that are intrinsic: the former involve awareness of long-term payoffs of our actions, while the latter raise fundamental questions of right and wrong.

Next are two chapters by Howard Raiffa, one from his classic *Art and Science of Negotiation* written twenty years ago and the other from his just published sequel, *Negotiation Analysis*. As might be expected from a pioneer in the formal modeling of decisions, his analysis is constructed around a so-called social dilemma, a situation in which each individual must decide whether to do something good for the group as a whole, albeit at some cost personally. Many economists conclude that only self-centered behavior is rational, even though it leaves everyone worse off. Raiffa, however, instead argues for a moral frame of reference, with virtue being its own reward. Better still, he says, when selfless acts are made visible, others are inspired to follow suit. His straightforward view recalls Mark Twain's injunction (1901), "Always do right. This will gratify some people, and astonish the rest."

Raiffa's chapters illustrate how disciplinary frames themselves are value laden. Roger Fisher, another negotiation luminary, describes in Chapter Four how professional roles can bias our approach to problem solving, challenging in particular the canard that lawyers can only act as hired guns. He urges attorneys instead to explicitly negotiate their relationships with clients, clarifying what they will and will not do in the name of effective representation. Fisher does not eschew all advocacy, but he stresses that lawyers are also counselors and quasimediators. Above all else, they must be models of responsible conduct (walk the talk, if you will). Fisher's chapter foreshadows other material in this book, specifically the parts on relationships and agents (Parts Four and Five).

Gerald Wetlaufer presents a different point of view in Chapter Five, one that is largely skeptical of the claims that Raiffa, Fisher, and others have made on behalf of the promise of integrative or mutual gains bargaining. Wetlaufer acknowledges that mutually beneficial trades are possible in some instances but believes that those are the exception, not the rule. Readers can judge for themselves whether he makes that case. The important question for our purposes is how our views of negotiation ethics are premised on assumptions about whether the world is primarily zero sum. If it is, then doing the right thing would always seem to come at personal cost.

Richard Shell reminds us in Chapter Six that some ethical standards are embodied in legal standards, notably the prohibition against fraud. When other parties reasonably rely on material misrepresentations we have made in the course of negotiation, they can sue us, nullify the agreement, and recover damages. In one sense, the law of fraud protects victims of unscrupulous behavior. In another sense, it promotes beneficial exchanges by lending credibility that whatever we promise will in fact be delivered.

Shell contends that compliance with legal standards is a minimum threshold. Honoring more rigorous unwritten norms may be necessary, though their specific definition may vary depending on whether one is an idealist, pragmatist, or someone who sees negotiation as a game. Reading through this book, you can consider which of those categories best suit you. You may find some ideas you encounter congenial and others challenging. If none of the models fits perfectly, the process of reflection still should help you identify your own coherent values and rules of thumb for doing the right thing at the bargaining table.

References

Cooley, M. *City Aphorisms, Fifth Selection,* New York, 1988. Quote obtained from www.bartleby.com/66/96/13596.html

Twain, M. *Card Sent to the Young People's Society, Greenpoint Presbyterian Church,* Brooklyn, N.Y., Feb. 16, 1901. Quote obtained from www.bartleby.com/66/29/62029.html

CHAPTER ONE

Three Ethical Issues in Negotiation

David A. Lax

James K. Sebenius

The agent for a small grain seller reported the following telephone conversation, concerning a disagreement over grain contracted to be sold to General Mills:

> We're General Mills; and if you don't deliver this grain to us, why we'll have a battery of lawyers in there tomorrow morning to visit you, and then we are going to the North Dakota Public Service [Commission]; we're going to the Minneapolis Grain Exchange and we're going to the people in Montana and there will be no more Muschler Grain Company. We're going to take your license.[1]

Tactics mainly intended to permit one party to claim value at another's expense inescapably raise hard ethical issues. How should one evaluate moves that stake out positions, threaten another with walkout or worse, misrepresent values or beliefs, hold another person's wants hostage to claim value at that person's expense, or offer an "elegant" solution of undeniable joint benefit but constructed so that one side will get the lion's share?

One approach to these questions is denial—to believe, pretend, or wish that conflict and questions of dividing the pie have no part in negotiation and hence such tactical choices are falsely posed: "If one really understood that the whole

---

We are particularly indebted to Howard Raiffa and to the discussion of ethics in his book *The Art and Science of Negotiation*.

process was effective communication and joint problem solving, one could dispense with any unpleasant-seeming tactics, except to think about responding to their use by nasty opponents." However, denying that conflict over process and results is an essential part of negotiation is badly flawed conceptually.[2] Or one can admit that there are hard ethical questions but deny they are relevant, as suggested by the following advice (Beckman, 1977) from a handbook on business negotiation:

> Many negotiators fail to understand the nature of negotiation and so find themselves attempting to reconcile conflicts between the requirements of negotiation and their own senses of personal integrity. An individual who confuses private ethics with business morality does not make an effective negotiator. A negotiator must learn to be objective in his negotiations and to subordinate his own personal sense of ethics to the prime purpose of securing the best deal possible for his principals.

Just as we are uncomfortable denying the reality of conflict in bargaining in order to evade ethical issues, it is scarcely more satisfying to admit that ethical issues exist but, following the author of the above remark, simply to assert that they are irrelevant. Instead, we find at least two kinds of reasons to be concerned with ethical issues in negotiation.[3]

Many people want to be "ethical" for intrinsic reason—apart from the effect of such choices on future encounters. Why? Variously: because it simply feels better, because one ascribes an independent value to acting "ethically" because it may be psychologically healthier, because certain principles of good behavior are taken as moral or religious absolutes, or for other reasons.[4] Yet it is often hard in negotiation to decide what actions fit these criteria, especially when values or principles appear to conflict.

Ethical behavior may also have instrumental value. One hears that "it pays to be ethical" or "sound ethics is good business," meaning that if a negotiator calculates correctly, taking into account the current and long-run costs of overly shrewd behavior, profits and benefits will be higher. The eighteenth century diplomat François de Callières (1716) made a more expansive version of this point:

> It is a capital error, which prevails widely, that a clever negotiator must be a master of the art of deceit. . . . No doubt the art of lying has been practiced with success in diplomacy; but unlike that honesty which here as elsewhere is the best policy, a lie always leaves a drop of poison behind, and even the most dazzling diplomatic success gained by dishonesty stands on an insecure foundation, for it awakes in the defeated party a sense of aggravation, a desire for vengeance, and a hatred which must always be a menace to his foe. . . . The negotiator will perhaps bear in mind that he will be engaged throughout life upon affairs of

diplomacy and that it is therefore his interest to establish a reputation for plain and fair dealing . . . [which] will give him a great advantage in other enterprises on which he embarks in the future.

Of course, such justifications of ethics in terms of prudence rely on the calculation of its benefits turning out the right way. "Cast thy bread upon the waters," the Bible says, "and it shall return to thee after many days." The harder case, however, is when ethical behavior does not seem to pay—even after correctly factoring in the long-term costs of reputation, credibility, how others may react, and any ill social effects. Then one is back to intrinsic justifications.

Assuming, however, that ethical issues are relevant to bargaining, for whatever reasons, three characteristic areas strike us as especially useful to discuss: the appropriateness of certain tactics, the distribution among the bargainers of value created by agreement, and the possible effects of negotiation on those not at the table (externalities).[5] Without elaborating the philosophical frameworks within which such questions can be more fully addressed, we offer some thought on making these kinds of inescapable ethical choices.[6]

TACTICAL CHOICE

The essence of much bargaining involves changing another's perceptions of where in fact one would settle. Several kinds of tactics can lead to impressions that are at variance with the truth about one's actual position: persuasive rationales, commitments, references to other no-agreement alternatives, calculated patterns of concessions, failures to correct misperceptions, and the like. These tactics are tempting for obvious reasons: one side may claim value by causing the other to misperceive the range of potentially acceptable agreements. And both sides are generally in this same boat.

Such misrepresentations about each side's real interests and the set of possible bargaining outcomes should be distinguished from misrepresentations about certain aspects of the substance of the negotiation (e.g., whether the car has known difficulties that will require repair, whether the firm being acquired has important undiscussed liabilities, and so on). This latter category of tactics, which we might dub "malign persuasion," more frequently fails tests of ethical appropriateness. Consider two such tests.

Are the "Rules" Known and Accepted by All Sides?

Some people take the symmetry of the bargaining situation to ease the difficulty of ethical choice. The British statesman Henry Taylor is reported to have said that "falsehood ceases to be falsehood when it is understood on all sides that the truth is not expected to be spoken." In other words, if these tactics are mutually accepted as within the "rules of the game," there is no problem. A good analogy can be found in a game of poker: bluffing is expected and thus permissible, while drawing a gun or kicking over the table are not. Yet often, the line is harder to draw.

For instance, a foreigner in Hong Kong may be aware that at least some tailors bargain routinely but still be unsure whether a particular one—who insists he has fixed prices—is "just bargaining." Yet that tailor may reap considerable advantage if in fact he bargains but is persuasive that he does not. It is often self-servingly easy for the deceiver to assume that others know and accept the rules. And a worse problem is posed if many situations are often not even recognized as negotiation, when in fact they exhibit its essential characteristics (interdependence, some perceived conflict, opportunistic potential, the possibility of explicit or tacit agreement on joint action).[7] When, as is often the case in organizational life, such less acknowledged negotiation occurs, then how can any "rules" of the game meet the mutual "awareness and acceptance of the rules" test?

Can the Situation Be Freely Entered and Left?

Ethicist Sissela Bok (1978) adds another criterion: for lying to be appropriate, not only must the rules be well understood, but the participants must be able freely to enter and leave the situation. Thus, to the extent that mutually expected, ritual flattery or a work of fiction involve "lying," there is little problem. To make an analogy between deception and violence: though a boxing match, which can involve rough moves, meets this criterion, a duel, from which exit may be impossible, does not.

Yet this standard may be too high. Bargaining situations—formal and informal, tacit and explicit—are far more widespread than many people realize. In fact, a good case can be made that bargaining pervades life inside and outside of organizations, making continual free entry and exit impractical. So if bargaining will go on and people will necessarily be involved in it, something else is required.

Other Helpful Questions

When it is unclear whether a particular tactic is ethically appropriate, we find that a number of other questions—beyond whether others know and accept it or may leave—can illuminate the choice. Consider several such questions:

Self-Image. Peter Drucker (1981) asks a basic question: When you look at yourself in the mirror the next morning, will you like the person you see? And there are many such useful queries about self-image, which are intended to clarify the appropriateness of the choice itself and not to ask about the possible consequences (firing, ostracism, etc.) to you of different parties being aware of your actions: Would you be comfortable if your co-workers, colleagues, and friends were aware that you had used a particular tactic? Your spouse, children, or parents? If it came out on the front page of the *New York Times* or the *Wall Street Journal*? If it became known in ten years? Twenty? In the history books?

Reciprocity. Does it accord with the Golden Rule? How would you feel if someone did it to you? To a younger colleague? A respected mentor? A member of your family? (Of course, saying that you would mind very much if it were done to another need not imply that the tactic is unethical; that person may not be in your situation or have your experience—but figuring out the reason you would be bothered can give a clue to the ethics of the choice.)

Advising Others. Would you be comfortable advising another to use this tactic? Instructing your agent to use it? How about if such advice became known?

Designing the System. Imagine that you were completely outside the setting in which the tactic might be used, but that you were responsible for designing the situation itself, the number of people present, their stakes, the conventions governing their encounters, the range of permissible actions, and so on. The wrinkle is that you would be assigned a role in that setting, *but* you would not know in advance the identity of the person whose role you would assume. Would you build in the possibility for the kind of tactics you are now trying to evaluate?[8] A simpler version of this test is to ask how you would rule on this tactic if you were an arbitrator, or perhaps an elder, in a small society.

Social Result. What if everybody bargained this way? Would the resulting society be desirable? These questions may not have obvious answers. For example, hard individual competition may seem dehumanizing. Yet many argue that precisely because competition is encouraged, standards of living rise in free-market societies, and some forms of excellence flourish.[9]

Alternative Tactics. Are there alternative tactics available that have fewer ethical ambiguities or costs? Can the whole issue be avoided by following a different tack, even at a small cost elsewhere?

Taking a Broader View. In agonizing over a tactic—for instance, whether to shade values—it is often worth stepping back to take a broader perspective.

First, there is a powerful tendency for people to focus on conflict, see a "zero sum" world, and primarily aim to enlarge their individual shares. Such an emphasis on "claiming" is common, yet it can stunt creativity and often cause significant joint gains to go unrealized. In such cases, does the real problem lie in the ethical judgment call about a tactic intended to claim value, or is it a disproportionate focus on claiming itself? If it is the latter, the more fruitful question may be how to make the other face of negotiation—moves jointly to "create" value—more salient.

Second, does the type of situation itself generate powerful tendencies toward the questionable tactics involved? Is it an industry in which "favors" to public officials are an "expected" means for winning good contracts? If so, evaluating the acceptability of a given move may be less important than deciding whether to leave the situation that inherently poses such choices or which actions could alter, even slightly, the prevalence of the questionable practices.

DISTRIBUTIONAL FAIRNESS

One reason that a tactical choice can be uncomfortable is its potential effect on the distribution of value created by agreement. If a "shrewd" move allows a large firm to squeeze a small merchant unmercifully or an experienced negotiator to walk away with all the profit in dealings with a novice, something may seem wrong. Even when the nature of the tactics is not in question, the "fairness" of the outcome may be.

This difficulty is inherent in negotiation. Since there is a bargaining set of many potential agreements that are better for each person than his or her respective alternatives to agreement, the value created by agreement must necessarily be apportioned. Ultimately, when all joint gains have been discovered and common value created, more value for one party means less for another. But just where should the value split be? This, of course, is the age-old problem of "distributive justice," of what a just distribution of rewards and risks in a society should be. In the same way that this is a thorny, unresolved problem at the social level, so it is for individual negotiators—even when less well-recognized.[10] And this is why the problem is so hard and does not admit easy answers.

A classic problem among game theorists involves trying to develop fair criteria to arbitrate the division of $200 between two people.[11] An obvious norm involves an even split of $100 for each. But what if one is rich and the other poor? More for the poor man, right? "Not at all!" protests the rich woman. "You must look at after-tax revenue, even if you want a little more to end up going to the poor man. Moreover, you should really try to equalize the amount of good done for each of us—in which case $20 to him will improve his life much more than $180 will mine. Or look at it the other way: ask who can better afford to *lose* what amounts—and he can afford to lose $5 about as much as I can $195. Besides, he is a wino and completely on his own. I will sign this pledge to give the money to Mother Teresa, who will use it to help dozens of poor people in India. After all, that poor man *was* rich just two weeks ago, when he was convicted of fraud and had all his money confiscated to pay back his victims."

Who "should" get what in a negotiated agreement? The preceding tongue-in-cheek discussion should not obscure the importance of distributional questions. Certainly negotiators argue for this solution or that on the basis of "fairness" all the time. But the rich woman's objections should underscore how fragile and divisive conceptions of equity may be. One person's fairness may be another's outrage.

And fairness not only applies to the process of bargaining but also to its underlying structure. Think of the wage "bargaining" between an illegal alien and her work supervisor who can have her deported at a moment's notice. Is such a situation so loaded against one of the participants that the results are virtually certain to be "unfairly" distributed?

Many times, by contrast, we will be comfortable answering that we do not care about the actual result, only that the process was within normal bounds, that the participants intelligent and well-informed enough, and that no one outside the negotiation was harmed by the accord.

EXTERNALITIES

A third broad question involving others who are not at the bargaining table deserves some mention. If the Teamsters Union, major trucking firms, and a "captive" Interstate Commerce Commission informally bargained and agreed on higher rates, what about the interests of the unrepresented public? How do the children's interests figure into a divorce settlement hammered out by two adversarial lawyers who only know that each parent wants custody? Or, suppose that a commission negotiates and decides to raise current social security benefits dramatically but pay for them by issuing very long-term bonds, the bulk of whose burden will fall on the next two generations?

It is often easy to "solve" the negotiation problem for those in the room at the expense of those who are not. If such parties cannot take part directly, one way to "internalize" this "externality" is to keep their interests in mind or to invite the participation or observation of those who can represent their interests, if only indirectly.[12] Deciding that the process could be improved this way may not be too hard, though the mechanics of representation can be trickier. Yet even with "proper" representation, what about the actual outcome? We are back to questions akin to those in the section on distribution.

There is another, more subtle, external effect of the way in which ethical questions in bargaining are resolved. It involves the spillover of the way one person bargains into the pattern of dealings of others. Over time, each of us comes to hold assumptions about what is likely and appropriate in bargaining interactions. Each tactical choice shapes these expectations and reverberates throughout the circles we inhabit. And many people lament that the state of dealings in business and government is such that behavior we might prefer to avoid becomes almost irresistible, since others are doing it and overly idealistic actions could be very costly.

CONCLUSION

The overall choice of how to negotiate, whether to emphasize moves that create value or claim it, has implications beyond single encounters. The dynamic that leads individual bargainers to poor agreements, impasses, and conflict spirals also has a larger social counterpart. Without choices that keep creative actions from being driven out, this larger social game tends toward an equilibrium in which everyone claims, engages constantly in behavior that distorts information, and worse.

Most people are willing to sacrifice something to avoid such outcomes and to improve the way people relate to each other in negotiation and beyond. The wider echoes of ethical choices made in negotiation can be forces for positive change. Each person must decide if individual risks are worth general improvement, even if such improvement seems small, uncertain, and not likely to be visible. Yet a widespread choice to disregard ethics in negotiation would mark a long step down the road to a more cynical, Hobbesian world.

Notes

1. *Jamestown Farmers Elevator, Inc.* v. *General Mills,* 552 F.2d 1285, 1289 (8th Cir. 1977).

2. We elaborate this point in Chapters Two, Six, and Seven of Lax and Sebenius (1986).

3. For an insightful, commonsense discussion of the reasons for being "moral," see Hospers (1961).

4. If certain precepts are taken as Kantian categorical imperatives or as otherwise correct in an absolute sense, regardless of the consequences (the strong deontological position), the decision problem may be easy—unless more than one such principle appears to conflict.

5. Of course, there are many ethical issues involved in bargaining beyond those treated here—for example: How should an attorney bargain on behalf of a client that she believes is guilty? Should a bargaining agent be solely guided by his principal's conception of her own interests? Even where the agent thinks he "knows better" or is more "expert"? Where one party psychologically "dominates" the other? How can one party "properly" represent a constituent group, especially where the interests of the group members diverge?

6. For a good informal discussion of these questions, especially the first, see Raiffa (1982).

7. For an extended discussion, see Chapter One of Lax and Sebenius (1986).

8. This discussion draws from Rawls (1971).

9. But the welfare theorems of economics—that prove that competition equilibria are Pareto optimal and that Pareto-optimal allocations of goods and services are competitive equilibria—assume that bargaining is Pareto efficient. The thrust of our argument about the "Negotiator's Dilemma" (see Lax and Sebenius, 1986) and the work of bargaining with incomplete information (see, for example, Chatterjee, 1982; Rubinstein, 1983; Cramton, 1983, 1984a, 1984b; and Myerson, 1985) is that bargained outcomes will tend to be inefficient since bargainers act on the temptation to misrepresent.

10. In fact, bargaining is a time-honored way of resolving this dilemma, just as pure markets, legislative action, and judicial ruling are in other spheres where distributive issues must be settled. See Lindblom (1977).

11. For a very clear look at how analysts have approached this kind of problem, see Raiffa (1982).

12. For a discussion of this problem in the context of public disputes, see Susskind and Ozawa (1983).

References

Beckman, N. *Negotiations*. San Francisco: New Lexington Press, 1977.

Bok, S. *Lying: Moral Choice in Public and Private Life.* New York: Vintage Books, 1978.

Chatterjee, K. "Incentive Compatibility in Bargaining Under Uncertainty." *Quarterly Journal of Economics,* 1982, *82,* 717–726.

Cramton, P. C. "Bargaining with Incomplete Information: An Infinite Horizon-Model with Continuous Uncertainty." Stanford Graduate School of Business Research Paper no. 680, 1983.

Cramton, P. C. "Bargaining with Incomplete Information: A Two-Period Model with Continuous Uncertainty." *Review of Economic Studies,* 1984a, *51,* 579–593.

Cramton, P. C. "The Role of Time and Information in Bargaining." Stanford Graduate School of Business Research Paper no. 729, 1984b.

de Callières, F. *On the Manner of Negotiating with Princes* (A. F. Whyte, trans.). Boston: Houghton Mifflin, 1919. (Originally published 1716.)

Hospers, J. *Human Conduct.* New York: Harcourt, 1961.

Lax, D. A., and Sebenius, J. K. *The Manager as Negotiator.* New York: Free Press, 1986.

Lindblom, C. E. *Politics and Markets.* New York: Basic Books, 1977.

Myerson, R. "Analysis of Two Bargaining Problems with Incomplete Information." In A. Roth (ed.), *Game Theoretic Models of Bargaining.* Cambridge: Cambridge University Press. 1985.

Raiffa, H. *The Art and Science of Negotiation.* Cambridge, Mass.: Harvard University Press, 1982.

Rawls, J. *A Theory of Justice.* Cambridge, Mass.: Harvard University Press, 1971.

Rubinstein, A. "A Bargaining Model with Incomplete Information." Unpublished manuscript, Department of Economics, Hebrew University. Jerusalem, 1983.

Susskind, L., and Ozawa, C. "Mediated Negotiation in the Public Sector." *American Behavioral Scientist,* 1983, *27,* 255–279.

CHAPTER TWO

Ethical and Moral Issues

Howard Raiffa

It's often said that dishonesty in the short run is a poor policy because a tarnished reputation hurts in the long run. The moral question is: Should you be open and honest in the short run because it is right to act that way, even though it might hurt you in the long run?

The hundreds of responses I have obtained to a questionnaire on ethical values are instructive. The distributions of the responses from students of business administration, government, and law are reasonable. But the students do not overwhelmingly say, "That sort of behavior may be borderline in my opinion for others, but is unacceptable to me." Most say, "If I were in that situation, I also probably would act in that borderline way"; and a few say, "I think that that behavior is unethical, but I probably would do the same." That's disturbing to me.

One student defended herself—even though the questionnaires were anonymous—by stating that most businesspeople in their ordinary activities are not subjected to those moral dilemmas. And although she reluctantly admitted that she would act in an unethical manner if she were unlucky enough to be in the position of the contractor who is being unmercifully squeezed, she would try her utmost not to get into such situations.

Let's abstract and simplify by looking at a simple laboratory exercise concerning an ethical choice. Imagine that you have to choose whether to act nobly or selfishly. If you act nobly, you will be helping others at your own expense; if you act selfishly, you will be helping yourself at others' expense. Similarly, those others have similar choices. In order to highlight the tension between helping yourself and helping others, let's specify that if all participants act nobly, all do well and the society flourishes; but regardless of how others act, you can always do better for yourself, as measured in tangible rewards (say, profits), if you act selfishly—but at the expense of others. Leaving morality aside for the moment, the best tangible reward accrues to you in this asocial game if you act selfishly and all others act nobly. But if all behave that way, all suffer greatly.

To be more concrete, suppose that you are one player in a group of 101, so that there are 100 "others." You have two choices: act nobly or act selfishly. Your payoff depends on your choice and on the proportion of the "others" who choose to act nobly (see Figure 2.1). If, for example, 0.7 of the others act nobly, your payoff is $40 when you act nobly and $140 when you act selfishly. Notice that regardless of what the others do, if you were to switch from noble to selfish behavior, you would receive $100 more; but because of your switch, each of the others would be penalized by $2 and the total penalty to others would be $200—more than what you personally gain. The harm you cause to others, however, is shared: you impose a small harm on each of many.

If the others can see that you are acting selfishly, then acting unselfishly may be your prudent action from a cold, calculating, long-term-benefit point of view.

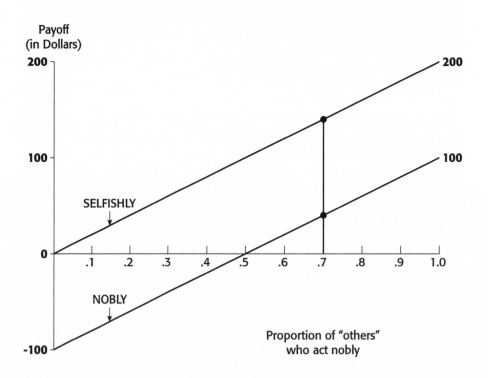

Figure 2.1 Payoffs for the Social Dilemma Game

Your good reputation may be a proxy for future tangible rewards. But what if the others (because of the rules of the game) cannot see how you, in particular, behave? Suppose that all anyone learns is how many of the others chose the selfish option?[1]

I learned about this game from Thomas Schelling, who dubbed it the "*N*-Person Prisoner's Dilemma Game," a direct generalization of that famous two-person game. In the literature, these games are called "social dilemmas" or "social traps," and are sometimes discussed under the heading of "the problem of the commons" or "the free-rider problem." Whenever anyone uses "the commons," there is a little less for everyone else. The "commons" could be a town green, common grazing land, a common river, the ocean, or the atmosphere. Overpopulating our common planet is a prime manifestation of this problem. Whenever we enjoy a public benefit without paying our due share, we are a "free rider." One variation of the free-rider problem is the noble-volunteer problem: Will a hero please step forward—and risk his or her life for the good of the many?

Subjects were asked to play this social dilemma game not for monetary payoffs, but as if there would be monetary payoffs. There might, therefore, be some distortion in the results—probably not much, but in any case the experimental results are not comforting. Roughly 85 percent of the subjects acted noncooperatively—acted to protect their own interests. Most subjects believed that only a small minority of the others would choose the cooperative (noble) act, and they saw no reason why they should be penalized; so they chose not to act cooperatively. They felt that it was not their behavior that was wrong, but the situation they were participating in. Unfortunately, many real-world games have these characteristics. A few subjects acted cooperatively because they were simply confused; but others—the really noble ones—knew exactly what was going on and chose to sacrifice their own tangible rewards for the good of the others, even though the others did not know who was acting for their benefit. If the rules of the game were changed to make "goodness" more visible, then more subjects would opt for the noble action—some, perhaps, for long-range selfish reasons. This suggests a positive action program: we should try to identify asocial games (social dilemmas) and modify the rules, if possible (which is easier said than done).

Now let's suppose that you are in a position to influence the one hundred others to act nobly by publicly appealing to their consciences. Do you need to influence all to follow your lead? No. You will get a higher monetary return for yourself by converting fifty selfish souls to the noble cause than by joining the

---

[1] In the laboratory version of the game I use less connotative terminology: "act cooperatively" instead of "act nobly" and "act noncooperatively" instead of "act selfishly." I'm sure that the mere labeling of these acts influences some behavior.

ranks of the selfish. But balancing tangible and intangible rewards, you might still prefer to act nobly if you could get, say, forty conversions; with fewer conversions, you might be sacrificing too much. Suppose that you are wildly successful: seventy-five others join your coalition. Say that seventeen of these would have acted nobly anyway; three are despicable poseurs who join the nobles but who will defect secretly; and fifty-five have actually been swayed by your moral pleadings. Now you not only have benefited financially, but you feel morally righteous as well. Unfortunately, your actions have also made it more profitable for the remaining twenty-five who have not joined your coalition. Each conversion adds $2 to the payoff of each of the others, including the selfish holdouts—they've been helped by your successful proselytizing. This may really bother some of the converted ones; it's unfair, they may argue, that the selfish, undeserving ones should profit from the noble actions of the majority. (A real-world analogue is the case where most of the nations of the world might agree not to catch blue whales, and because of this pact, it becomes easier for one noncooperating whaling country to find its prey.) Some of your converts may be so bothered to see that the undeserving are doing better than themselves that they may decide to defect. They may argue that the coalition is not working, when in absolute terms it may be working for them; but it may not be working in comparative terms. It rankles them that they are helping someone who is taking advantage of their noble behavior. So a few defect, and as a result, the coalition can easily come apart.

CHAPTER THREE

Negotiation Analysis

Howard Raiffa with John Richardson and David Metcalfe

THE MISPLACED MATTRESS

Imagine this scenario: One miserably hot afternoon, you are driving from Boston to Cape Cod. Traffic is crawling along a stretch of two-lane, one-way highway that usually presents no problem. Finally after an interminable time, you discover the trouble: a mattress is in the middle of the road; cars have to squeeze to one side to pass it. After you clear the problem, should you stop your car and move the mattress? There will be at least some inconvenience to you and possibly a bit of danger involved if you stop. "Why should I be the fall guy? Let someone else be the good guy. Anyway, I'm already late, because of the delay, for my appointment."

This scenario, concocted by Thomas Schelling, depicts another aspect of the social trap problem. What would you do? Would you stop and move the mattress?

It would be interesting to see how various cultural groups would react to this problem. A Mormon student we know claimed that if the mattress were on a highway in Utah it would be moved very quickly. It is part of the Mormon culture to try to do good for others, to take responsibility for the common cause. Would Japanese behave differently than Chinese or East Indians or Israelis or Kenyans or Swedes? How much are we individually willing to sacrifice for the good of others when we get no immediate tangible reward other than the self-satisfaction of doing good?

PERSONAL CHARITIES

Some give a lot to charity; others, in similar financial circumstances, give little. Foundations and personal philanthropy account for much of the support of medical, educational, and art institutions, as well as for support of the needy. As a society we should be proud of the amount of individual charitable giving. But the process is flawed, because there are many free riders who prefer to keep their money and let others support these causes, and because some causes do not adequately attract the support of the givers. One alternative, of course, is to depend less on charitable giving and more on governmental interventions for welfare and public institutions. The government would drain away some of the money from the givers and the nongivers (the free riders) and allocate it as it sees fit. The argument against the government's assuming the supporting role is that it involves too much bureaucracy and the government is not close enough to the needs of the people; better to administer welfare through the churches than through the government. It's not one or the other, of course, but mixtures of the two, and the U.S. government tilts more to the voluntary side than many of the European countries. Those governments tax more and spend more on welfare but perhaps not as much on medical research. The U.S. government provides generous tax exemptions for charitable giving, and this influences behavior.

SOME PERSONAL REFLECTIONS

Occasionally I find myself in the position exemplified by the n-person social trap: I can act to improve my immediate well-being a good deal, but only at the expense of hurting a lot of others a little bit and where the totality of damage to others is greater than my personal gains. For example, I drive my car and shun public transportation. As an analyst, I think about these issues. I'm not a purist, and my tradeoffs depend on the amount I'm being called upon to sacrifice and the totality of harm to others and how this collective harm is distributed.

I believe that most utilitarian calculations in situational ethics are too narrowly conceived. In a loose sense, all of us are engaged in a grandiose, many-person, social dilemma game, where each of us has to decide how much we should sacrifice to benefit others. The vast majority of us would like to participate in a more cooperative society, and all of us may have to make some sacrifice in the short run for that long-run goal. We have to calculate, at least informally, the dynamic linkages between our actions now and the later actions of others. If we are more ethical, it makes it easier for others to be more ethical. And as was the case in the multiperson social dilemma game, we should not become excessively distraught if there are a few cynical souls who will tangibly profit from our combined beneficent acts.

If you act to help others, you may hurt yourself in the short run; but if your act is visible to others, you may profit from it in the long run because of the cyclical reciprocities it may engender. In that sense, your noble-appearing action may be in your long-run selfish interest. Yet much traditional moral teaching holds that doing good should not be advertised.

I think we should not demean visible acts of kindness, even though in part they may be self-serving, because those actions may make it easier for others to act similarly, and the dynamics will reinforce behavior that is in the common interest. An action that represents a moderate sacrifice in the short run may represent only a very modest sacrifice in the long run, when dynamic linkages are properly calculated. Many people, including myself, are also willing to make small (long-run) sacrifices for the good of others, all things considered. The visibility of beneficent acts thus plays a dual role: it reduces the tangible penalties to the actor, and it spurs others to act similarly; these two facets then interact cyclically.

A student of mine who heard this sermonizing said, "All this sounds a bit cynical to me. I don't want to teach my children to make personal sacrifices with lots of visibility to entice others to do good. Goodness should be its own reward." And when I responded, "But why not exploit the contagion factor of doing good?" he quipped, "So when the box goes around in the movie theatre for muscular dystrophy, you want me to say in a loud voice to my date: 'Should I put in five or ten dollars, sweetie?'"

I should say that I also believe that empathizing with others should be reflected in your own utility calculations: a sacrifice in long-range tangible effects to yourself, if it is compensated by ample gains for others, could be tallied as a positive contribution to your cognitive utilitarian calculations. I guess that's just an analytical way of saying that doing good is its own reward. But doing good and getting others to do some seems even better.

CORE CONCEPTS

How much are you willing to sacrifice to help others? How should you trade off a tangible hurt to yourself for the benefit of society?

> The essence of the social dilemma is that each player has a dominant strategy, but when each acts rationally by choosing this strategy, the entire group suffers. Each player has a choice: do what makes sense selfishly, or make a personal sacrifice for the good of the whole. If they all make a sacrifice, then each will do better than if they had all acted selfishly. (Raiffa, Richardson, and Metcalfe, 2002)

This chapter has returned to the social dilemma game, but this time the focus was on not two parties but many. We have analyzed a simple, highly stylized social dilemma game with many players from a behavioral game theory perspective. Each of N players must choose either to cooperate (C) or to defect (D); the C's create wealth (at some expense to themselves) and the D's free-ride. Individual rationality leads to social irrationality, just as in the two-party version. Variations were considered: whether preplay communication is permitted (if so, some players could act as leaders and preach cooperation); whether the players know who is choosing what before or after choices are made; whether the game is repeated (allowing the possibility of temporal collusion).

References

Raiffa, H., Richardson, J., and Metcalfe, D. *Negotiation Analysis: The Science and Art of Collaborative Decision Making.* Cambridge, Mass.: Belknap Press, 2002.

CHAPTER FOUR

A Code of Negotiation Practices for Lawyers

Roger Fisher

Most ethical problems facing lawyers in a negotiation stem from a conflict of interest between the lawyer's obligation to the client (presumably to get the best deal) and two of the lawyer's other interests: behaving honorably toward others involved in the negotiation and self-interest in preserving reputation and self-esteem.

It is often asserted that a lawyer is obliged to bluff and deceive those on the other side to the extent that it is ethically possible to do so. Professor James White of Michigan has written, "In one sense the negotiator's role is at least passively to mislead his opponent . . . while at the same time to engage in ethical behavior." And, "Anyone who would maximize his potential as a negotiator must occasionally do things that would cause others to classify him as a 'trickster,' whether he so classifies himself or not" (White, 1984, pp. 118–119).

It may be possible to limit these ethical problems by conducting a preliminary negotiation between lawyer and client, clarifying the basis on which the lawyer is conducting the negotiation. The following two drafts are intended to stimulate discussion of this possibility. The first is in the form of a memorandum that a lawyer might give to a new client, and the second an attached draft code of negotiating behavior.

Memorandum to a New Client: How I Propose to Negotiate

Attached to this memorandum is a Code of Negotiation Practices for Lawyers. It has been prepared by lawyers and other professional experts in the negotiation process and is based on a draft first produced by the Harvard Negotiation Project at Harvard Law School.

I would like to obtain your approval for my accepting this code as providing the general guidelines for any negotiations I may conduct on your behalf. I would also like you to know that I will follow these guidelines in any negotiations that you and I may have with each other, for example over the question of fees. Finally, I commend the code to you because I think it provides useful guidance on how you, yourself, might wish to conduct negotiations with others, even though you are not a lawyer.

The reason I would like your approval of my following this code in my negotiations as your lawyer is to avoid any future misunderstanding. In addition, I would like to put to rest the canard that because I am a lawyer, I have a "professional" duty to you as my client to engage in sharp or deceptive practices on your behalf—practices that I would not use on my own behalf and ones that might damage my credibility or my reputation for integrity. Let me explain.

The Code of Professional Responsibility approved by the American Bar Association provides that a lawyer should advance a client's interest zealously. The Code of Professional Responsibility does little to clarify this standard, and the Bar Association has failed to adopt proposed changes that would more explicitly permit a lawyer to balance the duty to be a partisan on behalf of a client with the duty to adhere to ethical standards of candor and honesty.

The result is that in the absence of client approval to do otherwise, it can be (and has been) argued that a lawyer should conceal information, bluff, and otherwise mislead people on behalf of a client even (1) where the lawyer would be unwilling for ethical reasons to do so on his or her own behalf; and (2) where the lawyer's best judgment is that to do so is contrary to the public interest, contrary to wise negotiation practices, and damaging to the very reputation for integrity that may have caused the client to retain the lawyer.

It is no doubt possible that in a given case a lawyer may obtain a short-term gain for a client by bluffing, threatening, actively misrepresenting the extent of the lawyer's authority, what the client is willing to do, or other facts, or by engaging in browbeating or other psychological pressure tactics. Yet many lawyers and academic experts believe that a practice of trying to settle differences by such tactics is risky for clients, bad for lawyers, and bad for society.

I believe that it is not a sound practice to negotiate in a way that rewards deception, stubbornness, dirty tricks, and taking risks. I think it wiser for our clients, ourselves, and our society to deal with differences in a way that optimizes the chance of reaching a fair outcome efficiently and amicably; that rewards those who are better prepared, more skillful and efficient, and who have the better case as measured by objective standards of fairness; and that makes each successive negotiation likely to be even better. (This does not mean that a negotiator should disclose everything or make unjustified concessions.)

The attached code is intended to accomplish those goals.

I hope you will read it and approve my trying to adhere to it. I will be happy to discuss it with you now and at any time during negotiations. Some of the ideas underlying the Code are discussed in the book *Getting to Yes: Negotiating Agreement Without Giving In* by Roger Fisher and William Ury (Houghton Mifflin, 1981). If you would like, I would be happy to provide you with a copy.

A Code of Negotiation Practices for Lawyers

I. Roles

1. Professional. You and those with whom you negotiate are members of an international profession of problem solvers. Do not look upon those on the other side as enemies but rather as partners with whom cooperation is essential and greatly in the interest of your client. You are colleagues in the difficult task of reconciling, as well as possible, interests that are sometimes shared but often conflict.
2. Advocate. You are also an advocate for your client's interests. You have a fiduciary obligation to look after the needs and concerns of your client, to make sure that they are taken into account, and to act in ways that will tend to ensure that they are well satisfied. It is not enough to seek a fair result. Among results that fall within the range of fairness, you should press with diligence and skill toward that result that best satisfies your client's interests consistent with being fair and socially acceptable.
3. Counselor. Clients, motivated by anger or short-term considerations, sometimes act, and may ask you to act, in ways that are contrary to their own best interests. Another of your roles is to help your clients take long-term considerations properly into account, come to understand their enlightened self-interest, and to pursue it.
4. Mediator. Furthermore, a negotiator often has to serve as a mediator between a client and those on the other side. Two lawyers, negotiating with each other, sometimes best function as comediators, trying to bring their clients together.
5. Model of just behavior. Finally, as a lawyer and negotiator, you should behave toward those with whom you negotiate in ways that incorporate the highest moral standards of civilization. Your conduct should be such that you regard it as a praiseworthy model for others to emulate and such that, if it became known, it would reflect credit on you and the bar. You should feel no obligation to be less candid for a client than you would be for yourself, and should not behave in ways that would justifiably damage your reputation for integrity.

II. Goals

As a negotiator, your goal is a good outcome. Such an outcome appears to depend on at least seven elements:

1. Alternatives. The outcome should be better for your client than the best available alternative that could be reached without negotiating.

2. Interests. Your client's interests should be well satisfied. The interests of other parties and the community should be sufficiently satisfied to make the outcome acceptable to them and durable.

3. Options. Among the many possible outcomes, an agreement should be the best possible—or as near to it as can reasonably be developed without incurring undue transaction costs. Possible joint gains and mutually advantageous trade-offs should be diligently sought, explored, and put to use. The result should be an elegant solution with no waste. This means that it could not be significantly better for your client without being significantly worse for others.

4. Legitimacy. The outcome should be reasonably fair to all as measured by objective criteria such as law, precedent, community practice, and expert opinion. No one should feel "taken."

5. Communication. If negotiations are to reach a wise outcome without waste of time or other resources, there must be effective communication among the parties. Communication should not halt when one or more of the parties wants to express disagreement. Even when a given negotiation fails to produce satisfactory results, communication lines should remain open.

6. Commitments. Pledges as to what you will or won't do should be made not at the outset of a negotiation but after differences of perception, interest, and values are fully appreciated. Commitments should be mutually understood and carefully crafted to be realistic and easy to implement.

7. Relationship. Both the way each negotiation is conducted and its outcome should be such that in future negotiations, it will be easier rather than harder for the parties to reach equally good or better outcomes.

III. Some Good Practices

There is no one best way to negotiate—a way that is applicable to every issue, context, and negotiating partner. In many situations, whether haggling in a bazaar or negotiating a new union contract, customs and expectations may be so fixed that any benefit that might occur from negotiating in a different way would be outweighed by the transaction costs of trying to do so. Nevertheless, the general rules of thumb and seven-element framework for analysis that follow may help even the most seasoned negotiator to continue to learn from experience and to improve the tools at his or her disposal.

A. General Guidelines

1. Authority. You and your client should establish the extent of your authority in terms that are as clear as circumstances permit. This includes the scope of the subject over which you will be negotiating and your authority to discuss questions, develop recommendations, make procedural commitments, and make final commitments on behalf of a client. If a client approves your use of this Code, you have authority to discuss any issue raised by the other side; to seek

to develop a proposal that you and the other negotiators can conscientiously recommend; and, if in your judgment the circumstances so warrant, to commit your client to those terms. In almost all circumstances, however, even though you have such extensive authority, you will find it wise to obtain your client's approval of the terms of an agreement before it is finally accepted. Likewise, it is also prudent to let those with whom you are negotiating know at an early stage that that is your intention.

2. Commitment. As negotiations proceed there is often considerable uncertainty as to the degree of the parties' commitment to points on which agreement seems to have been reached. Matters drafted and tentatively accepted cannot be reopened without some cost. Accordingly, it is useful to remind your fellow negotiators from time to time of your understanding of the present status of points on the table. (For example: "My understanding is that we are now, without any commitment from either side, seeking to develop the terms of a possible agreement—terms that we both think might be acceptable." Or: "Our acceptance of this point is on the premise that we are able to reach agreement on all the other points in a package; if other points are not resolved to our mutual satisfaction either party is free to reopen this point.")

3. Two judges. Two negotiators are like two judges in that no decision will be reached unless they agree. A lawyer's skill in dealing with a judge is thus highly relevant to the way in which he or she should treat a fellow negotiator. (A negotiation is less like a quarrel and more like an appellate argument; less "You idiot! . . ." and more "Your honor . . .") If an argument has too little merit or is too extremely partisan in your favor to be advanced before a judge, then you should not advance such an argument in the context of a negotiation. Nor should you be less honest or candid than you would be in court with a judge. And, no matter how predisposed you may be, you should be as open to reasoned argument as you would want a judge to be.

B. In Pursuit of a Good Outcome

1. Develop a best self-help alternative. You should compare all proposed terms with your client's best alternative to a negotiated agreement. This means that you should understand the best that your client can do through unilateral action, self-restraint, agreement with some other party, or litigation. In a dispute, one standard with which to compare any proposed settlement is the expected value to your client of the litigation option. You should make a thoughtful and realistic assessment of the possible outcomes of litigation, including the human and financial costs, the uncertainty of result, and the damage to relationships that is often involved. You should not let any personal interest in trying a case, vindicating a position, enhancing a reputation, or earning substantial fees bias your judgment.

2. Clarify interests. You should come to understand fully the interests of your client, not simply the stated wants, but the underlying needs, concerns, fears and hopes. Do your best to make sure that the other side appreciates them. Make sure that you fully appreciate the other side's interests. One element of being

well prepared is to be able to present the other side's point of view more persuasively than they can—and to explain convincingly why you still differ.

3. Generate options. Create a wide range of options that you believe are reasonably fair and take account of the legitimate interests of all parties. Encourage joint inventing by the parties, without commitment, of possible ways to reconcile the differing interests involved. To aid the process of inventing possibilities, postpone the process of evaluating and deciding among them.

4. Maximize legitimacy. Develop your knowledge of the law, precedents, expert opinion, and other potential objective standards of fairness applicable to the matter under negotiation. Discover and arm yourself with fair standards that effectively protect your client's interests. Do extensive research on standards previously advanced or accepted by those on the other side. Persuasively present the case for criteria that are both fair and take full account of the interests of your client. Be open to persuasion, but be an effective advocate for those standards that are most favorable to your client's interests to the extent that legitimate arguments can be found for them. In a negotiation, as in a courtroom, discussing what is fair does not mean giving in to the other side's demands.

5. Communicate effectively. Listen. The more you know about the other side's thinking, the greater chance you have of being able to persuade them. Unless you know what is on their minds, you are shooting in the dark. Acknowledging good points is one way of encouraging good communication.

6. Commit carefully. Commitments should generally be made at the end of the negotiation, not at the beginning. To reduce the risk of having either side lock itself into a fixed position before it fully understands the problem, consider the desirability of preparatory discussions at which both sides take no position and advance no proposals. Both sides clarify interests and perceptions, generate options, and suggest possible standards for determining a fair outcome.

When you do make an offer, remain willing to examine any proposed change that (1) would make the proposal better for both sides; (2) would make it substantially better for either side without significantly damaging the interests of the other; or (3) would in your eyes make the proposed agreement objectively fairer. Likewise, you should be prepared and open to considering any counteroffer that meets the same standards.

7. Build relationships. Throughout a negotiation, you have two crucial relationships—with the other side and with your client. In addition, you must continue to live with yourself. A good relationship is built and maintained by adhering to some basic values:

   Be honest. Your obligation to your client never requires you to be dishonest. You must, of course, keep some matters confidential. Full disclosure is not expected or required.

   Keep promises. Honor commitments. The easiest way to keep all promises is to make very few. If circumstances are going to make it impossible or unreasonable to keep a commitment, be the first to let people know.

Consult. Nothing is more basic to a good working relationship than advance communication. A rule of thumb is ACBD: Always Consult Before Deciding on matters that will significantly affect others.

Be open. A policy of listening, learning, taking advice, and being flexible builds the kind of relationship that encourages joint problem solving.

References

Fisher, R., and Ury, W. *Getting to Yes: Negotiating Agreement Without Giving In.* Boston: Houghton Mifflin, 1981.

White, J. J. "The Pros and Cons of *Getting to Yes.*" *Journal of Legal Education,* 1984, *34*(1), 118–119.

CHAPTER FIVE

The Limits of Integrative Bargaining

Gerald B. Wetlaufer

Over the last fifteen years, many of us who study and teach negotiations have been strongly influenced by the possibilities of "win-win solutions," "getting to yes," "problem solving," "value creation," "expanding the pie," "non-zero-sum games," and "integrative bargaining."[1] Subject only to slight variations in use, these terms may best be understood in terms of the game theorists' distinction between "integrative" and "distributive" bargaining. Both terms describe circumstances in which two or more parties seek, through negotiation, to reach an agreement that will leave both parties better off than they would have been in the absence of the agreement. In distributive bargaining, any such agreement will create a single, definite amount of benefit, or "surplus," to be divided among the parties. It is a zero-sum, win-lose game in which the parties must divide a metaphorical "pie" of fixed size. In integrative bargaining, the amount of benefit available to the parties, and thus the size of the "pie," is not fixed but variable. In this sense, integrative bargaining is a non-zero-sum game presenting opportunities for "win-win" solutions. The distinction between integrative and distributive bargaining may be drawn in two ways: one focusing on the nature of the opportunities presented by various bargaining situations and the other on the differing tactics that may be appropriate to distributive and integrative bargaining.[2]

It is now conventional wisdom that opportunities for integrative bargaining are widely available, that they are often unrecognized and unexploited, and that as a result, both the parties to negotiations and society as a whole are worse off than would otherwise have been the case.[3] The failure to recognize and exploit these opportunities may reflect a failure of education, curable either by reading or by attending a course or seminar.[4] It may reflect the "I'm right, you're wrong, and I can prove it" style of discourse associated with a law school education and historically male modes of moral reasoning.[5] Or it may be the result of the negotiator's dilemma in which the open and cooperative tactics thought appropriate to integrative bargaining are systematically exploited and driven out by the more combative tactics generally associated with distributive bargaining— starting high, conceding slowly, concealing and misrepresenting one's own interests, arguing coercively, threatening, and bluffing.[6]

If the problem at hand is our failure to recognize and exploit opportunities for integrative bargaining, the solution, we are told, is to shift away from the tactics of distributive bargaining and toward the tactics appropriate to integrative bargaining: cooperation, openness, and truth telling.[7] Individual negotiators should embrace these tactics not because they are good or ethical or because they will help to build a better society, but instead because they will promote the individual's immediate pecuniary self-interest.

My essay has two purposes. One is to take a fresh look at the claims concerning the pervasiveness of opportunities for integrative bargaining. The other is to re-examine the argument that the tactics of cooperation, openness, and truthtelling are in the immediate pecuniary self-interest of the parties to a negotiation. In pursuing these objectives, I will seek to specify the exact nature of the self-interest and of the joint gains (or pie expansion) that are being invoked. I will then test certain claims regarding the circumstances that create opportunities for integrative bargaining. I will also assess the case that has, or has not, been made in favor of cooperation, openness, and truth telling.

I reach three conclusions. First, opportunities for integrative bargaining are not nearly as pervasive as is sometimes authoritatively asserted. Second, the claim that opportunities for integrative bargaining make good behavior a simple matter of rational, pecuniary self-interest is not nearly as strong as is sometimes claimed, both because opportunities for integrative bargaining are less pervasive than has been asserted and because, even when such opportunities may exist, the case for good behavior is weaker than has been claimed. Third, and accordingly, the case for good behavior cannot rest entirely on pecuniary self-interest.

DISTINCTIONS IN THE DOMAIN OF SELF-INTEREST

The first question to be asked is what exactly the proponents of integrative bargaining mean by "self-interest" when they say that identifying and exploiting opportunities for integrative bargaining are in the self-interest of the parties.

Specifically, do they mean the self-interest of the parties taken as an aggregate or the self-interest of each party taken individually? Do they mean pecuniary self-interest, or are they referring to some larger form of self-interest such as that discussed in the *Gorgias* (Plato, 1987) when Plato's Socrates asserts that the just man, even if he ends up with less wealth, is nonetheless better off than the unjust man? Finally, do they mean immediate self-interest or self-interest in the long run, which might refer to one's self-interest after the community learns about those who engage in sharp bargaining and after those persons suffer the adverse consequences of a bad reputation?

It seems clear to me that, despite an occasional lapse in clarity, the nature of "self-interest" invoked by the proponents of integrative bargaining is individual rather than collective, it is pecuniary, and it is immediate and thus independent of reputational or other iterative effects. It is self-interest measured in terms of a person's maximization of her total utility under the common game-theoretic assumptions that she gains no utility from benefits accruing to others (e.g., her adversary) and that she gains no utility from the experience of behaving in an ethical manner. Where either assumption is relaxed or where either of these latter forms of utility is assumed to be present, there is a case for cooperation, openness, and truth telling in all circumstances, including those that the game theorists tell us present opportunities only for distributive or win-lose bargaining. But that is not the argument offered by the proponents of integrative bargaining.

Similarly, the case for cooperation, openness, and truth telling that is made in the name of integrative bargaining must rest on something other than a person's interests in his continuing relationships or his reputation. While such interests may lead a negotiator to moderate his reliance on such distributive bargaining tactics as bluffs, misrepresentations, and threats, the existence of such interests is entirely independent of the possibility of integrative bargaining.

DISTINCTIONS IN THE DOMAIN OF JOINT GAINS

A good deal of confusion arises from the assertion that opportunities for "integrative" or "win-win" bargaining are distinguishable from opportunities for "distributive" or "win-lose" bargaining in that the former can "create value" and "expand the pie" while the latter cannot. Characterizing the distinction in this way causes confusion because, in fact, all opportunities for bargaining, including opportunities that are solely win-lose or zero-sum games, present opportunities to "create value" and to "expand the pie."

For purposes of clarification, I will distinguish three forms of value creation, only one of which constitutes an opportunity for integrative or win-win bargaining. The first of these forms is found where the pie can be made larger only in the sense that is true of all bargaining, including all bargaining that is merely distributive. In such circumstances, there is a zone of agreement (i.e., a range of possible agreement) within which both parties will be better off than they would have been in the absence of the agreement. Thus, in this minimal sense, purely distributive bargaining can be said to "create value" or "expand the pie." I shall call this "Form I" value creation. Though it involves the "creation" of value, Form I does not involve integrative bargaining and is not a situation in which the more open tactics associated with integrative bargaining will promote the immediate pecuniary self-interest of a party.

The same can also be said of opportunities for Form II value creation. Form II value creation is possible when there is one issue (e.g., the amount of money to be paid for some product), and one party cares more about that issue than does the other. This is a situation in which, assuming there is a range of possible agreements that would leave both parties better off, there is an opportunity for Form I value creation in that the aggregate benefits to the parties will vary depending on whether or not they can reach agreement. Also, and this is what distinguishes Form II value creation, this is a situation in which the aggregate benefits to the parties, the size of the pie, will vary across the range of possible agreements. Thus, the total value created by the agreement will be relatively large if most of that over which the parties are negotiating (e.g., surplus as measured in dollars) is captured by the party who cares more about that issue. Similarly, the total value created by the agreement will be relatively small if most of the surplus is captured by the party who cares less about that issue.

An opportunity for Form II value creation is not an opportunity for integrative bargaining because the possible agreements are arrayed along a single continuum such that any possible agreement is, in its relationship to any other, better for one party but worse for the other. One cannot move from any one possible agreement to any other possible agreement in such a way that both parties are made better off by the move. Nor can one even move from one possible agreement to another in such a way that one party is better off and the other is no worse off. Thus, Form II value creation, like Form I, does not involve integrative bargaining.

Only what I shall call "Form III" value creation offers an opportunity for integrative or win-win bargaining. Unlike Forms I and II, Form III value creation involves that kind of pie-expansion or value creation in which the parties can reach a range of different agreements, in which the size of the pie will vary across the range of possible agreements (also true of Form II), but in which some of those agreements leave both parties better off than do others. If there are some possible agreements that both parties would regard as better than others, then the size of the pie created by the agreement depends both upon parties' ability to reach some agreement (Form I value creation) and upon their wit and ability to arrive at one of the better agreements. It is in this sense that a situation presenting an opportunity for Form III value creation is a non-zero-sum game and an opportunity for integrative or win-win bargaining.[8]

ASSESSING CLAIMS CONCERNING THE NATURE AND PERVASIVENESS OF SIGNIFICANT OPPORTUNITIES FOR INTEGRATIVE BARGAINING

The proponents of integrative bargaining usually assert that opportunities for such bargaining are widely, if not universally, available (Lax and Sebenius, 1986). Lax and Sebenius, in the most important contribution yet made to our understanding of these matters, catalogue the opportunities for integrative bargaining. Their list includes differences between the parties in terms of (1) their interests,[9] (2) their projections concerning possible future events (Fisher, Ury, and Patton, 1991; Lax and others, 1985; Lax and Sebenius, 1986; Sebenius, 1992), (3) their willingness to accept risks (Fisher, Ury, and Patton, 1991; Lax and others, 1985; Lax and Sebenius, 1986; Sebenius, 1992), and (4) their time preferences regarding payment or performance (Fisher, Ury, and Patton, 1991; Lax and others, 1985; Lax and Sebenius, 1986; Menkel-Meadow, 1984; Sebenius, 1992). As we shall see, all four of these circumstances will sometimes, but only under certain further conditions and with certain important qualifications, afford opportunities for the parties to expand the pie through integrative bargaining. I will argue, however, that such opportunities are less pervasive and less important than is customarily suggested.

Lax and Sebenius also assert that opportunities for integrative bargaining exist whenever there are (5) "differences in capabilities" between the parties,[10] (6) possible economies of scale,[11] (7) considerations related to continuing relationships,[12] (8) differences in criteria for success (Fisher, Ury, and Patton, 1991; Lax and Sebenius, 1986), (9) differences in attitudes toward precedent and principle (Fisher, Ury, and Patton, 1991; Lax and Sebenius, 1986), or (10) differences in constituencies, personal and organizational situations, ideologies, and conceptions of fairness.[13] I conclude that none of these differences creates opportunities for integrative bargaining beyond the four already specified.

Differing Interests, Including Multiple Issues Differently Valued

We might begin with the situation in which the parties have differing interests and with the question whether, under all or some such circumstances, those differences in interests create opportunities for integrative bargaining. While I shall argue that opportunities for integrative bargaining do not exist in all such circumstances, they do appear to exist in some. Imagine, for instance, that a corporate plaintiff sues an airline, that the parties have been exploring the possibility of settlement, and that they have reached a tentative agreement on $80,000. Next assume that the defendant, just back from a seminar on win-win negotiation, proposes an in-kind settlement in which the defendant would provide the plaintiff with $120,000 worth of air travel. Because of the airline's high fixed costs and the frequency with which it carries empty seats, the cost to the airline will be only $30,000. Both parties find the in-kind settlement to be highly preferable to the cash agreement they had tentatively reached. In this sense, the parties have found themselves in a situation where there is a range of possible agreements and some of those agreements are better than others for both parties. Thus, there is an opportunity for Form III value creation and for integrative bargaining.

If this is a situation in which differences in the parties' interests present an opportunity for integrative bargaining, attention must be paid to a range of circumstances that appear similar to our example, yet do not present opportunities for integrative bargaining. One set of cases to be excluded from our category includes all exchange transactions in which two parties simply exchange one thing for another, say, for instance, money for a used car. We may assume, at a minimum, that such transactions occur only when the car is more highly valued by the buyer than by the seller. This difference in valuation, while it could be characterized as a difference in interests between the parties, does nothing more than create the possibility of a mutually beneficial agreement and, with that, the possibility of Form I value creation. It merely satisfies the minimal conditions necessary for distributive bargaining. It is distinctly not an opportunity for Form III value creation, and thus it is not an opportunity for integrative bargaining.

The same is true even if the parties differ in their valuation of both elements of the exchange transaction, as would be the case if the parties to our sales transaction differed not only with regard to the value of the car but also with regard to the value of money. Let us assume that the buyer is a hungry and practical man for whom every last dollar counts, for the simple reason that a dollar saved on the purchase of the car can be used to feed his hungry child. Assume further that the seller is an unworldly academic who firmly believes he must get something for his car but, beyond that point, cares not a bit for money. This is a situation in which the "size of the pie" may vary in two distinct ways. First, the pie will get larger and value will be created if the parties reach an agreement that leaves both parties better off than they would have been in the absence of that agreement. This is the Form I value creation we have just discussed. In addition, the size of the pie will vary depending upon the exact agreement that is reached. Thus, if the prospective buyer's reservation price (the price above which he cannot go) is $1,200 and the prospective seller's reservation price (the price below which he cannot go) is $800, an agreement could be reached at any amount between $800 and $1,200. But if the prospective buyer cares more about the money than does the prospective seller, there is an intelligible sense in which aggregate utility[14] will be higher at $800 than at $1,200, because the $400 that could have gone to either party has actually gone to the party who values it more. This is Form II value creation. But however important this opportunity for Form I and Form II value creation, it is not an occasion for integrative bargaining. From the perspective of the parties and their self-interest, this situation is in no respect win-win. There is no agreement as to the sales price, which, when compared to any other possible agreement, is better from the perspective of both parties. A party who in this situation engages in the tactics of integrative bargaining will find that his self-interest is systematically disserved by that choice of tactics.

If a simple exchange transaction cannot offer the sort of differing interests that may create opportunities for integrative bargaining, neither does a sales transaction involving multiple goods or services. Let us go now to a local car dealership where a prospective buyer has just reached a tentative agreement to buy a new sports car for $18,500, a price that is 10 percent below the sticker price. The salesman is offering to sweeten the deal by throwing in the deluxe sound system, normally priced at $870, for only $600. Our buyer, who has long dreamed of having such a system and is more than a little pleased with the negotiating prowess he has already shown, says, "$500 and you've got yourself a deal." The seller, whose costs for this system are only $300, responds with feigned admiration, "You're killin' me, but I'll do it." It is certainly true that both parties count themselves as better off than they would have been under their tentative agreement. But there is a serious question as to whether this really is a case of win-win bargaining, or whether it is instead a case in which two distributive bargains have simply been laid together.

We can approach this question by asking whether if both issues had been on the table at the beginning, the parties would have had the kinds of differing interests that would have made it possible to reach a range of possible agreements, some of which would have been better than others for both parties. The answer is "yes" only in the paltry sense that both parties count themselves better off if the transaction includes both the basic car and the deluxe sound system than they would have been if no agreement were reached or if that agreement included only the car. But that interest could just as well have been satisfied by two quite separate, and quite distributive, sales transactions. The seller has a reservation price both for the basic car and for the deluxe sound system, and his reservation price for the two of those combined is simply the sum of those separate reservation prices. The same is true of the buyer. There is, as we have already discovered, a range of possible agreements. But what is crucial is the fact that within that range, a move from any one possible agreement to any other will make one party better off and the other party worse off. This is what distinguishes distributive bargaining, and in these circumstances, the openness with respect to the parties' interests (as distinct from their reservation prices) merely points the way to further opportunities for distributive bargaining but not for integrative bargaining.

Having considered sales and exchange transactions both in their simple forms and when they involve the sale of multiple goods or services, our next example involves what I shall call the cross-selling of goods or services. An example is the purchase of a new car coupled with the "trade-in" of the old one. Both elements of this transaction may be perfectly sensible, not least because the dealer enjoys much easier access to a market for used cars than do his customers. But once it has been recognized that both parties may be better off entering into both elements of this transaction, the negotiation is purely distributive. Both parties have reservation prices both for the car they are buying and the car they are selling. Confusion is sometimes sown when the dealer claims to be "paying" more for the trade-in than it would appear to be worth, while in fact simply granting an additional discount from the list price of the new car. But the economic reality is that despite the presence of two products and the fact that they are being cross-sold, the bargaining between the parties is for a single dollar amount, and any dollar amount that will be better for one party will be worse for the other. Even here, there is an opportunity only for distributive bargaining.[15]

I close this litany of examples with one that seems, more clearly than these other cases, to present a situation in which the presence of multiple issues differently valued does create an opportunity for integrative bargaining. The example involves a divorce in which there are two issues: money and custody. We will assume, stereotypically, that one party is a work-at-home mom who cares more about custody and the other is a workaholic husband who barely knows his children but cares desperately about the things that money can buy. Then consider three possible agreements. In the first, the money is split down the middle, and custody is shared on a true fifty-fifty basis. In the second, the wife gets full and exclusive custody of the children, and the husband gets all of the money. And in the third, the wife gets all the money (which she doesn't want) and the husband gets custody of the children (whom he doesn't know). There is a Form III relationship among these three possible agreements. Under the first agreement, the parties reach a split-the-difference compromise on each of the two issues. Both parties will be better off than they would have been in the absence of an agreement, and thus we have Form I value creation. But as one moves from the first agreement (compromise on both issues) to the second agreement (wife gets the children, husband gets the money), both parties will regard themselves as better off than they would have been under the first agreement. And as one moves from the first agreement to the third agreement (wife gets the money, husband gets the children), both parties will see themselves as worse off than they had been under the first agreement. Accordingly, this is an opportunity for Form III value creation in that the size of the pie varies across a range of possible agreements and in which, for both parties, some of those agreements may be better than others.[16]

Differing Assessments as to Future Events: Differing Probabilistic Assessments of the Likelihood of Some Future Event or the Likely Future Value of Some Variable

Expanding the Pie. Lax and Sebenius next assert that differences in probabilistic assessments create opportunities for integrative bargaining (Lax and Sebenius, 1986). It would be more accurate, however, to say that these circumstances will sometimes present opportunities for a particular kind of integrative bargaining if, but only if, the parties are both willing to bet on their differing assessments. The differences being exploited here are differences in the parties' predictions concerning future events. More specifically, they are either differing probabilistic assessments of the likelihood of some future event (Lax and Sebenius, 1986; Lax et al., 1985) or differing assessments of the likely future value of some variable (Lax and Sebenius, 1986; Lax et al., 1985).

Negotiators may exploit these opportunities for integrative bargaining only through a contingent agreement. Differing probabilistic assessments of the likelihood of some future event create opportunities for contingent agreements in the form "if X, then A; if not X, then B." Differing assessments of the likely future value of some variable afford opportunities for contingent agreements in which some aspect of the agreement, probably price, is tied to the now indeterminate future variable. These agreements take the form, "We agree that A will be determined in accordance with some future value of X." This opportunity for integrative bargaining may be illustrated through three examples. First, the parties may have different assessments of the likelihood that some thing—in our example it will be a used car—will work. Second, they may have different assessments of the likely future price of a commodity. And third, they may have different assessments of the number of seats that will be sold for a recital. Notice that although all of these differing assessments involve matters directly relevant to the agreement the parties are seeking to make (the car, the commodity, and the recital), a contingent agreement could be reached that turned on different assessments unrelated to the transaction. Thus, an agreement concerning the sale of land could carry a price that was contingent on whether the Chicago Cubs win next year's World Series.

BETTING THE THING WILL WORK. A common example of an opportunity for integrative bargaining involves a situation in which the parties have, and then exploit, different assessments of the likelihood that some tangible device (e.g., a used car or a new technology) will work. Assume that Mr. Used Car Seller is trying to sell the car he has been driving for several years and that his reservation price is $2,200.[17] He is willing to sell the car for $2,200 or more, but not for less, than that amount. To state the matter more fully, he is willing to sell the car if and only if he receives in exchange either $2,200 or more or something that he currently believes is worth such an amount. At the same time, Ms. Used Car Buyer has looked at Mr. Seller's car and concluded that although it would suit her purposes, she can pay up to, but no more than, $2,000. Because she can only pay $2,000 and he must receive at least $2,200, there is no simple dollar amount that is acceptable to both parties. There is no zone of agreement and, as things now stand, no possibility of agreement.

It turns out, however, that there is a difference between the parties' expectations concerning the likelihood that the car will require major repairs. Mr. Seller believes the car is in great shape mechanically, and he is perfectly certain it will not require major repairs over the next two years. Ms. Buyer, for her part, has some reservations. Specifically, on the basis of a detailed mechanical inspection, she believes there is a 60 percent probability the car will need no major repairs but a 40 percent probability the cost of such repairs will be $1,000. Indeed, the $2,000 that Ms. Buyer is prepared to pay for the car already reflects the 40 percent probability that she will be paying $1,000 in major repairs. If that probability could be eliminated, she would be willing to pay $2,400 for the car.[18]

This additional information presents the possibility of a contingent agreement in which Ms. Buyer pays $2,300 for the car and Mr. Seller guarantees her against any major repair costs during the first two years. To Mr. Seller, the value of this transaction is $2,300 because he receives the purchase price ($2,300), and, in his mind, there is a zero percent probability that he will have to pay anything on his guarantee. Thus, taking everything into account, he still values this agreement at $2,300, which is $100 better than (higher than) his $2,200 reservation price. To Ms. Buyer, the expected total cost of this transaction is $2,300. That is $100 better than (lower than) what would have been her $2,400 reservation price if she were not required to bear what she believes to be the significant risk that the car will require major repairs. Absent a contingent agreement, there was no possibility of agreement at all. But once the parties identified and exploited the opportunity for a contingent agreement, a mutually advantageous transaction became possible. The possibility of a contingent agreement allows the parties to transform their situation from one presenting no zone of agreement to one presenting a sizable zone of agreement, thereby expanding the size of the pie.

BETTING ON THE FUTURE PRICE OF A COMMODITY. Another example of integrative bargaining involves the possibility that the parties can identify and exploit differing assessments of the likely future value of some variable. Typically, this variable is the likely future price of a commodity. Assume two people are bickering over the sale of two tons of a commodity to be delivered in two years. Ms. Commodity Seller's reservation price is $4,000, and Mr. Commodity Buyer's reservation price is $3,600.[19] At this point, no zone of agreement exists. Further assume, however, that Ms. Seller believes that in two years, the market price of the commodity will be relatively high ($2,200 per ton), and Mr. Buyer believes that the market price will be relatively low ($1,600 per ton). There is now the possibility of a contract based on the future market price of the commodity. For instance, the price of the two tons could be set at whatever proves to be the current market price of the commodity in two years. Ms. Seller would value this contract at $4,400, $400 better than (higher than) her $4,000 reservation price. Mr. Buyer would value this contingent contract at $3,200, which is $400 better than (lower than) his $3,600 reservation price. Both parties believe themselves to be significantly better off than they would have been had they entered a contract for a fixed dollar amount. Indeed, there is now a significant zone of agreement where once there had been none.

BETTING ON THE NUMBER OF SEATS THAT WILL SELL. A third example of integrative bargaining involves a negotiation between an opera singer and the owner of a concert hall. Assume Ms. Singer will not sing for less than $14,000, and Mr. Owner, having taken account of his expenses and the number of seats he believes he can sell, cannot offer anything more than $10,000. As long as the parties seek to negotiate an agreement for a fixed dollar amount, there is no zone of agreement. That is to say, there is no dollar amount that is, as it must be for Ms. Singer, at or above $14,000 and is also, as it must be for Mr. Owner, at or below $10,000.

Assume further, however, that the two parties hold different expectations about the number of seats that will be sold and that both are willing to bet on their assessment. Ms. Singer is utterly confident that 10,000 tickets will be sold, while Mr. Owner—burned too often when he has tried to sell high culture to the burghers of his city—is equally certain that only 4,000 tickets will be sold.

The integrative solution to this problem is to suggest a contingent agreement in which, for instance, Ms. Singer is paid $1.50 for every seat that is sold.[20] From her perspective, such a contract is worth $15,000 ($1.50 per seat times 10,000 seats), which is $1,000 better than (higher than) her $14,000 reservation price. From the perspective of Mr. Owner, the perceived cost of the agreement is $6,000 ($1.50 per seat times 4,000 seats), $4,000 better than (lower than) his $10,000 reservation price. Through integrative bargaining and a contingent agreement, the parties can enter a contract that leaves them both better off than they otherwise would have been in the absence of this agreement.

Some Differing Assessments of Future Events That Do Not Create Opportunities to Expand the Pie. Certain differences of this kind do not, at least as a practical matter, give rise to opportunities for integrative bargaining. For instance, if I am selling a car and the buyer believes the car will run fine, but I (the seller who ought to know) believe it will need major repairs, then the parties differ in their probabilistic assessment of the likelihood of some future event, yet no opportunity for integrative bargaining exists. In the normal course, the buyer will bear the risk of repair. If in this case we were to shift that risk to the seller through a guarantee, it would make the pie smaller, not larger. And if the buyer were to learn of the seller's differing assessment of the likelihood that major repairs would be required, she (the buyer) likely would revise her assessment and, accordingly, lower her reservation price. This difference does not create an opportunity to expand the pie, but rather only an opportunity to reduce its size. And if it is discovered, it will not enhance, but instead diminish, the possibility of agreement.

The same problems are potentially present in the commodities negotiation example. In that case, both the seller and the buyer were individually optimistic about how the world price would be moving. The seller thought the price would be relatively high (good news for sellers), and the buyer thought it would be relatively low (good news for buyers). If we reversed those assumptions and made the parties individually pessimistic about how the world price would be moving, then differing assessments of the likely future value of some variable would exist, but there would be no opportunity to fashion a contingent agreement that would expand the pie. Indeed, fashioning a contingent agreement in which each party bets on his own projection will cause the pie and the zone of agreement to become smaller, not larger.

Unless the Parties Are Willing to Bet, No Opportunity to Expand the Pie Exists. The point here is simple but important. There is nothing inherent about the possibility of placing a bet that would cause people, even people in business, to place that bet. Surely some are in the business of speculating and betting on their projections. Most, however, are in the business of providing goods and services at a reasonable price. Many, if not most, in this second group are not looking for opportunities to roll the dice. If, however, what is offered is an opportunity to bet on one's product (or invention), I assume the number of people willing to gamble will go up. But as a general matter, among businesspeople and others, those seeking out opportunities to bet on their projections are probably the exception and not the rule.

The Expansion of the Pie May Be Neither Stable nor Permanent. Thus far, I have demonstrated that opportunities for integrative bargaining are sometimes afforded by certain differing assessments concerning the likelihood of some future event or the likely value of some future variable. There is, however, one more difficulty that must be faced. This difficulty arises because there is only one mechanism by which these opportunities for integrative bargaining may be exploited—the contingent agreement—and we know from the beginning that the contingency we are exploiting ultimately will be eliminated.

At the moment in which the agreement is reached, the pie certainly appears to have expanded. But when the uncertainty is eliminated and the contingency resolved, the pie will likely resume its original size. If and when that happens, one party, or conceivably both, will find himself to be much worse off than he thought himself to be at the time he entered the agreement. Indeed, at least one party, and conceivably both, may be worse off than he would have been had he not entered into the agreement at all.

There are at least two situations that may result when the uncertainty is eliminated and the contingency resolved. In one, the agreement appears to expand the size of the pie, at least for a time, but the pie eventually returns to its original size, leaving one or both parties worse off than they had anticipated. If the realization of the contingency is good for one party, it will be bad for the other, and vice versa. In these cases, and the commodity transaction described above may be one of them, the realization of the contingency will cause the pie to return to its original size, and one or both of the parties will be worse off than they anticipated. Indeed, one or both parties may well be worse off than they would have been in the absence of an agreement. Thus, they may turn out to have violated their reservation price.

In the second situation, the agreement seems to expand the size of the pie, at least for a time, and the resolution of the uncertainty may or may not leave one or both parties worse off than they had anticipated. Here, the uncertainty may be resolved in a way that is good for both parties—or in a way that is good for one party without being bad for the other. The car sale and the concert contract described above are examples of this situation. In each of these negotiations, there is a risk that is relevant to the value of the transaction, but it is a risk that may never be realized. Thus, the car may require major repairs, and none of the tickets to the opera house may be sold. What distinguishes this second situation (the car sale and the concert contract) from the first (the commodity transaction) is that in the event the risk does not come to fruition, the party who was left bearing the risk will be better off while the other party is left no worse off. Under circumstances in which the contingency is of this kind, the size of the pie may shrink back to its original size (if the risk materializes) or it may not (if the risk does not materialize). This is, of course, a better situation than the first, in which the size of the pie will certainly shrink back to its original size.

Differing Preferences Regarding Risks

Differences in risk aversion may also create opportunities for integrative bargaining. I begin, however, by drawing a distinction between two parties' potentially dissimilar assessments of particular risks and two parties' potentially dissimilar aversions to risk. The previous section deals with the former, and we are here concerned with the latter.

If the parties to a negotiation have different aversions to risk and if the negotiation involves something that carries a risk, then there may (but also may not) be an opportunity for integrative bargaining in the sense that an agreement, reached without regard to the allocation of risk, may be modified so as to leave both parties better off. Such an opportunity will exist when, and only when, the preliminary agreement leaves the risk in the wrong hands. Under those circumstances, the party who is not left bearing the risk can be given the risk, the party who will thus get rid of the risk will be better off in more than the amount by which the party acquiring the risk will be worse off, and the party getting rid of the risk will be in a position to compensate the party acquiring the risk in an amount that will leave both parties better off than they were before the compensated shifting of the risk.

One can think of this as a special case of multiple issues differently valued. The object of the negotiation appears to be unitary, but on closer examination, it can be unbundled into, on the one hand, the concrete object of the negotiation (e.g., the car) and, on the other, a risk that someone must bear (e.g., the potential costs of repair). This may present an opportunity for what amounts to an insurance transaction. As usual, the solution is to arrange matters so that the concrete object of the negotiation goes to the party who values it more, and the risk goes to the party who assigns to that risk the lower negative value. He who avoids the risk is then in a position to compensate she who accepts the risk, and to do so in a way that leaves both better off than they would have been in the absence of its transfer.

There is then the question of whether all such differences constitute opportunities for integrative bargaining. They do not. Thus, if in the normal course of the negotiation the risk ends up with the party who assigns to it the lower negative value, the risk is already where it ought to be, and transferring it to the other party would not increase the aggregate value arising from the transaction but would instead decrease it. Such a transfer would not cause the pie to expand but rather to contract.

Differing Time Preferences Regarding Payment or Performance

Differences in time preferences regarding payment or performance sometimes create opportunities for integrative bargaining as well. The simplest way to demonstrate this potential is to assume that two parties have negotiated an agreement for the sale of property for $2,500, with payment and performance to take place in twelve months. Assume also that one of the parties cares about the time of payment, and the other does not. Under these circumstances, the parties can always expand the pie by altering the time of payment in accordance with the preference of the party who cares, or who cares more, about that aspect of the agreement.

Assume that the seller cares about the time of payment, preferring to be paid earlier rather than later, and that the buyer (who, if he cared, would prefer to pay later) is indifferent. Because $2,500 received today is worth more to the seller than the same amount received a year from now, making that amount payable today will cause the seller to see herself as better off than she would have been if payment were deferred. At the same time, the buyer, whom we have assumed to be indifferent as between paying now and paying later, counts himself as no worse off for the earlier payment. Under these circumstances, the pie is larger if the parties set the price at $2,500 payable today than if they were to set it at the same dollar amount payable in a year. If the roles are reversed such that the buyer prefers to pay later rather than earlier and the seller is indifferent about time of payment, then if the time of payment is set in accordance with the preference of the party who cares more—in this instance, the buyer—one party will see himself as better off, the other party will see herself as no worse off even in the absence of compensation, and the size of the pie will have expanded.

Lest we forget, there is no assurance that all of the additional wealth generated by the expansion of the pie will end up in the hands of the person who has the stronger preference about the time of payment. We have assumed that the other person is indifferent as to the time of payment, not as to the size of the payment. The person who is indifferent with respect to timing certainly might agree to the payment schedule preferred by the other party without asking anything in exchange. It is more likely, though, that he would ask for some compensation. And if he is a hard bargainer, there is in theory no reason why he might not capture the lion's share of the wealth generated by the change in the payment schedule.

I must remind the reader that, for purposes of demonstration and analysis, I have assumed that these negotiations were accomplished in two discrete stages. In the first stage, the parties engaged in distributive bargaining and reached a preliminary agreement, and in the second stage, they exploited the opportunity for integrative bargaining, expanded the pie, and divided the proceeds generated by that expansion. Realistically, there is no reason to expect the parties to proceed in such an artificially bifurcated way. Rather, we would normally expect to see a single, more or less continuous negotiation in which the parties divide the pie while seeking to identify and exploit opportunities to expand the pie.

Other Differences

Lax and Sebenius argue that in addition to the circumstances described above, there are a great many other situations, almost all of them "differences," that create opportunities to expand the pie through integrative bargaining. These include "differences in capabilities" between the parties, possible economies of scale, considerations related to continuing relationships, differences in criteria for success, differences in attitudes toward precedent and principle, or differences in constituencies, personal and organizational situations, ideologies, and conceptions of fairness. But none of these circumstances, except those that fall within one of the four categories already discussed, creates opportunities for integrative bargaining.

Differences in capabilities and possible economies of scale may create opportunities for joint gains, but not for the Form III gains that distinguish integrative bargaining. Rather, they create opportunities for the Form I joint gains that arise any time two parties enter into a mutually beneficial agreement. Such differences may create or expand the possibility of a distributive agreement by which both parties may make themselves better off than they otherwise would have been. But that is simply to say that these circumstances create an opportunity for bargaining. They do not create an opportunity for Form III joint gains and for integrative bargaining.

Considerations related to continuing relationships or to reputational effects may provide a negotiator with a good reason to be cooperative, to be open and truthful, or otherwise to moderate her reliance upon the tactics (e.g., misrepresentation) associated with distributive bargaining. But the fact that she has found reason to alter her tactics in the direction of cooperation, openness, and truth telling does not mean that she has done so because there exists an opportunity for Form III value creation. No such opportunity exists. Although the parties face a series of negotiations, nothing in this circumstance indicates the presence of anything other than Form I joint gains. It is certainly not a situation, as it must be for there to be an opportunity for integrative bargaining, in which the size of the pie may vary and in which both parties will be better off with some of the possible agreements than they would have been with others.

The remaining elements on the list—differences in criteria for success, attitudes toward precedent and principle, constituencies, personal and organizational situations, ideologies, and conceptions of fairness—may sometimes signal the presence of multiple issues differently valued. Thus, there may be situations in which there is an especially good chance that the parties can unbundle or disaggregate their interests, identify issues that are differently valued, and then engage in the appropriate form of integrative bargaining. When this occurs, the parties may find themselves in one of the four previously specified circumstances affording an opportunity for integrative bargaining. These differences do not, however, constitute additions to the catalogue of circumstances affording such opportunities.

ASSESSING CLAIMS THAT IT IS IN A BARGAINER'S SELF-INTEREST TO ENGAGE IN THE TACTICS OF COOPERATION, OPENNESS, AND TRUTH TELLING WHEN OPPORTUNITIES FOR INTEGRATIVE BARGAINING EXIST

A final claim that can now be evaluated is that opportunities for integrative bargaining necessarily imply that it is in a negotiator's immediate pecuniary self-interest to engage in the tactics of cooperation, openness, truth telling, honesty, and trust. First, I have demonstrated that opportunities for integrative bargaining, especially meaningful opportunities for integrative bargaining (e.g., where the pie may be made to expand and to stay expanded), exist within a narrower range of circumstances than sometimes has been claimed. Some of the differences cited by Lax and Sebenius simply do not create opportunities for integrative bargaining. Others, namely those involving different assessments regarding future events, create opportunities to expand the pie only if the parties are willing to bet on their projections. And even when the parties are willing to bet, there will be opportunities for integrative bargaining only some of the time and only in ways that will sometimes prove self-defeating in the sense that the pie may eventually return to its original size. If the pie shrinks back, one or both of the parties will be worse off than they had expected to be and, potentially, worse off than they would have been had they not entered the agreement. Other circumstances named by Lax and Sebenius—multiple issues differently valued, differing projections concerning future events, differing time preferences, differing levels of risk aversion—sometimes offer opportunities for integrative bargaining but sometimes do not. Although the general claim is made that opportunities for integrative bargaining provide a reason, based solely on immediate pecuniary self-interest, to engage in openness and truthtelling, those opportunities are considerably less pervasive than has been announced. Thus, this argument for openness and truthtelling is, in that degree, narrower and less persuasive.

Second, even within the range of circumstances in which there are significant opportunities for integrative bargaining, the bargainer must almost always engage in distributive bargaining as well. Therefore, it is in the bargainer's self-interest not just to adopt the tactics of openness and truth telling that are said to be appropriate to integrative bargaining, but somehow also to adopt the tactics of truth hiding and dissimulation that are said to be appropriate to distributive bargaining. However we might manage these incompatible tactics, this situation presents at most a weak and highly qualified argument for openness and truthtelling. Moreover, the argument for openness and truth telling is not an argument for openness and truth telling with respect to everything, but instead is limited to information useful in identifying and exploiting opportunities for integrative bargaining. Thus, an opportunity for integrative bargaining will present an occasion for a certain amount of truth telling with respect to one's relative interest in various issues (or one's projections about the future or aversion to risk) without also presenting even a weak argument for truth telling with respect to one's reservation price.

Finally, one should understand that a bargainer's self-interest is never promoted by disclosure for its own sake. Rather, what is in the bargainer's self-interest is discovering truthful information about the other side's interests and situation. Thus, what is true in distributive bargaining is also true where there are opportunities for integrative bargaining; the best possible position is to secure perfect information about the other side's position while disclosing nothing at all about one's own. Disclosure is rational and in a bargainer's self-interest only insofar as it may be essential to securing the information she needs. If she can secure that information without disclosure, whether through research or simply by getting the other side to spill the beans over drinks, there is no case for openness and truth telling. Moreover, as is also the case with distributive bargaining, if she can induce the other side to disclose because they wrongly think she is doing the same, it cannot be argued that her immediate, individual, and pecuniary self-interest would be advanced by a policy of openness and truth telling.

CONCLUSION

It seems clear that there has been a certain amount of overclaiming that has been done in the name of integrative bargaining. Thus, differences in capabilities, differences in resources, and economies of scale do not offer opportunities for integrative bargaining. They may create opportunities for Form I joint gains, but that merely makes them an opportunity for bargaining, not for integrative bargaining. Similarly, considerations related to continuing relationships or to reputational effects may be reasons to cooperate and to moderate one's reliance on distributive tactics, but do not present opportunities for integrative bargaining.

Moreover, some circumstances that actually afford opportunities for integrative bargaining do so in ways that, as a practical matter, cannot be exploited. This is certainly the case when the person selling the used car sees a greater probability that major repairs will be needed than does the buyer. It is probably also the case when the opera singer is less optimistic than the manager as to the number of tickets that will be sold. Further, some opportunities for integrative bargaining are of a kind that even if they can be exploited, expand the pie in a way that is inherently unstable and that ought to be avoided by people who do not want to bet that their judgment is better than the judgment of others. It is in the nature of those bets that someone will lose. When the uncertainty is eliminated and the pie shrinks back to its original size, the loser will not only be worse off than he expected to be, but he may also have violated his reservation price.

Finally, the claim that cooperation, openness, and truth telling are in the short-term pecuniary self-interest of negotiators—the claim that honesty is the best policy in this strong sense—requires a three-fold qualification. First, it must be qualified because that claim is dependent upon the opportunities for true Form III value creation through integrative bargaining, and those opportunities have been shown to be a good deal less common than has been asserted.

Second, the claim must be qualified because at most, it provides an argument for openness and honesty with respect to some matters but not with respect to others. And third, the claim must be qualified because in most circumstances presenting opportunities for Form III value creation, what matters is not the disclosure of one's own information but the discovery of information concerning one's adversary. In such circumstances, disclosure is useful when and only when it is the price that must be paid for discovery.

I do not mean to speak against cooperation, openness, and truth telling. To the contrary, I will speak in their favor. But little is gained by resting the case for these practices solely on the claim that opportunities for integrative or win-win bargaining are widely available and that as a result, these practices are generally warranted by a negotiator's own immediate pecuniary self-interest. That claim is both too strong and too weak: too strong because it is false in significant respects and too weak because it misses what may be the main point. Further, in missing that point, it surrenders to our preoccupation with pecuniary self-interest and contributes to the impoverishment of ethical discourse.

If there is a general case for cooperation, openness, and truth telling in negotiations, that case is multidimensional, and parts of it are expressly ethical. Certainly, because there are opportunities for integrative bargaining, a measure of openness and truth telling is sometimes warranted as a matter of a negotiator's immediate pecuniary self-interest. Similarly, a negotiator's long-term pecuniary self-interest may sometimes be served by openness and truth telling because of the costs that may be associated with a reputation for sharp dealing.[21] But it is also true that a negotiator's pecuniary self-interest is, at best, only a portion of his true self-interest. Thus, it may be in his true self-interest to accept some pecuniary costs for the sake of living in a community in which cooperation, truth telling, and ethical behavior are the norm. Moreover, Plato's Socrates may have been right when he argued that a person who has some combination of wealth and virtue may be happier and better off than a person who has more wealth but less virtue.[22]

There are, of course, times when considerations of ethics may call upon a negotiator to sacrifice a measure of self-interest, especially if the self-interest is pecuniary (Wetlaufer, 1990b). There are at least two ethical arguments that may induce a negotiator to moderate his claiming behavior, to cooperate, and to be truthful at least to the point of avoiding misrepresentation. One such argument, which has little appeal to me, is that ethics is the maximization of aggregate wealth or aggregate utility; that cooperation and truth telling will, even when they are not in a negotiator's pecuniary self-interest, promote the likelihood that the pie will expand and that wealth will be maximized and that therefore one ought to engage in a certain amount of cooperation, openness, and truth telling.[23] The other argument is grounded in the proposition that misrepresentation does unwarranted harm to others (Wetlaufer, 1990b).

I am left with the belief that Fisher, Ury, and Menkel-Meadow had it about right when they directed our attention toward the possibility of unbundling the parties' interests, identifying issues that might be valued differently, and then engaging in the appropriate form of integrative bargaining when multiple issues are differently valued. If there is an important and often unrealized source of joint gain, this appears to be it. Similarly, I conclude that the weakest of the four opportunities for integrative bargaining involves the exploitation of differing assessments regarding future events.[24] It certainly works well when someone who is selling refrigerators, computers, new cars, or audio-video equipment provides a warranty. The seller understands the risks to be minimal, and the buyer values the reassurance. Moreover, the seller is in the position to hold a large portfolio of risks, whereas the buyer is not. But apart from these very straightforward situations, which the market will almost surely have already put in place, this form of integrative bargaining generally seems to have little practical importance.

We have, in certain respects, allowed ourselves to be dazzled and seduced by the possibilities of integrative or "win-win" bargaining. That, in turn, has led to a certain amount of overclaiming. The reason, I think, is that if we hold these possibilities in a certain light and squint our eyes just hard enough, they look for all the world like the holy grail of negotiations. They seem to offer that which we have wanted most to find. What they seem to offer—though in the end it is only an illusion—is the long-sought proof that cooperation, honesty, and good behavior will carry the day not because they are virtuous, not because they will benefit society as a whole, but because they are in everyone's individual and pecuniary self-interest. But however much we may want "honesty" to be "the best policy" in this strong sense, the discovery of integrative bargaining has not, at least so far, provided that long-sought proof.

Perhaps the time has finally come to consider the possibility that this proof will always elude us, for the simple reason that the world in which we live does not, in this particular way, conform to our wishes. Even if there is just the chance that this is so, and it looks much more like a certainty than a chance, it would be appropriate to acknowledge the ultimate insufficiency of understanding self-interest in narrowly pecuniary terms. It would be appropriate to attend in a systematic way to the facts that even when it is contrary to our pecuniary self-interest, relationships matter; that we care about our reputations, not just for effectiveness but also for decency and good behavior; that we care about living in—and helping to create—communities in which pecuniary self-interest is not the only language that is spoken; and that Plato's Socrates may have gotten it right. And it would be appropriate to acknowledge the central importance of the ethical case against certain forms of competitive and self-interested behavior, especially those forms of behavior, central to the process of negotiations, that involve misrepresentations and other conduct that imposes harm on others.

Notes

1. See Walton and McKersie (1965); Fisher and Ury (1981); Pruitt (1981); Raiffa (1982); Menkel-Meadow (1983, 1984); Brett and others (1985); Lax and others (1985); Lewicki and Litterer (1985); Lax and Sebenius (1986); Susskind and Cruikshank (1987); Fisher, Ury, and Patton (1991). I know of no body of literature that has come together from so wide a range of disciplines and perspectives, and from such a diverse array of intellectual and professional communities, as does this one. In the end, however, it is a single and continuous body of work.

2. See Lax and Sebenius (1986). Some of the earliest contributions (see note 1) show opportunities for joint gain that are somewhat broader than the game theorists' understanding of integrative bargaining. Such opportunities include the game theorists' understanding of integrative bargaining, as well as the idea of principled negotiations and of negotiations under circumstances in which the parties have, and seek to promote, a shared interest in their long-term relationship. See, for example, Brett and others (1985) on principled negotiations defined by reference to objective criteria and long-term relationships; Fisher, Ury, and Patton (1991) on forms of integrative bargaining, principled negotiations, and long-term relationships; and Menkel-Meadow (1984) on forms of integrative bargaining and long-term relationships. Lax and Sebenius focus more narrowly on those forms of joint gain that fit within what I am calling the game theorists' understanding of integrative bargaining. The purpose of this chapter could be understood as clarifying the exact nature of the joint gains invoked by Lax and Sebenius, clarifying the exact circumstances in which those gains are available, and then assessing the case for cooperation, openness, and truth telling associated with those opportunities for capturing those joint gains. The case for cooperation, or at least the appearance of cooperation, in a long-term relationship is quite different from the case for cooperation associated with opportunities for integrative bargaining. The same can be said of the case for cooperation in connection with principled negotiations.

   Lax and Sebenius use the term *integrative bargaining* differently, or at least more narrowly, than others do. See Brett and others (1985) on using integrative bargaining primarily, if not exclusively, to refer to principled negotiations or to circumstances in which the parties share an interest in a long-term relationship. Neither of these uses comes within Lax and Sebenius's definition of the term. To minimize confusion, whenever I use the term *integrative bargaining* without quotation marks, I am using it as it is used by Lax and Sebenius.

3. See Lax and Sebenius (1986), asserting that opportunities for integrative bargaining—opportunities for "moves beyond simple agreement that benefit all parties" and in which "one's gain need not be the other's loss"—exist "much more frequently" than do bargaining situations that do not present such opportunities.

   Insofar as such terms as *problem solving* and *integrative bargaining* may sometimes refer to circumstances or tactics other than what Lax and Sebenius would describe as integrative bargaining, there is some risk of misunderstanding. For instance, Fisher, Ury, and Patton (1991) argue that a "major block to creative problem-solving lies in the assumption of a fixed pie: the less for you, the more for me. Rarely if ever is this assumption true . . . [because] there almost always exists the possibility of joint gain" (pp. 70–71). But their examples show that they are not just referring to circumstances presenting opportunities for Form III value creation (that is, opportunities for integrative bargaining), but also opportunities for Form I value creation (opportunities for presumptively distributive bargaining).

As to the claim that lost opportunities for integrative bargaining leave society as a whole worse off than it otherwise would have been, see Lax and others (1985) on demonstrating the risk of Pareto inefficiency and Sebenius (1992) explaining the likelihood of ex-post Pareto-inefficient agreements. See also Fisher, Ury, and Patton (1991) on contending that principled negotiation can help make the world a better place.

4. In addition to the courses that are being taught in law schools and business schools around the country, there are a number of organizations committed to the promulgation of information intended to make us better negotiators. Among them is the Harvard Negotiation Project, part of the Program on Negotiation at Harvard Law School. The list of scholars associated with that program is, to say the very least, prodigious. The National Institute for Dispute Resolution in Washington, D.C., performs similar work, as evidenced by its sponsorship of the collaborations that led to the publication of Brett and others (1985) and Lax and others (1985).

   As to the demand for books, courses, and workshops, the paperback copy of the second edition of Fisher, Ury, and Patton's *Getting to Yes* (1991) rightly proclaims itself "The National Bestseller." The cover goes on to explain that as of 1991, there were "more than two million copies in print in eighteen languages." For those who might like further evidence of the demand for this material, there is the business reply card, bound inside the back cover, for something called "Getting to Yes: The Video Workshop." It includes 130 minutes of videotape, 45 minutes of audiotape, a thirty-six-page Facilitator's Guide, six Viewer's Guides, and a copy of *Getting to Yes*. "The price of the complete Video Workshop, including all supplementary materials, is $2000."

5. See, for example, Menkel-Meadow (1984). See generally Menkel-Meadow (1985, 1988); Rhode (1993); Wetlaufer (1990a).

6. Lax et al. (1985); Lax and Sebenius (1986); Sebenius (1992). For value claimers, "Negotiation is hard, tough bargaining. The object of negotiation is to convince the other guy that he wants what you have to offer much more than you want what he has; moreover, you have all the time in the world while he is up against pressing deadlines. To 'win' at negotiating—and thus make the other fellow 'lose'—one must start high, concede slowly, exaggerate the value of concessions, minimize the benefits of the other's concessions, conceal information, argue force-fully on behalf of principles that imply favorable settlements, make commitments to accept only highly favorable agreements, and be willing to outwait the other fellow" (Lax and Sebenius, 1986, p. 32). See also Lax and others (1985); Sebenius (1992). Sebenius lists "holding valued issues 'hostage'" as a claiming tactic associ-ated with distributive bargaining. In fact, as I think he would agree, this tactic can

be brought to bear only when there are multiple issues differently valued. That is the classic opportunity for integrative bargaining.

7. Lax and Sebenius (1986, p. 32) recommend "openness, clear communication, sharing information, creativity, an attitude of joint problem solving, and cultivating common interests," cooperation, and "being open, sharing information about preferences and beliefs, not being misleading about minimum requirements, and so forth" (pp. 32, 38, 112–114). They note that "to create value, a negotiator needs *to learn* about her counterparts' interests and perceptions, to help them learn about hers, to *foster ingenuity and creativity,* and to *blunt the escalation of conflict*" (p. 113). They urge empathetic listening and clear communication for a posture that is "'side by side against the problem,'" for "brainstorming," for "'separating the people from the problem,'" for "being 'hard on the problem but soft on the people,'" for "allowing counterparts to vent emotions, avoiding insults and offensive mannerisms, holding meetings in pleasant neutral settings, avoiding threats and final offers, and helping counterparts to save face when necessary" (p. 113). See also Fisher, Ury, and Patton (1991), Lax and others (1985), and Sebenius (1992, on characterizing the difference in tactics as that between competition and cooperation).

8. There is an important distinction that may be drawn within the domain of Form III value creation, relating to the stability and permanence of the value created. This distinction will become clear when I discuss the particular circumstances that afford opportunities for Form III value creation.

9. See Lax and others (1985) and Lax and Sebenius (1986). Fisher, Ury, and Patton (1991) urge their readers to attend to "interests not positions." They express what can be understood as a preference for unbundling differently valued interests and then engaging in the form of integrative bargaining appropriate to situations in which there are multiple issues differently valued. Menkel-Meadow (1984) illustrates her argument with a series of examples that involve the unbundling or disaggregation of differently valued interests, integrative bargaining in the manner appropriate to multiple issues differently valued, and sometimes a final compromise. See also Pruitt (1981), explaining how log-rolling may occur only "when the parties have differing priorities across the issues at hand" (pp. 153–154); Susskind and Cruikshank (1987), generally treating multiple issues differently valued as the entire universe of opportunities for integrative bargaining; and Sebenius (1992), claiming that "differences in relative valuation suggest joint gain from trades or from 'unbundling' differently valued attributes" (pp. 18, 29).

10. Lax and Sebenius (1986) argue that there are opportunities for "value creation"— a term generally synonymous with integrative bargaining—when two parties have "complementary capabilities" or, more broadly, "differences in capabilities": "Just as differences in interest, probability, risk aversion, and time preference may imply gain, so may differences in capabilities, access to production opportunities, technologies, or abilities to convert resources physically" (p. 102). Menkel-Meadow (1984) offers an example in which a plaintiff is provided not with money but with a job. See also Lax and others (1985); Sebenius (1992); and Note (1996), citing in-kind settlements as an instance of integrative bargaining.

11. Lax and Sebenius (1986, pp. 111–112): "There do exist joint gains not deriving from differences or pure shared interests. With scale economies, two absolutely identical parties may reach agreement even where no common value is to be created." Also see Sebenius (1992).

12. A "kind of shared interest can come into play" when "a whole range of settlements" might further the parties' "identical interest" in their relationship (Lax and Sebenius, 1986, p. 109). See also Brett and others (1985). I have noted elsewhere the possibility that one party may care more than the other about the prospects of a future relationship and the corresponding possibility of strategic misrepresentations (Wetlaufer, 1990b).

13. In addition to the possibility of "dovetailing" differences related to "value, expectation, capacity, risk-bearing attitude, and time preference, . . . good negotiators can find ways to make use of many more differences—in the participants' criteria for success, in attitudes toward precedent and principle, in constituencies, in personal and organizational situations, in ideology, in conceptions of fairness, and so on. . . . [Indeed,] differences are as varied as negotiators. If recognized, this truth carries a profoundly optimistic message for the process of creating value" (Lax and Sebenius, 1986, p. 105). See also Fisher, Ury, and Patton (1991).

14. I am speaking here about aggregate utility and not about aggregate wealth. Some among the proponents of "law and economics" commit themselves not to the task of maximizing aggregate utility but to what they see as the more practical task of maximizing aggregate wealth (see, for example, Posner, 1992). They will be uncomfortable with this part of my analysis both because, from the perspective of aggregate wealth, they may be indifferent as to who received this $400 and also because they may be resistant to the very enterprise of interpersonal comparisons of utility. I understand the arguments they make and the level of their commitment to those arguments. If it is their position that the argument made in the text is either unintelligible or impermissible, I am simply unpersuaded.

15. A familiar classroom example involves a landlord and a tenant who have been dickering over the rent. The parties have reached a tentative agreement at $700, but the tenant is worried that he is overextending himself and that he really cannot afford to pay anything more than $650. Then the tenant, remembering his training in win-win bargaining, suggests that he would agree to mow the lawn every week if the landlord would reduce the rent to $640. The landlord, who had been paying a local lawn care service $75 per month, happily agrees. Through the introduction of the second issue (the lawn mowing), the parties have found a second agreement that is better for both parties than had been the first. But once the parties have identified the possibility of cross-selling the lawn mowing, the transaction is purely distributive. Every dollar by which the now-modified "rent" (actually rent plus mowing) moves up or down is a dollar by which one party is made better off and the other worse off.

16. In the classic textbook example, two brothers are quarreling over the household's last orange. Conceivably, either brother could end up with the entire orange or he could compromise and cut it in half. But if they understood that one brother wanted only to eat the fruit of the orange and that the other brother wanted only

to use the skin of the orange to zest a cake, they would understand that one could have the entire fruit while the other could have the entire skin. Thus, there is a possible agreement that would leave both parties significantly better off than they would have been had they simply cut the orange in half. Indeed, they could move from a 50–50 agreement to a 100–100 agreement in which they both obtained all of what they wanted. This is the purest case of a Form III integrative solution.

17. Assume more specifically that he has a buyer who is willing to pay him this amount for the car in a straight dollar transaction.

18. In other words, Ms. Seller now has two reservation prices. One, her reservation price for the car if she has to bear the risk of major repairs, is $2,000. The other, her reservation price if she does not have to bear that risk, is $2,400. The $400 difference between the two simply reflects her valuation of those risks at $(.40)($1,000)$.

19. For purposes of this example, assume that these reservation prices represent competing offers that are available to the respective parties.

20. There are a number of possible solutions to this problem, all involving contingent agreements of one form or another. In addition to the agreement in which Ms. Singer gets a fixed amount for each ticket sold, the parties may enter into an agreement in which she promises to pay Mr. Owner a certain amount in the event that the house does not fill (a guarantee). She could also be paid a certain amount of the price of each ticket sold over and above what he believes will be the number sold. Or they could agree that she simply will not be paid if the house does not fill.

21. See Brett and others (1985); Fisher, Ury, and Patton (1991); Menkel-Meadow (1984). Two cautions may be in order, however. First, what may matter most in this situation is the appearance of cooperation, openness, and truth telling. It is probably true here, as elsewhere, that a negotiator who can behave in a competitive manner while appearing to behave in a cooperative manner may, by strictly pecuniary standards, have the best of both worlds. Second, at least in the practice of law, some evidence suggests that a reputation for ruthlessness is not always contrary to one's pecuniary self-interest. We need not name names.

22. See Plato (1987). See also Bok (1978); Postema (1983—assuming throughout that one has an interest in one's own integrity and morality); and Editor's Note (1951), asserting that sharp dealing disregards "the duty everyone, including a lawyer, owes to himself to so conduct himself as not to lose his own self-respect."

23. Some may believe that justice or morality is nothing more than the maximization of aggregate wealth or of aggregate utility. See, for example, Posner (1992) and Sidgwick (1907). But even those who do not embrace these views still may see efficiency (and thus aggregate wealth) as a kind of public good. Accordingly, they may condemn hard bargaining, or at least lying, on the grounds that it can diminish the level of public trust and thus impair the efficiency with which we conduct our affairs. Arrow (1974); Bok (1978); Wetlaufer (1990b); and Dasgupta (1988). Exploring this idea is about as close as Fisher, Ury, and Patton (1991) come to an explicit statement of an ethical commitment.

24. Its weakness is in the fact that the "joint gains" are inherently unstable, that they may disappear in their entirety, that they are sometimes unavailable as a practical matter (because the differing projections are wrongly aligned), and because they are available—if that is not too strong a word—only to those who are looking to place a bet. It is also my experience that the significant weakness of these joint gains is easily exceeded by the difficulty of teaching, at least to arithmetic-phobic law students, the quantitative decision analysis that is necessary if one is to have one's bearings while seeking to exploit these opportunities for integrative bargaining. I find this to be the case even when working with a problem so well designed and well annotated as RCI, Inc. and Southeastern Electric as set out in Lax and others (1985).

References

Arrow, K. J. *The Limits of Organization.* New York: Norton, 1974.

Bok, S. *Lying: Moral Choices in Public and Private Life.* New York: Pantheon Books, 1978.

Brett, J. M., and others. *The Manager as Negotiator and Dispute Resolver.* National Institute for Dispute Resolution, 1985.

Dasgupta, P. "Trust as a Commodity." In D. Gambetta (ed.), *Trust: Making and Breaking Cooperative Relations.* New York: B. Blackwell, 1988.

Editor's Note. *Stanford Law Review,* 1951, *4,* 355–356.

Fisher, R., and Ury, W. *Getting to Yes.* Boston: Houghton Mifflin, 1981.

Fisher, R., Ury, W., and Patton, B. *Getting to Yes.* New York: Penguin Books, 1991.

Lax, D. A., and others. *The Manager as Negotiator: Curriculum Materials in Dispute Resolution for Decision Analysis and Economics.* National Institute for Dispute Resolution, 1985.

Lax, D. A., and Sebenius, J. K. *The Manager as Negotiator.* New York: Free Press, 1986.

Lewicki, R. J., and Litterer, J. A. *Negotiation.* 1985.

Menkel-Meadow, C. "Legal Negotiation: A Study of Strategies in Search of a Theory." *American Bar Foundation Research Journal,* 1983, *4,* 905.

Menkel-Meadow, C. "Toward Another View of Legal Negotiation: The Structure of Problem Solving." *UCLA Law Review,* 1984, *31,* 754–842.

Menkel-Meadow, C. "Portia in a Different Voice: Speculations on a Woman's Lawyering Process." *Berkeley Women's Law Journal,* 1985, *1,* 39.

Menkel-Meadow, C. "Feminist Legal Theory, Critical Legal Studies, and Legal Education or 'The Fem-Crits Go to Law School.'" *Journal of Legal Education,* 1988, *38,* 61.

Note. "In-Kind Class Action Settlements." *Harvard Law Review,* 1996, pp. 109, 810.

Plato, *Gorgias* (D. J. Zeyl trans.). Indianapolis: Hackett Pub. Co., 1987.

Posner, R. A. *Economic Analysis of Law.* (4th ed.). Boston: Little, Brown, 1992.

Postema, G. J. "Self-Image, Integrity, and Professional Responsibility." In D. Luban (ed.), *The Good Lawyer.* Totowa, N.J.: Rowman & Allanheld, 1983.

Pruitt, D. G. *Negotiation Behavior.* New York: Academic Press, 1981.

Raiffa, H. *The Art and Science of Negotiation.* Cambridge, Mass.: Belknap Press, 1982.

Rhode, D. L. "Missing Questions: Feminist Perspectives on Legal Education." *Stanford Law Review,* 1993, *45,* 1547.

Sebenius, J. K. "Negotiation Analysis: A Characterization and Review." *Management Science,* 1992, *38,* 18–38.

Sidgwick, H. *Methods of Ethics.* (7th ed.). London: Macmillan and Co., 1907.

Susskind, L., and Cruikshank, J. *Breaking the Impasse: Consensual Approaches to Resolving Public Disputes.* New York: Basic Books, 1987.

Walton, R. E., and McKersie, R. B. *A Behavioral Theory of Labor Relations.* New York: McGraw-Hill, 1965.

Wetlaufer, G. B. "Rhetoric and Its Denial in Legal Discourse." *Virginia Law Review,* 1990a, *76,* 1545–1598.

Wetlaufer, G. B. "The Ethics of Lying in Negotiations." *Iowa Law Review,* 1990b, *75,* 1219–1273.

CHAPTER SIX

Bargaining with the Devil Without Losing Your Soul

Ethics in Negotiation

G. Richard Shell

ETHICS COME FIRST, NOT LAST

Your attitudes about ethical conduct are preliminary to every bargaining move you make. Your ethics are a vital part of your identity as a person, and, try as you may, you will never be able to successfully separate the way you act in negotiations from the person you are in other parts of your life. That is "you" at the bargaining table as well as "you" in the mirror every morning.

Your personal beliefs about ethics also come with a price tag. The stricter your ethical standards, the higher the cost you must be willing to pay to uphold them in any given transaction. The lower your ethical standards, the higher the price may be in terms of your reputation. And the lower the standards of those with whom you deal, the more time, energy, and prudence are required to defend yourself and your interests.

I'll give you my bias on this subject right up front: I think you should aim high where ethics are concerned. Personal integrity is one of the four most important effectiveness factors for the skilled negotiator. Negotiators who value "personal integrity" can be counted on to negotiate consistently, using a thoughtful set of personal values that they could, if necessary, explain to others. This definition puts the burden on you as an individual—not me as judge—to construct your own ethical framework. I learned long ago that the best way to teach others about values is to raise tough questions, give people tools to think about them, then get out of the way.

Reasonable people will differ on ethical questions, but you will have personal integrity in my estimation if you can pass my "explain and defend" test after making a considered, ethical choice. After we have examined some ways of thinking about your own duties, we will look at how you can defend yourself when others use ethically questionable tactics against you.

THE MINIMUM STANDARD: OBEY THE LAW

Regardless of how you feel about ethics, everyone has a duty to obey the laws that regulate the negotiation process. Of course, bargaining laws differ between countries and cultures, but the normative concerns underlying these different legal regimes share important characteristics. I will look briefly at the American approach to the legal regulations of deception as an example of the way law works in negotiations, but basic principles of fairness and prudence in the bargaining conduct are global, not national.

American law disclaims any general duty of "good faith" in the negotiation of commercial agreements. As an American judge once wrote, "In a business transaction both sides presumably try to get the best deal. . . . The proper recourse [for outrageous conduct] is to walk away from the bargaining table, not sue for 'bad faith' in negotiations." This general rule assumes, however, that no one has committed fraud. As we shall see, the law of fraud reaches deep into the complexities of negotiation behavior.

There are six major elements of a fraud case. A bargaining move is fraudulent when a speaker makes a (1) knowing (2) misrepresentation of a (3) material (4) fact (5) on which the victim reasonably relies (6) causing damages.

A car dealer commits fraud when he resets a car odometer and sells one of his company cars as if it were brand new. The dealer knows the car is not new; he misrepresents its condition to the buyer; the condition of the car is a fact rather than a mere opinion, and it is a fact that is important ("material") to the transaction; the buyer is acting reasonably in relying on the mileage as recorded on the odometer when she buys the car; and damages result. Similarly, a person selling her business commits fraud when she lies about the number and kind of debts owed by the business.

Lies about important facts that go to the core of a deal are not unknown in business negotiations. But most negotiators don't need a lawyer or an ethicist to tell them that such misrepresentations ought to be avoided. These are cases of fraud, pure and simple. People who try to cheat you are crooks.

More interesting questions about lying come up on the margins of the law of fraud. What if the dealer says you had better buy the car today because he has another buyer ready to snatch the car away tomorrow? That may be a statement of fact, but is it material? It looks like Sifford's little lie about his catalogue price. [Earlier in the chapter, the author relates a story in which the late Darrell

Sifford, a Philadelphia newspaper columnist, is able to get a remarkable deal on a globe by lying to the store clerk, saying that he had seen the same globe in a catalogue for a lower price.] Assuming Sifford is innocent of legal fraud in the globe case, should we hold a professional car dealer to a different legal standard? Is the car dealer's lie about the other buyer fraudulent or just a form of creative motivation?

Suppose the seller does not state a fact but instead gives an artfully phrased opinion? Perhaps the person selling her business says that a large account debt "could probably be renegotiated" after you buy the firm. Could this opinion be deemed so misleading as to be fraudulent if the seller knows for a fact that the creditor would never consider renegotiation?

Let's look briefly at each element in the law of fraud and test where the legal limits lie. Surprisingly, though we would all prefer to see clear black and white rules outlining our legal duties, staying on the right side of the law often requires a prudent respect for the many gray areas that inevitably color an activity as widespread and multifaceted as negotiation. Knowing what the law is helps you stay within its boundaries, but this knowledge does not eliminate the need for a strong sense of right and wrong.

Element 1: Knowing

To commit fraud, a negotiator must have a particular state of mind with respect to the fact he or she misrepresents. The misstatement must be made "knowingly." One way of getting around fraud, therefore, might be for the speaker to avoid direct contact with information that would lead to a "knowing" state of mind.

For example, a company president might suspect that his company is in poor financial health, but he does not yet "know" it because he has not seen the latest quarterly reports. When his advisers ask to set up a meeting to discuss these reports, he tells them to hold off. He is about to go into negotiation with an important supplier and would like to be able to say, honestly, that so far as he knows the company is paying its bills. Does this get him off the hook? Perhaps. But many courts have stretched the definition of "knowing" to include statements that are, like the executive's in this case, made with a conscious and reckless disregard for their truth.

Nor is reckless disregard for truth the limit of the law. Victims of misstatements that were made negligently or even innocently may obtain relief in certain circumstances. These kinds of misstatements are not deemed fraudulent, however. Rather, they are a way of recognizing that a deal was based on a mistake.

Element 2: Misrepresentation

In general, the law requires a negotiator to make a positive misstatement before a statement is judged fraudulent. A basic legal rule for commercial negotiators is, "Be silent and be safe."

As a practical matter, of course, silence is difficult to maintain if one's bargaining opponent is an astute questioner. In the face of inconvenient questions, negotiators are often forced to resort to verbal feints and dodges such as, "I don't know about that" or, when pressed, "This is not a subject I am at liberty to discuss." When you choose to lie in response to a pointed question probing the strength of your bargaining position, you immediately raise the risk of legal liability. As we shall see below, however, some lies are not material, and the other party may be charged with a duty to discount the truth of what you tell them.

Surprisingly, there are circumstances when it may be fraudulent to keep your peace about an issue even if the other side does not ask about it. When does a negotiator have a duty to voluntarily disclose matters that may hurt his bargaining position? American law imposes affirmative disclosure duties in the following four circumstances:

1. *When the negotiator makes a partial disclosure that is or becomes misleading in light of all the facts.* If you say your company is profitable, you may be under a duty to disclose whether your used questionable accounting techniques to arrive at that statement. You should also update your prior statement if you show a loss in the next quarter and negotiations are continuing.

2. *When the parties stand in a fiduciary relationship to each other.* In negotiation actions between trustees and beneficiaries, partners in a partnership, shareholders in a small corporation, or members of a family business, parties may have a duty of complete candor and cannot rely on the "be silent and be safe" approach.

3. *When the nondisclosing party has vital information about the transaction not accessible to the other side.* A recent case applying this exception held that an employer owed a duty of disclosure to a prospective employee to disclose contingency plans for shutting down the project for which the employee was hired. In general, sellers have a greater duty to disclose hidden defects about their property than buyers do to disclose "hidden treasure" that may be buried there. Thus, a home seller must disclose termite infestation in her home, but an oil company need not voluntarily disclose that there is oil on a farmer's land when negotiating to purchase it. This is a slippery exception; the best test is one of conscience and fairness.

4. *When special codified disclosure duties, such as those regarding contracts of insurance or public offerings of securities.* Legislatures sometimes impose special disclosure duties for particular kinds of transactions. In the United States, for example, many states now require home sellers to disclose all known problems with their houses.

If none of these four exceptions applies, neither side is likely to be found liable for fraud based on nondisclosure. Each party can remain silent, passively letting the other proceed under its own assumptions.

Element 3: Material

Many people lie or deliberately mislead others about something during negotiations. Often they seek to deceive by making initial demands that far exceed their true needs or desires. Sometimes they lie about their bottom line. Perhaps, like Sifford, they embellish their story about why they are entitled to a particular price or concession.

Of course, initial demands and bottom lines may not be "facts" in the ordinary sense of the word. One may have only a vague idea of what one really wants or is willing to pay for something. Hence, a statement that an asking price is "too high" may not be a misrepresentation as much as a statement of opinion or preference.

Suppose, however, that an art gallery owner has been given authority by an artist to sell one of the artist's paintings for any price greater than $10,000. Is it fraud for the gallery owner, as part of a negotiation with a collector, to say, "I can't take less than $12,000"? In fact, she does have authority to sell the painting for anything above $10,000, so there has been a knowing misrepresentation of fact. Suppose the buyer says, "My budget for this purchase is $9,000," when she is really willing to spend $11,000? Same thing. The legal question in both cases is whether these facts are "material."

They are not. In fact, lies about demands and bottom-line prices are so prevalent in the bargaining that many professional negotiators do not consider such misstatements to be lies, preferring the term "bluffs."

Why? Such statements allow the parties to assert the legitimacy of their preferences and set the boundaries of the bargaining range without incurring a risk of loss. Misleading statements about bottom-line prices and demands also enable parties to test the limits of the other side's commitment to their expressed preferences.

The American legal profession has gone so far as to enshrine this practice approvingly in its Model Rules of Professional Conduct. These rules provide that "estimates of price or value placed on the subject of a transaction and a party's intention as to an acceptable settlement of a claim" are not "material" facts for purposes of the ethical rule prohibiting lawyers from making false statements to a third person.

There are thus no legal problems with lying about how much you might be willing to pay or which of several issues in a negotiation you value more highly. Demands and bottom lines are not, as a matter of law, "material" to a deal.

As one moves from bluffs about how much one wants to spend or charge toward more assertive, specific lies about why one price or another is required, the fraud meter goes up. One common way to back up a price demand, for example, is Sifford's "I can get it cheaper elsewhere" argument, used by consumers the world over. Negotiators often lie about their available alternatives. Is this fraudulent?

When a shopper lies to a storekeeper that she can get an item cheaper across town, the statement is not "material." After all, the seller presumably knows (or should know) at least as much about the value of what he is selling as the buyer does. If the seller wants to sell it for less than the asking price, who knows better than the seller what the right price is?

But suppose we switch roles. Suppose the seller lies about having another offer that the buyer has to beat? For example, take the following older, but still important legal case from Massachusetts.

A commercial landlord bought a building and negotiated a new lease with a toy shop tenant when the tenant's lease expired. The proprietor of the toy shop bargained hard and refused to pay the landlord's demand for a $10,000 increase in rent. The landlord then told the shop owner that he had another tenant willing to pay the $10,000 amount and threatened the current tenant with immediate eviction if he did not promptly agree to the new rate. The tenant paid but learned later that the threat had been a bluff; there had been no other tenant. The tenant successfully sued for fraud.

In another case, this time from Oklahoma, a real estate agent was held liable for fraud, including punitive damages, when she pressured a buyer into closing on a home with a story that a rival buyer (the contractor who built the house) was willing to pay the asking price and would do so later that same day.

What makes these lies different in a legal sense from the "I can't take less than $12,000" statement by the art gallery owner or the "I can get it cheaper elsewhere" comment by a shopper? I think the difference has to do with the fact that the victims in these cases were "little people"—small businesses and customers—who were being pressured unfairly by professionals. The made-up offers were "material" facts from the buyers' point of view. They were specific, factual, coupled with ultimatums, and impossible to investigate.

But I do not think a court would have reached the same result if both parties had been consumers or both sophisticated professionals. Nor would I expect to see results like this outside a wealthy, consumer-oriented country such as the United States. Still, it is worth noting that such cases exist. They counsel a degree of prudence on the part of professional sellers or buyers when dealing with the public.

Element 4: Fact

On the surface, it appears that only misstatements of objective facts are occasions for legal sanctions. Businessmen seeking to walk close to the legal line are therefore careful to couch their sales talk in negotiation as opinions, predictions, and statements of intention, not statements of fact. Moreover, a good deal of exaggeration or puffing about product attributes and likely performance is viewed as a normal aspect of the selling process. Buyers and sellers cannot take everything said to them at face value.

The surface of the law can be misleading, however. Courts have found occasion to punish statements of intention and opinion as fraudulent when faced with particularly egregious cases. The touchstone of the law of fraud is not whether the statement at issue was one of pure fact but rather whether the statement succeeded in concealing a set of facts the negotiator preferred to keep out of sight.

Suppose you are borrowing money from a bank and tell the bank as part of your application that you plan to spend the loan on new capital equipment. In fact, you are really going to pay off an old debt. Fraud? Possibly.

In the memorable words of a famous English judge, "The state of a man's mind is as much a fact as the state of his digestion." Lies regarding intention even have a special name in the law: promissory fraud. The key element in a promissory fraud case is proof that the speaker knew he could not live up to his promise *at the time the promise was made.* In other words, he made the promise with his fingers crossed behind his back. If you are the victim, you must also show that the other side's intention going into the deal went to its very heart—that is, that the statement of the intention was "material."

What about statements of opinion? Self-serving statements about the value of your goods or the qualifications of your product or company are the standard (legal) fare of the negotiating table. However, when negotiators offer statements of opinion that are flatly contradicted by facts known to them about the subject of the transaction, they may be liable for fraud. In one New York case, for example, the seller of a machine shop business opined to a prospective buyer that the buyer would have "no trouble" securing work from his largest customer. In fact, the seller was in debt to his customer, intended to pay off this debt from the proceeds of the sale to the buyer, and had virtually no work there due to his reputation for poor workmanship. The buyer successfully proved that the sale had been induced by the seller's fraudulent statement of opinion and collected damages.

What seems to matter in these cases is unfairness. If a statement of intention or opinion so conceals the true nature of the negotiation proposal that a bargaining opponent cannot accurately assess an appropriate range of values or risks on which to base the price, then it may be fraudulent.

Element 5: Reliance

Negotiators who lie sometimes defend themselves by saying, in effect, "Only a fool could have believed what I said. The other party had no business relying on me to tell him the truth—he should have investigated for himself."

As we saw in our discussion of lies about other offers, this defense works pretty well when both sides are on roughly the same footing. But when one side has a decided advantage, as does a professional buyer or seller against a consumer or small business, American courts are more sympathetic to the idea that the victim reasonably relied on the lie.

In addition, courts are sympathetic to those who, in good faith, rely on others to treat them fairly in the negotiation process and who have that trust violated by more powerful firms trying to steal their trade secrets and other information. There have been a number of cases, for example, allowing recoveries to independent inventors and others who disclosed trade secrets in the course of negotiations to sell their discoveries. The prospective buyers in these cases are typically big companies that attempted to use the negotiation process as a way of getting something for nothing. The prudent negotiator, however, always secures an express confidentiality agreement if secret information or business plans must be disclosed in the course of the information exchange process.

One trick that manipulative negotiators use to avoid liability after they have misstated important facts or improperly motivated a transaction is to write the true terms and conditions into the final written agreement. If the victim signs off on the deal without reading this contract, he will have a hard time claiming reasonable reliance on the earlier misstatements in a fraud case later on.

For example, suppose you negotiate the sale of your company's principal asset, an electronic medical device, to a big medical products firm. During the negotiations, the company assures you that it will aggressively market the device so you can earn royalties. The contract, however, specifically assigns it the legal right to shelve the product if it wishes. After the sale, it decides to stop marketing your product and you later learn the company never really intended to sell it; it was just trying to get your product off the market because it competed with several of its own.

In a case like this, a court held that the plaintiffs were stuck with the terms of the final written contract. The lesson here is clear: *Read* contracts carefully before you sign them, and question assurances that contract language changing the nature of the deal is just a technicality or was required by the lawyers.

Element 6: Causation and Damages

You cannot make a legal claim for fraud if you have no damages caused by the fraudulent statement or omission. People sometimes get confused about this. The other negotiator lies in some outrageous and unethical way, so they assume the liar's conduct is illegal. It may be, but only if that conduct leads directly to some quantifiable economic loss for the victim of the fraud. If there is no such loss, the right move is to walk away from the deal (if you can), not sue.

BEYOND THE LAW: A LOOK AT ETHICS

As you may have noticed, the legal rules that govern bargaining are suffused with a number of ethical norms. For example, professionals with a big bargaining advantage are sometimes held to a higher standard when negotiating with amateurs and consumers than they are when they approach others as equals. Parties that stand in special relationships to each other, such as trustees or partners, have heightened legal disclosure duties. Lies protecting important factual information about the subject of the transaction are treated differently from lies about such things as your alternatives or your bottom line. Silence is unacceptable if an important fact is inaccessible to the other side unless you speak up.

I want to challenge you to identify what *your* beliefs are. To help you decide how you feel about ethics, I will briefly describe the three most common approaches to bargaining ethics I have heard expressed in conversations with literally hundreds of students and executives. See which shoe fits—or take a bit from each approach and construct your own.

As we explore this territory, remember that nearly everyone is sincerely convinced that they are acting ethically most of the time, whereas they often think others are acting either naively or unethically, depending on their ethical perspective and the situation. Thus, a word of warning is in order. Your ethics are mainly your own business. They will help you increase your level of confidence and comfort at the bargaining table. But do not expect others to share your ethics in every detail. Prudence pays.

THREE SCHOOLS OF BARGAINING ETHICS

The three schools of bargaining ethics I want to introduce for your consideration are (1) the "It's a game" Poker School, (2) the "Do the right thing even if it hurts" Idealist School, and (3) the "What goes around, comes around" Pragmatist School.

The "It's a Game" Poker School

The Poker School of ethics sees negotiation as a "game" with certain "rules." The rules are defined by the law, such as the legal materials we covered above. Conduct within the rules is ethical. Conduct outside the rules is unethical.

The modern founder of the Poker School was Albert Z. Carr, a former special consultant to President Harry Truman. Carr wrote a book in the 1960s called, appropriately enough, *Business as a Game*. In a related article that appeared in the *Harvard Business Review,* Carr (1968) argued that bluffing and other misleading but lawful negotiating tactics are "an integral part of the [bargaining] game, and the executive who does not master [these] techniques is not likely to accumulate much money or power."

People who adhere to the Poker School readily admit that bargaining and poker are not exactly the same. But they point out that deception is essential to effective play in both arenas. Moreover, skilled players in both poker and bargaining exhibit a robust and realistic distrust of the other fellow. Carr (1968) argues that good players should ignore the "claims of friendship" and engage in "cunning deception and concealment" in fair, hard bargaining encounters. When the game is over, members of the Poker School do not think less of a player just because that person successfully deceived them. In fact, assuming the tactic was legal, they may admire the deceiver and vow to be better prepared (and less trusting) next time.

We know how to play poker, but how exactly does one play the bargaining "game"? Stripped to its core, it looks like this: someone opens, and then people take turns proposing terms to each other. Arguments supporting your preferred terms are allowed. You can play or pass in each round. The goal is to get the other side to agree to terms that are as close as possible to your last proposal.

In the bargaining game, it is understood that both sides might be bluffing. Bluffs disguise a weak bargaining hand, that is, the limited or unattractive alternatives you have away from the table, your inability to affect the other side's alternatives, and the arguments you have to support your demands. Unlike poker players, negotiators always attempt to disclose a good hand if they have one in the bargaining game. So the most effective bluffs are realistic, attractive, difficult-to-check (but false) alternatives or authoritative (but false) supporting standards. Experienced players know this, so one of the key skills in the bargaining game is judging when the other party's alternatives are really as good as he or she says. If the other side calls you on your bargaining bluff by walking away or giving you a credible ultimatum, you lose. Either there will be no deal when there should have been one, or the final price will be nearer to their last offer than to yours.

As mentioned, the Poker School believes in the rule of law. In poker, you are not allowed to hide cards, collude with other players, or renege on your bets. But you are expected to deceive others about your hand. The best plays come when you win the pot with a weak hand or fool the other players into betting heavily when your hand is strong. In bargaining, you must not commit outright, actionable fraud, but negotiators must be on guard for anything short of fraud.

The Poker School has three main problems as I see it. First, the Poker School assumes that everyone treats bargaining as a game. Unfortunately, it is an empirical fact that people disagree on this. For a start, neither the idealists nor the pragmatists (more on these below) think bargaining is a game. This problem does not deter the Poker School, which holds that the rules permit its members to play even when the other party disagrees about this premise.

Second, everyone is supposed to know the rules cold. But this is impossible, given that legal rules are applied differently in different industries and regions of the world.

Finally, as you know (having read about the legal treatment of fraud), the law is far from certain even within a single jurisdiction. So you often need a sharp lawyer to help you decide what to do.

The "Do the Right Thing Even If It Hurts" Idealist School

The Idealist School says that bargaining is an aspect of social life, not a special activity with its own unique set of rules. The same ethics that apply in the home should carry directly into the realm of negotiation. If it is wrong to lie or mislead in normal social encounters, it is wrong to do so in negotiations. If it is OK to lie in special situations (such as to protect another person's feelings), it is also OK to lie in negotiations when those special conditions apply.

Idealists do not entirely rule out deception in negotiation. For example, if the other party assumes you have a lot of leverage and never asks you directly about the situation as you see it, you do not necessarily have to volunteer information weakening your position. And the idealist can decline to answer questions. But such exceptions are uncomfortable moments. Members of the Idealist School prefer to be candid and honest at the bargaining table even if it means giving up a certain amount of strategic advantage.

The Idealist School draws its strength from philosophy and religion. For example, Immanuel Kant said that we should all follow the ethical rules that we would wish others to follow. Kant argued that if everyone lied all the time, social life would be chaos. Hence you should not lie. Kant also disapproved of treating other people merely as the means to achieve your own personal ends. Lies in negotiation are selfish acts designed to achieve personal gain. This form of conduct is therefore unethical. Period. Many religions also teach adherents not to lie for personal advantage.

Idealists admit that deception in negotiation rarely arouses moral indignation unless the lies breach the trust between friends, violate a fiduciary responsibility, or exploit people such as the sick or elderly, who lack the ability to protect themselves. And if the only way you can prevent some terrible harm like a murder is by lying, go ahead and lie. But the lack of moral outrage and the fact that sometimes lying can be defended does not make deception in negotiations right.

Idealists strongly reject the idea that negotiations should be viewed as "games." Negotiations, they feel, are serious, consequential communication acts. People negotiate to resolve their differences so social life will work for the benefit of all. People must be held responsible for all their actions, including the way they negotiate, under universal standards.

Idealists think that the members of the Poker School are predatory and selfish. For its part, the Poker School thinks that idealists are naïve and even a little silly. When members of the two schools meet at the bargaining table, tempers can flare.

Some members of the Idealist School have recently been trying to find a philosophical justification for bluffs and bottom lines. There is no agreement yet on whether these efforts have succeeded in ethical terms. But it is clear that outright lies such as fictitious other offers and better prices are unethical practices under idealist principles.

The big problem for the idealists is obvious: their standards sometimes make it difficult to proceed in a realistic way at the bargaining table. Also, unless adherence to the Idealist School is coupled with a healthy skepticism about the way other people will negotiate, idealism leaves its members open to exploitation by people with standards other than their own. These limitations are especially troublesome when idealists must represent others' interests at the bargaining table.

Despite its limitations, I like the Idealist School. Perhaps because I am an academic, I genuinely believe that the different parts of my life are, in fact, a whole. I aspire to ethical standards that I can apply consistently. I will admit that I sometimes fall short of idealism's strict code, but by aiming high I hope I am leaving myself somewhere to fall that maintains my basic sense of personal integrity.

I confess my preference for the Idealist School so you will know where I am coming from in the discussion. But I realize that your experience and work environment may preclude idealism as an ethical option. That's OK. As I hope I am making clear, idealism is not the only way to think about negotiation in ethical terms.

The "What Goes Around Comes Around" Pragmatist School

The final school of bargaining ethics, the Pragmatist School, includes some original elements as well as some attributes of the previous two. In common with the Poker School, this approach views deception as a necessary part of the negotiation process. Unlike the Poker School, however, it prefers not to use misleading statements and overt lies if there is a serviceable, practical alternative. Uniquely, the Pragmatist School displays concern for the potential negative effects of deceptive conduct on present and future relationships. Thus, lying and other questionable tactics are bad not so much because they are "wrong" as because they cost the user more in the long run than they gain in the short run.

As my last comment suggests, people adhere to this school more for prudential than idealistic reasons. Lies and misleading conduct can cause serious injury to one's credibility. And credibility is an important asset for effective negotiators both to preserve working relationships and to protect one's reputation in a market or community. This latter concern is summed up in what I would call the pragmatist's credo: what goes around comes around. The Poker

School is less mindful of reputation and more focused on winning each bargaining encounter within the rules of the "game."

What separates the Pragmatist School from the Idealist School? To put it bluntly, a pragmatist will lie a bit more often than will an idealist. For example, pragmatists sometimes draw fine distinctions between lies and hard-core facts of a transaction, which are always imprudent (and often illegal), and misleading statements about such things as the rationales used to justify a position. A pragmatic car salesman considers it highly unethical to lie about anything large or small relating to the mechanical condition of a used car he is selling. But this same salesman might not have a problem saying, "My manager won't let me sell this car for less than $10,000," even though he knows the manager would sell the car for $9,500. False justification and rationales are marginally acceptable because they are usually less important to the transaction and much harder to detect as falsehoods than are core facts about the object being bought and sold.

Pragmatists are also somewhat looser within the truth when using so-called blocking techniques—tactics to avoid answering questions that threaten to expose a weak bargaining position. For example, can you ethically answer, "I don't know," when asked about something you do know that hurts your position? An idealist would refuse to answer the question or try to change the subject, not lie by saying, "I don't know." A pragmatist would go ahead and say, "I don't know," if his actual state of knowledge is hard to trace and the lie poses little risk to his relationships.

THE ETHICAL SCHOOLS IN ACTION

As a test of ethical thinking, let's take a simple example. Assume you are negotiating to sell a commercial building, and the other party asks you whether you have another offer. In fact, you do not have any such offers. What would the three schools recommend you do?

A Poker School adherent might suggest a lie. Both parties are sophisticated businesspeople in this deal, so a lie about alternatives is probably legally "immaterial." But a member of the Poker School would want to know the answers to two questions before making his move.

First, could the lie be easily found out? If so, it would be a bad play because it wouldn't work and might put the other side on guard with respect to other lies he might want to tell. Second, is a lie about alternatives the best way to leverage the buyer into making a bid? Perhaps a lie about something else—a deadline, for example—might be a better choice.

Assuming the lie is undetectable and will work, how might the conversation sound?

BUYER: Do you have another offer?

POKER SCHOOL SELLER: Yes. A Saudi Arabian firm presented us with an offer for $_____ this morning, and we have only forty-eight hours to get back to it with an answer. Confidentiality forbids us from showing you the Saudi offer, but rest assured that it is real. What would you like to do?

How would an idealist handle this situation? There are several idealist responses, but none would involve a lie. One response would be the following:

BUYER: Do you have another offer?

IDEALIST SELLER 1: An interesting question—and one I refuse to answer.

Of course, that refusal speaks volumes to the buyer. Another approach would be to adopt a policy on "other buyer" questions:

BUYER: Do you have another offer?

IDEALIST SELLER 2: An interesting question, and one I receive quite often. Let me answer you this way. The property's value to you is something for you to decide based on your needs and your own sense of the market. However, I treat all offers with the greatest confidence. I will not discuss an offer you make to me with another buyer, and I would not discuss any offer I received from someone else with you. Will you be bidding?

Of course, this will work for an idealist only if he or she really and truly has such a policy—a costly one when there is another attractive offer he or she would like to reveal.

A final idealist approach would be to offer an honest, straightforward answer. An idealist cannot lie or deliberately mislead, but he is allowed to put the best face he can on the situation that is consistent with the plain truth:

BUYER: Do you have another offer?

IDEALIST SELLER 3: To be honest, we have no offers at this time. However, we are hopeful that we will receive others soon. It might be in your interest to bid now and take the property before competition drives the price up.

How about the pragmatists? They would suggest using somewhat more sophisticated, perhaps deceptive blocking techniques. These techniques would protect their leverage in ways that were consistent with maintaining work relationships. Once again, assume that the buyer has asked the "other offer" question and there are no other offers. Here are five ways a pragmatist might suggest you block this question to avoid an out-and-out factual lie about other offers while minimizing the damage to your leverage. Some of these blocking techniques would work for idealists too:

- *Declare the question out of bounds:* "Company policy forbids any discussion of other offers in a situation like this." Note that, if untrue, this is a lie, but it is one that carries less risk to your reputation because it is hard to confirm. If there really is such a company policy, an idealist could also use this move to block the question.

- *Answer a different question:* "We will not be keeping the property on the market much longer because the market is moving and our plans are changing." Again, if untrue, this statement is a mere lie about a rationale that troubles pragmatists less than idealists.

- *Dodge the question:* "The more important question is whether we are going to get an offer from you—and when."

- *Ask a question of your own:* "What alternatives are you examining at this time?"

- *Change the subject:* "We are late for our next meeting already. Are you bidding today or not?"

Blocking techniques of this sort serve a utilitarian purpose. They preserve some leverage (though not as much as the Poker School) while reducing the risk of acquiring a reputation for deception. Relationships and reputations matter. If there is even a remote chance of a lie coming back to haunt you in a future negotiation with either the person you lie to or someone he may interact with, the pragmatists argue that you should not do it.

So—which school do you belong to? Or do you belong to the school of your own, such as "pragmatic idealism"? To repeat, my advice is to aim high. The pressure of real bargaining often makes ethical compromisers of us all. When you fall below the standard of the Poker School, you are at serious risk of legal and even criminal liability.

BARGAINING WITH THE DEVIL: THE ART OF SELF-DEFENSE

Regardless of which school of bargaining ethics you adopt, you are going to face unscrupulous tactics from others on occasion. Even members of the Poker School sometimes face off against crooks. Are there any reliable means of self-defense to protect yourself and minimize the dangers? This section will give you some pointers on how to engage in effective self-defense against unethical tactics at the bargaining table.

Maintain Your Own Standards—Don't Sink to Theirs

It is tempting to engage in tit for tat when the other side uses unethical tactics. We get angry. We lose perspective and start down the unethical path ourselves.

Avoid this trap. First, no matter what school of bargaining ethics you adhere to, you need to keep your record clean both to maintain your self-respect and to avoid gaining a reputation for slippery dealing. Second, as soon as you begin acting unethically, you lose the right to protest other people's conduct. Their behavior may give you a legitimate claim to extract concessions, or it may form the basis for a legal case. Once you join them in the gutter, you forfeit your moral and legal advantage.

Table 6.1 is a tool to keep yourself out of trouble with deception. You'll have to decide for yourself whether the advice passes muster under your personal ethical standards. So far as I know, all of the alternatives are legal, so Poker School adherents who find themselves in a tight spot in which a lie will not work should feel free to use them. Pragmatists usually prefer to avoid lies if relationships matter, so these will be helpful to them too. Idealists can use any of these that involve telling the truth in a way that does not mislead or deflecting a question with an obvious, transparent blocking maneuver.

Remember, there is no commandment in negotiation that says, "Thou shalt answer every question that is asked." And as an aspiring idealist, I have found it useful to follow this rule: *Whenever you are tempted to lie about something, stop, think for a moment, and then find something—anything—to tell the truth about.* If the other side asks you about your alternatives or your bottom line, deflect that question and then tell the truth about your goals, expectations, and interests.

A Rogue's Gallery of Tactics

As my final offering on this topic, here is a list of the more common manipulative tactics you will encounter at the bargaining table:

- Decide which school of bargaining ethics you belong to.
- Determine whether you can use your relationships to offset the dangers of unethical conduct by others involved in the transaction.
- Probe, probe, probe. Do not take what you hear at face value.
- Pause. Remember that you do not have to answer every question.
- Do not lie. Instead, find a way to use the truth to your advantage.

We have seen some of these before, but I will summarize them again for ease of reference. Note that only some of them involve overt deception.

I do not label these unethical because most of them are well within the boundaries of the Poker School, and some can work even for pragmatists when there is no relationship problem in view.

Table 6.1. Alternatives to Lying

Instead of Lying About	Try This
Bottom line	Blocking maneuvers
	Ask about their bottom line.
	Say, "It's not your business."
	Say, "I'm not free to disclose that."
	Tell the truth about your goal.
	Focus on your problems or needs.
Lack of authority	Obtain only limited authority in the first place.
	Require ratification by your group.
Availability of alternatives	Initiate efforts to improve alternatives.
	Stress opportunities and uncertainties.
	Be satisfied with the status quo.
Commitment to positions	Commit to general goals.
	Commit to standards.
	Commit to addressing the other side's interests.
Phony issues	Inject new issues with real value or make a true wish list.
Threats	Use cooling-off periods.
	Suggest third-party help.
	Discuss use of a formula.
Intentions	Make only promises you can and will keep.
Facts	Focus on uncertainty regarding the facts.
	Use language carefully.
	Express your opinion.

SUMMARY

Ethical dilemmas are at the center of many bargaining encounters. There is no escaping the fact that deception is part of negotiation. And there is no escaping the importance people place on personal integrity in their dealings with others at the bargaining table. One ethical slip, and your credibility is lost, not just for one but for many deals. Effective negotiations take the issue of personal integrity very seriously. Ineffective negotiators do not.

How do you balance these two contradictory factors? I have presented three frameworks for thinking about ethical issues: the Poker School, the Idealist School, and the Pragmatist School. I personally think you are better off sticking to the truth as much as possible. I sometimes lose leverage as the price of this scruple, but I gain a greater measure of ease and self-respect as compensation.

Where you come out on bargaining ethics, of course, is a matter for you to decide. My only injunction to you is this: negotiators who value personal integrity can be counted on to behave consistently, using a thoughtful set of personal values that they could, if necessary, explain and defend to others.

References

Carr, A. Z. *Business as a Game.* New York: New American Library, 1968.

Carr, A. Z. "Is Business Bluffing Ethical?" *Harvard Business Review,* Jan.–Feb. 1968.

PART TWO

TRUTH TELLING
IN NEGOTIATIONS

Negotiation is about information: asking for it, giving it, analyzing it, and using it to forge agreements between two or more people who either want to or have to deal with each other to make something happen. Perhaps the most vexing issue in negotiation, and the most discussed one, is what duty or obligation we have to tell the truth in negotiation. To the extent that negotiation is widely regarded as a strategic enterprise where information is manipulated in order to persuade or induce one party to give the other party what it wants, many regard any obligation to be totally truthful in a negotiation as unrealistic or naive.

The view that there is a special culture of negotiation that conforms to game theorists' descriptions of negotiation as a strategic two-person game of imperfect or incomplete information (Schelling, 1960) in which the goal of individual maximization is best pursued by misleading the other party about what one really wants or is willing to accept is represented here in Chapter Eight in the classic "Machiavelli and the Bar" by commercial law professor James J. White. White has argued for many decades that we must take negotiation ethics as we find them, in the empirical world of negotiation as it currently exists, with expectations of dissembling, "puffing" (formally permitted by the lawyers' ethics rules), and no affirmative duty to disclose one's desires, intents, or bottom lines. White has suggested that any attempt to formally require or regulate a higher duty of candor would be ineffective because most negotiations occur in private, and there would be no way to know what the truth really was or what was really represented. To have formal rules that require candor, affirmative disclosures, and obligations of complete fair dealing and good faith, when they would be honored in the "cultural breach," would do a disservice to any rule system or regulatory scheme.

Over the years, many in both law and business (represented in some of the following chapters) have suggested that formal rules (whether professional ethics rules or laws of fraud and misrepresentation) should be more demanding of us as human beings, to reflect a higher morality of treating our fellow humans as ends, not means, in negotiation and to ensure that negotiation outcomes reflect the merits of the issues between the parties, not the power relations between the parties or the ability of skillful negotiators to manipulate, deceive, or dissemble.

Other than the formal legal prohibitions and remedies for fraud and misrepresentation in tort, contract, and specialized areas of law (regulated by state, not national, law), negotiators are relatively free to make their own decisions about how much to reveal and how much not to reveal. Thus, decisions about truth telling are both ethical or moral decisions and instrumental or strategic. What should I reveal to the other side? What benefit or harm will be caused by revelation of a particular fact, preference, need, or objective? What benefit or harm might be caused by not revealing something? Possible voiding of the agreement? Loss of reputation for future dealings, either between principals or their negotiating agents?

In the chapters in Part Two, commentators on truth telling, candor, and deception in negotiation reveal that how one approaches this issue invokes very foundational beliefs about human nature and the negotiation process. For J. Gregory Dees, Peter Cramton, Sissela Bok, and a more ambivalent Geoffrey Hazard, trust is an essential part of human dealings and should be a moral imperative, as well as strategic incentive, in negotiations. Without some trust, we cannot coexist or make deals happen. Without an expectation of some truth telling, candor, and disclosure, we cannot create the trust that is necessary for people to agree to do things together. So at varying levels of moral and practical justification, these authors suggest what the human incentives and obligations should be to treat others honestly and in good faith in negotiated interactions, and they propose both deontological (duty-based) and more practical behavioral and institutional suggestions for how to accomplish this. James J. White and Alan Strudler represent a different point of view, suggesting that some deception (at least about reservation prices and objectives) is actually necessary and produces more efficient outcomes for the parties. Geoffrey Hazard suggests that trustworthiness is necessary to both make transactions and resolve human disputes in lawsuits and elsewhere, but he is less sanguine that this can be policed by formal rules.

The chapters in Part Two reflect the current debates about what it is that negotiators hope to accomplish. When maximizing individual gain is the goal, it is clear that some deception or lack of candor may seem defensible to protect parties from being taken advantage of by the other side in the trades that occur in most negotiations. This view almost always assumes a two-party, one-issue (pricing) negotiation in which it is unlikely the parties will see each other again—the classic arms-length commercial (or litigation) bargain. More modern (and we would say enlightened) negotiation theorists have suggested that the possibility of multiple and complementary, not conflicting (Homans, 1961), desires, continued dealings, reputational concerns, need for predictability in enforcement of agreements, and a search for value and resource creation before or in lieu of resource allocation or division would suggest that a more open and trusting, as well as trustworthy, approach to facts and information (and objectives and values) in negotiation might be advisable from both instrumental and moral stances. Readers would be well advised to consider what assumptions the authors make about the negotiation process, its goals, and the contexts in which particular cases are situated when evaluating the claims made for relative honesty or deception.

In perhaps the most classic treatment of deception and truth telling, philosopher Sissela Bok in Chapter Seven turns the questions of efficiency and privacy on their heads. Writing at a time of massive public deception in the polity (the Watergate scandal) and clearly appropriate in our own times of corporate dissembling and lack of candor, Bok suggests that what goes on in private negotiations may affect (adversely) our public lives. Seeing deceit as a form of human violence or coercion that accumulates as more and more people find it defensible (whether from a reflexive protectionist stance or as an affirmative strategy), she urges us to think about the effects of deception on the deceived (the "other" side of a negotiation conceived of as us; see Mark Twain's *The War Prayer,* 2002) and on the rest of us. What is a world like where the presumption is one of distrust and arms-length suspicion of the other? How do we act when we assume that others are not telling us the truth? Defensiveness and reactive and accumulating deceptions infect the larger society in which deals are made and legal disputes are confidentially settled for nuisance value rather than on the merits. Bok asks us, as do Dees and Cramton, to imagine a world in which the presumptions might be reversed: Rather than assuming distrust and dishonesty, how can we create the conditions for developing mutual trust and a presumption (which can be argued against in appropriate cases) in favor of candor?

As you read these chapters on truth telling, it may be important to ask what happens when negotiators of different worldviews confront each other, whether the negotiation context makes a difference (could a used car salesman ever really be totally candid?), and what the best ways are to encourage whatever an optimal amount of truthful information exchange is (formal rules, economic incentives, change of customs or practices, and achievement of mutually advantageous outcomes).

References

Homans, G. C. *Social Behavior: Its Elementary Forms.* New York: Harcourt, Brace, 1961.

Schelling, T. *The Strategy of Conflict.* Cambridge, Mass.: Harvard University Press, 1960.

Twain, M. *The War Prayer.* New York: HarperCollins, 2002. (Originally published 1923.)

CHAPTER SEVEN

Truthfulness, Deceit, and Trust

Sissela Bok

Suppose men imagined there was no obligation to veracity, and acted accordingly; speaking as often against their own opinion as according to it; would not all pleasure of conversation be destroyed, and all confidence in narration? Men would only speak in bargaining, and in this too would soon lose all mutual confidence.
—Francis Hutcheson, *System of Moral Philosophy*

A great man—what is he? . . . He rather lies than tells the truth; it requires more spirit and quill. There is a solitude within him that is inaccessible to praise or blame, his own justice that is beyond appeal.
—Friedrich Nietzsche, *The Will to Power*

Lying, after all, is suggestive of game theory. It involves at least two people, a liar and someone who is lied to; it transmits information, the credibility and veracity of which are important; it influences some choice another is to make that the liar anticipates; the choice to lie or not to lie is part of the liar's choice of strategy; and the possibility of a lie presumably occurs to the second party, and may be judged against some a priori expectations; and the payoff configurations are rich in their possibilities.
—Thomas Schelling, "Game Theory and the Study of Ethical Systems"

LYING AND CHOICE

Deceit and violence—these are the two forms of deliberate assault on human beings.[1] Both can coerce people into acting against their will. Most harm that can befall victims through violence can come to them also through deceit. But deceit controls more subtly, for it works on belief as well as action. Even Othello, whom few would have dared to try to subdue by force, could be brought to destroy himself and Desdemona through falsehood.

The knowledge of this coercive element in deception, and of our vulnerability to it, underlies our sense of the centrality of truthfulness. Of course, deception—again like violence—can be used also in self-defense, even for sheer survival. Its use can also be quite trivial, as in white lies. Yet its potential for coercion and for destruction is such that society could scarcely function without some degree of truthfulness in speech and action.[2]

Imagine a society, no matter how ideal in other respects, where word and gesture could never be counted on. Questions asked, answers given, information exchanged—all would be worthless. Were all statements randomly truthful or deceptive, action and choice would be undermined from the outset. There must be a minimal degree of trust in communication for language and action to be more than stabs in the dark. This is why some level of truthfulness has always been seen as essential to human society, no matter how deficient the observance of other moral principles. Even the devils themselves, as Samuel Johnson said, do not lie to one another, since the society of Hell could not subsist without truth any more than others (Johnson, 1968).

A society, then, whose members were unable to distinguish truthful messages from deceptive ones, would collapse. But even before such a general collapse, individual choice and survival would be imperiled. The search for food and shelter could depend on no expectations from others. A warning that a well was poisoned or a plea for help in an accident would come to be ignored unless independent confirmation could be found.

All our choices depend on our estimates of what is the case; these estimates must in turn often rely on information from others. Lies distort this information and therefore our situation as we perceive it, as well as our choices. A lie, in Hartmann's words, "injures the deceived person in his life; it leads him astray" (Hartmann, 1932).

To the extent that knowledge gives power, to that extent do lies affect the distribution of power; they add to that of the liar and diminish that of the deceived, altering his choices at different levels.[3] A lie, first, may misinform, so as to obscure some objective, something the deceived person wanted to do or obtain. It may make the objective seem unattainable or no longer desirable. It may even create a new one, as when Iago deceived Othello into wanting to kill Desdemona.

Lies may also eliminate or obscure relevant alternatives, as when a traveler is falsely told a bridge has collapsed. At times, lies foster the belief that there are more alternatives than is really the case; at other times, a lie may lead to the unnecessary loss of confidence in the best alternative. Similarly, the estimates of costs and benefits of any action can be endlessly varied through successful deception. The immense toll of life and human welfare from the United States' intervention in Vietnam came at least in part from the deception (mingled with self-deception) by those who channeled overly optimistic information to the decision makers.

Finally, the degree of uncertainty in how we look at our choices can be manipulated through deception. Deception can make a situation falsely uncertain as well as falsely certain. It can affect the objectives seen, the alternatives believed possible, the estimates made of risks and benefits. Such a manipulation of the dimension of certainty is one of the main ways to gain power over the choices of those deceived. And just as deception can initiate actions a person would otherwise never have chosen, so it can prevent action by obscuring the necessity for choice. This is the essence of camouflage and of the cover-up—the creation of apparent normality to avert suspicion.

Everyone depends on deception to get out of a scrape, to save face, to avoid hurting the feelings of others. Some use it much more consciously to manipulate and gain ascendancy. Yet all are intimately aware of the threat lies can pose, the suffering they can bring. This two-sided experience which we all share makes the singleness with which either side is advocated in action all the more puzzling. Why are such radically different evaluations given to the effects of deception, depending on whether the point of view is that of the liar or the one lied to?

THE PERSPECTIVE OF THE DECEIVED

Those who learn that they have been lied to in an important matter—say, the identity of their parents, the affection of their spouse, or the integrity of their government—are resentful, disappointed, and suspicious. They feel wronged; they are wary of new overtures. And they look back on their past beliefs and actions in the new light of the discovered lies. They see that they were manipulated, that the deceit made them unable to make choices for themselves according to the most adequate information available, unable to act as they would have wanted to act had they known all along.

It is true, of course, that personal, informed choice is not the only kind available to them. They may decide to abandon choosing for themselves and let others decide for them—as guardians, financial advisers, or political representatives. They may even decide to abandon choice based on information of a conventional nature altogether and trust instead to the stars or to throws of the dice or to soothsayers.

But such alternatives ought to be personally chosen and not surreptitiously imposed by lies or other forms of manipulation. Most of us would resist loss of control over which choices we want to delegate to others and which ones we want to make ourselves, aided by the best information we can obtain. We resist because experience has taught us the consequences when others choose to deceive us, even "for our own good." Of course, we know that many lies are trivial. But since we, when lied to, have no way to judge which lies are the trivial ones and since we have no confidence that liars will restrict themselves to just such trivial lies, the perspective of the deceived leads us to be wary of all deception.

Nor is this perspective restricted to those who are actually deceived in any given situation. Though only a single person may be deceived, many others may be harmed as a result. If a mayor is deceived about the need for new taxes, the entire city will bear the consequences. Accordingly, the perspective of the deceived is shared by all those who feel the consequences of a lie, whether or not they are themselves lied to. When, for instance, the American public and world opinion were falsely led to believe that bombing in Cambodia had not begun, the Cambodians themselves bore the heaviest consequences, though they can hardly be said to have been deceived about the bombing itself.

An interesting parallel between skepticism and determinism exists here. Just as skepticism denies the possibility of knowledge, so determinism denies the possibility of freedom. Yet both knowledge and freedom to act on it are required for reasonable choice. Such choice would be denied to someone genuinely convinced—to the very core of his being—of both skepticism and determinism. He would be cast about like a dry leaf in the wind. Few go so far. But more may adopt such views selectively, as when they need convenient excuses for lying. Lies, they may then claim, do not add to or subtract from the general misinformation or "unfreedom" of those lied to. Yet were they to adopt the perspective of the deceived, such excuses for lying to them would seem hollow indeed. Both skepticism and determinism have to be bracketed—set aside—if moral choice is to retain the significance for liars that we, as deceived, know it has in our lives.

Deception, then, can be coercive. When it succeeds, it can give power to the deceiver—power that all who suffer the consequences of lies would not wish to abdicate. From this perspective, it is clearly unreasonable to assert that people should be able to lie with impunity whenever they want to do so. It would be unreasonable, as well, to assert such a right even in the more restricted circumstances where the liars claim a good reason for lying. This is especially true because lying so often accompanies every other form of wrongdoing, from murder and bribery to tax fraud and theft. In refusing to condone such a right to decide when to lie and when not to, we are therefore trying to protect ourselves against lies which help to execute or cover up all other wrongful acts.

For this reason, the perspective of the deceived supports the statement by Aristotle: "Falsehood is in itself mean and culpable, and truth noble and full of praise."[4]

There is an initial imbalance in the evaluation of truth-telling and lying. Lying requires a reason, while truth-telling does not. It must be excused; reasons must be produced, in any one case, to show why a particular lie is not "mean and culpable."

THE PERSPECTIVE OF THE LIAR

Those who adopt the perspective of would-be liars, on the other hand, have different concerns. For them, the choice is often a difficult one. They may believe, with Machiavelli, that "great things" have been done by those who have "little regard for good faith." They may trust that they can make wise use of the power that lies bring. And they may have confidence in their own ability to distinguish the times when good reasons support their decision to lie.

Liars share with those they deceive the desire not to be deceived. As a result, their choice to lie is one which they would like to reserve for themselves while insisting that others be honest. They would prefer, in other words, a "free-rider" status, giving them the benefits of lying without the risks of being lied to. Some think of this free-rider status as for them alone. Others extend it to their friends, social group, or profession. This category of persons can be narrow or broad, but it does require as a necessary backdrop the ordinary assumptions about the honesty of most persons. The free rider trades upon being an exception, and could not exist in a world where everybody chose to exercise the same prerogatives.

At times, liars operate as if they believed that such a free-rider status is theirs and that it excuses them. At other times, on the contrary, it is the very fact that others do lie that excuses their deceptive stance in their own eyes. It is crucial to see the distinction between the free-loading liar and the liar whose deception is a strategy for survival in a corrupt society.[5]

All want to avoid being deceived by others as much as possible. But many would like to be able to weigh the advantages and disadvantages in a more nuanced way whenever they are themselves in the position of choosing whether to deceive. They may invoke special reasons to lie—such as the need to protect confidentiality or to spare someone's feelings. They are then much more willing, in particular, to exonerate a well-intentioned lie on their own part; dupes tend to be less sanguine about the good intentions of those who deceive them.

But in this benevolent self-evaluation by the liar of the lies he might tell, certain kinds of disadvantage and harm are almost always overlooked. Liars usually weigh only the immediate harm to others from the lie against the benefits they want to achieve. The flaw in such an outlook is that it ignores or underestimates two additional kinds of harm—the harm that lying does to the liars themselves and the harm done to the general level of trust and social cooperation. Both are cumulative; both are hard to reverse.

How is the liar affected by his own lies? The very fact that he knows he has lied, first of all, affects him. He may regard the lie as an inroad on his integrity; he certainly looks at those he has lied to with a new caution. And if they find out that he has lied, he knows that his credibility and the respect for his word have been damaged. When Adlai Stevenson had to go before the United Nations in 1961 to tell falsehoods about the United States' role in the Bay of Pigs invasion, he changed the course of his life. He may not have known beforehand that the message he was asked to convey was untrue, but merely to carry the burden of being the means of such deceit must have been difficult. To lose the confidence of his peers in such a public way was harder still.

Granted that a public lie on an important matter, once revealed, hurts the speaker, must we therefore conclude that every lie has this effect? What of those who tell a few white lies once in a while? Does lying hurt them in the same way? It is hard to defend such a notion. No one trivial lie undermines the liar's integrity. But the problem for liars is that they tend to see most of their lies in this benevolent light and thus vastly underestimate the risks they run. While no one lie always carries harm for the liar, then, there is risk of such harm in most.

These risks are increased by the fact that so few lies are solitary ones. It is easy, a wit observed, to tell a lie, but hard to tell only one. The first lie "must be thatched with another or it will rain through." More and more lies may come to be needed; the liar always has more mending to do. And the strains on him become greater each time—many have noted that it takes an excellent memory to keep one's untruths in good repair and disentangled (de Montaigne, 1595; Plass, 1959). The sheer energy the liar has to devote to shoring them up is energy the honest man can dispose of freely.

After the first lies, moreover, others can come more easily. Psychological barriers wear down; lies seem more necessary, less reprehensible; the ability to make moral distinctions can coarsen; the liar's perception of his chances of being caught may warp. These changes can affect his behavior in subtle ways; even if he is not found out, he will then be less trusted than those of unquestioned honesty. And it is inevitable that more frequent lies do increase the chance that some will be discovered. At that time, even if the liar has no personal sense of loss of integrity[6] from his deceitful practices, he will surely regret the damage to his credibility which their discovery brings about. Paradoxically, once his word is no longer trusted, he will be left with greatly decreased power— even though a lie often does bring at least a short-term gain in power over those deceived.

Even if the liar cares little about the risks to others from his deception, therefore, all these risks to himself argue in favor of at least weighing any decision to lie quite seriously. Yet such risks rarely enter his calculations. Bias skews all judgment, but never more so than in the search for good reasons to deceive. Not only does it combine with ignorance and uncertainty so that liars are apt to overestimate their own good will, high motives, and chances to escape detection; it leads also to overconfidence in their own imperviousness to the personal entanglements, worries, and loss of integrity which might so easily beset them.[7]

The liar's self-bestowed free-rider status, then, can be as corrupting as all other unchecked exercises of power. There are, in fact, very few "free rides" to be had through lying. I hope to examine those exceptional circumstances where harm to self and others from lying is less likely, and procedures which can isolate and contain them. But the chance of harm to liars can rarely be ruled out altogether.

Bias causes liars often to ignore the second type of harm as well. For even if they make the effort to estimate the consequences to individuals—themselves and others—of their lies, they often fail to consider the many ways in which deception can spread and give rise to practices very damaging to human communities. These practices clearly do not affect only isolated individuals. The veneer of social trust is often thin. As lies spread—by imitation, or in retaliation, or to forestall suspected deception—trust is damaged. Yet trust is a social good to be protected just as much as the air we breathe or the water we drink. When it is damaged, the community as a whole suffers, and when it is destroyed, societies falter and collapse.

We live at a time when the harm done to trust can be seen firsthand. Confidence in public officials and in professionals has been seriously eroded. This, in turn, is a most natural response to the uncovering of practices of deceit for high-sounding aims such as "national security" or the "adversary system of justice." It will take time to rebuild confidence in government pronouncements that the Central Intelligence Agency did not participate in a Latin American coup or that new figures show an economic upturn around the corner. The practices engendering such distrust were entered upon, not just by the officials now so familiar to us, but by countless others, high and low, in the government and outside it, each time for a reason that seemed overriding.

Take the example of a government official hoping to see Congress enact a crucial piece of antipoverty legislation. Should he lie to a congressman he believes unable to understand the importance and urgency of the legislation yet powerful enough to block its passage? Should he tell him that unless the proposed bill is enacted, the government will push for a much more extensive measure?

In answering, shift the focus from this case taken in isolation to the vast practices of which it forms a part. What is the effect on colleagues and subordinates who witness the deception so often resulting from such a choice? What is the effect on the members of Congress as they inevitably learn of a proportion of these lies? And what is the effect on the electorate as it learns of these and similar practices? Then shift back to the narrower world of the official troubled about the legislation he believes in and hoping by a small deception to change a crucial vote.

It is the fear of the harm lies bring that explains statements such as the following from Revelation (22:15), which might otherwise seem strangely out of proportion: "These others must stay outside [the Heavenly City]: dogs, medicinemen, and fornicators, and murderers, and idolaters, and everyone of false life and false speech."[8] It is the deep-seated concern of the multitude that speaks here; there could be few contrasts greater than that between this statement and the self-confident, individualistic view by Machiavelli: "Men are so simple and so ready to obey present necessities, that one who deceives will also find those who allow themselves to be deceived."

DISCREPANT PERSPECTIVES

The discrepancy of perspectives explains the ambiguity toward lying which most of us experience. While we know the risks of lying and would prefer a world where others abstained from it, we know also that there are times when it would be helpful, perhaps even necessary, if we ourselves could deceive with impunity. By itself, each perspective is incomplete. Each can bias moral judgments and render them shallow. Even the perspective of the deceived can lead to unfounded, discriminatory suspicions about persons thought to be untrustworthy.

We need to learn to shift back and forth between the two perspectives and even to focus on both at once, as in straining to see both aspects of an optical illusion. In ethics, such a double focus leads to applying the Golden Rule: to strain to experience one's acts not only as subject and agent but as recipient, sometimes victim. And while it is not always easy to put oneself in the place of someone affected by a fate one will never share, there is no such difficulty with lying. We all know what it is to lie, to be told lies, to be correctly or falsely suspected of having lied. In principle, we can all readily share both perspectives. What is important is to make that effort as we consider the lies we would like to be able to tell. It is at such times of choice and judgment that the Golden Rule is hardest to follow. The Muslim mystic Al-Ghazali recommended the shift in perspectives in the following words: "If you want to know the foulness of lying for yourself, consider the lying of someone else and how you shun it and despise the man who lies and regard his communication as foul. Do the same with regard to all your own vices, for you do not realize the foulness of your vices from your own case, but from someone else's."[9]

The parallel between deception and violence as seen from these two perspectives is, once again, striking, for both violence and deception are means not only to unjust coercion but also to self-defense and survival. They have been feared and circumscribed by law and custom when seen from the perspective of those affected by lies and by assaults. In religion and in ethics alike, they have been proscribed, and advice has been given on how to cope with the oppression in their wake.

But they have also been celebrated through the ages when seen from the perspective of the agent, the liar, the forceful man. The hero uses deceit to survive and to conquer. When looked at from this point of view, both violence and deceit are portrayed with bravado and exultation. Nietzsche and Machiavelli are their advocates, epic poetry their home. See, for example, how Athena, smiling, addresses Odysseus in the *Odyssey:*

Whoever gets around you must be sharp
and guileful as a snake; even a god
might bow to you in ways of dissimulation.
You! You chameleon!
Bottomless bag of tricks! Here in your own country
would you not give your stratagems a rest
or stop spellbinding for an instant?

You play a part as if it were your own tough skin.
. . . .
No more of this, though. Two of a kind, we are,
contrivers, both. Of all men now alive
you are the best in plots and story telling.
My own fame is for wisdom among the gods—
deceptions, too.[10]

THE PRINCIPLE OF VERACITY

The perspective of the deceived, then, reveals several reasons why lies are undesirable. Those who share it have cause to fear the effects of undiscovered lies on the choices of liars and dupes. They are all too aware of the impact of discovered and suspected lies on trust and social cooperation. And they consider not only the individual lie but the practice of which it forms a part, and the long-term results which it can have.

For these reasons, I believe that we must at the very least accept as an initial premise Aristotle's view that lying is "mean and culpable" and that truthful statements are preferable to lies in the absence of special considerations. This premise gives an initial negative weight to lies. It holds that they are not neutral from the point of view of our choices; that lying requires explanation, whereas truth ordinarily does not. It provides a counterbalance to the crude evaluation by liars of their own motives and of the consequences of their lies. And it places the burden of proof squarely on those who assume the liar's perspective.

This presumption against lying can also be stated so as to stress the positive worth of truthfulness or veracity.[11] I would like to refer to the "principle of veracity" as an expression of this initial imbalance in our weighing of truthfulness and lying. It is not necessarily a principle that overrides all others or even the one most frequently appealed to. Nor is it, obviously, sufficient by itself— witness the brutal but honest regime or the tormentor who prides himself on his frankness. Rather, trust in some degree of veracity functions as a foundation of relations among human beings; when this trust shatters or wears away, institutions collapse.[12]

Such a principle need not indicate that all lies should be ruled out by the initial negative weight given to them, nor does it even suggest what kinds of lies should be prohibited. But it does make at least one immediate limitation on lying: in any situation where a lie is a possible choice, one must first seek truthful alternatives.[13] If lies and truthful statements appear to achieve the same result or appear to be as desirable to the person contemplating lying, the lies should be ruled out. And only where a lie is a last resort can one even begin to consider whether or not it is morally justified. Mild as this initial stipulation sounds, it would, if taken seriously, eliminate a great many lies told out of carelessness or habit or unexamined good intentions.

When we try to move beyond this agreement on such an initial premise, the first fork in the road is presented by those who believe that all lies should be categorically ruled out. Such a position not only assigns a negative weight to lies; it sees this weight as so overwhelming that no circumstances can outweigh it. If we choose to follow that path, the quest for circumstances when lying is justified is obviously over.

Notes

1. See Dante, *The Divine Comedy: Inferno,* trans. Charles S. Singleton, Princeton, NJ: Princeton University Press, 1940, canto II, p. III), where Dante characterizes force and fraud as the two forms of malice aiming at injustice. See also Frye (1976).

2. But truthful statements, though they are not meant to deceive, can, of course, themselves be coercive and destructive; they can be used as weapons, to wound and do violence.

3. The discussion that follows draws on the framework provided by decision theory for thinking about choice and decision making. This framework includes the objectives as they are seen by the decision maker, the alternatives available for reaching them, an estimate of costs and benefits associated with both, and a choice rule for weighing these.

4. Aristotle (1934, bk. 4, chap. 7). For a discussion of Aristotle's concept of truth, see Wilpert (1940).

5. While different, the two are closely linked. If enough persons adopt the free-rider strategy for lying, the time will come when all will feel pressed to lie to survive.

6. The word *"integrity"* comes from the same roots which have formed *"intact"* and *"untouched."* It is used especially often in relation to truthfulness and fair dealing and reflects, I believe, the view that by lying, one hurts oneself. The notion of the self-destructive aspects of doing wrong is part of many traditions. See, for example, the *Book of Mencius.* "Every man has within himself these four beginnings [of humanity, righteousness, decorum, wisdom]. The man who considers himself incapable of exercising them is destroying himself." See Severy (1971) and Dobson (1963).

7. For a discussion of bias and "opportunistically distorted beliefs," see Myrdal (1968).

8. "Dogs" is taken to mean "heathens" or "sodomites"; and Noonan (1970, p. 9) argues that the word *pharmakoi,* here translated as "medicine men," referred to those who procured abortions and prescribed abortifacient drugs.

9. Watt (1953, p. 133). Al-Ghazali allowed, however, lies for the necessary and praiseworthy goals where no truthful alternatives exist. See Keddie (1963).

10. Homer (1961, p. 251). Compare Nietzsche (1954), *The Will to Power* (p. 293), "A thousandfold craftiness belongs to the essence of the enhancement of man" and "On Truth and Lie in an Extra-Moral Sense."

11. While such a principle is not as frequently stressed as others, it has been vigorously defended. Cicero stated, "The foundation of justice, moreover, is good faith—that is truth and fidelity to promises and agreements" (*De officiis* I. 7. 23, 1913, p. 25). Hutcheson (1968) stated the "general law of veracity" in his *System of Moral Philosophy,* published posthumously in 1755. Price (1948), takes veracity to be one of the sources of duty. Rashdall (1924) mentions a "Principle of Veracity" in his *Theory of Good and Evil* (bk. 1, p. 192). Ross (1930) emphasized "duties of fidelity," which include an undertaking not to lie, in *The Right and the Good.* And Warnock, in his recent book, *The Object of Morality* (1971), stresses the need for a principle of nondeception.

    For some the principle is supported by religious evidence, while for others intuition supports it, and for still others, the weight of past experience.

12. The function of the principle of veracity as a foundation is evident when we think of trust. I can have different kinds of trust: that you will treat me fairly, that you will have my interests at heart, that you will do me no harm. But if I do not trust your word, can I have genuine trust in the first three? If there is no confidence in the truthfulness of others, is there any way to assess their fairness, their intentions to help or to harm? How, then, can they be trusted? Whatever matters to human beings, trust is the atmosphere in which it thrives.

13. Compare Nozick (1968). See also McCormick (1973) and the discussion of Pareto optimality: the state of affairs when there does not exist an alternative action that is at least acceptable to all and definitely preferred by some.

References

Aristotle. *Nicomachean Ethics* (H. Rackham, trans.). London: William Heinemann, and Cambridge, Mass.: Harvard University Press, 1934.

Cicero. *De officiis* (W. Miller, trans.). Cambridge, Mass.: Harvard University Press, and London: William Heinemann, 1913.

Dobson, W.A.C.H. (trans.). *Mencius.* Toronto: University of Toronto Press, 1963.

Frye, N. *The Secular Scripture: A Study of the Structure of Romance.* Cambridge, Mass.: Harvard University Press, 1976.

Hartmann, N. *Ethics,* New Brunswick, N.J.: Transaction Publishers, 2002, 2:282.

Homer. *Odyssey* (R. Fitzgerald, trans.). New York: Doubleday, 1961.

Hutcheson, F. *System of Moral Philosophy.* New York: Augustus M. Kelley, 1968. (Originally published 1755.)

Johnson, S. *The Adventurer.* In W. J. Bate (ed.), *Selected Essays from* The Rambler, Adventurer, and Idler. New Haven, Conn.: Yale University Press, 1968. (Originally published 1753.)

Keddie, N. "Sincerity and Symbol in Islam." *Studia Islamica,* 1963, *19,* 45.

McCormick, R. *Ambiguity in Moral Choice.* Milwaukee, Wis.: Marquette University Press, 1973.

de Montaigne, M. "Des Menteurs." In *Essais.* Paris: Impr. nationale éditions, 1998.

Myrdal, G. *Objectivity in Social Research.* New York: Pantheon, 1968.

Nietzsche, F. *Nietzsche* (W. Kaufmann, trans.). New York: Viking Press, 1954.

Noonan, J. Jr. *The Morality of Abortion.* Cambridge, Mass.: Harvard University Press, 1970.

Nozick, R. "Moral Complications and Moral Structures." *Natural Law Forum,* 1968, *13,* 1–50.

Plass, E. M. (comp.). *What Luther Says: An Anthology.* St. Louis, Mo.: Corcordia Press, 1959.

Price, R. *A Review of the Principal of Ethics* (D. Raphael, ed.). Oxford: Clarendon Press, 1948. (Originally published 1758.)

Rashdall, H. *Theory of Good and Evil.* (2nd ed.). New York: Oxford University Press, 1924.

Ross, W. D. *The Right and the Good.* Oxford: Clarendon Press, 1930.

Severy, M. (ed.). *Great Religions of the World.* Washington, D.C.: National Geographic Society, 1971.

Warnock, G. J. *The Object of Morality.* London: Methuen, 1971.

Watt, W. M. *The Faith and Practice of Al-Ghazali.* London: Allen and Unwin, 1953.

Wilpert, P. "Zum Aristotelischen Warheisbegriff." *Phil Jahrbuch de Görresgesellschaft,* *53,* 1940, 3–16.

CHAPTER EIGHT

Machiavelli and the Bar

Ethical Limitations on Lying in Negotiation

James J. White

Upon the enactment of the Model Rules of Professional Conduct, published ethical norms will for the first time give explicit consideration to the lawyer's behavior in the process of negotiation. Rules 4.1, 4.2, and 4.3 deal with negotiation. Although the Canons, the interpretations of the Canons, and the Disciplinary Rules and Ethical Considerations gave tangential consideration to negotiating,[1] none of the Disciplinary Rules or Ethical Considerations explicitly considered negotiation apart from the process of litigation or counseling. The mere recognition of negotiation as a separate process worthy of unique rules is a large step. The purpose of this paper is to address the general question of truthfulness as that question is faced in Rule 4.2.[2]

The difficulty of proposing acceptable rules concerning truthfulness in negotiation is presented by several circumstances. First, negotiation is nonpublic behavior. If one negotiator lies to another, only by happenstance will the other discover the lie. If the settlement is concluded by negotiation, there will be no trial, no public testimony by conflicting witnesses, and thus no opportunity to examine the truthfulness of assertions made during the negotiation. Consequently, in negotiation, more than in other contexts, ethical norms can probably be violated with greater confidence that there will be no discovery and punishment. Whether one is likely to be caught for violating an ethical standard says nothing about the merit of the standard. However, if the low probability of punishment means that many lawyers will violate the standard, the standard becomes even more difficult for the honest lawyer to follow, for by doing so he may be forfeiting a significant advantage for his client to others who do not follow the rules.

The drafters appreciated, but perhaps not fully, a second difficulty in drafting ethical norms for negotiators. That is the almost galactic scope of disputes that are subject to resolution by negotiation. One who conceives of negotiation as an alternative to a lawsuit has only scratched the surface. Negotiation is also the process by which one deals with the opposing side in war, with terrorists, with labor or management in a labor agreement, with buyers and sellers of goods, services, and real estate, with lessors, with governmental agencies, and with one's clients, acquaintances, and family. By limiting his consideration to negotiations in which a lawyer is involved in his professional role, one eliminates some of the most difficult cases but is left with a rather large and irregular universe of disputes. Surely society would tolerate and indeed expect different forms of behavior, on the one hand, from one assigned to negotiate with terrorists and, on the other, from one who is negotiating with the citizens on behalf of a governmental agency.[3] The difference between those two cases illustrates the less drastic distinctions that may be called for by differences between other negotiating situations. Performance that is standard in one negotiating arena may be gauche, conceivably unethical, in another. More than almost any other form of lawyer behavior, the process of negotiation is varied; it differs from place to place and subject matter to subject matter. It calls, therefore, either for quite different rules in different contexts or for rules stated only at a very high level of generality.

A final complication in drafting rules about truthfulness arises out of the paradoxical nature of the negotiator's responsibility. On the one hand, the negotiator must be fair and truthful; on the other, he must mislead his opponent. Like the poker player, a negotiator hopes that his opponent will overestimate the value of his hand. Like the poker player, in a variety of ways he must facilitate his opponent's inaccurate assessment. The critical difference between those who are successful negotiators and those who are not lies in this capacity both to mislead and not to be misled.

Some experienced negotiators will deny the accuracy of this assertion, but they will be wrong. I submit that a careful examination of the behavior of even the most forthright, honest, and trustworthy negotiators will show them actively engaged in misleading their opponents about their true positions.[4] That is true of both the plaintiff and the defendant in a lawsuit. It is true of both labor and management in a collective bargaining agreement. It is true as well of both the buyer and the seller in a wide variety of sales transactions. To conceal one's true position, to mislead an opponent about one's true settling point, is the essence of negotiation.

Of course, there are limits on acceptable deceptive behavior in negotiation, but there is the paradox. How can one be "fair" but also mislead? Can we ask the negotiator to mislead, but fairly, like the soldier who must kill, but humanely?

TRUTH TELLING IN GENERAL

The obligation to behave truthfully in negotiation is embodied in the requirement of Rule 4.2(a) that directs the lawyer to "be fair in dealing with other participants." Presumably the direction to be fair speaks to a variety of acts in addition to truthfulness and also different from it. At a minimum, it has something to say about the threats a negotiator may use,[5] about the favors he may offer,[6] and possibly about the extraneous factors other than threats and favors which can appropriately be used in negotiating.[7] As I have suggested elsewhere, each of these issues has important ramifications, and each merits independent consideration by the drafters of the Model Rules and by lawyers. In this paper I ignore those questions and limit my consideration to the question of truth telling.

The comment on fairness under Rule 4.2 makes explicit what is implicit in the rule itself by the following sentence: "Fairness in negotiation implies that representations by or on behalf of one party to the other party be truthful." Standing alone, that statement is too broad. Even the Comments contemplate activities such as puffing, which in the broadest sense are untruthful.[8] It seems quite unlikely that the drafters intend or can realistically hope to outlaw a variety of other nontruthful behavior in negotiations. Below we will consider some examples, but for the time being, we will consider the complexity of the task.

Pious and generalized assertions that the negotiator must be "honest" or that the lawyer must use "candor" are not helpful.[9] They are at too high a level of generality, and they fail to appreciate the fact that truth and truthful behavior at one time in one set of circumstances with one set of negotiators may be untruthful in another circumstance with other negotiators. There is no general principle waiting somewhere to be discovered, as Judge Alvin B. Rubin seems to suggest in his article on lawyers' ethics.[10] Rather, mostly we are doing what he says we are not doing: hunting for the rules of the game as the game is played in that particular circumstance.

The definition of truth is in part a function of the substance of the negotiation (Bok, 1978). Because of the policies that lie behind the securities and exchange laws and the demands that Congress has made that information be provided to those who buy and sell, one suspects that lawyers engaged in Securities and Exchange Commission (SEC) work have a higher standard of truthfulness than do those whose agreements and negotiations will not affect public buying and selling of assets. Conversely, where the thing to be bought and sold is in fact a lawsuit in which two professional traders conclude the deal, truth means something else. Here, truth and candor call for a smaller amount of disclosure, permit greater distortion, and allow the other professional to suffer from his own ignorance and sloth in a way that would not be acceptable in the SEC case. In his article, Rubin recognizes that there are such different perceptions among members of the bar engaged in different kinds of practice, and he suggests that there should not be such differences.[11] Why not? Why is it so clear that one's responsibility for truth ought not be a function of the policy, the consequences, and the skill and expectations of the opponent?[12]

Apart from the kinds of differences in truthfulness and candor which arise from the subject matter of the negotiation, one suspects that there are other differences attributable to regional and ethnic differences among negotiators.[13] Although I have only anecdotal data to support this idea, it seems plausible that one's expectation concerning truth and candor might be different in a small, homogeneous community from what it would be in a large, heterogeneous community of lawyers. For one thing, all of the lawyers in the small and homogeneous community will share a common ethnic and environmental background. Each will have been subjected to the same kind of training about what kinds of lies are appropriate and what are not appropriate.

Moreover, the costs of conformity to ethical norms are less in a small community. Because the community is small, it will be easy to know those who do not conform to the standards and to protect oneself against that small number. Conversely, in the large and heterogeneous community, one will not have confidence either about the norms that have been learned by the opposing negotiator or about his conformance to those norms.

The differences that may result in perceptions about "truth and candor" often come to the surface in my negotiations seminar at the Michigan Law School, where there will be students from all parts of the country, from large and small cities, and from a variety of ethnic backgrounds. One such seminar involved a discussion between two students who had engaged in a mock negotiation that had been heated and had resulted in an unsatisfactory outcome for both. Each student had grown up in Manhattan; one was black, the other was Jewish. Their discussion in the seminar about their personal reactions to negotiation, about their experience as children and young adults in the art of negotiation, and about their personal reactions to it was illuminating. The Jewish student, one of the best in the class, was more at ease with the negotiation process, more comfortable with the ambiguity it produced, and more experienced as a negotiator. The black student, also a good student, reported that an extended negotiation without some event to relieve the tension caused him tremendous anxiety. He reported that his youthful negotiations were short and often concluded in explosive behavior. For example, if there were an argument about where two groups would play baseball (on my lot or yours), the typical negotiation would last a few minutes and, if it were not quickly resolved, would be concluded by a fight. At the conclusion of that fight, the game would be played on the winner's lot. Although the anecdote does not show systematic ethical differences between the two students, it does reveal systematically different attitudes about the negotiation process as a whole, and there is no reason to believe that there are not similar and systematic differences about the appropriate level of candor and honesty among the various ethnic and regional subgroups in our society. That is not to say that one norm is correct, only that the rules of the game played by one group are not the same as the rules played by another.

If the Comments or the body of the Model Rules are to refer to truthfulness, they should be understood to mean not an absolute but a relative truth as it is defined in context. That context in turn should be determined by the subject matter of the negotiation and, to a lesser extent, by the region and the background of the negotiators. Of course, such a flexible standard does not resolve the difficulties that arise when negotiators of different experience meet one another. I despair of solving that problem by the promulgation of rules, for to do so would require the drafters of these rules to do something that they obviously could not wish to do. That is, unless they wish to rely on the norms in the various subcultures in the bar to flesh out the rules, they will have to draft an extensive and complex body of rules.

FIVE CASES

Although it is not necessary to draft such a set of rules, it is probably important to give more than the simple disclaimer about the impossibility of defining the appropriate limits of puffing that the drafters have given in the current Comments.[14] To test these limits, consider five cases. Easiest is the question that arises when one misrepresents his true opinion about the meaning of a case or a statute. Presumably such a misrepresentation is accepted lawyer behavior both in and out of court and is not intended to be precluded by the requirement that the lawyer be "truthful." In writing his briefs, arguing his case, and attempting to persuade the opposing party in negotiation, it is the lawyer's right and probably his responsibility to argue for plausible interpretations of cases and statutes which favor his client's interest, even in circumstances where privately he has advised his client that those are not his true interpretations of the cases and statutes.

A second form of distortion that the Comments plainly envision as permissible is distortion concerning the value of one's case or of the other subject matter involved in the negotiation. Thus, the Comments make explicit reference to "puffery" (American Bar Association, 1980). Presumably they are attempting to draw the same line that one draws in commercial law between express warranties and "mere puffing" under section 2–313 of the Uniform Commercial Code.[15] While this line is not easy to draw, it generally means that the seller of a product has the right to make general statements concerning the value of his product without having the law treat those statements as warranties and without having liability if they turn out to be inaccurate estimates of the value. As the statements descend toward greater and greater particularity, as the ignorance of the person receiving the statements increases, the courts are likely to find them to be not puffing but express warranties.[16] By the same token, a lawyer could make assertions about his case or about the subject matter of his negotiation in general terms, and if those proved to be inaccurate, they would not be a violation of the ethical standards. Presumably such statements are not violations of the ethical standards even when they conflict with the lawyer's dispassionate analysis of the value of his case.

A third case is related to puffing but different from it. This is the use of the so-called false demand. It is a standard negotiating technique in collective bargaining negotiation and in some other multiple-issue negotiations for one side to include a series of demands about which it cares little or not at all.[17] The purpose of including these demands is to increase one's supply of negotiating currency. One hopes to convince the other party that one or more of these false demands is important and thus successfully to trade it for some significant concession. The assertion of and argument for a false demand involves the same kind of distortion that is involved in puffing or in arguing the merits of cases or statutes that are not really controlling. The proponent of a false demand implicitly or explicitly states his interest in the demand and his estimation of it. Such behavior is untruthful in the broadest sense, yet at least in collective bargaining negotiation, its use is a standard part of the process and is not thought to be inappropriate by any experienced bargainer.

Two final examples may be more troublesome. The first involves the response of a lawyer to a question from the other side. Assume that the defendant has instructed his lawyer to accept any settlement offer under $100,000. Having received that instruction, how does the defendant's lawyer respond to the plaintiff's question, "I think $90,000 will settle this case. Will your client give $90,000?" Do you see the dilemma that question poses for the defense lawyer? It calls for information that would not have to be disclosed. A truthful answer to it concludes the negotiation and dashes any possibility of negotiating a lower settlement even in circumstances in which the plaintiff might be willing to accept half of $90,000. Even a moment's hesitation in response to the question may be a nonverbal communication to a clever plaintiff's lawyer that the defendant has given such authority. Yet a negative response is a lie.

It is no answer that a clever lawyer will answer all such questions about authority by refusing to answer them, nor is it an answer that some lawyers will be clever enough to tell their clients not to grant them authority to accept a given sum until the final stages in negotiation. Most of us are not that careful or that clever. Few will routinely refuse to answer such questions in cases in which the client has granted a much lower limit than that discussed by the other party, for in that case an honest answer about the absence of authority is a quick and effective method of changing the opponent's settling point, and it is one that few of us will forego when our authority is far below that requested by the other party. Thus, despite the fact that a clever negotiator can avoid having to lie or to reveal his settling point, many lawyers, perhaps most, will sometime be forced by such a question either to lie or to reveal that they have been granted such authority by saying so or by their silence in response to a direct question. Is it fair to lie in such a case?[18]

Before one examines the possible justifications for a lie in that circumstance, consider a final example recently suggested to me by a lawyer in practice. There the lawyer represented three persons who had been charged with shoplifting. Having satisfied himself that there was no significant conflict of interest, the defense lawyer told the prosecutor that two of the three would plead guilty only if the case was dismissed against the third. Previously those two had told the defense counsel that they would plead guilty irrespective of what the third did, and the third had said that he wished to go to trial unless the charges were dropped. Thus, the defense lawyer lied to the prosecutor by stating that the two would plead only if the third were allowed to go free. Can the lie be justified in this case?[19]

How does one distinguish the cases where truthfulness is not required and those where it is required? Why do the first three cases seem easy? I suggest they are easy cases because the rules of the game are explicit and well developed in those areas. Everyone expects a lawyer to distort the value of his own case, of his own facts and arguments, and to deprecate those of his opponent. No one is surprised by that, and the system accepts and expects that behavior. To a lesser extent, the same is true of the false demand procedure in labor-management negotiations where the ploy is sufficiently widely used to be explicitly identified in the literature. A layman might say that this behavior falls within the ambit of "exaggeration," a form of behavior that while not necessarily respected is not regarded as morally reprehensible in our society.

The last two cases are more difficult. In one, the lawyer lies about his authority; in the other, he lies about the intention of his clients. It would be more difficult to justify the lies in those cases by arguing that the rules of the game explicitly permit that sort of behavior. Some might say that the rules of the game provide for such distortion, but I suspect that many lawyers would say that such lies are out of bounds and are not part of the rules of the game. Can the lie about authority be justified on the ground that the question itself was improper? Put another way, if I have a right to keep certain information to myself and if any behavior but a lie will reveal that information to the other side, am

I justified in lying? I think not. Particularly in the case in which there are other avenues open to the respondent, should we not ask him to take those avenues? That is, the careful negotiator here can turn aside all such questions and by doing so avoid any inference from his failure to answer such questions.

What makes the last case a close one? Conceivably it is the idea that one accused by the state is entitled to greater leeway in making his case.[20] Possibly one can argue that there is no injury to the state when such a person, particularly an innocent person, goes free. Is it conceivable that the act can be justified on the ground that it is part of the game in this context, that prosecutors as well as defense lawyers routinely misstate what they, their witnesses, and their clients can and will do? None of these arguments seems persuasive. Justice is not served by freeing a guilty person. The system does not necessarily achieve better results by trading two guilty pleas for a dismissal. Perhaps its justification has its roots in the same idea that formerly held that a misrepresentation of one's state of mind was not actionable, for it was not a misrepresentation of fact.

In a sense, rules governing these cases may simply arise from a recognition by the law of its limited power to shape human behavior. By tolerating exaggeration and puffing in the sales transaction, by refusing to make misstatement of one's intention actionable, the law may simply have recognized the bounds of its control over human behavior. Having said that, one is still left with the question, Are the lies permissible in the last two cases? My general conclusion is that they are not, but I am not nearly as comfortable with that conclusion as I am with the conclusion about the first three cases.

Taken together, the five foregoing cases show me that we do not and cannot intend that a negotiator be "truthful" in the broadest sense of that term. At the minimum, we allow him some deviation from truthfulness in asserting his true opinion about cases, statutes, or the value of the subject of the negotiation in other respects. In addition, some of us are likely to allow him to lie in response to certain questions that are regarded as out of bounds, and possibly to lie in circumstances where his interest is great and the injury seems small. It would be unfortunate, therefore, for the rule that requires "fairness" to be interpreted to require that a negotiator be truthful in every respect and in all of his dealings. It should be read to allow at least those kinds of untruthfulness that are implicitly and explicitly recognized as acceptable in his forum, a forum defined both by the subject matter and by the participants.

MANDATORY DISCLOSURE

Model Rule 4.2(b) requires the lawyer "to disclose a material fact known to the lawyer, even if adverse, when disclosure is . . . necessary to correct a manifest misapprehension of fact or law resulting from a previous representation made by the lawyer or known by the lawyer to have been made by the client." Elsewhere the rules make clear that one must make such a disclosure even though he is disclosing facts that would otherwise be privileged and that he would otherwise be prohibited from disclosing because of Rule 1.7. The rule is clear and explicit; it unequivocally resolves conflict between client confidentiality and disclosure. For that, the drafters should be commended.[21] More important, the drafters are right.

To those who value the privilege more highly than the drafters and who think it sacrilegious to suggest that a lawyer should disclose his client's confidence, consider the anomalies that result if the lawyer is not required to speak up. Assume, for example, that the lawyer for a tenant has negotiated a $2,000 settlement with the landlord's lawyer. Assume that the dispute arose when the tenant's apartment was burglarized and that the settlement was based on the assertion by the tenant that the landlord was negligent in maintaining the locks. Assume, however, that the settlement was based on figures that had been relayed orally by the tenant client to his lawyer. Subsequently the tenant brings a receipt showing that a missing stereo was purchased for $200, although the tenant has now altered the receipt to show a $1,500 purchase price. The $2,000 settlement offer was based on that altered price. Obviously the landlord's lawyer would not have offered a $2,000 settlement had he known that the stereo was worth only $200 and not $1,500. It is a material misrepresentation that would allow any agreement to be overturned on the grounds of fraud or mistake. Would it not be anomalous, then, if the rule said to the lawyer, "You must accept this settlement or at most you can resign, but because these were privileged documents and privileged information, you may not disclose them to the other side"? Such a rule would require a lawyer to facilitate an agreement that, if the facts were known, would be unenforceable. Rule 4.2 would require the lawyer to come forward and to tell the other side the stereo's true price.

Consider two other cases where the rule will come into play. One is the situation in which a client has stated certain facts on a deposition and then concedes to his lawyer that they are not true, or it comes to the lawyer's attention by other means that they are not true. In such circumstances the lawyer would have to disclose that to the opposing party.[22] The same rule would apply if at an early stage in a negotiation, one party had relied on a case that was subsequently overruled or on a statute that was repealed.[23]

There are two difficulties with the rule; one of them may be a major difficulty. First and least important is to determine how to measure when a "manifest misapprehension" has occurred. Consider, for example, the case widely used in mock negotiation by lawyers and law students in which a mechanic testifies on the deposition that his customer (the father of a child who was killed in an auto accident after the mechanic worked on the car) did not request that the mechanic check the brakes but asked only for a "general checkup" of the car.

Subsequently, the mechanic comes to his lawyer and states that he "remembers" that the father of the dead child did tell him to check the brakes. To me that has always seemed a straightforward case for this rule, one in which the witness lied initially, subsequently was overcome with remorse, and confessed to his lawyer. There is another plausible hypothesis that has been suggested to me by my colleague Andrew S. Watson, whose specialty is psychiatry and law, and by various lawyers who have negotiated the problem. That is the hypothesis that the mechanic testified truthfully the first time that he had in fact not been ordered to check the brakes, but that his sense of guilt at being even remotely connected with the death of the child caused him subsequently to believe incorrectly and to state inaccurately that he had been instructed to check the brakes. How is the lawyer to behave in such a case? If he adopts the latter interpretation, there is no misrepresentation and he need not come forward. If he adopts the former interpretation, the case falls squarely within 4.2(b). The rule will present a series of other line-drawing problems in determining whether or not the fact was "material" and in determining whether it "resulted" from a previous representation by the lawyer or his client. Finally, as in the hypothetical case, there will be the question of what is a manifest misapprehension. Doubtless these difficulties are inherent in any rules of the kind proposed, and if we are to have such a rule, we will have to tolerate substantial deviation in its application and use by lawyers based on their individual interpretations of these words.

A more troublesome difficulty with the rule, and one related to the first, is that it may be so widely violated that it ought not be enacted. It is my hypothesis that it is better to have no rule than to have one so widely violated as to be a continuing hypocrisy that may poison the application of the remaining rules. It is conceivable that Rule 4.2(b) is such a rule. In the first place, the rule runs up against the traditional and deep-seated idea that the lawyer has a single-minded commitment to his client's case. Like many of the rules it also conflicts with the lawyer's desire to win, with his own identification with his client's case. Of course, lawyers who are so bound up with their clients' cases are not exemplars, but the rules are designed to deal with the mine run as well as the exemplary lawyer. Thus, the rule calls on the lawyer not only to squeal on his client but, worse, to destroy a winner for himself and his client.

Of course, it is in the nature of compliance with ethical norms that one's self-interest is often injured, but there must be a trade-off between compliance and injury to one's self-interest. If the latter is too great, few will follow the rules. If any significant part of the rules is routinely violated by a majority of the bar, that in turn weakens the structure of all the rules and makes it difficult to sustain a commitment of the organized bar to following and enforcing those rules. Whether the proposed rule concerning revelations of clients' misstatements and misrepresentations is a rule that would be so widely violated that it should not be enacted, I cannot say. From presenting the problem I described above to several hundreds of lawyers and discussing that problem afterward, I am confident that a majority of the lawyers operating under today's rules would not reveal the fact that the client had recanted his deposition in a negotiation with the other party. My observation of those lawyers suggests that the most common position is one in which the lawyer will no longer use the mechanic's assertion affirmatively but will not admit that the mechanic has recanted the position he took on the deposition.[24]

Do these anecdotal data suggest that lawyers in general will not follow the rule? At least it should give pause. It is conceivable that lawyers would change their attitude if a rule as explicit and straightforward as the one proposed were enacted and if there were an effective means to inform the bar at large about such a rule.

In summary, I support Rule 4.2(b), but I think the drafters need to realize that by enacting that rule together with some of the others that are proposed, we are asking lawyers to deviate from the traditional American attitude that the lawyer is identified with his client's interest and is obliged to protect privileged information. Because such a rule asks the lawyer not only to act contrary to his selfish interests but also to violate the important psychological association with his client and his client's case, the drafters are undertaking a difficult chore. In their consideration of this rule, the drafters must take account of that question and of the probability that lawyers will be willing to conform to such a rule. If they conclude that a substantial minority of the lawyers who know such a rule will nevertheless violate it, that alone is sufficient basis for not enacting such a rule.

CONCLUSION

To draft effective legislation is difficult; to draft effective ethical rules is close to impossible. Such drafters must walk the narrow line between being too general and too specific. If their rules are too general, they will have no influence on any behavior and give little guidance even to those who wish to follow the rules. If they are too specific, they omit certain areas or conflict with appropriate rules for problems not foreseen but apparently covered.

There are other, more formidable obstacles. These drafters are essentially powerless. They draft the rules, but the American Bar Association must pass them, and the rules must then be adopted by various courts or other agencies in the states. Finally, the enforcement of the rules is left to a hodgepodge of bar committees and grievance agencies of varied will and capacity. Thus, the drafters are far removed from and have little control over those who ultimately will enact and enforce the rules. For that reason, even more than most legislators, drafters of ethical rules have limited power to influence behavior. This weakness presents a final dilemma and one they have not always faced as well as they should, namely, to make the appropriate trade-off between what is "right" and what can be done. To enact stern and righteous rules in Chicago will not fool the people in Keokuk. The public will not believe them, and the bar will not follow them. What level of violation of the rules can the bar accept without the rules as a whole becoming a mockery? I do not know and the drafters can only guess. Because of the danger presented if the norms are widely and routinely violated, the drafters should err on the conservative side and must sometimes reject better and more desirable rules for poorer ones simply because the violation of the higher standard would cast all the rules in doubt.

Notes

1. See, e.g., the American Bar Association Code of Professional Responsibility DR 7–102(A) and DR 1–102(A): "A lawyer shall not: . . . (4) engage in conduct involving dishonesty, fraud, deceit, or misrepresentation" (American Bar Association, 1979).

2. I note in passing one objectionable aspect of the proposed Rules that is unrelated to truthfulness. That is their gratuitous direction, in the introduction and Comments, about how to behave in negotiation. For example, the introduction has extensive discussion on what I would regard not as an ethical matter but as the substance of negotiating. It contains statements about the appropriate consideration of long-run as well as short-run interests, about whether one should behave in a "tough" or "hypertechnical" manner, and about other things that are matters of style, not of ethics. In my judgment, these are substantive negotiating questions that should be left to the judgment of the negotiator. They are not part of the responsibility of those making model rules for behavior in negotiation. One who is naturally a curmudgeon should not be thought less ethical than a person who is pleasant to deal with. One who is hypertechnical is not necessarily less ethical than a person who is willing to leave things to a handshake. Such discussion of style and substance of negotiation as opposed to the ethical behavior in negotiation seems gratuitous and inappropriate in the Model Rules and in the Comments to the Model Rules.

3. For a discussion of the circumstances that might justify a lie, even for one with an extraordinary commitment to truthfulness, see Bok (1978).

4. Karrass (1974, p. 23) states flatly that "bluffing is part of negotiating." Moreover, he instructs one to make offers that the opponent must refuse in order to make later offers look good by comparison. See also Karrass (1970).

5. It is obvious that threats are important parts of much negotiation—the threat to go to trial, the threat to go to war, the threat to do a variety of other acts. In itself, an implicit or explicit threat is often neither unethical nor illegal. But it is easy to think of threats that are either unethical or illegal or both. For example, a threat of

criminal prosecution in return for the settlement of civil litigation is normally thought to be both unethical and in violation of the criminal law. It would be useful to have someone outline the appropriate bounds of negotiating behavior here. For a consideration of some of the problems, see Joseph (1978).

6. See generally Edwards and White (1977). There we consider a variety of problems that deal with the questions of what favors are appropriate and what factors extraneous to the negotiation may properly be used. The favors one might offer to an opposing negotiator range all the way from a martini through a golf outing to some other form of entertainment that involves considerable expense. Of course, the ethical problem here is not unique to negotiation, but it is important for negotiators.

7. Lawyer writings on negotiation are full of instructions to time one's settlement offer to coincide with the opposing lawyer's need for money to pay his taxes or for the use of other factors extraneous to the negotiation itself. Obviously, many factors other than the objective merit of the opponent's case will be factors in the negotiation. An obvious example, unrelated to the merits of the case of the opposing party but one highly important in the negotiation, is the skill of the lawyer that the opposing client has hired. If he is the best trial lawyer in the city, the settlement value of his case will go up. If he is a lawyer known to be afraid of the courthouse, the settlement value will go down. Surely every lawyer would be expected to use that in negotiating a settlement, but if one takes a step or two beyond that simple calculation based on lawyer skill, one finds himself on uncertain ground. See also Edwards and White (1977).

8. See, for example: "A party is permitted to suggest advantages to an opposing party that may be insubstantial from an objective point of view. The precise contours of the legal duties concerning disclosure, representation, puffery, over-reaching, and other aspects of honesty in negotiations cannot be concisely stated. . . . It is a lawyer's responsibility to see that negotiations conducted by the lawyer conform to applicable legal standards, whatever they may be." From Comment to Rule 4.2 in American Bar Association (1980).

9. See, for example, Canon 22 of the Canons of Professional Ethics, in American Bar Association (1967): "The conduct of the lawyer before the Court and with other lawyers should be characterized by candor and fairness." See also Patterson and Cheatham (1971).

10. Rubin (1975) states his position as follows: "The lawyer must act honestly and in good faith. Another lawyer, or a layman, who deals with a lawyer should not need to exercise the same degree of caution that he would if trading for reputedly antique copper jugs in an oriental bazaar. It is inherent in the concept of an ethic, as a principle of good conduct, that it is morally binding on the conscience of the professional, and not merely a rule of the game adopted because other players observe (or fail to adopt) the same rule" (pp. 577, 589).

11. Rubin (1975) writes, "The esteem of a lawyer for his own profession must be scant if he can rationalize the subclassifications this distinction implies. . . . Lawyers from Wall Street firms say that they and their counterparts observe

scrupulous standards, but they attribute less morality to the personal injury lawyer, and he, in turn, will frequently point out the inferiority of the standards of those who spend much time in criminal litigation. The gradation of the ethics of the profession by the area of law becomes curiouser and curiouser the more it is examined, if one may purloin the words of another venturer in wonderland" (pp. 583–584).

12. Consider our hypothetical concerning distortion of the value of a piece of property in a negotiation with a lawyer who is presumed to know his business or, alternatively, with an aged and ignorant owner. The students in my negotiation seminar routinely will find exaggeration and distortion to be inappropriate when one is dealing with the layman, but to be at least ethical, if not wise, behavior when dealing with an opposing lawyer. See generally Edwards and White (1977).

13. For a consideration of some of the deviations in negotiating behavior arising out of cultural differences, consider the following excerpt from Hall and Whyte (1960, p. 5–12): "In Latin America, you should expect to spend hours waiting in outer offices. If you bring your American interpretation of what constitutes punctuality to a Latin-American office, you will fray your temper and elevate your blood pressure. For a forty-five-minute wait is not unusual—no more unusual than a five-minute wait would be in the United States. No insult is intended. . . . The time pie is differently cut, that's all.

". . . In America, we show good faith by ignoring the details. 'Let's agree on the main points. The details will take care of themselves.' Not so the Greek. He signifies good will and good faith by what may seem to you an interminable discussion which includes every conceivable detail. Otherwise, you see, he cannot help but feel that the other man might be trying to pull the wool over his eyes. Our habit, in what we feel to be our relaxed and friendly way, of postponing details until later smacks the Greek between the eyes as a maneuver to flank him.

"The American desire to get down to business . . . works to our disadvantage in other parts of the world. . . . The head of a large, successful Japanese firm commented: 'You Americans have a terrible weakness. We Japanese know about it and exploit it every chance we get. You are impatient. We have learned that if we just make you wait long enough, you'll agree to anything.'

". . . Not only is our idea of time schedules no part of Arab life but the mere mention of a deadline to an Arab is like waving a red flag in front of a bull. In his culture, your emphasis on a deadline has the emotional effect on him that his backing you into a corner and threatening you with a club would have on you."

14. "The precise contours of the legal duties concerning disclosure, representation, puffery, over-reaching, and other aspects of honesty in negotiations cannot be concisely stated." Comment to Rule 4.2, Model Rules (American Bar Association, 1980).

15. Section 2–313(2) of the Uniform Commercial Code reads in part as follows: "It is not necessary to the creation of an express warranty that the seller use formal words . . . but an affirmation merely of the value of the goods or a statement

purporting to be merely the seller's opinion or commendation . . . does not create a warranty." Put another way, puffing is permitted.

16. Compare *Wat Henry Pontiac Co.* v. *Bradley* (1949) (a statement about a used car to a woman who was to drive with her young child to visit her husband in the service was held an express warranty) with *Frederickson* v. *Hackney* (1924) (an extravagant statement to a wary farmer about the quality of a young bull was held not to be a warranty).

17. "A typical strategy used by most unions at one time or another is to bury two or three serious fringe objectives in a veritable mountain of fringe demands—as many as twenty-five, thirty, and more" (Peters, 1955, p. 165).

18. Curtis might have authorized a lie in this case and may well have justified it on the basis suggested: "It may be that it all depends on whether you are asked the question by someone who has a right to ask it. If he has no right to ask and if simple silence would, or even might, lead him to the truth, then, I believe your lawyer is in duty bound to lie. For the truth is not his, but yours. It belongs to you and he is bound to keep it for you, even more vigorously than if it were only his own" (Curtis, 1951, p. 3, 8). Bok (1978) waffles on these issues but would appear not to support a lie in such circumstances. Compare her discussion on p. 160 and that at pp. 167 and 171–173.

19. Consider a variation on the last case. Assume that the defense lawyer did not say explicitly that the two would plead only if the third were allowed to go free but simply said, "If you drop the charges against one, the other two will plead guilty." In that case, the lie is not explicit, but surely the inference that the defense lawyer wishes the prosecutor to draw is the same. Should that change the outcome?

20. See, for example, Rule 4.2(b)(2) and Rule 3.1(f) (American Bar Association, 1980).

21. Rule 1.7(b) provides: "A lawyer shall disclose information about a client . . . to the extent required by law or the Rules of Professional Conduct." The Comments refer explicitly to Rule 4.2, and the quoted language is apparently intended to resolve the conflict in favor of disclosure when the lawyer learns that his client has lied or otherwise misrepresented facts to the opposing side. See Comment on mandatory disclosure in the Model Rules (American Bar Association, 1980).

22. In this context, Rule 4.2 asks the lawyer to do no more than Rule 26(e) of the Federal Rules of Civil Procedure would require. Although that rule requires supplementation of a party's deposition when he "obtains information" that leads him to "know" that the earlier response was incorrect, it undoubtedly also includes cases in which the party lied in the first instance and thus "knew" all along that his response was incorrect. Rule 26(e) reads as follows: "A party who has responded to a request for discovery with a response that was complete when made is under no duty to supplement his response to include information thereafter acquired, except as follows:

"(2) A party is under a duty seasonably to amend a prior response if he obtains information upon the basis of which (A) he knows that the response was incorrect when made, or (B) he knows that the response thought correct when made is no longer true and the circumstances are such that a failure to amend the response is in substance a knowing concealment." See also section 2049 of Wright and Miller (1970).

23. One might argue that a representation about a case does not produce "a manifest misapprehension of . . . law resulting from a previous representation." A misapprehension, so the argument goes, results from the failure of the opposing lawyer to Shepardize the cases and to determine that the one relied on was subsequently overruled. I think that reads the rule too narrowly and that at least in cases in which there is a central case that one party has cited in the negotiations and has relied on, that party has an obligation upon its overruling on appeal to correct his opponent's understanding.

24. One rarely hears of a lawyer revealing a client's lie despite the current DR 7–102(B), which reads as follows: "A lawyer who receives information clearly establishing that (1) his client has, in the course of the representation, perpetrated a fraud upon a person or tribunal shall promptly call upon his client to rectify the same, and if his client refuses or is unable to do so, he shall reveal the fraud to the affected person or tribunal, except when the information is protected as a privileged communication" (American Bar Association, 1979).

Presumably the failure to come forward in this case would be justified by a lawyer's argument either that the information did not "clearly" establish that fraud had been perpetrated or that the information was privileged and thus could not be revealed. The rule is not clear because of the confusing cross-reference to DR 4–101, which authorizes a lawyer to reveal confidences or secrets "when permitted under Disciplinary Rules or required by law or court order."

Even if the lawyer concludes that he is not free to reveal his client's confidence because DR 4–101 limits DR 7–102(B), he should conclude that he could not use the lie affirmatively because to do so would violate DR 7–102(A)(2), (4), (5), and possibly other subsections.

Note in the hypothetical case I have assumed that the employee of an insured is nevertheless the "client" of the lawyer, whose fee will in fact be paid by an insurance company.

References

American Bar Association. *Opinions of the Committee on Professional Ethics with the Canons of Professional Ethics Annotated and Canons of Judicial Ethics Annotated.* Chicago: American Bar Association, 1967.

American Bar Association. Committee on Ethics and Professional Responsibility. *Model Code of Professional Responsibility and Code of Judicial Conduct.* Chicago: American Bar Association, 1979.

American Bar Association. Commission on Evaluation of Professional Standards. "Model Rules of Professional Conduct 89–90." Discussion draft. Chicago: American Bar Association, Jan. 30, 1980.

Bok, S. *Lying: Moral Choices in Public and Private Life.* New York: Pantheon Books, 1978.

Curtis, C. P. "The Ethics of Advocacy." *Stanford Law Review,* 1951, *4,* 38.

Edwards, H. T., and White, J. J. *Problems, Readings and Materials on the Lawyer as a Negotiator.* St. Paul, Minn.: West Publishing Co., 1977.

Frederickson v. *Hackney.* 159 Minn. 234, 198 N.W. 806 (1924).

Hall, E. T., and Whyte W. F. "Intercultural Communication: A Guide to Men of Action." *Human Organization,* 1960, *19,* 5–12.

Karrass, C. L. *The Negotiating Game: How to Get What You Want.* New York: Crowell, 1970.

Karrass, C. L. *Give and Take: The Complete Guide to Negotiating Strategies and Tactics.* New York: Crowell, 1974.

Livermore, J. M. "Lawyer Extortion." *Arizona Law Review,* 1978, *20,* 403.

Patterson, L. R., and Cheatham, E. E. *The Profession of Law.* Mineola, N.Y.: Foundation Press, 1971.

Peters, E. *Strategy and Tactics in Labor Negotiations.* New London, Conn.: Foremen's Institute, 1955.

Rubin, A. B. "A Causerie on Lawyers' Ethics in Negotiation." *Louisiana Law Review,* 1975, *35,* 577–589.

CHAPTER NINE

Promoting Honesty in Negotiation

An Exercise in Practical Ethics

Peter C. Cramton

J. Gregory Dees

*There is such a gap between how one lives and how one ought
to live that anyone who abandons what is done for what ought
to be done learns his ruin rather than his preservation.*
—Niccolo Machiavelli

*We must make the world honest before we can honestly
say to our children that honesty is the best policy.*
—George Bernard Shaw

If business ethics is to have a significant impact on business practice, many of us working in the field will need to take a more pragmatic approach to our craft (Dees and Cramton, 1991). Our work should help ethically sensitive business people establish stable institutional arrangements that promote and protect ethically desirable conduct, and it should help individuals to develop strategies for effective ethical behavior in a competitive and morally imperfect world. This paper is offered as one model of more practical business ethics.

To illustrate the model, we have selected the topic of deception in negotiation. Negotiation is a pervasive feature of business life. Success in business typically requires successful negotiations. It is commonly believed that success in negotiation is enhanced by the skillful use of deceptive tactics, such as bluffing,

We are grateful to Howard Stevenson and Tom Piper for comments and to the Harvard Business School, the National Science Foundation, and the Hoover Institution for support.

exaggeration, posturing, stage-setting, and outright misrepresentation. As White (1980, p. 927) candidly states, "The critical difference between those who are successful negotiators and those who are not lies in this capacity both to mislead and not to be misled." Some shrewd practitioners have advanced the art of deception beyond prudent concealment of preferences to more aggressive forms of strategic misrepresentation.[1]

Given the high value placed on honesty, the incentives for deception in negotiation create a serious moral tension for business people, as well as a public relations problem for business. The public relations problem is not new. In ancient Athens, Hermes, a trickster who stole his brother's (Apollo's) cattle on the day he was born and later lied about it, was the patron god of merchants. Anacharsis wrote in 600 B.C., "The market is the place set apart where men may deceive one another."

Not surprisingly, deception in negotiation is a widely discussed problem in business ethics. However, much of the attention has been devoted to the question of when (if ever) various deceptive tactics are ethically justified. Many writers have been highly critical of deception in business. Others, most notably Carr (1968) in his controversial piece on business bluffing, have argued that business has its own ethics, one that permits a wide range of deceptive practices that would not be acceptable outside of business.

We see little benefit from joining this debate. It is not our intent in this paper or our intent in Dees and Cramton (1991). Boatright's suggestion (1992) that our "mutual trust perspective" on practical ethics might best be understood as a two-tiered Hobbesian theory about the justification of deception misses our central point. We were not staking out a philosophical position, but rather attempting to articulate a deep-seated view reflected in the attitudes and behaviors of many negotiators with whom we have had experience. The point was to provide a backdrop for developing practical recommendations that negotiators might actually take up. Debating the possible philosophical justifications for different types of deception is intellectually engaging, but unlikely to have a direct impact on practice. How many negotiators would change their behavior when it is pointed out that their views are essentially Hobbesian and that Kant, who is regarded as a superior moral philosopher, would find them objectionable? Even if this claim were accompanied by a philosophical refutation of Hobbes and an explanation of Kant's categorical imperative, it seems doubtful that much negotiating behavior would change.

We also avoid the standard debate because it focuses too much attention on justification, obscuring the fact that behavior may be justified but nonetheless regrettable. A dramatic example is the killing of civilians during a war, even a just war. In some instances, it may be justified, but even when justified, it is regrettable. Rather than engaging in (perhaps unresolvable) philosophical debates about the exact conditions under which the killing of civilians is justified, it seems that one who is concerned about the loss of civilian life in war would be better served by putting resources and intellectual energy into developing political, economic, diplomatic, and military strategies that reduce the risk to innocent civilians.

Our premise is that outside of a few recreational contexts, deception is a regrettable feature of business negotiations, even when it is justified (or commonplace).[2] The Machiavellian gap between what is done and what (ideally) ought to be done is real when it comes to deception in business negotiations. A purely moralistic (or philosophical) response is likely to be ineffective. A Machiavellian response is likely to make things worse. In the spirit of Shaw, we prefer to explore means of constructively narrowing the gap, thereby making the world more honest.

ETHICS, OPPORTUNISM, AND TRUST

In an ideal world, people would do the right thing simply because it is right. In the world in which we live, morality is more complex. People often disagree about what is right. Even when a consensus on moral values is reached, many find that they do not consistently live up to moral standards. One reason for falling short is that most people place a high value on their own welfare. They may have moral ideals and commitments, but concern about personal well-being is a powerful motivating factor. It is more powerful for some than it is for others, but few can claim to be indifferent to it. Any significant gap between the demands of ethics and the urging of self-interest, narrowly defined,[3] creates incentive problems for individuals and for societies wishing to maintain high ethical standards. The problems arise on two levels.

At the first level are the direct incentive problems of opportunism and desperation. Problems of opportunism arise when individuals willingly violate ethical norms in order to pursue opportunities for private gain. They yield to temptation. Problems of desperation arise when individuals violate ethical norms to avoid personal loss or hardship. Even if we grant that most people place some intrinsic value on doing the right thing, as they see it, sometimes the risk or the temptation is just too great. Philosophers refer to this problem as "weakness of the will." Weakness of the will is not limited to moral deviants. Too often we are presented with evidence from our daily lives, from news stories, and from academic research[4] that well-educated, apparently normal individuals can be tempted or pressured into compromising ethical standards.

The effects of opportunism and desperation are magnified by a second-level problem concerning trust and fair play. One of the reasons people are willing to behave ethically, even when their personal welfare is at risk, is that they expect others to behave likewise. It seems unfair for individuals with weaker ethical commitments to prosper materially, especially at the expense of individuals with stronger commitments. An atmosphere of mutual trust appears to play an important role in grounding ethical behavior for many people.[5] Suspicion that others are profiting from misconduct can destroy that atmosphere and spoil the sense of satisfaction that might be gained from principled behavior. A sense of fair play can motivate individuals with strong ethical commitments to engage in what they would otherwise consider unacceptable behavior.

Individual integrity and social stability are difficult to maintain in a social setting in which there is serious conflict between ethics and personal welfare. Traditionally, moral philosophers have responded to this conflict in one of two ways. Some, particularly Kantians, acknowledge the gap between ethics and self-interest, but assert on philosophical grounds the dominance of moral considerations over those of personal welfare. Others argue that the gap is only apparent. By refining the definition of self-interest, they attempt to reconcile ethics and self-interest (Kavka, 1984). As philosophically interesting as these views are, neither holds much promise of improving conduct. Practical, not conceptual, solutions are needed.

INCENTIVES FOR DECEPTION IN NEGOTIATION

To illustrate the practical approach to ethical incentive problems, we have chosen to concentrate on the phenomenon of deception in negotiation. Negotiation offers a familiar setting in which individuals often feel a tension between ethics and self-interest. In particular, individuals frequently face a temptation to deceive the other party, in hopes of bettering the outcome for themselves.

We adopt the following definitions:

A *negotiation* is any situation in which two or more parties are engaged in communications, the aim of which is agreement on terms affecting an exchange, or a distribution of benefits, burdens, roles, or responsibilities.

Deception is any deliberate act or omission by one party taken with the intention of creating or adding support to a false belief in another party.[6]

Honesty is the absence of deception.[7]

Notice that lying is only one tactic that may be used to deceive a negotiation partner. Lying, strictly interpreted, requires making a false statement (or at least a statement believed to be false by its maker). The clever manipulation of verbal and nonverbal signals to create or support a false impression, without making a false statement, also counts as deception. Likewise, concealing information is a deceptive tactic if and only if the concealment is intended to create or support a false belief. In some cases, there is a fine line between allowing the other party to continue to hold a false belief and adding support to that belief.

To understand the incentives for deception in negotiation, we use some basic game theory[8] and a fictional world called Metopia. The simplified world of Metopia allows us to put aside temporarily some of the complexity of the real world in order to analyze the incentives for deception. Metopia is a world much like ours, but populated exclusively with rational, self-centered individuals. We adopt the standard definition of self-interest from economics:

> An action is in a party's *self-interest* if, given the party's beliefs at the time of decision, the action yields greater expected utility for the party than any other available action.

Metopians always act in their self-interest. Their interests are even more self-centered and material, focused on their own personal welfare. Metopians' preferences are independent of the preferences of others. They have no specific preferences about the process of the negotiation. In particular, Metopians do not have an independent preference for honesty or dishonesty in the process of negotiation. They feel no guilt about deception, nor do they enjoy fooling others. Metopians have no interest in the opinions of others, except to the extent that such opinions are likely to inhibit or enhance their ability to satisfy their self-centered interests. Finally, Metopians do not have any religious belief system that provides moral rewards and punishments. These features characterize the narrow conception of self-interest in Metopia.

OPPORTUNITIES FOR DECEPTION IN METOPIA

The basis for deception in Metopia is the presence of (real or perceived)[9] informational differences among the parties. Negotiators often have private information about the item under discussion, about their ability and willingness to take future actions, and about their own settlement preferences. Private information, however, does not always present a profitable opportunity for deception. Often it is more prudent to be honest. In general, an opportunity for A to profitably deceive B arises only when B believes A has information that is of value to B in determining B's negotiating position, B knows of no other cost-efficient way to get the information before making a commitment, and it is to A's advantage if B acts on false beliefs about the matter. The opportunity will depend in part on the kind of information in question.

Deception About the Matter Under Negotiation

It is common for at least one of the parties to have privileged access to information about the subject matter under negotiation. In an exchange, often the seller has the information advantage. The classic example is the seller of a used car who knows more about the history and mechanical condition of the car than the buyer does. Sometimes, however, the buyer has an advantage over an unsophisticated or uninformed seller. An example of this would be an art dealer buying a dusty old painting at a garage sale, or a real estate developer buying parcels of property for an unannounced development project. In a barter situation, both parties may have informational advantages about their side of the exchange. Information asymmetry is not limited to product exchanges. It is also common when the negotiation is about a service to be delivered, a benefit (or burden) to be distributed, or a right (or responsibility) to be assigned.

Even in Metopia, where negotiators recognize the other party's incentives to deceive, the possibility of deception can cause serious problems. For example, suppose a seller has private information about the quality, broadly interpreted, of the good being sold. The higher the quality, the more the good is worth to the buyer, and consequently the more the buyer is willing to pay. In a one-shot situation, the seller has an interest in overstating the product's quality. If the seller is believed, she can get a higher profit by overstating, assuming it is more costly to produce high quality goods than low quality goods. A Metopian buyer, therefore, will not believe statements that the good is of high quality, even when it is. Thus, the incentive to deceive about quality leads to Akerlof's "market for lemons" (1970). The buyer, not believing statements of high quality, is willing to pay only a low quality price. The seller is only willing to produce low quality goods, even if both are better off with the exchange of high quality goods at a high quality price.

Deception About Future Actions

Statements about future actions play a key role in many business negotiations. Such statements fall into two categories: threats and promises. Each of these presents an opportunity for deception about one's true intentions.

Threats are often used to place pressure on the other party to settle. They range from the simple threat of walking away from the negotiation to threats of causing harm to the other party. For instance, in a labor negotiation, management may threaten to close a plant if the union does not make concessions. Threats can be bluffed, but for a bluffed threat to work, it must be credible. Suppose A threatens B. The threat is credible if B thinks that it is in A's interest to carry out the threat if B does not comply. The success of the threat, then, depends on how well B can assess A's true incentives. In the above example, if labor does not have information about plant-by-plant profitability, management may get concessions by threatening to close the plant. B may not be able to tell a bluffed threat from a real one. Legitimate threats and warnings may be robbed of their informational content. Even if management offered to present labor with the financial information, labor would recognize management's incentive to present deceptive information. Without a reliable source of information, B may have to discount all of A's threats, legitimate or bluffed.

Promises are an essential element in most negotiations. Often one party performs, or makes an investment before the other. Even if the central exchange appears to be simultaneous, there may be understandings and expectations about future actions. Sellers may promise to protect buyers in certain contingencies, for instance, allowing the buyer to return clothing that does not fit. On the other hand, buyers may ask for credit and promise to pay sellers at a later date. In any case, a party making a commitment is likely to know much more about the probability of compliance than the party to whom the commitment is made. For instance, a computer manufacturer who is planning to go out of business, but wants to sell as much of her remaining stock as possible, might continue to offer a warranty that she knows she will not be in a position to honor. Again, lack of information about the true incentives, abilities, and resources of A, the party making the commitment, makes B vulnerable to deception. When A has an incentive to deceive, even A's good faith promises are not believed. It is difficult for A to credibly reassure B of A's willingness and ability to fulfill the promise.

Deception About Settlement Preferences

The third area of opportunity for deception in Metopia involves the settlement preferences of the negotiating parties. Settlement preferences include the negotiator's reservation price, time pressures, and the different values the negotiator places on specific terms of agreement. Sometimes it is useful to share these preferences if the sharing does not make one vulnerable to exploitation by the other. Yet, often, negotiators find it in their interest to misrepresent their preferences. They may want to conceal a weak bargaining position, or to give the appearance of making a concession when they are getting what they want.[10] It is possible for the other party to gather indirect evidence about these matters. For instance, if house buyer B discovers that house seller A has accepted a job in another part of the country and has made a deposit on a house there, this points to A's eagerness to sell. If rug seller A sells many of the same rugs, rug buyer B may be able to get a history of the prices A has accepted in the past as an indicator of how low A is willing to go. Nonetheless, individual negotiators generally have privileged access to information about their own settlement preferences.

To see why uncertainty about settlement preferences may lead to deception, imagine the negotiation process between two traders, A and B, where each party is uncertain about the strength of the other's bargaining position. Neither trader knows the other's values or outside opportunities, or how these values and opportunities change as time passes. The negotiation consists of a sequence of offers and counteroffers until someone finally accepts the other's offer. Agreement occurs at a point where the further benefits of bargaining (improved terms of trade) do not seem worth the costs to secure them (delayed agreement or a risk of disagreement). The parties bargain until the marginal cost of continuing exceeds the marginal benefit. B's net gain of continuing is based on her expectation about A's future concessions, which, in turn, is based on B's belief about the strength of A's bargaining position. To do well, A would like to persuade B to accept A's most recent offer by convincing B that only slight concessions will be made in the future. A natural justification for slight concessions in the future is a strong bargaining position—good outside opportunities and a lack of eagerness to reach agreement. Hence, A benefits from convincing B that her bargaining position is stronger than it truly is. A has an incentive to deceive B about any facts, beliefs, or values that might expose the weakness in A's position.

For this reason, bargainers in Metopia are skeptical of information that the other party presents that bears on that party's settlement preferences. This has its costs. To convince B of the strength of her position, A must take actions that a weaker A would not want to imitate, such as delaying agreement or risking disagreement, both of which involve bargaining inefficiencies. Indeed, so long as there is some uncertainty about whether gains from trade exist, some bargaining inefficiencies must occur regardless of the bargaining process adopted, if the parties act in their own self-interest and have only costly means of signaling strength.[11]

FACTORS INHIBITING DECEPTION IN METOPIA

One might think that Metopia would be riddled with attempted deception and bad faith, since Metopians exploit opportunities to misrepresent information in a negotiation. However, as Adam Smith observed, "The most notorious liar . . . tells the fair truth at least twenty times for once that he seriously and deliberately lies" (1759, p. 530). The same might be said of Metopians. Several mechanisms work to inhibit deception. Metopians would rationally invest in processes and mechanisms to protect themselves from deception and its untoward social consequences. Even potential deceivers recognize the effect that the possibility of deception has in undermining even their true statements. To create a climate of confidence that would facilitate negotiations, Metopians would investigate claims, construct contractual mechanisms to enforce honesty, and work to ease the availability of reputation information.

Ex Ante Verification

One remedy for the risk of deception is to verify claims and assumptions before making commitments that depend on those claims or assumptions. Negotiators could gather independent evidence themselves, or they might hire others to do it. Gathering it themselves is generally the most reliable method. However, an individual negotiator does not always have the expertise to verify claims efficiently. Accordingly, just as the use of house inspectors has become commonplace in residential real estate transactions, Metopians would employ auditors, testers, inspectors, and private detectives to verify the truth of claims made or implied in negotiations.[12]

One problem is that verification of every significant claim made in a negotiation would be quite costly. Often it would not be justified. Metopians would be creative in reducing the costs of verification. Two mechanisms for doing so are the use of economies of scale and random verification. It would be highly inefficient, for instance, for everyone buying a refrigerator to hire a private inspector to evaluate different models. However, because refrigerators are standard products, we would expect to see information gathered by a third party, who would sell it to those who need it. When economies of scale are not possible, Metopians could adopt random verification procedures to lower verification costs. This would work so long as the parties caught in a deceptive act could be punished harshly. For example, if the maximum penalty that A could apply to B is ten times B's individual net gain from deceiving A, then A's verifying information one out of ten times is sufficient to prevent deception by B. Verification is economical in this case, so long as the cost of verification is no more than ten times the net efficiency gain from honest behavior.

Contractual Mechanisms

Unfortunately, even with some creativity, ex ante verification is limited. Some claims are simply too difficult or too costly to test ex ante with any confidence. Claims about the long-term reliability of a new product typically fall into this category, as do many claims about actions to be taken in the future and about settlement preferences. In such cases, Metopians would develop contractual mechanisms to add credibility to claims made or implied in a negotiation.

Ideally, the mechanisms would be self-enforcing. However, such mechanisms are limited in their applicability and may be more costly than alternatives, even though the alternatives require third-party enforcement. Consequently, we would expect to find in Metopia systems of third-party enforcement and a high level of explicit contracting. The third parties could play a variety of roles, from holding collateral to adjudicating disputes and exacting settlements. Metopia would benefit from an analogue to our court system, with coercive authority. Although complete contracts in many negotiations would be impossible to write because of unforeseen contingencies, Metopians vulnerable to deception would press for clarity on important matters. Explicit claims are more easily verified to third parties. Ambiguity and vagueness make enforcement problematic.

Warranties. Warranties are one type of contractual device that would be used in Metopia to handle matters that are not subject to ex ante verification.[13] Warranties can be used to add credibility to claims about the item under negotiation that cannot be reliably or cost-effectively assessed until after the deal is struck: "Defective products will be replaced or repaired at the manufacturer's expense." They also can be used to make explicit and reinforce promises of future performance: "If we ever fail to plow the snow from your driveway before 7 A.M., your full year's service contract is free."[14] They can even provide some assurance regarding settlement preferences: "If we sell this item to anyone at a lower price within six months, or if you can find another dealer who will beat our price on the item, we will pay you double the difference."[15] Metopians would use warranties to shift the risks inherent in a negotiation from the recipient of the warranty to the provider of the warranty.

It is not easy to write an enforceable and cost-effective warranty in Metopia. To be enforceable, it needs to clearly specify the conditions under which it applies, the remedies available to the recipient, and the process for bringing the remedies about. Otherwise, it invites costly and hard-to-resolve disputes between self-interested Metopians. Cost-effectiveness depends on the nature of the warranty's specific provisions, the ability and the incentives for the provider to make good, and tendencies for opportunistic behavior on the part of the recipient. For instance, a manufacturer's warranty that allows for replacement or repair only when a manufacturing defect is detected may not be very effective in cases where it is difficult to determine whether a discovered defect is due to poor manufacture or misuse of the product by the buyer. A warranty that requires that the product be returned in person to a remote regional service center for lengthy evaluation and repair could well make the transaction costs involved in seeking remedy under the warranty so high as to make its application a nonissue. Likewise, a product service contract offered by a company with limited financial resources and a significantly understaffed service department provides little value to the buyer. On the other hand, an unconditional warranty of consumer satisfaction that is easy to invoke and offers generous remedies (e.g., "satisfaction guaranteed or all your money back, no questions asked") is likely to create opportunistic behavior on the part of self-interested Metopian consumers. They will buy products, get some valuable use out of them, and then make warranty claims.

Despite these difficulties, Metopians would work hard to construct enforceable and cost-effective warranties to secure their transactions, provide credibility to their claims, and reduce incentives for opportunism. Nonetheless, at its heart, a warranty is just another promise. Its credibility in a Metopian world rests on the availability of other enforcement mechanisms and on reputation effects (to be discussed shortly).

Bonds. Promises, including warranties, often need further reinforcement to be credible. Even if the promisor makes the promise in good faith, incentives can change before the promise is carried out. How can the promisee be reasonably confident of performance? Another way to provide credibility to claims about future action is to put in place mechanisms that will reinforce the promisor's incentives for good faith ex ante and compliance ex post. This can be done by posting a bond.

Posting a bond involves doing something at the time the deal is struck that allows the other party or a third party to either exact a penalty from a negligent promisor or compensate the harmed promisee if the promise is not kept. The most common form of bonding mechanism is collateral. The promisor gives the promisee, in effect, a contingent claim on some of the promisor's assets. If the promise is not fulfilled, the assets revert to the promisee. In some cases, the promisee will hold the assets until the promise is fulfilled, but this need not be the case if a credible third party can enforce the asset transfer when nonperformance is verified.

What if the promisor does not have assets to compensate the promisee for nonperformance? One way of handling this would be through insurance schemes. An insurer would evaluate promisors and charge a premium based on the insurance company's assessment of the probabilities of default. The insurer would pool premiums from a number of promisors to provide enough funds for paying expected claims. Such a scheme would have to be constructed carefully to avoid the problems of adverse selection and moral hazard. Another alternative for dealing with the problem of limited assets is the use of hostages. The agreement can be reinforced as long as the promisor has assets that she values as much as noncompliance with the promise. Hostages are items of value to the promisor that may not have value to the promisee. The incentive for compliance is the threat to destroy or transfer the hostages.

Creating the right bonding agreement is also difficult in Metopia.[16] A bond that requires too little from the promisor will result in nonperformance. A bond that provides too much value to the promisee may lead to a false claim of nonperformance, especially if the promisee is holding the collateral. Even with independent parties adjudicating disputes, it will be difficult to get the incentives just right for all three parties. Much rests on the reputation of the third party and the clarity of conditions for nonperformance. Nonetheless, we would expect to find Metopians constructing a wide variety of bonding arrangements to offset the problems raised by incentives to deceive.[17]

Contractual mechanisms, such as warranties and bonds, have limited application. In some cases, it will be impossible for Metopians to contract on relevant future actions. One reason it may not be possible is that one party's action may be unobservable to the other. Hence, the party may make false claims about the nonobservable action. For example, a consultant may be hired to complete a project that has uncertain time requirements, promising to work hard to complete the project in the shortest possible time. If the consultant's effort is unobservable to the client, the consultant may have an incentive to renege on the promise of concerted effort. Likewise, a group sharing a common resource may agree to use the resource efficiently, but if the group cannot monitor individual use of the resource, individuals may overuse it. The difficulty of verifying compliance may make it impossible to write a contract that induces the efficient level of effort (Holmstrom, 1979). Even if it is possible to write a complete contract, it may prove too costly to enforce the contract, because the actions—while observable to the deceived party—may not be easily verified to the third party attempting to enforce the contract. Furthermore, the effective application of contractual mechanisms often requires an independent third party with the right incentives. Finally, these mechanisms can be costly. They can complicate contract writing, tie up assets that could be profitably used elsewhere, and divert value to third parties who must be paid. If not constructed with great care, these contractual mechanisms can create new incentives for deceptive behavior.

Reputation Effects

To supplement ex ante verification and contractual mechanisms, Metopians would need to rely on reputation effects to induce honesty.[18] A person's reputation affects future opportunities by influencing the other's belief about what the person will do in the future. A negotiator with a reputation for being deceitful is likely to be disadvantaged in future negotiations. She may have a hard time finding negotiating partners, and when she finds them, they will be on their guard. This is not because Metopians are morally offended by deceit. It is simply that negotiations tend to go better, other things being equal, when one is dealing with a person who has a reputation for honesty to maintain. Thus, when deciding to deceive, a Metopian negotiator must consider not only the short-run consequence of the decision, but also how the decision affects her reputation and hence future negotiations.

Adam Smith (1759, p. 350) was aware of the power of reputation, commenting, "The prudent man is always sincere, and feels horror at the very thought of exposing himself to the disgrace which attends upon the detection of falsehood." Smith overstates the case. An intelligent Metopian will know that some attempts at deception pose greater risks to one's reputation than others. Reputation works best when claims are explicit, ex post detection is likely, and information about deceptive practices can be credibly communicated to the culprit's future negotiating partners.

Reputations in Ongoing Negotiations Between Two Parties. The setting in which reputation is most likely to be effective is that of two parties, A and B, who negotiate repeatedly over time. Suppose both parties have an incentive to deceive if a particular negotiation is considered in isolation. The incentive problem in an isolated negotiation is captured by the prisoner's dilemma game.

Each cell in the matrix gives the payoffs to A and B as a function of their choices. In this highly stylized representation, both parties decide independently whether to adopt a negotiation strategy based on open and honest communication or a strategy of deception. If both are honest, they find a point on the Pareto frontier that is both equitable and efficient (each gets 2). If both deceive, equity is preserved but efficiency is sacrificed (each gets 1). Finally, if one deceives an honest person, the deceiver gets the maximum payoff (3) and the honest person gets the worst payoff (0). A Metopian in the one-shot negotiation would choose to deceive, since it is a dominant strategy: deception is the preferred choice regardless of what the other person does. But if the parties face each other repeatedly in subsequent negotiations, the incentives change.

To see how reputations can work in our example, imagine that after each negotiation, there is a probability p that the relationship will continue for at least one more period.[19] In such a setting, each party can adopt a reputational strategy that supports honest behavior, such as the following: "I will be open and honest so long as you reciprocate with honest behavior, but if ever you deceive me, I will be deceitful forever after." Such a harsh and unforgiving strategy (Friedman, 1971) will prompt honest behavior provided the long-run benefit from honest behavior exceeds the short-run benefit that can be gained by deceiving an honest party. Assuming B is following the strategy above, A can get 2 in each period by being honest; whereas deceit would result in a payoff of 3 in the current period and a payoff of 1 in all future periods. The payoff from honesty then is $2(I + p + p^2 + \ldots) = 2/(1 - p)$; the payoff from deceit is $3 + (p + p^2 + \ldots) = 3 + p^1 + (I - p)$. It is better to be honest than to deceive so long as $2/(1 - p) > 3 + p/(1 - p)$, or $p \geq 1/2$. So long as there is at least a 50 percent chance that the parties will meet again, they are able to support honest behavior. The short-run benefit from deceiving an honest party is insufficient compensation for destroying a reputation for honesty.[20]

This story relies on the assumption that deception is uncovered after each negotiation and before any further encounters. What if deceptions are only occasionally observed? Can we still motivate honesty as self-interested behavior?

		B's Choice	
		Honest	Deceive
A's Choice	Honest	2, 2	0, 3
	Deceive	3, 0	1, 1

The answer (and analysis) is roughly the same as before: honest behavior can be sustained provided it is sufficiently likely that the parties will meet again and it is not too unlikely that a deception will be observed. Suppose each deception is detected with probability d. Is honesty better than a one-period deception? Honesty yields 2 in every period for an expected payoff of $2/(1 - p)$, whereas a one-period deception results in 3 in the current period and then either 1 or 2 thereafter, depending on whether the deception was detected, resulting in an expected payoff of $3 + p(d/(1 - p) + (1 - d)2/(1 - p))]$. Simplifying, we find that honesty is better than deception, so long as $p \geq 1/(1 + d)$. If there is a 50 percent chance of detection, then there must be a two-thirds chance of meeting again: if there is a 10 percent chance of detection, the continuation probability must be at least 10/11.

More interesting is the case where only a noisy signal of deception is observed. Reputations can help in this situation of imperfect observability. However, some punishment must take place even if no one is actually deceptive. Since deception cannot be distinguished from bad luck, both bad luck and deception must be punished. This unjust punishment might offend moral sensibilities in the real world, but Metopians would freely use it if it worked. One possible strategy is as follows: "If it is sufficiently likely that you have been honest in the last period, I will be honest this period; otherwise, I won't trust you for the next several periods, and then will revert to honesty." For a given continuation probability and level of noise in the observations of honesty, it is possible to specify exactly what "sufficiently likely" and "several" must be in order to support honesty as an equilibrium with this strategy.[21] There is some efficiency loss, since punishments occasionally are called for. However, to the extent that the continuation probability is large and the noise in observing defections is small, the efficiency loss will be small as well.

Continuing relationships provide an effective environment for using reputations to deter deception. However, we should note one limitation of this analysis. It assumes that the continuation probability is a given. But in fact a party's decision whether to continue the relationship may depend on what happened in the past. If there is a particular negotiation with unusually large stakes, it might make sense for a Metopian negotiator to adopt a "take the money and run" strategy: deceive the other and then move on to other things. This is precisely the strategy used by a double agent engaged in espionage (Sobel, 1985). For a time, the spy must gain the confidence of her superior by supplying accurate information, but when the value of deception is highest, the spy will double-cross her superior and move on.

Reputations Where Only One Party Has a Continuing Market Presence. Our story so far requires that the parties in the negotiation continue to interact with each other for an indefinite period. This seems plausible in a number of situations, such as negotiations between a firm and a regular supplier or between a manager and her immediate subordinate, but there are numerous situations where only one party is likely to be susceptible to reputation effects. This happens when one party continues to play an active role in a market, but does so with many one-shot (or infrequent) negotiating partners. A retail car dealer is an example of what we call an enduring negotiating party. The typical car buyer does not make car purchases frequently enough to develop much of a reputation. The dealer, however, provides an enduring presence to which a reputation can adhere.

Do reputation effects still work to induce honesty in these Metopian negotiations? They do only if the party that endures is also the party with the greatest opportunities for deception, and there is an efficient mechanism for conveying information about the enduring party's reputation in a credible way to future negotiating partners. In such cases, the threat of losing a good reputation prevents the enduring party from exploiting the other.

What if there is also some risk of the non-enduring party engaging in deception. For instance, the car buyer might pay for the car with a bad check. In our example of a one-shot negotiation, modeled as a prisoner's dilemma, both parties are at risk—each may be deceived by the other—so both parties must endure if reputation effects are to inhibit deception. If only one party endures, then nothing is to stop the non-enduring party from deceiving the enduring party. As a defensive measure, the enduring party might be forced to be deceptive as well. However, this undesirable result can be avoided if we modify the example so that the non-enduring party moves first (or, equivalently, that the non-enduring party's behavior is verifiable ex ante). For instance, the car dealer would not deliver the car until the buyer's check cleared the bank. In this case, the enduring party B is facing a sequence $(A_1, A_2, \ldots, A_n, \ldots)$ of A parties. B is not at risk, since she can condition her action on A's choice. Although each A only participates in one negotiation, so she cannot develop a reputation, she does observe the previous outcomes of others dealing with B; hence, she can condition her behavior on what B has done in the past. The following strategy by each A party will support honest behavior provided the future is sufficiently valuable to B: "I will be honest, so long as you have never deceived a previous A person. Otherwise, I will not trust you."

As before, we can introduce complications such as providing the A parties with only a noisy signal of B's behavior. The result is the same as with two enduring parties: to the extent each A party can observe B's past actions and so long as the future is sufficiently important to B, B will want to maintain a reputation for honesty. As before, we make the assumption that whether a party endures is a given. In reality, an enduring party might choose to leave a business. In this case, there would be an incentive for deception in the final transactions, provided that the non-enduring parties were in the dark about this termination decision. A case of this sort was mentioned earlier: the computer company offering warranties on its machines, even though it is secretly planning to go out of business.

Reputations in One-Shot Negotiations. But what if neither party is likely to have a continued presence in a given negotiation market and the parties are likely to be negotiating together only a single time? This is the case of the principals in many civil litigation cases. Can reputations be used to reduce the incentive for deception? The answer is clearly no, if we cannot create something to carry the reputation, but often it is possible to create a reputation bearer.

Metopians might do this by hiring an enduring agent to perform the negotiation. Lawyers in a litigation case might serve this purpose. Even if the plaintiff and defendant are antagonistic adversaries, their lawyers may have established reputations for the efficient and equitable resolution of disputes. The lawyers' use of deceptive tactics is limited to the extent that such tactics would adversely affect their reputations. Similarly, when a firm hires an auditor to prepare a financial statement before a public stock offering, the firm is renting the reputation of the auditor to add credibility to the firm's statement to potential investors (Wilson, 1983). The firm cannot be trusted on its own, since deception would raise the proceeds from the offering. Hence, an auditor who maintains a valuable reputation for honest behavior is an essential ingredient of the transaction. In Metopia, we would expect to find a variety of reputational agents.

This strategy, however, is not always available. It may be difficult to motivate the agent to act in the principal's best interests. Divorce attorneys may be in an excellent position to settle rationally the dispute of an emotional and antagonistic couple, but if they are paid by the hour, their financial incentive may be to magnify the conflict. Alternatives such as a fixed-fee contract may not be feasible, since it exposes the attorneys to adverse selection (only the most time consuming conflicts may be submitted to an attorney for a fixed fee) and threatens the couple with moral hazard (the attorneys may shirk on their responsibility to find an efficient and fair settlement in favor of a quick settlement).

An alternative to the use of reputational agents when the parties to a negotiation are not likely to interact again is suggested by Kreps (1990). Suppose the party, A, that puts the other, B, at risk can buy a name that indicates honest behavior because past holders of the name have been honest. After buying the name, A decides whether to act honestly and then sells the name to another party. If the sale is delayed until A's honesty can be determined, the sale price of the name should depend on A's behavior. By acting honestly, A preserves the value of the name. Deceit would destroy the name's good reputation and hence its value. Viewing reputations as an asset that can be bought and sold enables the parties to make deals that require trust, even if they are involved in only a single negotiation. Of course, there are limits to this technique. It requires that the reputational names be protected and treated as property. Its effectiveness depends on the price of the name and on the probability that any deception would be detected before the name is sold. If the payoff from deception is too high relative to the cost and potential worth of the name, A will forfeit the investment in the name in favor of deception. It is important for B, the party at risk, to know how the name's value depends on A's behavior.

SUMMARY OF FACTORS AFFECTING DECEPTION IN METOPIA

Even in the self-centered world of Metopia, deception would be moderated by natural forces in a wide range of circumstances. To preserve fruitful transactions, Metopians will protect themselves (and their trading partners) from deception when they can do so in a cost-effective way. Since even the suspicion of deception can be harmful to potentially profitable negotiations, it is worthwhile for the negotiating parties to find means of reducing it.

Honesty, however, is not always the best policy by Metopian standards. Occasionally Metopians will be able to gain from deceptive tactics. Based on the analysis here, we would predict that in Metopia, other things equal, deception is more likely to be a problem when the following conditions hold:

- *Information asymmetry is great.* The greater the information disparity between the two parties, the more opportunity at least one of the parties has for profitable deception. Every negotiation involves some asymmetry. Each negotiator possesses some private information, such as information about her preferences or about her intentions to keep future commitments.

- *Verification is difficult.* Some questions, such as the physical condition of a simple, existing product, can be easily settled before the deal is consummated. Others, such as long-term maintenance costs for a new product, can only be confirmed afterward. And some, such as a party's reservation price, are difficult to ever confirm. Deception is more likely with matters that are most difficult to verify, such as the other party's preferences, their commitment to future actions, and long-term performance claims about the good under negotiation. Because it makes verification to a third-party difficult, deception is also more likely to occur when claims are made verbally without independent witnesses.

- *The intention to deceive is difficult to establish.* Deliberate deception is often hard to distinguish from a mistake or oversight. Deception is more likely when the deceiver has a plausible alternative explanation for her behavior. Deception about something one should clearly know is less likely than deception about matters for which one could innocently claim to be the victim of misinformation. Subtle forms of deception are more likely to occur than explicit lying. The use of negotiating agents may also make it difficult to detect intentional deception. The principal can claim that the deception was the result of poor communication or an unscrupulous negotiating agent who acted without authority. Finally, vague or sweeping claims that are open to alternative interpretations make it difficult to establish intentional deception. In such cases, a negotiator can more plausibly claim that she never meant to give a false impression.

- *The parties have insufficient resources to adequately safeguard against deception.*[22] Depending on the expected gains from the negotiation and the initial endowments of the negotiating parties, there will be limits on the resources available to protect the parties against deception. Warranties, collateral, hostages, and other insurance devices use up resources. They may be potentially useful but not sensible in transactions promising small gains. In larger, more risky transactions, the negotiators may have too few assets to create bonding devices sufficient to eliminate incentive problems.

- *Interaction between the parties is infrequent.* Deception is more likely in one-shot negotiations than in long-term relationships. The expectation of continued interaction provides negotiators with more time and a greater incentive to confirm the reliability of information provided or signaled by the other party. It also provides more opportunities for retaliation in future transactions.

- *Ex post redress is too costly.* If deception is uncovered after the deal is done, there may be means of seeking redress, either individually or through third parties. One could track down the offender and threaten harm unless adequate compensation is provided. Alternatively, one could take the offender to court. The deceived party may prefer such an effort, even when the costs of it exceed the expected compensation, if the action has enough reputation value. Aggressive action in one case may dissuade future negotiating partners from attempting deception. Sometimes, however, the costs and risks of seeking redress are too high,[23] even recognizing the reputation value. In other cases, such redress is not feasible because the deceived party has little leverage over the deceiver, the deceiver cannot easily be found, or the deception cannot be adequately demonstrated to a third party (a court or future negotiators).

- *Reputation information is unavailable, unreliable, or very costly to communicate.* When it is difficult to convey information about the past performance of negotiators, we can expect more deception. We should find less deception in small, close knit communities or in dense social networks than we do in large, loosely connected populations. Even in

Metopia, there may be situations in which handshake deals are possible, without formal contracting. We should also find less deception when there is a relatively low cost system for collecting and transmitting reputation information, such as a Better Business Bureau.

- *The circumstances are unusual in a way that limits inferences about future behavior.* Some instances of deception are unlikely to damage future negotiations because they occur in distinctly different circumstances. The question is whether future negotiating partners would regard a particular act of deception as relevant to predicting behavior in negotiations with them. For instance, deception in a game setting, such as bluffing in poker, may not be thought to have any bearing on expectations of behavior outside the game setting. Deception of an enemy or of an outsider may not affect negotiations with a friend or an insider.

- *One party has little to lose (or much to gain) from attempting deception.* The mechanisms discussed so far work only when each negotiator has expectations of a continuing economic life, places reasonably high value on future economic success, and has a reputation to protect. However, in some circumstances, a negotiator may not be concerned about the prospects of being caught at deception, provided she is not caught until after the deal is closed. The negotiator may have a reputation that is so bad that further deception would not hurt it. She may have a high discount rate, placing a low value on future transactions. She may be in desperate straits. Or the payoff from this one negotiation may be sufficiently high.

These above conditions represent rough guidelines about when Metopians have greater incentives for profitable deception. Whether to attempt deception in a given situation requires a complex assessment of expected costs, benefits, and risks.

REAL-WORLD DIFFERENCES

We have offered some specific hypotheses about incentives for deception in Metopia. To what extent do our findings about Metopia extend to the world we know? Human nature is not so simple or uniform as that of the Metopians:[24]

- *People are not as self-centered as Metopians.* They are capable of a wide range of sentiments and commitments not available to Metopians. Some of these sentiments work to promote honesty; others encourage more deception.

People often care about others. Most people have some benevolent motivations and ethical commitments. Individuals have sympathy for the pains of others and take pleasure in others' well-being. However, this care does not typically extend to all of humankind, but only to a referent group (Hirschleifer, 1982). The size and nature of that group vary significantly from person to person. The care also varies in intensity, depending on such things as the closeness of the relationship with the other person. In addition to this passive care for others, people care about how they affect others (Arrow, 1974). They generally do not want to cause harm, and do want to cause pleasure or satisfaction. Individuals typically do not want to benefit from the misfortune of others, even when they have not caused the misfortune (Nagel, 1975).

Beyond concerns about the welfare of others, most have internalized rules of behavior so that they feel pangs of conscience, guilt, or shame when they resort to certain objectionable behaviors such as deception. They have preferences about how they act as well as preferences about the results of their actions. Many take pride in their sense of personal integrity. They take offense at any suggestion that they are not trustworthy. On a social level, people feel and express moral approbation and disapprobation about the behavior of others, even when the other's behavior is not a direct threat to them. They are willing to incur costs to shame, ostracize, and punish others who engage in questionable behavior.

On the other hand, people also have preferences that may encourage deception. Benevolence and moral commitments typically have limits. People are concerned about their own well-being and generally place more weight on their own welfare than on that of others. Furthermore, people tend to be competitive. Relative standing matters. People want to win, to do better than their peers. The harm they are willing to commit on their way to winning may be limited—each will draw the line somewhere—but many are willing to cause harm to have an advantage. For many people, moral commitments are contingent upon a belief that others share the same commitments. Many individuals, especially in competitive settings, are moral pragmatists, willing to do their part, but concerned not to be taken as a sucker or a fool. At the extreme, some people actually appear to take pleasure in harming other parties in a negotiation. People can carry grudges and vendettas beyond reason. They are capable of malevolence and spite. Some even take a particular pleasure in successful deception. The evidence for this is the large number of games where bluffing and deception play a role in the enjoyment of the game and in determining success. Some individuals carry the thrill of fooling others out of the game setting into other more serious negotiations.

- *People are not as smart as Metopians.* Individuals in the real world vary more in their ability to make rational calculations. None reaches the level of intelligence found in Metopians. Consequently, people are more likely to make mistakes in reasoning about the costs and benefits of deception. Some opportunities for self-interested deception will be missed as a result of such mistakes. Also, because of the common affliction of myopia, the bias toward clear short-term gains, some individuals will see opportunities for deception even when they would disappear with a longer view. Hume (1751) identified the risk of opportunism by frail humans. Of those who attempt to selectively use deception only when it appears to be in their self-interest, he says, "While they purpose to cheat with moderation and secrecy, a tempting incident occurs, nature is frail, and they give into the snare, whence they can never extricate themselves, without total loss of reputation, and the forfeiture of all future trust and confidence with mankind." Hume identifies a real risk, but exaggerates the repercussions of getting caught in a deception. As Bhide and Stevenson (1990, p. 129) observe, "Even unreconstructed scoundrels are tolerated in our world as long as they have something else to offer."

Because of the limits of human rationality and intelligence, judgments of trust may be made hastily, without adequate supporting evidence. In some cases, individuals will not appreciate the powerful incentives for deception. As a result, individuals may be gullible and believe others when it would be more reasonable to discount their claims. This opens the door to more deception. However, sometimes people err in the other direction and exhibit more distrust than is rational. Bad experience in a negotiation can make people cynical about the trustworthiness of others. They may ignore the structural differences from one negotiation to the next, irrationally distrusting the other party regardless of the incentives. Such a person is likely to overinvest in protective measures.

What can we conclude from these differences? The main lessons can be summarized briefly. In the real world, mutual benevolence, moral commitment, and mutual trust are available as tools for promoting honesty in negotiations. However, there is so much variation in individual moral attitudes, characters, and abilities that it is hard to develop strategies for promoting honesty that are robust. People do not wear their characters on their sleeves. Negotiators often face significant uncertainty about the trustworthiness of the party on the other side of the table. The chances for honesty depend not only on the structural conditions that permit self-interested deception in Metopia, but also on the psychological forces in individuals and in the communities in which they live. A benevolent person supported by a community that reinforces that benevolence is less likely to engage in opportunistic deception than a Metopian would be. A more competitive person from a community of competitive persons is more likely to be deceptive. In either case, how the individual behaves may be a function of that individual's attitudes toward and expectations of the other party in the negotiation.

Despite the differences, we believe that the Metopian model presents a useful starting point for thinking about the problem of deception in real-world negotiations. Self-interest plays an important role in the real-world. Reputation, verification, and contractual mechanisms are viable means of reducing the inefficiencies caused by deception and providing a basis for trust.

PROMOTING HONESTY IN NEGOTIATION

Given that deception is a regrettable feature of negotiations, both morally and practically, what can be done by ethically concerned people to promote more honesty? Before describing individual strategies, it is useful to review how existing institutional arrangements work to support honesty.

SOCIAL AND INSTITUTIONAL SUPPORT

Those who think social engineering for ethics is unwise or unnecessary should reflect on the many institutions (public and private) that already exist with this end in mind. Many of the mechanisms that we noticed in Metopia are part of standard practice in the real world.[25] Individuals deciding on strategies for promoting honesty should be aware of the support mechanisms already in place to promote honesty and trust. This is not to say that further institutional improvement is impossible. Something may be learned by reflecting on the strengths and weaknesses of existing mechanisms. Entrepreneurial extensions and innovations (both in the public and private sectors) may be possible.

Legal and Regulatory Protection

The most obvious social support mechanism is government enforcement of norms. Not only do we have civil and criminal law, but we have in this country elaborate regulatory mechanisms. Regulators not only set rules, but also do the research that individual consumers could ill afford. Examples of legal and regulatory protections are numerous. On the federal level, they range from the effort of the Federal Trade Commission to control deceptive advertising, to the Food and Drug Administration to screen medications before they can be sold to the public, and the National Labor Relations Board to adjudicate disputes between business and organized labor. State governments, for instance, enact "lemon" laws to protect car buyers and seller disclosure requirements to protect house buyers. One can debate the effectiveness and efficiency of any of these mechanisms, but they are clearly intended to help reduce deception in the marketplace.

In commercial negotiations, contract law is an important source of support for policing deception in negotiation. Negotiators should understand potential legal remedies and protections relevant to their negotiations. They are more extensive than many negotiators realize.[26] Unfortunately, the civil law is a rather blunt instrument for the enforcement of norms. For it to be effective, negotiators need to be aware of its provisions, the deceptive behavior needs to be verifiable in a court of law, and the parties must be willing to spend the resources (time and money) to seek remedies.

In addition to governmental regulation and adjudication, industries often have their own regulatory mechanisms. Sometimes it is in the interest of an industry to provide assurance of honorable dealings with its customers, suppliers, employees, and the communities in which it does business. For instance, in the securities industry, a form of arbitration is used to settle disputes between brokers and their clients. A negotiator should know whether any relevant industry regulations or dispute resolution procedures apply.

Institutional Sources of Reputational Information

In addition to formal adjudication mechanisms and regulatory agencies, negotiators may have access to formal sources of reputational information. Two prominent examples of this are better business bureaus and credit rating bureaus. Better business bureaus keep records of customer complaints and can provide this information to potential customers. Credit rating bureaus provide information on past payment performance of individuals. Negotiators also can gain access to legal and news databases that contain information on prior legal actions against the other party. These and other reputational databases may help negotiators decide with whom to do business. With information technology advancing, the costs of maintaining reputational databases should decline, and their use should increase.

These institutionalized reputational databases are controversial. Questions have been raised about the completeness and accuracy of the information they dispense. Reputations may be unfairly ruined. Parties whose reputations are threatened may not be given a fair opportunity to rebut the allegations or to make a case for extenuating circumstances. These databases may provide inaccurate, thin, or inappropriate information. The challenge for these sources is to maintain the integrity of their information. The challenge for users is to keep in mind that the information is imperfect.

Independent Rating and Evaluation Services

There have arisen several private organizations that test products, survey consumers, rate company performance, and provide other information to potential buyers. These organizations capitalize on the economies of scale associated with product and service evaluation. By serving a large customer base, they can afford to engage in research that would be too costly for an individual.

One such organization is Consumers Union, the publisher of *Consumer Reports* magazine. This organization evaluates products and services offered to consumers and makes the information available in its publications. Among other things, it provides information on dealer costs for new cars, price ranges for used cars, and information on the reliability and maintenance costs of various makes. Customers can use this information to make inferences about a car dealer's reservation price or to challenge any misleading assertions about the reliability of the car. Because Consumers Union is independent of manufacturers, it has credibility with buyers that manufacturers making quality claims about their own products would not have. Other examples of this sort of service are J. D. Power and Associates' customer satisfaction indexes, Lipper Analytical Services' mutual fund rating service, Underwriters Laboratory's certification of electrical safety, Moody's and Standard and Poor's bond ratings, and A. M. Best's ratings of the financial strength of insurance companies. By providing an independent source of hard-to-get information, these organizations make it difficult for sellers to deceive about product quality, company financial strength, or the satisfaction of previous customers. Sometimes independent evaluators will even provide guarantees, as with the Good Housekeeping Seal of Approval. Of course, these services work most effectively in large markets. For many commercial negotiations, sufficient economics of scale are not present to justify the creation of such an organization.

Third-Party Professionals

Negotiators often have access to professionals to assist in specific negotiations. They may be used to act as reputational agents, assess important facts, or arbitrate disputes. Industries that are organized in part for this role include lawyers, accountants, arbitrators, investment bankers, and engineers. The challenge in using third parties is in assessing their qualifications and aligning their incentives properly.

Professional associations often have mechanisms for improving information and incentives, thereby reducing the risk to the buyer of third-party services. For instance, lawyers have strong norms to faithfully represent their clients' interests. These norms are supported by codes of ethics, which are enforced by the state's bar association. The bar also sets minimum quality standards.

Standardized Contractual Mechanisms

Norms are also established in certain industries to provide standard protections that go beyond legal requirements. Products and (increasingly) services often come with warranties. The use of collateral to secure certain types of loans against repayment risks is also a common institutionalized practice.

Affiliations and Credentials

It is also common in some industries for individual businesses to join together under a common name or to purchase the rights to use a name for reputational purposes. Sears sells the use of its name to building contractors who install fencing, aluminum siding, and other home improvements. Consumers who trust Sears and believe Sears stands behind the contractor's work may be more willing to trust a Sears affiliated contractor than an independent contractor with whom they will deal only once. In industries with many independent practitioners, industry associations can play a similar role. They provide members with a certification of credibility. Examples include Chartered Life Underwriter, Certified Financial Planner, and Certified Public Accountant. These designations assist consumers in evaluating the level of professional expertise, and perhaps the ethics of practitioners. Even when a specific designation or certification process is not involved, affiliation with a reputable industry group, such as the Better Business Bureau or Chamber of Commerce, may provide some sense of trustworthiness.

Society has been remarkably creative in developing mechanisms to promote honesty and secure business transactions from the risks of deception. However, these institutional safeguards are not present, nor are they effective, in all arenas of negotiation. Sometimes individual negotiators have to develop strategies for promoting honesty and for protecting themselves from opportunism.

Notes

1. For a description of a variety of deceptive practices in everyday business, see Blumberg (1989).

2. For more argument on this point, see Dees and Cramton (1991).

3. We invoke a narrow notion of self-interest specifically to avoid two dangers inherent in broader notions. One danger is reflected in the meaningless conception of self-interest characterized by revealed preference theory, according to which even the most blatant self-sacrificial behavior is by definition self-interested. Sen (1977) exposes the weaknesses inherent in this definition. The other danger is that posed by some philosophers (see Kavka, 1984) who wish to broaden the notion of self-interest in a specific way so as to guarantee that ethical behavior is self-interested. Ethical behavior becomes its own reward. Both of these views trivialize real incentive problems.

PROMOTING HONESTY IN NEGOTIATION 133

4. For instance, an example of academic research in this vein is presented by Baiman and Lewis (1989), who conducted an experiment in which they found that although subjects exhibited some resistance to lying, modest monetary incentives were sufficient to overcome this resistance in a large number of cases.

5. This mutual trust perspective on morality in practice is developed further in Dees and Cramton (1991).

6. Although our definition is quite broad, it excludes unintended deception, even where that deception could be foreseen and prevented. Such deception raises interesting issues, but to discuss them would be a diversion from our main objective. For detailed treatments of some definitional complexities, see Chisholm and Feehan (1977) and Fried (1978).

7. Some would suggest that honesty requires the disclosure of all relevant information, even when withholding that information would not qualify as deception on our account. We prefer to distinguish between honesty (the absence of deliberate deception) and candor (complete openness). For simplicity of analysis, we choose to focus on the former.

8. This may seem problematic, because the standard assumptions of game theory imply that deception is never successful. Game theory assumes that the agents are intelligent and rational. As a result, agents recognize when deception is in another's self-interest and are not misled. By not allowing gullible negotiators, we understate the incentives to deceive. Nonetheless, game theory provides a rigorous and consistent framework for thinking about incentive problems.

9. For simplicity, we speak of one party having information that could be concealed, misrepresented, or truthfully shared. Technically, however, deception can occur even when the deceiver has no private information. It is enough that the other party to the negotiation believes that the first party has valuable private information.

10. This latter strategy is effective on issues where one party expects a conflict of interest when none exists. In a study of experienced and naive negotiators, Thompson (1990, p. 88) found that successful, experienced bargainers disguised their compatible interests to feign "making a concession for the purpose of gaining on another issue."

11. This is a rough statement of a theorem due to Myerson and Satterthwaite (1983). Cramton, Gibbons, and Klemperer (1987) show how the theorem depends on the distribution of the ownership rights when many parties share ownership. For an analysis of the inefficiencies caused by private information in dynamic bargaining models, see, for example, Cramton (1992). Kennan and Wilson (1993) provide a survey of the literature on bargaining with private information.

12. For now, we set aside the problem of contracting with these third parties in Metopia. In order to assure the reliability of a third-party verifier, Metopian negotiators would have to use the same mechanisms that they use for promoting honesty in their primary negotiations.

13. Under the broad heading of warranties, we are including any promise to make an adjustment to the terms of exchange (provide a full or partial refund, repair or

replace a product, etc.) based on what happens after the deal is consummated. This includes warranties against defects, performance guarantees, guarantees of satisfaction, price guarantees, and cancellation or refund policies.

14. For a discussion of the value of service guarantees, see Heskett, Sasser, and Hart (1990).

15. It should be noted that price guarantees can have the effect of reducing price competition rather than assuring low prices.

16. See Kronman (1985) for a discussion of the limitations of these devices in the absence of third-party enforcement. Though we allow a role for third parties, the basic structure of his arguments still applies.

17. We do not mean to suggest that warranties and bonds only serve to reduce incentives for deception. Even with universal due diligence and good faith, some uncertainties will remain in most negotiating contexts. These devices can be used to provide for a more efficient allocation of the associated risk.

18. See Fudenberg (1992) and Pearce (1992) for surveys of reputational models in game theory.

19. Alternatively, p could denote the discount factor in an infinitely repeated game or more generally the product of the discount factor and the continuation probability. In all cases, the analysis is the same.

20. More forgiving punishments, such as tit-for-tat (see Axelrod, 1984), work as well. Indeed, so long as the continuation probability is more than 5,090, assuming detection is certain, tit-for-tat sustains honest behavior, since $2 + 2p \geq 3 + 0p$ for all $p \geq 1/2$. Dixit and Nalebuff (1991) suggest an even more forgiving strategy that takes into account the goodwill that might build up over time. In gaming experiments, Deutsch (1973) found that a defensive but nonpunitive strategy could be quite effective in inducing cooperation.

21. See Porter (1983) for a detailed analysis of this strategy or Abreu, Pearce, and Stacchetti (1986) for an analysis of the optimal collusive strategy.

22. For a more general discussion of limited transaction resources in the context of contract law, see Maser and Coleman (1989).

23. See Maser and Coleman (1989) for a discussion of the costs and risks of third-party intervention.

24. Several of the differences we discuss are in Etzioni (1988).

25. We concentrate here on secular mechanisms relevant to all in our pluralistic society. However, we would be remiss if we failed to note the importance of religion in inspiring and reinforcing the moral conduct of many individuals. Religion often relies not only on inspiration and moral exhortation but also on powerful incentive systems, including monitoring of behavior by an all-knowing third party. For a discussion of the importance of moral retribution in religion, see Green (1988).

26. See Shell (1991a, 1991b) and Farnsworth (1987) for discussions of the extent to which contract law applies to opportunism and fair dealing in the precontractual stages of negotiation.

References

Abreu, D., Pearce, D., and Stacchetti, E. "Optimal Cartel Equilibria with Imperfect Monitoring." *Journal of Economic Theory,* 1986, *39,* 251–269.

Akerlof, G. A. "The Market for 'Lemons': Quality Uncertainty and the Market Mechanism." *Quarterly Journal of Economics,* 1970, *84,* 488–500.

Arrow, K. J. "Gifts and Exchanges." *Philosophy and Public Affairs,* 1974, *1,* 343–362.

Axelrod, R. *The Evolution of Cooperation.* New York: Basic Books, 1984.

Baiman, S., and Lewis, B. "An Experiment Testing the Behavioral Equivalence of Strategically Equivalent Employment Contracts." *Journal of Accounting Research,* 1989, *27,* 1–20.

Bhide, A., and Stevenson, H. H. "Why Be Honest If Honesty Doesn't Pay." *Harvard Business Review,* Sept.–Oct. 1990, pp. 121–129.

Blumberg, P. *The Predatory Society: Deception in the American Marketplace.* New York: Oxford University Press, 1989.

Boatright, J. R. "Morality in Practice: Dees, Cramton, and Brer Rabbit on a Problem of Applied Ethics." *Business Ethics Quarterly,* 1992, *2,* 63–73.

Carr, A. Z. "Is Business Bluffing Ethical?" *Harvard Business Review,* Jan.–Feb. 1968, pp. 143–159.

Chisholm, R., and Feehan, T. D. "The Intent to Deceive." *Journal of Philosophy,* 1977, *74,* 143–159.

Cramton, P., Gibbons, R., and Klemperer, P. "Dissolving a Partnership Efficiently." *Econometrica,* 1987, *55,* 615–632.

Cramton, P. C. "Strategic Delay in Bargaining with Two-Sided Uncertainty." *Review of Economic Studies,* 1992, *59,* 205–225.

Dees, J. G., and Cramton, P. C. "Shrewd Bargaining on the Moral Frontier: Toward a Theory of Morality in Practice." *Business Ethics Quarterly,* 1991, *1,* 135–167.

Deutsch, M. *The Resolution of Conflict: Constructive and Destructive Processes.* New Haven, Conn.: Yale University Press, 1973.

Dixit, A. K., and Nalebuff, B. J. *Thinking Strategically: The Competitive Edge in Business, Politics, and Everyday Life.* New York: Norton, 1991.

Etzioni, A. *The Moral Dimension: Toward a New Economics.* New York: Free Press, 1988.

Farnsworth, E. A. "Precontractual Liability and Preliminary Agreements: Fair Dealing and Failed Negotiations." *Columbia Law Review,* 1987, *87,* 218–293.

Fried, C. *Right and Wrong.* Cambridge, Mass.: Harvard University Press, 1978.

Friedman, J. W. "A Noncooperative Equilibrium for Supergames." *Review of Economic Studies,* 1971, *38,* 1–12.

Fudenberg, D. "Explaining Cooperation and Commitment in Repeated Games." In J. J. Laffont (ed.), *Advances in Economic Theory: Sixth World Congress.* Cambridge: Cambridge University Press, 1992.

Green, R. M. *Religion and Moral Reason: A New Method for Comparative Study.* New York: Oxford University Press, 1988.

Heskett, J. L., Sasser, W. E., Jr., and Christopher, W. L. *Service Breakthroughs: Changing the Rules of the Game.* New York: Free Press, 1990.

Hirschleifer, J. "Evolutionary Models in Economics and Law: Cooperation Versus Conflict Strategies." In P. H. Rubin and R. O. Zerbe, Jr. (eds.), *Research in Law and Economics,* 4. Greenwich, Conn.: JAI Press, 1982.

Holmstrom, B. "Moral Hazard and Observability." *Bell Journal of Economics,* 1979, *10,* 74–91.

Hume, D. *An Enquiry Concerning the Principles of Morals.* Oxford: Clarendon Press, 1975. (Originally published 1751.)

Kavka, G. S. "The Reconciliation Project." In D. Copp and D. Zimmerman (eds.), *Morality, Reason, and Truth.* Lanham, Md.: Rowman and Allanheld, 1984.

Kennan, J., and Wilson, R. "Bargaining with Private Information." *Journal of Economic Literature,* 1993, *31,* 45–104.

Kreps, D. M. "Corporate Culture and Economic Theory." In J. Alt and K. Shepsle (eds.), *Perspectives on Positive Political Economy.* Cambridge: Cambridge University Press, 1990.

Kronman, A. T. "Contract Law and the State of Nature." *Journal of Law, Economics, and Organization,* 1985, *1,* 5–32.

Maser, S. M., and Coleman, J. L. "A Bargaining Theory Approach to Default Provisions and Disclosure Rules in Contract Law." *Harvard Journal of Law and Public Policy,* 1989, *12,* 637–709.

Myerson, R. B., and Satterthwaite, M. A. "Efficient Mechanisms for Bilateral Trading." *Journal of Economic Theory,* 1983, *28,* 265–281.

Nagel, T. "Comment." In E. S. Phelps (ed.), *Altruism, Morality, and Economic Theory.* New York: Russell Sage Foundation, 1975.

Pearce, D. "Repeated Games: Cooperation and Rationality." In J. J. Laffont (ed.), *Advances in Economic Theory: Sixth World Congress.* Cambridge: Cambridge University Press, 1992.

Porter, R. H. "Optimal Cartel Trigger Price Strategies." *Journal of Economic Theory,* 1983, *29,* 313–338.

Sen, A. "Rational Fools: A Critique of the Behavioural Foundations of Economic Theory." *Philosophy and Public Affairs,* 1977, *6,* 317–344.

Shell, G. R. "Opportunism and Trust in the Negotiation of Commercial Contracts: Toward a New Cause of Action." *Vanderbilt Law Review,* 1991a, *44,* 221–282.

Shell, G. R. "When Is It Legal to Lie in Negotiations?" *Sloan Management Review,* Spring 1991b, 93–101.

Smith, A. *The Theory of Moral Sentiments.* Indianapolis: Liberty Classics, 1976. (Originally published 1759.)

Sobel, J. "A Theory of Credibility." *Review of Economic Studies,* 1985, *52,* 557–574.

Thompson, L. "An Examination of Naive and Experienced Negotiators." *Journal of Personality and Social Psychology,* 1990, *59,* 82–90.

White, J. J. "Machiavelli and the Bar: Ethical Limitations on Lying in Negotiation." *American Bar Foundation Research Journal,* 1980, *4,* 926–934.

Wilson, R. "Auditing: Perspectives from Multiperson Decision Theory." *Accounting Review,* 1983, *58,* 305–318.

CHAPTER TEN

On the Ethics of Deception in Negotiation

Alan Strudler

The truth can get in the way of a good deal. So many people lie, dissimulate, and otherwise fail to tell the truth in negotiation.[1] In this paper I will focus on the case of deception about "reservation price," that is, a person's bottom-line price, the price such that she would walk away from a negotiation rather than accept a worse price. I will maintain that despite the commonsense moral presumption against deception more generally, some deception in negotiation, including lies about one's reservation price, may be morally acceptable. When things go well, such deception is a signaling and symbolic device that even strangers, people who neither know nor trust one another, can use to work their way to a reasonable and mutually advantageous agreement in an otherwise risky environment.[2] In some circumstances, I will maintain, one may lie in negotiation without incurring a reason to feel moral regret or embarrassment. I will also maintain that these circumstances are quite limited in scope. By explaining why deception about one's reservation price may be acceptable in negotiation, I hope to improve the prospects for understanding why deception about material facts is wrong.

A good deal of empirical evidence suggests that ordinarily, a bargaining opponent's perception of one's reservation price serves to anchor her expectations

---

For helpful comments, I thank David Wasserman, Michael Slote, Jim Kuhn, Eric Dietrich, Greg Dees, Tom Carson, and the members of an audience at the Wharton School. The usual disclaimers apply.

about the negotiation's outcome (Carnevale and Pruitt, 1992; Raiffa, 1982). Other things being equal, it is therefore in the seller's interest to convey a high reservation price and in the buyer's interest to convey a low one.[3] Suppose, then, that I am buying a new car and wish to sell my old car, for which I have found a potential buyer, Jane. Suppose, also, that the least I could reasonably take for it, and hence my reservation price, is $5,000; anything less, I would be better off trading the car in. If I convince Jane that my reservation price is $5,500 rather than $5,000, then she is likely to make me a better offer than she would if she believed that my reservation price were $5,000. Lying may help achieve this effect. It follows, of course, that if I, as seller, tell the truth about my modest reservation price, and Jane, as buyer, lies about hers, I increase the risk of coming out behind. This hardly seems an attractive consequence of honesty. The question thus presents itself why I should put myself at this gross disadvantage. When, if ever, may I lie or otherwise engage in deception about my reservation price?

Several recent writers look to the ethics of self-defense as a model for understanding the ethics of deception in negotiation (Carson, 1993; Dees and Cramton, 1991). Their idea, very crudely put, is that deception in negotiation is best understood in terms of a person's right to defend herself against the possibility of wrongful or potentially harmful conduct by her bargaining opponent. I will argue that focus on the norms of self-defense makes much negotiation seem far too sleazy. Without suggesting that negotiation may typically be understood in purely cooperative terms, I will argue that appeal to norms of self-defense gets perverse results in cases where deception in negotiation seems otherwise morally acceptable. When deception in negotiation makes sense, it is ordinarily not as a way of fending off a prospective attacker or wrongdoer, but instead because of its promise as a mutually beneficial solution to a problem confronted by negotiators who, for morally benign reasons, cannot trust each other. Ordinarily deception is wrong because of the way that it harms the deceived or interferes with access to information essential to autonomous choice-making. Deception in negotiation, in certain contexts, I will suggest, will be wrong in neither of these ways.

A STRATEGY OF SELF-DEFENSE

As a historical matter, one strange example, which seems on the surface removed from problems in negotiation, has proved an attractive target for moral philosophers and casuists interested in self-defense: the case of deceiving a prospective murderer about the whereabouts of his intended victim. Not surprisingly, several philosophers agree that it is acceptable to deceive a murderer because, as a person who would use the truth toward an evil end, he has no right to the truth (see Sedgwick, 1991; Vuillemin, 1982; Chisholm and Feehan, 1977). This view may be regarded as expressing the idea that wrongdoers such as murderers or liars, by virtue of their wrongdoing forfeit or waive some of their rights to be treated as we treat innocent persons.

Even though murder is so plainly a worse evil than anything at issue in a run-of-the-mill business negotiation, the analogy may be tempting. If one may deceive to prevent murder, perhaps one may also do so to defend against lesser wrongs. In cases where one confronts a bargaining foe who would deceive in order to gain an advantage for himself, for example, that foe threatens a wrong not as serious a matter as murder but a wrong nevertheless: his deception may serve to produce for him an unfair bargaining advantage. If you respond to this deception by deception of your own, this may remove his wrongful advantage. One might also regard the deceptive bargainer as by his action forfeiting or waiving certain rights to truthfulness that people ordinarily enjoy. Once a person forfeits or waives these rights, it may seem, we may deceive him if we wish.

Interpretations of deception in negotiation as a defensive strategy have been developed recently in insightful pieces by Carson (1993) and by Dees and Cramton (1991). These authors, I think, cover the most promising candidates for the self-defensive interpretation of deception, and examining the strengths and weaknesses of these interpretations will make it plainer what we should expect from an interpretation of deception that does not rely on the norms of self-defense. In the remainder of this section, I focus on the arguments by Dees and Cramton; in the subsequent section, I consider Carson's argument; in the final section, I develop the elements of an alternative interpretation of deception in negotiation.

Dees and Cramton (1991) are concerned with the norms that underlie "defensive dishonesty" in negotiation (p. 148). They emphasize that in negotiation, people seek ways to limit their exposure to the risk that a bargaining opponent will exploit information about settlement preferences to gain strategic advantage, and argue the dishonesty is an accepted tactic for defending oneself against a potentially dishonest bargaining opponent.

On the basis of their own observations of practitioners from the business and legal communities, Dees and Cramton claim to have identified the following norm, which they maintain guides decisions of practitioners about when to deceive in negotiation: *"Mutual Trust Principle:* It is unfair to require an individual to take a significant risk or incur significant cost out of respect for the moral rights of others, if that individual has no reasonable grounds for trusting that the relevant others will (or would) take the same risk or make the same sacrifice" (1991, p. 144).[4]

How does the Mutual Trust Principle apply to cases of deception in negotiation? Return to the negotiation over the sale of my car. As far as I know, Jane may lie to me about her reservation price; hence I lack reasonable grounds to trust Jane to take the risk of telling me the truth about her reservation price. The conditional clause in the Mutual Trust Principle (the clause which begins, "if that individual has no reasonable grounds") is therefore satisfied. It follows, according to the consequent clause in the principle (which begins, "It is unfair to require an individual to take a significant risk"), that it is unfair to require me to take a risk out of respect for the rights of Jane. The relevant risk here is that which I would undertake by not lying to Jane. Thus, the Mutual Trust Principle allows me to lie to Jane.

Dees and Cramton (1991) do not endorse the Mutual Trust Principle. In fact, a focus of their work is explaining how we may change the environment of negotiation so that we will trust one another more, and the principle will not apply. Nonetheless, Dees and Cramton believe that the Mutual Trust Principle provides a more realistic depiction of morality as it functions in practice than is provided by the more idealistic principles often advanced in business ethics writings.[5] They realize that the Mutual Trust Principle demands relatively little of people, but seem to think that the modesty of the principle is a constraint that writers in business ethics must accept if they want their work to be relevant to business practice.

How plausible is the Mutual Trust Principle? Not very. My skepticism about the principle applies not merely to its validity as part of a minimally decent conception of morality, but also to its relevance to an explanation of ordinary business conduct. The principle seems to allow one to do anything to one's opponent, no matter how horrible, so long as one thinks that the opponent will do the same horrible thing. Even if it is unreasonable to expect business practitioners (or professors) to behave like saints, I think it also unreasonable to suppose that their morality (or ours) ordinarily sinks quite this low.

Perhaps a fictional example will illustrate the implausibility of the Mutual Trust Principle. Suppose that Smith and Jones are competitors in the software industry. Each possesses a trade secret that the other wants. Smith is a scurrilous competitor who would do anything, perhaps even physically harm an opponent to get ahead. Suppose, now, that Jones thinks that he can get away beating Smith's secret out of him and that if he does not do so, he will not get Smith's secret. According to the Mutual Trust Principle, it seems that it would be acceptable for Jones to do so because Jones does not trust Smith to accept the risk of not beating the secret out of him: Jones reasonably believes that Smith cannot be trusted, that he would attack given the opportunity. Because the Mutual Trust Principle would license plainly vicious behavior such as this beating, it strikes me as unfair to practitioners to ascribe acceptance of the principle to them. (If you are bothered by the unrealistic character of the assault example, consider another: fraud, or lies about a material aspect of something being negotiated. Suppose you think that your bargaining opponent would lie to you about fundamental issues of the software you are negotiating about: then according to the Mutual Trust Principle, you may lie to her about these fundamental issues of quality. You may engage in material fraud. But plainly that is morally wrong, so the Mutual Trust Principle must be rejected.)

How would Dees and Cramton respond to the case of Smith and Jones? One possibility is that they would suggest that although the case confirms that the Mutual Trust Principle does not capture the conception of ideal morality which forms the subject matter of academic moral philosophy, it casts no doubt on the idea that the principle forms part of the pragmatic perspective of business and law that concerns them. It may seem hard to dispute these claims about the role of the Mutual Trust Principle as part of the practitioner's perspective, at least insofar as Dees and Cramton base them on observational evidence which they alone possess. If they claim to have simply "observed" people acting in accordance with the Mutual Trust Principle, and we were not at the scene when the observations occurred, we seem in a weak position to doubt the veracity of their perception. On the other hand, the "fact" that people act in accordance with the Mutual Trust Principle hardly seems like the sort of thing that one simply observes. Acceptance of principles is less something that one simply observes than it is a manner of explanation: one explains a particular set of behaviors by saying that people who behaved in that way probably do so because they embrace a set of principles. The question thus arises whether it might be plausible to ascribe acceptance of this principle to the practitioners with whom Dees and Cramton may have worked. It seems doubtful that any group of practitioners Dees and Cramton, professors at two of the nation's leading universities, are likely to encounter would be sympathetic to the idea that it is acceptable for Jones to beat Smith's secrets out of him. Because the Mutual Trust Principle endorses action that ordinary practitioners would find abhorrent, it is a mistake to attribute its acceptance to them.

The implausibility of the Mutual Trust Principle arises, then, not merely because the principle fails to conform to the philosopher's abstract conception of ideal morality but also because the principle is not realistic: it does not reflect the norms that practitioners embrace. One point of the Mutual Trust Principle is to enable Dees and Cramton to provide practitioners with advice that is more practically relevant than that which they receive from business ethics writers who embrace a more idealistic and less pragmatic perspective than do Dees and Cramton. Because the Mutual Trust Principle is at odds with even ordinary business morality, however, it is unclear why advice based on it should be practically valuable. If their prescriptions for practitioners assume the credibility of principles that practitioners reject, practitioners will not find their prescriptions cogent.

It seems safe to grant Dees and Cramton the idea that it is important to make the business environment more trustworthy. Nonetheless, we are left with hard problems about the ethics of deception in negotiation. These problems are confronted not merely by idealists and saints, but by ordinary people making practical decisions in the business world. When, if ever, is it acceptable to lie or otherwise deceive one's bargaining opponent? Practical advice on how to make deception less useful and therefore less tempting does not advance our understanding of how to act when deception is useful.

As Dees and Cramton suggest, the fact that another person cannot be trusted seems plainly relevant in deciding how one may, as a moral matter, behave toward him. How does the fact that a person cannot be trusted not to deceive you about his settlement preferences in negotiation bear on the issue of whether you deceive him regarding your settlement preferences?

The principle that Dees and Cramton consider, the Mutual Trust Principle, suggests that one may engage in an otherwise morally unacceptable action against another person merely because that person cannot be trusted not to engage in a similar action. I have urged that this principle is too permissive. The task remains of establishing the relevance of the fact that another person might deceive you in negotiating to questions of how you may treat him.

A MORE RESTRAINED STRATEGY OF SELF-DEFENSE

Thomas Carson (1993) suggests that deception in negotiation may be justified by appeal to principles of self-defense. When my bargaining opponent is mis-stating her settlement preferences and she will thereby harm me unless I deceive her, then I may deceive her. On Carson's view, defensive dishonesty is justified only when it is necessary to protect oneself against harmful deceptions of one's bargaining opponent. This emphasis on necessity is a traditional component in theories of self-defense.[6]

Carson's approach faces serious problems. One such problem, which he recognizes but too easily dismisses, is making sense of how the necessity requirement in self-defense can apply to cases of deception. It is not plain when, if ever, dishonesty is necessary in negotiation. In many negotiations, the necessity of deception must be assessed in light of the fact that one may withdraw from the deal by ending negotiations or taking one's business elsewhere: at times, one has acceptable alternatives to negotiation, and it seems that the defense of necessity would not apply, but it also seems acceptable to dissimulate about one's reservation price.

Suppose, for example, that I go to a flea market where I encounter a merchant Brown, who offers me a valuable watch at a reasonable price. I know that he has been selling the same watch to others for 20 percent less, and that I can, and I am expected to, bluff him down to the lower price. Like most other people who have bought a watch here, I can get a better price by lying about my own bottom-line price. Does the right to self-defense allow me to do so?

It seems clear that it is permissible to bluff Brown down by lying about my reservation price. But it is not clear that it is "necessary," in any sense to self-defense, for me to do so. As Carson acknowledges, sometimes there are alternative ways available to achieve the aim one is after in bargaining. One may walk away from the deal and take it up with someone else. Suppose that Green, the shopkeeper down the block, is selling the watch at a no-haggling fee of $100. Then I may just break off negotiation with Brown and buy the watch from the other shopkeeper at no significant added cost to myself. In that event, it hardly seems necessary to lie in order to get what I want. Now, as Carson correctly observes, in many cases a person may lack an acceptable alternative to carrying through with a negotiation. Union members involved in bargaining over a labor contract will standardly lack the option of breaking off talks and moving to a new employer, and even in many cases of negotiating over the price of a particular object like a vase, it may be unreasonably costly for a person to seek another person with whom to make a deal. One may not know that the object will be available elsewhere, or the costs of finding such an object may be high enough so that one reasonably refuses to bear them. Carson invokes cases of these sorts to suggest that the necessity requirement in self-defense can often be satisfied, and that self-defense therefore possesses significant explanatory value for cases of deception in negotiation. But I wish to maintain, first, that there are many cases where deception seems as legitimate as it ever does in negotiation, but where there is no necessity requirement, and second, that considerations of necessity aside, appeals to self-defense cannot capture the complexity of moral reasoning that occur when deception seems acceptable in negotiation.

Return to my negotiation with Brown over a watch. On the self-defense view, if I can lie about my bottom-line price, it is because doing so is necessary as a means of protecting myself. In the case as we are conceiving it, however, the necessity evaporates when I learn of Green's watch sale down the street. In a paradigmatic case of self-defense, my right of self-defense does not seem subject to these vicissitudes. Suppose, for example, that I catch somebody in the act of attempting to steal my priceless heirloom. I know that once he leaves my property, he will leave the country and I will never see the heirloom again, but that I can stop him and retrieve the property by using some force. My right of self-defense, which extends to personal property, allows me to use force—or at least the threat of it—to defend my rights in the property, and it does so in part because force is necessary in the circumstances. Suppose, now, that I discover that the use of force is no longer necessary because a policeman has arrived and is blocking the only escape path the thief might take. It is no longer necessary for me to use force. And I therefore have no right to do so. The case of deception in negotiation is quite different. Once I discover that the watch is for sale at a better price down the street, it does not end my right to make false statements about my bottom-line price. In deciding whether to bluff, I need not consider whether doing so is necessary to protect myself. Deception in negotiation does not seem like self-defense.

Another reason to deny that the right to engage in deception in negotiation can be understood in terms of the right of self-defense that arises from considering the broad scope of the right to self-defense. No doubt there are limits on what one can do in self-defense. One's self-defensive measure must be somehow proportional to the value of what one is defending. It is excessive to kill somebody to prevent him from stealing carrots from your garden, even if the only weapon that you have available is an anti-tank gun and thus the only way that you can defend your property is by killing the person against whom you wish to defend yourself. On the other hand, it seems clear that the right of self-defense allows you to use a variety of means to defend yourself; you are not restricted to defending yourself through the same means used by your attacker. If someone threatens you with force, you are not restricted to responding in-kind. You might instead defend yourself with lies. For example, if someone points a gun at you and says "Your money or your life," you need not make a similar threat to defend yourself. If your assailant is stupid and gullible, for example, you might defend yourself by falsely telling him that the police are about to arrive, or that you have no money, or some other falsehood. If self-defense indeed allows responses that are not in-kind and we are to understand the right to deceive as an instance of the right to self-defense, then there is no reason that one should be restricted when defending oneself against deception in negotiation to using deception. In particular, there is no reason that one might not defend oneself with force. Hence, if you confront a bargaining opponent who can read through your lies but who shrinks at the prospect of force, however minimal the force, it may be that the only way that you can defend yourself is by threatening force or perhaps even by using force against her. In principle you can, for example, use force—perhaps slapping or pinching your bargaining opponent—to get Brown to lower the price of the vase we encountered earlier at the flea market. In that event, if the right to deceive in negotiation may be understood in terms of the right of self-defense, it follows that you are permitted to use force, or at least the threat of it, against Brown, a plainly absurd result.[7]

IS DECEIT WRONG?

Carson (1993) asserts categorically,[8] as do Dees and Cramton (1991), that deception (particularly lying) in negotiation involves conduct which is at least prima facie wrong. Indeed, Dees and Cramton must regard deception in bargaining as more than prima facie wrong. They maintain that it is always regrettable (Cramton and Dees, 1993). It should follow, on their view, that the presumptive wrongness of deception is not something that can be wholly rebutted by self-defensive considerations such as those provided by the Mutual Trust Principle. Instead, even when a person has on balance good reasons to go forward with deception in negotiation, a trace of wrongness remains to taint her action, and this wrongness, it would seem, forms a basis for a person to regret her action. But I will suggest that no plausible case be made even for the prima facie wrongness of deception.[9]

Reasons to think that deception is presumptively wrong are naturally divided into three categories. First, deception may undermine trust; second, it may cause economic harm; and third, it may violate Kantian strictures against using a person as a mere means.

Consider, first, the argument from trust. It suggests that deception in negotiation is presumptively wrong because of its adverse impact on the prospects for trust; deception, one may argue, tends either to erode trust or to stand in the way of building trust. It strikes me that in many ordinary cases of negotiation, this argument from trust gets the causal arrow backward. Deception occurs because of a lack of trust and not vice versa. Recall the case with which we started my negotiation with Jane about the selling price of my car. When I say that I couldn't possibly sell the car for less than $5,000, it is because, at the start of our negotiation, I do not trust her with the truth about my selling price. Similarly, we may suppose, she does not trust me. Neither of us expects the other to tell the truth about price. Neither of us is taken by surprise by the fact that the other is exaggerating about price. It might be, however, that if each told the other about our reservation prices, that would enhance the trust we feel for each other. But not necessarily. In his outstanding book on negotiation, Howard Raiffa (1982) advises people that not even after a successful negotiation, one should not tell the other party about one's reservation price. The implication is that such information will only be a source of resentment. A person will be happier not knowing exactly how much better the negotiation might have gone for his side. If explicit information about reservation price causes resentment, it might also detract from the environment of trust. In any case, it seems plain, that as a matter of fact, there are ways, other than truthfulness about reservation price, to enhance trust.

After we get through the initial ritual of exaggeration and settle down to business, we may demonstrate to each other the reliability of character that will form the basis of trust. Whether or not deception in negotiation erodes trust is, I will suggest, an empirical question. Its answer depends on what happens, as a matter of fact, after the deception occurs. When deception occurs as a predictable part of a process that solves a recalcitrant problem confronted by the parties to a negotiation, it seems at least possible that it will enhance rather than erode trust: deception may be a mutually advantageous tool. Indeed, I will later argue that when deception in negotiation is acceptable, it is precisely because it plays this kind of constructive role.

How about the argument from economic harm? It suggests that deception is presumptively wrong because of the harm it causes. I think it helpful to distinguish between two interpretations of this argument. The first interpretation appeals to losses sustained as a result of deception; the second appeals to benefits missed as a result of deception. Consider, now, the interpretation in terms of losses sustained. Because these losses are hard to measure, this argument is hard to assess. It may help to consider it in the more concrete context of the negotiation between Jane and me regarding the sale of my car. One might regard the negotiation as wasteful because our bickering about prices (our initial offers) that neither of us take seriously wastes our time. If we imagine that Jane and I are both handsomely paid people, this waste of time would be economically costly. Or perhaps more seriously, if we imagine that negotiators are acting on behalf of large firms and employing large staffs, then the number of valuable hours wasted increases, as does the economic waste. Since misrepresentation always implies negotiation effort expended to get past the exaggeration and to the truth, perhaps it is always wasteful in this sense.

The interpretation of the argument from economic harm just sketched strikes me as unconvincing for two separate reasons. The first reason concerns the narrowness of the harm alleged. Of course, misrepresentation in negotiation has its costs. Everything that people do has costs. This is a trivial consequence of the fact that our time is valuable. To judge whether an action is wasteful, therefore, it does not suffice to show that it has costs. It is also required to measure these costs against the costs of alternative actions, and to take into account the advantages that flow from the action. In the car deal, if Jane gets a good car at a fair price and I get near what my car is worth, the advantages we enjoy as a result of a successfully completed negotiation may more than outweigh the disadvantages of the costs of deceptive negotiation. Deception about reservation price is a normal and expectable part of haggling. If we had to spend some time haggling over the price of the car, that may be reasonable, especially if such haggling makes a deal in the end more likely. It might have been better if we could have arrived at our final price without haggling, but that is unrealistic. For that matter, it might be better in some ideal sense if we could make economic exchanges without incurring any transaction costs. But we can't. We must haggle to conclude deals. Deception about reservation price is part of one way to haggle. Such deception is not harmful unless people would generally be better off without it. It is an empirical question whether people would be better off. In my capacity as armchair sociologist, it strikes me as plausible that sometimes people would, and sometimes people would not, gain as a result of deception in negotiation. In any event, it is a non sequitur to maintain that because some costs attach to deception in negotiation, it is so harmful that it amounts to a wrong.

Another complaint about the costs of deception focuses not on losses attained but on benefits or opportunities missed. Because of deception in negotiation, I might be willing to make concessions that are valuable to you, but resist doing so only because you do not let me know that they are valuable. This possibility is most realistic in cases of "integrative" bargaining, in which negotiation determines not only how the pieces of a pie are to be distributed but how large the pie will be (see Lewicki, Litterer, Minton, and Saunders, 1994). Consider a variant on a standard example of an integrative problem. Imagine that you and I are battling over the division of a blueberry pie. So long as the issue is just "how much" each of us gets, it is a distributive issue. Our negotiation is a "win-lose": the more you get, the more I lose, and vice versa. Hence, all things being equal, since we share a powerful passion for this pie, we might expect to arrive at the agreement of dividing the pie down the middle and giving half to each of us, a distributive solution. Our negotiation becomes integrative, and not merely distributive, when we look for mutually advantageous ways of dividing the pie. Now suppose it turns out that I hate blueberry filling but love crusts and that you have the complementary tastes. Obviously we do best for ourselves if you take the inside and I take the outside of the pie, the optimal integrative solution. Although the case of the pie is a bit silly, there are other cases where integrative reasoning seems important. In a car sale, for example, people may vary in the degree to which they care about price, warranty, delivery time, financial terms, etc. By getting to know the idiosyncratic features of your bargaining opponent's preferences, you may be able to work out an advantageous agreement. The prospects for such an agreement may seem bleak, however, if the parties take a strategic view of information about settlement preferences. If I desperately need a warranty and you can provide one at little cost, for example, I may not want you to know my plight, out of fear that you will use information about it to force me to make large concessions on price. But if you do not know how much I want the warranty, you may not bother to offer it. Given enough mutual misunderstanding about one another's bargaining preferences, it is easy to imagine that the agreement we finally reach falls short of optimality. Without some plain and true talk about what each of us actually wants, it may seem that we must rely on guesswork to fashion an agreement; because there may thus be many elements in a distributive bargaining set, there may be many more ways to guess wrong than to guess right, it seems, therefore, that in many typical distributive bargaining problems, it is more likely that we would guess wrong than right.

I do not wish to deny, of course, that sometimes it is harmful or even wrong to engage in deception about one's settlement preferences. Yet it is important not to be taken in by overly simple generalizations. There is no reason to think that strategic misrepresentation at the beginning of the bargaining process, even if it sometimes worsens the odds for a successful integrative bargaining solution, will always do so. Indeed, I will soon urge that such misrepresentations are mutually beneficial even for opposing negotiators, and that understanding just how this is so is key to understanding the norms of deception in negotiation. But first I wish to point out a more elementary reason that arguments which purport to establish the wrongness of deception by appeal to the harm of deception cannot succeed.

Much negotiation occurs as part of competitive economic activity. Because such competition requires the expenditure of effort and resources, it is always and obviously, in some important sense, costly. Moreover, in negotiation which is not purely integrative, that is, in distributive negotiation, competition occurs. And some people lose. In a free market system, this kind of economic loss, even if harmful to some, cannot coherently be regarded as wrongful. When Ford, in its competition with General Motors, increases its market share at the expense of General Motors' market share, Ford harms General Motors, but does not wrong General Motors. Of course, this is not to suggest that economic harm, or harm that occurs as part of economic competition, is never wrongful. Gratuitous or sadistic economic harm may be wrong, for example, as might harm that arises from unfair or exploitative practices. But it cannot suffice to establish the wrong of an action in negotiation to show that the action causes economic harm. Instead, it must be shown that the victim had a right not to be harmed in that particular way. It follows that the attack on deception in terms of the harm that it causes is in important respects a non-starter. No discussion of harmful consequences per se can explain the norms of deception in negotiation.

If arguments from harm cannot establish the wrongness of deception in negotiation, how might one try to establish it? One might, following Dees and Cramton, take a Kantian tack and suggest that such deception "would seem to violate the Kantian injunction against treating others as means only" (Dees and Cramton, 1991, p. 138). But I see no reason to think that deception in negotiation need treat a person as a means only. Consider how one Kantian, Alan Donagan, voices the complaint against lying more generally: "In duping another by lying to him, you deprive him of the opportunity of exercising his judgment on the best evidence available to him. It is true that the activities of a lying busybody may sometimes bring about a desirable result; but they do it by refusing to those whom they manipulate the respect due to them" (Donagan, 1977, p. 189).

The passage by Donagan is useful because it states how lying and other forms of deception may treat a person in ways that compromise Kantian strictures against treating a person as a mere means—it compromises a person's ability to make a fully informed decision. When this ability is compromised, so too is a person's autonomy compromised, which is a mark of moral wrongness. It does not suffice to justify such compromise, Donagan suggests, that the victim of a lie gains some advantage or "desirable result." It is, on this Kantian view, ordinarily wrong to bring about even an attractive result by wrongful means. The question we now face is whether deception in negotiation need violate these Kantian constraints. By manipulating the information that people get and providing false information, must lies or other forms of deception in negotiation compromise individual autonomy? I will suggest not.[10]

Let me illustrate with an example of a failed negotiation. A few years back I went to Madrid for an extended stay. Two weeks after I arrived, I had to move from a hotel to an apartment. There were about ten boxes that I needed to move from the hotel, and I was confident that a taxi could handle the job, since one had done so for the trip from the airport to the hotel. Because there was no taxi to be seen near the hotel, I had to go a few blocks to find one. When we arrived at the hotel, he feigned shock at the sight of the boxes and said that they were far too many for him to carry. I told him that I would expect to pay "extra" because of all the boxes, but he just shook his head, declaring again that there were too many boxes. (The apparent message was that no amount of money I would be likely to have could suffice to compensate him for this trip, that reservation price was out of my reach.) At that point, I gave him the money for the fare on his meter and said that I would find some other way to get the boxes to my apartment. (I ended up renting a car.) He looked incredulous and said, *"Con usted no se puede razonar,"* meaning, roughly, that it was hopeless reasoning with me. At this point, I finally realized that his declaration of the impossibility of moving the boxes was simple posturing, that he expected me to know this, and that I was being viewed as foolish for wasting both our time by refusing to bargain. I felt too perplexed to continue; he left, cursing me. Because I did not understand how to reasonably respond to the lies he told (or false suggestions he made) about his "reservation price," we could not get our negotiation started. As I learned from my dealings with many merchants during the course of my stay in Spain, it would have been to the mutual advantages of the taxi driver and me if I had spent more time trying to elicit a price from him, or if I had simply offered my own price. My guess about his behavior, in retrospect, is that by suggesting that the move was impossible, he was just trying to dramatize its difficulty, a necessarily lengthy performance, which he hoped would establish that his fare should be very high.

A person more sophisticated in Castilian ways than I would no doubt have succeeded in getting the taxi to take the boxes to the apartment. Such a Castilian passenger need not have had her autonomy impugned nor otherwise wronged by the lies of the taxi driver. At the outset of the negotiation, the parties would know that they can expect lies. One factor suggesting that neither party's autonomy is compromised is that they can get the information that they need to make a good deal, including information about the range of the other's bottom-line price, even if the process by which they get it is a bit tortured. Between competent buyers and sellers, lies about reservation prices, while an obstacle to the truth, are an easily enough surmountable obstacle so that they need not compromise autonomy. If both parties openly have the option to lie, then so long as people are generally aware of the relevant conventions and expectations about making false statements, reliance on what is said will be restrained, but the deceptive statements will have value. They can be used as a basis for making inferences and guesses; they can be used to express commitment to a price range or to the idea that one has something quite valuable to offer (Gulliver, 1979). By seeing how people respond to counter-offers, you can make a reasonable judgment about what their reservation price really is. Deception thus may be a trial balloon that you expect to have shot down, but whose destruction can be instructive for both you and your opponent. Deception about one's reservation price, then, can form part of an indirect process of communication, a process that is advantageous because it is less risky than more direct communication. Even if the process is nothing to which one consents, it may nonetheless be fair: it may solve a problem, shared by both negotiators, of exposure to the risk that one's opponent will exploit truthfulness about reservation price, and it may do this in a way that gives each negotiator a reasonable chance of enjoying the benefits of the solution.[11]

There is an argument that a Kantian should not be impressed with the fact that the Castilian customer can talk her way past the lies of the taxi driver, however. Lots of lies, especially white lies, can be neutralized by the epistemically diligent. It does not follow that these lies are not wrongly manipulative. If, for example, in order to get your political support, I lie to you about whether I served in Vietnam, my lie is something that you could, through diligence, uncover. It does not follow that the lie doesn't violate autonomy. It merely follows that, because of your diligence, you successfully defend your autonomy against my attack. I act manipulatively, but my manipulation fails. Is it the same in negotiation? I think not. The conventions of deception are often clear. The symmetry of informational opportunity preserves autonomy. Even if you resent the idea of going through the process, you are on notice about the necessity of doing so if you want to make a good deal. Thus, you are in a good position to exercise your informed choice. While in the war records case, my aim is to keep the truth from you entirely, in a normal negotiation such as the used car sale case, I expect you to arrive at some reasonable picture of my bottom-line price as part of the process of the give and take of negotiation.

One should not exaggerate the benign character of these deceptions. I do not wish to claim that their sole function is to communicate in a more safe manner that which one might simply state if it were safe to do so. Obviously they may also serve the strategic advantage of the deceiving negotiator and they may even make the negotiators so mad the negotiations break down and both parties lose. While negotiators who lie or otherwise deceive about their reservation price expect their opponents to gain some knowledge of this price through the give and take of negotiation, they also expect, hope, and try to make it the case that their opponent does not discern exactly what that price is. But from the perspective of respect for individual autonomy, even this expectation need not signal anything illicit. The amount of information one needs to make an intelligent and informed choice—a requirement of respect for autonomy—varies with the nature of the choice made. I may make an intelligent and informed choice to buy a lottery ticket without knowing whether this particular lottery ticket is worthless or the winner, so long as I know, roughly, the odds that it is the winner. There is nothing wrong with a lottery agent selling a ticket that he knows is a loser, so long as the lottery itself and the distribution of tickets are fair (although such lotteries are discouraged because it is too hard to keep them free of the appearance and reality of corruption). In a typical negotiation such as the car sales negotiation, what matters is that negotiators have access to enough information about an opponent's reservation price so that it is possible to bargain toward a fair price. So long as that much information is available, I see no reason to think that a competent buyer's autonomy need be compromised by lies or other deception about bottom-line price.

Suppose, then, that deception about reservation prices need not be wrong either on the ground that it compromises autonomy or that it is somehow harmful. Why do it? Are there affirmative reasons to think that it might be morally acceptable?

The practical advantages of deception are clear. Deception about reservation price can be valuable. When things go well, such deception is a device people who neither know nor trust one another can use to work their way to a reasonable agreement. As became clear in the discussion of the car sale case at the beginning of this paper, if you state the truth about your reservation price you may take an unreasonable risk, especially if your bargaining opponent exaggerates hers. Often the outcome of a negotiation is to split the difference between prices on the table, and these prices may be a function of perceived reservation prices. Misrepresentation of one's reservation price may enhance prospects for communication while limiting exposure to certain kinds of risk.

To this point, I have framed the argument about deception in merely negative terms, criticizing the view that ordinarily such deception is morally unacceptable. But plainly a closely related positive position can be made. In the brief remainder of this paper, I will sketch that position, which I will call the Mutual Advantage View. In doing so, I have the limited purpose of demonstrating the possibility of a distinctive and attractive alternative rationale for a practice of modest deception in negotiation. I will leave for another occasion, not so much focused on criticizing other approaches, a full defense and articulation of Mutual Advantage View.

The mutual advantage in the Mutual Advantage View arises from the fact that the possibility of deception helps solve the problem of communication shared by the parties to a negotiation; it thus produces an important benefit, namely provides a safe device for indirect communication that both parties may find useful. The moral credentials of a limited practice of deception in negotiation are not exhausted by the size of the benefit flowing from the practice, however. The practice may also be fair: in circumstances where negotiating parties are competent and have reason to know about the existence of conventions permitting limited deception, each party has a fair and equal opportunity to safely get information about his opponent's reservation price, and neither party is likely to gain a large advantage over the other.[12] A fair and mutually advantageous practice that allows people to negotiate, while limiting the risk they face, has strong moral credentials.

Plainly there are some similarities between the rationale for deception rooted in self-defense and the Mutual Advantage rationale. Both protect against certain kinds of risk. But the strategy of self-defense interprets deception as a means of fending off attacks from prospective wrongdoers or harmdoers, while the Mutual Advantage approach suggests that at least sometimes, deception serves the more constructive role of an indirect means of communication that fairly solves a mutual problem. These distinguishing characteristics of the Mutual Advantage rationale suggest some normative implications. The Mutual Advantage rationale differs from the self-defense rationale in ways that make Mutual Advantage both more permissive and less permissive than self-defense. For example, self-defense does not allow you to engage in deception unless you reasonably feel threatened that your opponent may deceive you. Here, the Mutual Advantage approach is more permissive because it allows you to initiate deception, so long as the possibility is fair (and hence mutually understood by the involved parties) and potentially mutually advantageous. To see how Mutual Advantage can be less permissive than self-defense, recall the case of my negotiation with Brown about the purchase of a watch. The self-defense rationale would allow me to use force or engage in material fraud against Brown, if "necessary," in order to get a fair price on the watch. Nothing in the Mutual Advantage approach supports such action because these actions are too likely to produce one-sided benefits.

CONCLUSION

My aim in this paper has been to urge that Mutual Advantage shows more promise than self-defense as an approach to understanding the norms of deception in negotiation. Plainly, a full vindication of the Mutual Advantage approach would require more than the sketch I have developed here. More must be said about how much and when a person may deceive, how much and when a person may disclose, the distinction between lying and other forms of deception, the source of the value of deception under the Mutual Advantage approach, deception about matters other than reservation price, fairness, and other issues.

Notes

1. While there may be important moral differences between lies and other willful lapses in truth, I do not believe that these differences matter for this paper, and considerations of economy will lead me for the most part to ignore them. Thus,

while it seems plausible that the standards for justifying a lie will be more difficult than for other forms of deception, I won't examine such issues here. In any event, my position on the distinction between lies and other forms of deception really becomes potentially relevant only in the final portion of this paper, where I sketch my own positive view. If one objects to lumping together lies and other forms of deception, one might, in that section, take my discussion to concern only deception other than lies, though I do not think such modesty is necessary. Indeed, I regard the arguments explored in that section as adequate to vindicate some lies as well as many other deceptive acts. Similarly, I do not believe that it is necessary to explore the nuances of the proper definition of "lying." Instead, I will simply assume the well-known definition used by Sissela Bok (1978) of a lie as "any intentionally deceptive message which is stated" (p. 14).

2. As John Boatright (1992) observes, apparently acceptable deception about reservation prices may also occur within an environment of trust. I am, however, here especially interested in the role of deception where trust is a problem. In any case, Boatright's observation introduces complications that I cannot address here. For useful discussion of the morality of deception in environments in which trust exists, see Nyberg (1993).

3. Indeed, Robert H. Frank (1988, p. 165) goes so far as to say that "the art of bargaining, as most of us eventually learn, is in large part the art of sending misleading messages about [reservation prices]." And Richard Shell (1991, p. 93) points out that the perceived importance of deception in negotiation goes beyond issues of reservation price: "In simple, distributive, bargaining, when someone asks, 'What is your bottom line?' few negotiators tell the truth. They dodge, they change the subject or they lie. In more complex, multi-issue negotiations even relatively cooperative negotiators often inject straw issues or exaggerate the importance of minor problems in order to gain concessions on what really matters."

4. In the same context, they also invoke the Efficacy Principle. But I do not see how it makes a difference for the cases that concern us. The Efficacy Principle provides, "It is unfair to require an individual to take a significant risk, or incur a significant cost out of respect for the moral rights of others, if the action that creates the risk or cost is unlikely to have its beneficial effect, or if it would benefit only those who would not willingly incur the same risk or cost" (Dees and Cramton, 1991, p. 144).

5. But see Boatright (1992) for a strong argument that Dees and Cramton underestimate the power of ordinary moral theory for handling these cases.

6. It is not clear what position, if any, Dees and Cramton take on necessity. They do not address the issue explicitly. Perhaps they think that a necessity requirement is somehow implicit in their analysis. Perhaps they deny a necessity requirement.

7. But I do not believe Carson would find this result objectionable.

8. Carson's position on this issue is complex, however. He maintains that "hardened negotiators" should not be regarded as lying to one another because they do not warrant the truth of what they say to one another (Carson, 1993, p. 323). Indeed, Carson would deny that many apparently false statements about one's settlement

preferences are prima facie wrong. His reason for holding this view is that he thinks that "hardened negotiators" mutually consent to deception. I think that his position here is quite interesting and worthy of a much more substantial discussion than I can undertake in a paper not wholly devoted to his view. My response to him would be to argue that his use of the notion of consent is illegitimate because the relevant consent is mere fiction: no actual consent occurs in the cases that interest us, and the temptation to appeal to consent expresses a concern that any deception in negotiation must occur within a practice that is in relevant respects fair. I feel free to evade full discussion of these issues now, however, because Carson himself says that his position on the ethics of misstating one's reservation price is independent of his views about whether "hardened negotiators" should be regarded as lying about their settlement preferences (Carson, 1993). Indeed, he characterizes these views on lying and consent as merely "speculative," and thinks it important to consider the ethics of deception in negotiation apart from questions about the criteria for lying (Carson, 1993).

9. Many philosophers seem to hold that it is intuitively plain, at least after we consider how firm our intuitions remain after reflecting on a variety of cases, that lying and many other forms of deception are at least prima facie wrong. They would hold that no special argument, apart from reflection about intuitions on the cases, need be made for the relevant claim of prima facie wrongness. Indeed, this seems to be Carson's view. But because it strikes me as far from self-evident that lying is always even prima facie wrong, I think it worth exploring whether there are any good reasons for supposing it always to be prima facie wrong.

10. While the moral considerations I discuss can be used to defend, in certain limited circumstances, both lies and other forms of deception, I do not wish to argue for the claim that they are morally equivalent. Here I only wish to assert that the same kind of considerations can be cogently adduced in support of lies and other forms of deception. As I suggested earlier, while it seems plausible that the standards for justifying a lie will be more difficult than for other forms of deception, I will not examine such issues here.

11. For a fuller discussion of how one might respect an individual's autonomy without getting an individual's consent, see Strudler and Wasserman, "The First Dogma of Deontology: Quinn on Doing and Allowing," *Philosophical Studies*, vol. 80, (Oct. 1995) pp. 51–67.

12. It is the sort of practice that passes a hypothetical social contract test: reasonable business professionals and lawyers might endorse it in advance for handling hard negotiating problems. The practice thus possesses one important indicia of fairness, even though it is plainly not feasible for people to actually endorse (or consent to) such a practice when entering a negotiation.

References

Boatright, J. R. "Morality in Practice: Dees, Cramton, and Brer Rabbit on a Problem of Applied Ethics." *Business Ethics Quarterly*, 1992, *2*, 63–73.

Bok, S. *Lying: Moral Choices in Public and Private Life.* New York: Pantheon Books, 1978.

Carnevale, P. J., and Pruitt, D. G. "Negotiation and Mediation." *Annual Review of Psychology,* 1992, *43,* 531–582.

Carson, T. "Second Thoughts About Bluffing." *Business Ethics Quarterly,* 1993, *3,* 318–341.

Chisholm, R., and Feehan, T. D. "The Intent to Deceive." *Journal of Philosophy,* 1977, *74,* 143–159.

Cramton, P. C., and Dees, J. G. "Promoting Honesty in Negotiation: An Exercise in Practial Ethics." *Business Ethics Quarterly,* 1993, *4.*

Dees, J. G., and Cramton, P. C. "Shrewd Bargaining on the Moral Frontier: Toward a Theory of Morality in Practice." *Business Ethics Quarterly,* 1991, *1,* 135–167.

Donagan, A. *The Theory of Morality.* Chicago: University of Chicago Press, 1977.

Frank, R. H. *Passions Within Reason.* New York: Norton, 1988.

Gulliver, P. H. *Disputes and Negotiations: A Cross-Cultural Perspective.* Orlando, Fla.: Academic Press, 1979.

Kerman, J., and Wilson, R. "Bargaining with Private Information." *Journal of Economic Literature,* 1993, *31,* 45–105.

Lewicki, R. J., Litterer, J. A., Minton, J. W., and Saunders, D. M. *Negotiation.* Burr Ridge, Ill.: Irwin, 1994.

Nyberg, D. *The Varnished Truth: Truth Telling and Deceiving in Ordinary Life.* Chicago: University of Chicago Press, 1993.

Raiffa, H. *The Art and Science of Negotiation: How to Resolve Conflicts and Get the Best Out of Bargaining.* Cambridge, Mass.: Harvard University Press, 1982.

Sedgwick, S. "On Lying and the Role of Content in Kant's Ethics." *Kant-Studien,* 1991, *82,* 42–62.

Shell, G. R. "When Is It Legal to Lie in Negotiations?" *Sloan Management Review,* Spring 1991, 93–101.

Strudler, A., and Wasserman, D. "The First Dogma of Deontology: Quinn on Doing and Alllowing." *Philosophical Studies,* 1995, *80,* 51–67

Vuillemin, J. "On Lying: Kant and Benjamin Constant." *Kant-Studien,* 1982, *73,* 413–424.

CHAPTER ELEVEN

Deception and Mutual Trust

A Reply to Strudler

J. Gregory Dees

Peter C. Cramton

Deception in negotiation has long been an intriguing topic for business ethicists. Strudler has added to the intrigue by proposing what for many ethicists will seem to be a counter-intuitive view: that some forms of deception in business negotiation are morally neutral or even benign. Strudler's approach is not simply a reaffirmation of Albert Carr's thesis (1968) that business has its own ethics. Rather, Strudler offers a novel analysis of negotiation tactics.

In presenting his views, Strudler follows a time-honored tradition of an author preparing readers for his own views by first purporting to uncover fatal flaws in alternative theories. Since the reader does not have the earlier work freshly in mind or readily at hand, the author's characterization of the earlier theory is decisive. Readers end up believing that anyone with an ounce of moral decency could not have seriously put forward the earlier theory and conclude any new theory would be an improvement. Having lowered the bar, the author, in this case Strudler, jumps over it with apparent ease.

Since we have the distinction of being Strudler's first victims, we have taken a special interest in his paper. Strudler casts our "Mutual Trust Perspective" (Dees and Cramton, 1991) as a kind of Dr. Jeckyll/Mr. Hyde theory. On one hand, he portrays us as uptight prudes who cluck moral disapproval over something as trivial as the deceptions engaged in by a Madrid taxi driver hoping to

---

We are deeply grateful for the suggestions and advice provided by Jaan Elias.

extract an extra commission for carrying heavy boxes. On the dark side, Strudler describes us as wild-men who would cheer-on violent, paranoid software entrepreneurs looking to beat the living daylights out of one another in order to gain trade secrets. Naturally, we believe that he has got us wrong. We also think that his theory is fatally flawed, even harmful. However, we will resist the temptation to respond with a caricature of Strudler's work. Such a strategy is not likely to be effective in this case since readers probably have Strudler's views freshly in mind and, if not, could easily check our claims by turning a few pages. The principle of self-defense may justify an unfair counter-attack, but the context prohibits it.

Strudler was not the first to raise questions about our work (see Boatright, 1992; Gibson, 1994), but he is the most aggressive in his critique. We are flattered by the attention, but disappointed that our arguments have not been universally compelling. While the critical response has convinced us that we need to be clearer about our claims and that we could improve on our earlier works, our central convictions remain unshaken. In response to Strudler's paper, we will explain why deception is a morally regrettable feature of business negotiations, and why the Mutual Trust Perspective is a reasonable working hypothesis.

DECEPTION, SIGNALING, AND MORAL REGRET

On one point, Strudler's interpretation of our work is correct. We do object to his contention that deception in negotiation, even deception about one's reservation price, is morally benign and not a cause for regret. Though we do not hold the extreme view he attributes to us, we believe that "outside of a few recreational contexts, deception is a regrettable feature of business negotiations, even when it is justified (or commonplace)" (1993, p. 361). For us, "morally regrettable" has a precise definition: a practice is morally regrettable if the world would be a better place with less of it and a worse place with more. Our thesis is that it would be good if parties to a negotiation reduce deception through some feasible and fair method. Despite Strudler's arguments to the contrary, we believe this is not limited to deception about material facts but also is true for deception about settlement preferences (including reservation prices). We acknowledge settlement preference deception may be hard to prevent, detect, police, or punish; nonetheless it is regrettable. Indeed, we fear that Strudler's arguments alleviate the moral pressure to find techniques to increase trust and reduce deception in this area.

Strudler's argument for deception fails because it rests on two conflations. The first involves the very notion of deception. Strudler mixes the idea of a deliberate deception intended to mislead with the idea of making false statements in order to signal useful information. As we explicitly defined the term, *deception* involves "the *intention* of creating or adding support to a false belief in anther party" (1993, p. 362, emphasis added). By contrast, Strudler's false statements (which he labels "lies") are meant as a "signaling and symbolic device" (p. 795) to help negotiators reach a mutually beneficial agreement. It is true that among sophisticated negotiators who are skilled at decoding one another's statements, what Strudler describes may occur—with little harm being done. But it is hard to count these "lies" as instances of intentional deception, since they are not expected to mislead, and in fact do not mislead. The power of Strudler's argument and examples rests on blurring this distinction.

Even though false statements that signal useful information may be used to strike mutually beneficial bargains, making such statements can hardly be counted as a socially desirable practice. In these negotiations, the signals are usually noisy at best, decoding is more of an art than a science, and conveying the truth even when you desperately want to can be very difficult. Verbal fencing between skilled business negotiators may lead to inefficiencies. Contexts in which the decoding scheme is so precise and the negotiation so well-choreographed as to avoid these problems are rare indeed. Think of the challenges in decoding inflated letters of recommendation.

If Strudler means to include deliberate attempts to mislead in his account of deception, it is even more difficult to see how negotiations could be "mutually advantageous." True, negotiations that involve deception sometimes end up in mutually advantageous agreements, but that hardly supports the belief that the deception was in any way instrumental to achieving the result. Strudler fails to demonstrate a causal link between deceptive strategies and the eventual settlement; he seems to believe that the only alternative to his version of negotiations is the failure to reach an agreement.

Strudler underestimates the costs of deception, even when an intentional effort fails to mislead. Current theory and empirical studies show that attempts at deception are costly (see Kennan and Wilson, 1993). Private information about settlement preferences creates incentives for deception, which leads to inefficiencies. Negotiators often take costly actions in order to convince rivals of the truth. For example, a firm may endure a costly strike in order to convince workers that it is unable to pay a high wage. Deceptive activities generally lead to increased bargaining costs, increased post-agreement monitoring costs, and missed opportunities for those mutually advantageous agreements that Strudler prizes so highly. How many people have walked away from potentially mutually advantageous deals either because of frustration with the negotiating process, or because they came to believe (falsely) that no agreement was possible?

Furthermore, Strudler never fully envisions the fallout from successful deception. Successful deceptions often involve gaining a person's trust during the negotiation process only to abuse it; the deception is, in essence, a broken promise. When both parties are trying to do the same thing to one another, we may not cry too much for the losers, especially if they are equally skilled. Nonetheless, we may still find the nature of the process to be unfortunate, even offensive.

Strudler might counter that deception often allows both parties to leave the negotiation believing they got a good deal, even when they did not by any objective standards. On this point, Howard Raiffa (1982) counsels that it is not a good idea to reveal one's reservation price after a deal has been struck. While Strudler cites Raiffa's statement as support of his view, it may simply be sound advice for avoiding further confrontation. Telling someone that they have been duped is not honesty, it is a taunt. Anyone who has supervised negotiation exercises has seen the indignation and outrage expressed by students who have agreed to settlements far above their opponent's reservation price. Even when these settlements are technically "mutually advantageous," the students' reactions generally contain a judgment of their opponent's tactics that is hardly "morally benign." Raiffa's advice cuts sharply against Strudler, not in his favor. If reservation-price deception were benign, why not reveal? The manipulative character of deception is morally problematic, even when a deceived negotiator leaves feeling good about an unwise agreement. It would be perverse to place a positive moral value on this sort of false consciousness, as pleasant as it may be at the time.

For these reasons, we regard deception about settlement preferences as morally regrettable, even when it may be locally (individually) justified. We may all marvel at the ability of people to make a successful end out of a poor process, but this in no way makes the process less regrettable. Strudler offers no compelling invisible-hand type of argument linking attempts at deception to better negotiation outcomes. If he had one, it certainly would be a breakthrough.

Strudler's second conflation involves the notion of moral regret. He fails to make the distinction between "wrongdoing" on the part of an individual and a practice being "morally regrettable" from the standpoint of society. As the much analyzed prisoner's dilemma shows, this distinction is crucial since individuals may be held blameless for defecting (i.e. deceiving), even though this course of action is not socially optimal. In his article, Strudler concentrates on whether individual negotiators should be regarded as wrongdoers in order to judge if the behavior is socially desirable or not. For instance, in contrasting his view with ours, Strudler states, "When deception in negotiation makes sense, it is ordinarily not as a way of fending off a prospective attacker or wrongdoer, but instead because of its promise as a mutually beneficial solution to a problem confronted by negotiators who, for morally benign reasons, cannot trust each other" (p. 796). However, neither party need be a wrongdoer for the practice of deception to be regrettable—people can engage in regrettable social practices for "morally benign reasons" from their own standpoint. As we argue below, Strudler's inability to distinguish between levels of analysis also leads to his mischaracterization of the Mutual Trust Principle.

Our primary objection to Strudler is that we believe it is a good thing to reduce deception in negotiation, including settlement issue deception. What most troubles us about his view is that it provides a rationale for business negotiators to neglect the valuable process of building trust and reducing wasteful efforts to mislead. In this regard, Strudler functions as an apologist for the status quo. His view justifies a system of commercial transactions that encourages and rewards deceptive skill. Fortunately, the history of economic development seems to show progress on the other side, as practices (money-back guarantees, etc.) and institutions (Better Business Bureaus, etc.) are developed to help reinforce trust (see Cramton and Dees, 1993, for a discussion of practical devices for reducing deception). These practices and institutions even are beginning to have a bearing on reservation prices. For instance, many appliance stores offer price guarantees, many auto dealers offer no-haggle pricing, and third parties offer information (e.g., the dealer's invoice price on a car) that can help consumers determine a seller's reservation price.

MUTUAL TRUST, PRUDENCE, AND MORAL PROGRESS

Strudler acknowledges the importance of trust in understanding deception in negotiation, but he rejects the Mutual Trust Perspective (MTP) we proposed in 1991. No doubt, the MTP could use some clarification, refinement, and improvement, and it will certainly offend some people who would urge unconditional commitment to moral principles. However, when it is placed into its proper context, we believe that it still serves its purpose. We proposed the Mutual Trust Perspective to capture how people who are neither saints nor scoundrels might justify otherwise questionable conduct in morally ambiguous contexts. The original statement of the central principle went as follows: *"Mutual Trust Principle:* It is unfair to require an individual to take a significant risk or incur a significant cost out of respect for the interests or moral rights of others, if that individual has no reasonable grounds for trusting that the relevant others will (or would) take the same risk or make the same sacrifice" (p. 144).

At the heart of Strudler's attack on the MTP is an example that purports to demonstrate how the MTP could not be "part of a minimally decent conception of morality" or an appropriate interpretation of business behavior (pp. 797–798). The example involves the case of software entrepreneurs Jones and Smith, the latter "a scurrilous competitor who would do anything, perhaps even physically harm an opponent to get ahead." Strudler then argues that the MTP would justify Jones administering a beating to Smith, or Jones engaging in material misrepresentation (fraud) against Smith, in order to get Smith's trade secrets. Since such behavior is obviously well beyond the bounds of permissible business behavior, Strudler rejects MTP. In the process, he mischaracterizes MTP as a "self-defense" explanation for deception in negotiation. While we do refer to "defensive deception," Strudler's definition of self-defense goes well beyond, placing MTP in the same category as views "expressing the idea that wrongdoers such as murderers or liars, by virtues of their wrongdoing, forfeit or waive some of their rights to be treated as we treat innocent persons" (p. 796).

We find Strudler's attack inventive, but his interpretation of MTP is wildly different from what we originally intended. Both the characterization and the example wrench MTP out of its context and misstate the central thesis of our work. The focus in MTP is as much on the circumstances of the negotiation as on the character of the other party. In introducing MTP, we said that the principle "points to a consideration about *the specific social context* in which actions are taken that can serve, other things being equal, to undermine obligations derived from ideal moral reasoning" (1991, p. 144, emphasis added). The MTP is *not* concerned with "self-defense," in Strudler's sense. It is not based on any idea of moral wrongdoing by others but simply on the lack of reasonable grounds for trust in a specific social context. It does not presuppose that inherent moral rights are forfeited by anyone, since the absence of trust in these contexts undermines the very notion of rights.

Boatright (1992) made much of the similarity between MTP and Hobbes's "two-level theory that makes allowances for imperfect conditions in which trust is lacking" (p. 70). Like Hobbes, MTP suggests goodwill is conditional, since moral commitment requires a social context in which an individual has reasonable grounds for trusting others before making the same commitment. The principal difference between the MTP and Hobbes is that the MTP envisions trust emerging not in the one fell swoop of a Leviathan, but by incremental and evolutionary efforts to "tame" various domains of human activity. In these domains, trust is built through a variety of imperfect mechanisms and the state of nature is conquered inch by inch. Where the social context has not followed trust to be built, moral obligations weaken because of the sense of "fair play" expressed in the MTP. Each transaction between individuals takes place in a number of different domains, some "tamed" and others not. Moral obligations in "untamed" domains may be noble, but they are often futile.

To better understand how Strudler's example does an injustice to the MTP, it is best to reconstruct what led us to posit the MTP. We began not with a principal but a puzzle: Why is deception about settlement preferences (reservation prices) condoned, while deception in many other areas is condemned? How do individuals who consider themselves decent and moral justify these deceptive behaviors? As one explanation of this puzzle, we argued that negotiators felt that while some types of deception were indeed "tamed" by social norms, laws, and third-party institutions, for other matters, the negotiators were still in a Hobbesian state of nature—what we termed a "Hobbesian frontier." In particular domains (e.g., reservation prices) people invoked something like the Mutual Trust Principle because of the difficulty in establishing trust, not because their opposite numbers are bad people who had forfeited their rights. People adopted the MTP because they were unwilling to sacrifice their personal interests to moral principles without grounds for trusting that others would make the same sacrifice.

The MTP does not (and certainly was not intended to) imply that you can do anything to a person that the person might be willing to do to you if they had the opportunity. In the example Strudler offers, Jones would have called the police, since physical coercion is a "tamed" area—case closed. MTP does not license Jones to resort to physical violence or fraud. These behaviors are not on the Hobbesian frontiers, at least not in our relatively stable society. One might imagine societies less "tame" than ours in which individuals may feel justified in resorting to these more aggressive forms of behavior. However, in his example, Strudler has not constructed such a context.

Strudler's example fails on other grounds as well. The Mutual Trust Principle specifically states that it is "unfair to require an individual to take a *significant risk* or incur a *significant cost*" in the absence of reasonable grounds for trusting the other person. Strudler's examples are weak in showing significant risks and costs to Jones if he refrains from beating or defrauding Smith. Failing to get Smith's trade secret is not a significant "cost" to Jones. Though the line can be hard to draw analytically, gaining a benefit is intuitively different from avoiding a significant cost or risk. As a benchmark, we propose comparing the risks and costs of doing business in similar conditions, but where reasonable grounds for trust are present. The issue is whether the absence of trust in a domain significantly increases the costs and risks associated with unilateral moral restraint. As Strudler defines the case, this sort of incremental risk or cost does not seem to be present. That is, Jones would face a legitimate competitive risk from Smith and his trade secrets, even if Smith were trustworthy.

Strudler may not be the only one to misread MTP in this way. Therefore, we should restate the core principle to include the emphasis on social context that we elaborated in our previous articles:

Revised Mutual Trust Principle: Obligations to refrain from specific kinds of morally regrettable conduct are diminished (perhaps eliminated) for an individual when the following two conditions are present: (1) the individual is operating in a trust-deficient social context, and (2) refraining from the regrettable conduct would cause the individual to bear significant incremental risks or incur significant incremental costs.

A *trust-deficient social context* is a domain of human interaction in which participants lack reasonable grounds for trusting relevant others not to engage in morally regrettable conduct.

Incremental costs and risks are those that would not be present if the individual were in a context with grounds for trust and could reasonably rely on others to refrain from the regrettable conduct.

Whether an obligation is diminished or eliminated may depend on the severity of the risks and costs associated with unilateral moral restraint. No doubt, this formulation is still imprecise and open to debate. However, it is sufficient to serve the purpose for which it is intended.

THE CHARACTER OF OUR ENTERPRISE

To be fair, what confused Strudler and may confuse others, particularly those not familiar with our prior work, is that the character of MTP differs from traditional approaches in business ethics. MTP favors a pragmatic balance between the calls of morality and prudence over the idealism of most business ethics. The kind of conditional goodwill described by MTP may seem strange and unsavory, because unilateral moral action is both more familiar and admirable to ethicists.

The development of MTP also differed from the development of most moral theories. Rather than being a view derived from first principles and tested against our highest (arm-chair) moral intuitions, it was derived from our conversations with business negotiators, lawyers, and students in negotiation classes. When these informants expressed a reluctance to be honest when they could not trust the other side to be equally honest, we formulated MTP to capture the ethics of people who consider themselves to be reasonably moral yet feel justified acting in a regrettable fashion. Rather than a finely nuanced normative dictum, we see the MTP as a building block in a larger program of pragmatic business ethics. It shows us how we might help improve practice when we cannot effectively sway people toward unilateral moral commitment with philosophical arguments. It points to the lever of trust.

We embarked on this course of development in order to speak effectively to business practitioners and to offer them actionable advice that they might take seriously. We believe that one important goal of business ethics as a field is to promote constructive change in business practices. This is not the only legitimate goal, but it seems essential if business ethics is to hold its own relative to other fields in business (e.g., marketing, strategy, finance, etc.). In exploring how business ethics could be most effective, our attention was brought to a disconnection between some of the moral theories that ethicists were relying on in their research and what we were hearing in conversations with practitioners. We began to wonder if F. H. Bradley might not be right in his observation about the limits of theoretical ethics: "The man who can give moral advice is the man of experience, who, from his own knowledge and by sympathy, can transport himself into another's case; who knows the heart and sees though moral illusion; and the man of mere theory is in the practical sphere a useless and dangerous pedant" (Bradley, 1927, p. 226).

Bradley did not convince us to give up the search for theory, but he encouraged us to try to develop a more sympathetic understanding of actual practices. We took advice from Anette Baier's interpretation of David Hume's perspective on applied ethics: "The brief for 'applied' philosophy which we get from Hume, then, is one that directs the philosopher to learn from the non-philosophers before presuming them to advise them." Following Baier, we sought to "become less of an intellectual judge and more of an apprentice participant" (1985, p. 39).

The MTP was an early attempt to articulate what we were hearing in our relationships with practitioners. Nothing that we have seen or heard in the past few years has undermined our confidence in the spirit of MTP and its value as a working hypothesis. We could spend more time trying to refine it, but we think this would be less valuable than spending the same time helping practitioners use the core ideas of this theory to devise practical solutions to moral problems. This theory allows us to speak to practitioners in a way that is both sympathetic and constructive. It is neither an apology for current practices nor a criticism. By helping business people find ways to build trust and lower the risks and costs of moral restraint, we thought we could have a greater positive impact on business practice than we could have debating the finer points of the morality of deception in negotiation.

Admittedly, even with the modifications suggested here, the MTP might not hold up to empirical research. As both Strudler and Boatright (1992) point out, MTP is an empirical matter and could be subject to standard systematic study, refinement, and perhaps refutation. Though we have not amassed systematic evidence for the MTP, we openly welcome empirical research. As we stated in our first paper, "Many questions remain about the Mutual Trust Perspective. The theory clearly needs to be fleshed-out in more detail. Empirical work is needed to provide a better understanding of how this perspective is reflected in practical decision making. We need to find out whether people normally think and act like moral pragmatists, as we characterize them" (1991, p. 160). Some potentially relevant work is being done on this score (see Tenbrunsel, 1995), but the results that we have seen so far are not conclusive with regard to the role of trust in justifying deception in negotiation. Even acknowledging that point, we see little harm done by focusing our work on building trust in business negotiations.

This kind of constructive, practitioner-oriented approach to business ethics is relatively new. We do not claim to have fully worked out its shape and character, and we welcome like-minded souls to push this type of work further. What we envision is an interdisciplinary approach that would weave philosophy, morality, social science, common sense, and business experience together to provide practitioners with guidance that speaks directly to them and that provides practical advice. This new research program would focus more on strategies for constructive action and less on judgmental evaluation. This approach would take seriously how business people think. The key questions are: How do we learn from and work with business people who are not likely to be persuaded by philosophical arguments, who may well lose patience with the qualifications and abstractions that form a central part of our disciplinary heritage? How do we provide constructive advice rather than simply condemning or excusing their actions? Moral theory can help point to the direction for improvement, but it alone cannot provide the road map or strategy for getting there.

CONCLUDING COMMENTS

To return to the central point of this paper, the core of our argument regarding deception in negotiation is this:

1. Contrary to Strudler's thesis, the world would generally be better off with less deception in negotiation, including deception about settlement preferences.

2. Philosophical arguments about the moral value of honesty are not likely to persuade many practitioners to change their behavior, and arguments that justify or excuse deception may reinforce a regrettable practice.

3. The practice of deception in negotiation rests, in large part, on the absence of social mechanisms to secure mutual trust and on perceived risks and costs associated with unilateral moral restraint.

4. The most promising avenue for reducing undesirable deception is to give business people the conceptual and practical tools for building trust and securing their interests.

The bulk of our second paper (1993) was devoted to presenting those concepts and tools, using the literature of game theory and negotiation to develop our points. We hope that interested readers will read our earlier work and decide for themselves whether Strudler's approach to the problem of deception is superior.

References

Baier, A. "Doing Without Moral Theory?" In S. G. Clarke and E. Simpson (eds.), *Anti-Theory in Ethics and Moral Conservatism.* Albany: State University of New York Press, 1985.

Boatright, J. R. "Morality in Practice: Dees, Cramton, and Brer Rabbit on a Problem of Applied Ethics." *Business Ethics Quarterly,* 1992, *2,* 63–75.

Bradley, F. H. *Ethical Studies.* New York: Oxford University Press, 1927.

Carr, A. "Is Business Bluffing Ethical?" *Harvard Business Review,* 1968, 46(1), 143–152.

Cramton, P. C., and Dees, J. G. "Promoting Honesty in Negotiation: An Exercise in Practical Ethics." *Business Ethics Quarterly,* 1993, *3*(4), 359–394.

Dees, J. G., and Cramton, P. C. "Shrewd Bargaining on the Moral Frontier: Toward a Theory of Morality in Practice." *Business Ethics Quarterly,* 1991, *1,* 135–167.

Gibson, K. "Harmony, Hobbes and Rational Negotiation: A Reply to Dees and Cramton." *Business Ethics Quarterly,* 1994, *4*(3), 373–381.

Kennan, J., and Wilson, R. "Bargaining with Private Information." *Journal of Economic Literature,* 1993, *31*(1), 45–104.

Raiffa, H. *The Art and Science of Negotiation: How to Resolve Conflicts and Get the Best Out of Bargaining.* Cambridge, Mass.: Harvard University Press, 1982.

Strudler, A. "On the Ethics of Deception in Negotiation." *Business Ethics Quarterly,* 1995, *5*(4), 795–812.

Tenbrunsel, A. "Justifying Unethical Behavior: The Role of Expectations of Others' Behavior and Uncertainty." Unpublished doctoral dissertation, Northwestern University, 1995.

CHAPTER TWELVE

The Lawyer's Obligation to Be Trustworthy When Dealing with Opposing Parties

Geoffrey C. Hazard, Jr.

The present regulation of lawyers' trustworthiness is modest. The Code of Professional Responsibility, in DR 7–102(A)(5), provides that "in his representation of a client, a lawyer shall not . . . knowingly make a false statement of law or fact" (American Bar Association, 1977). This provision might be characterized as a minimalist formulation of the law of disclosure. It prohibits only misrepresentation and requires no affirmative disclosure. It is limited to statements of "fact" as distinguished from evidence, indications, portents, opinions, possibilities, or even probabilities of which the lawyer may be aware. It is limited to matters that are false as distinguished from those of which the lawyer is skeptical or even suspicious.

The Code of Professional Responsibility contains two other provisions that augment this basic rule. Yet these standards also fail affirmatively to require a high level of trustworthiness in dealing with opposing parties. The first, DR 7–102(A)(3), provides that a lawyer shall not "conceal or knowingly fail to disclose that which he is required by law to reveal" (American Bar Association, 1977). This provision clearly does not go far in the direction of a disclosure requirement. Instead of specifying the matters that must be revealed, it incorporates by reference general requirements laid down by the law at large. Thus, rules such as those imposed on lawyers by securities regulations require affirmative revelations.[1] The law of fraud as generally understood requires revelation where necessary to correct a material misstatement when the lawyer has become aware of an inaccuracy.[2]

The second relevant provision is DR 7–102(B)(1), which provides that "a lawyer who receives information clearly establishing that . . . his client has, in the course of the representation, perpetrated a fraud upon a person . . . shall promptly call upon his client to rectify the same, and if his client refuses . . . he shall reveal the fraud to the affected person . . . except when the information is protected as a privileged communication" (American Bar Association, 1977).

In light of the exception in the last clause, it is doubtful whether the provision can ever be operative (Hazard, 1978). Even if it could be operative, it only applies to fraud and even then only when the fraud is "clearly" established. Thus the disclosure required by DR 7–102(B)(1) is little more than that required for lawyers to escape complicity in their clients' fraud. If so, the provision is redundant in light of DR 7–102(A)(7),[3] and the net requirement of the Code of Professional Responsibility is that lawyers avoid fraudulent representations. Such a precept falls far short of requiring trustworthiness.

Comparison may be made between these provisions and those promulgated by the American Bar Association Commission on Evaluation of Professional Standards, familiarly known as the Kutak Commission. Its provision on this subject, in the Commission's Proposed Final Draft, May 30, 1981, is as follows:

Rule 4.1 *Truthfulness in Statements to Others*
In the course of representing a client a lawyer shall not:
  (a) Knowingly make a false statement of fact or law to a third person; or
  (b) Knowingly fail to disclose a fact to a third person when:
    (1) In the circumstances failure to make the disclosure is equivalent to making a material misrepresentation;
    (2) Disclosure is necessary to prevent assisting a criminal or fraudulent act, as required by Rule 1.2(d); or
    (3) Disclosure is necessary to comply with other law.[4]

Proposed Rule 4.1(a) corresponds to DR 7–102(A)(5)and proposed Rule 4.1(b)(1) is a corollary. Proposed Rule 4.1(b)(2) corresponds to DR 7–102(A)(7). Proposed Rule 4.1(b)(3) corresponds to DR 7–102(A)(3). The only other difference between Proposed Rule 4.1(b) and the provisions of the present Code of Professional Responsibility concerns the question of preserving client confidences. The present code does not explicitly determine whether the disclosure requirement of DR 7–102(A)(3) operates when the required disclosure will reveal adverse information about the client—as it almost inevitably will. The term *"confidences"* in the present code, however, probably does not include information that effectuates a fraud (Wigmore, 1961; American Bar Association, 1908). The Comment to proposed Rule 4.1 clarifies this point.

Upon careful consideration, it thus is clear that the Kutak Commission's proposed rules on trustworthiness do little to alter the status quo as set forth in the

Code of Professional Responsibility. Yet the commission considered and ultimately rejected a more sweeping proposal. Its discussion draft of January 30, 1980, included the following formulation (American Bar Association, Commission on Evaluation of Professional Standards, 1980):

4.2 Fairness to Other Participants

(a) In conducting negotiations a lawyer shall be fair in dealing with other participants.

(b) A lawyer shall not make a knowing misrepresentation of fact or law, or fail to disclose a material fact known to the lawyer, even if adverse, when disclosure is:

  (1) Required by law or the Rules of Professional Conduct; or

  (2) Necessary to correct a manifest misapprehension of fact or law resulting from a previous representation made by the lawyer or known by the lawyer to have been made by the client [American Bar Association, Commission on Evaluation of Professional Standards, 1980].

Proposed paragraph (a) went well beyond the fraud standard, prescribing a general requirement that lawyers be "fair." This certainly encompasses a concept of truthful representations. On the other hand, paragraph (b) restates DR 7–102(A)(5) and subparagraph (b)(1) does not depart radically from the present code. Subparagraph (b)(2) parallels the *Restatement (Second) of Agency* (1957, sec. 348, comment c), which provides that under certain circumstances, if a lawyer does not correct a manifest misapprehension on the part of the opposing party, the lawyer could incur civil liability. Furthermore, the lawyer would probably be guilty, under existing legal principles, of the ethical offense of "assisting" the client in "illegal" conduct (Hazard, 1981).

The idea underlying the Kutak Commission's original proposal was not very complicated: the lawyer, as the instrument of a transaction, should be the guardian of its integrity (Rubin, 1975, p. 591). The proposal did not purport to hold lawyers strictly liable for the integrity of transactions or even burden them with a duty of reasonable care. Their only duty was to disclose facts of which an opposing party was obviously ignorant and which might affect the integrity of the transaction.[5]

Much more fundamental objections were leveled at the proposal, particularly at the requirement that lawyers be "fair." Many members of the commission and certainly the Reporter were surprised at the vehemence of the objections. *"Vehemence"* is the correct word, since much more heat than light was forthcoming in the reaction to the proposal. The commission's surprise was compounded because the proposal seemed appropriate to the lawyer's role and appeared to reflect one interpretation of the lawyer's duty as established in the decisional law (Kutak, 1980).

Although the explanation of the bar's aversion to the January 1980 proposal is complex, some concerns can be identified. First, many members of the bar do not realize or are unwilling to accept the fact that the law at large applies to lawyers (Hazard, 1978). Perhaps these members of the bar believe an immunity attaches to lawyers against the civil liabilities imposed by the law on other intermediaries such as real estate brokers or securities underwriters. More subtly, perhaps lawyers recognize that the law at large applies to them but do not wish to be accountable for that obligation in the context of professional discipline.

Still subtler concerns were involved. The fundamental difficulty appears to stem from the lack of a firm professional consensus regarding the standard of openness that should govern lawyers' dealings with others and the lack of settled and homogeneous standards of technique in the practice of law (White, 1980). This lack of consensus indicates that lawyers, at least nationally, do not share a common conception of fairness in the process of negotiation. The lack of this consensus means that lawyers lack the language to express norms of fairness in negotiation and the institutional means to give effect to these norms.

The underlying disagreement about standards of fairness is not difficult to understand. Lawyers' standards of fairness are necessarily derived from those of society as a whole (White, 1980), and sub-cultural variations are enormous. At one extreme lies the "rural God-fearing standard," so exacting and tedious that it often excludes the use of lawyers. At the other extreme stands "New York hardball," now played in most larger cities using the wall-to-wall indenture for a playing surface. Between these extremes are regional and local standards and further variations that depend on the business involved, the identity of the participants, and other circumstances.[6] Against this kaleidoscopic background, it is difficult to specify a single standard that governs the parties and thus a correlative standard that should govern their legal representatives.

The second area of disagreement concerns professional technique. Lawyers differ widely in the technical sophistication they expect of themselves and of others with whom they deal (Laumann and Heinz, 1977). As a result, their expectations regarding their own or their opponents' knowledge in the context of a given transaction may vary widely. Among practitioners having a very high level of technique, it is expected that a lawyer has carefully investigated and compiled relevant information, is familiar with recent developments in applicable law, recognizes all tax implications of a transaction, and anticipates secondary transactions likely to be involved in the transaction at hand. At another level of technique, lawyers may use a standard form for a transaction and hope for a satisfactory result.[7]

Professional transactions within any given level of technique proceed according to implicitly understood conventions that allay all but ordinary anxiety on the part of the lawyers. Professional transactions that combine diverse levels of technique pose much greater difficulties. Lawyers accustomed to less sophisticated techniques are understandably fearful that they will be outmatched or even hoodwinked, with the possibility of loss to their clients and humiliation or even worse for themselves.

Lawyers accustomed to more sophisticated techniques have a correlative but perhaps less apparent dilemma. First, signs of bumbling on the other side cannot necessarily be taken at face value; there is such a thing as country-slickering and it occurs even in the city. Second, sophisticated lawyers are at risk precisely because of their technical sophistication. High-level technicians recognize aspects of transactions that lawyers of lesser sophistication may overlook. But what is to be done with that knowledge? If it is withheld, the transaction becomes vulnerable to rescission because of the lawyer's nondisclosure. The lawyer's professional competence, if not fully deployed for the benefit of the opposing party, thus becomes a potential infirmity for the transaction.[8] Conversely, if the lawyer's competence is deployed for the benefit of the opposing party, where does the deployment properly stop, short of a takeover of the transaction and assumption of responsibility for the interests of both parties?[9]

In the ebb and flow of practice, lawyers can and do adjust to these exigencies. The high level technicians deal with each other with circumspection but confidence. Lawyers in other strata of the professional community have their own conventions. When levels are crossed, the less sophisticated lawyer must decide whether to trust the opponent or to associate someone else, research into the night, or perhaps even abort the transaction. The more sophisticated lawyer must decide whether to risk later recriminations about the transaction if the bargain is too hard, whether to make particular disclosures to protect the deal but at the risk also of killing the deal, or whether to handle the transaction for both sides.

This range of possibilities is difficult to govern by regulation. A rule based on the premise that the legal profession is substantially homogeneous in technical sophistication would put the technically sophisticated lawyer in a hopeless dilemma when dealing with an unsophisticated opposing counsel. Such a lawyer could straightforwardly be a partisan of his own client unless it became evident that the other side was inadequately represented. But in that case, the superior technician would have to assist the other side to guard against the risk of a subsequent charge of nondisclosure or fraud. Yet until a transaction is well underway, a lawyer cannot know which course of action is required. At the same time, the lawyer who is unsophisticated or is simply acting according to his idea of the applicable conventions of openness would be in jeopardy of giving away his client's position. Thus, in a situation where the opposing lawyers differ substantially in technical sophistication, a rule requiring reciprocal disclosure could not yield genuine reciprocity.

On the other hand, it would be practically impossible to formulate a general rule that accounts for variations in technical sophistication. Consider the difficulties with the concept of specialization and with the definition of specialization once the concept was accepted (Fromson, 1976) or with the problem of "incompetence" among the trial bar (Smith, 1980). Could we imagine rules of disclosure that were based on a distinction between type A lawyers and type B lawyers? Anyone who is sanguine about overcoming these difficulties should try drafting the criteria by which to differentiate the technically sophisticated practitioner from the bar at large.

In light of these constraints, legal regulation of trustworthiness cannot go much further than to proscribe fraud. That is disquieting but not necessarily occasion for despair. It simply indicates limitations on improving the bar by legal regulation (Schwartz, 1980).

Notes

1. For example, under securities regulations, lawyers are required to make certain disclosures in their representation of corporate clients. See 15 U.S. Code sec. 77www (1976); Lipman (1974).

2. See *Restatement (Second) of Torts* (1976). Cf. *Restatement (Second) of Agency* (1957, sec. 348; agent subject to tort liability for fraudulent representation made on behalf of principal).

3. DR 7–102(A)(7) provides that "in his representation of a client, a lawyer shall not . . . [c]ounsel or assist his client in conduct that the lawyer knows to be illegal or fraudulent" (American Bar Association, 1977).

4. American Bar Association, Commission on Evaluation of Professional Standards (1981). Proposed Rule 1.2(d) provides as follows: "A lawyer shall not counsel or assist a client in conduct that the lawyer knows or reasonably should know is criminal or fraudulent, or in the preparation of a written instrument containing terms the lawyer knows or reasonably should know are legally prohibited, but a lawyer may counsel or assist a client in a good faith effort to determine the validity, scope, meaning, or application of the law."

5. In this regard, use of the term *material facts* in the January 1980 proposal would have been more precise.

6. These were brought home to me dramatically when I entered the practice of law in Oregon after attending law school in New York City.

7. See, for example, *Lucas* v. *Hamm,* 56 Cal. 2d 583, 364 P.2d 685, 15 Cal. Rptr. 821 (1961), 46. This consideration became pivotal in the Kutak Commission's decision to withdraw proposed Rule 4.1(a) of the Discussion Draft, Jan. 30, 1980.

8. This consideration became pivotal in the Kutak Commission's decision to withdraw proposed Rule 4.1(a) of the Discussion Draft, Jan. 30, 1980.

9. See 329 U.S. at 516 (Jackson, J., concurring) ("Discovery was hardly intended to enable a learned profession to perform its functions either without wits or on wits borrowed from the adversary").

References

American Bar Association. *Canons of Professional Ethics, No. 37.* Chicago: American Bar Association, 1908.

American Bar Association. *ABA Code of Professional Responsibility.* Chicago: American Association, 1977.

American Bar Association. Commission on Evaluation of Professional Standards. "Model Rules of Professional Conduct." Discussion Draft, Jan. 30, 1980.

American Bar Association. Commission on Evaluation of Professional Standards. "Model Rules of Professional Conduct." Proposed Final Draft, May 30, 1981.

Fromson, T. "The Challenge of Specialization: Professionalism at the Crossroads." *New York State Bar Journal,* 1976, *48.*

Hazard, G. *Ethics in the Practice of Law.* New Haven: Yale University Press, 1978.

Hazard, G. "How Far May a Lawyer Go in Assisting a Client in Conduct That Might Be Illegal?" *University of Miami Law Review,* 1981, *669.*

Kutak R. J "Evaluating the Proposed Model Rules of Professional Conduct." *American Bar Foundation Research Journal,* 1980, *1016, 1021,* n. 22.

Laumann, E., and Heinz, J. "Specialization and Prestige in the Legal Profession: The Structure of Deference." *American Bar Foundation Research Journal,* 1977, *1,* 155–216.

Lipman, F. "The SEC's Reluctant Police Force: A New Role for Lawyers." *New York University Law Review,* 1974, *49,* 437.

Restatement (Second) of Agency. § 1957.

Restatement (Second) of Torts. § 1976.

Rubin, A. B. *A Causerie on Lawyer's Ethics in Negotiations,* 35, La. L. Rev. 577 (1975).

Schwartz, M. L. "The Death and Regeneration of Ethics." *American Bar Foundation Research Journal,* 1980, 953–960.

Smith, "Peer Review: Its Time Has Come." *American Bar Foundation Research Journal,* 1980, *66,* 4.

White, J. J. "Machiavelli and the Bar: Ethical Limitations on Lying in Negotiation." *American Bar Foundation Research Journal,* 1980, *926, 927.*

Wigmore, J. *Treatise on Evidence.* § 2298 (McNaughton Rev. 1961 8c Supp. 1980).

CHAPTER THIRTEEN

Curtailing Deception

The Impact of Direct Questions on Lies and Omissions

Maurice E. Schweitzer

Rachel Croson

Deception in organizations represents a significant managerial challenge (Grover, 1993a; Grover and Hui, 1994) across a broad range of functional areas (Jones, 1991). Available examples range from inflated Medicare claims in Florida ("Hospital Chain . . . ," 1998) to misrepresentation of repair work throughout Sears' automotive unit in California ("Getting Your Car . . . ," 1992; "Sears Gets . . . ," 1992). One managerial activity particularly prone to deception is negotiations. For example, in recent lawsuits, Textron was accused by its union of lying during labor negotiations (*Textron* v. *United Automobile,* 1998), Digital Equipment Corporation was accused of lying during pretrial negotiations (*Digital* v. *Desktop Direct,* 1994), and Woolworth was accused of misrepresenting the amount of asbestos in a building during the negotiation of a lease (*Century 21 Inc.* v. *F. W. Woolworth Co.,* 1992).

Negotiators have both incentives and opportunities to mislead others (Lewis and Saarni, 1993). For example, negotiators who use deception often benefit by increasing their power (Lewicki and Robinson, 1998), their perceived power (Shapiro and Bies, 1994), and profits (Chertkoff and Baird, 1971; O'Connor and Carnevale, 1997). Of course, there are costs to using deception. These costs, however, are often uncertain and delayed, and even when deception is detected, the costs can be mitigated by providing explanations perceived to be adequate and honest (Shapiro, 1991).

Opportunities for deception are created by two factors: First, the existence of private and asymmetric information and second, the difficulty people have detecting deception. Since few untrained people can detect lies (DePaulo, 1988; Ekman and O'Sullivan, 1991; Ekman and Friesen, 1974; DePaulo and DePaulo, 1989), negotiators have ample opportunities to mislead others. Further, since people are generally overconfident in their ability to detect deception (Ekman and O'Sullivan, 1991), negotiators are likely to underestimate the magnitude of this problem.

Despite the importance of deception in negotiations, surprisingly few prescriptions for contending with deceptive practices exist. Fisher, Ury, and Patton (1991) suggest that negotiators "learn to spot particular ploys that indicate deception," and then "raise the issue explicitly and question the tactic's legitimacy" (p. 130). Detecting lies, however, is very difficult. To help detect lies, Thompson (1998) recommends three specific strategies: testing the consistency of information by asking many questions, insisting on negotiating in person, and asking for proof such as documentation when possible. In this paper, we investigate a related, but different approach to curtailing deception. We investigate the impact of asking direct questions on lying behavior. We consider the most blatant type of misrepresentation, lies about material facts, and examine the role of direct questions in mitigating deception. The first study measures actors' propensity to deceive friends and strangers when asked or not asked a direct question. The second study extends this investigation by identifying the impact of direct questions on lies of omission and lies of commission.

TYPES OF DECEPTIVE BEHAVIOR

Deceptive practices have been classified along several dimensions. In early work, Bok (1978) distinguishes between misleading *statements,* which she defines as lies, and misleading *omissions,* which she defines as deception. In this paper we distinguish between lies of omission and lies of commission but use the terms *deception* and *lying* interchangeably.

DePaulo et al. (1996) develop a taxonomy of lies, and classify lies according to their content, motivation, magnitude, and referent (whether the lie is about the liar, another person, objects, or event). Lewicki and Stark (1996) analyze subjects' evaluations of eighteen ethically questionable negotiation tactics, and categorize these into five "appropriateness" categories. We draw from this literature, and classify types of deception according to the information misrepresented. These categories include lies about a reservation price, lies about interests, bluffs (making false threats or promises), and lies about material facts. Unlike prior work on deception, we focus our investigation on lies about material facts.

ACCEPTABILITY OR DECEPTIVE PRACTICES IN NEGOTIATION

Despite the routine occurrence of deception in negotiations, there is little agreement among experts on the extent to which deception is appropriate. Some scholars recommend that negotiators avoid "bluffing" (Dees and Cramton, 1991; Fisher, Ury, and Patton, 1991), while others claim that deception is a normal (Lax and Sebenius, 1986; Wokutch and Carson, 1993) and in some cases an integral (Carr, 1968) part of the negotiation process.

More often, however, scholars have made distinctions between types of deception that are and are not acceptable. These distinctions have been based upon the type of information concealed, the type of deceptive practice used, and whether or not the deception involves a statement or an omission. For example, Wokutch and Carson (1993) argue that it is worse to lie about an issue about "which other parties have a right to know than one about which they have no right to know" (p. 502). Others ethicists have argued that lies about one's reservation price are acceptable, while lies about material facts are not (Strudler, 1995).

In related empirical work, negotiators typically consider lies about one's reservation price to be acceptable, but consider fabrications about material facts to be unethical (Anton, 1990), inappropriate (Lewicki and Stark, 1996), and unacceptable (Lewicki, Saunders, and Minton, 1997; Lewicki and Robinson, 1998). The practice of bluffing has been more difficult to categorize. Bluffs have been rated as unacceptable in some studies (Lewicki and Stark, 1996; Lewicki and Robinson, 1998), but acceptable in others (Anton, 1990). Kronzon and Darley (1999) find that perceptions of conflict and deception are moderated by identification. For example, subjects who identify with the deceiver rate deception as more acceptable than those who identify with the target.

Advice for negotiators echoes this confusion. Prescriptions regarding the use of deception range from Raiffa's recommendation (1982) that negotiators deal honestly with each other to Wokutch and Carson's claim (1993) that lying in negotiations is justified in most cases. Lax and Sebenius (1986) suggest that negotiators consult a list of questions, such as "What if everyone bargained this way?" to guide their own behavior.

EXPERIMENTAL STUDIES OF DECEPTION IN NEGOTIATION

A number of studies have examined self-reports of deceptive practices and identified important determinants of deception. These studies find that individual characteristics such as nationality (Lewicki and Robinson, 1998), education, religion (Maier and Lavrakas, 1976), gender, and work experience (Robinson,

Lewicki, and Donahue, 1997), as well as contextual factors such as relationship considerations (Maier and Lavrakas, 1976; Haidt and Baron, 1996) affect a negotiator's propensity to lie. These results are consistent with behavioral models of deception (Lewicki, 1983) and unethical behavior (Hegarty and Sims, 1978; Trevino, 1986; Grover, 1993a; Grover, 1993b; Grover and Hui, 1994).

A few experimental studies have also examined deception in negotiations. Tenbrunsel (1998) investigates the role of incentives in misrepresentation of a forecast, and finds that larger incentives increase the likelihood of misrepresentation. O'Connor and Carnevale (1997) examine misrepresentation of a common value issue in a negotiation task, and find that negotiators in 28 percent of the dyads misrepresent their interests. In other experimental work, Shapiro (1991) investigates negotiators' reactions to deception. Her findings reveal that negotiators who use deception can mitigate negative reactions by providing explanations which are perceived to be adequate and honest. Taken together these studies illuminate important antecedents and consequences of lying, but offer little advice for contending with deception.

STUDY 1

The first study investigates self-reported lying behavior of subjects asked to assume the role of a prospective seller of a used car. The questionnaire scenario describes a car with a transmission problem that will need work but does not require immediate attention. A prospective buyer takes the car for a test drive but does not detect the problem. Consequently, the buyer would reasonably assume that the car is mechanically sound. In this questionnaire, subjects are asked how likely they would be to reveal this problem to a friend and to a stranger who asks or does not ask about the mechanical condition of the car.

Hypotheses

Our first hypothesis explores the relationship between asking questions and deception. We expect subjects who are asked a direct question to be less likely to use deception than subjects who are not asked a direct question. We develop this expectation based upon three assumptions. First, we assume that people can choose to lie by omission, lie by commission, or reveal the truth. Second, we assume that most people would prefer to lie by omission than by commission. Third, we assume that direct questions force people to articulate a response, and choose between telling a lie by commission and revealing the truth.

The key assumption underlying this hypothesis is that people will be more reticent to mislead someone by commission than omission. Prior work has demonstrated that people judge commissions more seriously than omissions (Spranca, Minsk, and Baron, 1991) and that emotional reactions to adverse outcomes are stronger when these outcomes result from action than when they result from inaction (Kahneman and Tversky, 1982). In addition, intentionality is easier to judge for acts than for equivalent omissions, and both individual decision makers and the law attach greater responsibility to actions (Baron, 1992; Shell, 1991). Consequently, if direct questions foreclose the option of lying by omission we expect direct questions to curtail the overall use of deception:

Hypothesis 1a: When asked a direct question, subjects will be less likely to use deception than when they are not asked a direct question.

We also propose the alternative hypothesis: that asking a direct question will actually increase the use of deception. In this case, we consider the possibility that direct questions increase anxiety, and that respondents will choose to tell lies to resolve this anxiety. We assume that asking questions creates tension and conflict, and that one approach for resolving this tension is the use of deception. In support of this mechanism, Hample (1980) found that most lies were responsive and unplanned. Liars were "suddenly faced with a lie-provoking problem" (p. 41) that triggered the use of deception. This process explanation is echoed in Grover's model of lying (1993a) in organizations involving "individual distress that can be relieved by lying" (p. 481). A separate literature has also demonstrated that leading questions can evoke misinformation. In an extreme example of this process, leading questions can be used to elicit false memories (see Loftus, 1997; Garven, Wood, Malpass, and Shaw, 1998). Consequently, we consider the alternative hypothesis.

Hypothesis 1b: When asked a direct question, subjects will be more likely to use deception than when they are not asked a direct question.

Our second hypothesis investigates the relationship between deception and solidarity. Brown (1965) describes dimensions of relationships, and defines a solidarity dimension to represent the intimacy of a relationship. Hamilton and Sanders (1981) extend this concept and define solidarity across a range of relationships. Close or "status" relationships involve intimate associations such as familial ties. At the opposite extreme, remote or "contract" relationships involve limited and temporary relationships such as a one-time interaction with an anonymous clerk.

Although friends may be more likely to tell altruistic lies, we expect friends to be less likely to lie about a material fact in a transactional negotiation. An exposed lie in this context will have greater consequences for friends, such as harming a future relationship and disrupting a social network. Even if a lie escapes detection, friends are likely to suffer stronger feelings of regret and guilt. In previous work, Haidt and Baron (1996) found that friends are held more responsible than strangers.

It is also easier to lie to strangers. Strangers are less sensitive to nonverbal and verbal cues (Anderson, Ansfield, and DePaulo, 1999) and are consequently less likely to detect deception. Strangers are also less likely to detect deception in the future since a liar is less likely to reveal information to a stranger at a future point in time:

Hypothesis 2: Subjects will be more likely to deceive strangers than friends.

We also consider the role of ethics education in curtailing lying behavior. Ethics education may impact actual professional behavior (Duska, 1991), and in experimental work, ethics education has been linked to advances in moral development (Jones, 1989). Ethics education has become more prevalent in business schools (Schoenfeldt, McDonald, and Youngblood, 1991), and we examine its impact on the use of deception in this setting.

Hypothesis 3: Subjects who have taken a course in ethics will be less likely to use deception than those who have not taken a course in ethics.

Method

We recruited eighty graduate students from a southern university in the U.S. to complete one of four versions of a questionnaire for course credit.

A total of twenty subjects completed each of the four versions, which were identical except for the order of the treatment conditions. The questionnaire began with the following introduction:

Suppose you are planning to move, and must sell your current car—a 1990 Honda Civic (4 door, automatic transmission, and sun roof). You have taken good care of the car and believe it to be in decent condition. Recently, though, you have had some transmission trouble. Your mechanic told you that the car will eventually need some work, but that the problem does not require immediate attention—the car seems to run perfectly fine most of the time.

After reading this introduction, subjects were asked to rate the likelihood that they would tell a prospective buyer about the transmission problem on an 11-point scale (1 = certainly would not tell, to 11 = certainly would tell) under each of four conditions. The order in which these questions were asked created a two-by-two design for the treatment conditions of a buyer who is either a friend or a stranger and a buyer who either asks or does not ask about the mechanical condition of the car. All four treatment conditions are presented here in brackets:

A potential buyer, Jon, has just come to look at the car. [Jon is a friend of yours, and you expect to keep in touch with him after you move/ Jon is a stranger you just met and you do not expect to ever see him again.] Jon took the car out for a test drive, and the car performed without a problem.

a. Suppose Jon [asks you/does not ask you] about the mechanical condition of the car. How likely would you be to tell him about the transmission problem?

The questionnaire concluded by asking subjects their age, gender, whether or not they had ever taken a course in ethics, and the number of times they had been involved in selling and buying a used car.

Results

Since each subject rated the likelihood that they would reveal the transmission problem under four treatment conditions, we conducted a repeated measures analysis of variance to analyze responses. Presentation order did not significantly influence responses, and consequently we combine results across versions for the remainder of the analysis.

The average respondent's age was 26.6, and fifty-two (65 percent) of the respondents were male. A second repeated measures analysis of variance revealed no significant gender differences [$F(1, 78) = 1.63$, ns], and we combined results across gender as well.

Almost all of the subjects admitted that they might mislead a prospective buyer under some conditions. Only six respondents (7.5 percent) claimed that they would certainly tell a prospective buyer about the car trouble in each of the four cases.

We next computed the total number of times a subject had bought or sold a used car. On average, each respondent had been involved in a total of 2.94 used car transactions. A third repeated measures analysis of variance revealed no significant differences across levels of experience with buying or selling a used car [$F(12, 67) = .88$, ns]. This suggests that the experience of buying or selling a used car did not moderate lying behavior in this case.

In the condition involving a stranger who neglects to ask about the mechanical condition of the car, twenty subjects (25 percent) claimed that they would certainly not tell a stranger about the transmission problem, and only six subjects (7.5 percent) claimed that they certainly would tell. However, when the situation involves a friend who inquires about the mechanical condition of the car, a total of forty-nine subjects (61.25 percent) claimed that they certainly would reveal the transmission problem, and no subjects admitted that they certainly would not reveal the problem.

Figure 13.1 reports average responses for each of the four cases. Subjects were most likely to reveal the mechanical problem to friends who asked, next most likely to tell friends who did not ask, third most likely to tell strangers who asked, and least likely to tell strangers who did not ask. These differences were statistically significant; the Wilks' lambda from a repeated measures analysis of variance produced an $F(3, 74) = 51.53$, $p < .001$. Separate multivariate analyses of variance determined that friendship mattered [Wilks' λ $F(2, 75) = 505.67$, $p < .001$], asking mattered [Wilks' lambda $F(2, 75) = 283.47$, $p < .001$], and that there was an interaction between the two [Wilks' lambda $F(2, 75) = 16.93$, $p < .001$] suggesting that asking benefits strangers more than it does friends.

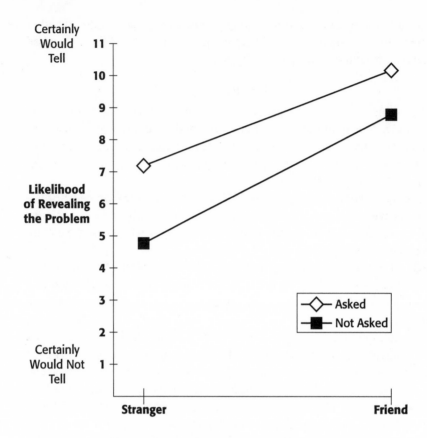

Figure 13.1. Average Likelihood of Revealing a Mechanical Problem

The results support hypothesis la (subjects were less likely to lie when asked a direct question) and hypothesis 2 (subjects were less likely to lie to friends).

The interaction between friendship and asking probing questions may be explained by a ceiling effect. For example, several subjects selected an "11 on the 11-point scale when asked if they would reveal the transmission problem to a friend who did not ask about the mechanical condition of the car. These subjects were unable to rate themselves as even more likely to reveal the problem to a friend who did ask. To investigate this explanation we conducted a second set of repeated measures analyses of variance that "excluded subjects who selected any extreme-scale values. This reduced the sample to twenty-two subjects, and results from this analysis revealed that friendship mattered [Wilks' lambda $F(2, 17)$ = 218.53, p < .001] and asking mattered [Wilks' lambda $F(2, 17)$ = 90.25, p < .001], but we did not find an interaction between the two [Wilks' lambda $F(2, 17)$ = .42, ns].

Surprisingly, we found no support for hypothesis 3. There were no differences between the responses of the forty-two (52.5 percent) subjects who had taken an ethics course and those of the thirty-eight (47.5 percent) subjects who had not taken an ethics course. As Figure 13.2 depicts, respondents who had taken an ethics course were slightly less likely to lie, but this difference did not approach significance; results from a repeated measures analysis of variance comparing those who had to those who had not taken an ethics course yielded an $F(1, 78) = .04$, *ns*.

Discussion of Study 1

These results describe the self-reported propensity of subjects to lie in a negotiation context. A vast majority of subjects admitted that they might or would certainly mislead a prospective buyer about a mechanical problem with a car. By design, negotiator's private information in this scenario constitutes a material

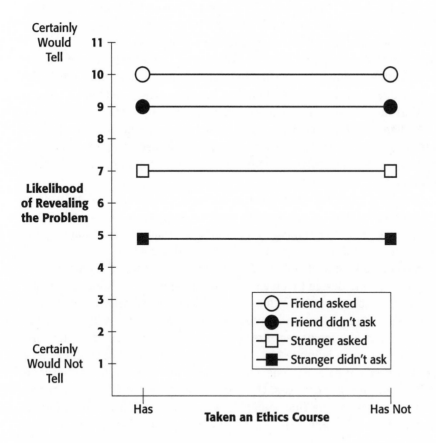

Figure 13.2. Average Response and Ethics Education

fact, and the prevalence of deception in this study is surprising in light of prior work which has demonstrated that negotiators consider lies about material facts to be unacceptable (Anton, 1990; Lewicki and Stark, 1996; Lewicki, Saunders, and Minton, 1997). The difference between prior findings and our results may be explained by a difference in context, a difference in subject population, or a difference in elicitation method. Context influences the acceptability of deception (Lewicki, 1983; Lewicki, Litterer, Minton, and Saunders, 1994), and task frame has been demonstrated to influence behavior (Neale, Huber, and Northcraft, 1987). Subjects in this study may have been more likely to lie because the benefits from lying were more explicit or because the context of a used car cued a greater propensity to lie. In addition, demographic characteristics may have influenced evaluations. Even though both prior work and this study involved graduate students, the two populations were drawn from different universities with different demographic compositions.

Subjects reported that they were more likely to disclose the problem when they were asked a direct question. This finding supports the premise that subjects are less comfortable misleading others by commission than omission, rather than the hypothesis that asking questions creates conflict that ultimately increases the use of deception. Subjects also reported a higher propensity to disclose the problem when the prospective buyer was a friend than when the prospective buyer was a stranger. Friends in this case may be held more responsible for lies that cause harm. This result may be domain specific, and in other contexts where social norms dictate misrepresentation, friends may be held less responsible for deception, or may even be expected to use deception. Although we found an interaction between omission and friendship in our initial analysis, this result can be explained by a ceiling effect.

Suprisingly, subjects who had taken a course in ethics were just as likely to lie as subjects who had not. This result does not suggest that ethics education cannot improve moral thinking, but rather indicates that the ethics training this population received did not influence behavior in this context.

Our second study extends our investigation by addressing three limitations of Study 1. First, the design involved self-reported measures. Subjects may act differently when actually faced with a direct question. The tension created when someone asks a direct question in a face-to-face negotiation, as in our second study, may evoke a different set of responses than those reported in this one. Second, the first study is limited by its application to a used car context. The context of a used car sale may cue specific behaviors that are not representative of behavior in other contexts. Our second study uses a different, transactional context. Third, the first study does not distinguish between lies of omission and lies of commission. This limitation is also addressed in our second study.

STUDY 2

The focus of Study 2 is the impact of direct questions on deceptive behavior, and this experiment extends our investigation in several ways. First, the experiment involves a negotiation task designed to measure behaviors rather than intentions. Second, the experiment involves a domain different from a used car context. Third, this study distinguishes between types of deceptive practices. Specifically, we are able to observe both lies of omission and lies of commission in this experiment.

The second study describes a negotiation experiment involving the sale of a used computer with a faulty hard drive. The seller knows about the problem with the drive and also knows that the buyer is unaware of the problem. Through the course of negotiation sellers can either lie about this information, conceal this information by omission, or reveal this information to the buyer. Deception in this study is measured by coders who analyzed audio-taped recordings of the negotiation process.

Hypotheses

In this section we identify manipulation checks about the interventions and hypotheses about the relationship between asking questions and deception. The structure of Study 2 lacks the control of Study 1, and we were concerned that buyers in this negotiation would fail to ask enough questions. Since the focus of the experiment is the relationship between questions and deception, we designed interventions to prompt buyers to ask questions.

We designed three treatment conditions to influence the number of questions buyers asked. In the strong and moderate treatments, buyers were prompted to consider information they did not know, and to list questions they should ask prior to negotiating. We expect this intervention to increase the salience of missing information (Slovic, Fischhoff, and Lichtenstein, 1987) and prompt buyers to ask additional questions. That is, we expect buyers who are prompted to list questions prior to negotiating to ask more questions than buyers who are not prompted to list questions.

The strong treatment condition also included a list of potential problems with purchasing a used computer. We expect this information to highlight the amount of missing information and influence the nature and number of questions buyers ask. Specifically, we expect buyers in the strong treatment condition to ask more questions than buyers in the moderate treatment condition.

We next consider the relationship between asking questions and deception. In some negotiation contexts, negotiators have a positive obligation to disclose information. In these cases, omissions may constitute fraud. For example, if a negotiator sells an item with a hidden defect that a prudent buyer would not be able to identify through the course of a normal or routine inspection, the seller has an obligation to disclose the problem. We propose the following model of hypotheses for subject behavior for revealing or concealing this type of information. Subjects may choose to truthfully reveal the information, actively lie about the information by commission, or avoid the topic and lie by omission. Note that avoiding the topic in this case constitutes a lie of omission.

We expect subject behavior to be influenced by direct questions as depicted by Figure 13.3. When buyers ask a direct question, sellers choose between revealing information and misstating a fact (lying by commission). In this case, we assume that sellers are not able to deflect the question or avoid the topic. Effectively, we assume that when buyers ask a direct question they foreclose the seller's option to lie by omission. When buyers do not ask a direct question, sellers choose between revealing the information and lying by omission. Of course, sellers could lie by commission even when they are not asked a direct question, but we expect sellers to favor lies of omission for both rational (Shell, 1991) and irrational (Spranca, Minsk, and Baron, 1991) reasons. Consequently, when sellers are not asked a direct question we do not expect to observe lies of commission. For these same reasons, we expect deception to be more prevalent when buyers do not ask a direct question, and we propose our first hypothesis:

Hypothesis 1: Subjects will be more likely to reveal a material problem when asked a direct question than when not asked.

This framework also suggests that subjects will not tell lies of omission when they are asked a direct question. We assume that deflecting a direct question is either too difficult or itself tantamount to answering the question, and propose our second hypothesis:

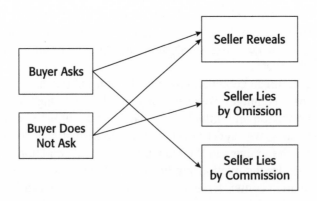

Figure 13.3. Linking Direct Questions and Deception

Hypothesis 2: Subjects will be less likely to lie by omission when asked a direct question than when not asked.

Since we expect subjects to favor omissions to commissions when they are not asked questions and to be unable to lie by omission when asked a direct question, we propose our third hypothesis:

Hypothesis 3: Subjects will be more likely to lie by commission when asked a direct question than when not asked.

Method

Participants and Design. A total of 148 participants were recruited from negotiation courses to role-play a case involving the sale of a used computer. There was no overlap in subjects between the first and second study. Participants were randomly paired and assigned to the role of either buyer or seller. The case was conducted during the first week of the semester before significant relationships or reputations could develop. We recruited 148 subjects from two different schools of business. One hundred subjects were recruited from a large eastern university and 48 subjects were recruited from a large southern university.

All sellers received the same information. In particular, sellers know that the computer had a "sticky" hard drive, which was prone to crashing. Sellers also knew that buyers were unaware of this problem.

Buyers were randomly assigned to one of three between-subject treatment conditions labeled strong, moderate, or weak. The strong treatment condition informed buyers that previous research has found that most buyers fail to ask enough questions. Buyers were then prompted to think carefully about information that they did not know about the computer, and list questions they should plan to ask before making an offer. This treatment condition then listed advantages and disadvantages of purchasing a used computer such as one would find in a consumer guide. This list included leading information for the buyer noting that one drawback to purchasing a used computer is "a lack of information about infrequent crashes or other mechanical problems."

The moderate treatment condition was similar to the strong treatment condition, and also prompted buyers to list questions they should ask during their negotiation. This moderate treatment condition, however, did not include the list of advantages and disadvantages contained in the strong treatment condition. The weak treatment condition was a filler task that asked buyers to list questions they would ask their favorite celebrity. While all three treatment conditions prompted buyers to generate a list of questions, only the strong and moderate conditions prompted buyers to generate negotiation-related questions.

Negotiation Task. The negotiation task involved a buyer and a seller for a used computer with a "sticky" hard drive. As part of their private information, sellers were told:

> When you first purchased the machine (for $2,700), it worked beautifully. In the past couple of months, however, you have had to take it in for service 3 times! Apparently, the 1.2 gig hard drive (which is a large hard drive) has a problem and is prone to crashing. When this happens, you have had to reload EVERYTHING onto the machine. Fortunately, you have kept copies of ALL your important documents, and while this problem has been merely annoying to you, it would pose a serious problem to an unsophisticated user. Since the machine came with a 1 year warranty (which expired 2 weeks ago), all previous repairs to the machine have been free, but you know that the repair shop has not been able to correct this "sticky" hard drive.

Thus, sellers knew that the hard drive periodically crashes and that the repair shop has been unable to correct this problem. Sellers also knew that the buyer did not detect this problem during a quick test run of the computer:

> So far, you have not had much luck selling the machine. One buyer, however, did come by yesterday to check it out and the computer ran without a problem. At that time, they did not ask any questions, only turned the machine on, ran Word and Excel for a couple of minutes and left.

In contrast, buyers were told nothing about the machine's specific problems. Instead, all buyers were told:

> Your friend (an undergraduate computer science major) recommended that you buy a used computer. He said that most computers, if they have problems, break down during the first year, and that if you can find a computer which has been previously owned for at least a year with no problems, it is likely to be a reliable machine.

And later . . .

> You decided to check this machine out since its features would suit your needs. Yesterday, when you went to check out the machine, you turned it on, ran Word and Excel for a couple of minutes, and everything seemed to be in working order. Thus buyers knew general information about the computer and that a quick test run of the computer revealed no problems.

Procedures and Measures. Participants were given approximately twenty minutes to read and prepare the case material. Buyers and sellers were then paired and negotiated the case without a time limit. Each negotiation was recorded with an audio tape, and at the conclusion of each negotiation, subjects completed an agreement sheet and a post-negotiation questionnaire.

We collected both outcome and process measures from each negotiation. The outcome measures include agreements if any, and the final prices as reported in the final agreement sheets. Process measures were collected from the audio recordings of each negotiation. Two raters, blind to the purpose of the study and blind to the hypotheses, independently coded each recording. Raters measured the number of non-price-related questions buyers asked, whether or not buyers asked about the mechanical condition or reliability of the computer, the number of reliability related questions buyers asked, what information sellers revealed about the computer problem, and the length of the negotiation.

Raters' evaluations were consistent. Reliability measures computed from the Spearman-Brown prophecy formula (Nunnally and Bernstein, 1994) produced values of .96 for the number of questions buyers asked, .95 for whether or not buyers asked about the mechanical condition, .95 for the number of reliability related questions buyers asked, .75 for the information sellers revealed, and .97 for the length of the negotiation. A third rater, also blind to the purpose of the study and treatment conditions, independently coded cases involving rater disagreement. This process produced a single set of codes for each negotiation.

We also collected data from the post-negotiation questionnaire of each participant. These questionnaires asked participants questions including general demographic information and their perceptions of the negotiation process.

Results

All of the 148 participants completed the exercise. The average participant's age was 25.3 (SD = 4), with 2.9 (SD = 3.1, median = 3) years of full-time work experience. Most of the participants (66.9 percent) were male, and most dyads reached an agreement. The average final price was $1,350 ($SD$ = 89), with eight dyads failing to reach agreement.

Subject Pool Effects and Manipulation Checks. Our first set of analysis investigates potential differences between the two university populations in our subject pool. We conduct Ordinary Least Squares (OLSQ) regression and logistic regression analyses using process measures and outcomes as dependent measures, and treatment condition and university (a dummy variable) parameters as independent variables. We find no differences between the two university populations across process measures and outcomes; across all models, parameter estimates for the university variable are small and insignificant. Consequently, we combine data from both populations for the remainder of the analysis.

Analysis of variance reveals that treatment condition significantly influenced the number of questions buyers asked [$F(2, 72)$ = 7.10, p < .01]. Bonferroni corrected pairwise comparisons (for a group alpha = .05) reveals that buyers asked significantly fewer questions in the weak treatment than in the moderate and strong treatments. We did not find a significant difference between the number of questions asked in the strong treatment and in the moderate treatment.

The percentage of buyers who asked about the reliability of the computer in particular demonstrated a similar pattern. Tests for equality of proportions reveal that buyers in the moderate treatment were more likely to ask about the reliability of the computer than were buyers in the weak treatment. This result approached statistical significance ($p = .053$), but other differences were not significant.

As described by Table 13.1, buyers in both the moderate and strong treatments asked more questions and were more likely to ask about the reliability of the computer, but we found no significant differences between the negotiation processes of buyers in the moderate and strong treatments. We suggest some possible explanations for these results in the discussion section.

Sellers' Claims. The main variable of interest in this study is the seller's claim regarding the working condition of the computer. We group sellers' claims into three categories: sellers either revealed the problem (revealed), lied to conceal the problem (commission), or made no mention of the problem (omission). The revealed problem category includes statements such as "The computer has a problem" and "The computer has a problem that may persist." The commission category includes statements such as "The computer has no problem" and "The computer had a problem, which is now fixed." The omission category includes cases where the seller made no mention of the reliability or working condition of the computer. In Exhibit 13.1 we list actual examples of the types of questions buyers asked and the responses sellers gave.

Table 13.2 describes the negotiation process in terms of whether or not buyers asked about the reliability (or mechanical condition) of the computer and sellers' claims. Our main result is that sellers' claims were significantly influenced by whether or not buyers asked about the reliability of the computer $\chi^2 (2) = 54.37, p < .0011$.

Table 13.1. Questions Asked by Treatment Condition

Process Measures	Treatment Condition		
	Weak	Moderate	Strong
Number of questions asked (average)	5.56	9.56	8.35
Percentage asked about reliability	76.0	92.0	83.3
Number of dyads	25	25	24

Exhibit 13.1. Excerpts from the Negotiation Process: Example Questions and Answers

When Sellers Revealed the Problem

Example 1

Buyer: Has anything gone wrong with the computer while you've had it?
Seller: Well the problem that I've been working on is the hard drive. And it crashes every now and then.
Buyer: So if it crashed I could lose some of my data?
Seller: It is possible to lose data, but what I do is back up all my data. Everybody who runs a computer backs up the data.

Example 2

Buyer: Have you had to use your warranty to fix anything?
Seller: Once in a while it used to crash. And that was kind of a problem, which is why I've been very good at making sure I have all the software. In case it ever crashes, you've got all the software.
Buyer: When you say crash, what do you mean?
Seller: Ah, I'm not sure why it crashed. That's why, you know, I took it in.
Buyer: When it crashes, what did you lose? I'm concerned. What did you have to do?

When Sellers Lied by Commission

Example 3

Buyer: Have you had any problems with the computer in the past? Is there anything I need to be concerned about?
Seller: Well, I've been happy with it. It works relatively well for me. It's no longer under warranty. But it's been a great computer for me.
Buyer: Now is there anything, any part of the computer, that you would need to take with you? Or is the whole thing for sale?
Seller: No, basically everything is for sale. The way you saw it, you can take it. All the programs are loaded. It has a hard drive. You know the monitor—it's a great monitor.

Example 4

Buyer: Have you had any problems with the computer? I mean, anything out of the ordinary?
Seller: No nothing, nothing major actually. You know from time to time, you clean up things, but nothing major. It was just like, ah, like, ah, regular maintenance.
Buyer: Regular maintenance?
Seller: Yes.
Buyer: Have you added any new hardware where you had to open up the computer? Like to install like a modem or install a CD-ROM? Or did it come with all that?
Seller: It came with all that. It was fully packaged. It was all set.
Buyer: So you haven't opened it up?
Seller: No. No need to do that.

Table 13.2. Asking Questions and Information Exchange

	Buyer Asked	
Seller's Action	Yes	No
Revealed	38 (61 percent)	0 (0 percent)
Omission	0 (0 percent)	9 (75 percent)
Commission	24 (39 percent)	3 (25 percent)
Total	62	12

When buyers did ask about the reliability of the computer, sellers either revealed the problem or concealed the problem with a lie of commission. When buyers did not ask about the reliability of the computer, sellers either lied by omission or lied by commission, stating that the computer had no problem. In no case did a seller reveal the computer problem when the buyer failed to ask about the reliability of the computer.

Confirming our first hypothesis, sellers were significantly more likely to reveal the problem when buyers asked them about the reliability of the computer than when buyers did not ask them about the reliability of the computer. When buyers asked a direct question about the reliability of the computer, they were informed of the problem 61 percent of the time. When buyers did not ask about the reliability of the computer, they were informed of the problem 0 percent of the time ($p < .001$ in a test for equality of proportions).

Confirming our second hypothesis, sellers were more likely to lie by omission when they were not asked a direct question than when they were asked a direct question. When buyers asked a direct question about the reliability of the computer, none of the sellers avoided the topic and said nothing about the condition of the computer. When buyers did not ask a direct question, 75 percent of the sellers avoided the topic and said nothing about the condition of the computer ($p < .001$ in a test for equality of proportions).

Consistent with our third hypothesis, sellers were more likely to lie by commission when they were asked a direct question than when they were not asked a direct question. When buyers asked about the reliability of the computer, 39 percent of the sellers lied by commission. When buyers did not ask about the reliability of the computer, 25 percent of the sellers lied by commission. This difference, however, was not statistically significant.

These results are consistent with our main hypotheses and generally consistent with the framework depicted in Figure 13.3. We were surprised, however, by the behavior of sellers who were not asked direct questions. None of these sellers revealed the problem, and some of these sellers volunteered lies of commission.

Negotiated Outcomes. We next examine the relationship between negotiated outcomes and the claims sellers made. Although in most negotiations, buyers and sellers reached an agreement based solely upon price, five negotiated agreements included warranties (e.g., "a thirty-day return policy") and eight negotiated outcomes resulted in no agreement. As expected, negotiated agreements were most likely to include warranties when sellers revealed the problem, but even then only four agreements included warranties. When sellers lied by commission, one agreement included a warranty, and when sellers lied by omission, none of the agreements included a warranty. When sellers revealed the problem, lied by commission, and lied by omission, four, two, and two of the negotiations resulted in no agreement, respectively. In our analysis of the relationship between sellers' claims and final prices, we excluded negotiated outcomes that included warranties or resulted in no agreement.

To examine the relationship between sellers' claims and final prices, we conducted an analysis of variance. We modeled final price as a function of the information condition and identified a significant information effect [$F(2, 57) = 4.77$, $p = .01$]. When sellers revealed the problem, the average final price was $1,338 ($SD = \$65$); when sellers lied by commission, the average final price was $1,349 ($SD = \$57$); and when sellers lied by omission, the average final price was $1,419 ($SD = \$70$). A Bonferroni-corrected paired comparisons (with a group alpha $= 0.05$) revealed that final prices were significantly lower when sellers revealed the problem than when they lied by omission and significantly lower when sellers lied by commission than when they lied by omission. Although final prices were higher in the commission condition than the revealed condition, they were not significantly higher.

We conducted additional analysis of the negotiations involving lies of commission. In these cases, sellers' lies may or may not have convinced buyers about the reliability of the computer. To gauge the degree to which buyers remained suspicious about the condition of the computer, we measured the number of reliability related follow-up questions buyers asked after sellers told lies of commission (e.g., "So, what you're saying is you've never had a problem?"). The number of reliability related, follow-up questions buyers asked ranged from zero to seven, with a median of one. We conducted a median split of the final price data according to the number of follow-up questions buyers asked. We found that average final prices were significantly lower when buyers asked more than one follow-up question, $1,326 ($SD = 43.4$) than when they asked only one or no follow-up questions, $1,371.5 ($SD = 57.1$), $t(21) = 2.12, p < .05$.

Discussion of Study 2

We extended Study 1 by separately examining lies of omission and lies of commission in a transactional negotiation context. We found a direct relationship between buyers' questions and sellers' use of deception. When sellers were not asked a direct question, none of them revealed the problem. Most sellers told lies of omission, while others told lies of commission. When sellers were asked a direct question, none of them deflected the question. Instead, most sellers who were asked a direct question revealed the problem. Sellers told lies of commission (e.g., "The computer is in perfect condition") in both cases, but were more likely to tell lies of commission when asked a direct question.

We were surprised to observe lies of commission when sellers were not asked a direct question. While most sellers in this context chose to tell lies of omission rather than lies of commission, a result consistent with the omission bias literature (Spranca, Minsk, and Baron, 1991), there were several exceptions. We suspect that the face-to-face nature of this experiment created anxiety for some subjects and prompted them to tell lies of commission. This finding is consistent with prior work which has found that face-to-face communication may harm the negotiation process by enabling disputants to employ aggressive tactics such as facial gazing (Carnevale, Pruitt, and Seilheimer, 1981; Carnevale and Isen, 1986).

We also found that final prices were higher when sellers lied by omission than when they lied by commission. We suspect that in many cases, sellers' lies of commission were not effective in assuaging buyers' suspicions. In general, the relationship between deception and negotiated outcomes may be complicated. For example, less effective negotiators may be more likely to use deception than skilled negotiators, who do not need to use deception to achieve successful outcomes. In addition, poor negotiation performance itself may increase the likelihood that negotiators will resort to deception.

Prescriptively, results from this study suggest that disputants should prepare for negotiations by thinking about relevant information they do not know and listing questions they should ask before making an offer. In this study, these steps increased the number of questions buyers asked. Ultimately, this preparation may increase a negotiator's likelihood of asking relevant questions, learning important information, and attaining better outcomes.

GENERAL DISCUSSION

This paper describes the effect of asking direct questions on the incidence and nature of deception. Almost every subject in our first study admitted that they might use deception in a negotiation, and almost half of the sellers in our second study actually used deception in a negotiation task. Across both studies subjects were less likely to use deception if they were asked a direct question.

These results highlight the importance of deception to the negotiation process, and have direct application to negotiation practice and deception theory. Prescriptively, these results suggest that negotiators should anticipate both lies of omission and lies of commission. To curtail their risk of being deceived by omission, negotiators should increase the number of direct questions they ask. To do this, negotiators can take several steps prior to a negotiation to increase the number of pertinent questions they ask. Specifically, negotiators should think about missing information and generate a list of relevant questions. Although we found lies of commission to be less effective than lies of omission, negotiators should also take steps to protect themselves against lies of commission. For example, negotiators should routinely verify relevant claims and obtain written guarantees.

The focus of these recommendations is different than most of the advice previously given to help people contend with deception. Most recommendations focus on methods for *detecting* deception. For example, prior work has recommended showing interest in lies to provoke liars to embellish their fabrications (Stiff and Miller, 1986) or staring at a liar to increase anxiety, which might lead to greater leakage of information (Ford, 1996). While these measures may work in some cases, a substantial body of research has demonstrated that it is extremely difficult to detect lies (DePaulo, 1988; DePaulo, Stone, and Lassiter, 1985; Ekman and O'Sullivan, 1991; Ekman and Friesen, 1974; DePaulo and DePaulo, 1989).

While prior work has found that asking questions facilitates information sharing in integrative tasks (Thompson, 1991), this study demonstrates that asking direct questions facilitates information sharing in distributive tasks by curtailing overall deception. The influence of asking questions on deception, however, is complicated. While asking direct questions significantly reduces the likelihood of being told a lie of omission, asking questions may increase the likelihood of being told a lie of commission. Results from this work suggest that negotiators prefer to lie by omission than commission, and that asking direct questions restricts a negotiator's ability to tell lies by omission. Future work should extend this investigation to explore negotiator preferences and perceptions about types of deception. Future work should also explore the relationship between different types of questions and the information exchange process. For example, future work could build on Lewicki, Litterer, Minton, and Saunders's categorization (1994) of negotiation questions and link types of questions to types of deception. Other distinctions among questions may also matter. For example, specific questions (e.g., "How are the brakes?") may be more effective than general questions (e.g., "How reliable is the car?"), and open questions (e.g., "Have you had a problem?") may be more effective than confirming questions (e.g., "You haven't had a problem, have you?"). In some cases, however, asking questions may have unintended consequences, such as revealing information about one's own beliefs, preferences, and interests.

Results from this work also suggest that negotiators should be particularly wary when negotiating with strangers. In this study, negotiators were more likely to lie to strangers than to friends. Strangers in this case were defined as people with whom the seller had not had a past relationship and with whom they had no expectation of a future relationship. In some cases, expectations of past and future interaction may be disentangled, and future work should explore this and other aspects of social relationships on the deception decision process.

Deception in organizations represents a fundamental, but relatively understudied problem. Although negotiators encounter deception on a routine basis, existing research offers little advice for contending with deceptive practices. Results from this work demonstrate that negotiators can use the communication process to moderate lying behavior. Further work remains in developing our understanding of the deception communication process and in developing additional methods for managing deception.

References

Anderson, D., Ansfield, M., and DePaulo, B. "Love's Best Habit: Deception in the Context of Relationships." In P. Philippot, R. Feldman, and E. Coats (eds.), *The Social Context of Nonverbal Behavior.* Cambridge: Cambridge University Press, 1999.

Anton, R. J. "Drawing the Line: An Exploratory Test of Ethical Behavior in Negotiation." *International Journal of Conflict Management,* 1990, *1,* 265–280.

Baron, J. "The Effect of Normative Beliefs on Anticipated Emotions." *Journal of Personality and Social Psychology,* 1992, *63,* 320–330.

Bok, S. *Lying: Moral Choice in Public and Private Life.* New York: Pantheon, 1978.

Brown, R. *Social Psychology.* New York: Free Press, 1965.

Carnevale, P. J., and Isen, A. "The Influence of Positive Affect and Visual Access on the Discovery of Integrative Solutions in Bilateral Negotiation." *Organizational Behavior and Human Decision Processes,* 1986, *37,* 1–13.

Carnevale, P. J., Pruitt, D., and Seilheimer, S. "Looking and Competing: Accountability and Visual Access in Integrative Bargaining." *Journal of Personality and Social Psychology,* 1981, *40,* 111–120.

Carr, A. Z. "Is Business Bluffing Ethical?" *Harvard Business Review,* 1968, *46*(1), 143–153.

Century 21 Inc. v. *F. W. Woolworth Co.,* 181 A.D. 2D 620. (New York, 1992).

Chertkoff, J. M., and Baird, S. L. "Applicability of the Big Lie Technique and the Last Clear Chance Doctrine in Bargaining." *Journal of Personality and Social Psychology,* 1971, *20,* 298–303.

Dees, G. I., and Cramton, P. C. "Shrewd Bargaining on the Moral Frontier: Toward a Theory of Morality in Practice." *Business Ethics Quarterly*, 1991, *1*, 135–167.

DePaulo, P. J. "Research on Deception in Marketing Communications: Its Relevance to the Study of Nonverbal Behavior." *Journal of Nonverbal Behavior*, 1988, *lZ* 253–273.

DePaulo, P. J., and DePaulo, B. M. "Can Deception by Sales Persons and Customers Be Detected Through Non-Verbal Behavioral Cues?" *Journal of Applied Social Psychology*, 1989, *19*, 1552–1577.

DePaulo, B. M., and others. "Lying in Everyday Life." *Journal of Personality and Social Psychology*, 1996, *70*, 979–995.

DePaulo, B. M., Stone, J. I., and Lassiter, G. D. "Deceiving and Detecting Deceit." In B. R. Schlenker (ed.), *The Self and Social Life*. New York: McGraw-Hill, 1985.

Digital v. *Desktop Direct*, 114 S. Ct. (Washington, D.C., 1994).

Duska, R. F. "What's the Point of a Business Ethics Course?" *Business Ethics Quarterly*, 1991, *1*, 335–354.

Ekman, P., and Friesen, W. V. "Detecting Deception from Body or Face." *Journal of Personality and Social Psychology*, 1974, *219*, 288–298.

Ekman, P., and O'Sullivan, M. "Who Can Catch a Liar?" *American Psychologist*, 1991, *246*, 913–920.

Fisher, R., Ury, W., and Patton, B. *Getting to Yes. Negotiating Agreement Without Giving In.* (2nd ed.). New York: Penguin Books, 1991.

Ford, C. V. *Lies! Lies! Lies!!! The Psychology of Deceit.* Washington, D.C.: American Psychiatric Press, 1996.

Garven, S., Wood, J. M., Malpass, R. S., and Shaw, J. S. "More Than Just Suggestion: The Effectiveness of Interviewing Techniques from the McMartin Preschool Case." *Journal of Applied Psychology*, 1998, *80*, 347–359.

"Getting Your Car Fixed Without Getting Fleeced." *Money*, Dec. 1992, p. 138.

Grover S. L. "Lying, Deceit, and Subterfuge: A Model of Dishonesty in the Workplace." *Organization Science*, 1993a, *4*, 478–495.

Grover, S. L. "Why Professionals Lie: The Impact of Professional Role on Reporting Accuracy." *Organizational Behavior and Human Decision Processes*, 1993b, *55*, 251–272.

Grover, S. L., and Hui, C. "The Influence of Role Conflict and Self-Interest on Lying in Organizations." *Journal of Business Ethics*, 1994, *13*, 295–303.

Haidt, J., and Baron, J. "Social Roles and the Moral Judgment of Acts and Omissions." *European Journal of Social Psychology*, 1996, *26*, 201–218.

Hamilton, V., and Sanders, J. "The Effects of Roles and Deeds on Responsibility Judgements: The Normative Structure of Wrongdoing." *Social Psychology Quarterly*, 1981, *44*, 237–254.

Hample, D. "Purposes and Effects of Lying." *Southern Speech Communication Journal*, 1980, *44*, 33–47.

Hegarty, W., and Sims, H. P. "Some Determinants of Unethical Decision Behavior: An Experiment." *Journal of Applied Psychology,* 1978, *63,* 451–457.

"Hospital Chain to Pay $4.7 Million." *Los Angeles Times,* Aug. 20, 1998, p. A16.

Jones, T. "Can Business Ethics Be Taught? Empirical Evidence." *Business and Professional Ethics Journal,* 1989, *8,* 73–93.

Jones, T. "Ethical Decision Making by Individuals in Organizations: An Issue-Contingent Model." *Academy of Management Review,* 1991, *16,* 366–395.

Kahneman, D., and Tversky, A. "The Psychology of Preferences." *Scientific American,* 1982, *246,* 160–173.

Kronzon, S., and Darley, J. "Is This Tactic Ethical? Biased Judgements of Ethics in Negotiation." *Basic and Applied Social Psychology,* 1999, *21,* 49–60.

Lax, D. A., and Sebenius, J. K. "Three Ethical Issues in Negotiation." In R. J. Lewicki, J. A. Litterer, J. W. Minton, and D. M. Saunders (eds.), *Negotiation.* Burr Ridge, Ill.: Irwin, 1986.

Lewicki, R., Litterer, J., Minton, J., and Saunders, D. *Negotiation.* Buff Ridge, Ill.: Irwin, 1994.

Lewicki, R., and Robinson, R. "Ethical and Unethical Bargaining Tactics: An Empirical Study." *Journal of Business Ethics,* 1998, *17,* 665–682.

Lewicki, R. J. "Lying and Deception: A Behavioral Model." In M. H. Bazerman and R. J. Lewicki (eds.), *Negotiating in Organizations.* Thousand Oaks, Calif.: Sage, 1983.

Lewicki, R. J., Saunders, D. M., and Minton, J. W. *Essentials of Negotiation.* Boston: Irwin, 1997.

Lewicki, R. J., and Stark, N. "What Is Ethically Appropriate in Negotiations: An Empirical Examination of Bargaining." *Social Justice Research,* 1996, *9,* 69–95.

Lewis, M., and Saarni, C. (eds.). *Lying and Deception in Everyday Life.* New York: Guilford Press, 1993.

Loftus, E. "Creating False Memories." *Scientific American,* 1997, *277,* 70–75.

Maier, R. A., and Lavrakas, P. J. "Lying Behavior and the Evaluation of Lies." *Perceptual and Motor Skills,* 1976, *42,* 575–581.

Neale, M., Huber, V., and Northcraft, G. "The Framing of Negotiations: Contextual Versus Task Frames." *Organizational Behavior and Human Decision Processes,* 1987, *39,* 228–241.

Nunnally, I. C., and Bernstein, I. H. *Psychometric Theory.* New York: McGraw-Hill, 1994.

O'Connor, K., and Carnevale, P. "A Nasty but Effective Negotiation Strategy: Misrepresentation of a Common-Value Issue." *Personality and Social Psychology Bulletin,* 1997, *23,* 504–515.

Raiffa, H. *The Art and Science of Negotiation.* Cambridge, Mass.: Harvard University Press, 1982.

Robinson, R. I., Lewicki, R. I., and Donahue, E. M. "Extending and Testing a Five Factor Model of Ethical and Unethical Bargaining Tactics: Introducing the SINS Scale." Working paper, Harvard University, 1997.

Schoenfeldt, L., McDonald, D., and Youngblood, S. "The Teaching of Business Ethics: A Survey of AACSB Member Schools." *Journal of Business Ethics*, 1991, *10*, 237–241.

"Sears Gets Handed a Huge Repair Bill." *Business Week*, Sept. 14, 1992, p. 38.

Shapiro, D. L. "The Effects of Explanation on Negative Reactions to Deceit." *Administrative Science Quarterly*, 1991, *36*, 614–630.

Shapiro, D. L., and Bies, R. J. "Threats, Bluffs, and Disclaimers in Negotiations." *Organizational Behavior and Human and Decision Processes*, 1994, *60*, 14–35.

Shell, R. G. "When Is It Legal to Lie in Negotiations?" *Sloan Management Review*, 1991, *32*(3), 93–101.

Slovic, P., Fischhoff, B., and Lichtenstein, S. "Facts Versus Fears: Understanding Perceived Risk." In D. Kahneman, P. Slavic, and A. Tversky (eds.), *Judgement Under Uncertainty: Heuristics and Biases.* Cambridge, U.K.: Cambridge University Press, 1987.

Spranca, M., Minsk, E., and Baron, J. "Omission and Commission in Judgment and Choice." *Journal of Experimental Social Psychology*, 1991, *27*, 76–105.

Stiff, J. B., and Miller, G. R. "Come to Think of It . . . : Interrogative Probes, Deceptive Communication, and Deception Detection." *Human Communication Research*, 1986, 12, 339–357.

Strudler, A. "On the Ethics of Deception in Negotiations." *Business Ethics Quarterly*, 1995, *5*, 805–822.

Tenbrunsel, A. "Misrepresentation and Expectations of Misrepresentation in an Ethical Dilemma: The Role of Incentives and Temptation." *Academy of Management Journal*, 1998, *41*, 330–339.

Textron v. *United Automobile*, 118 S. Ct. 1626 (Washington, D.C., 1998).

Thompson, L. "Information Exchange in Negotiation." *Journal of Experimental Social Psychology*, 1991, *27*, 161–179.

Thompson, L. *The Mind and Heart of the Negotiator.* Upper Saddle River, N.J.: Prentice-Hall, 1998.

Trevino, L. "Ethical Decision Making in Organizations: A Person-Situation Interactionist Model." *Academy of Management Review*, 1986, *11*, 601–617.

Wokutch, R. E., and Carson, T. L. "The Ethics and Profitability of Bluffing in Business." In R. J. Lewicki, J. A. Litterer, J. W. Minton, and D. M. Saunders (eds.), *Negotiation.* Burr Ridge, Ill.: Irwin, 1994.

PART THREE

BARGAINING TACTICS

G od is in the details—. Or is it, the devil's in the details?[1] Both versions of
the adage apply in negotiation. Our goodness is not defined by whatever
we profess in the abstract but rather is enacted step by step in each of the
small things that we do at the bargaining table. Aspiring to high standards is
one thing. Living up to them can be devilishly hard.

Do we tell the truth, the whole truth, or merely something like the truth? Do
we meet where it is convenient for our counterparts or insist on meeting on our
own turf? Are we comfortable issuing ultimatums or with upping our demands
during the course of negotiation? All of these decisions are tactical in the sense
that they involve actions in service of larger substantive, relational, and reputational goals. Even standing alone, however, they reflect what (if anything) we
feel we owe others with whom we deal—assuming that we have even paused
to consider the implications of our behavior.

The chapters in Part Three describe familiar negotiation tactics, many of the
hard-bargaining variety. What constitutes a dirty trick, of course, is in the eye
of the beholder. What I see as merely clever, you may regard as venal. What
you do to defend yourself looks like escalation to me. Our interpretations
depend on our relationship. If it is strained and you have taken days to respond
to my proposal, I may assume that you are making me sweat. By contrast, if we
are on good terms, I may worry that you are simply overworked.

David Lax and James Sebenius (1983) have suggested a version of Gresham's Law in negotiation: just as bad money drives out good in the economy, aggressive tactics may dominate collaborative moves. Robert Axelrod's provocative work on the evolution and complexity of cooperation (1984, 1997) offers the more optimistic possibility that in ongoing relationships, at least, negotiators may restrain themselves from using dirty tricks. That said, many negotiators seem to function tactically, taking one step at a time, not contemplating how their moves will be read by counterparts or whether they are playing the right game.

Not all of the chapters in Part Three address the ethical propriety of hardball tactics or their effectiveness, for that matter. Readers should examine their own standards and other chapters in this book to determine the appropriate boundaries. Are they contingent on context and the bargaining style of others?

We begin with a classic article by Michael Meltsner and Philip Schrag, "Negotiating Tactics for Legal Services Lawyers." It was written thirty years ago, when for the first time, neighborhood-based legal services programs were expanding to provide legal assistance on a broad scale to low-income people. Many of the young lawyers in these programs were high on idealism but inexperienced when it came to dealing with slumlords, shady lenders, and employers who made their business out of ignoring job safety and minimum wage laws. The Meltsner and Schrag piece was published in the *Clearinghouse Review,* the newsletter of the national legal services program. It gave its readers a short course on the bargaining ploys that they were likely to encounter in representing their disadvantaged clients. The *Clearinghouse Review* "received so many requests over the years to use this article in training materials and manuals" (Meltsner and Schrag, 1989) that it reprinted the article sixteen years later for a new generation of readers, the only time it had ever printed an article twice.

The article was as misunderstood and derided by the academy as it was popular with poverty lawyers. Some critics believed that the tactics it described were unethical and that Meltsner and Schrag were tacitly advocating their use,[2] despite the authors' explicit statements that they did not endorse the propriety of these tactics and that they wanted legal services lawyers at least to be able to recognize when these tactics were being used by their adversaries (Rubin, 1975; Stulberg, 2002; Editors, 2002). Others expected that positional bargaining tactics would be "counterproductive" (Menkel-Meadow, 1984). These commentators, writing in the wake of Fisher and Ury's great work of 1981, *Getting to Yes,* may not have taken sufficient account of the fact that the legal services lawyers' negotiations often involved zero-sum battles with nonrepeat players over small sums of money (such as creditors' claims for the balances due on installment contracts), where, Meltsner and Schrag believed, multi-issue negotiations to "get to yes" were less likely to be feasible. We urge our readers to consider the extent to which tactics like these may be effective and whether some or all of them can sometimes be justified, particularly if they are used not to advance personal self-interest but the interest of others.

Chapter Fifteen, from James Freund's *Smart Negotiating,* draws on its author's extensive experience as an attorney representing large corporations. It advocates more aggressive tactics than might be found in *Getting to Yes,* though it identifies lines that should not be crossed. As with many of the other chapters in this book, readers should consider whether the argument it makes is on moral or utilitarian grounds.

The studies explored in Chapter Sixteen by Roy Lewicki and Robert Robinson examine the attitudes of M.B.A. students on where ethical lines should be drawn. There is strong consensus on some issues, but opinion is split on others. Some of that division may be attributable to differing assumptions that respondents made about the context in which the tactics might be used, though there simply may be disagreement in other instances. If ethics are the embodiment of broadly accepted social norms, can negotiators justifiably ignore precepts that are not endorsed by a strong majority of their peers?

Chapter Seventeen, by Albert Carr, written more than thirty years ago, remains a classic in the field partly because of the critical response it has continued to trigger. Carr argued that negotiation is a game much like poker and that people who play it should understand that bluffing is to be expected. Among other things, Carr illustrates the power of metaphor both to illuminate our reasoning and to constrain it. If Carr had imagined negotiation as a dance rather than a card game, would his conclusions about bluffing have been different?

Notes

1. The quotation is attributed to the eminent architect Ludwig Mies van der Rohe ("On Restraint in Design," 1959). Gloria Steinem (1994) is credited with a different corollary: "God may be in the details, but the goddess is in the questions. Once we begin to ask them, there's no turning back."

2. The editors of the *Ohio State Journal on Dispute Resolution* (Volume 18, Issue 1, 2002) later concluded that "the text of the [Meltsner and Schrag] article does not support Professor Stulberg's characterization of it."

References

Axelrod, R. *The Evolution of Cooperation.* New York: Basic Books, 1984.

Axelrod, R. *The Complexity of Cooperation.* Princeton, N.J.: Princeton University Press, 1997.

Editors. "Response to Prof. Joseph B. Stulberg." *Ohio State Journal on Dispute Resolution,* 2002, *18*(1).

Fisher, R., Ury, W. *Getting to Yes.* Boston: Houghton Mifflin, 1981.

Lax, D., and Sebenius, J. *The Manager as Negotiator.* New York: Free Press, 1983.

Meltsner, M., and Schrag, P. G. "Negotiating Tactics for Legal Services Lawyers." *Clearinghouse Revie*w, 1989, *23,* 858.

Menkel-Meadow, C. "Toward Another View of Legal Negotiation: The Structure of Problem-Solving." *UCLA Law Review,* 1984, *31,* 754–832.

"On Restraint in Design." *New York Herald Tribune,* June 28, 1959, http://www.bartleby.com/cgi-bin/texis/webinator/sitesearch?query= God+is+in+the+details.&db=db&filter=colQuotations&Submit=Go.

Rubin, A. B. "A Causerie on Lawyers' Ethics in Negotiation." *Louisiana Law Review,* 1975, *35,* 577–593.

Steinem, G., 1994, http://www.bartleby.com/66/20/55720.html.

Stulberg, J. P. "Book Review: That May Work in Practice, but Will It Work in Theory?" *Ohio State Journal on Dispute Resolution,* 2002, *17,* 499–461.

CHAPTER FOURTEEN

Negotiating Tactics for Legal Services Lawyers

Michael Meltsner

Philip Schrag

egal services and public interest lawyers probably spend as much time negotiating on behalf of their clients as they do litigating cases, but relatively little has been written on the tactics and techniques of negotiation. Yet it is plain that whether lawyers are sparring about the wording of a stipulation, a decree, or a model statute, the outcome depends not only on the relative strengths of the parties, but on their perceived strengths, styles, and methods of negotiation.

Settlement negotiations in commercial cases are usually dominated by a single issue: the size of a financial award. Public interest cases, on the other hand, commonly involve proposed injunctive relief. The settlement process in such cases is likely to be complex, primarily because the agreement which emerges from negotiations will involve a range of discrete issues, each one of which may be traded off in return for another. For example, an affirmative action plan to end racial and sexual discrimination at an industrial plant will involve dozens of issues, including the number and percentage of persons of particular races and sexes to be hired at different job levels, guarantees with respect to promotion, back pay for persons discriminated against in the past, alterations in company testing procedures, changes in the language of the company's labor advertising, implementation schedules, reporting requirements, and counsel fees.

This article catalogues several successful negotiating tactics. Of course, not every tactic described is appropriate for every negotiation; the use of each depends on the particular case and especially upon the perceived relative strengths of the parties during the bargaining process. In general, a party who appears to himself and to his adversary to be strongly desirous of negotiations is less able to use the more powerful tactics set forth. Even the attorney who must negotiate from a position of perceived weakness should be familiar with the tactics that may be used against him, so that he may defend himself as best he can.

This list of tactics is not intended to endorse the propriety of every one of them, but there can be no doubt of their efficacy in appropriate situations. All of these techniques are commonly used by lawyers, and the attorney who chooses to abjure one because it is ethically dubious should at least learn to recognize and to understand the device so that he can defend against it. The more "tricky" of these ploys are used most commonly in urban centers, where lawyers are not likely to be negotiating repeatedly with the same adverse attorneys who will eventually recognize their favorite tactics. Lawyers who have to deal with each other in case after case are more likely to conduct an open, straightforward discussion than those who may never negotiate with each other again.

PREPARATORY TACTICS

1. *Arrange to negotiate on your own turf.* Whenever possible, insist that the meeting be held in your office or in another setting where you will feel more comfortable than your adversary, and where he will be at a psychological disadvantage because he has had to come to you. The importance of the setting to a negotiation was brilliantly (if hyperbolically) portrayed by Charlie Chaplin in his famous film *The Great Dictator.* Hitler (played by Chaplin) has invited Mussolini to Germany to decide whether Germany or Italy will invade a neutral country. Hitler's aides arrange for Mussolini to enter Hitler's office by a door at an end of the room, far from the führer's desk. Mussolini will have to walk a great distance to reach Hitler and, of course, will feel small in the enormous office. The aides also constructed an extremely low chair for Mussolini, so that, when seated, he will have to look up at Hitler. But Mussolini takes Hitler by surprise. He enters by the back door, calmly sits on Hitler's desk, and looks down at Hitler. The two dictators then adjourn to a barber shop, where they compete with each other during the negotiations by continually raising their respective barber's chairs to achieve additional height.

Some neighborhood poverty lawyers who negotiate with attorneys for banks, realty corporations, and other large firms have added a new twist to the "home base" tactic by attempting to maneuver their adversaries into entering the ghetto, sometimes for the first time in their lives. Their fears for their physical safety and their shock at viewing local housing conditions may reduce their bargaining effectiveness.

Negotiating in your own office has some specific practical advantages as well. If agreement is reached, it gives you the option of calling in your secretary and dictating a memorandum of agreement on the spot; you may not desire to do this, but the option is *yours*. You save traveling time and impose its cost on your adversary. And you have the opportunity, seconds after the meeting has been completed, to dictate a precise memorandum to your files relating the detailed information your adversary disclosed during the session.

2. *Balance or slightly outnumber the other side.* Attempt to ascertain or estimate the number of persons the other side is bringing to the meeting, and do your best to ensure that your side is represented by at least the same number of persons, and possibly one additional person. In a bargaining session where two negotiate against one, or three against two, the side with fewer representatives is usually at a disadvantage in that it will tire more readily and will be less able to control the flow of discussion. There is also a tendency in a bargaining situation to reach a compromise evenly balanced among the views of all participants, even if two of the participants are on one side and one on the other, so the active presence of additional bargainers materially affects the outcome. On the other hand, an adversary who feels cornered because he is substantially outnumbered may feel too insecure to bargain seriously. Be prepared therefore to justify the presence of additional representatives on the ground that they have technical expertise necessary to successful completion of the settlement.

3. *Time the negotiations to advantage.* When one side wants to get the discussion over with quickly, it usually loses. If you perceive that your adversary is anxious to settle quickly (or to avoid protracted discussion because his client is only paying a set fee), arrange to negotiate when you can spend a lot of time at it (e.g., when you have a whole day clear), when your adversary is pressed for time, or when one of you has so little time that, after enough discussion to whet your adversary's appetite, negotiations must be adjourned for a week or two. You may find that under these conditions, your adversary makes major concessions to avoid further loss of time. Some lawyers make it a point to schedule negotiations with government attorneys at 4:00 P.M., on the assumption that civil service lawyers expect to go home at 5:00 P.M. and will bargain much more quickly and carelessly at that hour than they would in the morning. Similarly, a lawyer who is not used to working on weekends will probably negotiate more poorly on a Saturday or Sunday than during the week.

4. *Know the facts thoroughly.* Unless he is deliberately unprepared so that the negotiations will be delayed, an unprepared lawyer is usually at a severe disadvantage. He will constantly have to apologize for his ignorance, and his apologies often create a subtle pressure to concede points as to which his adversary

is better informed. In addition, an unprepared lawyer may feel inner pressure to compromise because he does not wish to reveal his ignorance by participation in an extended discussion.

5. *Lock yourself in.* This is a risky but powerful prenegotiation tactic and should be used only with the greatest care. In cases that have attracted public attention, an attorney can increase his bargaining power by announcing publicly a position from which he will not retreat so that his adversary knows that he will lose face if he does in fact retreat. Then the attorney can convincingly say that aspect of his position is nonnegotiable. Attorneys who use this tactic sometimes have their bluff called and may, in fact, have to make a concession and then explain the retreat to their clients.

6. *Designate one of your demands a "precondition."* If the other side wants to talk (e.g., if it requested the negotiations), a lawyer can often improve the chances of a favorable outcome by calling one of his demands a "precondition" to negotiations. If the precondition is met, he starts out with a psychological advantage, a substantive gain, and fewer items which are subject to compromise in the discussions that follow. Even if the precondition pertains only to action during the negotiations themselves—for example, that neither party will speak to the press until their conclusion—the temporary resolution of certain issues is likely to set a pattern for the eventual settlement.

INITIAL TACTICS

7. *When it is in your interest, make the other side tender the first offer.* The party making the first offer suffers the disadvantage of conceding that it really wants to settle. Furthermore, it may make an offer that actually concedes more than the other side thought it could get at the end of the negotiating process. The attorney who receives such a surprising offer will declare his shock that so little is being tendered and will demand much more. One surprisingly successful technique for evoking the first offer is to remain silent. Few people can tolerate more than a few seconds of silence during a negotiation; most feel compelled to say something to break the ice. Or you might simply say to your adversary, "Why don't you start by giving us an idea of your position." There are situations, however, where by making the first offer a party advantageously sets the agenda for the entire discussion. The negotiations may never leave the questions raised initially; other questions, which may be the weakest from your point of view, will fall into place as part of a general wrap-up of the deal.

8. *Make your first demand very high.* Outrageously unreasonable demands become more justifiable after substantial discussion. Even if an initially high demand is rejected, it makes a subsequent demand that is almost as high appear to be a more reasonable compromise. The negotiator who opens with a reasonable compromise is likely to be pushed to a worse settlement than he could

have obtained by harder bargaining. Nevertheless, some demands are too out-rageous to make. They will encourage your adversary to believe that you are not seriously interested in bargaining despite your protestations to the contrary.

9. *Place your major demands at the beginning of the agenda.* There seem to be "honeymoon" periods, in which negotiators make compromises more freely, at the outset of negotiations and at their conclusion. By forcing your adversary to deal at the outset, when he wants most to compromise, with the items of greatest interest to you, or at the end, when he has invested many hours or weeks of time in negotiating and wants a return on his investment, you can improve your client's position.

10. *Make the other side make the first compromise.* There is a psychological advantage in benefiting from the first concession. Studies indicate that losers generally make the first concessions in negotiating a dispute.

TACTICS GENERALLY

11. *Use two negotiators who play different roles.* The famous "Mutt and Jeff" technique, in which police use one friendly and one nasty interrogator to extract a statement from a reluctant defendant, works well in negotiation. Two lawyers for the same side feign an internal dispute concerning their position; one takes the hard line, offering almost no compromise, while the other appears to desire to make small concessions, and occasionally he prevails. Lawyers adverse to such a team frequently grasp at the marginal concessions because they seem substantial in relation to the position of the hard-liner.

12. *Invoke law or justice.* To a surprising extent, lawyers are impressed with the citation of authority, and laymen tend to be overwhelmed by a reference to a case or statute. If your adversary seems to react to it, quote or advert to legal authority as often as possible, particularly if you can assert that the position you urge is legally compelled, or that the one he desires is either legally prohibited or at least troublesome. If the other side seems to desire an end to the discussions more than you do, lengthy analytical discussion of cases and statutes is also a good way to kill time without disclosing any facts about your client's case. If the law is not on your side, avoid using it. Instead, invoke more general principles of justice, or whatever other kind of authority (e.g., public pressure) seems to support your position.

13. *Be tough—especially against a patsy.* "Unfortunately, when one party is conciliatory and the other cantankerous, the imbalance usually favors the competitive player in the short run" (Karrass, 1970, p. 130).

14. *Appear irrational where it seems helpful.* This is a dangerous but often successful tactic. An adversary who is himself an expert negotiator can be thrown off base considerably by a lawyer who does not seem to play the same game, for example, one who seems to behave irrationally. Premier Nikita

Khrushchev significantly increased the deterrent power of the relatively small Soviet nuclear force by banging his shoe on the table at the United Nations in 1960; he gave the impression of being somewhat imbalanced—a man who might unleash nuclear weapons upon even a slight provocation.

15. *Raise some of your demands as the negotiations progress.* The conventional model of negotiation contemplates both sides lowering their demands until a compromise is finally reached. But the highly successful negotiator backtracks; he raises one of his demands for every two concessions he makes and occasionally reopens for further discussion topics that everyone thought had been settled and laid aside. This tactic not only reduces the aggregate concession he makes, but it makes the other side want to finish the negotiation quickly before he stiffens his position any more or retracts the concessions he had made. The party who desires to finish quickly has two strikes against him.

16. *Claim that you do not have authority to compromise.* You can make a topic nonnegotiable by persuading your adversary that you do not have, and cannot obtain, the authority to go beyond a certain point. The freshman negotiator sometimes makes the mistake of trying to impress the other side with his authority; the expert modestly explains that he has very little authority, and that his client is adamant. (Of course, the client's supposed adamancy stops just at the point of the minimum concessions the lawyer thinks he need make.) The lawyer should not bring his client with him to the negotiation unless he has a clear understanding of why he is doing so; he exposes himself to the real danger that his adversary will go over his head to the client himself, and he gives up the power to invoke his client's instructions as a reason for refusing to agree to a particular demand.

17. *Clear the agreement with your client before signing it.* Before you reach final agreement, you will want to consult with your client. Checking with the client is not only an obligation that you owe to him, it is an important bargaining tactic. It enables you to delay the proceedings while you check, and it gives you a chance to consider any errors you might have made before you sign.

POST-NEGOTIATION TACTICS

18. *Make your adversary feel good.* Never gloat over the terms of a settlement. Not only is such behavior boorish, but it may provoke an adversary to reopen negotiations or to adopt a different and stronger negotiating posture the next time you deal with him. If you can do so with candor, feel free to tell opposing counsel what a hard bargain he drove and what a good job he did for his client. If you meet an adversary and his client together, tell the client what a good job his lawyer did for him. This may please the client, but it certainly will please the lawyer and perhaps make him look forward to doing business with you

again. A humble attitude toward the results of settlement negotiations is more than a form of gamesmanship. It is, after all, the exceptional negotiation where the lawyer feels totally confident that he has obtained the most favorable terms possible. A common experience of negotiators is the sudden realization after a settlement has been reached that even more favorable terms might have been obtained with a firmer approach.

19. *After agreement has been reached, have your client reject it and raise his demands.* This is the most ethically dubious of the tactics listed, but there will be occasions where a lawyer will have to defend against it or even employ it. After laboring for hours, days, or weeks to work out a settlement, a negotiator is likely to be dismayed by the prospect of the agreement falling through. As a result, his adversary may be able to obtain last minute concessions. Such a strategy can boomerang; it may so anger an adversary that he simply refuses to bargain, even though bargaining is still in his interest, or he may fight fire with fire by increasing his own demands.

20. *Promptly reduce the agreement to writing yourself.* Unless the terms of settlement are reduced to writing, a lawyer can never be certain that he has an agreement. Counsel may be laboring under a mistaken impression that they have settled when in fact they have not resolved all of the questions that divided them. Reduction of terms to writing is an effective means of discovering whether there is actual agreement. Not only is the written instrument evidence of the agreement, but the formulation of its terms will tend to govern the conduct of the parties in the future. Quite often the terms that have been agreed upon will be subject to differing interpretations, some of which favor your side, some of which favor your adversary's side. You should, therefore, volunteer to undertake the labor of drafting the agreement. By doing so, you can choose language which reflects your interpretation of the terms agreed upon. Just as a diner who seriously wishes to pick up a check will usually end up paying, a lawyer who insists on drafting an agreement will usually prevail. Lawyers are not exceptional in preferring to avoid unnecessary work, particularly the tedious work of drafting documents. "After all," you might observe to your adversary, "this is only the first draft." If you draft the document, the other side should be given an opportunity to correct it and to discuss any language not faithfully incorporating the agreement that has been reached. But many lawyers are not thorough editors, so the opportunity to write the first draft becomes the power to choose critically important language. If an adversary writes the first draft, you should be prepared to go over it line by line, and, if necessary, to rewrite every word.

Reference

Karrass, C. L. *The Negotiating Game.* New York: Crowell, 1970.

CHAPTER FIFTEEN

Smart Negotiating

How to Make Good Deals in the Real World

James C. Freund

I don't intend to explore the legal implications of lying. You should know, however, that if you induce your counterpart to make a deal by fraudulently misrepresenting a material fact—and assuming his reliance on your misrepresentation is justified—then he can hold you liable for damages. Even under lesser circumstances, the resulting contract may be voided. In addition, lawyers who negotiate for clients are subject to certain ethical rules, which can lead to disciplinary action for violations. But even if this weren't the case, I would urge you to shun lying like the plague. It violates all precepts of fair dealing between responsible individuals.

I believe most right-minded people share that sentiment—at least in theory. The problem, however, is something that lies at the core of negotiating. The fact is that many of your actions and statements are designed to mislead your counterpart, to facilitate an inaccurate assessment on his part. You want your counterpart to believe you're more immovable on price than you really are. You don't want him to realize the relative unimportance to you of the point you're about to concede, so that your concession will motivate him to make a substantial move on another front. But where should you draw the line?

POSING THE ETHICAL ISSUE

Most of us engage in some forms of puffery. Sellers exaggerate the value of what's being sold. Buyers feel no compunction about overstating the firmness of their latest bid. Lawyers inflate the strength of their client's case. This sort of

212

hype is viewed as part of the game; everyone expects it, and the system accepts such behavior. At the other extreme, misrepresentations of fact that relate directly to what's being bought and sold are clearly off limits. You can't put zircons into a Tiffany box, move the odometer back ten thousand miles, or concoct a nonexistent account receivable.

On the other hand, many phony rationales are used to justify positions taken in negotiations (for instance, the reason stated by one party as to why he can't give a certain protection requested by the other). This is what I call "creative motivation." I don't encourage this sort of thing, but the reality is that it's generally condoned on the theory that one side isn't entitled to see the inner workings of the other side's mind. So, be warned, negotiators: take nothing at face value, and examine closely all ostensible rationales.

The questions that create a dilemma for the negotiator usually relate to matters that are collateral to the subject matter of the negotiation. They don't go to the quality of what's being bought and sold; rather, they relate to the leverage factors that affect the bargaining between the parties—such as Mr. Cellar's need to sell quickly and the unavailability of other alternatives.

Say that, as Cellar, you were to lie blatantly in response to Ms. Byre's question about other bidders, inventing another buyer who is ready, willing, and able to pay $180,000 on the spot. On hearing your reply, Byre panics and concludes an immediate deal at $190,000. Put aside any legal question; do you feel you've done something wrong? I do—and I bet you do, too. That's not a proper way to negotiate. Still, a less blatant response, hinting obliquely in the same direction, might enable you to rationalize any feelings of misbehavior.

I wish I could provide you with an all-purpose guideline on what's permissible and what's not, but I can't. In the end, like so many other aspects of negotiation that depend on good judgment, this one comes down to your own sense of what's appropriate. I will pass along, however, something that has been suggested as a legal test and that also works pretty well on a practical basis. The key is whether the deception causes some unfairness in the bargaining situation. Put another way, does the nature of what's said make it likely that the speaker will succeed in deceiving the listener? This may turn on whether the listener was justified in relying on the false statement. As a result, the more specific the statement ("I have another buyer at $180,000"), the more likely it crosses the line into "no-no" territory: when the remark is less precise ("My house is a real steal at $200,000"), chances are it will be considered puffing or simply the speaker's own opinion.

BLOCKING TECHNIQUES

So, Mr. Cellar, what should you do when that assertive Ms. Byre demands answers to tough questions about your need for funds and the presence of other buyers? The method you use has to block the flow of harmful information but not give your counterpart reason to infer the bad news from your response. Ruling a particular query out of bounds, for instance—"None of your business!"—runs the risk that Byre will infer from your sensitivity that she has struck pure gold. And even though she can never be as sure of her surmise as when you've revealed the truth, she may still proceed on the basis of that inference.

Surely, however, you can do better than that. We've all watched an adroit politician bob and weave around the questions of a skilled reporter. Here, your interrogator is likely to be considerably less adept and might even feel uneasy at pressing the inquiry. You may get away with ignoring the funds question entirely, if not by silence, then by changing the subject ("By the way, let me show you the handy ice maker in the refrigerator").

But since silence and non sequiturs also risk generating a negative inference, a better tack may be to deflect the inquiry, channeling your reply into a less sensitive area. Typical of this genre is the response that purports to answer the question but in fact addresses a different one. For instance, on the "other buyers" query, you might reply, "Funny you should ask. The broker was just saying the other day that this would be a perfect house for a doctor who has his office at home."

You can also provide a general answer to a specific question. For example, in responding to an inquiry about your "new home," a reply such as "Obviously, I'll have to live somewhere—I'm not about to take to the streets" may get you off the hook. This also illustrates, by the way, the use of sarcasm or hyperbole, which can be an effective technique with a less than persistent questioner. Specific answers to general questions may also derail the line of inquiry.

A frequently effective riposte is to proffer your own question back to the interrogator, particularly one that probes an area your counterpart might not want to discuss. On the funds question, for instance, you might turn the spotlight onto Ms. Byre's sources of financing. Showing that two can play at this game may ease the pressure of her direct inquiry.

Generally, my own preference is to take an assertive tack. On the "other buyers" issue, if I were Cellar—and assuming that a person of means recently expressed interest in the house (although hasn't yet made an offer)—I might say, "I don't have a firm offer at this time. But I do have a potential purchaser who, if he decides to buy, is clearly capable of paying $200,000. Are you willing to take the risk that I'll pass up your much lower bid for a possible higher offer?"

Or if I had no nibbles at all and therefore decided to rule the "other buyers" question out of order, I might couple it with a warning along these lines: "I don't want to get into that. Make up your mind, on the merits of the property. I'm telling you"—and here I would slow down and emphasize each word—"it . . . will . . . take . . . $200,000 . . . to . . . buy . . . this . . . house."

On the "paying for another house" question, I might try something that concedes the need for speed (which, after all, I won't ultimately be able to disguise) but attempts to point Byre in a different direction as to why the need exists. Perhaps something like this: "I love this house. It was a wrench for me to decide to sell it. But now that I've decided, I want it to happen quickly. You'd be well advised to get me signed, sealed, and delivered before I change my mind and take it off the market."

SENDING BLUE-CHIP AND BARGAINING-CHIP MESSAGES

To achieve credibility, you have to start by dividing your positions on the issues into categories similar to those I've outlined, or at least into two camps: what some people call the "blue chips" (including both immovable and staunch postures) and the "bargaining chips" (covering both malleable and pliant positions). Then you can begin to send different messages on each.

In order to be credible on the blue chips, you have to convey a sense of the importance you ascribe to them right from the outset and consistently throughout the negotiation. If you don't start early, your resolute attitude may come across as a manufactured afterthought. As the moment of truth nears, you can't suddenly elevate to deal-breaker status a point you treated casually in the early rounds. Inconsistency undermines the aura of credibility you're trying to create. Conversely, while you never want to suggest the relative unimportance of bargaining chips—or else you'll get no credit for giving them up—there are ways to imply that you don't hold them in the same esteem as the blues.

So, in our example, Peter ought to state his immovable position on "no consulting with the competition" in unmistakable terms at the first meeting: "If I'm going to hire you, Connie, it will only be if you promise not to do any work for those other guys, who are out there every day trying to eat my lunch." If she agrees right off the bat, fine. If not, then Peter is well advised to keep returning to the issue until she realizes he means business. In fact, Peter can buttress his posture by refusing to discuss other issues until this one is resolved.

Likewise, Connie should stress her staunch "standard payment schedule" issue the first time the question of money comes up, emphasizing that it wasn't just devised for this particular job: "My fee would be $25,000, Peter. In accordance with my standard practice, 50 percent of the fee is payable when I undertake the assignment." If, instead, she broaches the $25,000 without mentioning that she wants 50 percent down, when she finally gets around to mentioning it, the payment schedule may seem less inviolate than the amount of money (even though in her mind it's more so). If Peter balks at the terms, Connie shouldn't let the issue fester, but ought to engage in a spirited and reasoned defense of her position.

A negotiator who takes an immovable or staunch position should articulate a solid rationale to justify it. Peter's "exclusive" point is more than just antipathy for his competitors; it's good business. If Connie recommends efficiencies that result in reduced expenses, thereby allowing Peter to drop his pizza prices—and giving him a vital edge over the competition—he doesn't want Connie helping them figure out how to match the cuts. For her part, Connie should attempt to make decent rebuttal arguments, explaining how her services are custom-tailored for each client, the disparate nature of these seemingly competitive businesses, and so on. Negotiation often comes down to a battle of cogency. The more logical your arguments in support of a point, the greater your chances of resolving it on satisfactory terms.

How about the bargaining chips? Connie's fee isn't cast in stone; it differs for each job she undertakes, depending on the size of the company and the scope of the assignment. Still, she shouldn't start off with a lame attempt at justification or an apology for the amount. One simple sentence, "My fee is $25,000," sets an appropriate tone.

Peter's reaction—a sharp intake of breath, followed by rapid side-to-side shaking of the head—is predictable. "That's awfully steep," he says. "I'm just a small businessman, not one of those big-city outfits." The issue is joined. How should Connie handle this situation?

First, she has to walk a fine line between not appearing too rigid, which runs the risk of blowing the deal, and not seeming to pull numbers out of the air. One technique is to hint that movement is possible without actually moving. "Look, Peter, if you want to use my services, I have the feeling we'll be able to work out the price. Let's talk first about some of these other items." Perhaps the other items will furnish tradeoff material. In any event, the ultimate price will be a function of the scope of the assignment, which remains to be worked out.

On a pliant issue, I'll often send an implicit signal that I'm prepared to negotiate as a way of sharpening the distinction between it and a blue chip. So, for example, when Connie replies that she would be happy to come back after six months if she were paid for her time, Peter could say almost playfully, "But Connie, you're *too* well paid up-front. I need to figure out a way to get more for my money."

WHEN YOU'RE BLUFFING

Now we move from candor to fiction. Your "this is it" posture, after all, could be bogus. And the question that you and every negotiator has to face is whether you should bluff.

Bluffs are clearly a staple of bargaining. When they relate to your position on an issue (as contrasted with when they involve misrepresentations of fact), they're not ethically repugnant. And they can be effective. Still, I don't usually like to bluff. The reason is that a bluff has three possible outcomes, two of which are adverse to the bluffer—not good odds, in my book.

Let's say that Connie takes a "firm" position that $25,000 is the minimum she's willing to accept for the job. In fact, she would do it for $20,000, if necessary. The positive outcome for Connie is that Peter believes her, acquiesces, and signs up at $25,000. But assume he calls her bluff, stating firmly, "In that case, we have no deal." If he's believable, and Connie realizes she won't get the job for $25,000, she'll be forced to lower her price. Although she can try to put the best face on this (linking the reduction to a diminution in the scope of the assignment, for example), her credibility may be impaired for the balance of the negotiation.

Now if that were the only risk to bluffing, I might favor it as a technique. At least in a situation where the bluffer is credible and the other side has few options, the prospect of prevailing could outweigh the potential loss of credibility. But there's another possibility too: namely, that Peter will, in fact, believe Connie's bluff. However, because he's unwilling to pay that much, he will simply decide not to use her services, without giving Connie a chance to reduce her price.

The classic case here is the buyer who bluffs on his "top price," only to wake up the next day with the property having been sold to a third party at a somewhat higher price—but one that the bluffer would have been willing to pay. It's this fear of succeeding with the bluff but then having it blow up in your face that makes me consider the risks of bluffing generally unacceptable.

If you decide to ignore my counsel and bluff anyway, here are a few thoughts that might be of help:

- Save your bluff for a significant issue. Once exposed as a bluffer, you are unlikely to have another chance, so do not squander it on something unimportant.

- Bluff at the end of the process rather than at the start, where it presumptively lacks credibility.

- Make your bluff appear consistent with something you have been saying all along.

- Try to come up with a plausible explanation for why there's no give in your position.

- If possible, couple your bluff with a show of flexibility on some other issue. It is a good way to highlight that your firm position is something special.

- Execute your bluff in such a manner that if the other side believes you but is not willing to go along, you'll have a shot at backing down before the deal is aborted.

- If you're forced to back down, have a "changed circumstances" story ready to go in order to mitigate any harm to your credibility.

DEALING WITH WHAT MIGHT BE A BLUFF

Now let's look at a "this is it" position from the other side of the table. How can you tell if your counterpart is bluffing? Should you accept his "final" position as final? If he threatens that dire consequences will flow from your nonacquiescence, does he mean it?

Pretend, for these purposes, that you're Connie, and it's Peter's position on exclusivity that's at issue. You can live with his insistence that you not go after the business of the other pizza chains. Still, you would much rather have that flexibility if the point isn't as important to Peter as he's making it sound.

There's no surefire answer to dealing with a possible bluff, which is just why negotiating is such a tantalizing occupation. Basically you're making an educated guess, the kind you constantly rely on in other areas of life. Afterward, there will be plenty of time for self-congratulation or serious second-guessing. And sometimes, when you don't call the bluff, you'll never know whether it was real or not.

Here's the threshold question to ask yourself in this kind of situation: If Peter is not bluffing, will I give in on the point? If—unlike the case here—this occurs over an issue on which you are unwilling to accept Peter's position, then you wouldn't have to fret over whether he's bluffing or not. You must call the bluff, since the only chance of a deal occurring is for Peter to retreat. When this is the case, I prefer to do it quietly, with conviction but without any fuss or acrimony. Connie might say, "If this is your final position on the matter, Peter, which I sincerely hope it's not, then we're just not going to be able to do business." Peter should be under no illusion that Connie might later soften her stance.

It's a lot tougher, of course, when your answer to the threshold question is that if Peter isn't bluffing, you're prepared to yield the point, albeit reluctantly. That's the case here, and were you then to take that "sorry, no deal" posture, you would be bluffing. If it then turns out that Peter's position is genuine, you may lose everything. That's a chance I seldom want to take.

The technique I advise using here turns on your answer to a second question to ask yourself: Do I think that Peter is bluffing? Granted, you can't be sure, but you should be able to make an educated guess. If necessary, call a time out in the negotiations, in order to try to develop further information that bears on the credibility of Peter's position.

Let's say you don't think Peter is bluffing. You might then test the rigidity of his position by nibbling around the edges. Suggest various compromise formulations that if rejected still leave you positioned for ultimate acquiescence, without fear of losing the deal. For example, you can say that you "assume" Peter wouldn't mind your consulting for the other chains several years down the road, after he has had his head start. If you can get Peter to buy this exclusion, then you might try out a concept that frees you sooner, as long as you don't provide the other chains with advice similar to what you'll be giving to Peter. In such ways, you may be able to erode Peter's position, even though a frontal assault would have proved unavailing.

This method, however, fails to transmit a signal of your own resolve, which is the key ingredient needed to overcome a bluff. So if you suspect that Peter is bluffing, you should try to convey firmness coupled with some receptivity to an honorable compromise (but not capitulation). You can't, however, go as far as in the "sorry, no deal" scenario, which ought to be reserved for when that's really the case. It's a middle-of-the-road stance, with a slightly greater risk of losing the deal than in the prior formulation, but a risk you're willing to run because you believe Peter is bluffing.

So your posture might run along the following lines: "Peter, I'm simply not going to forgo forever the ability to take on any assignment from the other pizza chains. You wouldn't want to pay the amount of fee I'd have to charge to justify that! On the other hand, I fully understand the point you're making about wanting to gain an advantage over the competition as a result of my efforts. Let's see if we can come up with a formulation that protects your legitimate business interests, but doesn't unnecessarily restrict my freedom of action."

CREDIBILITY WRAP-UP

Keynote

The third basic skill of the smart negotiator centers around credibility—the ability to make his counterpart believe that he means what he says. At the same time, you have to make an accurate assessment of your counterpart's credibility. If you suspect that the other side is bluffing on an important point, you must send a signal of your own resolve in order to test the bluff, even if your actual level of resolve isn't quite so absolute. If your counterpart is bold enough to bluff, anything less on your part will only encourage his pretense.

Blunder

My candidate here is the bluff that's so effective it causes the other side (which isn't negotiating under the pressure of necessity) to call off the deal, even though the bluffer would have been willing to agree to the other side's final terms. Only take a chance bluffing about an issue when, if the bluff doesn't work, you'll have the opportunity to pull it off the table.

Lapse

Too often we take our own credibility for granted and don't make any buttressing effort. It's almost as if we assume that everyone will consider us as honest and straightforward as we know we are! But a safer assumption for you to make is that your counterpart will be just as concerned with whether you're bluffing as you are with whether he is. Don't forget, in these environs, a certain amount of suspicion and doubt come with the territory.

CHAPTER SIXTEEN

Ethical and Unethical Bargaining Tactics

An Empirical Study

Roy J. Lewicki

Robert J. Robinson

Negotiations are an interesting arena in which to study ethical decision making regarding honesty. First, negotiation is a pervasive activity in management contexts. In his study of key management roles, Mintzberg (1973) reported that managers spend a significant portion of their time either negotiating for things that are important to them, or resolving disputes among others in the workplace. Second, and more importantly, those who have written about effective negotiation strategies have often suggested that some types of dishonest behavior may be appropriate or even necessary to be an effective negotiator (see Lewicki, 1983; Carson, 1993; Cramton and Dees, 1993; Lewicki, Litterer, Minton, and Saunders, 1994; Lewicki and Stark, 1994, for reviews).

The purpose of the study reported in this paper was to examine judgments about the perceived ethical appropriateness of using selected tactics in managerial negotiations. The paper first examines the nature of negotiation and the challenges it poses for those who wish to act ethically. We explain the development of a questionnaire used to measure the perceived ethical appropriateness of selected tactics, and the results we obtained from two large samples of management students. The implications of these results will be explored for understanding how these tactics are perceived in negotiations, and for future research on the conditions under which these tactics may be used.

We thank Eileen Donohue for her help on the statistical analyses and two anonymous reviewers for their helpful critique.

221

THE NEGOTIATION CONTEXT

Lax and Sebenius (1986) define negotiation as "a process of potentially opportunistic interaction by which two or more parties, with some apparent conflict, seek to do better through jointly decided action than they could otherwise" (p. 11). Lewicki, Litterer, Minton, and Saunders (1994) state that a negotiation situation has the following parameters: (1) two or more parties who are interdependent, (2) a conflict of interest, (3) the parties are attempting to use one or more form of influence to obtain a "better" set of outcomes, and (4) the parties expect that there will be some "give and take," or concession making, to resolve their conflict.

Given either definition, it should be clear that in an effort to define and achieve a resolution to their conflict, and to achieve the best possible outcome for their side, each party must make the best possible case for his or her preferred solution, and move the opponent away from his or her preferred solution. These requirements may motivate an individual to violate contemporary ethical standards—in other words, to not do the right thing—by employing inappropriate influence tactics in order to gain the others' compliance. The purpose of this paper is to explore how negotiators perceive and make distinctions among the variety of marginally ethical tactics which may be available to them.

ETHICAL DECISION MAKING AND NEGOTIATION

We propose that dishonesty in negotiation is primarily concerned with problems of lying and truth telling.[1] Information is one of the most dominant sources of power (French and Raven, 1959)—particularly in negotiation (Lewicki, Litterer, Minton, and Saunders, 1994). Information control enhances negotiator power (Pfeffer, 1993). Since negotiation is primarily a process of exchanging and communicating this information in a persuasive manner, the opportunities for unethical conduct are ones of dishonest communication. Negotiators must decide how open and direct to be about their true settlement preferences, how to manage potential access to privileged communication, and how open to be about future and intended actions (threats and promises).

We propose that negotiators, when deciding whether to use tactics which may be less than fully ethical, evaluate these tactics on a continuum of "ethically appropriate" to "ethically inappropriate." Tactics at one end of this continuum are judged as being ethically acceptable and are commonly used in negotiation, even if they do require a small degree of deception or dishonesty. Tactics at the other end of the continuum are judged as ethically inappropriate and difficult to defend or justify. Between these two end points is a middle ground, or "gray area," in which tactics may be viewed as marginally unethical, justifiable under some circumstances but not others, and unclear as to their ethical appropriateness.

Our interest in this paper is to determine how negotiators perceive and discriminate among the range of available tactics. Much of the research literature (see below) proposes "categories" of dishonest actions, based on factors such as (1) the type of dishonesty involved; (2) the magnitude of the dishonesty; (3) the consequences (severity) of the dishonest action; or (4) the justifiability of the dishonest action. Our intent is to determine whether empirical methods for aggregating a group of unethical tactics through factor analysis can improve our understanding of the categories of tactics and their use.

CLASSIFICATIONS OF NEGOTIATING TACTICS

Lewicki (1983) proposed a model of lying and deception in negotiation. Drawing from Bok (1978) and her study of truth telling in medicine, lying was defined as "any intentionally deceptive message which is stated" (p. 13). Lewicki argued that the primary purpose of lying in negotiation is to increase the liar's power over the opponent through false or misleading information. Lies function to misinform the opponent, to eliminate or obscure the opponent's choice alternatives, or to manipulate the perceived costs and benefits of particular options that the opponent may wish to pursue. In negotiation, lies take several forms:

1. *Misrepresentation of position to an opponent.* The negotiator distorts his or her preferred settlement point. An individual intending to purchase an automobile may tell the seller that he can only afford $3,000, when in fact he is willing to spend up to $4,000. Misrepresentation is perceived as necessary in order to create a rationale for the opponent to make concessions. In an early study of misrepresentation, Chertkoff and Baird (1971) demonstrated that negotiators who made extreme demands (significantly above or below their preferred settlement point) were more likely to have opponents give in to these demands and to achieve highly favorable settlements.

2. *Bluffing.* The negotiator falsely states his or her intentions to perform some act. Bluffs can generally be described as false promises and false threats. A false promise (general form: if you do X, I will reward you) might be a commitment to reward an individual later if the opponent complies with our request now. A false threat (general form: if you don't do X or if you do Y, I will punish you) might be a stated intention to walk out if the opponent does not make appropriate concessions. In both cases, the actor never intends to follow through on the stated consequences.

3. *Falsification.* A third form of lying is the introduction of erroneous, incorrect information as though it were true. Examples include erroneous and misleading financial information, certifications of "proof," or false warranties

and guarantees. Whether spoken or printed, falsification attempts to use erroneous information to change the opponent's position by distorting the facts themselves.

4. *Deception.* A fourth form of lying is deception. Deception attempts to manipulate the opponent's logical and inferential processes in order to lead the opponent to an incorrect conclusion or deduction. First, negotiators may only present part of the relevant information and not "tell everything." An individual negotiating for a job may list several prestigious employers on his résumé without indicating that he only worked for those firms a short period of time. Deception also occurs when negotiators assemble a collection of arguments that lead the opponent to the wrong conclusion. A negotiator may give every indication she will support a particular course of action without explicitly proclaiming her endorsement of that action. When the endorsement is not forthcoming, she may claim that she did not lie—but she did not tell the whole truth either.

5. *Selective disclosure or misrepresentation to constituencies.* This final form of lying occurs in situations where other parties—in addition to the opponent— are involved in the negotiating relationship. The primary difference is in the target audience. Negotiators may misrepresent the events which occur at the negotiating table to their constituencies or may misrepresent the constituents' desires to the opposing negotiator.

As stated earlier, the purpose of this paper is to determine how negotiators evaluate a more complex array of negotiating tactics, all of which require deception and dishonesty. A repertoire of deceptive negotiation tactics was generated (see below); each tactic was then evaluated on a scale of ethical appropriateness in negotiation and likelihood that the respondent would use the tactic. Ratings of appropriateness of tactics were also subjected to a factor analysis to determine the dimensions which might underlie the aggregate of items. Once these results were obtained, data were collected at a second research site. This data collection offered the researchers a much larger sample on which to verify the reliability of their results. It also offered the opportunity to determine whether a different population might view the tactics differently or represent different underlying factors.

STUDY 1

The research subjects were 320 M.B.A. students enrolled in an academic course on negotiation (the data were collected in multiple iterations of the course over a two-year period) at Ohio State University (OSU). Each student completed the questionnaire at the beginning of the course. A demographic profile of the sample is presented in Table 16.1.

Table 16.1. Comparative Demographics of Ohio State University and Harvard Samples

	Harvard	Ohio State
Age	26.2	26.1
Gender		
Female	28.7%	29.7%
Male	71.3%	70.3%
U.S. citizen?		
No	30.5%	28.1%
Yes	69.5%	71.9%
Race		
White	69%	59.4%
Black	6%	12.5%
Asian/Hispanic/N.A.	25%	28.1%
Years full-time work experience	4.30	3.90

Research Questionnaire

The eighteen tactics selected were taken from a larger list, compiled from a number of research and practitioner-oriented publications on strategy and tactics in negotiation. Two criteria were used in creating the list. First, the tactic had to be a relatively common one which could be used in a variety of negotiation situations, i.e., it was not unique to any one negotiation context (e.g., real estate, buying an automobile) or type of dishonesty (e.g., bluffing, falsification, etc.). Second, the tactics had to differ in the apparent "magnitude" of the dishonesty involved. The Lewicki (1983) categories were used as a rough guide in paring down the list to eighteen items; however, the list of items was not intended to specifically mirror the Lewicki (1983) categories.[2] Preliminary drafts of the questionnaire were presented to managers who negotiate extensively; they suggested wording modifications and changes to refine the eighteen-item version used in this study.

The questionnaire asked each respondent to rate the perceived ethical appropriateness of using the tactic in negotiation[3] and the likelihood that they would use each of the eighteen tactics in a negotiation. All respondents were asked to judge from the following perspective: "You are about to enter into a negotiation. You will be negotiating for something which is very important to you and your business." No information about the negotiation context (the negotiator's own personal motivations, the specific issue being negotiated, information about the opponent, the relationship between the parties, or other contextual factors) was provided which might temper or shape the rating of the tactics. Respondents rated how appropriate each tactic was, and how likely they would be to use the tactic in this situation (scale range = 1–7, with higher ratings indicating greater perceived appropriateness or likelihood).

Results

First, descriptive statistics were computed to determine the means and standard deviations for the appropriateness and likelihood ratings of each tactic. The tactic means were then ordered by decreasing perceived appropriateness and are presented in Table 16.2.

Examination of this table indicates that there are some minor differences between the order of the appropriateness and likelihood ratings (e.g., item 4 was rated third highest for appropriateness but second highest for likelihood), but the overall distributions of ratings are highly similar. The differences between the means for a subject's rated appropriateness and likelihood ratings were small (the average difference between means was 0.2, and no item means differed by more than 0.5 of a rating point), indicating that in most cases, the appropriateness of an item was closely related to the likelihood of its being used.

Table 16.2. Appropriateness and Likelihood Ratings of Tactics

Tactic Number and Description	Mean Appropriateness	SD	Mean Likelihood	SD
6. Gain information about an opponent's negotiating position and strategy by "asking around" in a network of your own friends, associates and contacts.	6.10	1.47	6.04	1.59
5. Make an opening demand that is far greater than what one really hopes to settle for.	5.84	1.48	5.62	1.65
4. Hide your real bottom line from your opponent.	5.75	1.58	5.07	1.52
13. Convey a false impression that you are in absolutely no hurry to come to a negotiation agreement, thereby trying to put more time pressure on your opponent to concede quickly.	5.37	1.79	5.22	1.86

Tactic Number and Description	Mean Appropriateness	SD	Mean Likelihood	SD
3. Lead the other negotiator to believe that they can only get what they want by negotiating with you, when in fact they could go elsewhere and get what they want cheaper or faster.	4.28	1.70	4.31	1.78
10. Make an opening offer or demand so high (or low) that it seriously undermines your opponent's confidence in his/her own ability to negotiate a satisfactory settlement.	4.18	2.03	3.73	2.01
16. Intentionally misrepresent the nature of negotiations to the press or your constituency in order to protect delicate discussions that have occurred.	3.41	2.01	3.43	2.05
12. Talk directly to the people whom your opponent reports to, or is accountable to, and try to encourage them to defect to your side.	3.18	1.92	2.93	1.77
7. Gain information about an opponent's negotiating position by paying friends, associates, and contacts to get this information for you.	3.07	1.90	2.77	1.83
18. Intentionally misrepresent factual information to your opponent when you know that he/she has already done this to you.	2.94	2.00	3.35	2.12
9. Gain information about an opponent's negotiating position by cultivating his/her friendship through expensive gifts, entertaining, or "personal favors."	2.83	1.71	2.80	1.79

continued

Table 16.2. Appropriateness and Likelihood Ratings of Tactics (continued)

Tactic Number and Description	Mean Appropriateness	SD	Mean Likelihood	SD
17. Intentionally misrepresent the progress of negotiations to the press or your constituency in order to make your own position or point of view look better.	2.61	1.69	2.82	1.79
14. Threaten to make your opponent look weak or foolish in front of a boss or others to whom he/she is accountable.	2.35	1.59	2.33	1.54
11. Talk directly to the people whom your opponent reports to, or is accountable to, and tell them things that will undermine their confidence in your opponent as negotiator.	2.20	1.43	2.13	1.50
2. Promise that good things will happen to your opponent if he/she gives you what you want, even if you know that you can't (or won't) deliver those good things when the other's cooperation is obtained.	2.20	1.43	2.39	1.45
1. Threaten to harm your opponent if he/she doesn't give you what you want, even if you know you will never follow through to carry out that threat.	2.10	1.87	2.15	1.83
8. Gain information about an opponent's negotiating position by trying to recruit or hire one of your opponent's key subordinates (on the condition that the key subordinate bring confidential information with him/her).	2.02	1.41	1.98	1.42
15. Intentionally misrepresent factual information to your opponent in order to support your negotiating arguments or position.	1.99	1.43	2.44	1.55

Further analysis revealed substantial similarities among the items on the appropriateness and likelihood dimensions. Examination of the distributions suggested that the ratings could be best grouped into three categories: appropriate and likely to use (four tactics—6, 5, 4, 13), inappropriate and unlikely to use (twelve tactics—16, 12, 7, 18, 9, 17, 14, 11, 2, 1, 8, 15), and a "middle range" (the remaining two tactics—3 and 10). The same items fell into the same three categories for both scales. The high average intercorrelation (0.7) between the appropriateness and likelihood scales leads us to believe that the likelihood scale provided no additional information about how the tactics were viewed, and thus we decided to drop consideration of these ratings from subsequent analyses.

Factor Analysis of the Items

Having shown that the tactics were perceived as discernibly different from each other, the next step was to determine whether the tactics clustered together in some meaningful way. A factor analysis was performed on the appropriateness ratings to determine the emergent structure of the items. A principal components analysis with a varimax rotation was used. This is the least complicated of factoring procedures and has the advantage of using all of the item score variance. Only factor loadings with absolute value of 0.40 and above on any factor were considered (Rummel, 1970; Stevens, 1992).

Table 16.3 presents the results of the principal components analysis of the appropriateness item scores. Using the criterion of an eigenvalue greater than 1.0, five factors were extracted and rotated, accounting for 63.2 percent of the total variance.

The first factor, "Misrepresentation of Information," included items 15, 16, 17, and 18. The commonality in these items is that the negotiator is explicitly lying about some form of information, either to one's opponent or one's constituency.

The second factor was "Traditional Competitive Bargaining." The five items in this factor were examples of common techniques employed during traditional distributive bargaining situations (see Karrass, 1974; Lewicki, Litterer, Minton, and Saunders, 1994). This factor consisted of tactics 4, 5, 6, 10, and 13—including hiding one's real bottom line, making very high or low opening offers, and gaining information by asking among one's contacts and associates.

The third factor, "Bluffing," included items 1, 2, and 3. The commonality in these items is that all attempt to make your opponent believe that you are in control of consequences which you do not in fact control.

The fourth factor, "Manipulation of Opponent's Network," involves attempting to weaken your opponent's position through influencing his or her associates or constituency. Items 11, 12, and 14 load on this factor.

The final factor, named "Inappropriate Information Gathering," included items 7, 8, and 9. These tactics require gaining information about your opponent's negotiating position by employing various tactics generally viewed as unacceptable in traditional bargaining situations.

Table 16.3. Principal Components Analysis with Varimax Rotation for Appropriateness Ratings

Appropriateness Item	Rotated Factor Loadings[a]				
	1	2	3	4	5
18. Misrepresent information when opponent has	0.773				
17. Misrepresent to press to look better	0.764				
16. Misrepresent to press to protect	0.756				
15. Misrepresent to support position	0.696				
5. Make demand greater than hoped for		0.798			
4. Hide real bottom line from opponent		0.635	0.402		
13. Give impression that you aren't in hurry		0.582			
6. Gain information by "asking around"		0.614			0.406
10. Make offer to undermine confidence		0.495			
2. Promise good things you can't deliver			0.852		
1. Falsely threaten to harm opponent			0.760		
3. Make other believe must deal with you			0.657		
11. Reduce confidence of other's superiors				0.826	
14. Threaten to make look foolish to boss				0.746	
12. Encourage other's boss to defect				0.704	
8. Gain information by recruiting other's subordinates				0.721	
9. Gain information through cultivating friendship					0.673
7. Gain information by paying your associates					0.672

Note: Factor labels: (1) Misrepresentation of Information. (2) Traditional Competitive Bargaining. (3) Bluffing. (4) Manipulation of Opponent's Network. (5) Inappropriate Information Gathering.

[a]Only loadings with absolute ratings higher than 0.400 are reported.

Two tactics loaded on two factors, which made the analysis slightly more difficult to interpret. Item 4, "hide real bottom line from opponent," loaded on Traditional Competitive Bargaining (Factor 2) and Bluffing (Factor 3).

Although it is unfortunate that the tactic double-loaded, "hiding one's real bottom line" is, in fact, both an aspect of bluffing and part of the dynamics of traditional competitive bargaining. Similarly, item 6, "gain information by asking around in the opponent's network," loaded strongly on Traditional Competitive Bargaining (Factor 2) and Inappropriate Information Gathering (Factor 5). This tactic is also consistent with both the more narrow information-gathering process and with the broader scope of tactics used in the more traditional distributive bargaining process.

Table 16.4 presents the results of a maximum likelihood analysis of the Appropriateness ratings. This analysis is somewhat more tolerant of variance in the item ratings and seeks the "best" factor solution. It is traditionally used as a confirmatory factor analytic procedure.

This analysis reveals that the basic five-factor solution is maintained and the dual loadings of items 4 and 6 disappear. The items are slightly reordered within the factors, and Factors 4 and 5 exchange one item in the "network negotiation" clusters. However, the overall pattern strongly suggests that there are five clear factors in this group of items.

STUDY 2: VERIFICATION OF THE FACTOR STRUCTURE AND EXAMINATION OF DEMOGRAPHIC DIFFERENCES IN SCALE RATINGS

After establishing the structure of these five factors with the OSU sample, an opportunity to collect further data at a different institution created an occasion to pursue several research objectives. First, the additional data would create a significantly larger sample, permitting the researchers to replicate the factor analysis and have more confidence in the factor pattern. The second research site also offered the opportunity to explore whether students at that institution viewed the tactics differently (our hunch, based on stereotypical impressions of the competitiveness of the students, was that Harvard students might view the tactics as more ethically acceptable across the entire range of tactics). Finally, this second data collection offered the opportunity to link tactic ratings to demographic variables not collected in the first sample, such as age, gender, national origin, and self-reported views of their conflict management disposition as aggressive or cooperative.[4]

Table 16.4. Maximum Likelihood Analysis with Rotation for Appropriateness Ratings

Appropriateness Item	Rotated Factor Loadings[a]				
	1	2	3	4	5
17. Misrepresent to press to look better	0.819				
16. Misrepresent to press to protect	0.744				
18. Misrepresent information when opponent has	0.563				
15. Misrepresent to support position	0.522				
5. Make demand greater than hoped for		0.764			
13. Give impression that you aren't in hurry		0.596			
6. Gain information by "asking around"		0.507			
10. Make offer to undermine confidence		0.454			
4. Hide real bottom line from opponent		0.412			
2. Promise good things you can't deliver			0.877		
1. Falsely threaten to harm opponent			0.698		
3. Make other believe must deal with you			0.493		
11. Reduce confidence of other's superiors				0.758	
12. Encourage other's boss to defect				0.598	
14. Threaten to make look foolish to boss				0.595	
9. Gain information through cultivating friendship				0.591	
8. Gain information by recruiting other's subordinates					0.545
7. Gain information by paying your associates					0.447

Note: Factor labels: (1) Misrepresentation of Information. (2) Traditional Competitive Bargaining. (3) Bluffing. (4) Manipulation of Opponent's Network. (5) Inappropriate Information Gathering.

[a]Only loadings with absolute ratings higher than 0.400 are reported.

Method

736 first year M.B.A. students at Harvard Business School (HBS) were asked to complete a questionnaire at the beginning of a required course on managerial negotiation. The questionnaire requested demographic information and data about previous negotiation experience and also presented the same eighteen negotiation tactics given to the Ohio State University (OSU) sample. Two factor analyses—one with the HBS student data and one with the combined OSU-HBS students—were performed (one analysis determined whether the HBS sample differed from the OSU sample, and the second determined whether the results of the combined sample differed from either individual sample). The results of these factor analyses are presented in Table 16.5.

Table 16.5. Factor Analysis: Consolidation of OSU and HBS Students

Factor (Number and Description)	OSU Sample (n = 364)		HBS Sample (n = 736)		Combined (n = 1,100)	
	Items	Factor Loading	Items	Factor Loading	Items	Factor Loading
1. Misrepresentation	17	0.774	17	0.797	17	0.788
of Information	16	0.756	16	0.777	16	0.759
	18	0.765	15	0.669	18	0.728
	15	0.696	18	0.668	15	0.702
2. Traditional Competitive	5	0.798	5	0.717	5	0.743
Bargaining	13	0.614	10	0.692	4	0.649
	6	0.582	13	0.658	13	0.618
	10	0.495	4	0.606	10	0.583
	4	0.635	-	-	-	-
3. Bluffing	2	0.853	1	0.754	2	0.790
	1	0.760	2	0.731	1	0.760
	3	0.657	3	0.512	3	0.576
4. Misrepresentation of	11	0.826	11	0.680	11	0.796
Opponent's Network	12	0.704	8	0.669	14	0.657
	14	0.746	9	0.575	12	0.627
	-	-	12	0.571	-	- -
	14	0.463	-	-	-	- -
5. Inappropriate Information	9	0.673	6	0.806	7	0.773
Gathering	8	0.673	7	0.726	6	0.620
	7	0.720	-	-	9	0.618
	-	-	-	-	8	0.538

Results

The analysis in Table 16.5 reveals that there is a close correspondence between the factors discovered in the two samples. The combined factor analyses, performed on a total sample of 1,056 responses, also produced five factors, all consistent with and supportive of the initial analyses from the OSU sample. From here on, our discussion refers to the factors from the combined samples and are shown in the last column of Table 16.5.

OSU versus HBS M.B.A. Students. As shown in Table 16.6, HBS M.B.A. students emerged as somewhat more accepting of the entire group of negotiation tactics in general compared to their OSU counterparts. On four of the five factors, HBS M.B.A. students were significantly more accepting of the tactics in question (the differences on Factor 5 are only marginally significant, however). Only on Factor 3—misrepresenting an opponent's network—were there no differences between the samples.

It is interesting to speculate on the source of these differences between the two samples. On the one hand, both groups of students completed the questionnaire at the beginning of academic courses on negotiation, before they had the opportunity to experiment with these tactics themselves, observe others experimenting with the tactics, and experience the results of using them with classmates. On the other hand, the results confirmed our own naive stereotypic judgments that HBS students would be more comfortable with the ethicality of both "acceptable" (Factor 2) and "unacceptable" (Factors 1, 4, 5) tactics. Some of these differences may be due to the demographic and attitudinal differences noted below; additional variance may be attributed to parameters not collected for this research, such as personality differences between applicants to the two schools, academic talent and aptitude, as well as the type of professional work experience participants had before returning to business school or intended professional position after graduation. We did not collect systematic data on the two student populations to permit direct comparisons. Therefore, the explanatory power contributed by these other differences remains an agenda item for future research.

Women versus Men. There is a long history of research related to the impact of gender on approaches to negotiation. The stereotypical view is that men are more competitively selfish and more willing to engage in hard bargaining, while women are more cooperative and fair-minded. Watson (1994) challenged this stereotypical view, evaluated the theoretical underpinnings of the assumption, and provided an excellent review of past empirical research. Her conclusions are that the gender differences noted in past research are largely an artifact of power and status differences between genders in U.S. culture and that additional data about perceived power, status, opponent, and context are critical to truly

Table 16.6. Comparison of Various Groups on the Five Factors

Group	N	Factor 1: Misrepresentation of Information	Factor 2: Traditional Competitive Bargaining	Factor 3: Misrepresentation to Opponent's Network	Factor 4: Bluffing	Factor 5: Inappropriate Information Gathering
Harvard M.B.A.s	736	3.30*	5.61*	2.71	2.90*	3.56***
OSU M.B.A.s	364	2.67	5.2	2.80	2.52	3.43
Females	206	3.15	5.56	2.45	2.40	4.54
Males	528	3.36***	5.63	2.81*	2.80*	4.84*
Aggressives	160	3.63*	5.91*	3.11**	2.85*	4.89
Cooperatives	573	3.21	5.52	2.54	2.64	4.72
Noncitizens	203	3.27	5.36	2.83***	2.58	4.84
U.S. citizens	527	3.32	5.70*	2.67	2.73***	4.73
Asians	62	3.19	5.28[a]	3.85	2.82[A]	4.84
Eastern Europeans	11	3.32	5.11[ab]	2.76	1.98[a]	4.95
Latin Americans	36	3.27	5.16[a]	2.94	2.52	4.96
Middle Easterners	11	3.64	5.95[A]	3.27[A]	2.53	5.32
U.S. and U.K.	517	3.36	5.69[B]	2.66[a]	2.73[A]	4.73
Western Europeans	65	3.20	5.40	2.91	2.55	4.67

For the final sets of results, means with uppercase superscripts are significantly larger than means with corresponding lowercase superscripts. Preliminary data analysis indicated that U.S. and U.K. subjects were essentially similar in all aspects of their views on negotiation tactics. For the purpose of these analyses, these two categories have therefore been combined.

*$p < 0.1$. **$p < 0.05$. ***$p < 0.01$.

understanding how women may interpret the appropriateness of particular strategies and tactics.

Within the HBS sample, the data reveal that men were significantly more accepting of the tactics on four of the five factors. Interestingly, however, the two groups did not diverge on Factor 2—Traditional Competitive Bargaining—suggesting that women (at least in this sample) are as willing as their male counterparts to use these tactics when they are in traditionally competitive contexts, but have greater reservations than men about using the other kinds of tactics. Following Watson's findings (noted above) and given that most of the situational cues (status, power, opponent, and context) needed to truly distinguish male-female differences were absent in this study, our findings require replication in more clearly delineated situations which specify these cues.

Aggressiveness versus Cooperativeness. As part of the initial questionnaire and before they were asked to respond to the eighteen tactics, subjects were asked (a forced choice question) to categorize themselves as either "aggressive" or "cooperative" in negotiation situations.[5] As can be seen in Table 16.6, only 160 students (21.8 percent of the sample) classified themselves as aggressive; the remainder identified themselves as cooperative. The distinction proved predictive: on four of the five factors, self-rated aggressive subjects were more accepting of the tactics than their cooperative counterparts. Only on Factor 5— Inappropriate Information Gathering—did the two sides show similar acceptance of the tactics.

U.S. Citizens versus Noncitizens. The sizable non-U.S. citizen population at HBS allowed a direct comparison between U.S. and non-U.S. M.B.A.s (for a further breakdown, see below). Examination of Table 16.6 reveals that U.S. citizens emerge as somewhat more tolerant of certain kinds of tactics than noncitizens. On two factors—Traditional Competitive Bargaining and Bluffing—U.S. citizens are significantly more accepting of such tactics. This difference is greatest for Traditional Competitive Bargaining ($p < 0.01$), which raises the interesting possibility that American negotiators may, while following their own accepted ethical dictates, in certain instances be perceived as less ethical by their international counterparts. On the other hand, U.S. citizens are significantly less accepting of the tactics in Factor 3—Misrepresentation to an Opponent's Network—than their international brethren. The norm in the United States of not spreading stories and slander about someone, particularly to their network of friends and formal reports, appears to be stronger in the United States than elsewhere. Indeed, when one puts the unusual normative model on its head and asks, in effect, "How do the negotiating ethics of U.S. citizens differ from the rest of the world?" it is possible to imagine somewhat different prescriptions being made for how we train our managers. Instead of seeing "foreign" cultural norms as odd and necessary to appease, we may want to consider the idiosyncratic nature of American ethical mores.

Different International Groups. One-way analyses of variance of the factors across international groupings revealed some interesting distinctions.[6] On Factor 2—Traditional Competitive Bargaining—people from the Middle East emerged as significantly more accepting of such tactics than Asians, Eastern Europeans, and Latin Americans. U.S. respondents were also more accepting of such tactics than Eastern Europeans (the implications of this for U.S. entrepreneurs entering the ex-communist bloc nations should be clear). Interestingly, and amplifying on the discussion in the previous paragraph, on Factor 3—making Misrepresentations to an Opponent's Network—U.S. subjects are least accepting and are significantly less accepting than Middle Eastern respondents. On Factor 4—Bluffing—Americans and Asians are more accepting than Eastern Europeans.

Ethnic Groups. A final comparison was done on the HBS M.B.A. sample, using only U.S. subjects (not shown in Table 16.6). The categories were African American, Asian, Hispanic/Latino, and white. No differences were observed except for Factor 5—Inappropriate Information Gathering. On this factor, Hispanic/Latino subjects were more accepting of the tactics (5.58) than were Asians (4.57) or whites (4.71) (all p values < 0.05). To our knowledge, no research has been done on negotiation ethics which specify international or ethnic groups by which we can benchmark these findings.

DISCUSSION OF BOTH STUDIES

In this study, respondents to a questionnaire were asked to evaluate a set of ethically marginal negotiation tactics. These tactics were derived from reviewing several trade books and seminars that present a normative, competitive approach on "how to negotiate" (Karrass, 1974), as well as talking with experienced negotiators about incidents which they considered "unethical."

The results indicate that even though all tactics raise some questions about ethicality and appropriateness, the respondents have rather strong and consistent beliefs about which tactics are acceptable and which ones are unacceptable. Four tactics are generally seen as ethically "appropriate" (ratings of 5.0 or above), twelve tactics are seen as ethically "inappropriate" (ratings of 3.0 or below), and two tactics are seen as "marginal" (ratings between 3.0 and 5.0).

One conclusion that can be drawn from these data is that negotiation tactics are not seen as moral absolutes. Both the means and standard deviations of appropriateness and likelihood suggest that most respondents rated the tactics at different points along the dimensional scales and perceived the tactics quite differently.

Surprisingly, only two of the eighteen tactics (tactic 3—misleading an opponent—and tactic 10—making a "high ball" or "low ball" offer) fall within some "gray area" of marginal appropriateness. We expected that more of these tactics would be seen as marginal. Admittedly, this result may be an artifact by virtue of the method we use for determining "marginality"—i.e., selecting these two tactics from the middle of the scale based on their average ratings, rather than explicitly asking respondents to directly allocate the tactics to redefined categories labeled "appropriate," "marginal," and "inappropriate." In fact, the complete aggregation of tactics may be viewed as marginal, since we did not present tactics to respondents which were clearly "fully honest and disclosing," nor did we include many tactics that would constitute outright lying, cheating, and stealing in their most flagrant forms. As a result, the demand characteristics of the rating task may have forced a greater number of tactics into the "appropriate" and "inappropriate" categories than would otherwise occur. Further data collection and analysis, as well as a larger repertoire of tactics from the complete range, may help explain this distribution.

Factor Analyses

The factor analyses also demonstrate patterns which are interesting and interpretable. These patterns are remarkably robust across the two university samples. Second, the factor pattern does match—to some degree—the different types of truth distortion suggested in Lewicki (1983).

Factor 1, "Misrepresentation of Information," includes four tactics in which information is distorted in some manner to a "significant other" in negotiation—either the opponent (tactics 15 and 18) or the media (tactics 16 and 17). While the tactics differ in the reasons why they are performed—justification of position, retribution against an opponent, preserving confidentiality, or face saving—and while the respondents define sharp differences in the perceived appropriateness of the tactics, the common theme of misrepresentation unites them. Factor 1 clearly parallels the "falsification" category in Lewicki (1983). Overt and explicit statement of false factual information is viewed as one type of judgment in the decision process about which tactics to use in negotiation.

Factor 2, "Traditional Competitive Bargaining," represents an aggregation of traditionally accepted tactics in distributive negotiation—hiding a bottom line (4), making inflated opening demands (5), securing information about your opponent (6), undermining an opponent's confidence (10), and stalling or delaying negotiation progress (13). These tactics are frequently advocated as necessary to successful competitive negotiation (Cohen, 1980; Karrass, 1974). Respondents view these tactics less in regard to the types of deception involved than as common to a distinct style of negotiating. This factor is more difficult to relate to the

Lewicki (1983) model in that the factor does not represent a "type" of dishonesty (e.g., bluffing, falsification, etc.), but a cluster of those tactics which are in the "appropriate" range of things to do in negotiation (given this set of items). Given the prototypical model of distributive negotiation (Walton and McKersie, 1965; Lewicki and Litterer, 1985), the tactics are generally oriented toward maintaining the secrecy of one's own position, sending out false cues that will throw the opponent "off the track" and thwarting the attempted secrecy of the opponent.

The third factor, "Bluffing," includes three tactics which use deception to force an opponent into dealing with the negotiator directly. These might be labeled as the common bag of negotiator "dirty tricks": false threats (1), false promises (2), and cutting off an opponent's options to pursue objectives elsewhere (3). Again, these tactics differ strongly in perceived appropriateness and likelihood of use; tactic 3 is seen as marginal, while 1 and 2 are clearly inappropriate. However, they are united in their common intent to use power to pressure the opponent to comply with the negotiator directly, either by stating false threats and promises or narrowing the opponent's perceived choice options. This category rather strongly mirrors the "bluffing" category proposed by Lewicki (1983).

Factor 4, "Manipulation of Opponent's Network," represents a class of negotiation tactics in which the objective is to undermine the negotiator's support system in his or her constituency—talking to the boss or network and undermining the negotiator's support (11), encouraging erosion of his support through defections (12), or threatening to embarrass the opponent (14). Most negotiators understand the implicit (or often explicit) pressures on them by constituents to appear strong and competent, and the powerful impact that a negative evaluation can have on loss of face (see Brown, 1968; Lewicki, Litterer, Minton, and Saunders, 1994). While the brief scenario that we painted for the respondents contained no items specifically addressing the ethical concerns of the relationship between a negotiator and a constituency, this factor clearly indicates that the broader relationship with others, "outside" the boundaries of 1:1 negotiations, can become a key consideration in ethical judgments. This factor appears to parallel the category of lying described as "selective disclosure or misrepresentation to constituencies" in the Lewicki (1983) model.

Finally, the fifth factor was named "Inappropriate Information Gathering." This factor includes those items that address various forms of "bribery" (7, paying for information about an opponent), "paying informants" (8, recruiting an opponent's constituents to your side), and "seduction" (9, gaining information in exchange for gifts, favors, etc.). The commonality in these tactics is not one of truth distortion, but of "cheating" the informal rules of negotiation by paying for information which one would otherwise not have available to him or her. This was not a category of items which was proposed by the Lewicki (1983) model; however, that model only proposed categories of lying (violations of truth telling) in negotiation. This category, therefore, represents a cluster of items that emerged through the broad process of identifying the original list of tactics for this study. It also indicates that respondents clearly discriminate differences in the social exchange process by which information is obtained and distributed in negotiation; "paying" for information or for leverage in negotiation, particularly when it should be available "free," is discernible as an inappropriate class of negotiation tactics. All of these tactics are seen as inappropriate, some clearly more than others.

Demographic Differences

The differences noted in the Harvard sample as a function of institution, gender, nationality, and self-perceived personality style are interesting. Each of these findings is briefly reviewed and discussed below. However, a full and complete understanding of these findings requires significant methodological refinement of the data collection process and a fuller specification of negotiation context, opponent, relationship to opponent, etc., before we can truly determine the meaning and import of any of the differences noted.

Institutional Differences

Since there appears to be no significant difference in any of the demographic differences presented in Table 16.6, the institutional difference findings—that Harvard students tend to embrace four of the five factor groups more than Ohio State students—appears to be attributable to other sources of difference. These differences could include differences in academic qualifications for the institution, differences in personality such as aggressiveness or competitiveness (obtained for Harvard students but not OSU students), type of past work experience, the "institutional culture" of each school, or the point at which students are measured within their graduate education (Harvard students completed this course in the spring of their first year, while OSU students take the course as an elective in their second year). Our own speculation on these findings leads us to conclude that the general aggressiveness of Harvard students would be greater than Ohio State students, compounded by a greater competitiveness in the Harvard Business School student culture. Other recent research (Trevino, Butterfield, and McCabe, 1998; Lewicki, Poland, Minton, and Sheppard, 1997) has documented the strong impact of perceived organizational culture on dispositions to behave dishonestly, and our findings with regard to the sample differences could be explained by the different cultural norms. Future research on negotiator ethics may necessitate the measurement of perceived cultural context as a determinant of what tactics are seen as appropriate.

Gender

The differences in ratings as a function of gender results appear to confirm trends in many other studies on gender differences in conflict management: that women tend to be more cooperative and fair-minded. While women did not disagree with men on the "appropriateness" of traditional competitive bargaining tactics, they were more conservative than men on the evaluation of all other tactics. This finding would suggest that women draw a sharper delineation between those tactics which are somewhat dishonest but nevertheless appropriate for competitive negotiation versus those tactics which are clearly inappropriate to use. However, as noted above, Watson's findings (1994) suggest that reliable interpretation of gender differences must take into account a number of situational variables not measured in this study.

Nationality and Ethnicity

The current research revealed differences in the ratings of tactics between U.S. citizens and noncitizens, differences as a function of various world regions, and differences among U.S. ethnic groups. Similar to the results reported above for academic institution and gender, there are a large number of factors that might account for these differences—cultural expectations, expectations of the negotiation context, etc. We discussed each of the results in the above section and noted that the absence of benchmark data creates the opportunity for extensive cross-cultural exploration of how these tactics are viewed and used.

Self-Reported Personality Orientation

Finally, respondents in the Harvard sample who reported themselves as "aggressive" were more likely to see the tactics as appropriate (in four of the five categories) than those self-rating as cooperative. What is interesting about this result is that individuals, depending upon whether they classify themselves as aggressive or cooperative, exhibit differential thresholds of tolerance for the various tactics and appear to intuitively understand their own relative threshold. The findings are certainly not surprising, given that they are consistent with much other research on the role of personality and motivational orientation on the disposition that negotiators take to the bargaining process (see Lewicki, Litterer, Minton, and Saunders, 1994, for one review). Yet as this review points out, a full understanding of the role of personality variables requires an understanding of how those variables interact with the contextual parameters of the situation (opponent, negotiating problem, culture, etc.). Thus, even though we know that aggressive negotiators may be more likely to employ these tactics, future research will need to embed these tactics in a specific context to fully understand their use.

Limitations and Implications for Future Research

This study has some obvious and clear limitations. First, evaluations of the tactics, and the subsequent impact these evaluations have on scale ratings and factor loadings, may be affected by the words used to describe the tactic. Despite a major effort to employ language which is neutral and describes the behavioral act in nonevaluative terms, phrases such as *"intentionally misrepresent," "threaten,"* and *"undermine"* are not neutral terms. Research on the rationalization and justification of controversial or unpopular behavior (Staw, 1979; Bies, 1989) indicates that the manner in which behavior is labeled and explained contributes greatly to the evaluation of that action and willingness to perform it. Subsequent research may wish to experiment with the labels used to describe these behaviors, as different labels may lead to different evaluations of selected tactics.

Second, the study measures perceptions and intentions rather than actual behavior. The questionnaire study creates demand characteristics for respondents to state what they would do rather than observing what they actually do. Even though respondents were assured anonymity, we can expect that these demand characteristics probably skewed responses toward presenting a more "ethical" face to the world than might be otherwise observed.

Third, greater parsimony should be sought in the approach to developing the comprehensive list of tactics used in this research. A recent paper (Lewicki and Stark, 1994) suggests that this may be achieved by exploring the convergence (or lack thereof) of three different ways to think about marginally ethical negotiation tactics: proposed frameworks (Lewicki, 1983; Anton, 1990; Carson, 1993; Cramton and Dees, 1993), broader "explorations of honesty in the workplace" (Murphy, 1993), and lists of tactics derived from examining the practitioner literature. In an effort to achieve convergence among these approaches, recent work (Robinson, Lewicki, and Donohue, 1996) developed a comprehensive list of tactics that reflected a clearer conceptual approach to deceptive negotiating tactics and a broader list of sample items. However, factor analysis of this broader tactical array yielded the same identical factors as those reported in this study. Thus, we are quite confident that the clusters of tactics presented here are robust and durable.

Fourth, the data collected for this paper were from a U.S. student population. We do not see this as inappropriate, since these students (on average) have extensive work experience (Table 16.1), come from careers where negotiation was a significant activity (sales, marketing, real estate, banking, consulting, etc.), and expect to be returning to those same work environments following graduation. Yet we cannot deny that different results may be obtained from different samples representing different occupational groupings (see Anton's 1990 findings with clergy), and future research may pursue these benchmarks with other populations.

Finally, as noted many times in the discussion of our findings, there are several clear areas for future research. Most significant, we have noted that the judgments of tactic appropriateness were made outside a specific negotiation context. Respondents were asked to place themselves in a situation which was highly sterile and permitted them a great deal of latitude in defining the situation (their objectives, the nature of the other person, the issues at stake, etc.). Earlier papers (Lewicki, 1983; Lewicki Litterer, Minton, and Saunders, 1994) have reviewed research and suggested a number of personality and situational factors which might enhance or reduce the likelihood of using these tactics. For example, Lewicki and Spencer (1991) reported that negotiators were more likely to use the tactics when they anticipated that the other would behave competitively and far more likely to use the tactics when the relationship with the opponent was perceived to be short term rather than long term. Similarly, our own work has shown that the self-reported personality orientation of a negotiator can affect his or her judgments, as can cultural orientation and context. Future research should explore selected situational variables which are most likely to enhance or reduce the perceived appropriateness of tactics and likelihood of their use. This may include power differences, expectations of the other and the context, and the strengths of one's preferences to achieve objectives at any cost.

Notes

1. This may seem obvious to many, but good definitions of the scope of honesty are not readily available. The dictionary defines *honest* as "not given to lying, cheating, stealing or taking unfair advantage," suggesting that honesty encompasses respect for the truth, for rules, and for property. Murphy (1993) defines honesty "in terms of the extent to which individuals and groups in organizations abide by consistent and rational ethical principles related to obligations to respect the truth" (p. 9), suggesting that the definition applies only to standards of truth telling, but then immediately proceeds to elaborate on the deterioration of honesty in the workplace with examples of employee theft, corporate corruption, résumé fraud, etc.

2. Lewicki derived the categories used in the 1983 paper from earlier writing on different types of lying and deception (particularly Bok, 1978). There was no reason to presume that these categories were either comprehensive or exhaustive of the repertoire of dishonest negotiating tactics; therefore, the repertoire of tactics should not be bound by these categories.

3. "Appropriateness" was selected as a dimension because in earlier pilot studies, requesting subjects to rate the tactics as "ethical" caused consternation among some respondents who wanted the researchers to define "ethical" before they made their judgments. Asking respondents to define terms such as *"appropriate"* created no such problem.

4. The demographic data reported on the Ohio State sample in Table 16.1 accurately describes the demographics of this sample, but these data were not collected in a manner permitting them to be used to divide the sample into subgroupings based on age, gender, etc.

5. Although this forced choice produced the interesting results described here, subsequent studies will allow respondents to rate themselves (7-point scales) on both dimensions.

6. Only groups with numbers large enough for analyses (more than ten) were
   included here.

References

Anton, R. J. "Managing Conflict Before It Happens: The Role of Accounts." In M. A.
Rahim (ed.), *Managing Conflict: An Interdisciplinary Approach*, 83–91. New York:
Praeger, 1990.

Bok, S. *Lying: Moral Choice in Public and Private Life.* New York: Pantheon Books, 1978.

Brown, B. R. "The Effects of Need to Maintain Face on Interpersonal Bargaining."
Journal of Experimental Social Psychology, 1968, *4*, 107–122.

Carson, T. "Second Thoughts About Bluffing." *Business Ethics Quarterly*, 1993, *3*(4).

Chertkoff, J. M., and Baird, S. L. "Applicability of the Big Lie Technique and the Last
Clear Chance Doctrine in Bargaining." *Journal of Personality and Social Psychology*,
1971, *20*, 298–303.

Cohen, H. *You Can Negotiate Anything.* Secuacus, N.J.: Lyle Stuart, 1980.

Cramton, P. C., and Dees, J. G. "Promoting Honesty in Negotiation." *Business Ethics
Quarterly*, 1993, *3*(4).

French, J.R.P., and Raven, B. "The Bases of Social Power." In D. Cartwright (ed.),
Studies in Social Power. Ann Arbor, Mich.: Institute for Social Research, 1959.

Karrass, C. *Give and Take: The Complete Guide to Negotiating Strategies and Tactics.*
New York: Crowell, 1974.

Lax, D. A., and Sebenius, J. K. *The Manager as Negotiator.* New York: Free Press,
1986.

Lewicki, R. J. "Lying and Deception: A Behavioral Model." In M. H. Bazerman and
R. J. Lewicki (eds.), *Negotiating in Organizations.* Beverly Hills, Calif.: Sage
Publications, 1983.

Lewicki, R. J., Litterer, J., Minton, J., and Saunders, D. *Negotiation* (2nd ed.). Burr
Ridge, Ill.: Richard D. Irwin, 1994.

Lewicki, R. J., Poland, T., Minton, J., and Sheppard, B. H. "Deviance as Dishonesty: A
Typology of Workplace Dishonesty and Key Contributing Factors." In R. J. Lewicki,
R. Bies, and B. H. Sheppard (eds.), *Research on Negotiation in Organizations.* JAI
Press, 1997.

Lewicki, R. J., and Spencer, G. "Ethical Relativism and Negotiation Tactcs: Factors
Affecting Their Perceived Ethicality." Paper presented at the Academy of
Management, Miami, Aug. 1991.

Lewicki, R. J., and Stark, N. "What's Ethically Appropriate in Negotiations: An
Examination of Negotiation Ethics." *Social Justice Research*, 1994, *9*(1), 69–95.

Mintzberg, H. *The Nature of Managerial Work,* New York: Harper & Row, 1973.

Murphy, K. R. *Honesty in the Workplace.* Pacific Grove, Calif.: Brooks/Cole, 1993.

Pfeffer, J. *Managing with Power.* Cambridge, Mass.: Harvard Business School Press, 1993.

Robinson, R. J., Lewicki, R. J., and Donohue, E. *Extending and Testing a Five Factor Model of Ethical and Unethical Bargaining Tactics: Introducing the SINS Scale.* Paper presented to the International Association of Conflict Management, Ithaca, N.Y., 1996.

Rummel, R. J. *Applied Factor Analysis.* Evanston, Ill.: Northwestern University Press, 1970.

Staw, B. "Rationality and Justification in Organizational Life." In B. M. Straw and L. L. Cummings (eds.), *Research in Organizational Behavior* 2, 45–80.

Stevens, J. *Applied Multivariate Statistics for the Social Sciences,* (2nd ed.). Hillsdale, N.J.: Lawrence Erlbaum Associates, 1992.

Trevino, L. K., Butterfield, K. D, and McCabe, D. L. "The Ethical Context in Organizations: Influences on Employee Attitudes and Behavior." *Business Ethics Quarterly,* 1998, *8*(3), 447–476.

Walton, R. E., and McKersie, R. B. *A Behavioral Theory of Labor Relations.* Ithica, N.Y.: ILR Press, 1965.

Watson, C. "Gender Differences in Negotiating Behavior and Outcomes: Fact or Artifact?" In A. Taylor and J. Beinstein-Miller (eds.), *Conflict and Gender,* 191–210. Cresskill, N.J.: Hampton Press.

CHAPTER SEVENTEEN

Is Business Bluffing Ethical?

Albert Z. Carr

A respected businessperson with whom I discussed the theme of this article remarked with some heat, "You mean to say you're going to encourage managers to bluff? Why, bluffing is nothing more than a form of lying! You're advising them to lie!"

I agreed that the basis of private morality is a respect for truth and that the closer a businessperson comes to the truth, the more he or she deserves respect. At the same time, I suggested that most bluffing in business might be regarded simply as game strategy—much like bluffing in poker, which does not reflect on the morality of the bluffer.

I quoted Henry Taylor, the British statesman who pointed out that "falsehood ceases to be falsehood when it is understood on all sides that the truth is not expected to be spoken," an exact description of bluffing in poker, diplomacy, and business. I cited the analogy of the criminal court where the criminals are not expected to tell the truth when they plead "not guilty." Everyone from the judge down takes it for granted that the job of the defendant's attorneys is to get their client off, not to reveal the truth; and this is considered ethical practice.

I reminded my friend that millions of businesspeople feel constrained every day to say yes when they secretly believe no and that this is generally accepted as permissible strategy when the alternative might be the loss of a job. The essential point, I said, is that the ethics of business are game ethics, different from the ethics of religion.

He remained unconvinced. Referring to the company of which he is president, he declared: "Maybe that's good enough for some businesspeople, but I can tell you that we pride ourselves on our ethics. In thirty years, not one customer has ever questioned my word or asked to check our figures. We're loyal to our customers and fair to our suppliers. I regard my handshake on a deal as a contract. I've never entered into price-fixing schemes with my competitors. I've never allowed my sales force to spread injurious rumors about other companies. Our union contract is the best in our industry. And, if I do say so myself, our ethical standards are of the highest!"

He really was saying, without realizing it, that he was living up to the ethical standards of the business game—which are a far cry from those of private life. Like a poker player, he did not play in cahoots with others at the table, try to smear their reputations, or hold back chips he owed them.

But this same fine man, at that very time, was allowing one of his products to be advertised in a way that made it sound a great deal better than it actually was. Another item in his product line was notorious among dealers for its "built-in obsolescence." He was holding back from the market a much-improved product because he did not want it to interfere with sales of the inferior item it would have replaced. He had joined with certain of his competitors in hiring a lobbyist to push a state legislature, by methods that he preferred not to know too much about, into amending a bill then being enacted.

In his view these things had nothing to do with ethics; they were merely normal business practice. He himself undoubtedly avoided outright falsehoods—never lied in so many words. But the entire organization that he ruled was deeply involved in numerous strategies of deception.

PRESSURE TO DECEIVE

Most executives from time to time are almost compelled, in the interests of their companies or themselves, to practice some form of deception when negotiating with customers, dealers, labor unions, government officials, or even other departments of their companies. By conscious misstatements, concealment of pertinent facts, or exaggeration—in short, by bluffing—they seek to persuade others to agree with them. I think it is fair to say that if the individual executives refuse to bluff from time to time—if they feel obligated to tell the truth, the whole truth, and nothing but the truth—they are ignoring opportunities permitted under the rules and are at a heavy disadvantage in their business dealings.

But here and there business managers are unable to reconcile themselves to the bluff in which they play a part. Their consciences, perhaps spurred by religious idealism, trouble them. They feel guilty; they may develop an ulcer or a nervous tic. Before any executives can make profitable use of the strategy of the bluff, they need to make sure that in bluffing they will not lose self-respect or become emotionally disturbed. If they are to reconcile personal integrity and high standards of honesty with the practical requirements of business, they must feel that their bluffs are ethically justified. The justification rests on the fact that business, as practiced by individuals as well as by corporations, has the impersonal character of a game—a game that demands both special strategy and an understanding of its special ethics.

THE POKER ANALOGY

We can learn a good deal about the nature of business by comparing it with poker. While both have a large element of chance, in the long run the winner is the individual who plays with steady skill. In both games ultimate victory requires intimate knowledge of the rules, insight into the psychology of the other players, a bold front, a considerable amount of self-discipline, and the ability to respond swiftly and effectively to opportunities provided by chance.

In poker it is right and proper to bluff a friend out of the rewards of being dealt a good hand. In the words of an excellent poker player, former President Harry Truman, "If you can't stand the heat, stay out of the kitchen." If one shows mercy to a loser in poker, it is a personal gesture, divorced from the rules of the game.

Poker has its special ethics, and here I am not referring to rules against cheating. The players who keep an ace up their sleeves or who mark the cards are more than unethical; they are crooks, and can be punished as such—kicked out of the game or, in the Old West, shot. In contrast to the cheat, unethical poker players are those who, while abiding by the letter of the rules, find ways to put the other players at an unfair disadvantage. Perhaps they unnerve them with loud talk. Or they try to get them drunk. Or they play in cahoots with someone else at the table. Ethical poker players frown on such tactics.

Poker's own brand of ethics is different from the ethical ideals of civilized human relationships. The game calls for distrust of the other fellow. It ignores the claim of friendship. Cunning deception and concealment of one's strength and intentions, not kindness and openheartedness, are vital in poker. No one thinks any worse of poker on that account. And no one should think any the worse of the game of business because its standards of right and wrong differ from the prevailing traditions of morality in our society.

DISCARD THE GOLDEN RULE

That most businesspeople are not indifferent to ethics in our private lives, everyone will agree. My point is that in their office lives they cease to be private citizens; they become game players who must be guided by a somewhat different set of ethical standards.

The point was forcefully made to me by a midwestern executive who has given a deal of thought to the question: "So long as businesspeople comply with the laws of the land and avoid telling malicious lies, they are ethical. If the law as written gives individuals a wide-open chance to make a killing, they'd be fools not to take advantage of it. If they don't, somebody else will. There's no obligation on them to stop and consider who is going to get hurt. If the law says they can do it, that's all the justification they need. There's nothing unethical about it. It's just plain business sense."

"WE DON'T MAKE THE LAWS"

Wherever we turn in business, we can perceive the sharp distinction between its ethical standards and those of the churches. Newspapers abound with sensational stories growing out of this distinction:

- We read one day that Senator Philip A. Hart of Michigan has attacked food processors for deceptive packaging of numerous products (1966).

- The next day there is a congressional to-do over Ralph Nader's book, *Unsafe at Any Speed* (1965), which demonstrates that automobile companies for years have neglected the safety of car-owning families.

- Then another senator, Lee Metcalf of Montana, and journalist Vic Reinemer show in their book *Overcharge* (1967) the methods by which utility companies elude regulating government bodies to extract unduly large payments from users of electricity.

These are merely dramatic instances of a prevailing condition; there is hardly a major industry at which a similar attack could not be aimed. Critics of business regard such behavior as unethical, but the companies concerned know that they are merely playing the business game.

Among the most respected of our business institutions are the insurance companies. A group of insurance executives meeting recently in New England was startled when their guest speaker, social critic Daniel Patrick Moynihan, roundly berated them for "unethical" practices. They had been guilty, Moynihan alleged, of using outdated actuarial tables to obtain unfairly high premiums. They habitually delayed the hearings of lawsuits against them in order to tire out the plaintiffs and win cheap settlements. In their employment policies they used ingenious devices to discriminate against certain minority groups (1967).

It was difficult for the audience to deny the validity of these charges. But these managers were business game players. Their reaction to Moynihan's attack was much the same as that of the automobile manufacturers to Nader, of the utilities to Senator Metcalf, and of the food processors to Senator Hart. If the laws governing their businesses change, or if public opinion becomes clamorous, they will make the necessary adjustments. But morally they have in their view done nothing wrong. As long as they comply with the letter of the law, they are within their rights to operate their businesses as they see fit.

Violations of the ethical ideals of society are common in business, but they are not necessarily violations of business principles. Each year the Federal Trade Commission orders hundreds of companies, many of them of the first magnitude, to "cease and desist" from practices which, judged by ordinary standards, are of questionable morality but which are stoutly defended by the companies concerned.

In one case, a firm manufacturing a well-known mouthwash was accused of using a cheap form of alcohol possibly deleterious to health. The company's chief executive, after testifying in Washington, made this comment privately: "We broke no law. We're in a highly competitive industry. If we're going to stay in business, we have to look for profit wherever the law permits. We don't make the laws. We obey them. Then why do we have to put up with this 'holier than thou' talk about ethics? It's sheer hypocrisy. We're not in business to promote ethics. Look at the cigarette companies for God's sake! If the ethics aren't embodied in the laws by those who made them, you can't expect business people to fill the lack. Why, a sudden submission to Christian ethics by business managers would bring about the greatest economic upheaval in history!"

It may be noted that the government failed to prove its case against him.

CAST ILLUSIONS ASIDE

The illusion that business can afford to be guided by ethics as conceived in private life is often fostered by speeches and articles containing such phrases as, "It pays to be ethical," or, "Sound ethics is good business." Actually this is not an ethical position at all; it is a self-serving calculation in disguise. The speaker is really saying that in the long run a company can make more money if it does not antagonize competitors, suppliers, employees, and customers by squeezing them too hard. That is true, but it has nothing to do with ethics.

I think it is fair to sum up the prevailing ethical attitude as follows: We live in what is probably the most competitive of the world's civilized societies. Our customs encourage a high degree of aggression in the individual's striving for success. Business is our main area of competition, and it has been ritualized into a game of strategy. The basic rules of the game have been set by the government, which attempts to detect and punish business frauds. But as long as a company does not transgress the rules of the game set by law, it has the legal right to shape its strategy without reference to anything but its profits. If it takes a long-term view of its profits, it will preserve amicable relations, so far as possible, with those with whom it deals. A wise businessperson will not seek advantage to the point where he or she generates dangerous hostility among employees, competitors, customers, government, or the public at large. But decisions in this area are, in the final test, decisions of strategy, not of ethics.

THE INDIVIDUAL AND THE GAME

Individuals within a company often find it difficult to adjust to the requirements of the business game. They try to preserve their private ethical standards in situations that call for game strategy. When they are obliged to carry out company policies that challenge their conception of themselves as ethical managers, they suffer.

It disturbs them when they are ordered, for instance, to deny a raise to a manager who deserves it, to fire an employee of long standing, to prepare advertising that they believe to be misleading, to conceal facts that they feel customers are entitled to know, to cheapen the quality of materials used in the manufacture of an established product, to sell as new a product that they know to be rebuilt, to exaggerate the curative powers of a medicinal preparation, or to coerce dealers.

There are some fortunate executives who, by the nature of their work and circumstances, never have to face problems of this kind. But in one form or another the ethical dilemma is felt sooner or later by most businesspeople. Possibly the dilemma is most painful not when the company forces the action on the executives but when they originate it themselves—that is, when they have taken or are contemplating a step which is in their own interests but which runs counter to their early moral conditioning. To illustrate:

- The manager of an export department, eager to show rising sales, is pressed by a big customer to provide invoices that, while containing no overt falsehood that would violate a U.S. law, are so worded that the customer may be able to evade certain taxes in his or her homeland.

- A company president finds that an aging executive, within a few years of retirement and his or her pension, is not as productive as formerly. Should the executive be kept on?

- The produce manager of a supermarket debates whether to get rid of a lot of half-rotten tomatoes by including one, with its good side exposed, in every tomato six-pack.

- A chief executive officer is asked by company directors to comment on a rumor that the CEO owns stock in another company with which the CEO placed large orders. The CEO could deny it, for the stock is in the name of a son-in-law and the CEO has earlier formally instructed the son-in-law to sell the holding.

Temptations of this kind constantly arise in business. If executives allow themselves to be torn between a decision based on business considerations and one based on their private ethical codes, they expose themselves to grave psychological strain.

This is not to say that sound business strategy necessarily runs counter to ethical ideals. They may frequently coincide; and when they do, everyone is gratified. But the major tests of every move in business, as in all games of strategy, are legality and profit.

The business strategist's decisions must be as impersonal as those of a surgeon performing an operation—concentrating on objective and technique, and subordinating personal feelings.

All sensible businesspeople prefer to be truthful, but they seldom feel inclined to tell the whole truth. In the business game truth telling usually has to be kept within narrow limits if trouble is to be avoided. The point was neatly made a long time ago (in 1888) by one of John D. Rockefeller's associates, Paul Babcock, to Standard Oil Company executives who were about to testify before a government investigating committee: "Parry every question with answers which, while perfectly truthful, are evasive of bottom facts." This was, is, and probably always will be regarded as a wise and permissible business strategy.

FOR OFFICE USE ONLY

Executives' family lives can easily be dislocated if they fail to make a sharp distinction between the ethical systems of the home and the office—or if their families do not grasp that distinction.

An illustration of this comes from a southern sales executive who related a conversation at a time when a hotly contested political campaign was being waged in the state:

"I made the mistake of telling my family that I had had lunch with Colby, who gives me about half my business. Colby mentioned that his company had a stake in the election. Then he said, 'By the way, I'm the treasurer of the citizens' committee for Lang. I'm collecting contributions. Can I count on you for a hundred dollars?'

"Well, there I was. I was opposed to Lang, but I knew Colby. If he withdrew his business I could be in a bad spot. So I just smiled and wrote out a check then and there. He thanked me and we started to talk about his next order. Maybe he thought I shared his political view. If so, I wasn't going to lose any sleep over it.

"I should have had sense enough not to tell my family about it. They hit the ceiling. They said they were disappointed in me. They said that I should have stood up to Colby.

"I said, 'Look, it was an either-or situation. I had to do it or risk losing the business.'

"My spouse came back at me with, 'I don't believe it. You could have been honest with him. You could have said that you didn't feel you ought to contribute to a campaign for a man you weren't going to vote for. I'm sure he would have understood.'

"I said, 'You're way off the track. Do you know what would have happened if I had said that? Colby would have smiled and said, 'Oh, I didn't realize. Forget it.' But in his eyes from that moment I would be an oddball, maybe a bit of a radical. He would have listened to me talk about his order and would have promised to give it consideration. After that I wouldn't hear from him for a week. Then I would telephone and learn from his secretary that he wasn't ready to place the order. And in about a month I would hear through the grapevine that he was giving his business to another company. A month after that I'd be out of a job.'

"My spouse was silent for a while and then said, 'Something is wrong with business when a manager is forced to choose between family security and moral obligation. It's easy for me to say you should have stood up to him—but if you had you might have felt you were betraying your family. I'm sorry that you did it, but I can't blame you. Something is wrong with business!'"

Families may see decisions in terms of moral obligation as conceived in private life; executives may see them as a matter of game strategy.

PLAYING TO WIN

Some business managers might accept serious setbacks to their business careers rather than risk a feeling of moral cowardice. They merit our respect—but as private individuals, not businesspersons. When the skillful players of the business game are compelled to submit to unfair pressure, they do not castigate themselves for moral weakness. Instead, they strive to put themselves into a strong position where they can defend themselves against such pressures in the future without loss.

To be a winner, a manager must play to win. This does not mean that he or she must be ruthless, cruel, harsh, or treacherous. On the contrary, the better their reputation for integrity, honesty, and decency, the better their chances of victory will be in the long run. But from time to time, all business managers, like all poker players, are offered a choice between certain loss or bluffing within the legal rules of the game. If they are not resigned to losing, if they want to rise in the company and industry, then in such a crisis they will bluff—and bluff hard.

Every now and then one meets a successful manager who has conveniently forgotten the small or large deceptions practiced on the way to fortune. "God gave me my money," old John D. Rockefeller once piously told a Sunday school class. It would be a rare tycoon in our time who would risk the horse laugh with which such a remark would be greeted.

In the last third of the twentieth century even children are aware that if managers have become prosperous in business, they have sometimes departed from the strict truth in order to overcome obstacles or have practiced the more subtle deceptions of the half-truth or the misleading omission. Whatever the form of the bluff, it is an integral part of the game, and the executive who does not master its techniques is not likely to accumulate much money or power.

References

Babcock, P. Memorandum to J. D. Rockefeller, 1888.

Metcalf, L., and Reinemer, V. *Overcharge.* New York: McKay, 1967.

Nader, R. *Unsafe at Any Speed.* New York: Gromman, 1965.

New York Times, Nov. 21, 1966.

New York Times, Jan. 17, 1967.

PART FOUR

NEGOTIATING RELATIONSHIPS

Negotiation with others offers us the prospect of better outcomes than we can achieve by acting entirely on our own. In crafting deals, we can find mutual advantage in efficiently trading items that we value differently. In resolving disputes, we spare ourselves the uncertainty and costs, monetary and otherwise, of protracted conflict. We succeed, however, only if our preferred result is also satisfactory to the other party. We need their assent (and they need ours). We thus can see others as partners in a joint enterprise or as opponents, standing in the way of what we believe is justly ours.

Preserving or enhancing a relationship is often an important goal in negotiation, though there is not a simple trade-off with other objectives. Pressing hard for a good price does not necessarily tax a relationship with a vendor, just as conceding on price does not always win a customer's loyalty. Money alone cannot buy us love.

Lax and Sebenius (1983) described the economic tension between creating and claiming in negotiation, specifically how the steps necessary for generating joint gains are often subverted by tactics aimed at securing one's own share. This tension has relational implications, of course, though some are subtle and counterintuitive.

If both parties engage in aggressive claiming behavior, their relationship may be strained, although that is not always the case. In some settings, haggling is a social ritual. People expect the seller to start with an outrageous price and the buyer to feign lack of interest. Short-circuiting that process by putting a reasonable figure on the table deprives people of the chance to play a familiar, if time-consuming, game. At the other end of the spectrum, research indicates that although friendly negotiations often quickly produce agreement, the outcomes tend to be less creative and beneficial than those reached at arm's length. Friends who bend over backward not to strain their relationship may concede too quickly on things that are really important to them and thus fail to expand the pie.

Mnookin, Peppet, and Tulumello (2000) have noted that many negotiators feel a tension between what they term *empathy* and *assertiveness,* a sense that we must choose one or the other: "After all, if I agreed with *your* view I wouldn't have *mine!* Conversely, if I try to assert myself in this negotiation, it's going to be tough to demonstrate an understanding of how you see things. Our views are just fundamentally different. If I advocate for mine, I can't advocate for yours. It's one or the other, not both" (pp. 50–51). This is an age-old question, of course. As Hillel the Elder counseled, "If I am not for myself, who will be? If I am only for myself, who am I?"

In some respects, it is odd to designate one part of this book to the ethical implications of relationships, as negotiation is fundamentally a relational process. Every chapter in the book deals with relationships, often explicitly. We have highlighted three chapters here because they give attention to issues that are treated only in passing elsewhere.

Jonathan Cohen provocatively argues in Chapter Eighteen that negotiation, whether it is between friends or adversaries, should entail an ethic of respect. Readers should consider whether respect is a universal attitude or culturally bound. Chapter Nineteen is from *Everyday Negotiations: Navigating the Hidden Agendas in Bargaining,* by Deborah Kolb and Judith Williams. One of the central themes of their book is the importance of establishing connection in negotiation, though not at the price of making unreciprocated concessions and accommodations. Kolb and Williams maintain that without this connection, the parties cannot really pursue their enlightened self-interest. In Chapter Twenty, Eleanor Holmes Norton examines the ethics of the bargaining process and compares different norms that might be invoked. Although she addresses a legal audience, the issues that it illuminates apply to negotiation generally.

References

Lax, D., and Sebenius, J. *The Manager as Negotiator.* New York: Free Press, 1983.

Mnookin, R. H., Peppet, S. R., and Tulumello, A. S. *Beyond Winning: Negotiating to Create Value in Deals and Disputes.* Cambridge, Mass.: Belknap Press, 2000.

CHAPTER EIGHTEEN

The Ethics of Respect in Negotiation

Jonathan R. Cohen

There is no doubt that negotiation is a human encounter that poses ethical challenges. By my estimation, the four most commonly discussed topics among practitioners and scholars of negotiation are:

- Deception (for example, can one make statements which, although literally true, are designed to mislead?)

- Disclosure (for example, must a seller volunteer information about a product's nonapparent defects?)

- Fairness (for example, must negotiation surpluses be divided evenly?)

- Fidelity (for example, do the agent's interests align with his principal's?)[1]

Yet there is a fifth, and perhaps more foundational, ethical challenge in negotiation: respect. Respect relates to each of the other four categories, but is both prior to and distinct from them.

One way to begin an assessment of this ethical domain is to ask, "What distinguishes negotiation from other forms of human interaction?" A core difference is that in negotiation each party tries to get the other party to do something,

---

This article is based upon Cohen (2001), which explores ethics of respect in negotiation with particular attention to legal negotiations.

or at least explores that possibility. When negotiating, the other party is a potential means to one's ends.

Using the language of Martin Buber (1970), in negotiation we are drawn toward reducing the other party from a "Thou" to an "It." This gives rise to the object-subject tension: When negotiating, how does one reconcile the impulse to treat the other party as a mere means with the general ethical requirements for treating people?

This tension is difficult because it is ultimately irreducible. In negotiation, one's counterpart is both a means to one's ends and a human being. (Even when one negotiates with an organization's representative, that representative is a person, and usually representings [sic] the interests of persons.)[2] One cannot simply pretend that the other side's instrumentality does not matter—that, after all, is why the parties are negotiating with them. Nor does the positive fact of the other party's instrumentality eliminate the moral fact of her or his humanity. Usually one may do whatever one likes to get an object to do one's ends. No one objects to a cook banging a jar's lid on a table to loosen it. When people are the means, however, the ethical requirements are different.

THE DIGNITY OF EACH PERSON

Most moral and religious traditions require that people be seen and treated as beings with fundamental dignity. An implication of that view is that ethical negotiation requires one to respect the fundamental dignity of the other party. (We can see here the connection between respect and traditional negotiation ethics topics.) Is it wrong to lie to people or to treat them unfairly? If it is, then unless compelling justification can be given—and usually it cannot—it remains wrong to do so in negotiation.[3] But what does it mean to respect the fundamental dignity of another, to try to see and treat a person as a person rather than as a mere object? Consider two illustrative examples, the first from outside the negotiation realm and the second from within it.[4]

My father-in-law directs the medical staff of a nursing home. As part of staff training, he periodically interviews a home resident who so consents in front of the entire staff. He asks that resident to share parts of his or her life history, and not just medical history, with the staff. The residents' responses are often remarkable, if not inspirational. Why did my father-in-law institute this practice? "My goal," he writes, "is to show the staff that residents had rich and varied lives prior to their admission to the nursing home."[5] He wanted the nursing home employees, including himself, to see the residents as people rather than as mere combinations of medical ailments.

Now consider an example from negotiation. Three years ago, my wife and I were moving South and looking to buy our first home. After a morning of house hunting with a local realtor ("Bev"), all three of us went to a moderately priced restaurant for lunch. At the end of the meal, a bill of roughly twenty dollars arrived. My wife and I offered to divide the bill with Bev in proportion to what we had ordered, but she would not hear of it.

"Oh no," said Bev, "I'll pay for it."

"Why don't you pay for your part, and we'll pay for ours?" I replied.

"No," said Bev, "let me pay the whole check."

"You don't have to pay for us," I said. "We should at least pay for ourselves."

"Don't be silly," said Bev. "You're new in town. Once you move into your new house, you can have me and my husband over for dinner."

"Okay, then," I said.

What was going on? Was Bev simply demonstrating southern hospitality or did she want to make us feel beholden to her, thereby increasing the chances that we would keep her as our realtor?[6] As I consented to let Bev pay, both possibilities ran through my mind, as did the thought that if Bev was insisting on paying in order to make us feel indebted, then we should not feel indebted by her act. There was little doubt that Bev was acting respectfully, but to know whether she actually was being respectful or manipulative, one needed to know her intent.

Respect is frequently defined in terms of adhering to a prescribed set of external actions, such as shaking hands, addressing a person by her proper title, or arriving on time for appointments. While such matters of etiquette and courtesy are no doubt important, the root of respect lies deeper. At its core, respect is best understood not as a set of acts (a noun) but as a process (a verb). As the word itself indicates, "re-spect" is the process we undertake when we "look again" to see the fundamental dignity of the other party. Respect lies in fostering an internal psychological stance that recognizes the other party's personhood. It is that process of attempting to see the other party not merely as a means to one's ends but also as a person that is critical to ethical negotiation.

BUT WHAT IF . . .

At this point, readers may raise a variety of objections. Consider three. First, some may ask, "But what if I don't respect the other party? What if I know that the other party is a revolting character based on the harms he has done to me? Surely I'm not ethically bound to like someone whom I dislike?" Such a view highlights the value of understanding respect as an incremental process—of making an incremental effort to see the fundamental dignity of the other party. When one likes the other party, that process is easy. The challenge is to respect people you don't like. Recall the words of the late Israeli prime minister Yitzhak Rabin: "Peace you don't make with friends, but with very unsympathetic enemies" (Katz, 1995).

Further, the reason one is bound to respect the other party rests not on how he has treated you, but on the basis of the other party's personhood. How the other party treats you defines him, but how you treat the other party defines you. The other party's disrespect of you does not justify your disrespect of him. As the children's maxim states, "Two wrongs don't make a right." It is unrealistic to expect parties in conflict to like one another. In most negotiation settings, however, it is not unrealistic to expect the parties to at least attempt to respect the human dignity of one another.

Second, others may assert, "If I respect the other party and the other party doesn't respect me, I will be strategically disadvantaged. Surely I am not ethically bound to negotiate in a way that lets them, the other party, take advantage of me." The second sentence of this assertion is sensible. If one is obligated to respect others, surely one is obligated to respect oneself. Self-respect requires that one defend oneself from being misused.[7] Recall the order of Rabbi Hillel's three famous questions, "If I am not for myself, who will be for me? If I am for myself alone, what am I? And if not now, when?" Before one should be concerned with the welfare of others, one should be concerned with one's own welfare. However, the premise of this line of objection—that respecting the other party is strategically disadvantageous—is highly suspect.

Although there are exceptions, respecting the other party in negotiation usually works to one's advantage rather than disadvantage, for the more the other party feels respected, the more receptive the other party will be to reaching agreement. For example, empirical studies of legal negotiations by Williams (1983) and Schneider (2000) indicate that lawyers who treat other lawyers ethically and respectfully are consistently seen as more effective negotiators than those who do not. As a seasoned attorney said to me, "I cannot think of a single case I negotiated where treating the other side with respect worked to my client's harm." Such strategic efficacy does not provide a moral justification for respecting the other party. However, it helps refute on its own terms the claim that respecting the other party will be strategically disadvantageous.

Third, some may claim, "Negotiation *should* be a process where each party thinks only of himself and sees the other party solely as a means, for efficient outcomes result when parties pursue their self-interest." Supporters of this free market view might point to Adam Smith's famous statement (1976, p. 18), "It is not from the benevolence of the butcher, the brewer or the baker that we expect our dinner, but from their regard to their own self-interest. We address ourselves not to their humanity but to their self-love, and never talk to them of our own necessities but of their advantages."[8]

Others may invoke concepts like consent: "The parties all know how the game of negotiation is played. It's a dog-eat-dog activity, but when one enters the arena, one consents to the rules." Still others may point to the agent's duty of fidelity to his principal. Recall Lord Brougham's (1874) depiction of the lawyer as a zealous advocate: "An advocate, in the discharge of his duty, knows but one person in all the world, and that person is his client. To save that client by all means and expedients, and at all hazards and costs to other persons, and, among them, to himself, is his first and only duty; *and in performing this duty he must not regard the alarm, the torments, the destruction which he may bring upon others*" (Yarn, 2001, emphasis added).

These arguments too can be challenged empirically, for they also rest on the suspect premise that respecting the other party will be to one's strategic detriment. However, even if one accepts this suspect empirical premise, these arguments fail for other reasons. Free market ideology by itself does not reveal the ethical and legal limits under which self-interest may be pursued. For example, all recognize that a coercive act like threatening to slit someone's throat unless he signs a document constitutes an unethical and illegal negotiation tactic. Profitable actions are not always ethical actions. The other claims also wilt under scrutiny. There is little reason to suppose that when entering negotiations most parties consent, either explicitly or implicitly, to being disrespected.

As to the justification based on the agent's role (such as zealous advocacy by lawyers), just as it is wrong for principals to disrespect one another in direct negotiations, so too it is wrong for their agents to disrespect one another.[9] What is wrong for principals to do directly does not become right when delegated to their agents.

IN CONCLUSION

The structure of negotiation presents a basic ethical tension. In negotiation, the other party is both a means to one's ends and a person. This object-subject tension may lead many negotiators to disregard the personhood of the other party and treat the other party merely as a means. They should not. As human beings, parties within negotiation deserve to be treated with respect.

The good news is that this is not a situation where ethical behavior need be self-sacrificing; indeed, respecting the other party usually helps prompt that party's cooperation. The challenge and the moral duty are clear: when negotiating, one must remember that the other party is not just a means but also a person. What is wrong to do to another person is not excused by the act of negotiation.

Notes

1. For a survey of this literature, see Cohen (2001).

2. On the challenges of agency in negotiation, see Mnookin and Susskind (1999).

3. Some may ask whether this duty of respect is subsumed by the other commonly recognized negotiation ethics topics of deception, disclosure, fairness and fidelity. The negotiation with Bev, discussed later in this article, reflects a type of potential wrongful manipulation not well captured by these other categories. Another example not well captured by these traditional topics is Boulwarism (beginning the negotiation with a take-it-or-leave-it offer, thereby precluding the other party's voice in the negotiation and treating that party like a voiceless object rather than a subject). See Cohen (2001) for further discussion.

4. For further discussion of both of these examples, see Cohen (2001).

5. See Singer (2001).

6. There are other possibilities too. Perhaps the norm among realtors in the community was to pay for such lunches. I limit my discussion to the two possibilities above for expository purposes.

7. Fox (1996) describes the difficulty of self-advocacy in negotiation for many. Mnookin, Peppet, and Tulumello (2000) highlight the need for both empathy and assertiveness for effective negotiation.

8. Similarly, Friedman (1970) argues that businesses should focus solely on profit maximization and ignore "social responsibilities." Note that Smith was less of a free market, laissez-faire economist than he is often thought to be, for he recognized ethics along with self-interest as a central human concern. See Sen (1987).

9. See Luban (1988), Applbaum (1999), and Cohen (2001).

References

Applbaum, A. I. *Ethics for Adversaries: The Morality of Roles in Public and Professional Life.* Princeton, N.J.: Princeton University Press, 1999.

Buber, M. 1970. *I and Thou* (W. Kaufman, trans.). New York: Scribner, 1970.

Cohen, J. R. "When People Are the Means: Negotiating with Respect." *Georgetown Journal of Legal Ethics,* 2001, *14,* 739–802.

Fox, E. L. "Alone in the Hallway: Challenges to Effective Self-Representation in Negotiation." *Harvard Negotiation Law Review,* 1996, *1,* 85–111.

Friedman, M. "The Social Responsibility of Business Is to Increase Its Profits." *New York Times Magazine,* Sept. 13, 1970, p. 32.

Katz, L. M. "Reluctant War Hero Led Israel to Peace." *USA Today,* Nov. 6, 1995, p. 1A.

Luban, D. *Lawyers and Justice.* Princeton, N.J.: Princeton University Press, 1988.

Mnookin, R. H., Peppet, S. R., and Tulumello, A. S. *Beyond Winning: Negotiating to Create Value in Deals and Disputes.* Cambridge, Mass.: Harvard University Press, 2000.

Mnookin, R. H., and Susskind, L. E. (eds.). *Negotiating on Behalf of Others: Advice to Lawyers, Business Executives, Sports Agents, Diplomats, Politicians, and Everybody Else.* Thousand Oaks, Calif.: Sage, 1999.

Schneider, A. "Perception, Reputation and Reality: An Empirical Study of Negotiation Skills." *Dispute Resolution Magazine,* 2000, *6*(4), 24–28.

Sen, A. *On Ethics and Economics.* Oxford: Basil Blackwell, 1987.

Singer, K. "Resilience." *Patient Care,* July 30, 2001, p. 5.

Smith, A. *An Inquiry into the Nature and Causes of the Wealth of Nations* (E. Canham, ed.). Chicago: University of Chicago Press, 1976. (Originally published 1776.)

Williams, G. R. *Legal Negotiation and Settlement.* St. Paul, Minn.: West Publishing, 1983.

Yarn, D. H. "The Attorney as Duelist's Friend: Lessons from the Code Duello." *Case Western Law Review,* 2000, *51*(6), 69–113.

CHAPTER NINETEEN

Everyday Negotiation

Navigating the Hidden Agendas in Bargaining

Deborah M. Kolb

Judith Williams

We stress the skill required to manage the relational dimension of negotiation because too often empathy or concern for others is treated as an inherited or natural disposition, not an acquired one. It's considered a predilection you either have or don't have. Folk wisdom also tells us that women are inclined to emphasize relational needs and men individual criteria in their dealings with other people. A fallout of this common misperception is that men *and* women may avoid efforts to get connected. They see in connected moves not the strength that comes from employing relational skills but a weakness that can lead to demands for concessions and to accommodation.

The notion that connection leads to concession or accommodation blocks real engagement in two ways:

- Differences never get fully aired or appreciated when one party expects the other to sacrifice self-interests or feels obliged to do so.

- Collaborative overtures can be misconstrued as signs of weakness rather than components integral to reaching solutions that all parties consider fair.

Both traps are self-defeating, but there is a simple way to avoid them. You can engage in a dynamic kind of relationship building that is inextricably yoked to successful advocacy. Connection and advocacy do not cancel each other out. On the contrary, one does not happen without the other. You connect in a negotiation by engaging your counterpart, not by giving in to demands just to make him or her feel good.

GETTING READY TO LISTEN TO THE OTHER PERSON

As we prepare for negotiation, our focus is naturally on ourselves—what we want and what we need to do to better our chances of success. But there is a danger in this single-mindedness. We can become so engrossed in our take on the situation that we lose sight of the person we are negotiating with—except as a means to our ends or as a stumbling block in our way. Once into the negotiation, it is inevitable that we process whatever happens through that filter. A certain deafness sets in. We edit out what we don't want to hear and listen to what is said with a fixed script in mind. We make attribution errors that have us ascribing good intentions to ourselves but not to others. We create self-fulfilling prophecies.

Any two people will give different (sometimes wildly different) accounts of the same event. Naturally when we tell our stories, we are the heroes and heroines. Our story puts our spin on the events, conveniently editing out facts that don't fit. Typically we cast ourselves as virtuous, always doing the right thing. What we want is always reasonable and well deserved. The other person is greedy, inflexible, or domineering, focused only on the short term. We have done all the heavy lifting, finishing the proposal or going the extra mile to satisfy the client. The other one is the free rider. But what is true of our stories is also true for the other person's. To influence others in negotiations, you need to accept that they are equally convinced of their interpretation. You may disagree with their slant, but it is never wrong in their eyes.

Approaching a negotiation as a compilation of stories carries a distinct advantage. Each story is told from a specific point of view and never includes every detail. Stories are filled with gaps, laced with contradictions and puzzling inflections. As we listen to the other person, we learn from those gaps and contradictions. Stories don't trade in certainties. They deal with "maybe" and "what if," not statements of fact. Because stories admit no rights and wrongs, but depend on different but legitimate points of view, they weave together both the stream of feelings and the stream of thought that meet to make decisions in a negotiation.

As you consider a situation from various perspectives, you force yourself to entertain other explanations for why people might be acting the way they are. With a more complex story line, it is easier to see how those behaviors are linked. Often common concerns emerge with unexpected clarity, while differences in priorities become the building blocks of an agreement.

HOW CIRCULAR QUESTIONING WORKS

Conventional wisdom on negotiation has it that negotiators pursue "enlightened self-interest" when they take into account the needs of others. This is the notion of doing good for your counterpart *and* doing good for yourself. But enlightened solutions require enlightenment. Just as effective advocacy begins with you, with a positive attitude, connection emerges from a willingness and a curiosity to hear your counterpart's side of the story. It grows out of a belief that agreement depends on the wider understanding that comes from free exchange. This conviction grounds how you relate to the other party. It forces you to suspend belief or at least resist drawing premature conclusions—about the situation or your counterpart's motivations.

Step 1: Look at Your Story

It is important to start this restorying process with you and your feelings. Examining your own story in depth can reveal aspects you have been ignoring or refusing to see. Once you are aware of these missing segments, you have the tools at hand to do some self-imposed editing. Once you are clear on your story—what is missing and what is legitimately included—you can look for what is included in his or her version and what just might be missing.

Step 2: Look at the Other Person's Story

The tendency to get wedded to your own perspective is one of the major barriers to effective negotiation. It's simply too easy to become enamored of personal opinions. Operating in a closed world of our making, we tell ourselves we are right and the other person is wrong. We explain our reasons and don't ask questions about theirs. Talking but not listening, we fail to pick up cues that what we are saying is not being heard. Over half of the information conveyed in personal interactions and on which we make decisions in a negotiation is nonverbal, yet we often fail to use these cues.

Taking a hard look at how the other person might view a situation often brings these overlooked cues to the surface. More important, as you consider his or her side of the story, you generally have to revise your initial explanation of what is going on. How people view a problem depends on *their* experience, not yours.

To get inside the other person's story, you must suspend your interpretation, particularly when it comes to his or her motives. If we are operating with the best intentions, the other person, we figure, must be out to undermine us. But just as there are always two sides to every story, there can be similarly benign explanations for the motivations behind the other party's actions. Until and unless events offer proof to the contrary, it is a good idea to assume that your counterpart is acting in good faith and is not out to undercut you.

Otherwise you shut down communication and prevent any real understanding from emerging.

Step 3: Look for Links Between Stories

These final questions in the sequence help you understand the extent to which the other person's behavior may be prompted by your actions. Rather than pursuing some malevolent or unreasonable plan, the other party may be reacting to the way you are treating him or her. When we have a fixed idea in our head about a person's interests and concerns, we cannot help but process everything she says or does through that filter.

Working out the plausible stories on each side of the table forces you to probe your initial reactions and find more charitable explanations for the other person's actions. You have to tell another story. Soon you reach the stage of maybe—maybe he means something else, maybe she has another reason for what she's doing. When you think about the good reasons for your counterpart's actions, you uncover previously hidden but sensible accounts that are possible for what he does or what she says. From there, it is a short transition to "what if"—what if I did something else? What if I gave her the benefit of the doubt and responded more positively? A single "what if" always contains the promise of additional options, other ways that the plot you construct together can play out.

How you solve your differences links with how you treat each other. Efforts to connect with your counterpart encourage more open participation. The goal is to get people to share their experience with you so that you are not running blind on your own impressions. But unless they have some signal, some confidence, that they are being heard, that you appreciate their concerns, they will be reluctant to share them with you. It is not just information you are after. You want to build rapport and trust so that, together, you can engage in a dialogue. Many negotiations start out with opposing sides squared off. When you connect with the other person, you alter this dynamic.

ENGAGING YOUR COUNTERPART

However important it is to uncover hidden fears or perceptions, unfortunately as negotiators we often get locked into habits that work against collaboration. Efforts that appear mutual on the surface are anything but when we pay attention to the other party's reactions only to test how far we can push. These relational efforts may increase the odds that our demands will be heard and met, but mutual needs don't have much chance to surface. Being nice in an effort to manipulate the outcome is as transparent as being tough.

Even when you are genuinely interested in the other person's thinking and feelings, he or she may question your sincerity. Negotiators need more than pleasantries to respond to your efforts. It takes some convincing, some active demonstration that goes beyond the perfunctory or the expedient, to override these doubts. You have to *show* the other person that you appreciate his or her point of view. It is not enough simply to *think* you are being empathetic. Those thoughts must be translated into action, and that task can be difficult.

Appreciation is key to drawing out a counterpart's concerns (Cooperrider and Srivastva, 1987). When you appreciate the other party's concerns, his situation, or the face she presents to the world, you open the negotiation to the nuanced perceptions that that person brings. Appreciation conveys the importance you place on these differing perspectives and the opinions, ideas, and feelings that shape them.

Just as you must position yourself positively in the shadow of negotiation to be heard, you must also take steps to position your counterparts so they can tell their side of the story. By legitimately feeling and showing appreciation—for their situation, feelings, and ideas—you encourage them to elaborate, to fill in the gaps in your understanding:

- Appreciate the other person's situation. Your counterpart has a better sense of her situation than you can ever hope to have. By openly soliciting her views, you validate them (and her). You show her that they are important to you and to how the negotiation comes out.

- Appreciate the other person's feelings. How your counterpart feels about you and the negotiation often drives his behavior. Those feelings are communicated through nonverbal cues as well as actual comments. Pick up on them and acknowledge the emotions that the other party carries into a negotiation.

- Appreciate the other person's ideas. If the other party puts out an idea, build on that contribution. Just holding the idea up for consideration shows her that you value what she has to say even though you might not agree.

- Appreciate the other person's face. Give your counterpart room to maneuver. No one likes to be backed into a corner with no visible or acceptable means to retreat.

Appreciation needs to be made explicit. No matter how convinced we are that we appreciate our counterpart's predicament, unless we make him or her aware of that appreciation, doubts linger about the value those opinions or perspectives carry. So long as those doubts remain, the other party hesitates to tell his or her side of the story. Appreciation validates that story. When a bargainer's story is valued, when he or she is valued, a more complex account emerges.

In many conversations, opinions or ideas are heard sequentially with everybody competing to be heard. By contrast, when what Deborah Tannen (1993) calls "cooperative overlapping" structures the conversation, opinions are considered in relation to one another and get revised as the participants make new contributions. Each person builds on what went before. Everyone is both an empathetic critic of other people's ideas and a participant with his or her own opinions. However definite these ideas may be at the beginning they evolve through the exchange and commentary. The process is one of constant looping back, deliberately soliciting ideas, without making a decision. In an appreciative conversation those options and ideas do not remain distinct. Choices are not kept separate, to be selected or discarded. One idea builds on another.

When we pick up on a counterpart's ideas or comments, we shift the negotiation from a yes-no, up-down decision to a process that weighs which ideas work best for everyone. Appreciating the other party's suggestions, building on them, we break down the resistance to new ideas. With multiple possibilities rather than two mutually exclusive ones, we increase our chances of reaching agreement.

LIMITS TO GETTING CONNECTED

Whether and to what extent a mutually respectful give-and-take can be nurtured is often difficult to judge. But for collaboration to have a chance, you have to begin a negotiation assuming that it is at least a possibility. If and when you discover that the other party is playing a different game, you can shift course to protect yourself.

Where real inequalities exist, it is difficult to talk about connection. Bargainers with the least power are almost always the ones who pay the most attention to the other person's feelings and opinions. There is little reciprocity. They monitor the other side and then use responsiveness to get what they want. Connection, in fact, has been called the weapon of the weak. Connection, however, is more than a weapon of the weak. Despite the uneasy relation between connection and power, connection can actually be used to create power in a negotiation—but it is shared power. Without an appreciation of multiplicity, an ability to listen, or a capacity to suspend judgment, dialogue and discovery are next to impossible.

References

Cooperrider, D., and Srivastva, S. "Appreciative Inquiry in Organizational Life." *Research in Organizational Change and Development*, 1987, 1.

Tannen, D. "Rethinking Power and Solidarity in Gender and Dominance." In D. Tannen (ed.), *Gender and Conversation Interaction.* New York: University Press, 1993.

CHAPTER TWENTY

Bargaining and the Ethics of Process

Eleanor Holmes Norton

The pervasive use of bargaining is reason enough for an examination of bargaining ethics. Negotiation is used more often than any other discrete dispute resolution or problem-solving process.[1] Bargaining is an essential process in everyday life; in many situations, particularly common business deals, there are no real alternatives. However, negotiation is critical to both dispute resolution and consensus building alike. In addition, the versatility of bargaining makes it useful in resolving issues of all kinds and dimensions, whether matters of global importance, such as nuclear arms limitations, or of personal concern, such as custody following divorce. Not surprisingly, however, interest in negotiation has been primarily in strategy, divorced from ethical, legal, and other implications.

In legal disputes, in particular, ethical issues combine with the unstructured nature of the process to make negotiation susceptible to criticisms that have sometimes been made of other alternatives to litigation. Negotiation, like other forms of informal dispute resolution, raises controversial questions of whether power or status, in the absence of formal adjudication, may impinge upon outcomes. When the unique ethical questions that surround negotiation are added, these power and status disparities may be exacerbated. Without lawyers, judges, courts, and law, disputants are not assured of a principled resolution. Whether in disputes or in transactions, the poor, poorly informed, or those otherwise disadvantaged in relation to their opponents often will not have the protection of the law and its institutions. Unequal bargaining power may impinge unfairly upon the outcome of a negotiation, not only for disadvantaged parties but for others who, in a particular negotiation, are less powerful than their opponents. Erosion of public law and of the rights it protects could occur in a system of private bargaining of disputes, which is not exposed to public scrutiny.[2] Developing areas of the law, especially those affecting poor and other disadvantaged disputants, could be truncated.[3] Individuals might be more inclined to settle their claims, leaving in place systemic problems affecting others similarly situated. Settled disputes or negotiated transactions might be more difficult to make final and to enforce. These problems can only be exacerbated by indeterminate ethics in negotiation.

An analysis of the ethics of bargaining must take account of an extraordinary variety of behaviors, contexts, and goals. These complicated interactions give rise to visions of ethics that are subjective and inconsistent. Truthfulness and fairness, two core ethical values, are both extolled and ridiculed in bargaining. Attempts to unravel dilemmas and to avoid abuses, such as misrepresentation, too often must proceed case by case without any coherence. Often there is confusion as to whether particular tactics are undesirable because they are unethical or because they are distasteful. Ad hoc and sometimes inconsistent prescriptions for appropriate ethics do not help. This experience reveals the need for an understanding of how common ethical notions fit this special process. In the end, a negotiating ethic is unlikely to prove useful unless it is at once functional and ethically sound. This challenge requires an analysis that begins with the process itself.

This article takes the view that the structural features of bargaining and the dynamic of the process support an analytical model that helps to explain how ethical values operate in a private, adversarial market process controlled by the parties. The model developed here suggests that minimal truthfulness and fairness are functional ethical norms inherent in bargaining. The truthfulness and fairness associated with the process do not meet aspirational standards, but the practices that result do meet the minimal ethical requisite of an agreement. These practices also account for the universality and longevity of the process despite the absence of a consensus concerning an aspirational ethic. The resulting functionalism links bargaining ethics to the function they perform without assuming that the ethics that result are sufficiently aspirational in sorting out deception and unfairness. Thus, the functionalist model is not offered as an alternative to aspirational approaches. Rather, the assumption is that an adequately articulated aspirational ethic for bargaining must be preceded by an understanding of how the process operates in the face of ethical challenges.

IDENTIFYING NEGOTIATION ETHICS

Challenges of the Process

In many areas of human endeavor practice and principle are often estranged. But the distance between practices that are commonly used and acceptable ethical standards is particularly great in negotiation. Much of the estrangement can be attributed to practices that some negotiators regard as purely strategic and necessary for bargaining or to practices that are viewed as essential to represent a client with the requisite dedication.

Negotiation is dominated by process and technique, unguided by any specific consensus as to how ethical standards and norms should be applied to a process that tolerates the disguising of intentions and the use of pressure tactics. The paradigm for this article is traditional hard bargaining using offers and counteroffers because it is probably the most commonly used bargaining strategy. Some forms of bargaining, of course, are more benign and eliminate many ethical concerns. Even in the most cooperative and problem-solving approaches, however, there are usually some oppositional exchanges in which deception and pressure play a role. Consequently, normal ethical standards are sometimes abandoned in negotiations the way they are driving. Just as people enclosed in their cars sometimes behave toward strangers on the road as they would not toward the same individuals in a social setting, people do not always bargain the way they live. A lawyer who would tell the whole truth in court might tell a half-truth if the same matter were being resolved in the privacy of negotiations. The difference between the lawyer's ethics in court and at the negotiating table cannot be explained entirely by the presence or absence of judicial and written authority or by the lawyer's personal ethics. Ethics in bargaining, as in other human activities, are conditioned in part by personal character, belief systems, and other idiosyncratic features. However, unique characteristics of the bargaining process itself also influence the difference between ethics at the negotiating table and in other areas of life.

Identifying the features of the bargaining process that influence bargaining ethics is critical to understanding and arriving at appropriate bargaining ethics. If indispensable elements of the negotiating process demand particular modifications in ethical norms, such as truthfulness, this would be acceptable, assuming that (1) society regards bargaining as an indispensable activity that must continue, (2) bargaining itself is not unethical, and (3) the deviations from ethical norms can be justified by reference to acceptable criteria.

Certainly, the first two criteria are met. Bargaining is an indispensable activity.[4] Negotiated agreements are necessary to the functioning of societies that range from simple to complex in their organization.[5] To the extent that negotiations prevent war or other violence, bargaining contributes to the preservation of societies themselves. Societies without cash economies or formal judicial systems may be even more dependent on negotiated solutions than societies that use consciously organized and formal means to effect exchange, achieve agreements, and resolve disputes. Industrial and technological societies are patently dependent upon negotiated dealings. Whether the rapid trading in the stock market, the complex transactions in which corporations are merged, or the delicate negotiations that surround personal and family matters, it is difficult to imagine substitutes for negotiated transactions and resolutions. Second, bargaining itself is ethical. No process, universally accepted and pervasively practiced in some form in and among societies throughout the world, could have survived without ethical condemnation or criticism if the process itself contradicted commonly understood ethical norms.

The third question, whether there are acceptable criteria that would justify deviations from ethical norms is the subject of this article. Modifications in ethics should not be accepted easily because there are always costs, including the possibility of a more general erosion of ethical standards. Society has recognized exceptions from ethical norms, however, where justifications have been demonstrated. We accept modifications in ethical norms for lawyers and doctors in certain circumstances, for example. Both must withhold information others would be required to divulge. These exceptions are recognized as essential to assure the loyalty, unfettered exchange of information, and trust necessary for adequate representation in the case of lawyers and adequate medical treatment in the case of doctors.

Ethical Standards in Negotiation: Truthfulness and Fairness

Truthfulness and fairness are part of the respect for others that ethical standards are meant to encourage. The opportunities for departure from these ideals that regularly occur during bargaining capture the essential tension between negotiating opponents. The standard of truthfulness may be diluted because of the temptation to misrepresent, considering the value of information in achieving the most advantageous result. Notwithstanding the ideal of fairness, strong pressure may be placed on an opponent in order to achieve the desired result.

Truthfulness connotes the authenticity of the information conveyed. Without truthfulness, human relations would be impossibly cumbersome, because nobody could be believed and the trust essential to the accomplishment of all tasks would be impossible. In much the same way, truthfulness is vital to negotiations, but there are additional reasons for its necessity in this context. First, the assumption of truthfulness underlies the choice of negotiation by the parties; the parties would be unlikely to choose negotiation without the belief that the process would result in an agreement that would be carried out according to its terms. Second, each party to a negotiation needs information that may be possessed by only one of them. Third, the validity of the agreement itself is premised on truthfulness; an agreement based on false information may be declared fraudulent and therefore unenforceable.

Yet, the concept of truthfulness in negotiation raises unique ethical questions because in most circumstances candor is not necessarily required. Ethical clarity is taxed in a process in which both truthfulness and deception have standing. The legal doctrine of misrepresentation requires that the facts under negotiation be true.[6] However, puffing as to these facts is legal,[7] and aspects of puffing have recently been recognized as a specific exception to an attorney's ethical responsibility to be truthful. Deception may include a wide range of practices, from withholding information that need not be shared to misrepresentation that can invalidate an agreement. Between these poles are many deceptive practices: for example, an offer of inaccurate information concerning settlement price or concerning whether one is prepared to sue rather than settle at the terms offered; and silence concerning an important piece of information. The legitimacy, even necessity, of at least some deception in many traditional modes of bargaining makes it difficult to apply ordinary ethical notions of truthfulness in a systematic fashion. The available evidence confirms the notion that truthfulness is a particular source of ethical tension in negotiation.

Fairness is the core value of desserts as measured against specific norms or stated rules, systems, or values.[8] *Fairness* is a generic term more akin to *justice* than to specific ethical conduct, such as truth telling.[9] Fairness encompasses truthfulness as well as almost all other ethical values, since a person may gain an unfair advantage because of nearly any ethical violation. What constitutes fairness thus depends on the system of values or rules from which it is derived. For example, in a country whose people have chosen primogeniture, it is not unfair for land to be passed to the first son, rather than to the oldest daughter or to all the siblings equally.[10] Rather, equal division of property or division regardless of sex would be unfair, because both would violate that society's belief in primogeniture. Even within a society with shared values, however, there may be large variations in conceptions of fairness. In our society, most people would agree that accepting an essay into a contest several days after the deadline is unfair, because the late entrant has been given an unearned advantage not available to others and thus has profited from a violation of the applicable rules. But the same people might disagree about whether it is fair to award a lifetime ten-point advantage on a civil service exam to veterans that would give them a preference, long after their military service, over nonveterans who score better on examinations. Like these circumstances, bargaining inevitably raises issues of fairness. For bargaining, however, the rules are not clear from the societal values the way they are for primogeniture and the essay contest. Bargaining ethics are more analogous to the lifetime ten-point veterans' preference, where people are divided on the fairness of the practice. As a practical matter, the standard of fairness is decided by the parties in the context of each negotiation.

Despite the absence of concrete generic standards for an assessment of fairness in bargaining, there is consensus in law that an unfair agreement that results from abusive tactics or practices should not be honored. As used in this article, bargaining is unfair when coercive practices are used or when an unconscionable outcome results.[11] The coercive practices that are of concern here are abusive because they determine or influence bargaining outcomes by displacing natural or acceptable phenomena such as market forces, the relative strength of the issues, or the skill of the parties. Such practices rob the bargain of fairness.

As applied to negotiation, unfairness, like deception, is a troublesome concept, because in some instances a pressure strategy may be legitimate. In bargaining, it may be acceptable to pressure an opponent to agree to terms that she would like to avoid. Yet, when inappropriate pressure is applied, unfairness may result and the bargain may be unconscionable. For example, an agreement that was made under duress might be found to be unconscionable. A contemporary and controversial example that raises the issue of the limits on pressure is a threat to put a civil rights matter through the costly litigation process unless the plaintiff's attorney relinquishes her statutorily prescribed fees as part of the settlement.[12]

The blurred lines between ethical and unethical deception and between appropriate and unfair pressure are compounded by factors unique to negotiation. Ethical issues proceed from the frequent assumption in bargaining that pressing for advantage is the point of the process; from the need to differentiate tactical devices, such as bluffing, from unethical behavior such as misrepresentation; from the absence of clear and systematic criteria for addressing the difference between the two; and from the necessity that the parties, in the absence of specific guidance or of a monitor, find their own way to ethical bargaining. Because common bargaining practices do not always coincide with the universe of ethics outside the process, the differences need to be explained and justified.

THE ETHICS OF PROCESS: A MODEL FOR UNDERSTANDING NEGOTIATION ETHICS

When negotiators encounter ethical dilemmas in bargaining, often neither their own ethical standards nor any other frame of reference seems sensible or useful. How should a negotiator decide when truthfulness is required? Is the misrepresentation of the true price at which one would sell a product ethical? Why or why not? Take the negotiated sale of a used set of barbells as an example. If someone may misrepresent her settlement point as $100 when it is actually $50, may she misrepresent the information on which the settlement point is based, such as the original purchase price? What about claiming that the barbells are of high quality when, according to *Consumer Reports,* they are actually of middle or low quality? Suppose that the negotiator has decided that she can settle for as low as $50, if necessary, because she used the new barbells about ten times after she purchased the set. Is the prospective buyer entitled to this information? Should it be offered only if asked? May it be misrepresented if asked? Apart from truthfulness, what of fairness? Suppose the seller discovers that the buyer has no idea what barbells should cost and does not ask what the seller paid for them? Should the seller volunteer this information? Should she ask for twice as much as she might from a more experienced buyer and use hard-sell or arm-twisting techniques?

Aspirational Approaches to Negotiation Ethics

The difference in approach among aspirational ethics is especially clear-cut between the first two alternatives. At one end, universalism presses negotiation ethics closer to universal ethical norms. At the other end, traditionalism embodies the view that the uniqueness of the bargaining process requires a special ethic necessarily incongruent with universal norms. Traditionalism regards the negotiator's self-interest as the preeminent guidepost. In contrast, universalism approaches ethics as a priori truths or precepts toward which to press bargaining ethics.

Pure statements of universalism or traditionalism are rare, especially views that either explicitly or implicitly encompass negotiation. Judge Alvin Rubin, in his expression of a universalist vision,[13] and Charles Curtis, in his stark traditionalism,[14] are perhaps the closest and most serviceable to the analysis undertaken here.

Universalism largely rejects special "rules" tied to the individual's role in society or its processes (Rubin, 1975). Implicit in this vision is the assumption that societal rather than individual interests should be the center of gravity in negotiation. In Rubin's universalist conception, for example, a lawyer's societal obligations require that negotiators act honestly and in good faith toward their negotiating opponents and that they refrain from doing anything unconscionably unfair. The radicalism inherent in a universalist negotiating ethic is especially clear in Rubin's formulation. He believes that lawyers enjoy a monopolized professional position because they serve society's interest in "the just termination of disputes," not because of the interests of their clients.

Universalism is critical to negotiation ethics. It injects societal interests where individualism might otherwise eclipse all considerations except self-interest. The influence of universal standards can act against the distortions created by the pressure of partisan self-interest. If the negotiator (or, as the case may be, the negotiator's client) represents the highly partisan individualism associated with self-interest, the negotiator's opponent may be said to represent society's interest in ethical dealings.

Universalism does not help in distinguishing among these dilemmas. For example, Rubin (1975) argues for a duty of candor, including voluntary disclosure during negotiations, because "honesty implies not only telling [the] literal truth but also disclosing the whole truth" (pp. 582, 589–591). What, then, is the point of the strategic dealings that are the modus operandi of the process? The credibility of a negotiation ethic is weak when it fails to distinguish between actually assisting an opponent, by offering information she should be expected to seek for herself through bargaining techniques, such as bargaining for information (the original price of the barbells), and misrepresenting factual information (that the barbells are used).

The universalist concern with responsibility toward a negotiating opponent insinuates societal interests into the process, while the bargaining mentality is instinctively individualistic. A bargaining ethic that would substantially elevate society's interests thus contradicts the central individualist impulse of negotiation. Like legal ethics, negotiation ethics must always contend with the resiliency of partisan interests.

Traditionalism, a specialized ethic that is based on zero-sum self-interest, is an alternative that specifically rejects universalism. Classical bargaining using offers and counteroffers can thus be viewed as traditionalist. In the legal system, traditionalism is expressed in the oppositional stance assumed by lawyers with clients against others with adverse interests and is justified by the need for intense loyalty in order to adequately represent a client. This need is easiest to justify in the criminal justice system, where the loss of life or liberty can occur, and where the Sixth Amendment requirement of the assistance of counsel and other constitutional safeguards specifically reinforce client loyalty. However, client loyalty also is required in civil and nonlitigatory matters, where the intensity of the lawyer-client relationship is often as great as in criminal matters. Because traditionalism is the dominant ideology of the legal profession, expressions of this view are common. A classic statement by Charles Curtis (1951) portrays legal representation as a game the lawyer must play as well as she can, just as negotiation is often viewed as a game which allows actions that otherwise would not be tolerated. In the traditionalist view, the vicarious nature of the lawyer's work elevates his responsibility to his client and lowers his obligation to others. Instead of imposing a higher standard of responsibility toward opponents drawn from conventional ethics, as the universalist does, the traditionalist posits a higher responsibility toward clients drawn from the principle of client loyalty (Curtis, 1951). This standard allows the lawyer to lie for a client when he could not justify lying for himself.

Particularly as applied to unpoliced partisan bargaining, the special lawyer's ethic can easily take an extreme form. Curtis (1951), for example, concedes that a lawyer may not deceive the court, but believes that the lawyer's obligation to his client is so overriding that "it may be a lawyer's duty not to speak" (p. 9).

The difference between universalism and traditionalism is fundamental. A universalist such as Rubin (1975) begins with one of the central ideas of normative ethics—that, minimally, the lawyer cannot do for a client what the lawyer could not do for himself in negotiations. In contrast, the traditionalist, drawing upon the traditional ethics of the adversary system, presses legal ethics to their outer limits to reach the contrary conclusion (Curtis, 1951). For Curtis (1951), this means that a lawyer must use "a lower standard than he would if he were acting for himself, and lower, too, than any standard his client himself would be willing to act on, lower, in fact, than anyone on his own" (p. 6).

Thus, universalism and traditionalism address specific ethical problems in negotiation in contradictory ways. On lying and deception, they often represent irreconcilable ethics. The universalist principle adopted by Rubin (1975, p. 589)—"the lawyer must act honestly and in good faith" (p. 589)—would, for example, require a lawyer to disclose information during negotiation, even if his opponent did not make the relevant inquiry.[15] Not only must a lawyer refrain from fraud or deception that would invalidate the settlement; he is held to an affirmative standard of honesty and good faith as a consequence of his privileged status as a professional. The strict traditionalist, on the other hand, is equally clear in the opposing view, expressed by Curtis (1951) in its starkest form, that "freedom from the strict bonds of veracity" is one of the "chief assets of the profession" (p. 9). Curtis concludes unabashedly that, "one of the functions of the lawyer is to lie for his client" (p. 9).[16]

The analogies to nonlegal bargaining are inescapable. In negotiation, as in the legal process, partisanship and adversarial dealings are assumed; the burden on each party is to extract the most favorable outcome. Universalism does not make room for strategic avenues to truthfulness. Traditionalism elevates the partisanship that assists a client to the status of an ethic that all but dominates other values.

Neither universalism nor traditionalism can be satisfactorily imposed on negotiation because they do not take account of the special features of the negotiation process. Universalism imposes a near-conventional ethic that would convert truthfulness and fairness into mandatory principles, displacing much of the role and function of strategy.[17] Traditionalism would import the classic lawyer's ethic, although values comparable to the lawyer's ethic and the constitutional basis for traditionalism in the legal system are not present. While the attorney-client relationship that is at the root of traditionalism does not exclude an obligation to others, the extraordinary primacy of the client makes traditionalism a weak source for the ethics that would guide adversaries in negotiation.

Between the paradigmatic extremes of universalism and traditionalism are two clear possibilities. One is to find a basis for compromise within existing systems of ethics; the other, to abandon altogether the search for principles drawn from theory and to fix upon the common denominator of existing practices as the basis for articulating ethical standards.

One compromise between the paradigmatic extremes of universalism and traditionalism is a relativist ethic, which would seek to maintain elements of both of these aspirational paradigms. The distinction between litigation and nonlitigation might be the basis for a functional departure that would support a special negotiating ethic. The distinction has some appeal because it has long been accepted, both in the British legal system, which recognizes a division between barristers and solicitors, and in American legal culture, in which zealous (traditionalist) advocacy is identified most often with the courtroom lawyer. From the classic division of functions between the advocate and the counselor, a matching set of ethical rules might be developed that identifies ethics with function.

As a practical matter, however, the distinction between litigation and nonlitigation is an inadequate basis for deriving a functionally valid negotiating ethic. Litigators face their opponents outside the court, without the presence of a judge, more often than in formal proceedings. For example, the taking of depositions approximates courtroom activity but occurs without the presence of an arbiter. Moreover, the parties to litigation most often resolve their conflicts in private negotiations, despite the fact that the matter is initially filed in court.

It is difficult to justify a different ethic for resolving the same matter if the operative distinction comes down to the site at which resolution results, or the presence or absence of a judge, or even the traditional legal requirements associated with various types of courtroom advocacy.

The final approach, pragmatism, would use the data of negotiation experience itself—the practices acceptable in a given community—as the basis for a negotiation ethic. Pragmatism is grounded neither in ethical principles nor in an existing ethic such as the traditionalism of the client-oriented adversary process. Lowenthal offers the clearest expression of pragmatism: "the range of acceptable agreements for experienced negotiators in the field in question" (Lowenthal, 1988, p. 105). Different ethics would apply according to the skill and sophistication of each opponent. Accordingly, a lawyer could misrepresent his client's bottom line when dealing with a lawyer who uses such a practice, but not with one who does not. The factual context would be central to a determination of ethical responsibility in negotiation (pp. 107–108).[18]

Pragmatism advances the analysis of bargaining ethics by facing the multidimensional complexity of a process whose ethic need not be derived from classical aspirational sources alone. Data from bargaining experience are the major ingredient in pragmatist ethics. Rather than assume that societal ethical norms can be made to fit ethics in bargaining, as universalism does, or that classical adversarial notions can solve ethical dilemmas, as traditionalism does, or that advocacy of the same matter in different settings can yield an acceptable ethic, as relativism does, pragmatism forthrightly embraces prevailing experience. Negotiation would be moderated by whatever ethical standards are revealed by widespread practices (Lowenthal, 1988, p. 94).

Pragmatism has an initial appeal because it disavows abstraction in favor of concrete ethical experience (Lowenthal, 1988, p. 94). Moreover, a contextual approach to ethics, calibrated to existing norms in negotiation, would serve a number of useful purposes. By insinuating data from experience, the search for appropriate ethics would become a factual, not merely a theoretical, exercise. The concreteness of existing experience would be helpful in addressing the difficult practical problems inevitably associated with an ethic for a flexible, multipurpose process. Although it harbors aspirational aims, pragmatism looks to a revealed ethic; thus it suits a process in which ethics must be perceived as sufficiently connected to process realities to avoid being discarded or ignored. Because negotiations are self-monitored, an ethic that is linked to known or accepted practices is likely to be credible and acceptable.

These benefits, however, do not overcome serious flaws in the pragmatic approach to negotiation ethics. Pragmatism rests on the comfortable assumption that ethical standards from existing experience are adequate. Yet we cannot be certain that common practice is an appropriate ethical guidepost, because of the difficulty of gathering data to confirm the assumption on which pragmatism depends.

One may hypothesize that most negotiators aspire to truthfulness and fairness, but in the absence of evidence, it is not possible to know the extent to which they manifest these values in actual negotiations. The available information concerning bargaining ethics is not comforting. Embracing existing ethical norms in negotiation without knowing what these norms are may condone low ethical standards.[19] As a threshold matter, locating ethical norms in negotiation is a formidable task. Existing bargaining practice must be discovered, discussed, and articulated.[20]

Moreover, pragmatism presents serious methodological problems. For example, how much documented experience showing deviation from truthfulness or fairness should determine that deviation is ethical? Must there be a showing that virtually everyone would extract substantially more from an inexperienced than from an experienced negotiator before this practice is interpreted to be acceptable? What of issues on which the data are inconclusive? Reliance on existing practices raises confounding threshold issues of identification and evaluation.

The likelihood is that pragmatism would be overwhelmed by the task it sets for itself. It would be far too onerous and complicated to adopt a system of bargaining ethics that depended upon data concerning a large number of bargaining practices. Even if a pragmatist methodology could reduce the applicable bargaining practices on which it relies to a manageable number, such simplification of varied and complex practices might be subject to serious methodological criticism.

These four approaches, in part because of an insufficient focus on the operational features of the bargaining process, do not adequately satisfy the demands of a workable aspirational ethic for bargaining. Each, however, offers relevant insights. Universalism insists that negotiators not allow the special responsibilities of partisan advocacy to distort their ethical obligations. Without diminishing the importance of universalist aspirations, however, long and instructive experience with legal ethics cautions that there are limits to the usefulness of universal ethical rules in a specialized process. The need to accommodate individualist notions of partisan protection inherent in our legal system has produced a special lawyer's ethic. Similar partisan considerations are at work in bargaining.

Traditionalism most closely approximates the instinctive partisanship of classical competitive negotiations. In legal matters, traditionalism stresses both the right of the individual to partisan loyalty from an attorney and the importance of the adversarial system in obtaining justice. No such overriding values characterize generic negotiations. What remains, therefore, is partisanship, a virtually instinctive characteristic that needs no reinforcement in negotiation ethics. The legal system, in which the partisan posture has been submitted to detailed analysis,[21] teaches that partisanship brings ethical pressure. Unexposed to public monitoring, traditionalism would intensify the private struggle that the unpoliced bargaining process already encourages.

Relativism is useful in the search for an appropriate negotiation ethic because it directs attention to the actual purposes such an ethic would serve. Probing the function of a given aspect of legal practice is useful to the search for a feasible bargaining ethic. However, relativism that goes no further than the classic division between advocates and nonadvocates obscures the possibility that in negotiations, the two may harbor as many similarities as differences.

Pragmatism offers experience rather than theory as the basis for a bargaining ethic. However, the absence of systematic data revealing existing bargaining ethics seriously impedes this approach. If experience with bargaining ethics could be satisfactorily documented, pragmatism might point toward an ethic that is sensible, coherent, and practical. Even then, however, pragmatism would not ameliorate unethical practice if it rested on the lowest common denominator of ethical experience. In any case, pragmatism raises unprecedented methodological difficulties in determining how, and even whether, to credit existing experience as a legitimate basis for a bargaining ethic.

A Functionalist Model for Negotiation Ethics

Functionalism is a model that provides a way to analyze and test the ethics of the bargaining process as it operates through the bargaining techniques used by negotiators. Functionalism therefore differs from static models that are self-contained systems. For example, functionalism differs from aspirational approaches in its goals and in its focus. Its goals are descriptive and analytical, not aspirational. Its focus is on the process of bargaining, not on external ethical criteria or systems. Instead of looking first to ethical principles or systems to guide bargaining ethics, functionalism begins by analyzing the negotiation process itself in order to understand the challenges posed by the process for normative ethical conceptions. This is the logical place to begin the search for the appropriate ethic for an activity that is both specialized and unique. Although there are many modes of bargaining, they share generic characteristics. This section first identifies some basic characteristics found in the varied approaches to negotiation. It then develops an ethical model that takes account of these characteristics.

Structural Features of Negotiation

BARGAINING AS A FREE-FORM MARKET PROCESS. Bargaining is a self-regulated process in which parties with different goals engage in strategic dealings until they agree upon an outcome, or until one or more of them decides that agreement cannot be reached. However, this process has no prescribed form or rules. It is what the parties agree it is and may be conducted in any way that they decide. Bargaining, a self-directed market process, assumes that the parties will monitor the truthfulness and fairness of that process.

To assure ethical dealings, negotiators have no choice but to rely on the resources of the negotiation process itself. These resources are the great assortment of bargaining techniques that fuel the process and give it its free-form market characteristics. The strategic actions used to achieve negotiation goals are laced with ethical dilemmas. For example, a prospective buyer may give an evasive answer rather than respond directly to questions designed to discover why his company is seeking a parcel of land. He avoids deception, but his response is highly strategic. Suppose he then offers a price well below market level, and the seller feels that she is being treated unfairly. To elicit a response she considers more appropriate, the seller may threaten to call off negotiations. The buyer is not sure if this is her true intention, but he raises his price and the bargaining continues. The seller's threat may have been a bluff that falsified her real intentions, but it has resulted in an offer that is closer to the fair market value of the land. Such ambiguous approaches to truth and fairness are tolerated in bargaining, and the more appropriate price put forward by the buyer after the bluff is an important reason this is so. The seller's bluff was a strategic response that brought an increased offer from what might have resulted in an unfair price. The buyer's deception—the low price—was also a bluff, but it elicited a strategic response from the seller—calling off negotiations—which effectively addressed the deception. The higher price offered in response corrected for the original deception and the resulting price is closer to fair market value and therefore more likely to be considered fair. The difficulty, of course, is that even if responses that aid in setting a fair market price may be considered ethical, there is no guarantee that the bargaining process will always elicit functionally ethical responses.

Ethical dilemmas in bargaining begin with the virtually unsupervised responsibility the parties assume for ethical conduct in an unstructured setting.

Decisions concerning ethics, like those concerning strategy, assume the autonomy of the decision maker. One way to appreciate the market character of negotiation is to contrast negotiation, which is self-regulated, with courtroom expectations, in which ethical rules are explicitly elaborated and enforced. The central figure in the formal justice system is the judge, the neutral charged with dispensing justice. The judge regulates the formal, visible legal process, applying its laws, rules, and protocol. Armed with the power of contempt, the authority to refer to disciplinary proceedings, and other institutional and statutory powers,[22] the judge enforces ethical standards for relations between opponents and order and respect for the law and the court.

Bargaining is one of the few market processes that, as a practical matter, must be almost entirely self-regulated. There is no practicable way to monitor the process, and unless a lawsuit is brought to enforce or challenge an agreement, ethical abuse usually cannot be uncovered or addressed. The parties make strategic decisions consistent with their interests, including decisions concerning the ethics of their actions. The most important effect of self-regulation is to place greater responsibility on the parties to make ethical decisions.

BARGAINING AS AN ADVERSARIAL PROCESS. Like its market features, the adversarial posture in negotiation is a structural characteristic. An adversarial posture is necessary in bargaining to protect and advance the parties' interests, including their interests in ethical treatment. However, the viability of an adversarial setting depends on its ability to enforce ethical standards such as truthfulness and fairness. In litigation, enforcement of ethical standards occurs through judicial oversight. In negotiation, the parties enforce ethical standards in part through the assumption of a posture which is technically adversarial even when cooperative or problem-solving bargaining strategies and tactics are used. This posture facilitates the search for truthful information, helps guard against injurious disclosures, and helps prevent treatment that could prejudice a party's interests. The bargaining relationship remains adversarial throughout the process because, however benign or cooperative, the setting is a contest where something of value is at stake.

The adversarial posture is sometimes obscured during bargaining because negotiators often must act in seemingly contradictory ways. They must be resolute to protect self-interest, but accommodating to invite agreement. They must be determined to win acceptance of their positions, but compromising to avoid the breakdown of discussions. Negotiators often assume these postures—resolve and accommodation—interchangeably and act spontaneously in response to, or in anticipation of, an opponent's actions. The two roles may be played in any proportion, with one often predominating or even displacing the other. Nevertheless, the inevitable partisanship of parties with adverse interests, each seeking a solution favorable to himself, produces a structural adversarial role. In seeking truthfulness and fairness, the parties use the adversarial posture just as they do in deploying bargaining strategy. Although negotiation is often viewed as more gentle and less adversarial than litigation, labor strikes, or other oppositional actions,[23] negotiation has all the adversarial potential of litigation and similar contests but few of the restraints.

Bargaining between lawyers is the paradigm for the adversarial posture. However, as with laypeople who negotiate, lawyers will bring greatly varying degrees of adversarial intensity to the process. Nevertheless, the interest of a client, like the self-interest of ordinary negotiators, assures that the basic character of the relationship is always in some respect adversarial.

The tendency of the adversarial stance to encourage actual adversarial relations and to intensify the desire to win may increase the pressure to behave unethically. A desire to win can lead to a desire to prevail by any means, including lying and unfairness. However, such behavior is not a necessary function of the adversarial posture. In bargaining, the adversarial stance is a posture, not a description of the variety of actions it may encompass. The posture requires partisanship, not its excesses. The structural necessity for partisanship in bargaining is self-interest (or, for lawyers, client loyalty). The purpose of ethics, however, is to curb excessive self-interest and to encourage regard for the rights of others.

In bargaining, unlike in litigation, there is often a built-in brake on unbridled self-interest. Whatever oppositional stance negotiators assume, successful bargaining almost always entails some measure of compromise. Thus, if adversarial relations sometimes intensify ethical pressure, the need for compromise may reduce it.

BARGAINING TECHNIQUES: STYLE, STRATEGY, AND TACTICS. The adversarial posture is structural because it is inherently oppositional; but it is expressed through the style, strategy, and tactics negotiators adopt. These I call bargaining techniques. Negotiators use bargaining techniques to obtain truthful information and to assure fairness, just as they use these techniques to advance other negotiation goals.

The use of tactical and strategic techniques to accomplish ethical goals is unavoidable in bargaining. In a private, self-policed market process, there is no practical way to police ethical decisions from outside the process. Strategic decisions, however, are self-enforcing. In the barbells hypothetical, volunteering truthful information about the original price paid for the barbells, in an attempt to persuade an opponent that the offer to sell is set at a good price, is a strategic decision. But so is the use of deception in withholding this information and demanding a price much higher than the price one is willing eventually to accept. While strategy and tactics do not always accomplish their intended goals, the responses they engender from opponents often signal the need for further strategic maneuvers in order to elicit more accurate information or fairer treatment. Ethical decisions, no less than other decisions made during bargaining, depend on such needs.

Ethical issues often are so embedded in the adversarial structure of bargaining, as well as in the bargaining techniques used, that ethics and strategy are difficult to disentangle. For example, putting only one firm "take it or leave it" offer on the table and refusing to compromise is an inflexible strategy showing resolve; however, generally this strategy is not considered unfair or unethical because an opponent may use bargaining ingenuity to address the strategy, such as proposing concessions in exchange for modifications in the offer or bluffing by asserting an unwillingness to continue to bargain under these circumstances. To be fair, a strategy need not be conciliatory and it need not be easily countered. If the strategy is too rigid or severe, it may not succeed. It may instead precipitate the breakdown of discussions or an equally rigid reaction from an opponent. The use of the single, firm offer in particular inhibits the exchange that often facilitates agreement, and for this reason a bargaining strategy based on one inflexible offer is seldom used. This strategy does not leave sufficient room for accommodation, a feature that is normally necessary to reach an agreement. Thus, the use of only one, firm offer is atypical, not because it is unfair, but because it is at odds with elements of the bargaining process, such as reciprocity, exchange, and accommodation.

Bargaining is a complex process dominated by the subjective motivations and goals of the parties. The highly individual, often spontaneous, and sometimes emotional responses which account for bargaining strategy seldom lend themselves to systematic application. In a single negotiation, a person may open with distributive strategy demanding concessions, may then engage in integrative suggestions that increase the possibility of mutual gain, may again use distributive bargaining to extract more of this mutual gain for herself than her opponent, and may end by splitting the remaining issues down the middle, in a return to cooperative integrative bargaining.

PROCESS FEATURES, GOALS, AND ETHICS: A FUNCTIONALIST HYPOTHESIS. This section discusses a functionalist model of ethics that relies on the features of the bargaining process that have been identified in this article. The model is useful as an analytical tool to explain how the structure of the bargaining process, together with the bargaining techniques used by the parties, operate to produce an ethic that identifies the minimally acceptable forms of truthfulness and fairness that have sustained negotiation for centuries as a widely accepted process. This section shows how the model uses the structural characteristics of the negotiation process analyzed in the preceding section to arrive at assumptions concerning truthfulness and fairness. Then, to test the functionalist model, the discussion turns to an analysis of a recent change in professional standards for lawyers in negotiation that allows some misrepresentation in bargaining. This test demonstrates the analytical characteristics of the model, whose function is to offer a way to evaluate objectively practices that otherwise are judged subjectively or according to particular preferences or philosophies of bargaining.

The assumptions of the functionalist model may be summarized as follows:

1. Bargaining is indispensable to the functioning of society.
2. The fundamental purpose of bargaining is to achieve a valid agreement.
3. Practices that threaten the validity of an agreement violate the fundamental purpose of the process.
4. Bargaining is an adversarial market process in which willing opponents use partisan strategic dealings (bargaining techniques) to arrive at accurate information and to obtain fair treatment.

These assumptions underlie the use of the internal resources of the process to achieve truthfulness and fairness in bargaining. The result is a minimal but functional ethic. This ethic is best understood through an explanation of its operation to induce truthfulness and fairness and through an analysis of appropriate illustrations.

Truthfulness is important in negotiations because it encourages trust between opponents and thus facilitates agreement. However, adherence to the ethical standard of truthfulness in bargaining does not require a negotiator to abandon the assumptions of the process. Parties to a negotiation may use bargaining techniques, including strategic dealings, in order to arrive at accurate information concerning factual matters and the true intentions of an opponent, as well as to limit information offered to an opponent.

False information is not usually recognizable as a bargaining technique and therefore closes off the opportunity for an opponent to arrive at accurate information through the use of his own bargaining techniques. Thus, giving false information in a negotiation violates the assumption that bargaining techniques will elicit accurate information. False information also undermines the basic purpose of the bargaining process, to achieve a valid agreement. However, false information necessary for a mode of bargaining to occur is an exception because of the assumption that bargaining is necessary to the functioning of society. Generally, though, information that is necessary for bargaining to occur is also recognizable as a bargaining technique. Such false information does not threaten the validity of an agreement because it may be uncovered during the course of bargaining through the use of bargaining techniques so as to facilitate the eventual discovery of more accurate information. Thus, deceptive offers and counteroffers, as well as settlement point deception may be considered either bargaining techniques that invite counter-techniques or false information that is necessary for a form of bargaining to occur. The withholding of the name of a principal, however, cannot be uncovered readily through the use of bargaining techniques and therefore can be justified only as necessary for bargaining to occur. Often deceptive exchanges are not misrepresentations as the term is commonly understood because the true asking price or the settlement point may become clear to the parties only as a result of the process of bargaining itself.

Several examples may be helpful to show how the assumptions apply to truthfulness. Avoiding a direct answer is a bargaining technique when it limits information to an opponent without undermining the validity of an agreement. Failing to volunteer information is a bargaining technique when it limits information to an opponent unless, for example, silence about the particular facts undermines the validity of the agreement. Other examples of bargaining techniques are puffing concerning the quality of goods and bluffing concerning calling off negotiations. The process assumes that negotiators will use partisan strategic dealings to arrive at truthful information, and that the statements made will not keep opponents from using bargaining techniques to arrive at truthful information. Such deceptive information is not inconsistent with the assumptions of the process. When it is offered in such a way as to allow strategic responses that can arrive at more accurate information, it is necessary for bargaining to occur.

Fairness is also important in negotiations. Like truthfulness, it encourages trust between opponents and thus facilitates agreement without requiring a negotiator to abandon the assumptions of the process. Fairness is not a single concept but covers many abuses that can be judged only in the context in which they occur. For example, a lawyer in negotiations with another lawyer may take actions that might be considered unfair only if taken against a layperson. Many practices may be distasteful but not unfair, because they do not violate the assumptions of the process. For example, a strong negotiator may lower the asking price of a weak opponent, because the process assumes that willing opponents can depend on bargaining techniques to assure fair treatment.

Functionalism is not a test characterized by mathematical accuracy, but it is useful because it requires that departures from truthfulness and fairness in negotiation be justified in a manner consistent with explicit and objective assumptions of the bargaining process. Functionalism explains how the internal dynamic of the process sorts out gross deception and unfairness in order to protect the process from the invalidation of an agreement. A minimal ethic derived from the process itself is the result. Functionalism is not an aspirational ethic, but its descriptive mission endows it with an objectivity that can help discipline the search for an aspirational ethic that will have more than subjective appeal.

At the same time, the most serious shortcoming of functionalism is its ethical minimalism. Objective functionalist process criteria lack a deep moral dimension. At best, the minimalism of functionalism can separate etiquette from ethics and distinguish the distasteful from the disallowed and the inadvisable from the impermissible.

LAW AND THE FUNCTIONALIST MODEL: A CASE STUDY

Misrepresentation and Functionalism

Recall the important assumption that truthfulness is a functional necessity in bargaining. Negotiators need truthful information in order to forge an enforceable or acceptable bargain. At the same time, accurate information is often so valuable that it becomes the basic currency of bargaining.

Unconscionability and Functionalism

Fairness is a difficult concept to apply. Unlike misrepresentation, it lacks the concreteness and objectivity of specific violations. Sometimes in negotiation it is difficult to determine whether a harsh outcome to one party has resulted from her opponent's unethical action, or whether bargaining techniques, skill, or more favorable market conditions are responsible for the unfair results. The latitude that a market process allows makes difficult the application of principled judgments concerning fairness.

Moreover, fairness is an encompassing idea that can reach any and all ethical abuses, including misrepresentation and some forms of deception.[24] In judging pure issues of fairness in negotiation, then, what remains is conduct not encompassed by other conceptions of bargaining abuse. The concept of fairness, however, has little practical meaning apart from a specific set of rules or circumstances to which that concept is linked. There are no rules or circumstances for fairness that fit the entire expansive range of generic negotiations. Consequently, courts have judged fairness in negotiation on a case-by-case basis. Without specific rules or principles against which to decide each case, courts seldom find unfairness in bargaining.[25] Intervention by courts to judge the complex circumstances of each negotiation would compromise an inherent assumption of the process—that willing opponents will arrive at a fair solution using bargaining techniques. Thus, judicial intervention on fairness grounds has been largely limited to marginal or extreme situations in relation to the ordinary circumstances surrounding negotiation.

Drawing upon the doctrine of unconscionability, I argue in this section that, in the absence of statutory law or some other societal frame of reference, freedom of contract inhibits the institution of a definitive notion of fairness in bargaining. A generic definition of fairness would displace the legitimate operation of market forces and bargaining techniques in many situations. Thus, fairness in negotiation is exceedingly deferential to the bargaining process, validating functionalist assumptions that the strategic dealings of the parties are the primary tools available to control unfairness. I conclude that an aspirational ethic for bargaining should give special attention to issues of fairness, because functionalist assumptions about bargaining allow fairness a very limited mediating role.

Functionalism and Legal Regulation in Bargaining

Labor and Collective Bargaining. Collective bargaining in the United States is a virtual case study of a statutory approach to problems of truthful information and fairness in negotiations. Labor negotiations involve a high degree of statutory regulation compared with most areas of bargaining. Yet even in the statutory approach taken, functionalist principles that defer to the negotiation process predominate. This section argues that the statutory scheme that regulates both the sharing of truthful information and good-faith bargaining is deliberately deferential to the bargaining process.

REGULATION OF TRUTHFULNESS IN COLLECTIVE BARGAINING. The National Labor Relations Act (NLRA) does not specifically bar misrepresentation during bargaining; but its implicit requirement that negotiators disclose information necessary or relevant to the collective bargaining process (Gorman, 1976) and to the processing of grievances is necessarily a deterrent to some unethical deception. Mandatory disclosure has important strategic consequences that run counter to functionalism because in unregulated negotiations the parties would have to bargain for the information. The duty to disclose information known only to one party has important strategic consequences in collective bargaining. By strengthening bargaining leverage, especially for unions in search of resources for wages and benefits, mandatory disclosure has significant potential to affect the outcome of negotiations.

FAIRNESS AND GOOD FAITH IN COLLECTIVE BARGAINING. Earlier, we saw that since legal doctrine is of little use, fairness in bargaining is particularly dependent on the techniques used by the parties. This section argues that for all of its ostensible concern with fairness, labor law leaves this goal largely to the bargaining process as well, in keeping with functionalist assumptions.

In labor law, fairness issues are defined as elements of good-faith bargaining. The infrequency today of good-faith violations found on the basis of egregious bargaining strategy alone follows from the statutory recognition that the regulation of bargaining may affect bargaining results.[26] The choice and the use of strategy are left to the parties in order to avoid influencing the outcome. The flat bar in section 8(d) against interpreting the obligation to bargain collectively to mean that agreement or concession is expected reinforces the traditional bargaining prerogatives of the negotiators. Section 8(d), in turn, leads back to traditional bargaining mores, where freedom of contract is the rule, and to functionalist bargaining assumptions, where bargaining techniques supply the safeguard against unfairness.[27]

Divorce and Domestic Relations Law. Divorce law, like labor law, acknowledges strong policy concerns for truthfulness and fairness because important equitable issues are inherent in child custody, property distribution, and other family issues. Nevertheless, confronted with marital bargaining, the law incorporates functionalist assumptions that truthfulness and fairness are to be achieved through the strategic dealings of the parties.

Today it is not uncommon to find offensive practices and results that have survived consensual contractual divorce and separation negotiations, even after court review (Sharp, 1984). One of the most contentious practices to emerge is threats of custody battles made solely to extract favorable settlement terms.[28] These threats are not actionable under the law of duress, no matter how coercive or involuntarily accepted, because threats to do a lawful act are legal. Another example is a division of property that leaves one spouse, usually the wife, with far less than the other as a result of consensual bargaining in which the husband may have greater knowledge and control of the marital assets. The courts generally treat deceptive custody threats and inequitable division of property as bargainable matters that parties should sort out in negotiations rather than as issues subject to law or ethics.[29]

The experience with marital bargaining is an unusually telling example of the force of functionalist assumptions in law. Faced with inequities in agreements and the weak bargaining position many women still have, courts most often have felt constrained by the imperatives of the negotiation process that produced these results. Even when there is deception and unfairness, judges have regarded techniques of bargaining as the appropriate tools for the protection of the parties.

Even when the national economic stakes are high, as in assuring labor peace through effective collective bargaining, intervention through law has occurred to assure discussion among the parties, not fairness. Even when the public policy concerns are deep, as with divorce and family matters, the explicit concern for fair treatment of the parties has not resulted in significant alterations in bargaining. Courts have used neither the unconscionability doctrine nor the concept of good faith to invalidate agreements that appear unfair or one-sided in divorce or labor bargaining. Nor has bargaining deception in negotiation been effectively monitored in divorce law or barred in labor bargaining.

Despite compelling concerns, the law has left parties in both areas to achieve truthfulness and fairness through manipulation of the bargaining process. In divorce, judicial power to upset unfair agreements has lain dormant or has been displaced by the contractual bargaining that has attended recent divorce reform. In labor bargaining, negotiators must provide some important information, but, in most vital areas, bargaining deception is unregulated. Further, government intervention to assure fairness, apparent in the early years of the labor statute, has been statutorily reduced. In both labor and divorce regulation, functionalist assumptions have been asserted. In negotiations in both these areas, as well as in other bargaining, structural characteristics of the process—partisanship, the parties' adversarial posture, and strategic and other bargaining techniques—have become the safeguards of truthfulness and fairness.

CONCLUSION

The private world in which most bargaining occurs creates its own set of conditions and often its own rules. The ethics of bargaining, however, must be reconciled with the ethics of the real world. Otherwise, bargaining ethics becomes a world unto itself, closed not only from public view but from public concern and criticism. In such a world the inequality that parties inevitably bring to the negotiating table might be accentuated. Power and resource disparities are tolerated in bargaining; ethics should be shared.

This article has argued with some irony that in the existing state of our understanding, bargaining ethics are premature. Ethics, the aspirational standards that should apply to bargaining, are the cart; this article has focused on the horse, the bargaining process itself, and has argued that an understanding of its internal ethical radar must precede efforts to impose an aspirational ethic.

This article does not claim that bargaining is a self-regulating process that can depend upon its own internal resources to produce ethical behavior. If this were true, bargaining ethics would present fewer dilemmas and would have less apparent need for aspirational standards. Nevertheless, the bargaining process does produce a minimal ethic. This is not because the process has a "conscience" but because the successful culmination of the process is an agreement which has not been undermined by deception and unfairness. As its own structural features operate using adversarial market and strategic dealings, the process encourages minimal levels of truthfulness and fairness. Often, depending upon the uses negotiators make of the features of the process and their own ethical standards, higher levels are achieved.

Building upon an analysis of these features, this article has offered a model for explaining how bargaining receives and disposes of ethical challenges. This model is called functionalism because it draws its assumptions about ethics from the way the process operates or functions. Because the purpose of bargaining is to achieve a valid agreement, the process guides the strategic maneuvers of the parties, at least minimally, to both seek and give accurate information and to accord and extract fair treatment.

Functionalism embodies the imperfections of a market process, including its ethical minimalism. Yet it operates to distinguish the minimal truthfulness the process requires from the deception it disallows, and to distinguish permissible pressure tactics from intolerable unfairness. At the same time, it is the minimalism of the ethic of the market process that impels the search for a higher ethic.

Nevertheless, the gross ethic of the process is remarkable considering the ethical ambiguities negotiation invites. Minimal truthfulness is necessary for a valid agreement, but absolute candor is not. Similarly, fairness is necessary for a valid agreement, but the use of distasteful pressure tactics between roughly equal parties is not unfair. The bargaining process allows the seller to ask twice as much from an inexperienced negotiator as from an average one. On the other hand, the strategic dealings that produce minimal truthfulness and fairness can also raise ethical values to ideal levels. The process is responsive to both high and minimal ethical standards.

Perhaps the best case for the functionalist explanation is law. Often law shapes its subject matter. Bargaining, however, has shaped law. In its rules and approaches, in common law and statutes, the law systematically defers to bargaining. It declines to bar misrepresentation unless reliance is justified; to forbid many forms of direct and deliberate deception; to force full disclosure; to penalize concealment unless there is active suppression; and to prohibit distasteful tactics unless the circumstances are such that a judgment of patent unfairness is unavoidable. Even when strong policy concerns have led to statutory standards for bargaining, they have been timid in approach and quick in retreat. In labor law, the NLRA regulates information sharing concerning certain terms, but tolerates deception in most communications; it requires good-faith bargaining, but defines it minimally to require only the passing of words. In divorce law, the paternalism of the law has quickly withdrawn to the safety of contractual freedom and has given free rein to the bargaining techniques of the parties to produce truthfulness and fairness.

The ethical endowments of the process also reveal its deficiencies. Bargaining requires more than ethics drawn from the minimal operational needs of the process. Just as this article has discussed ethics drawn from within, future work must now consider how external influences and aspirational ethics might be made to fit the negotiation process.

The next logical step is to submit bargaining ethics to broader discussion and innovation. Ethics has gone mostly unnoted in scholarly literature, although negotiation itself has drawn widespread public interest and seen escalated use of the process and a large increase in books and commentaries on the subject. In this climate of interest, exposing the ethics of negotiation to the sunlight is likely to have salutary effects. Broader discussion may encourage negotiators to reflect on their ethics. Self-criticism as well as more systematic criticism by negotiators, scholars, and analysts may promote more ethical bargaining. Negotiators would probably welcome written commentary or informed guidance.

Modes of negotiation that mitigate many ethical problems are becoming more widespread. A pervasive and multipurpose process such as bargaining, however, must accommodate legitimate strategies, tactics, and styles of all varieties, including classical positional bargaining that has been the paradigm for this article. Nevertheless, traditional distributive hard-bargaining and competitive approaches are increasingly making room for problem-solving negotiations and cooperative approaches. Such approaches in and of themselves displace many ethical concerns because problem solving is at odds with deception and unfairness. The popularization of problem-solving negotiation, such as Fisher and Ury's standard-based negotiation (1981), suggests an eagerness for innovation in bargaining that departs from classical models.

Quite apart from process-driven ethics or a wholesale aspirational ethic, bargaining reform is possible in critical areas. Bearing in mind the operational needs of the process, reform should be discrete to particular concerns. While a statutory approach to the bargaining process is an unlikely remedy for most ethical concerns, carefully constructed law can remedy particular problems in areas of special concern, as in the regulation of collective bargaining, without unduly encumbering the process.

These are steps that I believe can have a beneficial effect in the short term. Thus far, efforts to improve bargaining ethics have been an empty vessel. Thoughtful steps that begin to fill it, even preliminarily, are important because of the increasing numbers of new negotiators. If left unattended, the danger is that they and the countless others who use negotiation will perpetuate not only the process but also its unethical practices.

Whatever steps are taken, an aspirational ethic for bargaining remains an important challenge. No process can be self-sufficient in creating its own ethic. Truthfulness and fairness are values that derive their meaning from human experience and ideals. The development of a satisfactory aspirational bargaining ethic demands more systematic thinking not only about the process and its needs, but also about the needs of society. Such thinking might begin by focusing on the potential for an aspirational bargaining ethic in light of the functional requirements of the bargaining process.

Notes

1. See Perschbacher (1985).

2. See Delgado and others (1985); Edwards (1985); Fiss (1984) at 1084–1085; Higginbotham (1976).

3. See, for example, Amsterdam (1984).

4. See Strauss (1978). Strauss argues that "social orders are, in some sense, always negotiated orders" (p. 235).

5. See Gulliver (1979) (negotiation "virtually universal").

6. See Boshkoff (1984) ("A misrepresentation is an incorrect statement of fact"); Model Rules, Rule 4.1 and comment, 1983.

7. See Calamari and Perillo (1987).

8. Fairness and justice are pervasive themes in philosophy and literature. See, for example, Aristotle (1955): "What [the just man] will do is give each his proportionately equal share, whether he is himself one of the parties nor not"; Ritter (1933): "defining justice for individual as fulfillment of three parts of human soul—appetitive, spirited, and rational—and for society as performance by citizens of their duties and tasks"; Santas (1979): "justice is virtue, and virtue leads to happiness"; Confucius (1983): "Tzu-Kung asked saying, Is there any single saying that one can act upon all day and every day? The Master said, Perhaps the saying about consideration: 'Never do to others what you would not like them to do to you.'"

9. Rawls, J. "Justice as Fairness." *Philosophical Review,* 1958, *67,* 164–194.

10. However, primogeniture is clearly unfair when judged by other values, such as equality.

11. See Leff (1967), discussing procedural unconscionability (coercive behavior during bargaining) and substantive unconscionability (unfair results).

12. See *Evans* v. *Jeff D.* (1986): Civil Rights Attorney's Fees Awards Act does not require award of attorney's fees upon settlement but leaves issue to discretion of district court. Civil rights litigation often requires significant efforts by small firms whose fees are essentially contingent upon prevailing against large employers. Arguably, a settlement proposal that forces an attorney to choose between a favorable offer for her client and payment for work she has performed is an unethical "coercive waiver." This argument was recently rejected by a divided Supreme Court, but the Court left open the possibility that the same practice might be actionable in other circumstances. Professional ethics require that a lawyer consider only his client's best interests in receiving a settlement offer. See Model Rules (1983). Further, Rule 68 of the Federal Rules of Civil Procedure requires that if a party rejects an offer that is greater than the value of the verdict of trial, she is liable for her opponent's fees and costs. Settlement offers covered by this rule include those where a party offers a lump sum to settle an entire matter through a package offer to cover fees and costs. See *Marekle* v. *Chesney* (1985).

13. See Rubin (1975): discussion of negotiation ethics relying largely on normative ethical ideas. Similar views are expressed by others: see Lowenthal (1988) and Steele (1986). For a universalist view of a lawyer's more general obligations, see Frankel (1974).

14. See Curtis (1951). For a critique of traditionalism, see Drinker (1952). See also Frankel (1974).

15. Of course, there are instances where affirmative disclosure would be required. Suppose, for example, that the barbells were a year old but looked new, and a potential buyer in the course of negotiating discovered that the seller had neglected to remove the original price tag, which was still glued to the inside of the weight on one end. If the conversation made clear that the buyer was relying on the price stated on the tag in the mistaken belief that the barbells were recently purchased, the seller would have a duty to affirmatively disclose the fact that the price tag reflected the price a year ago when the barbells were new. This duty would arise because the seller, by leaving the price tag on the barbells, has affirmatively misled the potential buyer and must correct the impression she has created.

16. Curtis qualifies this view, indicating that the more particular a lawyer's statements are, the greater is her obligation to be truthful. Even here, however, deception is allowed as to "particulars which do not belong to him, but are his client's secrets" (p. 9).

17. For a classic illustration of divergent views, compare Shaffer (1987), arguing that autonomy encouraging diverse views is less important than the lawyer's moral influence on the client, with Freedman (1987), arguing that autonomy encouraging diverse views requires lawyer to support his client's view.

18. Lowenthal would alter the Model Rules to recognize this change explicitly (Lowenthal, 1988, p. 108).

19. One commentator argues that "lawyer-negotiators most strongly believe that they operate outside of the usual substantive law restraints and that they do not risk personal liability for their bargaining conduct in their dealings with adversaries and other third parties" (Perschbacher, 1985, p. 121).

20. See, for example, Guernsey (1982), calling for discussion and guidance beyond limited consideration of ethical issues provided by current law review articles, cases, and ethical opinions. Guernsey is skeptical that this process will produce consistent standards and believes that "varying standards . . . reinforce less ethical practices" (p. 101) and inhibit ethical changes that should be made in existing conventions. He would resist variated pragmatist ethics because he believes that different minimum standards of ethics and competence would be to the detriment of clients.

21. See, for example, Hazard and Hodes (1985), analyzing broad range of rights and duties applicable to lawyers who practice in "the real world."

22. See, for example, Federal Rules of Civil Procedure, p. 11 (mandatory sanctions for attorneys or litigants filing *pro se* who sign court pleadings and other papers not well grounded in fact or law); 28 U.S. Code sec. 1927 (Supp. 1986) (attorneys filing unreasonable and vexatious multiple civil and criminal proceedings may be

personally subject to excess costs, expenses, and attorneys' fees); Fed. R. App., p. 38 (court may award damages for frivolous appeals); 28 U.S.C.A. sec. 1912 (Subsection G, Notes of Decision) (1982) (any party or attorney subject to damages including attorney fees for frivolous appeals). A similar pattern of sanctions is also found in state court rules. See, for example, Md. Cts. & Jud. Proc. Code Ann. rule 1–311 (1989) (providing sanctions for filing groundless or dilatory pleadings) and rule 1–341 (imposing costs on attorneys acting in bad faith). Judges also have the authority to begin disciplinary proceedings against attorneys. See *In re Application for Discipline of Canby* (1984) (ordering reprimand for attorney entering plea on behalf of defendant while knowingly using defendant's false name).

23. See, for example, Williams (1983): settlements perceived as producing more amicable outcomes and relationships between parties.

24. See *David* v. *Kolb* (1978): contract obtained through false representation found unconscionable.

25. See Sharp (1984).

26. See *National Labor Relations Board* v. *American National Insurance Company* (1952): NLRB may not regulate terms or compel agreement; *Struthers Wells Corp.* v. *NLRB* (1983): statutory bargaining rights of employees do not preclude the employer from bargaining for exclusive control of labor-management decision.

27. Legislation Section 8(d) added to the NLRA by the Taft-Hartley Act.

28. See Sharp (1984) and Guhring (1981). Compare Mnookin and Kornhauser (1979), arguing that custody and money are necessarily linked in divorce bargaining because of parents' desires to trade them and because linkage facilitates enforcement without resort to court. The authors argue that the legal rules covering issues such as child support and division of marital property function as legitimate bargaining chips or "bargaining endowments" in the negotiation process. However, concern that judicial deference to the bargaining process eviscerates the effect of such rules could produce pressure for rules that in effect would regulate bargaining. Mnookin and Kornhauser concede that any bargaining theory must take into account the possibility of altruism and spite. However, their assumption that parents will be chiefly motivated by concern for their children may not be borne out as frequently as they assume. Critical to the authors' preference for "bargain[ing] in the shadow of the law" (p. 980) is the need to replace pervasive uncertainty and discretion in divorce law with more precise standards.

29. See Sharp (1984). See, for example, *Blalock* v. *Blalock* (1974): threat to take property disposition issues to court unless settlement made is not coercive; *In re Marriage of Lawrence* (1982): if custody threats constituted duress, separation agreements would be jeopardized regardless of preagreement negotiations.

References

Amsterdam, A. G. "Too Many Lawyers, Too Many Suits, Not Enough Justice." Remarks at the Proceedings of the Forty-Fifth Judicial Conference of the D.C. Circuit, May 21, 1984.

Aristotle. *The Ethics of Aristotle* (J. Thomson, trans.). Harmondsworth, Middlesex: Penguin Books, 1955.

Blalock v. *Blalock*. 51 Ala. App. 686, 689, 288 So. 2d 747, 748–749 (1974).

Boshkoff, D. *Sum and Substance of Contracts*. Inglewood, Calif.: Center for Creative Education Services, 1984.

Calamari, J., and Perillo, J. *Contracts*. (3d ed.). 1987.

Confucius. *The Analects* (A. Waley, trans.). New York: Vintage Books, 1983.

Curtis, C. P. "The Ethics of Advocacy." *Stanford Law Review*, 1951, *4*(3).

David v. *Kolb*. 263 Ark. 158, 563 S.W.2d 438 (1978).

Delgado, R., and others. "Fairness and Formality: Minimizing the Risk of Prejudice in Alternative Dispute Resolution." *Wisconsin Law Review*, 1985, pp. 1359–1404.

Drinker, H. "Some Remarks on Mr. Curtis' 'The Ethics of Advocacy.'" *Stanford Law Review*, 1952, *4*, pp. 349, 350–351.

Edwards, H. "Hopes and Fears for Alternative Dispute Resolution," *Willamette Law Review*, 1985, *21*, pp. 425, 438–440.

Evans v. *Jeff D.* 475 U.S. 717 (1986).

Fisher, R., and Ury, W. *Getting to Yes: Negotiating Agreement Without Giving In.* Boston: Houghton Mifflin, 1981.

Fiss, O. "Against Settlement." *Yale Law Journal*, 1984, *93*, 1073.

Frankel, M. "The Search for Truth—An Umpireal View." 31st Annual Benjamin N. Cardozo Lecture, delivered before the Association of the Bar of the City of New York. Dec. 16, 1974.

Freedman, M. H. "Legal Ethics and the Suffering Client." *Catholic University Law Review*, 1987, *36*, 331.

Gorman, R. A. *Basic Text on Labor Law: Unionization and Collective Bargaining.* St. Paul, Minn.: West Publishing Company, 1976.

Guernsey, T. "Truthfulness in Negotiation." *University of Richmond Law Review*, 1982, *17*, 99.

Guhring. "Family Law in Transition: Is the Law Changing Too Fast?" *Trial*, 1981, *17*, 28, 30.

Gulliver, P. *Disputes and Negotiations: A Cross-Cultural Perspective.* New York: Academic Press, 1979.

Hazard, G., and Hodes, W. *The Law of Lawyering: A Handbook on the Model Rules of Professional Conduct. 1*, Englewood Cliffs, N.J.: Prentice Hall Law & Business, 1985.

Higginbotham, A. L. "The Priority of Human Rights in Court Reform." Remarks at the National Conference on the Causes of Popular Dissatisfaction with the Administration of Justice, Apr. 7–9, 1976.

In re Application for Discipline of Canby. 355 N.W.2d 704 (Minn. 1984).

In re Marriage of Lawrence. 642 P.2d 1043 (Mont. 1982).

Leff, A. A. "Unconscionability and The Code—The Emperor's New Clause." *University of Pennsylvania Law Review,* 1967, *115,* 485.

Lowenthal, G. "The Bar's Failure to Require Truthful Bargaining by Lawyers," *Georgetown Journal of Legal Ethics,* 1988, *2,* 411.

Marekle v. *Chesney.* 473 U.S. 1 (1985).

Mnookin, R., and Kornhauser, L. "Bargaining in the Shadow of the Law: The Case of Divorce." *Yale Law Journal,* 1979, *88,* 950, 951, n. 3.

National Labor Relations Board v. *American National Insurance Company.* 343 U.S. 395, 404 (1952).

Perschbacher, R. "Regulating Lawyers' Negotiations." *Arizona Law Review,* 1985, *27,* 75, 76.

Rawls, J. "Justice as Fairness." *Philosophical Review,* 1958, *67,* 164–194.

Ritter, C. *The Essence of Plato's Philosophy* (A. Alles, trans.). London: George Allen & Unwin, 1933.

Rubin, A. "A Causerie on Lawyers' Ethics in Negotiation." *Louisiana Law Review,* 1975, *35,* 577.

Santas, G. *Socrates: Philosophy in Plato's Early Dialogues. The Arguments of the Philosophers.* London & Boston: Routledge and K. Paul, 1979.

Shaffer, T. "Legal Ethics and the Good Client." *Catholic University Law Review,* 1987, *36,* 319.

Sharp, S. B. "Fairness Standards and Separation Agreements: A Word of Caution on Contractual Freedom." *University of Pennsylvania Law Review,* 1984, *132,* 1399-1403.

Steele, W. "Deceptive Negotiation and High-Toned Morals," *Vanderbilt Law Review,* 1986, *39,* 1387.

Strauss, A. *Negotiations: Varieties, Contexts, Processes, and Social Order.* San Francisco: Jossey-Bass: 1978.

Struthers Wells Corp. v. *NLRB.* 721 F.2d 465, 469–471 (3d Cir. 1983).

Williams, G. *Legal Negotiations and Settlement.* St. Paul, Minn.: West Publishing Company, 1983.

PART FIVE

NEGOTIATION AND AGENTS

Perhaps because negotiation is so dynamic, anxiety producing, and increasingly dominated by professionals of various sorts (lawyers, brokers, and business and sports agents), many people prefer to hire others to do their negotiating for them. Having someone other than a principal conduct a negotiation is often thought advantageous because the negotiation agent will have greater expertise in the negotiation process itself, the particular substantive field or market where the negotiation is conducted, more personal contacts with similarly situated negotiators, a particular reputation (choose either "shark" for mergers and acquisitions or "cooperative" for finding financing for deals or settlements of lawsuits), and a good "professional distance" from the situation and all it calls for in strategic choices, decisions, and representations (Wheeler, 1999; Mnookin and Susskind, 1999).

Although the agent can provide superior knowledge and skill in particular negotiations, agents also present problems for the negotiation principal. While agents can often justify their behavior by a role morality that allows them (both legally and morally) to do that which a principal could not do for himself, agency relationships are also sometimes regulated by law (fiduciaries, specially regulated agents such as residential real estate brokers and securities dealers) and present more onerous obligations and responsibilities than principals have for themselves. There is, in fact, a specialized body of law, agency law (Salacuse, 1999; American Law Institute, 2003), which regulates much of what agents can do, such as when they can actually bind their principals without the principal's consent and what authority they do and do not have in particular settings. So sometimes agents may have both more or less "apparent authority" or power than it seems explicitly in a negotiation, and this may cause problems for both principals and those on the other side of the negotiation table. The use of agents has its pros and cons.

In addition, the incentives that agents have to do their work (such as contingent versus retainer payments, ongoing relationships with counterparts or competitors in the same field, multiple or repeat-play customers or clients in the same field) often separate them from their principals and present difficult conflicts of interests for both the agent and the monitoring principal. Consider the criminal defense lawyer who represents several defendants in the same matter or multiple defendants on the same day of negotiation with a particular prosecutor for plea bargaining. Although legal ethics require a lawyer to treat each client separately and to represent each client diligently (and, under some rules, "zealously"), repeat-player lawyers who interact often with each other have to be concerned about their reputations for truth telling and evidence evaluation. In the real world, there is no doubt that different clients will be compromised in different ways when multiple cases are on the table simultaneously (Uphoff, 1992). Similar dynamics may be operating when class action lawyers settle cases for an aggregate group of plaintiffs who will receive settlements that regress toward the mean rather than being individualized. Similarly, in the world of sports and entertainment representation, knowledge of the studio, media, team ownership structure, and salary structures may give agents superior knowledge and power (if they are representing multiple and much desired clients), but knowing that one is going to negotiate again with the same parties may temper the demands made in particular cases. If the agent knows he will continue to have many clients (as real estate brokers do, for example), there may be less incentive to work particularly hard for one. And where, as in real estate, the broker negotiators on both sides (sellers and buyers) make their commission only if a deal is made, they will have incentives to work together to create a deal, where principals might prefer to resist on a particular point or structure something other than a boilerplate clause.

Negotiation ethics for agents is particularly problematic because negotiating agents come from so many different fields of expertise, with different contexts and cultural understandings of what is appropriate in mergers and acquisitions, sports and movie contracts, stock, and residential real estate sales. Some professional negotiating agents are more regulated than others (lawyers and securities and real estate brokers, for example), and this raises questions and issues about what different agents, from different fields, do when they are in competition with each other. Issues of who actually has authority to make and accept offers or proposals and who has the power to act are sometimes not clear and may vary depending on the actual power relations between particular agents and principals. Thus, many negotiations with agents have internal behind-the-table negotiations between agents and principals and constituencies, in addition to the "across-the-table" negotiations of the "opposing" parties (Mnookin, Peppet, and Tulumello, 2000). Agent-principal negotiations are even more complicated when the principal is an organization, institution, or entity (government agency or union, for example) with many members or constituents who have to have internal negotiations before they can authorize an agent to speak for them. In the dynamism of changing information and offers and proposals in negotiations, how much agents have to or should consult with their constituents is also both an instrumental and ethical concern. Some agents prefer flexibility to enable them to be creative and offer solutions or to listen to the other side, but too much flexibility given to the agent (especially if the principal is not present) may hinder the principal's input into issues that are of great importance. The role of agent or representative in negotiation is thus a complex one, even if it is the norm in many kinds of negotiation. Clients, customers, and everyone else who has to negotiate have much to consider in deciding whether the use of an agent is going to be advantageous enough to balance out some of the additional costs and concerns that arise whenever someone else acts for the people with the real stakes in issue (Rubin and Sander, 1988).

We begin Part Five with a chapter from a thoughtful exploration of the specialized morality attributed to the professional role, particularly of those in "adversarial" professions (lawyers, politicians, businesspeople, journalists). In Chapter Twenty-One, Arthur Applbaum traces the moral justifications of a role and craft so well performed that Monsieur Henri Sanson, royal executioner and subsequent executioner for the various regimes of the French Revolution, can be morally acquitted of being a serial murderer because his killings were so professionally conducted and formally authorized by the law (as it changed from regime to regime). Applbaum draws the obvious analogies to others who suggest that their roles allow them to do what ordinary people cannot: lawyers who persuade with less than the truth, politicians who must compromise their own principles to govern the many, and businesspeople who owe a duty to maximize profits for legions of unknown shareholders who are not at the negotiating table. The claims of justifications for and resistance to role morality have a long history in moral philosophy (Luban, 1984; Wasserstrom, 1975; Goldman, 1980; Fried, 1976) and modern literature (Ishiguro, 1989). Can the actions taken in role (the soldier who may kill, the lawyer or seller who may exaggerate, the politician who may not keep promises with virtual impunity) be morally excused, permitted, or justified because we see a different morality in the role or the institution in which that role is embedded (the adversary legal system, the commercial market, the unfettered market of ideas)?

Negotiation agents, be they lawyers, brokers, or sports agents, justify their hardball tactics, their exaggerated offers and demands, their "slight" divergences from the truth by referencing the particular needs of their principals with inadequate knowledge, resources, or skills to play the games on the fields in which the games are located. Yet while many of us hire agents to do our "dirty" work, we often are uncomfortable with what they do on our behalf, and we often do not want to be on the receiving end of someone else's agent.

To consider some of the limits of the ethically free agent, we juxtapose the arguments of two lawyers—one a professor of legal ethics, Murray Schwartz (Chapter Twenty-Two), and the other a distinguished federal appeals court judge, Alvin Rubin (Chapter Twenty-Three)—who suggest that at least some agents, like lawyers, should in fact have enhanced moral duties and obligations when they negotiate on behalf of clients. Whether from an instrumental perspective (their own market in reputation) or because in fact the system requires that all play by the rules honorably, these writers suggest that agents should perhaps have greater obligations to speak the truth and deal fairly with negotiation counterparts. Schwartz, for example, turns White's argument that negotiations are private and therefore unregulable on its head by suggesting that precisely because legal negotiations are conducted in private, without the presence of a judge or third-party neutral, there should be a greater obligation to tell the truth than in open court with a judge and several law clerks who could ferret out the truth for themselves. In confidential and private quarters with only two negotiators present, Schwartz tells us that lawyers should be even more individually accountable for their actions. Similarly, Rubin suggests that lawyers, as agents, are offering their services based on their reputation for using words and truth and serving "justice." Even though applied to the needs of individual clients, lawyers should exercise their craft with a concern for the entire justice system and the tasks that lawyers perform more generally within it.

Whether agents should be judged by their own specialized role morality or the same ethical strictures or criteria of judgment we apply to nonspecialized negotiators is one of the hardest ethical dilemmas in assessing what is fair in negotiations. To the extent that context and conditions of negotiations differ, do we need more variable standards (or rules) by which we judge negotiators based on their roles, experience, and professional discipline? Should it matter that all negotiators, "professional" agents, and amateurs alike swim and act in the same negotiation pond?

References

American Law Institute. *Restatement (Third) of the Law of Agency* (D. DeMott, rptr.). Philadelphia: American Law Institute, 2003.

Fried, C. "The Lawyer as Friend: The Moral Foundations of the Lawyer-Client Relation." *Yale Law Journal,* 1976, *85,* 1060.

Goldman, A. "Business Ethics: Profit, Utilities, and Moral Rights." *Philosophy and Public Affairs,* 1980, *9*(3), 260–286.

Ishiguro, K. *The Remains of the Day.* New York: Vintage, 1989.

Luban, D. *The Good Lawyer: Lawyers' Roles and Lawyers' Ethics.* Totowa, N.J.: Rowman & Allanheld, 1984.

Mnookin, R. H., Peppet, S. R., and Tulumello, A. S. *Beyond Winning: Negotiating to Create Value in Deals and Disputes.* Cambridge, Mass.: Belknap Press, 2000.

Mnookin, R. H., and Susskind, L. (eds.). *Negotiating on Behalf of Others: Advice to Lawyers, Business Executives, Sports Agents, Diplomats, Politicians, and Everybody Else.* Thousand Oaks, Calif.: Sage, 1999.

Rubin, J. Z., and Sander, F.E.A. "When Should We Use Agents? Direct vs. Representative Negotiation." *Negotiation Journal,* 1988, *4*(4), 395–401.

Salacuse, J. "Law and Power in Agency Relationships." In R. H. Mnookin and L. Susskind (eds.), *Negotiating on Behalf of Others: Advice to Lawyers, Business Executives, Sports Agents, Diplomats, Politicians, and Everybody Else.* Thousand Oaks, Calif.: Sage, 1999.

Uphoff, R. J. "The Criminal Defense Lawyer: Zealous Advocate, Double Agent or Beleaguered Dealer?" *Criminal Law Bulletin,* 1992, *28*(5), 419–456.

Wasserstrom, R. "Lawyers as Professionals: Some Moral Issues." *Human Rights Quarterly,* 1975, *5,* 105–128.

Wheeler, M. "First, Let's Kill All the Agents!" In R. H. Mnookin and L. Susskind (eds.), *Negotiating on Behalf of Others: Advice to Lawyers, Business Executives, Sports Agents, Diplomats, Politicians, and Everybody Else.* Thousand Oaks, Calif.: Sage, 1999.

CHAPTER TWENTY-ONE

Professional Detachment

The Executioner of Paris

Arthur Isak Applbaum

*Saviours of the homeland, hereafter do not make such a hasty end of criminals
who fall into your clutches. Put it to those extreme patriots of excess that it
is no service to their fellow citizens to eradicate, by their slapdash zeal, the
only way to come at the root of the catastrophes that were then being prepared.
Put it to them that they owe me compensation for the executions of which
they have deprived me. Each of the heads of the four scoundrels, if my sword
had put them off their shoulders, would have been worth twenty écus to me.
Put it to them that the work would have been much more neatly done and
that a great many spectators would have enjoyed the spectacle of the sacrifice
of these vile victims, if the tragedy had been played at my theatre.
. . . And let these usurpers consider that they, much more than I, deserve
that ignominy with which I am myself visited. For it is not I who kill the
criminals who die beneath my blows; it is Justice that sacrifices them,
it is Justice that makes me the avenger of society. Should not this
appellation rather honour than abase me? . . . Will philosophy not
succeed in making my profession a glorious one?*
—Complaints of the Public Executioner Against Those Who Have Exercised
His Profession Without Having Served Out Their Apprenticeship

The executioner of Paris did not write these words, though the satirist who
did captured with dead-on accuracy and prescience much of what can be
reconstructed about how Charles-Henri Sanson, perhaps the least understandable figure of the French Revolution, understood himself and was
understood by his contemporaries.[1]

At the risk of causing squeamishness, I invite you to explore with me one
extraordinary professional career and the arguments from the morality of roles
that can be offered in its defense. The uneasiness this will cause is not merely
an affront to delicate feelings, for the claims that can be made on Sanson's

behalf strikingly resemble the claims about role morality that have been offered for the less sanguinary professions. By entertaining arguments in Sanson's defense, we might learn much about what sorts of claims about roles succeed. If these arguments are perverse when offered by Sanson, why are they not perverse when offered by lawyers, politicians, bureaucrats, journalists, and business executives in defense of actions that, if performed outside of their roles, would be morally wrong? If Sanson's defense fails, so might the defenses of other professional roles. The point of this chapter is to unsettle.[2]

THE "ARGUMENT OF THE GUILLOTINE"

Sanson's grandfather's father was appointed Louis XIV's headsman in 1688. The professional calling, with its art and science of torture, dismemberment, and death, was handed down through apprenticeship and regal reappointment to Charles-Henri. He began doing his father's work in 1751 and was formally appointed in 1778 by Louis XVI (who would come to observe his appointee's handiwork up close). Sanson formally passed the commission on to his son in 1795 (though the son clearly was active on the scaffold, and may have taken the lead, before then). All six of Sanson's brothers, along with uncles and cousins, were also executioners, holding commissions in Tours, Dijon, Provins, Versailles, Blois, Montpellier, Rheims, and Genoa around the time of the Revolution. The Paris post stayed in the family until 1847.[3]

For decades, Sanson and his assistants conscientiously attended to the punitive needs of the *ancien régime:* the lesser sentences of public exposure, branding, and various mutilations; the rare beheading of nobles, the more common hanging of commoners, the breaking of robbers at the wheel, the burning of heretics at the stake, and, for attempted regicide, one quartering (botched, because the lore had been lost).[4] But Sanson seamlessly adapted to both the Revolution and its new technology, the humane and ennobling machine proposed by the good Doctor Guillotin. He ministered with professional detachment to, in turn, common criminals under the constitutional monarchy, royalist "plotters" at the direction of the Paris Commune, the king upon conviction by the National Convention, the moderate Girondins when purged by the Jacobins, the extremist Hébertistes at the instigation of Danton, the indulgent Dantonistes after their denunciation by Robespierre, and Robespierre himself when finally outmaneuvered by the Thermidorians.

After the Terror, the possibility of a Sanson fired the imagination of many writers, and he has been posed, alternately, as both grotesque and tragic. In 1795, the writer and onetime Girondist legislator Louis-Sébastien Mercier (1929, p. 220) wonders in horror about the man he calls "that monster":

I should love to know what goes on in that head of his, and whether he considers his appalling duties simply as a profession. . . . How does he sleep after receiving the last words and the last glances of all those severed heads? . . . He sleeps well enough, we are told, and it may well be that his conscience is untroubled. . . . It is said that the queen apologized to him when, on the scaffold, she accidentally placed the tip of her foot on his. What were his thoughts then? The coins of the royal treasury were for a long time his living. What a man this Sanson is! He comes and goes just like anyone else. Sometimes he goes to the Théâtre du Vaudeville. He laughs, he looks at me. My head escaped him, but he knows nothing of that.[5]

But others, creating grotesqueries of their own, present him as a man of humane sensibilities in the fashion of the cult of Rousseau, a tragic figure caught between duty and sentiment, and beset by undeserved social stigmatization for doing what must be done. Such a portrayal is entirely consistent with the high-minded hopes of Guillotin and the penal reformers of 1789. More than two years before the first guillotine was built, two engravings, almost mirror images of one another, envision an execution scene. One shows the face of a delicate executioner turning his head away in sadness or pain as he cuts a rope to drop the blade.[6] In the other, we see the back of a dramatically posed and shaded executioner, head turned away from both us and the victim, one hand raised to cover his mouth or face as the other cuts the rope (Schama, 1989). This same averted gaze is reproduced, fancifully, in a German engraving of the guillotining of Louis XVI, thereby turning hope into historical fact.[7] By 1804, Joseph Joubert in his notebooks can cuttingly lampoon this attribution of sensitivity with the following anecdote: "'Where have you been, young misses?' 'Mummy, we went to see a guillotining; oh, my goodness, how that poor executioner suffered'" (Arasse, 1989, p. 128; see also Joubert, 1983). Apocryphal memoirs were written humanizing the monster, one penned in part by Balzac. Some of these tales, with a royalist bent, show an executioner who has more compassion for his victims and their loved ones than do his murderous masters.[8]

Despite the literary portrayals, neither Sanson the monster nor Sanson the sensitive heart accounts for what is known about how Sanson presented himself and how the political factions of the Revolution viewed him. Any reconstruction must offer a coherent explanation of two facts: first, every Revolutionary faction that gained momentary ascendancy viewed Sanson as a practitioner of a necessary profession; second, Sanson viewed himself precisely that way.

Let us begin with how Sanson was viewed. In a climate of continual unmasking, where charges of betraying the nation and the Revolution could be made to stick on the slightest pretext, where thousands were shaved by the "national razor" either to sate the mob's appetite for conspirators, to eliminate political rivals, or to exercise sincere revolutionary zeal, Sanson was the only citizen of Paris safely beyond the reach of his machine. Consider how extraordinary this is: the king's functionaries swing from the *lanternes,* the king's Swiss guard is hacked to bits, but the King's Executioner becomes Citizen Sanson, the king's executioner. More than 2,500 heads later, the remnant of moderates succeeds in deposing Robespierre, and the final purge begins, but not of Sanson. One hundred more heads fly off in the first three days of the Counter-Terror, but Sanson is still on the right side of the blade. Fouquier-Tinville, the Revolutionary Tribunal's prosecutor through the Terror, is reviled as a monster even by fellow Jacobin prisoners, but the question of Sanson's responsibility does not arise (Schama, 1989). At trial, the prosecutor pleads in vain, "I am the axe! One does not punish the axe!" (Kershaw, 1958). The only blameless tool, however, is Sanson. He officially retires in September 1795, over a year after the end of the Terror, and applies for a government pension. His son, "whose name is on the list of candidates capable of carrying out the duties"—indeed, his capabilities have been well demonstrated—is appointed to succeed the father without further comment (Lenôtre, 1929).

That Sanson would be immune from the virulent politics of his day—the only Parisian who could answer "the argument of the guillotine"—was not obvious at the outset. In December 1789, he was denounced by republican journalists, who reported that a royalist press was operating in the house of the executioner. Camille Desmoulins, one of the accusers, mischievously called Sanson a *bourreau,* a derogatory term connoting brutishness, whose use was banned by royal decree at Sanson's request. "I call a cat a cat, and Sanson the *bourreau,*" Desmoulins (1790) taunted. How much truth was in the charge of royalism is unknown, but, in any case, Sanson successfully sued for libel and extracted a public retraction (Lenôtre, 1929). (He would renew his acquaintance with Desmoulins on the scaffold when luck ran out for the Dantonistes; there is no mention of recusal due to conflict of interest.)

The failed attempt to discredit Sanson is to be viewed in light of the heady legislative activity that brought scrutiny to the office of the public executioner that winter. On December 1, 1789, Doctor Guillotin reintroduced his egalitarian and humane revisions of the penal code, which, if adopted, would transform Sanson's job. Guillotin's egalitarian principle, that like crimes be punished alike, without regard to rank or estate, was approved at once. Other provisions that protected the families of criminals from dishonor, eliminated confiscation of the property of the condemned, and returned the body to the family for burial were intensely debated and adopted the following month. The provision that called for decapitation in all capital crimes, and by means of "a simple mechanism," met with less success (Lenôtre, 1929, p. 14). Argued one doubting representative, "Rather than elevate the masses to the dignity of the block, we should reduce the nobility to the modesty of the gibbet" (Arasse, 1989, p. 14). Guillotin oversold his innovation in a breathless speech—"The mechanism falls like a thunderbolt, the head flies off, the blood spurts forth, the victim is no more"— and was met by laughter in the Assembly (Arasse, 1989, p. 17). The press lampooned Guillotin's enthusiasm but nonetheless was favorably disposed toward his idea.

Then, in late December 1789, a lingering question about the Assembly's Declaration of the Rights of Man and Citizen was debated: Were even Jews and Protestants to count as citizens? Could they vote, stand for election to the Assembly, participate in the Communes? Debate spread to other customary outcasts, the profession of actor and—now that a humane penal code was in the air—the profession of executioner. The citizen-aristocrat the comte de Clermont-Tonnerre argued for the rehabilitation of the executioner:

> Professions are either harmful or not. Those that are constitute a habitual infraction that the law should prohibit. Where they are not, the law must be consistent with justice, on which it is based. . . . We have simply to overcome a prejudice. . . . Whatever the law requires is good. It requires the death of a criminal. The executioner simply obeys the law. It is absurd that the law should say to a man: do that, and if you do it, you will be abhorrent to your fellow men [Arasse, 1989, p. 120].[9]

The abbé Maury disagreed: "The exclusion of public executioners is not founded on a mere prejudice. It is in the heart of all good men to shudder at the sight of one who assassinates his fellow man in cold blood. The law requires this deed, it is said, but does the law command anyone to become a hangman?" (Arasse, 1989, p. 120).

The Assembly settled the matter with a broad but oblique proclamation on December 24: "The eligibility of any citizen cannot be combated on any grounds for exclusion but those which arise from constitutional decrees" (Lenôtre, 1929, p. 219). Because executioners had never been legally excluded, they were, by implication, entitled to full citizenship.

Sanson, smarting from charges of royalism in the printing press affair, wanted a more explicit affirmation. He engaged a lawyer to lobby the Assembly with a petition on behalf of his profession. Worth quoting at some length, this extraordinary claim of civil rights for an ordinary civil servant is a marvelous tour through the republican sensibility—reason, triumphing over prejudice, will recognize the delicate virtues of an honorable profession:

> The words that are about to be read . . . express the just complaints of a body of men whom a blind prejudice has marked with the seal of infamy, and whose life is a perpetual endurance of humiliations, shame, and opprobrium—offences which in themselves demand suppression; they tell the grievances of men who are unfortunately indispensable, and who now, before the fathers of their country, bewail the injustice of their fellow-citizens and claim the imprescriptible rights that are derived from nature and the law. . . .

There is no question—whatever may be said to the contrary by an *obscure journalist,* who makes a habit of calumniating the members of the National Assembly, and its decrees, and the public—of deciding whether the Executioners of Criminal Judgments shall take their seats beside the mayors, or shall fill the places of the generals in command of National Guards in the different towns of the kingdom: irony dishonours the person who employs it, when his business is to discuss the status of a citizen and to combat the prejudice that disgraces him unjustly; but the questions to be decided are whether executioners be eligible for places in the Communes, whether they have consultative or deliberative votes in assemblies; and in short whether they have any status as citizens. That the question should be answered in the affirmative can only be a matter of doubt in those feeble minds whose judgment is subservient to the tyrannical empire of prejudices.

Executioners practise their profession *by right of office;* they hold it directly from the King; their commissions are sealed with the Great Seal; and, like those of officers, are only to be obtained on *a good and laudable report* of the individuals receiving them. . . .

There is certainly nothing to be found, differing from other offices, in the commissions of executioners; and in the formalities that precede their acceptance there is nothing to be found that dishonours them, or proves a lack of delicate feeling on their part [Lenôtre, 1929, pp. 220–222].[10]

Once the prejudice against executioners dies out, the appeal continues, "society would no longer be deprived of their enlightenment, their patriotism, and the example of their virtues" (Lenôtre, 1929, pp. 222–223).

Sanson requested an explicit declaration of citizenship for these honorable, enlightened, and virtuous professionals of delicate feeling; ever sensitive to his dignity, he also wanted reaffirmation of the royal decree banning the use of the term *bourreau.* What began after the summer lynchings as a pamphleteer's farce had become, by January 1790, a serious argument. Indeed, philosophy was making Sanson's calling into a glorious profession.

The executioner's argument did not convince the ironists, of course. Marat, whose incendiary journalism would later divert even more of Sanson's business to the *lanternes,* took a parting shot:

We cannot resist our desire to call the attention of our readers to a masterpiece of *sensibility,* taste, and learning. . . . The prejudice that dooms executioners to infamy is absolutely demolished in this Memorial, which cannot be read without *emotion;* and the National Assembly, to whom it is addressed, cannot fail to give a good reception to demands that have for their foundation the imprescriptible rights of man, and reason, and philosophy [Lenôtre, 1929, p. 226].

The Assembly, for its part, simply allowed its previous decrees on citizenship to stand.

With the press plot quashed and his full citizenship established, the executioner did not have his political impartiality publicly questioned again. From then on, Sanson projects the sensibility and self-image of a professional civil servant. He gives expert opinions about new technologies, takes care to clarify instructions with his superiors, and frets with increasing intensity about his budget as the demands of his office increased.

Having settled on decapitation as the method of execution for all, the National Assembly asked Sanson for his professional opinion about the need for a "simple mechanism." Sanson is insightful as only an expert can be. Freestyle beheading requires not only a skilled headsman, but a courageous victim. He worries that democratic citizens may not have the bearing that could be counted on in aristocrats, so if beheading is to be democratized, some mechanical standardization is advisable:

> For the execution to arrive at the result prescribed by the law, the executioner must, with no impediment on the part of the condemned man, be very skilful, and the condemned man very steadfast. . . .
> . . . How can one deal with a man who cannot or will not hold himself up? With regard to these humane considerations, I am bound to issue a warning as to the accidents that will occur if this execution is to be performed with the sword. It would, I think, be too late to remedy these accidents if they were known only from bitter experience. It is therefore indispensable, if the humane views of the National Assembly are to be fulfilled, to find some means by which the condemned man can be secured so that the issue of the execution cannot be in doubt, and in this way to avoid delay and uncertainty [Arasse, 1989, pp. 184–185].

Sanson was summoned to use the new machine on his former king and employer in January 1793. Much apocrypha has grown around this ironic reversal, but the reliable historical record reveals but two clues about Citizen Sanson's deportment. The day before the execution, he asks for clarification about his duties with bureaucratic precision and formality that betray neither emotion nor recognition of the transformative importance of the deed he is to perform the next morning:

> CITIZEN,
> I have just received the orders you sent me. I will adopt all the measures necessary to prevent any delay in carrying them out. The carpenter has been informed of the position required for the machine, which will be set up at the spot indicated.
> It is absolutely necessary that I should know how Louis will leave the temple. Will he have a carriage, or will it be in the vehicle ordinarily used for executions of this kind? After the execution, what will become of the dead man's body?
> Is it I or my assistants who must be at the temple at eight o'clock, as is stated on the order?
> In the case of it's not being myself who must bring him from the temple, what is the place and the exact point at which I am to be?
> Since all these things are not mentioned in the order it would be well if the citizen acting for the *procureur-syndic* [sic] of the department would supply me

as quickly as possible with this information, while I am engaged in giving all the orders necessary to ensure that everything shall be punctually carried out. . . .

Citizen SANSON,
                    Executioner of Criminal Sentences [Lenôtre, 1929, p. 226][11]

After the execution, a jubilant crowd is reported to have scrambled for scraps of cloth dipped in the king's blood and other souvenirs of regicide (Lenôtre, 1929). In a notice to the newspapers, Sanson huffily defends the propriety of his office against hopeful gossip that he could provide such mementos:

> I have this moment learnt that there is a rumour abroad to the effect that I am selling Louis Capet's hair, or causing it to be sold. If any of it has been sold, the infamous trade can only have been carried on by knaves: the truth is that I did not allow anyone connected with me to take away or appropriate the smallest vestige of it [Lenôtre, 1929, p. 106].

Sanson will neither hint at any sympathy for his victim nor pander to the patriotic zeal of the mob: he fulfills the duties of his position with utter professional detachment.

But not without complaint. Our anonymous satirist's charge about lost *écus* notwithstanding, the executioner had not been paid on a per capita basis. Until Turgot's tax reforms of 1775, he was supported through the right of *havage,* a toll on the city's merchants. In the last years of the *ancien régime,* he received a fixed sum plus expenses. The Revolution eliminated reimbursement for most variable expenses (Lenôtre, 1929). As the case load picked up, Sanson complained with increasing bitterness to his superiors that he was being driven into personal ruin.

Early on, he thought the logic of a simple accounting would move the authorities. Here are some of his expenses, detailed in a letter to the National Assembly in June 1790:

Expenses of the Executioner
Two of his brothers to whom he gives 600 *livres* each, to answer the magistrates and give orders to the servants when there are executions to be carried out at several places on the same day: 1,200

The building of three carriages and a tumbril: 300

For the rent of a house large enough for his family, his servants, his horses, carriages, and the utensils necessary to his position, the said house being situated so that he is able to carry out orders promptly: 4,800

Incidental Expenses
The expenses on the days when there are executions.

The utensils to be used at executions, which have to be constantly renewed.

If the executioner were expected to put the torture, or to act as carpenter, the following expenses would result from the work:

. For putting the torture, one extra servant [Lenôtre, 1929, pp. 96–98].

A year later, his financial situation worsening, he writes the public prosecutor:

The method of execution that is practised to-day is at least three times as expensive as the old method, over and above the increase in cost of all the necessaries of life.

The service of the numerous criminal tribunals forces me to employ a number of persons capable of fulfilling the orders I receive. Since I cannot personally be everywhere at once I must have people that I can depend upon. For the public still demands decency. It is I who pay for that. . . .

. . . I can only have recourse to yourself, Monsieur, to give orders that I may be paid the money due to me, otherwise it seems that the sacrifices I have made up to the present time, in order that the duties of my office might be correctly performed, will result in the total wreck of my life in this place and my inevitable ruin, by forcing me to abandon my post and my family after twenty-four years of such employment [Lenôtre, 1929, pp. 99–100].

Finally, in April 1794, at the height of the Terror, he writes an extraordinarily revealing letter to the minister of justice:

Neither the executioner of Paris, nor those in any part of the Republic, are expected to supply their own equipment, and the law is so clear and has so plainly intended to give them no expense that it enjoins upon the Government to pay their assistants.

The executioner in Paris, who is supplied with four assistants, employs seven, and has not too many of them in the present circumstances, in view of the immense amount of unremitting work that is laid upon him and his assistants. Day and night on their feet, whatever the weather may be, and not a single day of rest—work that might well disable the most robust! Is it possible for a man to live on 1,000 francs, especially in these days?

The executioner gives his four chief assistants 1,800 francs and lodging, which things they insist upon having; otherwise he would secure no one at all. Their duties must be taken into consideration, as well as the expenses in upkeep caused by their work; and it must be remembered that nothing but the desire of gain induces anyone to adopt this calling. . . .

. . . This post is supposed to be worth 17,000 *livres*—but when the cost of his assistants has been deducted, as well as all the different and numerous expenses that he pays out of his own pocket, it will be seen that he is very unlucky to have such a post. And indeed the executioner cares little for the post. He has fulfilled its duties for forty-three years. The overwhelming work that it entails makes him wish to bring his services to an end. . . .

. . . If it be found possible to get the work done more cheaply, that another man shall be entrusted with it, since he cannot undertake it any longer, and can do nothing but give it all up if he be not reimbursed, and if he fail to obtain justice [Lenôtre, 1929, pp. 124–126].

Sanson is not resigning, mind you—just demanding of the minister of justice a budget increase. This, just days after chopping off the head of a former minister of justice. Danton quipped on the scaffold to his quondam subordinate, "But do not forget, do not forget to show my head to the people: it is worth seeing" (Arasse, 1989, p. 113). The king, we see, was not Sanson's only bossicide, and this could not have been lost on his current boss. At the depths of the Revolutionary spiral of political paranoia, Sanson shows no fear that he himself may be the target of Revolutionary unmasking. Rather, he conveys a strong sense of injustice at being overworked and underpaid—somewhat like a physician newly subjected to cost-containment measures complaining that the terms of the profession have been unilaterally changed. What he does not show is a hint of revulsion at the carnage, a question about its evil, or a doubt about the political legitimacy of whatever faction has gained control of the machinery of justice that supplies his machine. With Mercier, we too wonder, what goes on in that head of his?

Something must go on in that head of his, because Sanson is forced to explain himself. The Terror was unmistakably both public and political, and was intended to be so. The scaffold was theater, the dripping head held aloft the main prop, and the Terrorists did not seek to hide the performance. Euphemistic distance was not possible for Sanson, who was wet with his deeds. We may conclude that his arguments, and the best arguments that can be made for him, are tendentious, but he cannot be oblivious to the need for justification.

What, then, is the best case that can be made in defense of Sanson and his role? In the tradition, until this moment disreputable, of penning fictional memoirs in his name, we take up his cause. Perhaps philosophy will succeed in making his profession a glorious one:

CIRCA 1799

LOUIS-SÉBASTIEN MERCIER: Ah, Monsieur Sanson. Taking in the theater, I see. Coming and going, just like everyone else. I hope you don't find my forwardness rude, but I have always wondered: what goes on in that head of yours?

CHARLES-HENRI SANSON: My, you look familiar . . . Of course! Mercier the writer. One of the fortunate ones. Too bad about Desmoulins, no? I am so relieved that the past is past. Naturally, it was not to my liking, but we cannot always choose our professional assignments.

I take it that you are wondering how I can detach people's heads for a living? I will tell you. It is my profession. The role of the Paris executioner has been handed down, father to son, from my grandfather's father to me, and will be passed on to my grandson. It is not, strictly speaking, a hereditary position, but one into which each successive generation has been initiated and that each has adopted as its vocation.

There are families with a tradition of doctoring, families with a tradition of soldiering, families that have handed down cheese making and wine making and all manners of art and trade. We are a family of professional executioners: that is what we do, and each generation seeks to do it better. It is our calling.

MERCIER: A professional calling! I suppose you are a professional in the loose way that "professional" can mean anything done for pay, so that there are professional beggars and gamblers. And nasty ways of earning a living may run in families, from thievery to tyranny. But to justify your horrible work, you must mean by "profession" and "tradition" more than a mere description of customary employment. You must make a moral claim: that the role of executioner is justified because executioners are committed to some ideal that is an interpretation of a valuable tradition of professional practice. But where are the ideals? What is valuable about your bloodstained lineage? You are simply hired killers! Madame Roland was right about you: "He does his job and he earns his money" [Levy, 1973].

SANSON: This charge of avarice is unseemly and unfair. Yes, I expect to get paid for what I do, and yes, I expect that the expenses I incur in my work will be reimbursed. But that does not distinguish the executioner from the lawyer or the physician, and I take it you do not deny that law and medicine are professions. I am much less a hired blade than the surgeon or lawyer. Money never enters into any decision of *mine* about whom to serve and how to provide service. Indeed, I have incurred large out-of-pocket losses because I refuse to compromise on quality. The Ministry of Justice may have been negligent in paying my expenses, but I would not work with a dull blade or stained baskets—that would have been unprofessional.

I agree that if a claim of professionalism is to have any moral force it has to refer to ideals and commitments, and that a claim of tradition must involve more than mere habit. But the role of executioner meets both requirements. We take great pride in our craft and hold ourselves to the highest ethical and technical standards that apply to our work. We have learned from our predecessors and teach our apprentices to value excellence in the practice, which reflectively adapts to both new technologies and new political sensibilities. I realize that from the outside you cannot always appreciate our commitments, so we must appear rather ghoulish, but that is either ignorance or prejudice on your part. I have come to expect such reactions: you know, one of the marks of a true profession is that excellent practice can only be judged by fellow practitioners. You are not an expert judge of a court opinion or of a surgical procedure; why do you think that you can appreciate the niceties of the executioner's craft? For example, you may have thought from his scream that it was cruel to rip Robespierre's bandage from his shattered jaw, but I assure you it was a mercy—the consequences of an obstructed blade are far worse than the moment of pain he suffered. To carry out the judgments of law with dependable precision, the executioner worries about dozens of similar details that are designed to treat the condemned, the spectators, and the law with precisely the respect that each is owed, in light of the circumstances. Another example: in the days when violent criminals were broken at the wheel, the judges in their wisdom would direct us in cases meriting leniency to secretly strangle the victim after the first blows. A deft maneuver, which even the judges did not fully appreciate: to give to the crowd the edifying spectacle that they wanted and, more to the point, needed, but also to spare the victim unnecessary pain. If the punishment is to fit the crime, we are the tailors. How to transport the victim to the scaffold? How and when to bind and shear? How much time to allow for leave-taking and last words? Who is to be handled roughly? Firmly? Gently? In short, how, in my stagecraft, to satisfy the competing demands of impartiality and particularity? I trust that Madame Roland, in the end, revised her disparaging opinion of me. I was foil to her much-noted grace and dignity on the tumbril and scaffold, and I even granted her brave and compassionate request to go after the trembling Simon François Lamarche, contrary to the standing rule of women first. But I neither expect you to understand my commitments nor to share them. You are not an executioner.

MERCIER: No doubt you possess a horrible expertise of sorts, and as a one-time torturer you must have exquisite sensitivity to pain and suffering. Those who call you brutal are mistaken: you are cruel, which requires thoughtfulness. But I fail to see why the employment of expert cruelty is a virtue. Yes, on occasion you employ your expertise to relieve indignity and suffering, but on other occasions you do the opposite—slapping Charlotte Corday's cheek.

SANSON: The assistant who pandered to the mob by insulting the head of Marat's assassin acted unprofessionally. He was severely reprimanded.

MERCIER: And always, you are methodically killing another human being. You will answer that I cannot understand because I am not one of you. But you cannot expect that your appeal to inaccessible knowledge will persuade me. How else can I evaluate your claims, except on grounds that we can share?

SANSON: You have not yet convinced me that my reasons must be reasons for you too, but for now I will grant your premise and, as I did before the National Assembly, appeal to Reason. Since I see that I will not succeed, just yet, in showing you that the profession of executioner is rich with its own goods and virtues, I will start from the outside, so to speak, and show why my role is a socially useful and necessary one. A just society requires laws and their enforcement, including criminal laws and punishments. Punishments are not self-inflicting—someone must impose them. A just society also requires that the enforcement of laws not be arbitrary or capricious. People may disagree about whether criminal judgments are just, including the executioner called upon to carry them out. These disagreements may be about the justice of the outcome in a particular case, about the justice of a proceeding, about the justice of a law, or about the justice of a form of punishment. But if law is to rule, the executioner must obey a division of labor between his office and the office of the tribunal. To allow personal views about the sentences I execute to interfere with my duty is to substitute arbitrariness for the rule of law. Whatever you think of my character for having chosen this work, whether or not you cringe at the prospect of shaking my hand, you must grant that I do not act unjustly.

MERCIER: Was it not unjust to mutilate human beings with hot pincers and burning sulphur? To apply bone-mangling tortures to extract confessions? To behead the political scapegoats of a tyrant? And was it not unjust to slaughter a few thousand Parisians convicted of imaginary offenses in sham proceedings?

SANSON: The best way to untangle the thicket of charges you make against me is to distinguish the several phases of my career. As you note, I have been torturer and headsman for a now despised monarchy and the instrument of summary justice for a now despised Revolutionary government. But I have also applied the death penalty in the most humane way that we know in ordinary criminal cases tried fairly under the laws of a democratically elected republic. Permit me to begin with this easiest case, and then perhaps I will be able to persuade you of the harder ones.

Recall the comte de Clermont-Tonnerre's eloquent defense of my rights as a citizen: whatever the law requires is good. The law requires the death of a criminal. By putting the criminal to death, the executioner simply obeys a good law. How can that make him bad? The penal code that established death by decapitation was enacted by a democratically elected legislature, and so has the force of law. The court that imposed this penalty on the violent robber Pelletier, the guillotine's first victim, rendered an impartial and fair reading of that law. How, then, can there be any moral stain on my hands and character for executing the judgment of the court? Would that not be unreasoned prejudice?

MERCIER: But Clermont-Tonnerre's argument is mistaken at almost every step. Whatever the law requires is not necessarily good, for even democratic lawmakers can enact horribly bad and unjust laws. The death penalty is arguably an example of an unjust law.[12] And even if the punishment is not unjust to its victim, to use one's hands to kill another human being is immoral. The abbé Maury was right: the law may require executions, but the law does not require anyone to be an executioner. What sort of man chooses such a gruesome trade?

SANSON: As for the first step, I concede that laws may be bad or unjust. If the revolutionary idea of *Vox populi, vox Dei* is taken to mean that democracy is by definition infallible, the idea is patently false. But the National Assembly did not err in maintaining the death penalty: to kill those who kill is both just retribution and necessary deterrence.

But what if one believes that the death penalty is not just? After all, the Milanese reformer Cesare Beccaria urged its abolition, and our great Voltaire, much to my dismay, agreed [Beccaria, 1986; Voltaire, 1777]. Marie Antoinette's brother, the Habsburg emperor Leopold, followed Beccaria's advice in Tuscany (and put some honest men out of work). One of the great ironies of the Assembly debates over the penal code is that Robespierre himself argued for an end to the practice. Still, one would need to acknowledge that enlightened philosophers and statesmen of our time have taken both sides. Our own legislature, of course, saw fit to retain the death penalty, and this German fellow Kant [1991] has recently written that, were a society to disband, justice would demand that it first execute its condemned prisoners. So there is considerable disagreement among democratic lawmakers and lovers of liberty about the justice of capital punishment. Am I then to appoint myself tyrant and substitute my own view about what the law should be for the view of the people? No. Let us revise Clermont-Tonnerre's first step: though whatever the law requires is not necessarily good or just, at least when there is reasonable disagreement about what is good or just, what the law requires is The Law. So interpreted, *Vox populi, vox Dei* is true: the decrees of the National Assembly, and the judgments of courts in accordance with those decrees, have legitimate authority.

Before the Revolution, you argued that magistrates should be lenient in imposing the death penalty. I have no objection, so long as they exercise no more discretion than allowed them by law. But the law allows no discretion for those of us who enforce the judgments of those magistrates. Even impartial judges under good and just laws can mistakenly render bad or unjust judgments. Are you suggesting that the jailer refuse to take custody of a mistakenly convicted prisoner? That the officer of the court refuse to enforce payment when the judge has erred in deciding a lawsuit? Surely not. What is the difference if the error has occurred at the point of legislation, rather than judgment? Either way, does the legitimate authority of the state not morally bind me to carry out its sentences?

As for the abbé Maury's view that, though I carry out the law, I am abhorrent because I have chosen to do so, it is a deeply confused position. True, the law does not prohibit all immoral behavior, so claiming an action is legal is not enough to show that it is moral. Those disreputable actresses in the Palais-Royal deserve their reputation. But the profession of executioner is not simply permitted by law; the law requires of the government that the tasks of the executioner be performed. It is incoherent to desire that capital punishment be executed and condemn the executioner.

MERCIER: Have you not desired those disreputable actresses, Monsieur de Paris?

SANSON: Touché. I was too quick to disparage my sister-citizens of the stage. Though I may consistently want them to be free of legal restriction and still condemn them, I cannot approve of my patronage but disapprove of their performance.

MERCIER: But why not? You, after all, are not putting on an immodest spectacle, you are merely enjoying those who do. You are not devoting a life to the frivolity of the theater, merely an evening. (As a playwright, I am far more vulnerable on this score than you!) So, too, citizens may with consistency applaud your performance on the scaffold, but damn *you* for what you have done with your hands, and abhor *you* for building a career out of the bones of your victims.

SANSON: Consistency? It strikes me as irrational prejudice. I act for the people in every sense of the word: in their name, for their benefit, and upon their direction. My actions are their actions. Every time I cut off a head, every citizen—or at least every citizen who approves of the death penalty—does so as well. If they are blameless, so am I. If I am blameworthy, so are they.

MERCIER: If I must choose, I choose the latter: the people share in your evil. If the abbé Maury is mistaken, it is not because the comte de Clermont-Tonnerre is correct, but because Diderot is. You left the great encyclopedist off your list of worthies who oppose the death penalty, perhaps because his reasoning is so damaging to your case. Remember what he thought of your profession: "The odious name of hangman is now, as it was in other days, a stigma upon the man who bears it, and so it will be as long as it denotes one who publicly strangles another man, or breaks him on the wheel. This fact is not now founded on public opinion, but on the overwhelming force of the instinct that abhors every murderer except the man who murders in self-defense; which proves incidentally that the death-penalty is contrary to nature and beyond the jurisdiction of society" [Lenôtre, 1929, p. 209].

Diderot does not argue that the death penalty treats the criminal unjustly (though it might). Rather, he argues that the wrongness of capital punishment follows "incidentally" from something else: the death penalty turns men into killers, and killers are abhorrent. Because, Monsieur Sanson, you are made morally odious by your profession, we may not ask you to practice it on our behalf. The act of execution is wrong, even if the consequence—dead criminals—is good. If Diderot is correct, your attempts to justify your work from the outside, by appeal to the social utility of what you do, are to no avail. Even if we grant your usefulness, and even if we grant that the criminal can claim no right to be spared, killing is odious *from the inside* (to use your terms), so we may not ask you to kill for us.

SANSON: I see now why you are called Diderot's ape, Monsieur Mercier. *Unjustified* killing is odious, I agree. But even your idol Diderot grants that killing in self-defense is justified, and so, the hands of one who so kills are *not* morally tainted. You and Diderot need to show why the killing of a criminal, if such a killing is both justly retributive and socially useful, is nonetheless unjustified. Do you consider abhorrent the courageous soldiers who defend the Nation against our enemies from without?[13] Of course not. Well, I defend the Nation against enemies from within. You cannot sustain the view you attribute to Diderot. If killing is always immoral, then killing in self-defense or war is also immoral. Pacifism is a consistent doctrine, but you are no pacifist. If killing in self-defense or in a just war is justified, you need to show why the death penalty is not justified. You cannot argue from some essential odiousness of the act, for you concede that the act is not always odious.

MERCIER: Monsieur Sanson, such concessions do not help you very much. Let us not forget that we have spoken of the easiest case only, where the death penalty is enacted by a democratic legislature and imposed by fair courts. Even if I grant that conditions can be stipulated under which your profession is not monstrous, those conditions held for a year or so at best during the constitutional monarchy and the first few months of the Republic. Enough of easy cases. One cannot forget that before the Revolution you were the instrument of a tyrannical monarchy. Despite the efforts of judicial reformers like Montesquieu and Malesherbes, the state and its various tribunals were often arbitrary in the administration of punishment. And until Louis XVI abolished the *question extraordinaire,* you and your assistants extracted confessions through grotesquely inhumane methods.

In some other time or place, one of your calling might have invoked loyalty to the king in defense. But such a claim in your case is preposterous, since you beheaded your king. You then promiscuously lent your services to every Revolutionary faction that held sway in Paris, mechanically carrying out the purges of each against its predecessors—and then had the effrontery to officiate throughout the Counter-Terror. If the king's justice was often rough, the Terror's justice was perverse: you murdered a few thousand innocents under changing cloaks of legality.

Obedience is no excuse for immorality, but you cannot even claim to have been obedient. You cannot hide behind authority when you show no allegiance to authority. At least that wretched public prosecutor, Fouquier-Tinville, was a loyal Jacobin. We reject his defense, *"Je suis la hache! On ne punit pas la hache!"* not because we deny that he indeed was the tool of others, but because following orders does not absolve an actor of moral responsibility. But whose tool are you? Better you should say, "I am the whore! One does not punish the whore!"

SANSON: Please, Monsieur Mercier, some civility. Have you forgotten that I too have all the rights of an active citizen? The axe defense is not one I claim. You have recently wondered about me, "What an instrument—what a man!" But that question misunderstands me in two ways. On the job, I am neither an instrument nor a man. Let me explain.

I am not a mere instrument, if by that you mean one who takes no responsibility for what his superiors demand of him. Indeed, I roundly reject any simple appeal to authority to justify my career, if such an appeal takes the form of "One must follow orders; I was ordered to kill; therefore, I must kill." I am not an instrument devoid of mind or conscience, but a *professional.* Professions are committed to the realization of important values. My profession is the guardian of a political value that is of utmost moral importance. Although the good sought by my profession is valuable for all of society and capable of being recognized as valuable by all subjects and citizens, this good cannot be pursued except from within my professional role or roles like it. To this good I have dedicated my life, and my practice as executioner has aimed at it through all the changing regimes to which you accuse me of whoring. My devotion is not to any one regime or political ideology, but to the good of *social order* and the stability and security it brings. By stability, I do not mean the stability of any regime or form of government, but of civilized life itself; and by security, I mean security from the random horror of murderous mobs. To realize the good of social order, my profession is committed to a simple principle: the state must maintain its monopoly over violence.

Danton understood this principle quite well, and was compelled by its necessity. Now remembered most for his heroic efforts to stop the Terror, as minister of justice and founder of the Committee on Public Safety he had as big a hand in starting the bloodletting as anyone. Recall his argument for the establishment of the Revolutionary Tribunal: "Let us be terrible so that the people will not have to be" [Schama, 1989, p. 707]. If the National Convention was to control the retributive violence of the mobs and the neighborhoods, it would have to use organized violence to do so. So those who condemn me for my *sang-froid* should consider the alternative: hot-blooded and hot-headed vigilante justice. It is not I who fret about losing business to the *lanternes;* all who fear murderous disorder do, or ought to. Desmoulins punned that I was *"le représentant du pouvoir exécutif,"* the representative of the executive power [Desmoulins, 1790, p. 389]. Though he meant this to be yet another joke at my expense, he spoke an important truth. In a time of great unrest and danger, my steadfastness on the scaffold projected to the people that there was always a government, and that it was in control. So, what you see as a life of murderous prostitution, I see as a life spent preserving order. As long as the people could depend on me to work my machine, Paris would continue to trust that the machinery of social organization, at the deepest level, would not break down. Were there serious failures of justice in the *ancien régime?* Of course. Was the Terror a perversion of justice? Of course. But basic social order, though less inspiring, is a precondition for justice. I have been the humble guardian of order all these years.

MERCIER: So you are actually a reactionary authoritarian, like that Savoyard exile we have been hearing about, Joseph de Maistre? He is said to think that the horror of you holds up the world![14]

SANSON: You seriously misunderstand me. The profession, as I have described it, takes no stand about the Revolution and its legitimacy. Nothing that I have said supports any particular form of government, but government simply. We fear social disintegration and the murderous fear it produces. I have heard that Maistre has likened my powers of retribution to God's. If I have heard rightly, this is both obscurantist poppycock and simplistic social science. My profession sustains order neither by acting as an agent of divine retribution nor by repressing crime through the fear of temporal punishment. If these were the primary purposes of our work, we would not be justified in enforcing sentences against the innocent. We serve order, not by deterring lawlessness through threat, but more subtly, by deterring the lawless punishment of lawlessness through trust.

MERCIER: You would massacre innocents in the name of order?

SANSON: In my official capacity, I would execute innocents condemned to death by a judicial process authorized by the existing regime, so long as the practice of execution contributed to the maintenance of the rudiments of social order. If it came to pass that the regime I served was incapable of preventing chaos, or that the practice of execution within such a regime made widespread social disorder more, rather than less, likely, then the continued practice of execution under such conditions would fail to provide the good to which it is committed. My work would no longer be justified, and conscience would force me to step down from the scaffold. But such invalidating conditions did not hold in the *ancien régime*. One could imagine the Terror progressing to the point where the machinery of state execution itself became destabilizing, but revolutionary politics reversed its disastrous course on the ninth of *Thermidor*. All of Paris (but the Robespierristes) were thankful that I was in place on the tenth to administer order-preserving justice. To be clear: I was not needed to kill Robespierre—any number of vengeful citizens were prepared to do that—but only I could *execute* him. So you see, I am a professional who mindfully practices his calling so long as such practice is valuable. I am no blind obedient or mere instrument.

MERCIER: And dare I ask how you are not a man?

SANSON: I knew that you would not let that pass. My detractors have attributed inhuman qualities to me, but I mean something else, of course. (Anyone who doubts my capacity for human feeling need only recall my tears on that sorrowful day when my youngest son fell to his death from the scaffold.) What I mean by saying that on the job I am not a man is that I do not act as a man simply. In exercising my professional duties I must set aside personal considerations. I naturally have views, held at varying degrees of certainty, about the guilt or innocence of my victims. I may personally admire or loathe those who come before me. I have my own views about the politics of the day. These are the views of Charles-Henri, man and citizen. But the executioner must set aside the reasons of Charles-Henri, for it is not Charles-Henri acting on the scaffold, but the Executioner of Criminal Sentences of Paris.

I do not mean simply that the executioner *may* not take personal considerations into account, but that the executioner *cannot,* and still be the executioner. Charles-Henri can commit murder, can massacre, as you put it. But only the executioner can perform an *execution.* The act of execution that the executioner performs on the scaffold does not exist apart from his professional role—it is constituted by it. You would not describe what a surgeon does as stabbing, what a lawyer does as robbing, or what a prosecutor does as kidnapping, would you?

MERCIER: No, not when acting as proper surgeons, lawyers, or prosecutors. But they are capable of failing to act properly, and then they may become villains. I don't doubt that when you act as a proper executioner what you do is described as execution. But you are also capable of employing your expertise and the trappings of your office to murder, just as a surgeon is capable of murder. That is precisely what you did in the Terror.

SANSON: Though I agree that it is possible for one with the name of a professional to violate the criteria that confer upon an action the description constituted by the professional practice, those criteria are *professional* criteria. *Medical* judgment distinguishes surgery from butchery. *Carnificial* judgment distinguishes executions from murder. I am tempted to say that only physicians are capable of exercising medical judgment, and likewise executioners, but I will refrain—I don't need to go that far to make my point. All that I need to establish is that, on the scaffold, to be a good executioner, I must employ the reasons of the Executioner of Criminal Judgments, not of Charles-Henri. And I have already explained that for good executioners, preserving the state's monopoly over violence is reason enough.

MERCIER: Did you think your sleight of tongue about the senses of "good" would slip past me? Why should a person be a "good" professional if "good" professionals commit horribly bad acts? One should be *morally* good, a good man, Charles-Henri. If a good professional must be a bad man, then it is immoral to be a good professional. Why on earth should a man ignore moral reasons that run against professional ones?

SANSON: I do not deny the possibility of a bad professional role that is not worthy of anyone's commitment. But that is a judgment made about the role itself, not particular actions the role requires. I have already explained to you why I believe that the role of executioner is worthy of a person's commitment, and you half-believe it yourself. Having made such a commitment to the role, I cannot then reject the reasons for action the role provides. Only if the overall justification fails is any particular performance no longer an "execution," but a murder. As I said, I am not an instrument. I must judge my role. But the judgment is of a life in a role, not the particular acts the role requires me to perform.

MERCIER: Why should you decide at that level of generality, if you could avoid doing evil by judging the goodness of particular acts?

SANSON: Because in acting on my personal judgments, I step out of my professional role. But only within my role can my actions be described as state execution. You ask me to cease to be the Executioner of Criminal Judgments and become Charles-Henri the serial murderer.

MERCIER: I'm baffled. No one is suggesting that personal morality demands that you kill in cases where the professional role forbids killing, but that personal morality sometimes forbids you from killing in cases where the professional role demands it!

SANSON: Ah, but think of how deciding to refuse a professional assignment transforms the assignments I do *not* refuse. If Charles-Henri may sometimes decide *not* to kill, then when he does perform an execution, Charles-Henri has decided *to* kill. For what reason? Not that it is the executioner's professional duty, for you would have professional duty defer to personal judgment. The reason must be that Charles-Henri personally believes the condemned deserves to die. But for his personal judgment, the prisoner would live (or at least not die by his hand). But who is Charles-Henri to decide who lives and who dies? The person who takes that upon himself is a private assassin, not a public executioner, and so necessarily undermines the good of social order.

When I said before that only an executioner can perform an execution, I was not quibbling about the definitions of words, but saying something important about the meaning of actions. Though all may hope that the good of order the executioner pursues is realized, and though there may be other practices in other positions that contribute to social order, only an executioner can pursue this good through violent means. For anyone other than the executioner to employ violence for the sake of reinforcing the state's monopoly over violence would be self-defeating. If I were to act on reasons that the role requires the executioner to ignore, I would cease to be the executioner. My performance would no longer be an act of the state. The purpose of my profession would be undermined, and I would become a murderous butcher. Therefore, Charles-Henri and his judgments must stay off the scaffold.

But all this talk after the theater has made me hungry. I know of a little place that serves the best Alsatian sausages in all of Paris. Will you dine with me? . . . You've turned green, my dear Louis-Sébastien. Are you a vegetarian?

The record breaks off here. Whether Mercier dined at the executioner's table is not known. Left on our table are a number of claims Sanson has made in defense of his professional role that deserve closer attention. We should attend, for Sanson's arguments do not look all that different from the arguments offered by lawyers, business executives, politicians, bureaucrats, journalists, and soldiers to justify their commitments to their professional roles when those roles ask them to act in ways that, if not for the role, would be wrong. If versions of these arguments do indeed justify the moral permissions to harm others that are claimed by these professions, why do they not work for Sanson? And if we are sure that they do not work for Sanson, should we not reconsider whether they work to justify less sanguinary professional roles?

Lawyers are not serial murderers, but Maistre's visitor from another planet might be forgiven if he described them as serial liars and thieves. He would observe that lawyers—good lawyers—repeatedly try to induce others to believe in the truth of propositions or in the validity of arguments that they themselves do not believe, and he would observe that lawyers—again, good lawyers—often devote their skills to advancing the unjust ends of rapacious clients. "Liar" and "thief," the good lawyer would retort, are either ignorant or malignant misdescriptions. But the arguments lawyers invoke to defend zealous advocacy echo all of the executioner's claims. Does "murderer" misdescribe Sanson?

Notes

1. This anonymous, satirical pamphlet (emphasis added) was published in reaction to the *lanterne* lynchings and the parading of heads on pikes that followed the storming of the Bastille in July 1789.

2. Several mentions in Simon Schama's cornucopian *Citizens: A Chronicle of the French Revolution* (1989) aroused my curiosity about Sanson. Schama generously responded to my request for further references.

3. See Lenôtre (1929). Lenôtre is a pseudonym for Louis Leon Théodore Gosselin.

4. See Arasse (1989). Though it often required exceptional cruelty, capital punishment did not demand much of the Paris executioner's time in the *ancien régime*. Diderot estimated that three hundred executions a year occurred in all of France (Kershaw, 1958). About 160 public executioners held commissions throughout France before the Revolution (Lenôtre, 1929). Out of a French population of about 25 million, some 600,000 lived in Paris (Mitchell, 1992). Even with generous allowances for the higher concentration of political cases tried in the capital, it is unlikely that Sanson inflicted the death penalty more than a couple of dozen times a year before the Revolution.

5. Mercier spent thirteen months in prison (Patterson, 1960).

6. *Machine Proposed to the National Assembly by Monsieur Guillotin for the Execution of Criminals,* Musée Carnavalet, Paris; reproduced in Arasse (1989, following p. 116).

7. *Execution of Louis XVI, King of France, 21 January 1793,* Musée Camavalet, Paris; reproduced in Arasse (1989, following p. 116).

8. Balzac had a hand in writing *Memoires pour servir à l'histoire de la Revolution française, par Sanson, exécuteur des arrêts criminels, pendant la Révolution* (1829). See Lenôtre (1929, p. 72).

9. Clermont-Tonnerre became one of the casualties of the August 10, 1792, massacre: he was shot and tossed from a window (Schama, 1989).

10. Sanson is debunking a legend that the commission of the executioner is thrown at his feet, symbolizing an untouchable status.

11. The *procureur-général-syndic* was the legal agent of the state—roughly the public prosecutor.

12. Mercier urged the sparing use of capital punishment but not outright abolition (Mercier, 1929).

13. Compare Joseph de Maistre (1971), who imagines asking a visitor from another planet to guess how the executioner and soldier are viewed on earth: "The one brings death to convicted and condemned criminals, and fortunately his executions are so rare that one of these ministers of death is sufficient for each province. As far as soldiers are concerned, there are never enough of them, because they kill without restraint and their victims are always honest men. Of these two professional killers, the soldier and the executioner, one is highly honored and always has been by all the nations who have inhabited up to now this planet to which you have come; but the other has just as generally been regarded as vile. Try to guess on which the obloquy falls" (p. 246).

14. "And yet all grandeur, all power, all subordination rests on the executioner: he is the horror and the bond of human association. Remove this incomprehensible agent from the world, and at that very moment order gives way to chaos, thrones topple, and society disappears. God, who is the author of sovereignty, is the author also of chastisement: he has built our world on these two poles" (Maistre, 1971, p. 192).

References

Arasse, D. *The Guillotine and the Terror* (C. Miller, trans.). London: Penguin Books, 1989.

Beccaria, C. *On Crimes and Punishments* (D. Young, ed. and trans.). Indianapolis: Hackett Publishing, 1986. (Originally published 1764.)

Desmoulins, C. *Révolutions de France et de Brabant.* c. Jan. 1790, no. 9.

Kant, I. *The Metaphysics of Morals.* (M. Gregor, trans.). Cambridge: Cambridge University Press, 1991. (Originally published 1797.)

Kershaw, A. *A History of the Guillotine.* London: John Calder, 1958.

Lenôtre, G. *The Guillotine and Its Servant* (Mrs. R. Stawell. trans.). London: Hutchinson, 1929. (Originally published 1893.)

Levy, B. *Legacy of Death.* Upper Saddle River, N.J.: Prentice-Hall, 1973.

de Maistre, J. *Les Soirées de Saint-Pétersbourg.* In J. Lively (trans.), *The Works of Joseph de Maistre.* New York: Schocken Books, 1971. (Originally published 1821.)

Mercier, L.-S. *The Picture of Paris Before and After the Revolution* (W. Jackson and E. Jackson, trans.). London: George Routledge and Sons, 1929.

Mitchell, B. R. *International Historical Statistics: Europe, 1750–1988.* New York: Stockton Press, 1992.

Patterson, H. T. *Poetic Genesis: Sébastien Mercier into Victor Hugo.* Geneva: Institut et musée Voltaire, 1960.

Schama, S. *Citizens: A Chronicle of the French Revolution.* New York: Random House, 1989.

Voltaire. *Commentaire sur le livre Des Delitis et des peines.* In C. Beccaria, *An Essay on Crimes and Punishments.* Charleston, S.C.: David Bruce, 1777. (Originally published 1766.)

CHAPTER TWENTY-TWO

The Professionalism and Accountability of Lawyers

Murray L. Schwartz

THE NONADVOCATE FUNCTIONS OF THE LAWYER

The task of finding principles of professional behavior and responsibility for the vast world outside the adversary system requires both a description of that world and an identification of those universal features within it that warrant the prescription of common principles. The description offered here takes the form of a typology of lawyers' functions which draws distinctions by reference to the adversary system. This reference is deliberate, since to the extent that lawyers' nonadvocate functions resemble those of the advocate, it may be reasonable to apply similar principles of professionalism and nonaccountability to both.

Typology of Nonadvocate Functions

The principal nonadvocate functions of the lawyer fall into three major categories: compelled negotiations, voluntary negotiations, and counseling.[1] Compelled negotiations may be further classified according to whether or not the agreement reached in the negotiations requires judicial approval.

Compelled Negotiations. Compelled negotiations are those in which either party can force the other to a third-party resolution. In other words, negotiations are compelled whenever the controversy is litigable if the parties fail to reach an agreement.

329

Compelled negotiations requiring judicial approval of the outcome would include plea bargains, settlements of the legal claims of minors, and settlements of class action suits. In negotiations of this type, the lawyer must play two roles. Prior to agreement, the role is similar to that of the advocate, in that the lawyer is to negotiate "zealously" on behalf of the client in opposition to the other party. In contrast to the adversary system, however, there is no tribunal before which the evidence and arguments are put for resolution of disagreements, nor is there a panoply of rules of professional behavior, although limited rules of process may govern such special procedures as mandatory pretrial settlement conferences.

Once the bargain has been reached, the functions change. There may be formal rules of process, and there is an impartial third party, the judge, to whom arguments and evidence are presented. At this point, the lawyers cease to be adversaries and take a common position in seeking the judge's approval of the bargain, in effect vouchsafing the fairness or correctness of the outcome.[2] The role of the lawyer has changed from that of "zealous" advocate for the client to that of advocate for the consensus.

Where the parties do not need judicial approval, the role of the lawyers is similar to that in the preagreement stage of negotiations which must be approved by a judge, with lawyers for both parties trying to maximize their clients' positions in the final resolution. The possibility of litigation if they fail to arrive at a settlement may force the lawyers to keep in mind the persuasiveness of their polar claims to a potential third-party arbiter, but by definition no tribunal sits to resolve disagreements between the parties. Once again, except where rules of process govern such procedures as compulsory pretrial settlement conferences, there are few professional rules of conduct.

Voluntary Negotiations. This category includes transactions which are not litigable if the parties fail to agree. For example, in the ordinary buy-sell agreement, if the buyer and seller do not reach an agreement as to the terms of the transaction, that is the end of the matter. No agreement will be forced on them by compulsory reference to a third-party arbiter.

The presence of two parties both attempting to maximize their respective positions resembles the structure of the adversary system. But here there are ordinarily no rules of procedure, no special rules of professional behavior, and no third-party tribunal.

Counseling. Examples of the counseling functions of a lawyer include preparing a will, drafting a general bill of sale for a merchant, and advising a client about the probable tax consequences of a proposed course of action.[3] The absence of an immediate second party in these situations leads to a significant difference in dynamics compared to the context of negotiations described above. In the context of counseling, there is no adversary to challenge the client's statement of the facts, to sharpen the issues, to seek clarification of positions, or point to countervailing considerations. Thus, all the major elements of the adversary system are lacking. There is no third-party tribunal, no adverse party, and no rules of procedure; the lawyer and the client are on their own.

Applicability of Advocate's Principles

Each of the contexts described above (with the exception of the latter stages of compulsory negotiations subject to judicial approval) lacks at least one essential element of the adversary system: the impartial arbiter. We must consider whether this basic difference renders the principles derived for the adversary system inapplicable in these other contexts.

In the adversary system, the presence of the impartial arbiter has two important effects. First, it assures that there is one—and only one—part of the system charged with the responsibility of reaching the correct decision under the law (here the impartiality is nonpartisanship and freedom from bias). Second, it makes it possible to entrust the parties with the presentation of issues, evidence, and arguments and with the challenges to them (here the impartiality is nonparticipation). The arbiter sees to it that the rules of the contest are followed, and then decides who has prevailed.[4] Putting one's best foot forward by stepping on the feet of the other side makes sense because of the presence of an impartial arbiter. That presence legitimates the zealous advocate model of the lawyer and all that it entails. Lawyers are justified in using methods and seeking results with which they may personally disagree because of faith in the ability of the arbiter to reach a correct decision.

Should these expectations of lawyer behavior change when the arbiter is removed? A simple parallel may be found in an athletic contest such as a basketball game. When a game is formally refereed, our expectations of the players and coaches are very different than in a "pick-up" game. In the refereed contest it is the referee's job to spot the fouls, to interpret and apply the rules, and to decide who has won. We therefore expect the coaches and players to argue, to the extent permitted, those positions which are in their own best interests. The pick-up game, on the other hand, requires self-policing, since by definition there is no referee. If each team is adamant in adhering to its position in any controversy, the game cannot proceed. The teams and coaches must, therefore, exercise more restraint in the pick-up game than in the refereed contest.

A similar comparison may be made between lawyers operating within and without the adversary system—removal of the arbiter leads to substantially different expectations of the other parties. Within the adversary system all proceedings are ultimately directed toward the impartial arbiter. The function of lawyers is to bring about a rough equality between the parties to aid the arbiter in making fair determinations. The lawyers assure that both sides follow the rules and that the best possible case is presented for each client.

Viewed in this light, the absence of the impartial arbiter in nonadversarial contexts has two distinct significances. The first is that there is no longer anyone to point to for ultimate resolution of disputes; the only point of contact is the other party, or, in counseling situations, the client. Attention is no longer focused on the arbiter. The second has to do with the social implications of removing the coercive impartiality of the state from the decision making processes. The absence of the arbiter moves the proceedings away from the theoretical conception of evenhanded justice.

Lawyers outside the adversary system face different environments and different expectations. It is therefore necessary to consider, independently of the parallel issues within the adversary system, what principles of professionalism and accountability should apply to the lawyer representing clients in a nonadvocate role.

THE PROFESSIONALISM OF THE NONADVOCATE LAWYER

Whatever other differences in role there may be for the lawyer serving in a nonadvocate capacity, the client's expectations of the lawyer would no doubt be the same as for the advocate. These expectations might warrant a Principle of Professionalism for the nonadvocate which would track closely the advocate's Principle of Professionalism. For example: *When acting in a nonadvocate capacity on behalf of a client, a lawyer must, within the established constraints upon professional behavior, attempt to achieve the client's objectives.*

It must be stressed that such a principle need not be derived solely from the advocate's principle proposed earlier, nor from the advocate's role. It could be derived independently from the nature of the lawyer-client relationship, which may present a set of general expectations regardless of context. But the problem nonetheless remains: since the advocate's principle was validated by the adversary system in which the advocate functions, the absence of that system may mean that a parallel principle for the nonadvocate, however derived, is not as readily or completely validated. The adversary system obliges the advocate to assist the client even though the means used or the ends sought may be unjust. Is the same obligation properly applied to the nonadvocate's professional conduct?

Two considerations suggest a negative answer. First, the basic difference between the environment of the adversary system on the one hand, and the range of nonadversary environments on the other, indicates that identical professional requirements might be inappropriate. Second, while the "established constraints upon professional behavior" for the advocate are specific and extensive, for the nonadvocate they are neither. The two general professional principles might therefore have to differ in order to compensate for the difference in the extent to which lawyers in the two roles are subject to special rules of professional behavior.

As a preliminary step in constructing an appropriate guide to professional behavior for the nonadvocate, consider the following alternative formulations:

1. When acting in a nonadvocate capacity on behalf of a client, a lawyer must, within the established constraints on professional behavior, attempt to achieve the client's objectives, unless to do so would require that the lawyer use unfair, unconscionable, or unjust, though not unlawful,[5] means or that the client achieve unfair, unconscionable, or unjust, though not unlawful, ends, in which event the lawyer *need not* accept or continue the representation.

2. When acting in a nonadvocate capacity on behalf of a client, a lawyer must, within the established constraints on professional behavior, attempt to achieve the client's objectives, unless to do so would require that the lawyer use unfair, unconscionable, or unjust, though not unlawful, means or that the client achieve unfair, unconscionable, or unjust, though not unlawful, ends, in which event the lawyer *must not* accept or continue the representation.

The first of these rules[6] presents the options currently afforded a lawyer functioning in a nonadvocate capacity under Ethical Considerations 7–8 and 7–9 of the ABA Code.[7] These options allow the lawyer either to go forward or to withdraw if the result the client seeks is morally unjust. The second rule would prohibit the lawyer from going forward; it has no counterpart in the Code of Professional Responsibility.[8] Note that neither rule permits the lawyer to subvert the client's interests without the client's consent—the lawyer's option is to decline or discontinue the representation.

The questions raised by these rules are most usefully discussed with reference to the second rule. The first, inasmuch as it creates an option for the lawyer, raises primarily issues of accountability which will be discussed later.[9] Moreover, if we grant that in the absence of the adversary system no overriding policy is advanced by a lawyer's use of unfair, unjust, or unconscionable means or by a client's obtaining such ends, it is worth considering why lawyers as a professional matter should not be prohibited from using their skills for these purposes even though their clients might wish them to do so.

The arguments against the kind of prohibition contained in the second rule fall into three categories: the first has to do with unfairness to lawyers, the second with the impact of such a prohibition on the integrity of the lawyer-client relationship, and the third with unfairness to the client.

Unfairness to Lawyers

One immediate objection is that terms like *"unfair," "unconscionable,"* or *"unjust"* are too vague to be used in a rule of professional responsibility. One lawyer's concept of unconscionability may be another's consummation devoutly to be wished. It would be unconscionable, the argument might run, to discipline a lawyer for behavior that others—but not the individual lawyer—might regard as unconscionable in retrospect.

Such terms, however, are familiar both to the substantive law and to the various professional codes, including the ABA Code of Professional Responsibility.[10] Indeed, in a sense Ethical Consideration 7–8 requires the nonadvocate to make just such a determination of "unjustness" since it permits the lawyer to withdraw when the client refuses to abide by the lawyer's advice and pursues a course of conduct the lawyer believes is "morally unjust."[11] Whether a lawyer in those circumstances does withdraw depends on a number of considerations, but a necessary condition is that the lawyer believes that the client's ends are unjust. Lawyers who take this aspiration of the bar seriously thus already are forced to make the very determinations which could be challenged as being measured by too vague a standard.

Another possible response to the argument of vagueness would be to define *"unconscionability"* not in terms of a lawyer's subjective assessment, but rather by reference to an objective body of law, that is, by measuring a lawyer's conduct against a standard of how others in similar circumstances would regard the proposed transaction. Courts are not unfamiliar with an "unconscionability" standard, and lawyers may refer to an existing body of law for an explanation of the term.[12] If the standard explicitly posed the question "Would a court of equity regard this course of action as 'unconscionable'?," the vagueness objection, though not eliminated, would have less force.

Closely related to the objection of vagueness is the objection that such a standard would be arbitrarily enforced or even be unenforceable. That objection has several facets.

First, the contribution of a lawyer acting in a nonadvocate capacity is must less visible than that of the advocate. In most cases, the lawyer's conduct will not surface at all. To impose discipline in the few cases where it does surface would be to create an arbitrary system of enforcement.

Second, use of such a standard may result in abusive discrimination against lawyers who represent unpopular causes or oppressed persons, or who themselves are for personal, political, or other reasons personae non gratae at the bar. Whatever safeguard against this kind of abuse is obtained by limiting the scope of the professional rule to criminal or fraudulent conduct is lost *pro tanto* by expanding its scope to reach other kinds of conduct. The argument is not without force. Its persuasiveness depends upon the extent to which the disciplinary process is seen as concentrating unfairly on these types of lawyers. Expanding the grounds for discipline necessarily increases opportunities for using enforcement as a harassment device.

On the other hand, it may well be that concepts like unfairness, injustice, and unconscionability are just as likely to run in favor of poor or oppressed clients as against them, for the concepts as substantive law have for the most part aided these groups. Confining the reach of the terms to established legal understandings could further reduce the possibility of discriminatory enforcement.

A third facet is the question of whether professional disciplinary and enforcement systems can handle such types of conduct. Imposition of discipline upon lawyers for criminal and fraudulent conduct, both of which are now professional violations, is rare. How much will be gained or lost by the addition of an "unconscionable" category?

In answering this question it is necessary to consider the functions of a professional code apart from actual enforcement. One such function is analogous to the use of the criminal law for deterrence. Although the incidence of actual professional discipline is, like the use of criminal sanctions, remarkably low, the existence of sanctions itself has a deterrent effect. Moreover, the professional code serves an important reinforcement function. It enables lawyers who do not want to assist clients in questionable transactions to decline on the grounds that the code does not permit them to go forward, and thus to avoid the unpleasantness of refusing to assist on a basis that is seen by the client as a personal condemnation. A professional code is also an informational document. It tells lawyers how to behave. More than one lawyer has wanted to know the answer to the question, "What should I do?," in circumstances which would be covered by the prohibitory rule being considered here.

Integrity of the Lawyer-Client Relationship

A different set of objections to a rule prohibiting a lawyer from using unconscionable means or pursuing unconscionable ends has to do with the integrity of the lawyer-client relationship.

First, there is the negative impact upon the trust and confidence necessary to that relationship if the lawyer is cast as the "conscience" of the client. Clients come to lawyers for help and assistance, not moral lectures, it may be said. Yet the aspiration of the bar now is for the lawyer "to point out those factors which may lead to a decision that is morally just as well as legally permissible. He may emphasize the possibility of harsh consequences that might result from assertion of legally permissible positions" (American Bar Association, 1976, EC 7-8). From the point of view of the client, there may be little difference between a mandatory rule and a mere permissive caution; a mandatory rule might, therefore, be expected to have only minimal impact upon the lawyer-client relationship.

At least as important is the objection that clients will not tell lawyers all that is relevant to the proposed course of action out of fear that the lawyer will conclude that the proposal is unconscionable and refuse to assist. This argument is similar to, and often confused with, the doctrine justifying a testimonial privilege for lawyer-client communications. Whether such client concerns are actually reflected in the extent to which clients make full and frank disclosure to their lawyers is unclear. There is evidence that professional and legal rules have little effect on the willingness or unwillingness of clients to talk to their lawyers. For example, Professor Uviller (1975) asserts that the testimonial privilege is rarely the factor that determines the client's decision to talk freely to the criminal defense lawyer. Lawyers may have more trouble convincing clients not to talk to other people than establishing open communications within the lawyer-client relationship. It is reported that defendants who have been given the *Miranda* warnings and admonished by their own lawyers not to talk with the police nevertheless do so to their own detriment.[13] The Code of Professional Responsibility now permits a lawyer to breach the confidence wall by disclosing the client's intention to commit a crime and the information necessary to prevent it (American Bar Association, 1976, DR 74-101(C)(3)). Yet how many clients are aware of this exception and because of it do not talk to lawyers about their criminal intentions? With respect to a different client group, in today's world of increased liability of corporate officers, directors, accountants, and lawyers, it is doubtful that lawyers will be satisfied with incomplete answers or clients will be willing to risk liability due to insufficient disclosure because of their concern that lawyers will refuse to aid in their proposed courses of action.

Suppose, however, that some clients will be less than fully candid out of fear of their lawyers' reluctance to proceed. How undesirable would that be? Presumably, there is a danger that the client who mistakenly believes that the lawyer will regard the proposed course of action as "unjust" will make incomplete disclosures and consequently will receive inadequate counsel. Yet the alternative of allowing lawyers to cooperate in bringing about unjust results may be too high a price to pay to relieve the minds of clients who have those concerns.

Finally, whatever the justification for the application of an evidentiary privilege to lawyer-client communications outside the context of litigation, a privilege that excuses lawyers from revealing what a client has told them need not oblige lawyers to behave as if they never heard the client's story. The testimonial privilege of the advocate stands upon a different footing than the nonadvocate lawyer's general obligation not to disclose the client's confidences; there is no necessary reason for the two to be treated as coextensive for these purposes. Thus, while it may be wrong to urge lawyers to reveal to the investing public confidences obtained from the client which might disclose the inaccuracy of a financial statement,[14] it is a different question whether the securities lawyer should continue to assist the client as if the information were accurate.

Unfairness to the Client

This third set of challenges to the proposed prohibitory rule derives from the claim of lawyers to preempt the field of negotiating and counseling under the doctrine of unauthorized practice. If that doctrine were rigidly enforced, only lawyers could perform these functions. Thus a rule that prohibited lawyers under any circumstances from assisting clients could result in depriving those clients of rights to which they are presumably entitled under the law.

There are two ways in which such a result would arguably be unfair to clients. One is that to deny a client assistance even though the transaction involved is neither criminal nor fraudulent would be to prohibit the client from reaching concededly legal objectives. The other is that to require that lawyers refrain from assisting clients when they view the proposed course of action as "unconscionable" is to run the danger of imposing the standards of an elite upon segments of the population that are not fairly represented at the bar, since lawyers are hardly a cross-section of the community in socio-economic, racial, ethnic, or political terms.

The first of these objections can be at least partly answered by acknowledging that not all outcomes which are neither criminal nor fraudulent are "legal." There is a range of agreements, for example, which, though they are neither criminal nor fraudulent, the law regards as either unenforceable or subject to rescission or reformation (Dobbs, 1973; Corbin, 1960). It would not be a great extension to generalize that body of law into a professional rule which limits the lawyer's ability to assist the client where the ends are unconscionable. Moreover, if what is regarded as "unconscionable" is limited to existing judicial interpretation of the term, the limitation upon those who would represent minority or indigent clients seems less severe. Indeed, as previously suggested, the standard could be more often a shield for protecting such clients from oppressive action than a sword to wield against them.

As the preceding discussion reveals, there are a number of legitimate objections to be made to a professional rule which would prohibit a nonadvocate lawyer from engaging in "unconscionable" conduct. But that discussion also points to an appropriate way to take the force out of those objections—to define the professional limitation in terms of a body of substantive law. This is the approach recommended here.

The proposed Professional Rule for the Nonadvocate reads:

(A) When acting in a professional capacity other than that of advocate, a lawyer shall not render assistance to a client when the lawyer knows or it is obvious that such assistance is intended or will be used:
  (1) to facilitate the client in entering into an agreement with another person if the other person is unaware
    (a) of acts known to the lawyer such that under the law the agreement would be unenforceable or could be avoided by the other person; or
    (b) that the agreement is unenforceable or could be avoided under the policy of the law governing such agreements; or

(2) to aid the client in committing a tort upon another person, provided
that this rule applies in business or commercial transactions only to
torts as to which it is probable that the other person will in the circumstances be unable to obtain the remedy provided by the law; or

(3) to allow the client to obtain an unconscionable advantage over another
person.

(B) For the purpose of this rule, "assistance" does not include advice to a
client that a particular course of action is not unlawful.

The general purpose of this rule is to prohibit a lawyer from assisting a client
to achieve an advantage over a third party which the law would regard as
illegitimate in that it would render an agreement unenforceable. The rule's
provisions are phrased in terms of existing substantive law.[15]

An important feature of the proposed rule, which significantly limits its reach,
is its *mens rea* requirement. It could be argued that the appropriate *mens
rea* element would be the "belief" of the lawyer; such a requirement is, in
fact, used in some of the Disciplinary Rules of the ABA Code of Professional
Responsibility (DR 7-101(B)(2), DR 7-106(C)(1), and DR 7-106(C)(2)). But the
phrase "knows or it is obvious that" also is used in the code, notably in the rules
under Canon 7 mandating that a lawyer represent the client "Within the Bounds
of the Law" (DR 7-102(A)(1)). The difference is not metaphysical. A lawyer may
believe that a proposed course of conduct is tortious, for example, but recognize
that there are reasonable arguments to the contrary. Such a situation is posited
by Disciplinary Rule 7-101(B)(2), which provides that a lawyer may—and
impliedly may not—"refuse to aid or participate in conduct that he believes to
be unlawful, even though there is some support for an argument that the conduct is legal." As long as the professional code permits lawyers to assist clients
when they believe (but do not know) that the client's proposed course of conduct is unlawful, it would be inconsistent to prohibit assistance in "lawful" but
unenforceable transactions where the lawyer merely believes but does not know
that the transactions would be unenforceable. The limitation of the *mens rea*
requirement in the proposed rule thus accords with existing provisions of the
ABA and also with the rule's reference to the substantive law.

Subsection (A)(1)(a) comprehends transactions in which the lawyer is aware
of a mistake made by the other party which, if it subsequently became known
to the other party and the matter were litigated, would render the agreement
unenforceable or avoidable. The position taken in the rule is that the client has
no "legal right" to a noncriminal or nonfraudulent result which would nonetheless be unenforceable or which could be avoided were a court to review the
transaction, and that, therefore, the client has no right to receive professional
assistance for this purpose. A lawyer has a professional responsibility to decline

to accomplish on behalf of a client that which the formal processes of the law themselves would not tolerate.[16]

To the extent that such a restriction precludes fraud and deceit, its substance is already incorporated in Disciplinary Rule 7-102(A)(7) of the current Code of Professional Responsibility: "A lawyer shall not counsel or assist a client in conduct that the lawyer knows to be illegal or fraudulent." The proposed rule goes further. By focusing on the other party's unawareness of facts which would render the transaction unenforceable, subsection (a) both avoids controversies over the definition of *"fraud"*[17] and also reaches transactions which are unenforceable on grounds other than fraud. For example, the proposed rule would apply where a unilateral mistake of one party known to the other results in a contract that does not reflect the "true intent" of the contracting parties (American Bar Association, 1976, DR 4-101(C)(3)).

Subsection (A)(1)(b) is addressed to those circumstances where all the parties are aware of the facts, but a court would nonetheless declare the agreement unenforceable or voidable because of an overriding social policy such as that underlying the Statute of Frauds. Where the other party, although aware of the facts, is unaware of the unenforceability or avoidability of the transaction, the rule would prohibit the lawyer from assisting the client to take advantage of that unawareness. Where the other party is aware of the unenforceability of the agreement but nevertheless desires to proceed—as, for example, in an industry practice of closing a deal with a handshake rather than a formal writing—the lawyer may assist the client. Of course, in today's world of professional liability, a lawyer who assists a client in entering into an unenforceable or voidable transaction without being aware or advising the client of that potential outcome would be risking a substantial lawsuit from the client.

The first clause of subsection (A)(2) ("to commit a tort upon another person") casts the professional responsibility of the lawyer in terms of substantive tort law. That law already imposes civil liability upon a lawyer who knowingly assists a client to commit a tort for which the client is liable to a third person.[18] No immediate reason appears why such a provision should not be incorporated in a professional code,[19] except perhaps in the circumstances addressed in the proviso. Certain types of conduct in the business and commercial world are classified as either torts or breaches of contract, depending upon the purposes of the classification (e.g., measure of damages, statute of limitations).

Inasmuch as a substantial, if not dominant, body of opinion would hold that there is nothing improper about an intentional breach of contract since the law provides ample remedies, it would be unfortunate to let the lash of professional rules fall upon the shoulders of a lawyer because a particular breach of contract happens to carry tortious implications. On the other hand, lawyers should not be immunized from professional liability for assisting in tortious conduct merely because for some purposes the tort could also be regarded as a breach of contract. The proviso in the rule therefore imposes restrictions on a lawyer's ability to assist a client to commit a tort even in the business and commercial world, but limits those restrictions to circumstances in which the tort remedy is not practicable.

Subsection (A)(3) of the proposed rule would bar a lawyer from assisting a client to gain "an unconscionable advantage over another person." At first glance, this subsection would seem to raise the objections to an unconscionability standard reviewed above. But its context takes much of the force from those objections—in a rule that refers to areas of substantive law, the term *"unconscionable"* is to be understood first of all as referring to means and ends which have been specifically condemned under that term in statutes and judicial opinions. Its applicability, then, depends not upon whether a lawyer personally regards the transaction as unconscionable, but rather upon an objective determination of whether the means and ends would be regarded as unconscionable under existing law. This interpretation of *"unconscionable"* is further mandated by the *mens rea* requirement of the rule: discipline is to be imposed only when the lawyer "knows or it is obvious that" the proposed conduct is unconscionable.

Yet at the same time as the *mens rea* requirement lends precision to the term *"unconscionable,"* it is flexible enough to adjust to future developments in substantive law. Judicial or legislative definitions of unconscionability would be included as they become clearly established. There is room, too, for developments of the concept in less traditional ways, for example, through the reflections of committees on professional ethics. Ethics committees might serve the noncoercive functions of a professional code—the reinforcing and informing functions—by responding to lawyers' inquiries about whether proposed behavior would result in an "unconscionable advantage" over another person.

Of course, it is open to question whether ethics committees composed of legal practitioners should have the authority to opine on issues of unconscionability where legislatures and courts have not yet spoken. But the suggestion may be less objectionable if it is seen as a device for evaluating lawyer tactics rather than as a means of determining the unconscionability of client objectives, for lawyers may possess special competence to assess the "procedural" conscionability of their own techniques of negotiating and counseling.

Assignment to ethics committees of the task of explicating "substantive" unconscionability is more difficult to justify. Is it fair to assume that a group of lawyers serving in an advisory capacity, drawing on well-accepted sources of law and their own familiarity with the customs of the community, will reach reasonable conclusions as to whether a proposed course of conduct is "unconscionable"? Would it be easier to endorse this approach if such committees were to include nonlawyers? At the least, it would be illuminating to lawyers to have designated bodies to advise them on matters of this kind. Promulgation of subsection (A)(3) with the understanding that the term *"unconscionable"* is somewhat openended would provide an opportunity to gain experience with this type of advisory committee.

Subsection (B) of the proposed rule is intended to distinguish between advising clients that their proposed course of action is not unlawful, which the rule would permit, and assisting clients in that course of action through active participation, which the rule would prohibit. The subsection may be unnecessary, for a lawyer would not face the problems contemplated by the rule until after determining that the proposed transaction was not unlawful.

Whatever the client's own moral standards, the client is entitled to expect an honest response from the lawyer. Thus, the proper response under the proposed rule to a client's unenforceable or avoidable, but otherwise lawful, proposal is for the lawyer to tell the client that although the proposal is not unlawful, professional standards prohibit the lawyer from assisting the client in pursuing that course of action.

THE ACCOUNTABILITY OF THE NONADVOCATE LAWYER

The proposed Professional Rule for the Nonadvocate is limited at least initially to those types of transactions that have been recognized by positive law as being unenforceable and unconscionable. The rule does not reach other areas of behavior which would be considered "immoral" or "unjust," and leaves open questions of the nonadvocate's accountability for the course of action chosen. In the earlier discussion of the advocate's role, it was argued that the effective operation of the adversary system required a Principle of Professionalism which obliges the advocate to proceed in ways and toward ends that might be morally questionable. A second principle was, therefore, appropriate to provide that the advocate who adheres to the Principle of Professionalism is neither legally, professionally, nor morally accountable for the means used or the ends achieved. Should there be a similar principle for the nonadvocate who adheres to the limitations imposed by the proposed professional rule? In other words, may the nonadvocate demur to a charge of accountability, particularly moral accountability, for assisting a client in immoral conduct which is not prohibited by substantive law nor by a professional rule?

The issue is highlighted by comparing the moral accountability of the lawyer under the current ABA Code of Professional Responsibility with that of the nonlawyer representative. Generally, the nonlawyer representative is viewed as an agent of the principal, and thus is held morally accountable for any result to which the representative substantially contributes. A defense of duress may be available to the representative where the principal has threatened to subject the agent to pain, punishment, or other sanction sufficient to overcome the fortitude of a reasonable person in those circumstances. The representative might also claim a defense of "replacement"—that nothing would have been gained by refusing the principal since the agent would have been easily replaced with a willing substitute—though this argument is singularly unpersuasive in moral terms.

In contrast, Ethical Considerations 7–8 and 7–9 of the Code of Professional Responsibility appear to claim immunity from moral accountability for all lawyers.[20] The key language in Ethical Consideration 7–8 is the admonition that "the decision whether to forego legally available objectives or methods . . . is ultimately for the client. . . ." Ethical Consideration 7–9 recognizes that actions "in the best interest of the client" may seem to the lawyer "to be unjust." Both ethical considerations permit but do not require the lawyer to withdraw in these circumstances.[21]

The provision that the lawyer may but need not withdraw necessarily implies that either decision is correct as a matter of professional as well as legal account-ability. With respect to moral accountability, if the provision may be read as taking any position at all on the issue, it is that as long as neither lawyer nor client does anything illegal, there is no moral accountability for the lawyer.

The stated purpose of the ethical considerations is to set forth principles that are "aspirational in character and represent the objectives toward which every member of the profession should strive" (American Bar Association, 1976, p. 1). Use of the word *"unjust"* in the code suggests an implicit recognition that there are problems of moral accountability. Thus, it is probably accurate to infer that by allowing the lawyer some latitude in deciding whether to withdraw, the code is attempting to provide the nonadvocate with the same immunity from moral accountability that it accords the advocate. At the very least, there is some-thing odd about a code of professional behavior which admonishes lawyers to attempt to prevent their clients from engaging in "unjust" conduct (impliedly conceding that this is an identifiable genus), and yet permits them to go for-ward without fear of reproach if the client is adamant.

Is there any reason why lawyers who have a right to withdraw should not be personally accountable for their conduct if they continue to pursue their clients' ends, merely because those ends are not proscribed by professional rule? For the advocate, the demands of the adversary system were sufficient to jus-tify moral nonaccountability. It is now necessary to consider whether in the absence of that system there are attributes inherent in the nonadvocate rule that independently justify an immunity for the lawyer which is not granted to lay representatives.

Much of the earlier discussion of the nonadvocate's professional rule is rel-evant to this question, particularly the implications of the first alternative ver-sion of the rule which, like the Code of Professional Responsibility, would allow the lawyer either to withdraw or to continue.[22] It will be recalled that the objections surveyed earlier fell into three categories: unfairness to the lawyer, damage to the integrity of the lawyer-client relationship, and unfairness to the client.

The objection of unfairness to the lawyer rested on grounds of vagueness and unenforceability. Such considerations are not germane to questions of moral accountability. Since neither formal sanctions nor external enforcement agencies are involved, issues of fair notice and arbitrary enforcement simply do not arise.

The second objection, that the integrity of the lawyer-client relationship would be impaired, was based on two independent concerns. The first was that the client would resent the lawyer's presenting himself as a moral rather than purely legal advisor. Yet, as was previously noted, the Code of Professional Responsibility already encourages lawyers to tell their clients when they think their proposals are unjust. Recognition that lawyers have a moral obligation to do so, and will be held morally accountable for their own conduct or the achievement of their clients' goals, is not likely to have any further significant impact upon the lawyer-client relationship.

Another concern about the integrity of the lawyer-client relationship was that the client might make insufficient disclosure out of fear that the lawyer would conclude that the proposal was unjust and withhold assistance. But since the proposed professional rule does not oblige the nonadvocate to withdraw when the proposals are unjust (rather than unenforceable or substantively unconscionable), the impact of accountability is no more than this: lawyers must be prepared to defend, if they choose to do so, the morality of their own behavior and of their clients' objectives.

The final objection was that it would be unfair to the client to allow or oblige the lawyer to refrain from activity that the lawyer thought unconscionable, since the effect might be to deny legal assistance to clients whose sense of justness did not conform to the legal profession's arguably limited norm. That objection is just as valid here. Lawyers might hesitate to represent such clients if they could be held morally accountable even for ends which are neither criminal, fraudulent, nor unconscionable in the sense of the professional rule.

It is, of course, precisely this fear which in the context of the adversary system justifies obliging advocates to proceed without regard to the morality of the client's ends or the lawyer's means even when they believe that what they are doing is unjust. To justify the same immunity for the nonadvocate, we would have to find a social need for the technical assistance of nonadvocates that would take priority over moral considerations—a special need of men and women to have available persons in whom they may freely confide and who are professionally obliged to put their clients' interests above their own scruples.

Such a need, and such a justification, have recently been claimed by Professor Charles Fried (1976). He argues that the moral justification for a lawyer's seemingly immoral behavior is analogous to the moral justification for one friend's behavior on behalf of another. Although the aptness of the analogy has been questioned, the core of the argument remains: the continued societal protection of the nonadvocate functions of the legal profession may depend in significant part upon the need for a morally insulated body of professionals who perform the social function of acting for others in this confidential, committed way. Professor Fried (1976) attempts further to justify nonaccountability by arguing that the lawyer's principal social function is to preserve the client's autonomy under the law (Dauer and Leff, 1977).[23] Without the lawyer's technical assistance, the argument goes, the client would suffer unjustified loss of autonomy since the client would no longer obtain all that the law allows. Practically all of Professor Fried's illustrations, however, especially of this second argument, are drawn from the context of litigation. The moral justification for enabling a client to obtain an immoral or unjust advantage when no third-party tribunal is available to review the transaction is far less clear.

From the standpoint of moral accountability, when a client seeks to retain a lawyer for help with a transaction, the lawyer may or may not believe that what is sought is immoral or unjust. A lawyer who does not believe that what is sought is immoral has no problem about proceeding; one who believes that what is sought is immoral still has a choice of whether to assist or not. The lawyer is not prohibited legally or professionally from assisting. The assignment of moral accountability means only that the lawyer who proceeds must answer to the charge of immoral behavior. That lawyer may not demur.

Consider, however, the worst case from the client's point of view that all reasonably available lawyers refuse to assist because they have concluded that the client's proposal entails immoral ends or means. How undesirable would that outcome be? In the advocate's context, such a result would undercut the important social policy of remitting disputes to the adversary system. Is there an equally important policy to be vindicated outside the adversary system?

Suppose that all machinists refused to accept employment in a factory manufacturing "Saturday-night specials" because they were generally opposed to the use of firearms or believed that the particular weapon, though not unlawful, was too dangerous to be sold. Could it be said that the manufacturer had been improperly deprived of a legal right to manufacture "Saturday-night specials"? To make this claim would imply a judgment that the right of the manufacturer to produce the weapon was superior to that of the employees not to produce it. In general, we do not make such judgments about individual behavior.

The problem becomes more acute when those who refuse to work are the only ones the law permits to work. This is the case with professions whose practitioners are licensed by the state—engineers, architects, lawyers. Should it be a condition of retaining a license to engage in these professions that the licensee forgo the right to refuse to aid a client in achieving ends that are not illegal, fraudulent, or "unconscionable"? Attaching such a condition to professional licenses would import into each of these fields a public utility obligation without the protective controls and regulations that normally accompany that obligation.[24] Yet failing to impose that obligation to serve, with its concomitant stance of neutrality or amorality, may violate an important affirmative political value. Particularly in the case of lawyers, compelling arguments can be made that no person should be unable to realize his or her legal rights because of an inability to procure the assistance of a licensed legal practitioner.

A compromise may be possible. Assume that all available lawyers refuse to assist in an undertaking because each has concluded that the proposed course of action is immoral or unjust and none wishes to assume moral accountability for immoral or unjust conduct. In that situation, there could be a group obligation to provide assistance, with the individual lawyer selected by lot, rotation, or special qualification, as is done in appointing counsel for an unpopular criminal defendant. The lawyer should then properly be able to claim immunity from moral accountability.

On the other hand, if it is clear from the outset that the client ultimately will be able to obtain the professional assistance needed to achieve the immoral end, there is little to be gained from holding lawyers morally accountable for voluntarily agreeing to assist. This could indeed argue for a general principle of moral nonaccountability for the nonadvocate similar to that which has been hypothesized for the advocate.

An ultimate resolution must turn on the balance to be struck between the social value of requiring nonadvocate lawyers to bear moral responsibility for their professional behavior and the political value of preventing government from exercising its licensing power in a way that frustrates citizens in the realization of their legal rights. In this light, the initial question of whether a nonadvocate should be granted the extraordinary insulation from moral accountability provided the advocate becomes clearer. The analysis outlined in this article suggests that the answer to the question should be negative, so long as it is recognized that the answer is based on an essentially political judgment that lawyers outside the adversary system should not be obliged to assist all clients as a condition of being licensed to practice law. Furthermore, this conclusion is conditioned upon the validity of the basic assumptions which have informed this discussion that every client is entitled to be told whether a proposed course of action is or is not unlawful (lawyers may properly claim immunity from moral accountability if that is all they do); that clients may proceed to undertake the proposed course of action without the professional assistance of lawyers; and that all that is required of lawyers is that they be prepared to justify their conduct in moral terms—they may not demur to a charge of immorality in their professional behavior as nonadvocates.[25]

Notes

1. For a comprehensive analysis of negotiations from a different perspective, see Eisenberg (1976).

2. It is interesting to speculate why there are controversies which require judicial approval even when the parties are in agreement about the resolution of the dispute. In the case of minors' settlements, the reason may be that the client is considered unable to make a reasoned decision whether to accept a specific bargain (or, in other words, that the system lacks trust in the attorney's ability to make the decision in the best interests of the client), so that the court must be the client's surrogate. In class actions, there is the added concern about the identity and representation of all those who may be affected by the outcome. In the case of plea bargains, that same distrust may apply to both defense counsel and prosecuting attorney; in addition, there is the possible consideration of an independent interest of society, which only the judge can vindicate.

3. In some situations, clearly, the counseling and negotiating functions of a lawyer overlap. A lawyer cannot negotiate very well without also counseling the client. The client must be advised of the positions to be taken and their probable consequences; the client must be given an opportunity to decide about terms and conditions of settlement or to decide whether the controversy is to be settled at all. For present purposes, however, counseling refers to a different lawyer activity, the lawyer as counselor outside the context of negotiation.

4. This analysis ignores the fact, of course, that one function of the arbiter is to review and alter the procedural and substantive rules themselves, as experience and changing circumstances seem to require. The exercise of this function depends upon the nature and level of the particular forum.

5. As used here, the meaning of the word *"unlawful"* is that given to it in the ABA Code of Professional Responsibility (American Bar Association, 1976). With respect to the conduct of the client, it means criminal or fraudulent. With respect to the conduct of the lawyer, it means criminal, fraudulent, or in violation of a disciplinary rule. Conduct that might be described as unfair, unjust, or unconscionable is not "unlawful" within this definition as long as it is neither criminal, fraudulent, nor a violation of a disciplinary rule. This is the necessary implication of the ABA Code of Professional Responsibility, EC 7–8 and 7–9, which urge the lawyer to request the client's permission to forgo unjust behavior, but leave the ultimate decision to the client and permit the lawyer to assist in the unjust behavior without incurring sanction. See also note 7.

6. The term *"rule"* is used here rather than *"principle"* because of the greater specificity of the proposals.

7. The ABA Code of Professional Responsibility (1976), EC 7–8 and 7–9, read as follows:

   "EC 7–8: A lawyer should exert his best efforts to insure that decisions of his client are made only after the client has been informed of relevant considerations. A lawyer ought to initiate this decision-making process if the client does not do

so. Advice of a lawyer to his client need not be confined to purely legal considerations. A lawyer should advise his client of the possible effect of each legal alternative. A lawyer should bring to bear upon this decision-making process the fullness of his experience as well as his objective viewpoint. In assisting his client to reach a proper decision, it is often desirable for a lawyer to point out those factors which may lead to a decision that is morally just as well as legally permissible. He may emphasize the possibility of harsh consequences that might result from assertion of legally permissible positions. In the final analysis, however, the lawyer should always remember that the decision whether to forego legally available objectives or methods because of non-legal factors is ultimately for the client and not for himself. In the event that the client in a nonadjudicatory matter insists upon a course of conduct that is contrary to the judgment and advice of the lawyer but not prohibited by Disciplinary Rules, the lawyer may withdraw from the employment."

"*EC 7–9:* In the exercise of his professional judgment on those decisions which are for his determination in the handling of a legal matter, a lawyer should always act in a manner consistent with the best interests of his client. However, when an action in the best interest of his client seems to him to be unjust, he may ask his client for permission to forego such action."

8. A prohibition of this kind has, however, been proposed by commentators. See, e.g., Rubin (1975).

9. See the text accompanying note 22.

10. See EC 7–8 and 7–9 in American Bar Association (1976). See also EC 1–5 ("morally reprehensible conduct") and EC 7–13 (duty of government lawyer to avoid "unfair litigation," "to seek justice," and not "to bring about unjust settlements or results").

11. See note 7.

12. See *Williams* v. *Walker-Thomas Furniture Co.* (1965). See also Uniform Commercial Code sec. 2–302 (unconscionability provisions).

13. See the review of three empirical studies in Kamisar, La Fave, and Israel (1974).

14. Compare Sommer (1974–1975) with "Statement of Policy Adopted by American Bar Association Regarding Responsibilities and Liabilities of Lawyers . . . " (1975).

15. References to substantive law are also used in the Code of Professional Responsibility (American Bar Association, 1976) in important rules. Thus, the prohibitions against unauthorized practice of law necessarily refer to the substantive law of unauthorized practice (DR 3–101); the definition of *"confidence"* is that information "protected by the attorney-client privilege under applicable law" (DR 4–101(A)) and the circumstances in which a lawyer may reveal such confidences expressly include the occasions on which a lawyer is "required by law" to do so; Canon 7 of the code consistently refers to the substantive or procedural law in defining the limits of a lawyer's behavior when representing a client: what lawsuits to file (DR 7–102(A)(2)), the lawfulness of client behavior (DR 7–102(A)(7)), concealment of what is required by law to be revealed (DR 7–102(A)(3)), perjury (DR 7–102(A)(4)), and making false statements of law or fact (DR 7–102(A)(5)).

16. This concept is not a new one. In Opinion 722 (1948), the Committee on Professional Ethics of the Association of the Bar of the City of New York stated that it would be unethical under the relevant canons for a lawyer to insert in a lease on behalf of a landlord a waiver of the defendant's right to a sixty-day period in which to cancel an agreed-upon rent increase, a waiver which had previously been held void as against public policy. See also New York County Lawyers' Association Committee on Professional Ethics (1913); *Stare* v. *Tate* (1971).

17. The New York State Bar Association (1977) added a new definition to the Code of Professional Responsibility as applicable to the New York bar: "'Fraud' does not include conduct, although characterized as fraudulent by statute or administrative rule, which lacks an element of scienter, deceit, intent to mislead, or knowing failure to correct misrepresentations which can be reasonably expected to induce detrimental reliance by another." See also New York State Bar Association Special Committee to Review the Code of Professional Responsibility (1976).

18. For example, *Roberts* v. *Ball* (1976); *Warner* v. *Roadshow Attractions Co.* (1942); *Hoppe* v. *Klapperish* (1947); *Hahn* v. *Wylie* (1976).

19. It is arguable that the word *"unlawful"* includes tortious conduct; if so, subsection (2) is at worst redundant.

20. See note 7.

21. EC 1–5, American Bar Association (1976), which states that a lawyer should "refrain from all illegal or reprehensible conduct," seems to apply to lawyers acting in nonlawyer roles and, to the extent that it does apply to professional behavior, gives way before the more specific provisions of EC 7–8 and 7–9.

22. See the text accompanying note 9.

23. But see Fried (1977).

24. It would also run counter to some traditional concepts which the legal profession still embraces: "A lawyer is under no obligation to act as advisor or advocate for every person who may wish to become his client" (American Bar Association, 1976, EC 2–26).

25. The difficulties with this conclusion may be aggravated in the case of a lawyer who, having undertaken a nonadvocate representation, is confronted with a client demand for assistance in a specific immoral or unjust activity. It is conceivable that abandonment of the client in some circumstances would amount to a greater injustice than that which the client seeks. If that is the case, the lawyer may decide that the moral calculus permits him to continue. The point is that the lawyer must confront the problem squarely and may not refuse to answer the question of the morality of the lawyer's behavior. The typology of lawyers' functions described earlier in the article may be relevant to the merits of the moral decision the lawyer makes in these circumstances: the further from the adversary system and its structural elements the lawyer's situation is, the heavier is the burden of supporting the morality of that lawyer's behavior.

References

American Bar Association. *ABA Code of Professional Responsibility.* Chicago: American Bar Association, 1976.

Association of the Bar of the City of New York. "Report by Special Committee on Lawyers' Role in Securities Transactions." *Business Law,* 1977, *32,* 1898–1899.

Corbin, A. L. *Corbin on Contracts: A Comprehensive treatise on the Working Rules of Contract Law.* 12 vols. Charlottesville, VA: Lexis Law Publishing (originally published by West), 1960–1962.

Dauer, E., and Leff, A. "Correspondence—The Lawyer as Friend." *Yale Law Journal,* 1977, *86,* 573. But see Fried. "Reply," *Yale Law Journal,* 1977, 86, 584.

Dobbs, D. *Handbook on the Law of Remedies.* St. Paul, Minn.: West Pub. Co., 1973.

Eisenberg, M. A. "Private Ordering Through Negotiation: Dispute-Settlement and Rule-Making." *Harvard Law Review,* 1976, *89,* 637.

Fried, C. "The Lawyer as Friend: The Moral Foundations of the Lawyer-Client Relation." *Yale Law Journal,* 1976, *85,* 1060.

Fried, C. "Reply." *Yale Law Journal,* 1977, *86,* 584.

Hahn v. *Wylie.* 54 App. Div. 2d 629, 387 N.Y.S. 2d 855 (1976).

Hoppe v. *Klapperish.* 224 Minn. 224, 28 N.W. 2d 780 (1947).

Kamisar, Y., La Fave, W., and Israel, J. *Basic Criminal Procedure* (4th ed.). St. Paul, Minn.: West Pub. Co., 1974.

New York County Lawyers' Association Committee on Professional Ethics. "Questions Respecting Proper Professional Conduct Submitted to the Committee with Its Answers." Question and Answer 27, p. 48, 1913.

New York State Bar Association Special Committee to Review the Code of Professional Responsibility. *Report No. 4.* Oct. 12, 1976.

Roberts v. *Ball, Hunt, Hart, Brown and Baerwitz.* 57 Cal. App. 3d 104, 128 Cal. Rptr. 901 (2d Dist. 1976).

Rubin, A. *A Causerie on Lawyers' Ethics in Negotiation,* 35 La. L. Rev. 577 (1975).

Sommer, A. A. "The Emerging Responsibilities of the Securities Lawyer." 1974–1975 Federal Securities Law Reports. *79,* 631, 1974–1975.

Stare v. Tate. 21 Cal. App. 3d 432, 98 Cal. Rptr. 264 (2d Dist. 1971).

"Statement of Policy Adopted by American Bar Association Regarding Responsibilities and Liabilities of Lawyers in Advising with Respect to the Compliance by Clients with Laws Administered by the Securities and Exchange Commission." *Business Law,* 1975, *31,* 543, 544.

Uviller, H. R. "The Advocate, the Truth, and Judicial Hackles: A Reaction to Judge Frankel's Idea." *University of Pennsylvania Law Review,* 1975, *123,* 1067, 1073.

Warner v. *Roadshow Attractions Co.* 56 Cal. App. 2d. I, 132 P.2d 35 (2d Dist. 1942).

Williams v. *Walker-Thomas Furniture Co.* 350 F.2d 445 (D.C. Cir. 1965).

CHAPTER TWENTY-THREE

A Causerie on Lawyers' Ethics in Negotiation

Alvin B. Rubin

*I asked him whether, as a moralist, he did not think that the practice of the law,
in some degree, hurt the nice feeling of honesty. JOHNSON: "Why no, sir, if you
act properly. You are not to deceive your clients with false representations of your
opinion: you are not to tell lies to a judge."*
—BOSWELL'S LIFE OF JOHNSON

The philosopher of Mermaid Tavern did not discuss the morality expected when lawyers deal with other lawyers or with laymen. When a lawyer buys or sells a house or a horse or a used car, he is expected to bargain. When he becomes a secretary of state—like Dean Acheson, or John Foster Dulles—or a governor, or a senator, or a congressman or a legislator, he will negotiate and compromise.

In such activities lawyers may be acting for themselves as principals, or they may be representing constituents. But they are not practicing their profession as attorneys-at-law. It may be assumed that the lawyer who is buying or selling a farm on his own behalf is expected to behave no differently from any other member of his society, that no special ethical principles command his adherence or govern his conduct. And while the lawyer-diplomat or lawyer-politician may conceive of himself as a professional, rather than as an amateur, he will not be practicing a profession, as that term is generally understood.

When the lawyer turns to his law practice and begins to represent his clients as attorney or advocate, he assumes the role of a professional. What constitutes a profession is difficult to define comprehensively, but all attempts include reference to a store of special training, knowledge, and skills and to the adoption of ethical standards governing the manner in which these should be employed. When acting as an advocate, the lawyer professes a complex set of ethical principles that regulate his conduct toward the courts, his own clients, other lawyers and their clients.

Litigation spawns compromise, and courtroom lawyers engage almost continually in settlement discussions in civil cases and plea bargains in criminal cases. We do not know what proportion of civil claims is settled by negotiation before the filing of suit, but it must be vastly greater than the number of cases actually filed. Neither does institution of suit mean an end to negotiations; 91 percent of all cases filed in the United States district courts for the fiscal year ending June 30, 1974, were disposed of prior to the beginning of a trial on the merits, most of them by some sort of negotiated compromise. In the same year only 15 percent of the defendants in criminal cases in the federal courts went to trial; 61 percent of the charges terminated in pleas of guilty or nolo contendere and 24 percent were nol grossed or dismissed for some other reason (Administrative Office of the United States Courts, 1973, 1974). In almost all of the cases that were disposed of without trials, there were likely negotiations of one kind or another, such as plea bargains or exchanges of information.

Although less than one-fourth of the lawyers in practice today devote a majority of their time to litigation, and most spend none at all in the traditional courtroom,[1] there are few lawyers who do not negotiate regularly, indeed daily, in their practice. Some lawyers who handle little conventional litigation persist in saying that they do not act as negotiators. If there are a few at the bar who do not, they are *rarae aves*. Patent lawyers, tax counselors and securities specialists and all those who perform the myriad tasks of office law practice may not dicker about the value of a case—though some assuredly do but they constantly negotiate the settlement of disputed items.

Neither the Code of Professional Responsibility nor most of the writings about lawyers' ethics specifically mention any precepts that apply to this aspect of the profession. The few references to the lawyer's conduct in settlement negotiations relate to obtaining client approval and disclosing potentially conflicting interests (American Bar Association, 1976, EC 7-7, EC 6-16, EC 5-17). It is scant comfort to observe here, as apologists for the profession usually do, that lawyers are as honest as other men (Bloom, 1968). If it is an inevitable professional duty that they negotiate, then as professionals they can be expected to observe something more than the morality of the market place.

In 1969, after five years of study, the American Bar Association, to which 192,000 of the nation's more than 300,000 lawyers belong, adopted a Code of Professional Responsibility, superseding the archaic Canons of Ethics. The Code has, with minor changes, been adopted in forty-nine states and the District of Columbia.[2] It purports to set forth the ethical standards that apply to the lawyer's professional conduct. It is lengthy and intricate. Its style is forbidding and is only slightly more lucid than the more formidable parts of the Internal Revenue Code. But its complex structure and apparent effort to be comprehensive induce the belief that it sets forth those general principles to which lawyers should adhere in every aspect of their professional engagements.

Its nine canons are preceptual; they purport to state "axiomatic norms," and to express "in general terms the standards of professional conduct expected of lawyers in their relationships with the public, with the legal system, and with the legal profession" (American Bar Association, 1976). From the Canons are derived 137 Ethical Considerations that are "aspirational in character." Both Canons and Ethical Considerations (EC) are reinforced by 38 mandatory Disciplinary Rules (DR), each with subparts, that set forth the sanctions for proscribed conduct. But these scriptures contain nothing that deals directly with the propriety of a lawyer's conduct or his ethical responsibilities when dealing as a negotiator with another lawyer, a layman or a government agency. Indeed, there are only a few texts that can be used to construct precepts by analogy.

The superseded Canons of Ethics contained a fine homiletic sentence: "The conduct of the lawyer before the Court *and with other lawyers* should be characterized by candor and fairness" (American Bar Association, 1976, emphasis added). The admonitions of duty to the court—at least in some respects—remain explicit and elaborated in the code; the general statement of a duty to other lawyers no longer appears.[3] The Code does not speak directly to the duty of a lawyer in dealing with laymen.

There are a few rules designed to apply to other relationships that touch peripherally the area we are discussing. A lawyer shall not (American Bar Association, 1976):

- Knowingly make a false statement of law or fact (DR 7-102(A)(5)).

- Participate in the creation or preservation of evidence when he knows or it is obvious that the evidence is false (DR 7-102(A)(6)).

- Counsel or assist his client in conduct that the lawyer knows to be illegal or fraudulent (DR 7-102(A)(7)).[4]

- Knowingly engage in *other illegal conduct* or conduct contrary to a disciplinary rule (DR 7-102(A)(8), emphasis added).

- Conceal or knowingly fail to disclose that which he is *required by law* to reveal (DR 7-102(A)(3), emphasis added).

In addition, he "should be temperate and dignified and . . . refrain from all illegal and morally reprehensible conduct" (American Bar Association, 1976, EC 1-5). The lawyer is admonished "to treat with consideration all persons involved in the legal process and to avoid the infliction of needless harm" (American Bar Association, 1976, EC 7-10). Taken together, these rules, interpreted in the light of that old but ever useful candle, *ejusdem generis,* imply that a lawyer shall not himself engage in illegal conduct, since the meaning of assisting a client in fraudulent conduct is later indicated by the proscription of other illegal conduct. As we perceive, the lawyer is forbidden to make a false statement of law or fact knowingly. But nowhere is it ordained that the lawyer owes any general duty of candor or fairness to members of the bar or to laymen with whom he may deal as a negotiator, or of honesty or of good faith insofar as that term denotes generally scrupulous activity.

Is the lawyer-negotiator entitled, like Metternich, to depend on "cunning, precise calculation, and a willingness to employ whatever means justify the end of policy?" (Lapham, 1974, p. 30). Few are so bold as to say so. Yet some whose personal integrity and reputation are scrupulous have instructed students in negotiating tactics that appear tacitly to countenance that kind of conduct. In fairness it must be added that they say they do not "endorse the propriety" of this kind of conduct and indeed even indicate "grave reservations" (Melstner and Schrag, 1974, p. 232) about such behavior; however, this sort of generalized disclaimer of sponsorship hardly appears forceful enough when the tactics suggested include (Meltsner and Schrag, 1974, pp. 236–238):

- Use two negotiators who play different roles. (illustrated by the "Mutt and Jeff" police technique; "Two lawyers for the same side feign an internal dispute . . .")
- Be tough—especially against a patsy.
- Appear irrational when it seems helpful.
- Raise some of your demands as the negotiations progress.
- "Claim" that you do not have authority to compromise [emphasis added].
- After agreement has been reached, have your client reject it and raise his demands.[5]

Another text used in training young lawyers commendably counsels sincerity, capability, preparation, courage and flexibility. But it also suggests "a sound set of tools or tactics and the know-how to use (or not to use) them." One such tactic is, "Make false demands, bluffs, threats; even use irrationality" (Freeman and Weihofer, 1972, p. 122).

Occasionally, an experienced legal practitioner comments on the strain the custom of the profession puts on conscience. An anonymous but reputedly experienced Delaware lawyer is quoted as saying, "The practice of tax law these days requires the constant taking of antiemetics" (Hawley, 1956, pp. 230, 235).

The concern of lawyers with problems that do not ostensibly involve either ethics or negotiations reveals assumptions regarding what attorneys assume to be professionally proper. Thus, the *American Bar Association News* (1974) suggests that a major problem is raised by the question, "Must Attorneys Tell All to Accountants?" The problem revolves around the growing demand by accountants auditing corporate books that they be informed by corporate lawyers when a mutual client is facing or could be facing contingent liabilities through involvement in potentially costly lawsuits, possible tax claims, and so on. This is not a negotiation situation, but the resistance to telling an auditor the truth about his client's affairs arises, we are told, "because revelations could weaken cases already in court" (p. 9). Since the disclosure would certainly not be admissible in evidence, we must assume that the apprehended "weakening" is a softening of settlement posture if the real truth were told.

Honesty, as the oath administered to witnesses makes clear, implies not only telling literal truth but also disclosing the whole truth. The lawyer has no ethical duty to disclose information to an adversary that may be harmful to his client's cause; most lawyers shrink from the notion that morality requires a standard more demanding than duty to clients. EC 4-5 prohibits a lawyer from using information acquired in the representation of a client to the client's disadvantage, and this, together with the partisan nature of the lawyer's employment, indicates to the practitioner that nondisclosure is both a duty to the client and consistent with ethical norms.

While the lawyer who appears in court is said to owe a duty to disclose relevant legal authorities even if they harm his client's position, he need not disclose, and indeed most would say that he must conceal, evidence damaging to the client's cause. This fine analysis of what a lawyer should reveal to the judge in court doubtless inspired the observation by the Italian jurist, Piero Calamandrei (1942), who, in his celebrated *Eulogy of Judges,* asked, "Why is it that when a judge meets a lawyer in a tram or in a café and converses with him, even if they discuss a pending case, the judge is more disposed to believe what the lawyer says than if he said the same thing in court during the trial? Why is there greater confidence and spiritual unity between man and man than between judge and lawyer?" (p. 39).

Let us consider the proper role for a lawyer engaged in negotiations when he knows that the opposing side, whether as a result of poor legal representation or otherwise, is assuming a state of affairs that is incorrect. Hypothesize: L, a lawyer, is negotiating the sale of his client's business to another businessman, who is likewise represented by counsel. Balance sheets and profit and loss statements prepared one month ago have been supplied. In the last month, sales have fallen dramatically. Counsel for the potential buyer has made no inquiry about current sales. Does L have a duty to disclose the change in sales volume?

Some lawyers say, "I would notify my client and advise him that *he* has a duty to disclose," not because of ethical considerations but because the client's failure to do so might render the transaction voidable if completed. If the client refused to sanction disclosure, some of these lawyers would withdraw from representing him in this matter on ethical grounds. As a practical matter, (i.e., to induce the client to accept their advice) they say, in consulting with the client, the lawyer is obliged to present the problem as one of possible fraud in the transaction rather than of lawyers' ethics.

In typical law school fashion, let us consider another hypothetical. L, the lawyer, is representing C, a client, in a suit for personal injuries. There have been active settlement negotiations with LD, the defendant's lawyer. The physician who has been treating C rendered a written report, containing a prognosis stating that it is unlikely that C can return to work at his former occupation. This has been furnished to LD. L learns from C that he has consulted another doctor, who has given him a new medication. C states that he is now feeling fine and thinks he can return to work, but he is reluctant to do so until the case is settled or tried. The next day L and LD again discuss settlement. Does L have a duty either to guard his client's secret or to make a full disclosure? Does he satisfy or violate either duty if, instead of mentioning C's revelation he suggests that D require a new medical examination?[6]

Some lawyers avoid this problem by saying that it is inconceivable that a competent LD would not ask again about C's health. But if the question as to whether L should be frank is persistently presented, few lawyers can assure that they would disclose the true facts.

Lawyers whose primary practice is corporate tend to distinguish the two hypotheticals, finding a duty to disclose the downturn in earnings but not the improvement in health. They may explain the difference by resorting to a discussion of the lower standards (expectations?) of the bar when engaged in personal injury litigation. "That's why I stay away from that kind of work," one lawyer said. The esteem of a lawyer for his own profession must be scant if he can rationalize the subclassifications this distinction implies. Yet this kind of gradation of professional ethics appears to permeate the bar.

Lawyers from Wall Street firms say that they and their counterparts observe scrupulous standards, but they attribute less morality to the personal injury lawyer, and he, in turn, will frequently point out the inferiority of the standards of those who spend much time in criminal litigation. The gradation of the ethics of the profession by the area of law becomes curiouser and curiouser the more it is examined, if one may purloin the words of another venturer in Wonderland.

None would apparently deny that honesty and good faith in the sale of a house or a security implies telling the truth and not withholding information. But the code does not exact that sort of integrity from lawyers who engage in negotiating the compromise of a lawsuit or other negotiations. Scant impetus to good faith is given by EC 7-9, which states, "When an action in the best interest of his client seems to him to be unjust, [the lawyer] may ask his client for permission to forego such action," for such a standard means that the client sets the ultimate ethical parameter for the lawyer's conduct. Neither is there much guidance for the negotiator in EC 7-10 (American Bar Association, 1976): "The duty of a lawyer to represent his client with zeal does not militate against his concurrent obligation to treat with consideration all persons involved in the legal process and to avoid infliction of needless harm." EC 7-27 also palters with the issue: "Because it interferes with the proper administration of justice, a lawyer should not *suppress* evidence that he or his client has *a legal* obligation to reveal or produce." In context, this obviously applies to the presentation of evidence before a tribunal and not to out-of-court conversations. It likewise begs our present inquiry, for the issue in regard to EC 7-27 is whether there is a "legal" rather than an ethical obligation to reveal or produce the evidence.

The professional literature contains many instances indicating that, in the general opinion of the bar, there is no requirement that the lawyer disclose unfavorable evidence in the usual litigious situation.[7] The *racontes* of lawyers and judges with their peers are full of tales of how the other side failed to ask the one key question that would have revealed the truth and changed the result, or how one side cleverly avoided producing the critical document or the key witness whom the adversary had not discovered. The feeling that, in an adversary encounter, each side should develop its own case helps to insulate counsel from considering it a duty to disclose information unknown to the other side. Judge Marvin Frankel (1975), an experienced and perceptive observer of the profession, comments, "Within these unconfining limits [of the Code of Professional Responsibility] advocates freely employ time-honored tricks and strategems to block or distort the truth" (p. 21).

The United States Supreme Court has developed a rule that requires the disclosure by the prosecutor in a criminal case of evidence favorable to the accused. But this is a duty owed by the government as a matter of due process, not a duty of the prosecutor as a lawyer. In all other respects in criminal cases, and in almost every aspect of the trial of civil cases, client loyalty appears to insulate the lawyer's conscience. Making fidelity to the client the ultimate loyalty and the client himself the authority served appears to sanction the abdication of personal ethical responsibility, a kind of behavior described by psychologist Stanley Milgrim in *Obedience to Authority* (1974). He discusses a series of experiments in which people are induced to inflict apparent physical pain on another person because someone in authority orders it. The lawyer permits obedience to the client's interest to provide the moral authority as well as the rationalized justification for his conduct.

Do the lawyer's ethics protest more strongly against giving false information? DR 7-102(A)(5), already quoted, forbids the lawyer to "knowingly make" a false statement of law or fact. Most lawyers say it would be improper to prepare a false document to deceive an adversary or to make a factual statement known to be untrue with the intention of deceiving him. But almost every lawyer can recount repeated instances where an adversary of reasonable repute dealt with facts in such an imaginative or hyperbolic way as to make them appear to be different from what he knew they were.

Interesting answers are obtained if lawyers are asked whether it is proper to make false statements that concern negotiating strategy rather than the facts in litigation. Counsel for a plaintiff appears quite comfortable in stating, when representing a plaintiff, "My client won't take a penny less than $25,000," when in fact he knows that the client will happily settle for less; counsel for the defendant appears to have no qualms in representing that he has no authority to settle, or that a given figure exceeds his authority, when these are untrue statements. Many say that, as a matter of strategy, when they attend a pre-trial conference with a judge known to press settlements, they disclaim any settlement authority both to the judge and adversary although in fact they do have settlement instructions; estimable members of the bar support the thesis that a lawyer may not misrepresent a fact in controversy but may misrepresent matters that pertain to his authority or negotiating strategy because this is expected by the adversary (Voorhies, 1967).

To most practitioners it appears that anything sanctioned by the rules of the game is appropriate. From this point of view, negotiations are merely, as the social scientists have viewed it, a form of game; observance of the expected rules, not professional ethics, is the guiding precept. But gamesmanship is not ethics.

Consider the problems raised when a lawyer represents a client before a government agency, for example the Internal Revenue Service. Here special rules are thought to be applicable. A formal opinion of the ABA Committee on Ethics (1965) states:

> In practice before the Internal Revenue Service, which is itself, an adversary party rather than a judicial tribunal, the lawyer is under a duty not to mislead the Service, either by misstatement, silence, or through his client, but is under no duty to disclose the weaknesses of his client's case. He must be candid and fair, and his defense of his client must be exercised within the bounds of the law and without resort to any manner of fraud or chicane (p. 690).

The committee states that a lawyer engaged in handling a case before the Internal Revenue Service is not held to the principles of ethics that would apply to litigation in court because he is dealing with the IRS, which is the representative of one of the parties. The lawyer has an "absolute duty not to make false assertions of fact" but this does not "require the disclosure of weaknesses in the client's case . . . unless the facts in the attorney's possession indicate beyond reasonable doubt that a crime will be committed. A wrong, or indeed sometimes an unjust, tax result in the settlement of a controversy is not a crime" (American Bar Association, 1965, p. 691). This kind of juxtaposition of the permissible and the criminal leads inevitably to the conclusion that all that is not criminal is acceptable.

A different distinction is drawn by Calamandrei (1942):

> The difference between the true lawyer and those men who consider the law merely a trade is that the latter seek to find ways to permit their clients to violate the moral standards of society without overstepping the letter of the law, while the former look for principles which will persuade their clients to keep within the limits of the spirit of the law in common moral standards (p. 62).

The courts have seldom had occasion to consider these ethical problems, for disciplinary proceedings have rarely been invoked on any charge of misconduct in the area. But where settlements have in fact been made when one party acted on the basis of a factual error known to the other and this error induced the compromise, courts have set releases aside[8] on the basis of mistake, or, in some cases, fraud.

In Louisiana "fraud" is defined as "an assertion of what is false, or a suppression of what is true" (Louisiana Civil Code, art. 1847(5)). Such assertion or suppression embraces "not only an affirmation or negation by words either written or spoken, but any other means calculated to produce a belief of what is false, or an ignorance or disbelief of what is true" (art. 1847(6)). This codification is much the same as the prevailing view at common law (Summers, 1968). It is embraced within the concept of good faith in the negotiation and performance of contracts under the Uniform Commercial Code (secs. 1-201, 1-203, 2-103). Obviously a contract negotiated on the basis of misrepresentation of fact may be set aside; there is precedent, too, for invalidating the release of a personal injury claim entered into as a result of misrepresentation of matters of law.[9] These authorities fix limits on the conduct of the principal whether he acts in person or through a lawyer.

The profession seldom confronts the necessity Vern Countryman and Ted Finman (1966) say the attorney-at-law must consider: "the need, if conflicting interests are to be protected, for the lawyer to serve as a source of restraint on his client, and, indeed, on himself" (p. 185). The lawyer is a professional because his role is not merely to represent his client as a mercenary in the client's war; he is also "a guardian of society's interests" (p. 186).

In an unpublished paper, Dean Murray L. Schwartz (1974), of the University of California Law School, succinctly proposed three possible standards of the relationship of the lawyer's value structure to that of his client:

1. A lawyer should do everything for his client that is lawful and that the client would do for himself if he had the lawyer's skill;

2. A lawyer *need not* do for his client that which the lawyer thinks is unfair, unconscionable or over-reaching, even if lawful;

3. A lawyer *must not* do for his client that which the lawyer thinks is unfair, unconscionable or over-reaching, even if lawful.

"It will be giving away no professional secrets," he continues, "to tell you that the first standard of behavior is the one that is largely applied in a contested judicial matter." He thinks that the second standard is "officially recognized as appropriate for non-litigated matters" though the authorities cited in this paper and my own experience make me think this observation overly generous to the profession. The third, he correctly finds, is "no part of official doctrine."

A lawyer should not be restrained only by the legal inhibitions on his client. He enjoys a monopoly on the practice of law protected by sanctions against unauthorized practice. Through a subpart of the profession, lawyer-educators, the lawyer controls access to legal education. He licenses practitioners by exacting bar examinations. He controls access to the courts save in those limited instances when a litigant may appear *pro se,* and then he aptly characterizes this litigant as being his own lawyer, hence having a fool for his client.

The monopoly on the practice of law does not arise from the presumed advantages of an attorney's education or social status: it stems from the concept that, as professionals, lawyers serve society's interests by participating in the process of achieving the just termination of disputes. That an adversary system is the basic means to this end does not crown it with supreme value. It is means, not end.[10]

If he is a professional and not merely a hired, albeit skilled hand, the lawyer is not free to do anything his client might do in the same circumstances. The corollary of that proposition does set a minimum standard: the lawyer must be at least as candid and honest as his client would be required to be. The agent of the client, that is, his attorney-at-law, must not perpetrate the kind of fraud or deception that would vitiate a bargain if practiced by his principal. Beyond that, the profession should embrace an affirmative ethical standard for attorneys' professional relationships with courts, other lawyers and the public: *The lawyer must act honestly and in good faith.* Another lawyer, or a layman, who deals with a lawyer should not need to exercise the same degree of caution that he would if trading for reputedly antique copper jugs in an oriental bazaar. It is inherent in the concept of an ethic, as a principle of good conduct, that it is morally binding on the conscience of the professional, and not merely a rule of the game adopted because other players observe (or fail to adopt) the same rule. Good conduct exacts more than mere convenience. It is not sufficient to call on personal self-interest; this is the standard created by the thesis that the same adversary met today may be faced again tomorrow, and one had best not prejudice that future engagement.

Patterson and Cheatham (1971) correctly assert that the basic standard for the negotiator is honesty. "In terms of the standards of the profession, honesty is candor" (p. 123). Candor is not inconsistent with striking a deal on terms favorable to the client, for it is known to all that, at least within limits, that is the purpose to be served. Substantial rules of law in some areas already exact of principals the duty to perform legal obligations honestly and in good faith. Equivalent standards should pervade the lawyer's professional environment. The distinction between honesty and good faith need not be finely drawn here; all lawyers know that good faith requires conduct beyond simple honesty.

Since bona fides and truthfulness do not inevitably lead to fairness in negotiations, an entirely truthful lawyer might be able to make an unconscionable deal when negotiating with a government agency, or a layman or another attorney who is representing his own client. Few lawyers would presently deny themselves and their clients the privilege of driving a hard bargain against any of these adversaries though the opponent's ability to negotiate effectively in his own interest may not be equal to that of the lawyer in question. The American Bar Association Committee on Ethics does not consider it improper for a lawyer to gain an unjust result in a tax controversy. Young lawyers, among the most idealistic in the profession, about to represent indigents, are advised that they be tough, especially against a patsy.

There is an occasional Micah crying in the wilderness: "One should go into conference realizing that he is an instrument for the furtherance of justice and is under no obligation to aid his client in obtaining an unconscionable advantage. Of course, in the zone of doubt an attorney may and probably should get all possible for his client" (Herrington, 1930, p. 795).

This raises the problem inevitable in an adversary profession if one opponent obeys a standard the other defies. As Countryman and Finman (1966) inquire, "How is a lawyer who looks at himself as 'an instrument for the furtherance of justice' likely to fare when pitted against an attorney willing to take whatever he can get and use any means he can get away with?" (p. 281).[11]

In criminal trial matters, *Brady* v. *Maryland* (1962) imposes constraints on the prosecutor as a matter of constitutional due process by requiring that he divulge evidence favorable to the accused. The only limitations in the Code of Professional Responsibility on sharp practice in plea bargaining are on the public prosecutor, who "shall make timely disclosure to counsel for the defendant . . . of the existence of evidence, known to the prosecutor or other government lawyer, that tends to negate the guilt of the accused, mitigate the degree of the offense, or reduce the punishment" (American Bar Association, 1976, DR 7-103(B)).

It is obvious, as has already been pointed out, that this does not stem from an ethical standard for lawyers but on the duty of the government, a duty the government's lawyer performs as alter ego for his employer.

While it might strain present concepts of the role of the lawyer in an adversary system, surely the professional standards must ultimately impose upon him a duty not to accept an unconscionable deal. While some difficulty in line drawing is inevitable when such a distinction is sought to be made, there must be a point at which the lawyer cannot ethically accept an arrangement that is completely unfair to the other side, be that opponent a patsy or a tax collector. So I posit a second precept: *The lawyer may not accept a result that is unconscionably unfair to the other party* (compare Summers, 1968).

A settlement that is unconscionable may result from a variety of circumstances. There may be a vast difference in the bargaining power of the principals so that, regardless of the adequacy of representation by counsel, one party may simply not be able to withstand the expense and bear the delay and uncertainty inherent in protracted suit. There may be a vast difference in the bargaining skill of counsel so that one is able to manipulate the other virtually at will despite the fact that their framed certificates of admission to the bar contain the same words.

The unconscionable result in these circumstances is in part created by the relative power, knowledge and skill of the principals and their negotiators. While it is the unconscionable result that is to be avoided, the question of whether the result is indeed intolerable depends in part on examination of the relative status of the parties. The imposition of a duty to tell the truth and to bargain in good faith would reduce their relative inequality, and tend to produce negotiation results that are within relatively tolerable bounds.

But part of the test must be in result alone: whether the lesion is so unbearable that it represents a sacrifice of value that an ethical person cannot in conscience impose upon another. The civil law has long had a principle that a sale of land would be set aside if made for less than half its value, regardless of circumstance (Louisiana Civil Code, art. 2589). This doctrine, called lesion beyond moiety, looks purely to result. If the professional ethic is caveat negotiator, then we could not tolerate such a burden. But there certainly comes a time when a deal is too good to be true, where what has been accomplished passes the line of simply a good deal and becomes a cheat.

The lawyer should not be free to negotiate an unconscionable result, however pleasing to his client, merely because it is possible, any more than he is free to do other reprobated acts. He is not to commit perjury or pay a bribe or give advice about how to commit embezzlement. These examples refer to advice concerning illegal conduct, but we do already, in at least some instances, accept the principle that some acts are proscribed though not criminal (American Bar Association, 1976): the lawyer is forbidden to testify as a witness in his client's cause (DR b-102(A); see also EC b-9 and DR s-101(D)), or to assert a defense merely to harass his opponent (DR 7-102(A)(1)); he is enjoined to point out to his client "those factors that may lead to a decision that is morally just" (EC 7-8). Whether a mode of conduct available to the lawyer is illegal or merely unconscionably unfair, the attorney must refuse to participate. This duty of fairness is one owed to the profession and to society; it must supersede any duty owed to the client.

One who has actively practiced law for over 20 years and been a federal trial judge for eight years knows that the theses he has set forth are vulnerable to charges that they are impractical, visionary, or radical. Old friends will shake their heads and say that years on the bench tend to addle brains and lead to doddering homilies.

But, like other lawyers, judges hear not only of the low repute the public has for the bench but also of the even lower regard it has for the bar. We have been told so in innumerable speeches but, more important, our friends, neighbors and acquaintances tell us on every hand that they think little of the morality of our profession. They like us; indeed some of their best friends are lawyers. But they deplore the conduct of our colleagues. This is not merely an aftermath of Watergate: it is, in major part, because many members of the public, not without some support in the facts, view our profession as one that adopts ethics as cant, pays lip-service to DR's and on behalf of clients stoops to almost any chicane that is not patently unlawful. We will not change that attitude by Law Days alone. It is to serve society's needs that professions are licensed and the unlicensed prohibited from performing professional functions. It is, inherent in the concept of professionalism that the profession will regulate itself, adhering to an ethos that imposes standards higher than mere law observance. Client avarice and hostility neither control the lawyer's conscience nor measure his ethics. Surely if its practitioners are principled, a profession that dominates the legal process in our law-oriented society would not expect too much if it required its members to adhere to two simple principles when they negotiate as professionals: negotiate honestly and in good faith; and do not take unfair advantage of another—regardless of his relative expertise or sophistication. This is inherent in the oath the ABA recommends be taken by all who are admitted to the bar: "I will employ for the purpose of maintaining the causes confided to me such means only as are consistent with truth and honor."[12]

Notes

1. This "fact" is derived from personal observation, conversation with lawyers, and discussions with managing partners of larger law firms, who usually report that about 25 percent of their lawyers are in the litigation section.

2. California adopted new Rules of Professional Conduct on January 1, 1975. They are based in part on the Disciplinary Rules of the new code but do not include the ethical considerations.

3. ABA Code of Professional Responsibility EC 7-38 speaks to the lawyer's relationship with other lawyers in litigation: "A lawyer should be courteous to opposing counsel and should accede to reasonable requests regarding court proceedings, setting continuances, waiver of procedural formalities and similar matters which do not prejudice the rights of his client." It concludes: "A lawyer should be *punctual* in fulfilling all professional commitments" (emphasis added).

4. Presumably this implies, a fortiori, that a lawyer must not himself do anything fraudulent.

5. Regarding the tactic of having the client reject the agreement and raise his demand, the authors add, "This is the most ethically dubious of the tactics listed here, but there will be occasions where a lawyer will have to defend against it or even to employ it" (p. 238).

6. "Plaintiff should disclose as much information as he possibly can without harming his own case" (Baer and Broder, 1967, p. 91).

7. "In ordinary litigious controversy the bar has been told that it is entitled and perhaps required to take a tough, unyielding attitude with respect to the revelation of distasteful evidence" (Maguire, 1962, p. 493). In a footnote, Maguire continues, "Instance after instance can be adduced. Williston, Life and Law 271–272 (1940) (refraining from correcting judge's statement of fact, although Mr. Williston did and his opponents did not know the truth); Opinion 309, NYCLA 708 (1933) (not improper to refrain from revealing presence in court of eye witness vital to case of client's opponent, a three year old child). . . . cf. Opinion 307, NYCLA 706 (1933) (not improper to refrain from warning witness whose testimony would be helpful to client that witness by testifying may expose himself to prosecution)."

8. See, for example, *Cole* v. *Lumbermens Mut. Cas. Co.* (1964).

9. Annot., 21 A.L.R.2d 272 (1952). See also Annot., 71 A.L.R.2d 82 (1960). In addition, there may be a tort claim against the person who induces the release. See Annot., 58 A.L.R.2d 500 (1958).

10. For a recent illuminating reappraisal of the adversary process as a means to truth, see Frankel (1975).

11. See also Mathews (1953), observing that in negotiation, a lawyer "endowed with shrewdness and a sportive sense of outmaneuvering his opponent" has "an opportunity to indulge his proclivity almost devoid of risk of detection" provided he limits himself to "sharp practice" and does not step over into fraud, coercion or violations of law "or public policy" (pp. 93, 95). See Note (1964).

12. Oath of Admission recommended by ABA, modeled after the one in use in the State of Washington.

References

Administrative Office of the United States Courts. *Annual Report of the Director of Administrative Office of the United States Courts.* Washington, D.C.: Administrative Office of the United States Courts, 1973.

Administrative Office of the United States Courts. *1974 Semi-Annual Report of the Director.* Washington, D.C.: Administrative Office of the United States Courts, 1974.

American Bar Association. *Opinions of the Committee on Professional Ethics,* Formal Opinion 314, Apr. 27, 1965, 690.

American Bar Association. *Canons of Professional Ethics.* Chicago: American Bar Association.

American Bar Association. *Code of Professional Responsibility.* Chicago: American Bar Association, 1976.

American Bar Association News, Sept. 1974.

Baer, H., and Broder, A. *How to Prepare and Negotiate Cases for Settlement.* Englewood Cliffs, N.J.: Prentice-Hall, 1967.

Bloom, M. *The Trouble with Lawyers.* New York: Simon & Schuster, 1968.

Brady v. *Maryland.* 373 U.S. 83 (1962).

Calamandrei, P. *Eulogy of Judges.* Princeton, N.J.: Princeton University Press, 1942.

Cole v. *Lumbermens Mut. Cas. Co.* 160 So. 2d 785 (La. App. 3d Cir. 1964).

Countryman, V., and Finman, T. *The Lawyer in Modern Society.* Boston: Little, Brown, 1966.

Frankel, M. "The Search for Truth—An Umpireal View." *Record of the Association of the Bar of the City of New York,* 1975, *30.*

Freeman, H., and Weihofer, H. *Clinical Law Training.* St. Paul, Minn.: West Publishing Co., 1972.

Hawley. "Morality v. Legality." *Pennsylvania Bar Association Quarterly,* 1956, 230, 235.

Herrington. "Compromise v. Contest in Legal Controversies." *American Bar Association Journal,* 1930, *16,* 795, 798.

Lapham, L. "The Easy Chair." *Harper's,* Nov. 1974, p. 30.

Louisiana Civil Code.

Maguire. "Conscience and Propriety in Lawyer's Tax Practice." *Tax Counselor's Quarterly,* 1962, *6,* 493.

Mathews. "Negotiation: A Pedagogical Challenge." *Journal of Legal Education,* 1953, *6,* 93, 95.

Melstner, M., and Schrag, P. *Public Interest Advocacy: Materials for Clinical Education.* 1974.

Milgrim, S. *Obedience to Authority.* New York: Harper & Row, 1974.

Note. *University of Pennsylvania Law Review,* 1964, *112.*

Patterson, L., and Cheatham, E. *The Profession of Law.* Mineola, N.Y.: Foundation Press, 1971.

Schwartz, M. "Moral Development, Ethics and the Professional Education of Lawyers." Unpublished paper, Oct. 14, 1974.

Summers, R. "'Good Faith' in General Contract Law and the Sales Provisions of the Uniform Commercial Code." *Virginia Law Review,* 1968, *54,* 195.

Voorhies. "Law Office Training: The Art of Negotiation." *Practical Lawyer,* 1967, *13*(4).

PART SIX

SOCIAL INFLUENCES AND IMPACTS

Much of the literature on ethics in negotiation treats the negotiators and their negotiation processes as if they exist in their own enclosed system. Ethical questions are to be decided in the moment of interaction with some counterpart across the table, perhaps with some forethought about the goals or purposes of the negotiation and some consideration of the relationships that already exist or might be created by the negotiation. But as we all know, negotiators come to any negotiation with their own histories, demographics, moral default positions, philosophies about social action, professional training, and a variety of other bargaining endowments or characteristics that may have no direct connection to the particular merits of the negotiation. We bring who we are to the negotiations we conduct.

While we eschew complicated philosophical debates about free will and determinism here, we do think that none of us is a totally free agent in what we choose to do in a negotiation. What the "right thing to do" is will depend on the circumstances of the matter and the prior relationships of parties and negotiators but also what social influences have affected the particular negotiators before they arrive at any particular negotiating event. The literature is replete with debates about whether such "predispositional" factors as race (Ayres, 1991), gender (Kolb and Coolidge, 1991; Kolb and Williams, 2000; Menkel-Meadow, 1994), culture (Avruch, 1998), nationality (Brett, 2001), or role (Walton and McKersie, 1965) affect negotiation behaviors, in terms of goals chosen, behaviors demonstrated, attributions made (Ross and Nisbett, 1991), and commitments to agreements. A much smaller part of this literature focuses on whether these dispositional factors also influence ethical choices as well as other negotiation behaviors. Are women more likely to reveal information and be honest (as part of a tendency to be more cooperative) than men? Are some nationalities more likely to tolerate deception and lack of candor? Do the powerful (whether defined by resources, physical strength, or political threats) take advantage of the weak? Do the weak feel more justified in "anything goes" because the ends justify the means when dealing with the more powerful? These are all empirical questions, largely unresolved by the contradictory studies that do exist (Rubin and Brown, 1975; Thompson, 2000; Menkel-Meadow, 2000; Frank, Gilovich, and Regan, 1993). Nevertheless, despite the lack of empirical clarity about demographic and other associations with negotiation behavior, people who negotiate make attributions about each other all the time, whether group attributions are accurate or not. Thus, assumptions, expectations, and perceptions about what we think we can expect from others affect the choices we make about how much information to share and how to approach others about assuming collaboration and joint gain goals versus assumptions of zero-sum scarce resource division.

In Chapter Twenty-Five, Frank, Gilovich, and Regan's study of economics majors' greater tendency to "defect" and "compete" is both interesting in itself and stands in as a proxy for discussion about other possible cultural or socialized differences that may affect negotiation choices and attributions we make of each other. What is perhaps most important for us to recognize as an ethical matter is that false attributions (of stereotyping, category mistake, or substitution of dispositional for situational factors in negotiation) can cause us to treat others inappropriately or to feel inappropriately treated by others in ways that may cause bad results in terms of agreements reached and how individuals may be treated in the process. As Scott Peppet suggests in Chapter Twenty-Seven, awareness and mindfulness of a range of issues, seemingly extraneous to the negotiation, may at least cause us to pay more explicit attention to these issues. Likewise, Kolb and Williams (2000) suggest that what is implicit in the "shadows" of negotiation (power relations, demographics that lead to stereotyped attributions, and expectations) should be dealt with more explicitly (and planned for) in negotiations.

Just as all negotiators are products of social influences antecedent to any negotiation, the effects of any negotiation have social impacts on both those involved in the negotiation itself and those affected by it. Many studies document the tendency of negotiators to seek fair outcomes or "fair divisions" in distributive equity terms in negotiation (Young, 1991; Brams and Taylor, 1996; Bazerman, 1998), in direct contrast to assumptions about individual gain maximization that fills so many popular books about negotiation (Cohen, 1980).

When and how negotiators seek to distribute resources fairly, rather than to compete or individually maximize, remains another unanswered empirical question about negotiation, but it is clearly one of the most important macro "ethical" questions to be asked, by both parties within a negotiation and those who stand outside a particular negotiation and attempt to evaluate its fairness.

"Fairness" may be measured in many ways, as years of philosophical debates about equality, equity, proportionality, and desert demonstrates. Negotiators will seldom agree a priori on what their own standards of fairness are, but merely raising the issue of whether we owe fellow negotiators some consideration of distributional fairness or justice in a negotiation is to raise ethical consciousness (and perhaps to change the "game" in "game theory"). In some cases, standards of fairness will be judged by legal or other objective criteria imposed by those outside (as well as inside) the process (Condlin, 1992; Nolan-Haley, 1996).

Beyond the parties who participate in a negotiation, most negotiations have consequences for others outside the negotiation. Whether thought about as humans or economically based "externalities," there are a whole host of people (and things) who will be affected by what is accomplished (or not) in any given negotiation. How absent parties (future generations in environmental disputes and negotiations, Susskind, 1981; children in divorce negotiations, Wallerstein and Kelly, 1980) are treated or accounted for in negotiations is a seldom discussed but often crucial issue in evaluating the effects and fairness of any negotiation process. And a related, but more often treated, question is how known third parties (whether formal beneficiaries or not) outside of negotiated deals should be considered when deals are struck that are known to affect them (investors, Langevoort, 1999; taxpayers, other employees, fellow citizens, Bok, 1978). What obligations, if any, do negotiators have to consider how what they do affects others? Where there is virtually no formal rule, regulation, or law that requires negotiators to consider others outside their private processes (unless what they do is otherwise unlawful or voidable), increasing attention is being paid to making more private negotiation settlements or agreements public so that their effects on public values (like health and safety) can be assessed (Luban, 1995; Menkel-Meadow, 1993) despite the general rule that negotiation results are usually private contracts. So issues of procedural and outcome transparency in some negotiation settings has been linked to efforts to assess publicly and evaluate the effects of negotiation on both known and "innocent" bystanders.

To the extent that negotiations are increasingly being managed or facilitated, in both public and private settings, by third-party neutrals such as mediators, who may be hired by the parties or by public entities, questions about the accountability of the parties to other absent parties involve not only the negotiators but their mediators as well. Here Lawrence Susskind, an experienced mediator, who has long argued for the accountability of third-party neutrals for

the outcomes they help produce, provides in Chapter Thirty-One three important reasons that third parties should be responsible to those not at the negotiating table: the precedential effects of even privately mediated matters, the
special role of ethics of leadership implicated in the actions of third-party neutrals, and the educational effects of demonstrating that better-quality solutions
can be obtained by processes, such as facilitated negotiations, that are conducted with the express goals of reaching an outcome that is as beneficial as
possible to all relevant stakeholders.

While we focus here primarily on domestic, business, commercial, legal, and
similar kinds of negotiations, it is useful to begin to imagine how these issues
of transparency, publicity, and effects on third parties are also being played out
in the international arena, in statecraft and diplomacy, world trade, war and
peace (Watkins and Rosegrant, 2001), and reconciliation efforts (Chayes and
Minow, 2003).

References

Avruch, K. *Culture and Conflict Resolution*. Washington, D.C.: U.S. Institute of Peace
Press, 1998.

Ayres, I. "Fair Driving: Gender and Race Discrimination in Retail Car Negotiations."
Harvard Law Review, 1991, *104*(4), 817–872.

Bazerman, M. Judgment in *Managerial Decision Making*. (4th ed.). New York: Wiley,
1998.

Brams, S. J., and Taylor, A. D. *Fair Division: From Cake Cutting to Dispute Resolution*.
Cambridge: Cambridge University Press, 1996.

Brett, J. M. *Negotiating Globally: How to Negotiate Deals, Resolve Disputes and Make
Decisions Across Cultural Boundaries*. San Francisco: Jossey-Bass, 2001.

Chayes, A., and Minow, M. *Imagine Coexistence: Peace and Reconciliation Between
Opposing Groups After Violent Mass Conflict*. San Francisco: Jossey-Bass, 2003.

Condlin, R. "Bargaining in the Dark: The Normative Incoherence of Lawyer Dispute
Bargaining." *Maryland Law Review*, 1992, *51*, 1–104.

Kolb, D., and Coolidge, G. "Her Place at the Table: A Consideration of Gender Issues
in Negotiation." In J. W. Breslin and J. Z. Rubin (eds.), *Negotiation Theory and
Practice*. Cambridge, Mass.: Program on Negotiation, 1991.

Kolb, D., and Williams, J. *The Shadow Negotiation: How Women Can Master the
Hidden Agendas That Determine Bargaining Success*. New York: Simon & Schuster,
2000.

Menkel-Meadow, C. "Public Access to Private Settlements: Conflicting Legal Policies."
Alternatives, 1993, *11*(3), 85–87.

Menkel-Meadow, C. "Portia Redux: Another Look at Gender, Feminism and Legal
Ethics." *Virginia Journal of Social Policy and the Law*, 1994, *2*(1), 75–113.

Menkel-Meadow, C. "Teaching About Gender and Negotiation: Sex, Truths and Videotape." *Negotiation Journal,* 2000, *16*(4), 357–375.

Nolan-Haley, J. "Court Mediation and the Search for Justice and Law." *Washington University Law Quarterly,* 1996, *74,* 47–102.

Ross, L., and Nisbett, R. *The Person and the Situation.* New York: McGraw-Hill, 1991.

Rubin, J. Z., and Brown, B. R. *The Social Psychology of Bargaining and Negotiation.* Orlando, Fla.: Academic Press, 1975.

Susskind, L. "Expanding the Ethical Obligations of the Mediator."

Susskind, L. "Environmental Mediation and the Accountability Problem." *Vermont Law Review,* 1981, *6,* 85–117.

Thompson, L. *The Mind and Heart of the Negotiator.* (2nd ed.). Upper Saddle River, N.J.: Prentice-Hall, 2000.

Wallerstein J., and Kelly, J. *Surviving the Breakup: How Parents and Children Deal with Divorce.* New York: Basic Books, 1980.

Walton, R., and McKersie, R. *A Behavioral Theory of Labor Negotiations.* New York: McGraw-Hill, 1965.

Watkins, M., and Rosegrant, S. *Breakthrough International Negotiation.* San Francisco: Jossey-Bass, 2001.

Young, H. P. "Fair Division." In *Negotiation Analysis.* Ann Arbor: University of Michigan Press, 1991.

CHAPTER TWENTY-FOUR

Lies for the Public Good

Sissela Bok

*"How then," said I, "might we contrive one of those opportune falsehoods
of which we were just now speaking, so as by one noble lie to persuade
if possible the rulers themselves, but failing that the rest of the city?"
. . . "While all of you are brothers," we will say, "yet God in fashioning
those of you who are fitted to hold rule mingled gold in their generation,
for which reason they are most precious—but in their helpers silver
and iron and brass in the farmers and other craftsmen."
. . . "Do you see any way of getting them to believe this tale?" "No, not these
themselves," he said, "but I do, their sons and successors and the rest of
mankind who come after." "Well," said I, "even that would have a good
effect in making them more inclined to care for the state and one another."*
—Plato, *The Republic*

*HUGO: And do you think the living will agree to your schemes?
HOEDERER: We'll get them to swallow them little by little.
HUGO: By lying to them?
HOEDERER: By lying to them sometimes. . . .
HOEDERER: I'll lie when I must, and I have contempt for no one.
I wasn't the one who invented lying. It grew out of a society
divided into classes, and each one of us has inherited it from
birth. We shall not abolish lying by refusing to tell lies, but
by using every means at hand to abolish classes.*
—Jean-Paul Sartre, *Dirty Hands*

Three circumstances have seemed to liars to provide the strongest excuse for
their behavior—a crisis where overwhelming harm can be averted only
through deceit, complete harmlessness and triviality to the point where it
seems absurd to quibble about whether a lie has been told, and the duty to particular individuals to protect their secrets. Times of crisis can expand into vast

practices where the harm to be averted is less obvious and the crisis less and less immediate; how white lies can shade into equally vast practices no longer so harmless, with immense cumulative costs; and how lies to protect individuals and to cover up their secrets can be told for increasingly dubious purposes to the detriment of all.

When these three expanding streams flow together and mingle with yet another—a desire to advance the public good—they form the most dangerous body of deceit of all. These lies may not be justified by an immediate crisis nor by complete triviality nor by duty to any one person; rather, liars tend to consider them as right and unavoidable because of the altruism that motivates them. I want to turn to this far-flung category.

The most characteristic defense for these lies is based on the benefits they may confer and the long-range harm they can avoid. The intention may be broadly paternalistic, as when citizens are deceived "for their own good," or only a few may be lied to for the benefit of the community at large. Error and self-deception mingle with these altruistic purposes and blur them; the filters through which we must try to peer at lying are thicker and more distorting than ever in these practices. But I shall try to single out, among these lies, the elements that are consciously and purposely intended to benefit society.

A long tradition in political philosophy endorses some lies for the sake of the public. Plato, in the passage quoted at the head of this chapter, first used the expression "noble lie" for the fanciful story that might be told to people in order to persuade them to accept class distinctions and thereby safeguard social harmony. According to this story, God himself mingled gold, silver, iron, and brass in fashioning rulers, auxiliaries, farmers, and craftsmen, intending these groups for separate tasks in a harmonious hierarchy.

The Greek adjective which Plato used to characterize this falsehood expresses a most important fact about lies by those in power: this adjective is *"gennaion,"* which means "noble" in the sense of both "high-minded" and "well-bred."[1] The same assumption of nobility, good breeding, and superiority to those deceived is also present in Disraeli's statement that a gentleman is one who knows when to tell the truth and when not to. In other words, lying is excusable when undertaken for "noble" ends by those trained to discern these purposes.

Rulers, both temporal and spiritual, have seen their deceits in the benign light of such social purposes. They have propagated and maintained myths, played on the gullibility of the ignorant, and sought stability in shared beliefs. They have seen themselves as high-minded and well-bred—whether by birth or by training—and as superior to those they deceive. Some have gone so far as to claim that those who govern have a right to lie (Sylvester, 1967). The powerful tell lies believing that they have greater than ordinary understanding of what is at stake; very often, they regard their dupes as having inadequate judgment, or as likely to respond in the wrong way to truthful information.

At times, those who govern also regard particular circumstances as too uncomfortable, too painful, for most people to be able to cope with rationally. They may believe, for instance, that their country must prepare for long-term challenges of great importance, such as a war, an epidemic, or a belt-tightening in the face of future shortages. Yet they may fear that citizens will be able to respond only to short-range dangers. Deception at such times may seem to the government leaders as the only means of attaining the necessary results.

The perspective of the liar is paramount in all such decisions to tell "noble" lies. If the liar considers the responses of the deceived at all, he assumes that they will, once the deceit comes to light and its benefits are understood, be uncomplaining, if not positively grateful. The lies are often seen as necessary merely at one stage in the education of the public. Thus Erasmus (1962), in commenting on Plato's views, wrote:

> He sets forth deceitful fictions for the rabble, so that the people might not set
> fire to the magistracy, and similar falsifications by which the crass multitude is
> deceived in its own interest, in the same way that parents deceive children and
> doctors the sick
>   . . . Thus for the crass multitude there is need of temporary promises, figures,
> allegories, parables . . . so that little by little they might advance to loftier things.

Some experienced public officials are impatient with any effort to question the ethics of such deceptive practices (except actions obviously taken for private ends). They argue that vital objectives in the national interest require a measure of deception to succeed in the face of powerful obstacles. Negotiations must be carried on that are best left hidden from public view; bargains must be struck that simply cannot be comprehended by a politically unsophisticated electorate. A certain amount of illusion is needed in order for public servants to be effective. Every government, therefore, has to deceive people to some extent in order to lead them.

These officials view the public's concern for ethics as understandable but hardly realistic. Such "moralistic" concerns, put forth without any understanding of practical exigencies, may lead to the setting of impossible standards; these could seriously hamper work without actually changing the underlying practices. Government officials could then feel so beleaguered that some of them might quit their jobs; inefficiency and incompetence would then increasingly afflict the work of the rest.

If we assume the perspective of the deceived—those who experience the consequences of government deception—such arguments are not persuasive. We cannot take for granted either the altruism or the good judgment of those who lie to us, no matter how much they intend to benefit us. We have learned that much deceit for private gain masquerades as being in the public interest. We know how deception, even for the most unselfish motive, corrupts and spreads.

And we have lived through the consequences of lies told for what were believed to be noble purposes.

Equally unpersuasive is the argument that there always has been government deception, and always will be, and that efforts to draw lines and set standards are therefore useless annoyances. It is certainly true that deception can never be completely absent from most human practices. But there are great differences among societies in the kinds of deceit that exist and the extent to which they are practiced, differences also among individuals in the same government and among successive governments within the same society. This strongly suggests that it is worthwhile trying to discover why such differences exist and to seek ways of raising the standards of truthfulness.

The argument that those who raise moral concerns are ignorant of political realities, finally, ought to lead not to a dismissal of such inquiries, but to a more articulate description of what these realities are, so that a more careful and informed debate could begin. We have every reason to regard government as more profoundly injured by a dismissal of criticism and a failure to consider standards than by efforts to discuss them openly. If duplicity is to be allowed in exceptional cases, the criteria for these exceptions should themselves be openly debated and publicly chosen. Otherwise government leaders will have free rein to manipulate and distort the facts and thus escape accountability to the public.

The effort to question political deception cannot be ruled out so summarily. The disparagement of inquiries into such practices has to be seen as the defense of unwarranted power—power bypassing the consent of the governed. In the pages to come I shall take up just a few cases to illustrate both the clear breaches of trust that no group of citizens could desire, and circumstances where it is more difficult to render a judgment.

EXAMPLES OF POLITICAL DECEPTION

In September 1964, a State Department official, reflecting a growing administration consensus, wrote a memorandum advocating a momentous deceit of the American public (Gravel, 1971). He outlined possible courses of action to cope with the deteriorating military situation in South Vietnam. These included a stepping up of American participation in the "pacification" in South Vietnam and a "crescendo" of military action against North Vietnam, involving heavy bombing by the United States. But an election campaign was going on; the president's Republican opponent, Senator Goldwater, was suspected by the electorate of favoring escalation of the war in Vietnam and of brandishing nuclear threats to the communist world. In keeping with President Johnson's efforts to portray Senator Goldwater as an irresponsible war hawk, the memorandum ended with a paragraph entitled "Special considerations during the next two months," holding that "during the next two months, because of the lack of 'rebuttal time' before election to justify particular actions which may be distorted to the U.S. public, we must act with special care—signaling to . . . [the South Vietnamese] that we are behaving energetically despite the restraints of our political season, and to the U.S. public that we are behaving with good purpose and restraint" (Vol. 3, pp. 556–559).

As the campaign wore on, President Johnson increasingly professed to be the candidate of peace. He gave no indication of the growing pressure for escalation from high administrative officials who would remain in office should he win; no hint of the hard choice he knew he would face if reelected.[2] Rather he repeated over and over again that "the first responsibility, the only real issue in this campaign, the only thing you ought to be concerned about at all, is: Who can best keep the peace?" (White, 1965, p. 373).

The stratagem succeeded; the election was won; the war escalated. Under the name of Operation Rolling Thunder, the United States launched massive bombing raids over North Vietnam early in 1965. In suppressing genuine debate about these plans during the election campaign and masquerading as the party of peace, government members privy to the maneuver believed that they knew what was best for the country and that history would vindicate them. They meant to benefit the nation and the world by keeping the danger of a communist victory at bay. If a sense of crisis was needed for added justification, the domino theory strained for it: one regime after another was seen as toppling should the first domino be pushed over.

But why the deceit, if the purposes were so altruistic? Why not espouse these purposes openly before the election? The reason must have been that the government could not count on popular support for the scheme. In the first place, the sense of crisis and threat from North Vietnam would have been far from universally shared. To be forthright about the likelihood of escalation might lose many votes; it certainly could not fit with the campaign to portray President Johnson as the candidate most likely to keep the peace. Second, the government feared that its explanations might be "distorted" in the election campaign, so that the voters would not have the correct information before them. Third, time was lacking for the government to make an effort at educating the people about all that was at issue. Finally, the plans were not definitive; changes were possible, and the Vietnamese situation itself very unstable. For all these reasons, it seemed best to campaign for negotiation and restraint and let the Republican opponent be the target for the fear of United States belligerence.

President Johnson thus denied the electorate any chance to give or to refuse consent to the escalation of the war in Vietnam. Believing they had voted for the candidate of peace, American citizens were, within months, deeply embroiled in one of the cruelest wars in their history. Deception of this kind strikes at the very essence of democratic government. It allows those in power to override or nullify the right vested in the people to cast an informed vote in critical elections. Deceiving the people for the sake of the people is a self-contradictory notion in a democracy, unless it can be shown that there has been genuine consent to deceit. The actions of President Johnson were therefore inconsistent with the most basic principle of our political system.

What if all governments felt similarly free to deceive provided they believed the deception genuinely necessary to achieve some important public end? The trouble is that those who make such calculations are always susceptible to bias. They overestimate the likelihood that the benefit will occur and that the harm will be averted; they underestimate the chances that the deceit will be discovered and ignore the effects of such a discovery on trust; they underrate the comprehension of the deceived citizens, as well as their ability and their right to make a reasoned choice. And, most important, such a benevolent self-righteousness disguises the many motives for political lying which could not serve as moral excuses: the need to cover up past mistakes; the vindictiveness; the desire to stay in power. These self-serving ends provide the impetus for countless lies that are rationalized as "necessary" for the public good.

As political leaders become accustomed to making such excuses, they grow insensitive to fairness and to veracity. Some come to believe that any lie can be told so long as they can convince themselves that people will be better off in the long run. From there, it is a short step to the conclusion that, even if people will not be better off from a particular lie, they will benefit by all maneuvers to keep the right people in office. Once public servants lose their bearings in this way, all the shabby deceits of Watergate—the fake telegrams, the erased tapes, the elaborate cover-ups, the bribing of witnesses to make them lie, the televised pleas for trust—become possible.

While Watergate may be unusual in its scope, most observers would agree that deception is part and parcel of many everyday decisions in government. Statistics may be presented in such a way as to diminish the gravity of embarrassing problems. Civil servants may lie to members of Congress in order to protect programs they judge important, or to guard secrets they have been ordered not to divulge. If asked, members of Congress who make deals with one another to vote for measures they would otherwise oppose deny having made such deals. False rumors may be leaked by subordinates who believe that unwise executive action is about to be taken. Or the leak may be correct, but falsely attributed in order to protect the source.

Consider the following situation and imagine all the variations on this theme being played in campaigns all over the United States, at the local, state, or federal level:

A big-city mayor is running for reelection. He has read a report recommending that he remove rent controls after his reelection. He intends to do so, but believes he will lose the election if his intention is known. When asked, at a news conference two days before his election, about the existence of such a report, he denies knowledge of it and reaffirms his strong support of rent control.

In the mayor's view, his reelection is very much in the public interest, and the lie concerns questions which he believes the voters are unable to evaluate properly, especially on such short notice. In all similar situations, the sizable bias resulting from the self-serving element (the desire to be elected, to stay in office, to exercise power) is often clearer to onlookers than to the liars themselves. This bias inflates the alleged justifications for the lie—the worthiness, superiority, altruism of the liar, the rightness of his cause, and the inability of those deceived to respond "appropriately" to hearing the truth.

These common lies are now so widely suspected that voters are at a loss to know when they can and cannot believe what a candidate says in campaigning. The damage to trust has been immense. I have already referred to the poll which found 69 percent of Americans agreeing, both in 1975 and 1976, that the country's leaders had consistently lied to the American people over the past ten years. Over 40 percent of the respondents also agreed that "most politicians are so similar that it doesn't really make much difference who gets elected" (1975, 1976).

Many refuse to vote under such circumstances. Others look to appearance or to personality factors for clues as to which candidate might be more honest than the others. Voters and candidates alike are the losers when a political system has reached such a low level of trust. Once elected, officials find that their warnings and their calls to common sacrifice meet with disbelief and apathy, even when cooperation is most urgently needed. Lawsuits and investigations multiply. And the fact that candidates, should they win, are not expected to have meant what they said while campaigning, nor held accountable for discrepancies, only reinforces the incentives for them to bend the truth the next time, thus adding further to the distrust of the voters.

Political lies, so often assumed to be trivial by those who tell them, rarely are. They cannot be trivial when they affect so many people and when they are so peculiarly likely to be imitated, used to retaliate, and spread from a few to many. When political representatives or entire governments arrogate to themselves the right to lie, they take power from the public that would not have been given up voluntarily.

DECEPTION AND CONSENT

Can there be exceptions to the well-founded distrust of deception in public life? Are there times when the public itself might truly not care about possible lies, or might even prefer to be deceived? Are some white lies so trivial or so transparent that they can be ignored? And can we envisage public discussion of more seriously misleading government statements such that reasonable persons could consent to them in advance?

White lies, first of all, are as common to political and diplomatic affairs as they are to the private lives of most people. Feigning enjoyment of an embassy gathering or a political rally, toasting the longevity of a dubious regime or an unimpressive candidate for office—these are forms of politeness that mislead few. It is difficult to regard them as threats to either individuals or communities. As with all white lies, however, the problem is that they spread so easily, and that lines are very hard to draw. Is it still a white lie for a secretary of state to announce that he is going to one country when in reality he travels to another? Or for a president to issue a "cover story" to the effect that a cold is forcing him to return to the White House, when in reality an international crisis made him cancel the rest of his campaign trip? Is it a white lie to issue a letter of praise for a public servant one has just fired? Given the vulnerability of public trust, it is never more important than in public life to keep the deceptive element of white lies to an absolute minimum, and to hold down the danger of their turning into more widespread deceitful practices.

A great deal of deception believed not only innocent but highly justified by public figures concerns their private lives. Information about their marriages, their children, their opinions about others—information about their personal plans and about their motives for personal decisions—all are theirs to keep private if they wish to do so. Refusing to give information under these circumstances is justifiable—but the right to withhold information is not the right to lie about it. Lying under such circumstances bodes ill for conduct in other matters.[3]

Certain additional forms of deception may be debated and authorized in advance by elected representatives of the public. The use of unmarked police cars to discourage speeding by drivers is an example of such a practice. Various forms of unannounced, sometimes covert, auditing of business and government operations are others. Whenever these practices are publicly regulated, they can be limited so that abuses are avoided. But they must be openly debated and agreed to in advance, with every precaution against abuses of privacy and the rights of individuals, and against the spread of such covert activities. It is not enough that a public official assumes that consent would be given to such practices.

Another type of deceit has no such consent in advance: the temporizing or the lie when truthful information at a particular time might do great damage. Say that a government is making careful plans for announcing the devaluation of its currency. If the news leaks out to some before it can be announced to all, unfair profits for speculators might result. Or take the decision to make sharp increases in taxes on imported goods in order to rescue a tottering economy. To announce the decision beforehand would lead to hoarding and to exactly the results that the taxes are meant to combat. Thus, government officials will typically seek to avoid any premature announcement and will refuse to comment if asked whether devaluation or higher taxes are imminent. At times, however, official spokesmen will go further and falsely deny that the actions in question will in fact take place.

Such lies may well be uttered in good faith in an effort to avoid harmful speculation and hoarding. Nevertheless, if false statements are made to the public only to be exposed as soon as the devaluation or the new tax is announced, great damage to trust will result. It is like telling a patient that an operation will be painless—the swifter the disproof, the more likely the loss of trust. In addition, these lies are subject to all the dangers of spread and mistake and deterioration of standards that accompany all deception.

For these reasons, it is far better to refuse comment than to lie in such situations. The objection may be made, however, that a refusal to comment will be interpreted by the press as tantamount to an admission that devaluation or higher taxes are very near. Such an objection has force only if a government has not already established credibility by letting it be known earlier that it would never comment on such matters, and by strictly adhering to this policy at all times. Since lies in these cases are so egregious, it is worth taking care to establish such credibility in advance, so that a refusal to comment is not taken as an invitation to monetary speculation.

Another form of deception takes place when the government regards the public as frightened, or hostile, and highly volatile. In order not to create a panic, information about early signs of an epidemic may be suppressed or distorted. And the lie to a mob seeking its victim is like lying to the murderer asking where the person he is pursuing has gone. It can be acknowledged and defended as soon as the threat is over. In such cases, one may at times be justified in withholding information—perhaps, on rare occasions, even in lying. But such cases are so rare that they hardly exist for practical purposes.

The fact that rare circumstances exist where the justification for government lying seems powerful creates a difficulty—these same excuses will often be made to serve a great many more purposes. For some governments or public officials, the information they wish to conceal is almost never of the requisite certainty, the time never the right one, and the public never sufficiently dispassionate. For these reasons, it is hard to see how a practice of lying to the public about devaluation or changes in taxation or epidemics could be consented to in advance, and therefore justified.

Are there any exceptionally dangerous circumstances where the state of crisis is such as to justify lies to the public for its own protection? We have already discussed lying to enemies in an acute crisis. Sometimes the domestic public is then also deceived, at least temporarily, as in the case of the U-2 incident. Wherever there is a threat—from a future enemy, as before World War II, or from a shortage of energy—the temptation to draw upon the excuses for deceiving citizens is very strong. The government may sincerely doubt that the electorate is capable of making the immediate sacrifices needed to confront the growing danger. (Or one branch of the government may lack confidence in another, for similar reasons, as when the administration mistrusts Congress.) The public may seem too emotional, the time not yet ripe for disclosure. Are there crises so exceptional that deceptive strategies are justifiable?

Compare, for instance, what was said and left unsaid by two United States presidents confronted by a popular unwillingness to enter a war: President Lyndon Johnson, in escalating the war in Vietnam, and President Franklin D. Roosevelt, in moving the country closer to participating in World War II, while making statements such as the following in his 1940 campaign to be reelected: "I have said this before, but I shall say it again and again and again: Your boys are not going to be sent into any foreign wars" (*Public Paper and Addresses . . .*, 1940, p. 517).

By the standards set forth in this chapter, President Johnson's covert escalation and his failure to consult the electorate concerning the undeclared war in Vietnam was clearly unjustifiable. Consent was bypassed; there was no immediate danger to the nation which could even begin to excuse deceiving the public in a national election on grounds of an acute crisis.

The crisis looming before World War II, on the other hand, was doubtless much greater. Certainly this case is a difficult one, and one on which reasonable persons might not be able to agree. The threat was unprecedented; the need for preparations and for support of allies great; yet the difficulties of alerting the American public seemed insuperable. Would this crisis, then, justify proceeding through deceit?

To consent even to such deception would, I believe, be to take a frightening step. Do we want to live in a society where public officials can resort to deceit and manipulation whenever they decide that an exceptional crisis has arisen? Would we not, on balance, prefer to run the risk of failing to rise to a crisis honestly explained to us, from which the government might have saved us through manipulation? And what protection from abuse do we foresee should we surrender this choice?

In considering answers to these questions, we must take into account more than the short-run effects of government manipulation. President Roosevelt's manner of bringing the American people to accept first the possibility, then the likelihood, of war was used as an example by those who wanted to justify President Johnson's acts of dissimulation. And these acts in turn were pointed to by those who resorted to so many forms of duplicity in the Nixon administration. Secrecy and deceit grew at least in part because of existing precedents.[4]

The consequences of spreading deception, alienation, and lack of trust could not have been documented for us more concretely than they have in the past decades. We have had a very vivid illustration of how lies undermine our political system. While deception under the circumstances confronting President Roosevelt may in hindsight be more excusable than much that followed, we could no more consent to it in advance than to all that came later.

Wherever lies to the public have become routine, then, very special safeguards should be required. The test of public justification of deceptive practices is more needed than ever. It will be a hard test to satisfy, the more so the more trust is invested in those who lie and the more power they wield. Those in government and other positions of trust should be held to the highest standards. Their lies are not ennobled by their positions; quite the contrary. Some lies—notably minor white lies and emergency lies rapidly acknowledged—may be more excusable than others, but only those deceptive practices which can be openly debated and consented to in advance are justifiable in a democracy.[5]

Notes

1. The *gennaion pseudos* has generated much controversy. Some have translated it as "pious fraud" and debated whether such fraud can be perpetrated. Thus, Hastings Rashdall (1924, bk I, p. 195) argued that such frauds would be justifiable "if (when *all* their consequences are considered) they were socially beneficial." Other translations are "royal lie" (Jowett), and "bold flight of the imagination" (Cornford). The latter represents an effort to see Plato as advocating not lies by the government but stories, and possible errors; an interpretation that is difficult to uphold in view of the other contexts in the *Republic* where lying is discussed, such as 389b: "The rulers of the city may, if anybody, fitly lie on account of enemies or citizens for the benefit of the state." For Plato to have endorsed lying by the state is very significant, as truth for him was opposed, not just to falsehood, but to unreality.

2. As early as March 1964, Lyndon Johnson knew that such a hard choice might have to be made. See the telephone transcript cited by Kearns (1976, p. 197).

3. A lie by an experienced adult in a position of authority about private matters that can be protected by a refusal to speak is therefore much less excusable than a lie by the school child described by Bonhoeffer (1965): too frightened by the bullying teacher to be able to stand up to him or think of a nondeceptive "way out" on the spur of the moment.

4. See Schlesinger (1973, p. 356): "The power to withhold and the power to leak led on inexorably to the power to lie . . . uncontrolled secrecy made it easy for lying to become routine." See also Wise (1973).

5. For discussion of lying and moral choice in politics, see Plato's *The Republic;* Machiavelli's *The Prince;* Grotius's *On the Law of War and Peace;* Krauss's fascinating compilation of answers by Condorcet and others in a contest sponsored by Frederick II in 1780; Weber (1946); and Walzer (1973).

References

Bonhoeffer, D. "What Is Meant by 'Telling the Truth'?" In Eberhard Bethge (ed.), *Ethics*, pp. 363–72. New York: Macmillan, 1965.

Cambridge Survey Research. 1975.

Cambridge Survey Research. 1976.

Erasmus. *Responsio ad Albertum Pium, Opera Omnia*. Hildesheim, 1962. (Originally published 1706.)

The Senator Gravel Edition. *The Pentagon Papers*. Boston: Beacon Press, 1971, *3*, 556–559.

Kearns, D. *Lyndon Johnson and the American Dream*. New York: HarperCollins, 1976.

Krauss, W. (ed.). *Est-il utile de tromer le peuple?* Berlin: Akademic-Verlag, 1966.

The Public Papers and Addresses of Franklin D. Roosevelt. Washington, D.C.: Government Printing Office, 1940.

Rashdall, H. *The Theory of Good Evil* (2nd ed.). New York: Oxford University Press, 1924.

Schlesinger, A. M., Jr. *The Imperial Presidency*. Boston: Houghton Mifflin, 1973.

Sylvester, A. "The Government Has the Right to Lie." *Saturday Evening Post*, Nov. 18, 1967, p. 10.

Walzer, M. "Political Action: The Problem of Dirty Hands." *Philosophy and Public Affairs*, 1973, *2*, 160–180.

Weber, M. "Politics as a Vocation." In M. Weber, *Essays in Sociology* (H. H. Gerth and C. W. Mills, trans.). New York: Oxford University Press, 1946.

White, T. H. *The Making of the President 1964*. New York: Atheneum, 1965.

Wise, D. *The Politics of Lying*. New York: Random House, 1973.

CHAPTER TWENTY-FIVE

Does Studying Economics Inhibit Cooperation?

Robert H. Frank

Thomas Gilovich

Dennis T. Regan

From the perspective of many economists, motives other than self-interest are peripheral to the main thrust of human endeavor, and we indulge them at our peril. In Gordon Tullock's (1976) words, "The average human being is about 95 percent selfish in the narrow sense of the term" (Mansbridge, 1990, p. 12).

In this paper we investigate whether exposure to the self-interest model commonly used in economics alters the extent to which people behave in self-interested ways. The paper is organized into two parts. In the first, we report the results of several empirical studies—some our own, some by others—that suggest economists behave in more self-interested ways. By itself, this evidence does not demonstrate that exposure to the self-interest model causes more self-interested behavior, since it may be that economists were simply more self-interested to begin with, and this difference was one reason they chose to study economics. In the second part of the paper, we present preliminary evidence that exposure to the self-interest model does in fact encourage self-interested behavior.

DO ECONOMISTS BEHAVE DIFFERENTLY?

Free-Rider Experiments

A study by Gerald Marwell and Ruth Ames (1981) found that first-year graduate students in economics are much more likely than others to free-ride in experiments that called for private contributions to public goods. In their experiments, groups of subjects were given initial endowments of money, which they were to allocate between two accounts, one "public," the other "private." Money deposited in the subject's private account was returned dollar-for-dollar to the subject at the end of the experiment. Money deposited in the public account was pooled, multiplied by some factor greater than one, and then distributed equally among all subjects. Under these circumstances, the socially optimal behavior is for all subjects to put their entire endowment in the public account. But from an individual perspective, the most advantageous strategy is to put everything in the private account. Marwell and Ames found that economics students contributed an average of only 20 percent of their endowments to the public account, significantly less than the 49 percent average for all other subjects.

To explore the reasons for this difference, the authors asked their subjects two follow-up questions. First, what is a "fair" investment in the public good? Of the noneconomists, 75 percent answered "half or more" of the endowment, and 25 percent answered "all." Second, are you concerned about "fairness" in making your investment decision? Almost all noneconomists answered "yes." The corresponding responses of the economics graduate students were more difficult to summarize. As Marwell and Ames wrote,

> More than one-third of the economists either refused to answer the question regarding what is fair, or gave very complex, uncodable responses. It seems that the meaning of "fairness" in this context was somewhat alien for this group. Those who did respond were much more likely to say that little or no contribution was "fair." In addition, the economics graduate students were about half as likely as other subjects to indicate that they were "concerned with fairness" in making their decisions.

The Marwell and Ames study can be criticized on the grounds that their noneconomist control groups consisted of high school students and college undergraduates, who differ in a variety of ways from first-year graduate students in any discipline. Perhaps the most obvious difference is age. As we will see, however, criticism based on the age difference is blunted by our own evidence that older students generally give greater weight to social concerns like the ones that arise in free-rider experiments. It remains possible, however, that more mature students might have had a more sophisticated understanding of the nuances and ambiguities inherent in concepts like fairness, and for that reason gave less easily coded responses to the follow-up questions.

Yet another concern with the Marwell and Ames experiments is not easily dismissed. Although the authors do not report the sex composition of their group of economics graduate students, such groups are almost always preponderantly male. The authors' control groups of high school and undergraduate students, by contrast, consisted equally of males and females.[1] As our own evidence will later show, there is a sharp tendency for males to behave less cooperatively in experiments of this sort. So while the Marwell and Ames findings are suggestive, they do not clearly establish that economists behave differently.

Economists and the Ultimatum Bargaining Game

Another study of whether economists behave differently from members of other disciplines is by John Carter and Michael Irons (1991). These authors measured self-interestedness by examining behavior in an ultimatum bargaining game. This simple game has two players, an "allocator" and a "receiver." The allocator is given a sum of money (in these experiments, $10), and must then propose a division of this sum between herself and the receiver. Once the allocator makes this proposal, the receiver has two choices: (1) he may accept, in which case each player gets the amount proposed by the allocator; or (2) he may refuse, in which case each player gets zero. The game is played only once by the same partners.

Assuming the money cannot be divided into units smaller than $0.01, the self-interest model unequivocally predicts that the allocator will propose $9.99 for herself and the remaining $0.01 for the receiver, and that the receiver will accept on the grounds that a penny is better than nothing. Since the game will not be repeated, there is no point in the receiver turning down a low offer in the hope of generating a better offer in the future.

Other researchers have shown that the strategy predicted by the self-interest model is almost never followed in practice: 50–50 splits are the most common proposal, and most highly one-sided offers are rejected in the name of fairness (Guth, Schmittberger, and Schwarze, 1982; Kahneman, Knetsch, and Thaler, 1986). Carter and Irons found that in both roles (allocator and receiver) economics majors performed significantly more in accord with the predictions of the self-interest model than did nonmajors.[2]

As always, questions can be raised about experimental design. In this case, for example, Carter and Irons assigned the allocator and receiver roles by choosing as allocators those who achieved higher scores on a preliminary word game.[3] Allocators trained in the marginal productivity theory of wages (that is, economics majors) might thus be more likely than others to reason that they were entitled to a greater share of the surplus on the strength of their earlier performance. But while not conclusive, the Carter and Irons results are again suggestive.

Survey Data on Charitable Giving

The free-rider hypothesis suggests that economists might be less likely than others to donate to private charities. To explore this possibility, we mailed questionnaires to 1,245 college professors randomly chosen from the professional directories of 23 disciplines, asking them to report the annual dollar amounts they gave to a variety of private charities. We received 576 responses with sufficient detail for inclusion in our study. Respondents were grouped into the following disciplines: economics (N = 75); other social sciences (N = 106); math, computer science, and engineering (N = 48); natural sciences (N = 98); humanities (N = 94); architecture, art, and music (N = 68); and professional (N = 87).[4] The proportion of pure free riders among economists—that is, those who reported giving no money to any charity—was 9.3 percent. By contrast, only 1.1 percent of the professional school respondents gave no money to charity, and the share of those in the other five disciplines who reported zero donations ranged between 2.9 and 4.2 percent.[5] Despite their generally higher incomes, economists were also among the least generous in terms of their median gifts to large charities like viewer-supported television and the United Way.[6]

On a number of other dimensions covered in our survey, the behavior of economists was little different from the behavior of members of other disciplines. For example, economists were only marginally less likely than members of other disciplines to report that they would take costly administrative action to prosecute a student suspected of cheating. Economists were slightly above average for the entire sample in terms of the numbers of hours they reported spending in "volunteer activities." And in terms of their reported frequency of voting in presidential elections, economists were only slightly below the sample average.[7]

Economists and the Prisoner's Dilemma

One of the most celebrated and controversial predictions of the self-interest model is that people will always defect in a one-shot prisoner's dilemma game. Table 25.1 shows the monetary payoffs in dollars to two players, X and Y, in a standard prisoner's dilemma. The key feature of such a game is that for each player, defection has a higher payoff irrespective of the choice made by the other player. Yet if both players follow this self-interested logic and defect, both end up with a lower payoff than if each cooperates. The game thus provides a rich opportunity to examine self-interested behavior.

We conducted a prisoner's dilemma experiment involving both economics majors and nonmajors. All groups were given an extensive briefing on the prisoner's dilemma at the start of the experiment and each subject was required to complete a questionnaire at the end to verify that he or she had indeed understood the consequences of different combinations of choices; in addition, many of our subjects were students recruited from courses in which the prisoner's dilemma is an item on the syllabus. Our subjects met in groups of three and each was told that he or she would play the game once only with each of the other two subjects. The payoff matrix, shown in Table 25.1, was the same for each play of the game. Subjects were told that the games would be played for

Table 25.1. Monetary Payoffs for a Prisoner's Dilemma Game

		Player X	
		Cooperate	Defect
	Cooperate	2 for X 2 for Y	3 for X 0 for Y
You	Defect	0 for X 3 for Y	1 for X 1 for Y

real money, and that confidentiality would be maintained so that none of the players would learn how their partners had responded in any play of the game.

Following a period in which subjects were given an opportunity to get to know one another, each subject was taken to a separate room and asked to fill out a form indicating a response (cooperate or defect) to each of the other two players in the group. After the subjects had filled out their forms, the results were tallied and the payments disbursed. Each subject received a single payment that was the sum of three separate amounts: the payoff from the game with the first partner; the payoff from the game with the second partner; and a term that was drawn at random from a large list of positive and negative values. None of these three elements could be observed separately, only their sum. The purpose of this procedure was to prevent subjects from inferring both individual and group patterns of choice. Thus, unlike earlier prisoner's dilemma experiments,[8] ours did not enable the subject to infer what happened even when each (or neither) of the other players defected.

In one version of the experiment (the "unlimited" version), subjects were told that they could make promises not to defect during the time they were getting to know each other, but they were also told that the anonymity of their responses would render such promises unenforceable. In two other versions of the experiment (the "intermediate" and "limited" versions), subjects were not permitted to make promises about their strategies. The latter two versions differed from one another in terms of the length of pre-game interaction, with up to 30 minutes permitted for the intermediate groups and no more than ten minutes for the limited groups.

For the sample as a whole there were a total of 267 games, which means a total of 534 choices between cooperation and defection. For these choices, the defection rate for economics majors was 60.4 percent, as compared to only

38.8 percent for nonmajors. This pattern of differences strongly supports the hypothesis that economics majors are more likely than nonmajors to behave self-interestedly ($p < .005$).[9]

One possible explanation for the observed differences between economics students and others is that economics students are more likely to be male, and males have lower cooperation rates. To control for possible influences of sex, age, and experimental condition, we performed the ordinary least squares regression reported in Table 25.2.[10] Because each subject played the game twice, the individual responses are not statistically independent. To get around this problem, we limited our sample to the 207 subjects who either cooperated with, or defected from, each of their two partners. The 60 subjects who cooperated with one partner and defected on the other were deleted from the sample. The dependent variable is the subject's choice of strategy, coded as 0 for "cooperate" and 1 for "defect." The independent variables are "econ," which takes the value 1 for economics majors, 0 for all others; "unlimited," which is 1 for subjects in the unlimited version of the experiment, 0 for all others; "intermediate," which is 1 for subjects in the intermediate version, 0 for all others; "limited,"

Table 25.2. Whole Sample Regression

Variable	Coefficient	Standard Error	t-Ratio
Constant	0.579127	0.1041	5.57
Econ	0.168835	0.0780	2.16
Limited	0.00	—	—
Intermediate	−0.091189	0.0806	−1.13
Unlimited	−0.329572	0.0728	−4.53
Sex	0.239944	0.0642	3.74
Class	−0.065363	0.0303	−2.16

$R^2 = 22.2\%$ R^2 (adjusted) $= 20.3\%$

$S = 0.4402$ with $207 - 6 = 201$ degrees of freedom

Source	Sum of Squares	df	Mean Square	F-Ratio
Regression	11.1426	5	2.229	11.5
Residual	38.9540	201	0.193801	—

Note: Dependent variable: cooperate is 0 and defect is 1.

which is the reference category; "sex," coded as 1 for males, 0 for females; and "class," coded as 1 for freshmen, 2 for sophomores, 3 for juniors, and 4 for seniors.

Consistent with a variety of other findings on sex differences in cooperation,[11] we estimate that, other factors the same, the probability of a male defecting is almost 0.24 higher than the corresponding probability for a female. But even after controlling for the influence of gender, we see that the probability of an economics major defecting is almost 0.17 higher than the corresponding probability for a nonmajor.

The coefficients for the unlimited and intermediate experimental categories represent effects relative to the defection rate for the limited category. As expected, the defection rate is smaller in the intermediate category (where subjects have more time to interact than in the limited category), and falls sharply further in the unlimited category (where subjects are permitted to make promises to cooperate).[12]

Note, finally, that the overall defection rate declines significantly as students progress through school. The class coefficient is interpreted to mean that with the passage of each year the probability of defection declines, on the average, by almost 0.07. This pattern will prove important when we take up the question of whether training in economics is the cause of higher defection rates for economics majors.

For subjects in the unlimited subsample, we found that the difference between economics majors and nonmajors virtually disappears once subjects are permitted to make promises to cooperate. For this subsample, the defection rate for economics majors is 28.6 percent, compared to 25.9 percent for nonmajors. Because the higher defection rates for economics majors are largely attributable to the no-promises conditions of the experiment, the remainder of our analysis focuses on subjects in the limited and intermediate groups. The conditions encountered by these groups are of special significance, because they come closest to approximating the conditions that characterize social dilemmas encountered in practice. After all, people rarely have an opportunity to look one another in the eye and promise not to litter on deserted beaches or disconnect the smog control devices on their cars.

When the choices are pooled for the limited and intermediate groups, both economics majors and nonmajors defect more often, but the effect is considerably larger for economists. In those groups, the defection rate was 71.8 percent for economics majors and just 47.3 percent for nonmajors, levels that differ significantly at the .01 level.

As part of the exit questionnaire that tested understanding of the payoffs associated with different combinations of choices, we also asked subjects to state reasons for their choices. We hypothesized that economists would be more inclined to construe the objective of the game in self-interested terms, and therefore more likely to refer exclusively to features of the game itself, while noneconomists would be more open to alternative ways of interpreting the game, and would refer more often to their feelings about their partners, aspects of human nature, and so on. Indeed, among the sample of economics students, 31 percent referred only to features of the game itself in explaining their chosen strategies, compared with only 17 percent of the noneconomists. The probability of obtaining such divergent responses by chance is less than .05.

Another possible explanation for the economists' higher defection rates is that economists may be more likely to expect their partners to defect. The self-interest model, after all, encourages such an expectation, and we know from other experiments that most subjects defect if they are told that their partners are going to defect. To investigate this possibility, we asked students in an upper-division public finance course in Cornell's economics department whether they would cooperate or defect in a one-shot prisoner's dilemma if they knew with certainty that their partner was going to cooperate. Most of these students were economics majors in their junior and senior years. Of the 31 students returning our questionnaires, 18 (58 percent) reported that they would defect, and only 13 that they would cooperate. By contrast, just 34 percent of noneconomics Cornell undergraduates who were given the same questionnaire reported that they would defect from a partner they knew would cooperate ($p < .05$). For the same two groups of subjects, almost all respondents (30 of 31 economics students and 36 of 41 noneconomics students) said they would defect if they knew their partner would defect. From these responses, we conclude that while expectations of partner performance play a strong role in predicting behavior, defection rates would remain significantly higher for economists than for noneconomists even if both groups held identical expectations about partner performance.

WHY DO ECONOMISTS BEHAVE DIFFERENTLY?

Economists appear to behave less cooperatively than noneconomists along a variety of dimensions. This difference in behavior might result from training in economics; alternatively, it might exist because people who chose to major in economics were different initially; or it might be some combination of these two effects. We now report evidence on whether training in economics plays a causal role.

Comparing Upperclassmen and Underclassmen

If economics training causes uncooperative behavior, then defection rates in the prisoner's dilemma should rise with exposure to training in economics, all other factors held constant. Recalling our earlier finding that defection rates for the sample as a whole fall steadily between the freshman and senior years, the question is thus whether defection rates fall to the same degree over time for economists as for noneconomists. We found that the pattern of falling defection rates holds more strongly for noneconomics majors than for economics majors in the no-promises subsample. For noneconomics underclassmen in this group (freshmen and sophomores), the defection rate is 53.7 percent, compared to only 40.2 percent for upperclassmen. By contrast, the trend toward lower defection rates is virtually absent from economics majors in the no-promises subsample (73.7 percent for underclassmen, 70.0 percent for upperclassmen). In other words, students generally show a pronounced tendency toward more cooperative behavior with movement toward graduation, but this trend is conspicuously absent for economics majors.[13]

Naturally, we are in no position to say whether the trend for noneconomists reflects something about the content of noneconomics courses. But the fact that this trend is not present for economists is at least consistent with the hypothesis that training in economics plays some causal role in the lower observed cooperation rates of economists.

Honesty Surveys

In a further attempt to assess whether training in economics inhibits cooperation, we posed a pair of ethical dilemmas to students in two introductory microeconomics courses at Cornell University and to a control group of students in an introductory astronomy course, also at Cornell. In one dilemma, the owner of a small business is shipped ten microcomputers but is billed for only nine; the question is whether the owner will inform the computer company of the error. Subjects are first asked to estimate the likelihood that the owner would point out the mistake; and then, on the same response scale, to indicate how likely *they* would be to point out the error if they were the owner. The second dilemma concerns whether a lost envelope containing $100 and bearing the owner's name and address is likely to be returned by the person who finds it. Subjects are first asked to imagine that they have lost the envelope and to estimate the likelihood that a stranger would return it. They are then asked to assume that the roles are reversed and to indicate the likelihood that they would return the money to a stranger.

Students in each class completed the questionnaire on two occasions: during the initial week of class in September, and then during the final week of class in December. For each of the four questions, each student was coded as being "more honest" if the probability checked for that question rose between September and December; "less honest" if it fell during that period; and "no change" if it remained the same.

The first introductory microeconomics instructor (instructor A) whose students we surveyed is a mainstream economist with research interests in industrial organization and game theory. In class lectures, this instructor placed heavy emphasis on the prisoner's dilemma and related illustrations of how survival imperatives often militate against cooperation. The second microeconomics instructor (instructor B) is a specialist in economic development in Maoist China who did not emphasize such material to the same degree, but did assign a mainstream introductory text. On the basis of these differences, we expected that any observed effects of economics training should be stronger in instructor A's class than in instructor B's. The results for these two classes, plus the class of noneconomists, are summarized in Figure 25.1, which shows the proportion of each class reporting a "less honest" result at the end of the semester than at the beginning. As the figure indicates, one semester's training was accompanied by greater movement toward more cynical ("less honest") responses in instructor A's introductory economics class than in instructor B's. Subjects in instructor B's class, in turn, showed greater movement toward less honest responses than did those in our control group of introductory astronomy students.

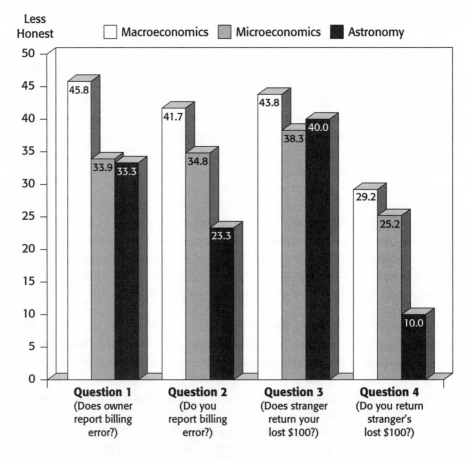

Figure 25.1. Freshmen Honesty Survey Results

It may seem natural to wonder whether some of the differences between the two economics classes might stem from the fact that students chose their instructors rather than being randomly assigned. Perhaps the ideological reputations of the two professors were known in advance to many students, with the result that a disproportionate number of less cynical students chose to take instructor B's course. However, the average values of the initial responses to the four questions were virtually the same for both classes. Moreover, even if students had differed across the two classes, this would not alter the interpretation of our findings, since the entries in Figure 25.1 record not the *level* of cynicism but the change in that level between the beginning and end of the course. Even if the students in Microeconomics A were more cynical to begin with, they became still more so during the course of the semester. This finding is consistent with the hypothesis that emphasis on the self-interest model tends to inhibit cooperation.

DISCUSSION

A variety of evidence suggests a large difference in the extent to which economists and noneconomists behave self-interestedly. We believe our survey of charitable giving and our prisoner's dilemma results lend additional support to the hypothesis that economists are more likely than others to free-ride.

Both of these exercises, however, also produced evidence that economists behave in traditionally communitarian ways under at least some circumstances. For example, economists reported spending as much time as others in volunteer activities, and were only marginally less likely than others to vote in presidental elections. Moreover, in the unlimited version of our prisoner's dilemma experiments, where subjects were allowed to promise to cooperate, economists were almost as likely to cooperate as noneconomists.

We also found evidence consistent with the view that differences in cooperativeness are caused in part by training in economics. This evidence is clearly less compelling than the evidence for a difference in cooperativeness. But it would be remarkable indeed if none of the observed differences in behavior were the result of repeated and intensive exposure to a model whose unequivocal prediction is that people will defect whenever self-interest dictates.

Should we be concerned that economics training may inhibit cooperation? Some might respond that while society would benefit if more people cooperated in social dilemmas, economists cannot be faulted for pointing out the unpleasant truth that self-interest dictates defection. One difficulty with this response is that it may be wrong. Several researchers have suggested that the ultimate victims of noncooperative behavior may be the very people who practice it (see, for example, Akerlof, 1983; Hirshleifer, 1987; Frank, 1988; and the essays in Mansbridge, 1990). Suppose, by way of illustration, that some people always cooperate in one-shot prisoner's dilemmas while others always follow the seemingly dominant strategy of defecting. If people are free to interact with others of their own choosing, and if there are cues that distinguish cooperators from defectors, then cooperators will interact selectively with one another and earn higher payoffs than defectors. Elsewhere we have shown that even on the basis of brief encounters involving strangers, experimental subjects are adept at predicting who will cooperate and who will defect in prisoner's dilemma games (Frank, 1988; Frank, Gilovich, and Regan, 1993). If people are even better at predicting the behavior of people they know well—a reasonable enough presumption—then the direct pursuit of material self-interest may indeed often be self-defeating.

In an ever more interdependent world, social cooperation has become increasingly important—and yet increasingly fragile. With an eye toward both the social good and the well-being of their own students, economists may wish to stress a broader view of human motivation in their teaching.

Notes

1. This was the case, in any event, for the groups whose sex composition the authors reported.

2. Kahneman, Knetsch, and Thaler (1986) report findings similar to those of Carter and Irons (1991): commerce students (the term used to describe business students in Canadian universities) were more likely than psychology students to make one-sided offers in ultimatum bargaining games.

3. This allocation procedure is described in a longer, unpublished version of Carter and Irons (1990).

4. The "other social sciences" category includes psychology, sociology, political science, and anthropology; "natural sciences" includes physics, chemistry, biology, and geology; "humanities" includes philosophy, history, English, foreign languages, and religion; and "professional" includes education, business, and nursing.

5. Although we do not have data on the gender of each survey respondent, gender differences by discipline do not appear to account for the observed pattern of free-ridership. For example, the natural sciences, which are also preponderantly male, had only one-third as many free riders as did economics.

6. The annual median gift of economists to charities is actually slightly larger, in absolute terms, than the median for all disciplines taken as a whole. But because economists have significantly higher salaries than do the members of most other disciplines, the median gift overstates the relative generosity of economists. To correct for income differences by discipline, we proceeded as follows. First, we estimated earnings functions (salary versus years of experience) for each discipline using data from a large private university. We then applied the estimated

coefficients from these earnings functions to the experience data from our survey to impute an income for each respondent in our survey. Using these imputed income figures, together with our respondents' reports of their total charitable giving, we estimated the relationship between income and total giving. (In the latter exercise, all economists were dropped from the sample on the grounds that our object was to see whether the giving pattern of economists deviates from the pattern we see for other disciplines.) We then calculated our measure of a discipline's generosity as the ratio of the average value of gifts actually reported by members of the discipline to the average value of gifts expected on the basis of the members' imputed incomes. The computed ratio for economists was 0.91, which means that economists in our sample gave 91 percent as much as they would have been expected to give on the basis of their imputed incomes.

7. In fairness to the self-interest model, we should note that there may be self-interested reasons for volunteering or contributing even in the case of charities like the United Way and public television. United Way campaigns, for example, are usually organized in the workplace, and there is often considerable social pressure to contribute. Public television fund drives often make on-the-air announcements of donors' names, and economists stand to benefit just as much as the members of any other discipline from being hailed as community-minded citizens. In the case of smaller, more personal charitable organizations, there are often even more compelling self-interested reasons for giving or volunteering. After all, failure to contribute in accordance with one's financial ability may mean outright exclusion from the substantial private benefits associated with membership in religious groups, fraternal organizations, and the like.

8. For an extensive survey, see Dawes (1980).

9. Because each subject responded twice, the 534 choices are not statistically independent, and so the most direct test of statistical significance, the chi-square test, is inappropriate for the sample as a whole. To overcome this problem, we performed a chi-square test on the number of subjects who made the same choice—cooperate or defect—in both of their games. There were 207 such subjects (78 percent of the sample). The pattern of results observed in this restricted sample is essentially the same as the one observed for the sample as a whole.

10. Because the conventional assumptions regarding the distribution of the error term are not satisfied in the case of linear models with dichotomous dependent variables, the standard ordinary least squares significance tests are not valid. In an appendix available on request from the authors, we report the results of models based on the probit and logit transformations. The statistical significance patterns shown by the coefficients from these transformed models are the same as for the ordinary least squares model. Because the coefficients of the ordinary least squares model are more easily interpreted, we report the remainder of our results in that format only.

11. See, for example, the studies cited in Gilligan (1982).

12. With the permission of subjects, we tape-recorded the conversations of several of the unlimited groups, and invariably each person promised each partner to cooperate. There would be little point, after all, in promising to defect.

13. A regression similar to the one shown in Table 25.2 confirms that this pattern continues to hold even when controlling for other factors that might influence defection rates.

References

Akerlof, G. "Loyalty Filters." *American Economic Review,* 1983, *73*(1), 54–63.

Carter, J., and Irons, M. "Are Economists Different, and If So, Why?" Working paper, College of the Holy Cross, Dec. 1990.

Carter, J., and Irons, M. "Are Economists Different, and If So, Why?" *Journal of Economic Perspectives,* 1991, *5*(2), 171–177.

Dawes, R. "Social Dilemmas." *Annual Review* of *Psychology,* 1980, *31,* 163–193.

Frank, R. H. *Passions Within Reason.* New York: Norton, 1988.

Frank, R. H., Gilovich, T., and Regan, D. T. "The Evolution of One-Shot Cooperation." *Ethology and Sociobiol*ogy, July 14, 1993, 247–256.

Gilligan, C. *In a Different Voice.* Cambridge, Mass.: Harvard University Press, 1982.

Guth, W., Schmittberger, R., and Schwarze, B. "An Experimental Analysis of Ultimatum Bargaining." *Journal* of *Economic Behavior and Organization,* December 1982, *3* (4), 367–388.

Hirshleifer, J. "On the Emotions as Guarantors of Threats and Promises." In Dupre, John (ed.), *The Latest and the Best: Essays on Evolution and Optimality,* 307–326. Cambridge, Mass.: MIT Press, 1987.

Kahneman, D., Knetsch, J., and Thaler, R. "Fairness and the Assumptions of Economics." *Journal of Business,* 1986, *59,* S285–S300.

Mansbridge, J. J. *Beyond Self-Interest.* Chicago: University of Chicago Press, 1990.

Marwell, G., and Ames, R. "Economists Free Ride, Does Anyone Else? Experiments on the Provision of Public Goods, IV." *Journal of Public Economics,* 1981, *15*(3), 295–310.

Tullock, G. *The Vote Motive.* London: Institute for Economic Affairs, 1976.

CHAPTER TWENTY-SIX

Half-Truths

Protecting Mistaken Inferences by Investors and Others

Donald C. Langevoort

A nice puzzle in the law of fraud has to do with the half-truth—a statement that is literally true but omits some material fact, thereby making it misleading. By all accounts, half-truths are actionable (*Restatement of Torts,* 1981; *Restatement of Contracts,* 1981). But exactly why this is so, or how we should decide when a true statement is deceptive in such a way as to give rise to liability, are questions that have received almost no critical attention.[1] Because half-truth claims are so frequently made in litigation, this leaves an unfortunate risk of confusing precedent.[2] Such confusion, in turn, causes people a good deal of trouble in knowing how to act (or advise their clients) free of legal risk, something particularly problematic given how often we are all tempted to be evasive.

The law's murkiness should not be surprising. Half-truths trigger a high level of both moral and social ambiguity. People often defend themselves against charges of deception by pointing out the technical accuracy of what they said, expecting significantly less blame if not total absolution.[3] If the listener inferred any more than what the statement actually said without seeking clarification, the victim deserves responsibility for assuming too much. In many settings, moreover, half-truths seem to be expected, or at least tolerated. Instructions to tell the "whole truth" notwithstanding, it is generally not considered perjury in a trial or deposition for a witness to give a technically true but evasive answer.[4] Nor is the whole truth expected of lawyers in advocacy settings.[5] In many highly adversarial business or legal negotiations (e.g., contested settlement talks), the baseline norm may not be an iota more than grudging technical accuracy.[6] Given such contingent societal expectations, the potential for misunderstanding legal obligations is all the greater.

Confusion aside, there is also an efficiency-based cause for concern. Though the law of nondisclosure is fluid and fuzzy, there is widespread recognition that parties to a negotiation are privileged to withhold at least some crucial information from the other, lest there be a disincentive to the socially beneficial production or discovery of that sort of information.[7] Yet the half-truth doctrine is sufficiently open-textured that it can apply and override this seemingly strong privilege almost any time a person opens his mouth. To address a subject at all can always lead to the argument that failure to address it fully was misleading.[8] And it is very difficult in any negotiation to avoid touching in some way or another on a subject that is material to the bargain.[9]

My primary interest in this subject stems from the important role that the half-truth doctrine—and the law of omissions and nondisclosures generally—plays under the federal securities laws. Again, there is no doubt that the doctrine applies.[10] Section 17(a)(2) of the Securities Act of 1933 explicitly bars persons from obtaining money or property by means of "any omission to state a material fact necessary in order to make the statements made, in the light of the circumstances under which they were made, not misleading" (U.S. Code sec. 77q(a)(2), 1997). Similar phrases appear in the express private rights of action for investors under Sections 11 (U.S. Code sec. 77k(a), 1997) and 12(a)(2) (U.S. Code 771(a)(2), 1997) of the Securities Act. In turn, the text from Section 17(a) was incorporated verbatim by the Securities and Exchange Commission (SEC) into what has become the most litigated antifraud prohibition of the securities laws, Rule 10b-5 under the Securities Exchange Act of 1934 (17 CFR sec. 240.10b-5, 1999). Courts are asked to apply these words scores of times each year, with particular frequency in cases where a company issues a press release or an executive grants an interview, commenting publicly on some topic. Does that comment trigger a duty to disclose to the investing public other important things company managers know about that subject, regardless of how confidential, sensitive, or embarrassing?

Judges regularly give answers one way or another,[11] but to date none has offered any grounded half-truth theory. Courts tend to declare something a half-truth or not—using exactly the same standard invoked under common law—and move on.[12] Yet a close reading of the cases suggests that the outcomes are often different: courts seem more inclined to dismiss half-truth claims in securities law settings, especially open-market cases, than in common law settings.

What follows is an effort to explain this divergence and thereby advance our understanding of the half-truth doctrine. Like nearly all subjects in the law of fraud, the half-truth resists anything approaching a bright-line restatement. But that should not deter us, for we do not expect an extraordinarily high level of determinacy in the law of fraud anyway. Fraud is about human discourse, which is necessarily contextual and fact-specific. What we can gain, however, is a better sense of the situations in which a person, having opened her mouth and begun to speak, can stop talking at a point short of complete candor. My sense is that some insight can be achieved by situating the half-truth on a continuum roughly half way between the duty to avoid affirmative misrepresentations and the more controversial and contingent duty to reveal hidden private information, both of which have received thoughtful attention in the economics literature. This, in turn, demands that the law seek to capture some sense of the "background norms" of communication in a particular setting—in other words, an assessment of what people are reasonably entitled to expect out of a particular speaker in terms of candor.

A fleshed-out conceptual understanding of the half-truth can then be used as the basis for a better articulation of corporate disclosure obligations under the securities laws. My main argument here is that there has been a failure to acknowledge explicitly the crucial differences that arise when information is publicized by corporations not directly for the benefit of investors, but for some other corporate reason. The proper inferences that investors should draw will vary depending on these differences. Hence, the divergence in outcomes between the common law cases and the open-market securities fraud cases is neither surprising nor unjustified. Indeed, what I will begin to develop is a metatheory of corporate discourse: what the law says about how investors should understand what firms are—or are not—saying when they speak. This theory, in turn, can also illuminate related questions such as when companies have a duty to update previously accurate statements and when a person who expresses excessive optimism violates Rule 10b-5.

COMMON LAW: THE ESSENCE OF THE HALF-TRUTH

The *Restatement (Second) of Torts* (1981) provides a standard definition of the half-truth doctrine. Section 529 says that a "representation stating the truth as far as it goes but which the maker knows or believes to be materially misleading because of the failure to state additional or qualifying matter is a fraudulent misrepresentation."[13] The *Restatement*'s first illustration of this rule is straightforward (see sec. 529). A is selling a tract of land to B and explicitly warns him that the city plans two streets that may lead to a small part of the land being condemned. That is true, but he omits reference to a third planned street that would have a far more severe adverse impact. A commits a fraud.[14]

This seems to be an easy case, and I take it as correct. But why? B could have asked if A knew of any related planned encumbrances and clarified the situation, but failed to do so. It also strikes me as too easy an example, not telling us whether the same result would follow, for example, if A knew not of another planned street by the city but some other comparably adverse action contemplated by a neighbor or private developer.

A number of facts about this hypothetical seem important. A's communication occurs in an arm's-length negotiation setting where A is volunteering information because he wants to induce B to pay a good price for the land. Presumably there were prior conversations about the nature and value of the property, and the information is being offered to B (and B alone) solely for its relevance to this transactional decision. A's disclosure also carries with it a fairly clear implication that the two streets are the only streets planned. I suspect that almost all people would see it that way unless already on notice (as with an adverse witness in a trial setting) that the person is not to be trusted in the first place. Indeed, the law of half-truths is all about determining what, if any, implication follows from one party's statements that would entitle the other party to rely without seeking further clarification. Here, it is hard to imagine any reason why A would volunteer information about the two streets but not the third except to lull B into a false sense of security. A seems to be taking advantage of an influence technique well known to psychologists and salespeople: disarming suspicions and building trust by divulging a fact that is contrary to his own self-interest.[15] This apparent manipulation bolsters the intuition that A's actions are wrongful.

Another important observation: Suppose A had said nothing at all about the two planned streets. Might he nonetheless have an affirmative duty to disclose the city's plans? Though we would want more facts here, the answer under contemporary common law—well recognized in a separate section of the *Restatement (Second) of Torts* (1981, sec. 529)—is that he could well have such a duty. Throughout this century, courts in many jurisdictions have expanded the category of affirmative disclosure duties to situations where the seller of real property knows of a material defect relating to value that is not discoverable by ordinary inquiry.[16] In other words, depending on the difficulty of discovery, it is possible that the half-truth aspect of this case is actually superfluous to the question of liability.

Why should B win here? Although I concede that intuitive notions of fairness and equity do drive much of the judicial decision-making in this area, invoking some economic analysis familiar to problems of contract bargaining helps to generalize from the foregoing.[17] Why do we have law barring affirmative misrepresentation in the first place? Why don't we say that reasonable people should always do their own "due diligence" investigation rather than rely on information provided by someone with an obviously conflicting interest? Putting aside the moral and paternalistic dimensions for a moment, the orthodox answer is that the law of fraud is efficient. It allows the less informed party to forego the costly and duplicative process of factual investigation and information discovery, thereby reducing transaction costs.[18] The law offers a credibility bond for the reliability of factual representations by the informed party.

It is not at all hard to extend this same logic to the half-truth. That is, it facilitates efficient transacting to say that the law will offer a credibility bond when a person speaks not only for the technical accuracy of the statement but also its natural and normal implication as a matter of ordinary communication (putting aside any expectations created by law). Language is inherently imprecise; it is not functional to force people to stop and analyze statements to see if there is some subtle limit or ambiguity that must be clarified. Indeed, it is impossible to distinguish cleanly between conventional misrepresentations and half-truths in the first place.[19] All words require some listener inference, some interpretive work, for comprehension.[20] There may be more inference occurring in a half-truth case, but not really a different sort of inference. A certain level of protection for reasonable inferences is thus appropriate. When the statement is clearly limited or restricted, on the other hand—so that there is a patent ambiguity to it—there should be no right to rely on any further implication. It is important to guard against the predictable tendency among listeners toward "wishful thinking" letting hope or greed, rather than reasonable deliberation, fill in the interpretive gaps of what was said.[21]

The task of determining the natural and normal implication of some statement is, like all questions of discourse, necessarily contextual. What a person derives from a statement depends on his or her frame of reference.[22] But some guidelines may be useful. If factual information is imparted in response to a question by the other party, an unqualified answer is a representation that the speaker has divulged not just accurately but completely, i.e., has provided all the information called for by the scope of the question. When information is simply volunteered (as in the *Restatement* illustration), it should normally be taken as an offer in lieu of the other party's independent fact gathering, and hence an implied representation that it contains all the information necessary to evaluate the particular subject in light of the purpose for which it apparently is being offered.[23] On the other hand, a party has the right to be nonresponsive even in a cooperative negotiation, or to couch a disclosure in terms that signal to the reasonable listener that additional inference is unwarranted. So long as the signals are not overly subtle, these conventions should be respected.[24]

There will be many borderline situations where the statement has a natural implication but not a clear one (i.e., reasonable people would disagree about the implication). Here is where I think the separate body of economics learning on affirmative disclosure obligations in the absence of a misrepresentation becomes useful. The goal of the law here is again to promote efficiency without chilling the incentive people have to produce or discover useful data. Intuitively, this suggests a line that compels disclosure of important but costly-to-obtain information, but with a prima facie privilege of nondisclosure for facts or inferences that are the product of something akin to skill or diligence. While that line by itself is plausible—indeed, it is the one suggested in Kronman's classic article on the subject[25]—the importance of information production incentives and the murkiness of relying on some kind of "diligence" exception (plus concerns about enforcement costs)[26] might lead instead to a presumption of a right to conceal except when it is fairly clear that the information is not legitimately proprietary.

Just as there is no clean distinction between classic misrepresentations and half-truths, neither is there one between half-truths and nondisclosure.[27] It is all still a continuum. Almost all nondisclosure cases arise in bargaining settings where there is indeed much said between the parties. Under these circumstances, what the court is being asked to do is determine what inferences the buyer can fairly draw from the seller's statements and omissions. Here the buyer's inferences may be more extensive—there is more interpretive work going on—but the difference is only in degree. To illustrate the difficulty of distinguishing clearly between half-truth and nondisclosure cases, consider *Brass v. American Film Technologies, Inc.* (1993). A large block of securities was being sold to a purchaser. The sellers failed to disclose that these were "restricted" securities under SEC rules, and hence illiquid for a period of time. The court found for the buyers (even though the information was on file at the SEC), and treated the case as one of pure nondisclosure. But much was said about the stock in question during the transaction. What was misleading was not the seller's silence but the set of representations about the value of the stock made in the course of negotiations. It would make just as much sense, if not more, to see it as a half-truth case.

This connection between the half-truth doctrine and affirmative disclosure duties is important. As we just saw, there is a well-recognized place in nondisclosure cases for a property-based privilege of "deserved informational advantage" as a limit on the duty to disclose. Similarly, a well-grounded normative theory of the half-truth should incorporate this privilege; it should accept that there both is and should be a "background norm" in commercial negotiations that permits a party to hide some items in his private stock of information. In the typical case where the informed party makes a factual statement that carries with it a reasonable (but not obvious) implication, the informed party should have a duty to add the additional or qualifying information to the extent that there is no compelling case for a nondisclosure privilege.[28] Under the half-truth doctrine, in other words, the willingness to speak on the subject assuages our concern about forcing disclosure of private information, causing us to move the line toward the disclosure duty even where there is some lingering ambiguity as to the extent of the implication.[29]

In those cases where there is a legitimate interest in exploiting the information, on the other hand, there is both an economic justification and a moral intuition for restraining the application of the half-truth doctrine. Parties to a negotiation do not normally assume that the other side will divulge its most sensitive private information. If the other side chooses to divulge, it is a sufficiently important event that we should listen reasonably carefully to what it is or is not saying. Implications should be drawn cautiously. But, when the subject being addressed is not likely to involve privileged information, it is fair to draw inferences more freely.

This strikes me as a helpful approach, but I want to consider a significant refinement. As noted at the beginning, there are some contexts in which the half-truth doctrine has little necessary place. If there is in fact little or no trust between two parties—a truly adversarial setting—it is difficult to justify the doctrine at all. At least ex ante, I suspect that in these settings, parties will often prefer a default rule of mere technical accuracy, with its reduced risk of ex post litigation. While I have seen no explicit statement in the case law that the half-truth doctrine adjusts downward to reflect a lack of trust between the parties, it should.[30]

Conversely, we should expect that negotiations characterized by a high degree of trust should lead to an upward adjustment: a broad half-truth doctrine, one with little privilege to conceal once a matter is addressed at all. In other words, addressing a matter would fully waive the privilege not to disclose. We would not need this in fiduciary settings, of course, for the relationship of trust and confidence triggers an affirmative duty to disclose that obviates any need to inquire into what was said or implied.[31] It would be interesting to see whether situations characterized by either a prior pattern of cooperation[32] or signals backed by strong reputational incentives that suggest a high likelihood of cooperation leads to a greater right to assume that a voluntary statement addressing a particular topic implies disclosure of all material known facts—sensitive or not—touching on it (something very close to an affirmative duty to disclose all material facts). Abstractly, it should, too, at least to the extent that the communication reinforced the expectation of openness and candor.[33] The thing that might reasonably deter a court from adopting such an approach is the ex post difficulty of assessing the level of trust in a particular relationship. There is admittedly some appeal to an across-the-board half-truth standard, with a diligence-promoting default bias on the side of discouraging negotiators from being too free in drawing inferences. But neglecting the presence of non-fiduciary trust comes at a considerable price in terms of the potential for exploitation, particularly by salespeople who are trained and experienced in its manufacture and distribution.[34]

We now have a better normative approach to the half-truth doctrine. It begins by assessing the normal inference that flows from a particular statement, and in a sizable middle ground takes account of both the proprietary character of the information and the level of trust established during the course of the relationship. With this, finally, it becomes somewhat easier to answer the question of whether, in the variation of the illustration given above, disclosure of the city's condemnation plans carries with it a duty to disclose known plans for comparable encumbrances.[35] To be sure, the inference is not an inevitable one. But given that this alternative information is not of a proprietary sort, the answer should be yes. I would be even more confident in this result if there is a good faith relationship between the parties. This approach helps us make sense out of the large number of cases in recent years that have employed the half-truth doctrine quite expansively.[36]

HALF-TRUTHS UNDER THE FEDERAL SECURITIES LAWS

Although it is not uncommon for the federal securities laws to be described as a "truth-telling" regime, that is itself a half-truth. Both by judicial and administrative action, corporations and investors are given substantial room to conceal crucial information from marketplace participants. This is driven by two related intuitions. One, noted earlier in the common law context, is to avoid the disincentive that might otherwise exist to discover new information if candor were truly the norm. The other is that business enterprises cannot survive in a competitive environment (and their investors will be harmed) if their most sensitive proprietary information is made public—and hence hand-delivered to their competitors. Thus, the background norm in securities law is not really one of complete truth-telling, but rather of an uneasy competition between disclosure duties and nondisclosure privileges.[37]

Unfortunately, neither Congress nor the SEC has ever sought to make clear what the affirmative disclosure duty is in most securities contexts.[38] They could (and should)[39] but have chosen not to. Consequently, the job has fallen to the courts to parse out these obligations under the law of fraud, and the half-truth doctrine has assumed more than its share of the burden as the vehicle for so doing. We should explore the way the doctrine has evolved with this background carefully in mind, for I suspect that this is the primary source for the apparent divergence in outcomes between common law and securities cases posited earlier.

Face-to-Face Settings

One context in which securities fraud disputes frequently arise is the face-to-face negotiation between two parties regarding, for example, the sale of a business, the private placement of securities, or a stockbroker's advice and recommendations. In these settings, the approach developed above works well in assisting with the application of the half-truth doctrine. Indeed, I would argue that in the brokerage context we can find evidence to support the view that the presence of trust (albeit short of a fiduciary relationship) influences how the half-truth doctrine is applied. An interesting conundrum in the law comes from the following. The Supreme Court has said that silence is not actionable under Rule 10b-5 absent a duty to speak, and such a duty normally arises only when there is a fiduciary relationship between the parties (*Chiarella* v. *United States,* 1980). Yet stockbrokers, at least, are still said to have an affirmative duty to disclose hidden risks, unusual markups, and conflicts of interest[40] and to only make recommendations of "suitable" securities.[41] This duty applies whether or not the relationship is fiduciary; the relationship between broker and customer, in the eyes of many courts, at least, often is not.[42]

Why this affirmative duty? The conventional answer is something called the shingle theory: that stockbrokers make an implied representation that they will deal fairly with their customers at all times.[43] But stated so baldly, this construct is a fiction. It is possible, however, to revise the shingle theory into a broad application of the half-truth doctrine: Once the broker has begun to address the merits of a particular investment, she assumes the duty to disclose all material information about it that would not otherwise be inferred by the customer. Information about unexpected risks and conflicts of interest is necessary in order to make the advice not misleading.[44]

Fraud-on-the-Market Cases

Mistaken Inferences in Market Settings. By the late 1960s, it became clear that privity is not required under Rule 10b-5 (17 C.F.R., sec. 240.10b-5, 1999). Rather, a person is liable to any purchasers or sellers who rely (actually or by presumption) on his intentionally false statements, so long as those statements were "reasonably calculated to affect the market price of an issuer's stock and to influence the investing public."[45] Obviously, that creates a broad scope of liability—and the consequent potential for extraordinary liability exposure in terms of the amount of out-of-pocket damages[46]—to anyone who speaks via public media on matters touching on particular securities. The entity most obviously at risk is the issuer of the securities in the course of its normal corporate disclosure and publicity. A vigorous policy debate has been occurring over the functionality of the current legal regime, which in many different ways invites extensive, expensive fraud-on-the-market litigation that may not be entirely merit-based.[47]

Courts regularly apply the half-truth doctrine in fraud-on-the-market cases as if the doctrine as articulated under the common law of fraud should be imported in unrefined form. But there are at least four stark differences in the way in which alleged half-truths occur in open market cases that should give us pause.

First, there is no bargaining between the parties. The most common fraud-on-the-market case comes from everyday corporate publicity. The company is neither buying nor selling its own securities. As such, we cannot draw the same inferences regarding the speaker's motivation or objective in offering information that we can in negotiations over the purchase of some kind of property, the setting in which nearly all the half-truth cases under common law arise. Nor can we so quickly invoke the standard justification for fraud, the desire to reduce transaction costs in these settings by simplifying the process of factual investigation, in the first place.[48]

Second (but related to the first), the kinds of communications are quite different from the direct representation observed in a negotiation. True, some fraud-on-the-market cases arise when it is clear that the speaker addressed her words to investors. Corporate filings with the SEC, most projections and estimates, and similar disclosures have investors as the natural and primary audience. But a surprisingly large number of cases involve more general corporate publicity, about product development,[49] for example, or significant strategic moves (mergers, restructurings, etc.).[50] These are the kinds of communications found in press releases and reported in the *Wall Street Journal* and other major business media. Here, the messages are typically directed at multiple audiences, of which investors are but one, and perhaps not the most obvious or important.[51] One suspects that most publicity about new products, for example, has potential customers and suppliers as the primary target audience. Organizational behavior studies suggest, moreover, that all forms of corporate publicity—including formal disclosure—must be structured with a careful eye to the impact on employees and other constituents that control important resources (e.g., the government).[52] In other words, a major contrast with face-to-face negotiations is that an investor reading some form of corporate publicity cannot assume that it was even generated to influence her investment decision. She might be a secondary or tertiary audience.

The third difference also follows from the use of mass media: the speaker loses some control over the content of the message. A press release, interview, or leak is reported by the media, which may distort the message either inadvertently (for example, simply in the process of cutting the material down to fit a four-paragraph story) or to sharpen the story as a way of making it more attractive to its readers.[53] This latter distinction applies, moreover, even when the company bypasses the press and speaks privately with one or more investment analysts as a means of communicating investment-related information.[54]

The fourth and final difference is that face-to-face negotiations usually occur with a view toward an exchange of money or property between the speaker and a particular party at a bargained-out price. The listener is taken as given: perhaps sophisticated, perhaps not. In contrast, open market fraud leads purchasers and sellers to trade in organized markets, where the ability of any given trader to affect the price at which the transaction occurs is minimal. If the market is characterized by a high level of efficiency, the orthodox assumption is that smart money dominates so that even if less sophisticated investors are fooled by some publicity, stock prices stay in line with assessments of fundamental value based on all publicly available information.[55] Hence the average investor, even if fooled, is not significantly harmed. This has led most courts to assume that the "listener" with respect to corporate publicity is the sophisticated, informed investor; less sophisticated traders may safely be ignored. This smart money can be deceived, of course, but it is not particularly easy.[56]

From these differences alone, we see that it will take much more thought to develop a coherent half-truth theory for open market corporate publicity. While this is surely so, I suspect that the basic structure we developed for face-to-face contacts works well as a starting point, even if we have to make adjustments to reflect certain of the distinctions.

The first difference—that there is no bargaining between the parties—is the easiest to deal with, at least if we buy into the conventional assumption that it is socially important to have fairly "accurate" stock prices.[57] No one doubts that corporate managers possess information that is crucial to securities pricing, or that they have an incentive to conceal or distort such information under certain circumstances.[58] Stock-based compensation, the desire to preserve control (avoiding proxy fights, institutional shareholder pressure, or hostile takeovers), and the ability of a high stock price to facilitate further capital raising or a program of corporate acquisitions all provide incentives to deceive, which are only partially offset by the corporate self-interest in a reputation for credibility. In this sense, communications directed at investors bear at least some resemblance to face-to-face representations. This would justify a duty of truthfulness under the "reasonably calculated" standard that would presumably include the obligation not to tell half-truths.

The more interesting difference is the second one—that the kinds of communications involved in fraud-on-the-market cases are quite different from the direct representation involved in negotiations—at least when investors are not the only or primary audience for the information. Take, for example, the half-truth aspect of *Backman* v. *Polaroid Corp.* (1990).[59] Polaroid was introducing a new "revolutionary" video product, Polavision, and the company knew that the project was faltering—sales were lagging behind internal estimates, and production had been temporarily halted. With such a high visibility innovation by a well-known manufacturer, the company was under immense pressure to disclose information. In the world of marketing, however, it is a common practice to "spin" product-related disclosure on the assumption that customers will run upon learning that other consumers are balking. Shelf-space will disappear. Morale among employees may suffer. Here, we have the well-known fear of risk disclosure becoming a self-fulfilling prophecy. Polaroid continued to feature Polavision in its disclosure, albeit with the indication that it was now being sold below cost. Was that a half-truth for failing to disclose the more serious evidence of adversity? The First Circuit said no.

I suspect that the court was right, and later will try to fit *Backman* into a more general theory of corporate half-truths. But we should take note here of the likelihood that an astute investor would recognize that this kind of disclosure was part and parcel of publicity directed largely at other audiences, under circumstances in which Polaroid had a natural incentive to bolster the product's chance of survival. As noted earlier, securities regulation has never sought to create an investor expectation that companies must reveal important competitive secrets—the background norm it creates is not one of absolute candor. Thus, even if the astute investor were to take factual claims at face value, she would not draw any strong inferences from disclosure that would be inconsistent with the company's marketing objectives. She would rely only on the limited technical accuracy of the statement, if that.[60] If other audiences were fooled into drawing inappropriate or unnecessary conclusions, so be it. Nor need this observation be limited to marketing "hype." As noted earlier, company executives have a strong incentive to style general corporate publicity to conform to a desirable image, the most common of which is one of confidence and control over its environment.[61] While there is no doubt a self-serving element to this,[62] image making is said to be necessary to capture desired resources for the firm from among a broad array of constituents, both internal and external. Displays of weakness, in other words, are to be avoided unless compelled. This, of course, creates a stark confrontation with the truth-telling dictates of the securities laws.[63]

In fact, however, we need not necessarily assume that anyone is fooled by biased corporate disclosure. In *Eisenstadt* v. *Centel Corp.* (1997), another case to be discussed more fully later, Judge Richard Posner made the plausible observation that corporate rhetoric has gradually evolved to a point where it has become the norm to use language that overstates corporate prospects. Listeners thus gradually learn the code. Once this happens, then all companies are effectively forced to conform. If a company does not use the overly optimistic rhetoric but instead tells the truth, the market will nonetheless assume that the disclosure is still in code and hence things must be that much worse. "Where puffing is the order of the day," Posner says, "literal truth can be profoundly misleading" (p. 746). (Posner does not, by the way, take this insight to its logical conclusion by suggesting that there should be Rule 10b-5 liability for telling the truth under such circumstances.)

That brings us to the fourth difference, the presence of the market. If we assume, as Posner does, that the market price is a proxy for consensus among informed expert investment analysts, then some happy conclusions follow. First, the analysts will be extremely smart consumers of corporate disclosures, alert to ambiguities, marketing hype, and boosterism, and fluent in code.[64] They will not jump to conclusions, and their careful interpretation of corporate disclosures will render harmless more foolish inferences by less savvy investors.

Second, a distinction between the open market and face-to-face negotiations that might otherwise seem troubling—the fact that investors who receive corporate publicity through the media cannot readily follow up to clarify ambiguities[65]—quickly disappears. Analysts regularly ask company officials, in private, what they meant or did not mean (assuming that the executives hadn't already warned them in advance about a forthcoming ambiguity).[66] In an efficient market, then, we would need at most a very narrow half-truth rule, one that protected only those inferences that even the expert, skeptical analyst would naturally draw. Arguably, the doctrine could even be done away with entirely.

This leads to an important insight. Our discussion of the common law half-truth doctrine was avowedly normative—we sought to build a limited place, justifiable on both economic and moral grounds, for certain kinds of concealment. If we assume that many investors are unsophisticated and that the unsophisticated can influence stock prices, then we run into a great difficulty to the extent that we try to create a comparable normative privilege. Unsophisticated investors presumably can be misled more easily by half-truths, for they may not understand the background norm of privileged concealment. There would thus be a socially dysfunctional distortion. But to the extent that market efficiency filters out the influence of the unsophisticated, this difficulty disappears. Savvy investors will (descriptively) make inferences with appropriate background expectations about the (normative) need for nondisclosure privileges. They will expect a sizable level of attempted concealment. In this sense, we can speak interchangeably about the proper normative regime and what sophisticated investors reasonably expect.

Mistaken Inferences in Noisy Markets. The hard half-truth questions arise mainly when we relax the assumption of market efficiency and entertain the possibility that less savvy "noise traders"[67] can have a sustained impact on market prices. That is a possibility that I take very seriously, and there is a good bit of learning that suggests that biases and emotions—sharpened by the self-interest of the securities industry and the financial press[68]—play a role in marketplace behavior.[69] Even Congress has acted to reduce corporate exposure caused by investor overreaction to bad news.[70] Unfortunately, we still do not have a well-developed theory of stock market behavior that would operate as an alternative to the efficient market hypothesis, from which we could make confident predictions about the impact on stock prices of inexpert inferences from investment-related disclosures. We simply have glimpses, such as the alleged manipulation of the price of Micron Corporation stock shortly after the celebrated manager of Fidelity's Magellan Fund reportedly made nonspecific statements about how enamored he was with Micron and other technology stocks.[71] In fact, according to the plaintiffs, Magellan was selling the bulk of its Micron holdings. That a savvy investor would have inferred from these reports that

Magellan was publicly disclosing its intent to buy more shares of Micron in advance of any actual purchases or gratuitously sharing its private stock of non-public information (the only good explanations for why one would buy based on this news) is hard to imagine. Yet the court sustained the omission claim.

If we relax the assumption of market rationality, we enter into a normative free fall, for we can then assume nearly any level of foolishness in drawing inferences. If we stick to our desire to deter corporate disclosures that distort the markets, we might then be left with a very broad scope to the half-truth duty in those instances where emotional reactions to what companies say are foreseeable. But how much relaxation, and thus how broad a scope, is impossible to gauge without a more fully developed alternative account of how stock markets behave.

At this point, I suspect, even a court skeptical of market efficiency on noise trading grounds is entitled to draw the line and say that whatever the descriptive reality, securities law should not, as a normative matter, go out of its way to protect foolishness and then simply invoke its own mental model of reasonable inference in assessing the line between reasonableness and gullibility, especially where strong confidentiality interests are at stake.[72] I would also offer a different but complementary thought. When noise trading theories have been put forward in the academic literature, they tend to be oversimplified to make them tractable. We do not yet have a richly textured effort to describe stock price bubbles (i.e., instances when unsophisticated investors push a stock's price above its fundamentally justifiable value for some sustained period of time). It would not surprise me, however, that were we to make a careful field study of all the individual purchase and sale decisions during any given time period, we would find that much of what drives the so-called noise is only loosely coupled with corporate disclosure and publicity. To be sure, highly salient disclosures will have a direct, perhaps excessive, impact. But aside from this level of news, what moves noise traders to purchase is a combination of influence activity by brokers, advisers, and the financial press—each of which has a strong incentive to find stocks with good "stories" to hype[73]—and the rumor-laced social contagion that comes as buyers share their trading activity with friends, family, and others.[74] Once a bit of momentum builds, more rational traders may add to the buying activity simply by betting that the noise will be sustained and that they can get out before the bubble pops.

If this is so, then we have a useful insight for securities litigation policy. Day-to-day corporate publicity and filings (as opposed to "big news") are probably not of great significance to the noise traders. There is a loose coupling, of course, insofar as brokerage and advisory firms and sophisticated journalists parse over the company's disclosures, and this affects their recommendations.[75] But we can bet that they are usually fairly savvy consumers of the information. If they pass on overdrawn inferences to the investors they influence, it is more likely because they have a deliberate self-interest in promoting those inferences than because they mistakenly read too much into the company's disclosures. And here, the causal link on which corporate liability would otherwise be grounded breaks.[76] It is hard to justify the full measure of fraud-on-the-market liability when the bubble is largely the product of third-party influence. Under these circumstances, the right proxy for gauging what inferences can fairly be drawn from relatively ordinary corporate disclosure would still be a fairly savvy audience of investment professionals. With respect to disclosures of higher saliency, it is admittedly harder to choose, and there is the risk that overestimating the savvy of the investing public in this effort will create opportunities for exploitation.[77] Whether that is bothersome from a policy perspective (or if so, how bothersome) moves us from analysis to ideology. Conventional securities regulation says that the unsophisticated deserve protection from the opportunistic: A more critical perspective might say that the costs associated with intervening help noise traders exceed whatever social benefit (if any) we might anticipate from the intervention, or that withholding assistance might encourage noise traders to be more careful. I doubt the latter,[78] but it is a conventional point that has to be considered.

So far, I have assumed that noise trading models describe an interplay between smart money and less sophisticated investors. We might still want to consider the further possibility that even the smart money is, at least in some cases, not quite as careful in its parsing of corporate publicity and disclosure as we have assumed, and more likely to draw unwarranted inferences.[79] My strong suspicion is that they are in fact savvy enough readers and listeners most of the time, but that there may be one exception: analysts who essentially fall in love with a stock and, by committing to its recommendation, resist coming to grips with bits of disconfirming data. This tendency is a strong psychological one, found in expert as well as nonexpert populations.[80] In other words, once an analyst commits to a stock, she may have a bias toward reading into corporate publicity and disclosures inferences that bolster the prior decision. She may be less likely to think of reasons why the disclosure might not support that inference. If so, we might want to readjust the half-truth approach back to something more closely resembling the less rigorous standard for face-to-face interactions in this one setting. But I am not convinced. In addition to the obvious difficulty of policing to see if these unusual conditions apply, one concern here is that we lose some of the ability the rigorous half-truth doctrine has to guard against harmful disclosures of competitive information. Another is that to the extent such confirmatory biases exist among analysts, they are likely to be even stronger among the company's managers, so that policing for cases of true fraud becomes all the more difficult (Langevoort, 1997a).

A Synthesis. The foregoing analysis muddies the waters, but not enough for me to abandon hope for a normative half-truth theory for open market fraud cases that is a step forward from the nontheory we have today. The following thus builds on the common law approach developed earlier, with modifications. As under that approach, the rule of thumb is to figure out whether it is reasonably likely that the person would have made the statement, under the circumstances, without an intent to deceive investors, and whether there is any normative justification for concealment. But in the fraud-on-the-market setting in particular, we do not want the question of whether the statement is a half-truth to be dependent on actual intent (an issue not readily susceptible to resolution in the earliest phase of the lawsuit).[81] The following three-part test, then, is really an objectified inquiry into materiality, with a "duty" twist.

First, a statement should be considered a half-truth if it is spoken or written in such a way that, in context, even a reasonably savvy investor would draw a natural—but materially mistaken—inference from it.[82] If there is palpable ambiguity or restraint in the statement itself, so that the savvy investor would be unsure what (if any) kinds of inference to draw, the statement is not actionable. In other words, the standard half-truth test applies, but more narrowly than in the typical common law setting.

Second, when the alleged inference is plausible from that same perspective but less than clear-cut, a statement made in the course of everyday corporate publicity should not be considered misleading if the information that was withheld was information that the company was entitled to protect as confidential or as a business secret within the background norms of securities regulation. Although we could do this on policy grounds alone, we need not. The notion here is that given the background norm of privileged information, an astute investor would not expect the company to divulge such sensitive information without a clear signal that it is doing so. Nor would the reasonable investor draw inferences from marketing and other kinds of statements designed largely for customer or employee audiences except where that inference is clear and unambiguous.

Third, and notwithstanding the foregoing, a statement that has a reasonable but false implication is actionable if made with specific intent to deceive investors.[83] Such intent may be alleged or proved by circumstantial evidence, but only if the evidence compellingly demonstrates that the speaker could not have been acting in good faith toward investors in speaking the way he did, but rather could only have done so in an effort to manipulate the price of the company's stock. In applying this latter test, a court would take account of factors such as the motive of the speaker, the substance and context of the statement, the likelihood of successful manipulation, and the apparent reason why the statement was made. This is a kind of analysis that courts perform quite often in securities cases.

To be sure, such analysis is not easy, especially when ruling on early motions by defendants to terminate a case, and no doubt will be applied unevenly by different judges. Yet I doubt that there is a pleasing alternative that is any more determinate. And, as noted earlier, I think it clear that many judges are already applying something resembling it. While the foregoing has by no means been articulated explicitly in the case law, it explains quite a number of holdings that otherwise seem curious and justifies the divergence between common law and securities law. For example (and in contrast to common law authority in face-to-face settings),[84] the release of accurate historic data does not trigger a fraud-based duty to disclose information in the company's possession that suggests that the past is not indicative of the future.[85] This is the essence of *Backman* v. *Polaroid Corp.* (1990), discussed earlier. Indeed, *Backman* is an example of the kind of situation where an intelligent investor would be very wary of drawing conclusions beyond the facts stated in the company's disclosures.[86] The company was launching a new product and was very concerned about not under-cutting it in the marketplace through adverse disclosure. Under these circumstances, the smart investor would assume that the company's publicity had a good dose of marketing spin, and that the company would be trying to maximize its competitive position by disclosing that (and only that) specifically required by law or demanded by some constituency.[87] For exactly the same reason, however, I am troubled by one of the best-known applications of the half-truth doctrines in recent years, the Ninth Circuit's suggestion in *In re Apple Computer Securities Litigation* (1989; Prentice and Langmore, 1994) that the company had a duty to disclose developmental problems with its highly touted Twiggy disk drive system simply because of a public statement that Twiggy "represents three years of research and development and has undergone extensive testing and design verification during the past year" (p. 1109).[88]

What of the Sixth Circuit's decision in *Levinson* v. *Basic* (1986),[89] a classic open market securities fraud case that produced the most important Supreme Court decision to date on open market securities fraud? Basic was in discussions with Combustion Engineering about a possible acquisition, providing Combustion with proprietary data and preparing its demands. Yet it denied in a press release that any "negotiations" were underway, and said it knew of no reasons for unusual market activity with respect to its stock. It repeated this denial later to stock exchange officials. This, of course, is a setting in which corporations in good faith wish to keep matters confidential: public awareness of merger negotiations can reduce their likelihood of success. Basic argued that what it said was technically true. The company did not actually know the reasons for the activity (though it no doubt strongly suspected it), and the discussions with Combustion might not technically be "negotiations" (see Kitch, 1995). The Sixth Circuit rejected the argument, taking note of the half-truth doctrine.

At first glance, this holding appears contrary to my approach insofar as it finds half-truth liability notwithstanding a fairly strong corporate secrecy need. But I find no real inconsistency. It takes a very awkward interpretation of either the word *"know"* or *"negotiation"* to consider Basic's response even technically accurate. Even sophisticated investors are unlikely to spot the ambiguity. Moreover, the background norm shifts considerably given that the company's statement was first made directly to investors, and then to exchange officials (for the benefit of the investing public) pursuant to the terms of a listing agreement that obligated the company to be candid when asked such questions. This is a far cry from generic corporate publicity, which should trigger more investor skepticism. These factors, I suspect, amply justify a finding of fraud notwithstanding the bona fide need for confidentiality.

Internal projections and estimates constitute another area where the foregoing approach has explanatory power. Such internal documents tend to be highly sensitive, based on varying assumptions about the future that often include the company's secret strategies. Courts have come close to saying that such internal estimates are immaterial per se unless they are substantially certain to occur (something rare).[90] This case law is hard to understand on these grounds. If materiality means that which a reasonable investor would likely consider significant, then such internal estimates should clearly pass the test (no doubt analysts like internal estimates very much, even if they do tend to discount some elements based on predictions of managerial optimism).[91] But these cases can more easily be understood in the context in which they typically arise: arguments that failure to release such estimates rendered the company's (usually more optimistic) public disclosure misleading. We will consider the misleading nature of optimistic statements generally later. For now, suffice it to say that given the proprietary nature of internal estimates, the savvy investor would not infer that the company would release them unless there is a very clear signal of a willingness to do so.

In one respect, however, the courts seem to have gone too far with respect to projections. The Ninth Circuit has suggested that a company can release for investors a public projection or estimate, but then conceal the fact that it has prepared one or more alternative projections or estimates, usually more pessimistic, which it is taking seriously internally.[92] While I can imagine some circumstances where that might be appropriate (e.g., where the concealed estimate is intentionally created using improbable assumptions, such as a worst-case scenario), my sense is that the public release of an estimate without qualification carries with it the fairly clear implication that the company believes it is the one most likely to occur.[93] The fact that it is but one of a number of plausible estimates being used by the company seems amply material, and its nondisclosure would be misleading.

EXTENDING THE THEORY TO OTHER KINDS OF OMISSION CASES UNDER RULE 10B-5

The Duty to Update

One of the most important and controversial exceptions to the rule that silence is not actionable absent a fiduciary-based duty to speak is the duty to update.[94] As articulated in the circuits that recognize the doctrine (principally the

Second[95] and Third[96]), a "forward-looking" corporate statement that is accurate when spoken but becomes false or misleading by virtue of subsequent facts triggers a duty to advise the investing public of those subsequent facts for as long as the earlier statement is still "alive" in the marketplace.[97] The intuition here is a simple one: a company has caused continuing reliance by investors by its voluntary forward-looking statement, and hence must rescue investors from the misimpression created by that statement in light of the subsequent facts.

Like the half-truth doctrine, this duty has its antecedent in the common law dealing with face-to-face negotiations.[98] If a negotiator asks the other party to disclose some fact and the other does so, there is likely to be reliance. If prior to the completion of the transaction the speaker discovers that the information is now false, then it seems fair and reasonable to compel a retraction. Indeed, it follows naturally from a transaction-cost-reducing objective. Just like the half-truth doctrine, however, similar reasoning becomes more problematic once we abandon privity and deal with general corporate publicity.

If we invoke the same kind of analysis of investor inference employed in the half-truth area, then a narrow and limited duty to update becomes more understandable. At first glance, it might seem odd that a savvy investor would ever assume from a prior correct statement that the company had undertaken a duty to warn should the information become unreliable, at least without its explicit assent to such a duty. But such assent might well be implied in one situation: where the issuer has made a statement that is styled or structured in a way that the intended audience is not only those making investment decisions right now but also those who will be making such decisions in the immediately foreseeable future.[99]

The best example of this would be an unrestricted statement, addressed to shareholders and other investors, of the company's commitment to a particular plan or policy. From this, we can make much more sense of the case law. In *In re Time Warner Inc. Securities Litigation* (1993), for instance, Time Warner had announced to disgruntled shareholders its intent to seek out one or more key strategic partners in order to pay off its short-term debt (incurred in fighting off a hostile takeover bid by Paramount) and position itself as a leading competitor in the entertainment and media business. It embarked on such a search but came up with little of significance. The company then began planning in earnest a very different strategy for dealing with the debt problem: a dilutive rights offering that was bound to reduce shareholder wealth. The court said that there could be a breach of the duty to update in failing to announce that the debt offering had been added as an alternative to the strategic alliance. On the other hand, there was no duty simply to update investors on the sorry progress of the talks with potential partners, short of actual cessation of those talks.

Both holdings make sense within our framework. The first is the specific kind of statement that was obviously intended as a formal announcement of company plans in response to a controversial situation not simply for the moment, but as a way of positioning the company for investors by announcing something of a commitment for the duration of the obvious problem it was facing. On the other hand, the reasonable investor would not expect ongoing revelation of the progress of the negotiations: It would be foolish to expect that of the company given the prejudice that might follow from premature disclosure. Such an implied promise, then, is not reasonably inferable.

Product announcements (e.g., research breakthroughs and patent applications) should rarely trigger the duty to update.[100] Here, again, we are in the realm of research, development, and marketing efforts in which a continuing duty is most likely to be prejudicial. This is consistent with the Second Circuit's decision in *San Leandro Emergency Medical Group* v. *Philip Morris Companies* (1996), in which the court limited Time Warner by refusing to find that Philip Morris had a duty to update its plans for pricing Marlboro cigarettes as the plans changed. Moreover, such announcements are ordinarily directed at multiple audiences, and savvy investors would also take that into account before assuming anything in terms of a commitment to make further announcements. However, there are a few scenarios where an analogy to *Time Warner* might be apt. If a company announces a reorganization of resources to make a particular product the central focus of the firm's efforts, for example, it should have to announce any abandonment or fundamental redirection of that commitment.[101]

General Statements of Optimism

Less than a decade ago, the leading treatise writers in securities regulation felt comfortable stating that the "puffing" doctrine under common law—that statements of opinion are not actionable when reasonable investors should see them as simple boosterism—"has all but gone the way of the dodo" (Loss and Seligman, 1991). Today, the puffing doctrine is alive and thriving as many courts immunize optimistic statements by companies, even when there are serious allegations that their managers were aware of adverse developments when they spoke.[102] The standard line here is that savvy investors know enough to recognize the habitual propensity of managers to put a positive spin on the company's prospects, and thus ignore it.

There is a close connection between the general optimism doctrine and the half-truth doctrine. Indeed, in many optimism cases, plaintiffs seem not to direct their attacks so much at the genuineness of the managers' optimism as their failure to disclose the adverse development as a qualifier to that optimism, i.e., facts necessary to make that optimistic statement not misleading.[103] If this is right, commonalities between the two doctrines should far dominate the differences.

I suspect that this is so, which leads me to conclude that the general optimism doctrine is founded on a good measure of common sense while simultaneously fearing that (like its close cousin, the "bespeaks caution" doctrine[104]) it can be taken too far if applied mindlessly.[105] We must begin with the recognition that because company officials have exclusive access to the most sensitive kinds of corporate data, they are an essential (if not unbiased) source of investment information.[106] If they are genuinely optimistic regarding the company's prospects, that is something a reasonable investor probably would take into account.[107] To say that smart investors simply assume that optimism is a facade and discount it is no more obvious than saying that smart investors never rely on brokers' recommendations because of their temptations to promote purchases and sales. That is simply not the case. The smart investor takes careful account of the management's reputation and whatever other information is accessible before putting much stock in their optimism, but then probably does factor the optimism into the total mix.[108] Occasionally, that can lead to deception.

Our half-truth framework can provide some help here. Expressions of optimism should not be actionable in those settings where hype is most commonplace: the kinds of statements made with customer and employee audiences largely in mind. As noted earlier, there is a strong incentive for companies to adopt public postures of invulnerability and confidence, especially in publicity relating to research, marketing, and other strategic initiatives. That is the kind of hype that should not affect a reasonably well informed marketplace, directly or indirectly.

Nor should a general statement of optimism be actionable simply because it does not reveal some known adversity, especially where there is a bona fide reason for keeping the adversity secret. Indeed, to the extent that there is a code here, a vague expression usually connotes that there are problems but that they are not seen as insuperable. This was the essence of Posner's decision in *Eisenstadt* v. *Centel Corp.* (1997), discussed earlier. Centel Corporation was auctioning off cellular properties, and private information suggested that the auction was running into significant problems. Nonetheless, the public disclosure was that the bidding process was going "very well" and "very smoothly" (p. 741). Posner suggested that there was no falsehood here given how savvy investors understand corporate discourse; the result would have been different, he said, had Centel's executives been aware of facts indicating an imminent disaster in the auction.

Posner's approach is surely correct: the issue, an empirical one, is how reasonable investors would understand the company's word choice. Note, however, that by admitting that the result could have changed under different factual circumstances, he is not taking the position that the language used by the company was inherently nonactionable (something, as we shall see, that other courts have indeed suggested). The emphasis is on appropriate inference, taken in context.[109] What I am bothered by is his conclusion that it is essentially beyond doubt that the informed investment community would treat Centel's "smoothly" statement to indicate nothing more than that officials were not certain that there would be an auction failure. That is possible, but not empirically self-evident. Posner's conclusion may be bolstered, however, by something he does not emphasize but that may be a crucial subtext to the opinion. Centel's statement no doubt was material to investors, but had to have been styled with a primary eye toward potential bidders for the cellular properties, from whom it wanted, in its shareholders' interests, to conceal any slow movement in the bidding. Given this obvious motive, the careful investor would not read too much (again, if anything) into such a vague expression.

This possibility aside, *Eisenstadt* is a good illustration of why courts should be cautious in applying the general optimism doctrine. It is no doubt true that if the management of a small company, with no established reputation, simply made optimistic remarks to an investor or business audience, investors would be unlikely to rely. That is indeed the setting in which many of these cases arise (see *Raab* v. *General Physics Corp.*, 1993). But suppose that a more established company was experiencing known difficulties, leading to substantial anxiety about the company's prospects. A statement that "we are optimistic that our performance this quarter will be in line with expectations"—though not unlike statements that some courts have dismissed as a matter of law as too general to be reliable—probably would be viewed as meaningful by sophisticated investors. A simple "we are optimistic," on the other hand, would probably convey little, and indeed confirm some adverse suspicions. In sum, context really is crucial.

This contextualism also makes it possible to reach egregious cases in the setting in which quite general statements of optimism are most likely to have a pernicious effect—when the investor community (analysts and all) has committed to a particular stock, creating a growing bubble, and thus is biased toward confirming prior impressions. Though such statements may not have much effect standing alone, they can enter the total mix of information as a means of deflecting more critical scrutiny from sophisticated investors, becoming "lulling" statements to an audience motivated to have the story be true. Optimistic statements would be barred at least in those circumstances where disastrous facts (though not mere adversity) appear.

CONCLUSION

We began this discussion by focusing on what seems, at first blush, to be a narrow topic: the half-truth, in both common law and securities law contexts. But it quickly became evident that this portion of the law of fraud is about regulating human and organizational discourse: who determines what meaning can properly be drawn from what someone says or does not say, and with what sort of guidance for making hard judgments about what was meant. For that reason, we could extend it in the securities law setting to other related questions like the duty to update and general statements of optimism—so long as we keep in mind (as courts have not always) the significant differences between face-to-face bargaining and general corporate publicity. It is possible, in other words, to say something systematic about mistaken inferences in the world of securities trading.

In the end, however, we must return to a point made earlier. The reason the half-truth, duty to update, and general optimism doctrines have taken on such significance in securities litigation is that neither Congress nor the SEC has ever been willing to try to articulate clearly an obligation on the part of corporate managers to divulge important information as it becomes material. Not surprisingly, courts have responded to this gap in an ad hoc fashion, creating the confusion noted at the outset. In response, securities lawyers tend to urge an abundance of caution whenever a matter must be discussed, and advise clients to be silent altogether so far as possible when there is a compelling need for secrecy.[110] Such advice has an obvious chill on the free flow of corporate information. And the ambiguity itself invites more and more litigation. There is little excuse for this opaqueness in legislative or administrative policy and de facto delegation to the judiciary.[111] An affirmative disclosure obligation could be articulated, even if there are undeniable challenges in devising such a requirement so as to avoid undue prejudice to legitimate confidentiality needs.[112] Were the gap to be filled, courts would have far less to struggle with under the fraud rubric in the first place and the subject of half-truths would for that reason alone become a good bit less troublesome.

Notes

1. Surveys of the law of misrepresentation and nondisclosure all spend time on the half-truth doctrine, but almost always by way of dicta and case illustration rather than any sustained effort at theoretical analysis of the half-truth as a distinctive problem. See, for example, James and Gray (1977), reviewing doctrine; Palmieri (1993), reviewing cases. The same is true in the securities context. See, for example, Cox, Hillman, and Langevoort (1997), commenting on a company's duty to disclose and on half-truths; Loss and Seligman (1991), discussing half-truths and common law and Securities and Exchange Commission fraud; Barnes and Bagley (1994), illustrating the kind of information a company must disclose through a fictional narrative; and Oesterle (1998), asserting that the right of nondisclosure appears to be dwindling, caused in part by the half-truth doctrine.

2. Compare *V.S.H. Realty Inc.* v. *Texaco Inc.* (1985), rejecting a motion to dismiss a half-truth claim under Massachusetts law when the seller disclosed some leaks in a storage facility but not others, and the seller stated that no governmental reports of defects had been received without noting that the Coast Guard was investigating

for leaks, with *Nei* v. *Burley* (1983), finding no half-truth when the seller of the property gave the buyer percolation test results but concealed the existence of a seasonal stream. Concurring and dissenting in *V.S.H. Realty,* Judge Breyer noted the tension between the court's conclusion and the *Nei* case.

3. I will allude here, but no more, to President Clinton's troubles arising from his deposition testimony and public statements regarding his affair. See Katz (1998), discussing President Clinton's misrepresentation issues and their relation to case law.

4. See *Bronston* v. *United States* (1973), holding that it is not perjury for a defendant to testify that his company had a Swiss bank account in the past while failing to say that he also had one in the past when asked whether he had ever had one because the statement, though unresponsive to the question, was literally true. In recent years, however, some courts have chipped away at *Bronston.* See, for example, *United States* v. *DeZarn* (1998), holding *Bronston*'s literal truth defense inapplicable where there was evidence that a witness's unresponsive answers were deliberately misleading.

5. See Model Rules of Professional Conduct (1983), Rule 3.3, explicating the rules of representations. The half-truth doctrine played a prominent role in the celebrated allegations by the Office of Thrift Supervision against the Kaye Scholer law firm in connection with its representation of a failed savings and loan entity. The firm's position, supported by an opinion it obtained from Professor Geoffrey Hazard, was that it was engaged in advocacy, and hence had wide latitude in making argumentative claims without a duty to divulge the entire truth. See generally Langevoort (1998), questioning whether the firm committed any actionable half-truths; Simon (1998), concluding that the charges against the firm were plausible and that the bar's response was disingenuous and irresponsible.

6. See White (1980), analyzing the difficulties in drafting ethical norms for negotiators. See generally Peters (1986), examining deception in the context of negotiation.

7. See Kronman (1978), attempting to reconcile the "unilateral mistake" and "withholding information" doctrines in contract law. See also *FDIC* v. *W. R. Grace and Co.* (1989), noting the existence of a duty to disclose where party "has without substantial investment on his part come upon material information"; Posner (1992), discussing fraud and its relation to contract rights. But see DeMott (1994), arguing that the fluidity of the law in this area makes any abstract synthesis difficult.

8. See, for example, *Pashley* v. *Pacific Electric Co.* (1944): "Even though one is under no obligation to speak as to a matter, if he undertakes to do so, either voluntarily or in response to inquiries, he is bound not only to state truly what he tells but also not to suppress or conceal any facts within his knowledge which will materially qualify those stated"; *Wirth* v. *Commercial Resources Inc.* (1981), "To reveal some information on a subject triggers the duty to reveal all known material facts."

9. Indeed, one might well argue that there is no such thing as "silence" in a business negotiation. All duty-to-disclose issues turn on what was said and implied, and whether nondisclosure was proper in light of the course of communication that went on between the parties. For a classic "buyer's nondisclosure" case that was really a half-truth holding, see *Zimpel* v. *Trawick* (1988), which holds that failure

to disclose to an elderly, sick woman that her land likely contained valuable oil deposits constituted fraud. See Strudler (1997) for an extensive discussion of *Zimpel* through which the author advocates a "deontological" account of nondisclosure law.

10. See, for example, *First Virginia Bankshares* v. *Benson* (1977), holding that a half-truth stating satisfactory insurance experience with a company while concealing suspicions that the company was filing bogus claims was actionable under common law fraud; Loss and Seligman (1991), noting that the seller need not state every fact that a prospective purchaser might like to know.

11. My sense from reviewing the case law is that most securities cases dealing with half-truths and omissions come before the judge in the context of a motion to dismiss for failure to state a cause of action or on a motion for summary judgment at a fairly early phase of the case. When cases go forward, they are most often settled. Hence, we find very few cases dealing with whether something is a half-truth that arise from later phases of litigation.

12. At least in the securities context, the subject of half-truths cannot be put aside as simply posing a question for the jury about the potential for the reasonable investor to be misled. That is the standard, to be sure, and it does involve a fact question (or a mixed question of law and fact). Technically, a court is supposed to dismiss the case prior to discovery and trial only if it is beyond question that no reasonable investor would have relied on the half-truth in question ("immateriality as a matter of law"). See, for example, *Fecht* v. *Price Co.* (1995), holding that fraud claims had been stated with the required degree of specificity. But judges have shown an inclination in securities fraud cases to make such determinations "as a matter of law." See, for example, *Shawmut Bank* v. *Kress Association* (1994), holding that an underwriter's failure to disclose a developer's principal's prior diversion of money to his other companies was not a material omission. Though often giving lip-service to the exclusive province of the fact finder, judges decide with some frequency that a reasonable investor could not possibly have been misled by the omission of some fact and thus dismiss a case before much discovery, if any, can occur. See generally Vanyo and Salceda (1995), outlining and analyzing potential mandates of the Private Securities Litigation Reform Act of 1995. Given this assertive judicial posture, the value of building a more coherent theory about mistaken inferences seems all the more self-evident.

13. See also *Restatement (Second) of Torts* (1981, sec. 551(2)(b)) establishing a duty to disclose information necessary to avoid partial and misleading statements.

14. The illustration is based on *Junius Construction Co.* v. *Cohen* (1931), which held that a vendor's misrepresentation in failing to warn a purchaser of an unopened street relieved the purchaser of liability on the contract.

15. See, for example, Cialdini (1993), illustrating the concept through a tale of a successful waiter.

16. See, for example, *Strawn* v. *Canuso* (1995), holding a real estate vendor liable for failing to disclose material facts regarding off-site conditions; *Ollerman* v. *O'Rourke Co.* (1980), holding that the vendor of a residential lot has a duty to a

"noncommercial" purchaser to disclose facts that are known to vendor. But see *Baskin* v. *Collins* (1991), holding that there is no duty to disclose governmental plans when such information was accessible to the plaintiff. Here, I am assuming some significant difficulty related to the discovery of the information.

17. See notes 6–8 and accompanying text.

18. There is, however, the limitation that enforcement of the antifraud rule be cost-effective. See generally Darby and Karni (1973), exploring the reasons for and determinants of false information to consumers.

19. For example, if a seller of a business discloses the beneficial owners but fails to disclose the equity-like role that finders had in the transactions, is that a conventional fraud (because the term *beneficial owner* implies something different) or a half-truth? See *SEC* v. *Great American Industries, Inc.* (1968), holding that a party to a business transaction is under a duty to disclose matters known to him to avoid being misleading.

20. See generally Holland, Holyoak, Nisbett, and Thagard (1986), discussing various kinds of inference, including analogy, representation of variability and uncertainty, generalization, and classical instrumental conditioning.

21. See Gilovich (1991). See also Lewis (1991), focusing on what appeals to customers, and O'Shaughnessy (1987), analyzing rationality in buying.

22. The relationship between inferences and frames of reference—and the resulting potential in terms of the ability to deceive—is the subject of Goffman's classic sociological text *Frame Analysis* (1974).

23. Hence, a rule of thumb here is to ask, from the perspective of the listener, why the information is being provided. If it is to obviate the need for independent investigation, that is fine. If it is because of some external compulsion (for example, mandatory disclosure), a willingness to volunteer anything more than what literally was said would be inappropriate. This also helps define the scope of a disclosure. We ask why the information is being offered (for example, to address a specific concern or to assure the listener that problems are not insuperable) in order to determine how far, if at all, the speaker must address related matters.

24. Again as a general matter, the expression of an intention or opinion should not trigger a duty to disclose further factual information. Such expressions may be actionable in and of themselves, however, if they are false and there is a right to rely on them.

25. Kronman's inclination is to compel the disclosure of all casually acquired material information. See Kronman (1978), arguing that in unilateral mistake cases, the party with knowledge is the one who can prevent mistakes with least expense; see also Brudney (1979), examining the extent to which silence should be prohibited in securities trading; Shavell (1994). But see Birmingham (1988), criticizing Kronman's economic analysis and arguing that he gets the law of unilateral mistake wrong.

26. A more conservative duty would also take account of human nature. If concealment is likely given social or cultural norms, then the task of policing nondisclosure cases will be fairly extensive. That might lead to limiting disclosure

obligations to the most serious instances. See Wonnell (1991), "Nondisclosure is tolerated only as a concession to human frailty that might render a duty to disclose ineffective." But there is evidence that courts today are being more aggressive in forcing disclosure than this point alone would indicate, even in arms-length business negotiations. See Palmieri (1993), asserting that courts recognize a general duty to disclose information during negotiations.

27. See note 10. In fact, most treatises assume that the half-truth doctrine is simply a species of actionable nondisclosure. See, for example, Keeton and Dobbs (1984).

28. Worth noting here are arguments by some notable legal scholars that there should be a privilege to lie about such proprietary matters. See Barnett (1992), arguing that the lack of disclosure in contracts is not fraudulent when the information relates only to the supply and demand for the resources in the contract; Levmore (1982), "The unfairness and inefficiencies of the buyer-explorer's dilemma suggest that the law ought to allow dishonest disclosure in cases in which the misinformation would only cause the misinformed party to behave as he would have without the information and in which it would be unfair—because of the cost and risk of extortion—to require disclosure of the informed party." But see DeMott (1994), arguing that Levmore's line of reasoning is unpersuasive because sometimes people do not know the extent to which they can do research. For a case driven heavily, no doubt, by sympathy for the victim, where the court found a defendant liable for a half-truth even though proprietary information was involved, see *Zimpel v. Trawick* (1988).

29. There is an analogy here to a conventional explanation for the moral obligation doctrine in contract law. We have substantial doubts about whether people should be able to recover in restitution against one another simply because they conferred a benefit on the defendant, in large part because we do not want to encourage officious intermeddling. But if the recipient makes a promise to pay, even if after the fact, our fears largely dissolve. Hence we enforce the promise even though it clearly lacks the element of a bargain.

30. I have argued (Langevoort, 1998), for example, that the Kaye Scholer law firm probably did not actually deceive the banking supervisors in making true but evasive claims in its representation of the Keating interests given the likely level of mutual suspicion in that relationship. An important qualification here, however, is that as a matter of policy, the law may want to limit the ability to conceal information in a particular setting. For example, it might want to say in civil discovery or banking regulation that there is a prima facie duty to disclose all material information, with only the most limited privileges (for example, the privilege against self-incrimination or the attorney-client privilege). If the law does this, then there is no reason for a narrow half-truth doctrine simply because of the presence of mistrust. The law has then created an expectation of candor. My discussion is aimed at the commercial context, where there is no such prima facie expectation of candor.

31. See, for example, *Vai v. Bank of America National Trust and Savings Association* (1961), finding a husband's failure to disclose fully and fairly material facts from

which he gained an advantage to be a breach of a fiduciary duty. For an interesting application of this in the pension fund area, see *Varity Corp.* v. *Howe* (1996),
in which the Court found insufficient candor by a corporation in discussing the
future of its pension plan with its employees.

32. All the more so if the prior pattern involved reliance, so that one or both parties
    has become dependent on the cooperation of the other. This, of course, is the kind
    of situation in contract law giving rise to a duty of good faith.

33. See Shell (1991), arguing that communication, especially when repeat dealings are
    likely, may form an emotional commitment to fairness and good faith; cf. Rose
    (1995), lamenting the inadequate attention to trust in legal studies. An analogy
    would be the holding in *Randi W.* v. *Muroc Joint Unified School District* (1997)
    that when a person voluntarily offered a letter of recommendation to a prospective
    employer, he has a duty to disclose evidence of known prior sexual misconduct,
    even if the letter does not clearly touch on that issue. In this example, the letter of
    recommendation clearly involves a cooperative, nonadversarial communication.

34. See generally Langevoort (1996a), discussing why brokers are tempted to mischar-
    acterize the risk level of an investment and why sophisticated investors may choose
    excessively risky investments. Along these same lines, the half-truth doctrine should
    be broadened when the alleged victims are unsophisticated and effectively tricked
    into expecting better disclosure than they actually receive. See *Emery* v. *American
    General Finance, Inc.* (1995), describing a half-truth situation where a loan company
    solicited unsophisticated borrowers to obtain additional credit without disclosing
    adequately that the consequence would be a refinancing of their initial loan at a
    much higher rate of interest—the practice of "loan flipping."

35. This does not mean that there would have to be disclosure of all material adverse
    information in the speaker's possession, but only that related to the topic dis-
    cussed. See *Watson* v. *Avon Street Business Center, Inc.* (1984), finding adequate
    disclosure and no half-truth where the seller told a prospective buyer about some
    roof damage but not about an unrelated defect. An even easier situation where
    there is no further duty to disclose based simply on what was said is where the
    statement warns the listener of the likelihood of hidden facts, on which the lis-
    tener fails to further investigate. See *Cara Corp.* v. *Continental Bank* (1992),
    holding the bank not liable for failing to disclose where it had no fiduciary rela-
    tionship to plaintiff and plaintiff did not rely on the nondisclosure.

36. See *Peerless Mills, Inc.* v. *AT&T* (1975), finding that in a business negotiation, reveal-
    ing high earnings for the previous six months triggered a duty to disclose additional
    adverse information about current period; *Nash* v. *Trustees of Boston University*
    (1990), finding fraud when a university professor told his current employer, as they
    were working out an early retirement agreement, that he was "negotiating" with
    another institution while omitting that he had all but accepted a job there; *Berger* v.
    Security Pacific Information Systems, Inc. (1990), finding a half-truth when a com-
    pany recruiting a new employee said that the company was highly solvent and had
    a secure future and omitted to disclose that the project for which the employee was
    being recruited was subject to a significant risk of defunding.

37. See generally Kitch (1995) (discussing the ways the securities laws and SEC rules try to give issuers some room to keep sensitive competitive information private); Mahoney (1995a) (same). Kitch rightly criticizes the SEC for not always being candid itself about the background norm, but it is presumably something that at least sophisticated investors understand well. For a judicial perspective, see *Roeder* v. *Alpha Industries* (1987), in which the court rejected a general affirmative duty to disclose material information in a corporation's possession.

38. Such a duty is implicit in certain settings, especially when the corporation or its insiders are buying or selling shares. See *Shaw* v. *Digital Equipment Corp.* (1996).

39. See notes 111 and 112 and accompanying text.

40. See *Chasins* v. *Smith, Barney and Co.* (1970); *Lieb* v. *Merrill Lynch, Pierce, Fenner and Smith* (1978). These affirmative disclosure decisions appear to have survived *Chiarella*. See, for example, *Grandon* v. *Merrill Lynch and Co.* (1998), holding that a private action under Rule 10b-5 exists against broker-dealers who charge undisclosed, excessive markups in municipal bonds; Cox, Hillman, and Langevoort (1997), citing cases holding that brokers must disclose risks and conflicts of interest.

41. See *O'Connor* v. *R. F. Lafferty and Co.* (1992), requiring the plaintiff to prove a broker's recommendation of unsuitable securities and scienter essential for a cause of action; *Leone* v. *Advest Inc.* (1985), holding that unsuitability states a cause of action under Section 10(b) and Rule 10b-5 where plaintiff alleges that a broker knowingly or intentionally chose unsuitable investments for the client.

42. See *Lieb* v. *Merrill Lynch, Pierce, Fenner and Smith.* (1978). Some courts, however, have said that the right to rely is not as robust where the customer is highly sophisticated. See, for example, *Banca Cremi S.A.* v. *Alexander Brown and Sons, Inc.* (1997).

43. See Karmel (1995), noting that older cases state that brokers impliedly represent that they will deal fairly with their customers.

44. See Langevoort (1996a): "The broker's duty is to couple a recommendation with any additional significant facts necessary to assess the nature and reliability of the broker's opinion" (p. 689).

45. *SEC* v. *Texas Gulf Sulphur Co.* (1968). See also *McGann* v. *Ernst and Young* (1996), finding an accounting firm liable on the basis of false information in an audit report because financial statements are one of the primary sources of information available to guide the decisions of the investing public; *In re Carter-Wallace Inc. Securities Litigation* (1998), finding that advertising in medical journals could constitute statements made "in connection with" a securities transaction; *In re Ames Department Stores Stock Litigation* (1993), finding misstatement in a prospectus and other misleading statements as potentially fraudulent, even where persons bringing suit were not purchasers in the public offering.

46. Under the "fraud-on-the-market" theory espoused in *Basic Inc.* v. *Levinson* (1988), traders in an efficient market enjoy a presumption of reliance, and hence do not have to prove even the awareness of the fraud. This, of course, expands the number of traders who can be part of the plaintiff class. In turn, if the plaintiff class succeeds, each trader is entitled to the difference between the trading price for the

securities and what they would have been worth had the truth been told. See Cox, Hillman, and Langevoort (1997), discussing the measure of damages in open market cases. On the policy problems here, see Mahoney (1992), who argues that fraud-on-the-market and precaution costs impose additional liability without additional social benefit or else divide up fixed recovery among a greater set of investors who do not necessarily require recovery.

47. See, for example, Grundfest (1994), contending that the Securities and Exchange Commission consistently seeks to avoid an enforcement action in "lower-quality" lawsuits "serving" as a basis for negotiating settlements with defendants unwilling to bear the risks and costs of a trial on the merits; Kraakman, Park, and Shavell (1994), investigating the fundamental relationship of shareholder suits to shareholder welfare; Langevoort (1996b), suggesting that damages should be capped in cases involving false or misleading corporate publicity and periodic due diligence filings in order to deter the rise of allegedly abusive litigation; "Symposium on the Private Securities Litigation Reform Act of 1995" (1996); Weiss and Beckerman (1995), suggesting that institutional investors should monitor the conduct of plaintiffs' attorneys as proxies for all members of plaintiff classes. The starting point for the concern about excessive litigation is the temptation to plaintiffs' lawyers that arise from the ability to sue companies for such large amounts of damages (with proportionate attorneys' fees) under circumstances where settlement by those companies is likely without much regard to the merits if the matter survives the early motions to dismiss. See Alexander (1991), arguing that lawsuits may have substantial settlement value regardless of the merits and generally are not influenced by expected trial decisions.

48. The common law, of course, allows a case of fraud to go forward even if it is a third party that is relying, subject to foreseeability limitations. See *Restatement (Second) of Torts* (1981, sec. 533). But this turns the doctrine into something very different, and my only point is that we should take account of the differences in assessing the standard of liability.

49. See, for example, *In re Apple Computer Securities Litigation* (1989). See generally Prentice and Langmore (1994), discussing Apple.

50. See, for example, *In re Time Warner Inc. Securities Litigation* (1993), holding that a corporate officer's enthusiastic statements about ongoing negotiations were not material misstatements where the negotiations were occurring and being undertaken in good faith, but that there could be a breach of the duty to update a particular previously announced plan or policy.

51. See generally Langevoort (1997a), examining whether the fact that company publicity reaches multiple audiences explains some fraud and deception.

52. See Pfeffer and Salancik (1978); Staw, McKechnie, and Puffer (1983). Deception directed at governmental authorities may be one of the less noticed triggers of fraud-on-the-market liability. See, for example, *Heit* v. *Weitzen* (1968), holding that a corporation's failure to disclose income from overcharges to government contracts was sufficient to meet the "in connection with" requirement of Rule 10b-5. Compare *Wielgos* v. *Commonwealth Edison Co.* (1989), finding that inaccurate

projections regarding the electric utility's ability to start up its nuclear power facilities could well have been directed at least in part at ratemaking authorities.

53. An interesting and troublesome body of law has evolved dealing with whether plaintiffs in fraud-on-the-market cases can base their allegations against the issuer on "unnamed" corporate sources in newspaper articles. See *Eisenstadt* v. *Centel Corp.* (1997), finding such allegations unacceptable on hearsay grounds; *In re Time Warner Inc. Securities Litigation* (1993), finding such allegations unacceptable on policy grounds. These cases recognize the important filtration role that newspapers play, though at the risk of eliminating the ability to police a common mechanism that companies use to speak to both the public and investors. The *Time Warner* court's suggestion that newspapers can generally be counted on to police companies for inaccurate statements seems particularly far-fetched.

54. See *Cooper* v. *Pickett* (1997), finding that a company can be liable for misleading investors if it misinforms analysts.

55. See *Basic Inc.* v. *Levinson* (1988), advocating the efficient open market hypothesis as a basis for the fraud-on-the-market doctrine. See generally Easterbrook and Fischel (1991).

56. I am, of course, well aware of the controversial nature of strong claims of market efficiency, and recognize that courts have not embraced the theory's teachings with uniform fervor. See *In re Time Warner Inc. Securities Litigation* (1993): "The laws of economics have not yet achieved the status of the law of gravity" (p. 271); Langevoort (1992), exploring the gulf between current economic literature and "the persistent, seemingly static, conception of market efficiency in the legal culture" (p. 854).

57. Compare Kahan (1992a), analyzing the desirability of removing different kinds of stock price inaccuracies, with Stout (1988), arguing that legal rules designed to improve market efficiency may result in social losses.

58. See Arlen and Carney (1992), examining the reasons that directors and officers conceal information; Gulati (1999), discussing labor market effects. Compare Langevoort (1997a), arguing that some corporate falsehoods are the product of cognitive biases rather than conscious intent. For purposes of this chapter, I will assume *arguendo* that the corporation is aware of the truth or falsity of its disclosure.

59. *Backman* v. *Polaroid Corp.* (1990). This case also considers the "duty to update." See note 97.

60. See the text accompanying notes 104–108.

61. See *Wielgos* v. *Commonwealth Edison Co.* (1989); *Heit* v. *Weitzen* (1968); Pfeffer and Salancik (1978); Staw, McKechnie, and Puffer (1983); see also Salancik and Meindl (1984), arguing that corporate managers manipulate information to give the impression that they are in control.

62. While maintaining an image of confidence and control can have a business justification, there is also an agency cost element to such attributions: the desire to perpetuate management control and perquisites. See Langevoort (1997a); Westphal and Zajac (1998).

63. As in the law of fraud generally (see note 28), there is an interesting literature debating whether the securities laws should permit lying in the interest of corporate secrecy. See, for example, Kahan (1992b), arguing that game theory analysis supports not imposing securities fraud liability for certain lies made in the context of negotiations; Ayres (1991), analyzing the Supreme Court's endorsement of the fraud-on-the-market theory in *Basic Inc.* v. *Levinson* (1988); Macey and Miller (1990), arguing that corporate information should not be disclosed if, in the directors' judgment, the disclosure would jeopardize the value of the firm's shares in the aggregate.

64. They will also, of course, have their own sources of information against which to check management's representations.

65. See notes 46–55 and accompanying text.

66. The process of selective disclosure is a prominent one with substantial debate about its propriety. Compare Fischel (1984), arguing that legal rules should not restrict the use of inside information by analysts, with Langevoort (1990), arguing for liberal rules for insider trading based on the role of the market analyst. Few doubt, however, that selective and favored treatment of analysts and other favored investors is commonplace. See, for example, Smith (1995).

67. *Noise trader* is the term often used in the finance literature to refer to those who trade in an uninformed fashion. See, for example, DeLong (1991).

68. See Stout (1995), arguing that brokers and institutional investment funds encourage trading.

69. This is still controversial, of course. Compare Langevoort (1992) with Romano (1998).

70. See Private Securities Litigation Reform Act of 1995, sec. 101(b), limiting damages in some securities litigation. See also Thompson (1996), evaluating the measure of recovery under the Private Securities Litigation Reform Act of 1995. Congress gave credit to a law review article (Lev and de Villiers, 1994) for the insight leading to the reform. See H.R. CONF. REP. NO. 104–369 at 42 n.25, reprinted in 1995 U.S.C.C.A.N. 730, 741 n.25.

71. See *In re Fidelity/Micron Securities Litigation* (1997). Specifically, the portfolio manager described Micron as still "relatively cheap."

72. This is not without danger, for I suspect that many judges impose an image of proper investor decision making that is quite unrealistic. See Langevoort (1995), arguing that judges tend to hold defendants to unrealistically high standards of behavior. My sense is that many judges overestimate the care with which even sophisticated persons approach such decisions.

73. See notes 52 and 53 and accompanying text; see also Mahoney (1995b), reviewing two explanations for excessive trading: noise trading and heterogeneous expectations.

74. See DiFonzo and Bordia (1997), observing the tendency of rumors to spread when an unusual event occurs that requires explanation; Klausner (1984), suggesting that "contagion theory" helps explain the actions of financial markets.

75. See *Panzirer* v. *Wolf* (1981), denying summary judgment where the plaintiff indirectly relied on a *Wall Street Journal* article that allegedly would have portrayed the company less favorably had its annual report been accurate.

76. Compare Fisher (1997), arguing that companies should not be liable for that portion of a stock price drop that reflects disappointment following analysts' overly optimistic biases or overstatements; Lev and de Villiers (1994), arguing that companies should not be liable for damages resulting from investors' overreactions.

77. That, for example, would be a worst-case reading of *In re Fidelity/Micron Securities Litigation* (1997). If the analyst was in a position to predict an emotional reaction to his disclosure, then money could have been made by the falsehood. This is not to say, however, that that is what happened. The facts are not fully consistent with such a planned market manipulation, particularly the timing of the publicity.

78. See Langevoort (1992), arguing that intervention via formal written disclosure is unlikely to affect those whose trading decisions do not reflect a careful deliberative process.

79. Within the noise trading literature, there is a segment that questions whether professional investors behave with the rationality we expect. See, for example, Daniel, Hirshleifer, and Subrahmanyam (1998), summarizing the literature modeling trader and analyst overconfidence; DeBondt and Thaler (1990), concluding that security analysts overreact to changes. This, in turn, blends into other explanations for why there might be biases here. See generally Carleton, Chen, and Steiner (1998), presenting an empirical examination of the agency costs associated with investment recommendations by national brokerage, regional brokerage, and nonbrokerage firm analysts.

80. See Langevoort (1997a); Tetlock, Skitka, and Boettgar (1989), finding empirical evidence that people who are accountable for and committed to a position will devote significant mental effort to justifying that position.

81. See note 11 and accompanying text.

82. See, for example, *In re Wells Fargo Securities Litigation* (1993), finding a bank's reporting of its loss loan reserves literally accurate but misleading; In re Discovery Zone Securities Litigation (1996), holding that a misimpression created by technically true disclosure about accounting procedures was actionable.

83. This is my one concession to the fear that noise trading does influence stock prices and that some corporate disclosures are sufficiently salient to have a direct influence on such traders.

84. See *Peerless Mills, Inc.* v. *AT&T* (1975), discussing alleged conversion of shares by the son of the owners of the company.

85. Of course, there might be a statutory or rule-based duty to do so in particular contexts. See notes 94–100 and accompanying text; see also *Shaw* v. *Digital Equipment Corp.* (1996), finding omissions and misleading statements actionable under Rule 10b-5; Note (1997), discussing Shaw.

86. The alleged half-truth in *Backman* v. *Polaroid Corp.* (1990) occurred in the company's SEC filings, making it slightly more problematic. But my sense is that

marketing hype is systematic throughout a company's publicity and that the relevance of this should not be overstated.

87. If there is a plain factual misrepresentation, the fact that it occurs in marketing materials does not bar the application of Rule 10b-5. See *In re Carter-Wallace Inc. Securities Litigation* (1998).

88. See generally Prentice and Langmore (1994), discussing Apple.

89. The Supreme Court's opinion dealt specifically with only two issues: the materiality of the merger negotiations and the reliance requirement under Rule 10b-5. See *Basic Inc.* v. *Levinson* (1988). It did not address the ultimate issue of whether Basic's statement was misleading.

90. See, for example, *Glassman* v. *Computervision Corp.* (1996), finding that the mere fact that the company's intraquarterly results lagged behind internal projections did not by itself create a duty to disclose that fact in a prospectus; *Starkman* v. *Marathon Oil Co.* (1985), stating that a corporation had no duty to disclose an outside consultant's asset valuation reports, which contained estimates of the value of unexplored oil and gas reserves based on highly speculative assumptions regarding the future path of oil and gas prices; Cox, Hillman, and Langevoort (1997).

91. See *In re Verifone Securities Litigation* (1992), holding that a corporation's prospectus was not misleading when it failed to sufficiently disclose difficulties that the corporation would be facing in marketing new products.

92. See *In re Lyondell Petrochemical Co. Securities Litigation* (1993). *In re Lyondell* is difficult to read because the court dealt with the actionability of the underlying statement (that the company would generate results at least matching 1988 levels) in an unpublished opinion. The published opinion deals more abstractly with the duty to disclose the internal projections.

93. Obviously, even if the half-truth doctrine were to apply, such forward-looking disclosure would be protected, perhaps excessively, by the safe harbor created by the Private Securities Litigation Reform Act of 1995. See 15 U.S. Code sec. 78u-4 (1997 and Supp. 1999). See generally Schneider and Dubow (1996).

94. See Cox, Hillman, and Langevoort (1997); Barnes and Bagley (1994); Oesterle (1998); Rosenblum (1991); Schneider (1989). See generally Bauman (1979), providing an earlier survey of the duty to update issue.

95. See *In re Time Warner Inc. Securities Litigation*, 9 F.3d 259, 266 (2d Cir. 1993), finding that a duty to update may arise if the original disclosure becomes misleading as a result of intervening events; see also *Ross* v. *A. H. Robins Co.*, 465 F. Supp. 904, 908 (S.D.N.Y. 1979), finding a duty to update if a voluntary statement becomes materially misleading in light of subsequent events), rev'd on other grounds, 607 F.2d 545 (2d Cir. 1979).

96. See *Weiner* v. *Quaker Oats Co.* (1997), holding that a corporation's earning growth projections did not support a duty to update; *Greenfield* v. *Heublein, Inc.* (1984), finding a duty to update if a voluntary statement becomes materially misleading in light of subsequent events.

97. By "alive" in the marketplace, courts mean an earlier statement on which investors are still reasonably relying. To qualify, such a statement would have to be sufficiently forward looking that it is reasonable to rely on it not simply at the moment it was made, but for some time thereafter. The Seventh Circuit has squarely rejected the existence of a duty to update. See, for example, *Stransky* v. *Cummins Engine Co.* (1995), holding that a company has no duty to update when it makes a forward-looking statement that turns out to be wrong. The First Circuit is muddied. In *Backman* v. *Polaroid Corp.* (1990), the court dismissed the case against Polaroid because even if the duty to update existed, it was not violated. See also note 59 and accompanying text. But the court spent some time giving reasons (for example, a chill on voluntary corporate disclosure) that such a duty might be unwise. See also Schneider (1990). But see *Evanowski* v. *Bankworcester Corp.* (1991), stating that a corporation's duty to update is limited to correcting specific information that is later rendered inaccurate.

98. See *Restatement (Second) of Torts* (1981, sec. 551(2)(c)), establishing the duty to disclose subsequently acquired information that would make a previous representation untrue; Page, Dobbs, Keeton, and Owen (1984); see also, for example, *Turnbull* v. *LaRose* (1985), imposing a duty to disclose under the law of fraud once the seller of the building learned that a major tenant was departing, even though the contract had already been signed.

99. This is reflected in Time Warner's insistence that information be forward looking in order to trigger the duty to update. See *In re Time Warner Inc. Securities Litigation* (1993); see also *In re Burlington Coat Factory Securities Litigation* (1997), emphasizing the connection between the duty to update and the company's implicit promise to disclose.

100. This is consistent with *Backman* v. *Polaroid Corp.* (1990).

101. A hard question is posed by *Weiner* v. *Quaker Oats Co.* (1997), where the court imposed a duty to update Quaker Oats's prior statement of corporate policy regarding its acceptable debt-to-total-capitalization ratio when it was negotiating a highly leveraged acquisition of Snapple Beverage Corporation. The court's basic intuition is right: such a statement of policy is the kind of representation that should trigger a duty to update. Nevertheless, it is difficult to see how the company could have revised its disclosure without defeating the confidentiality of the merger negotiations (a point the court recognized but rejected as irrelevant). My sense is that a savvy market participant would not take the company's capitalization statement as an implied promise to compromise an acquisition, but I accept the issue as a close one.

102. The seminal contemporary case on this subject is *Raab* v. *General Physics Corp.* (1993), in which the court found that predictions in an annual report about future earnings were not material. Today, Raab's progeny can be found in nearly every circuit. See generally O'Hare (1998), arguing that almost every federal circuit court has recently used the puffery defense to improperly insulate companies from liability for their misrepresentations; Roussel (1998). While this doctrine is well established, it is not easy to apply, for courts are also insistent that specific

statements of optimism are actionable. See *In re Apple Computer Securities Litigation* (1989), holding that projections and general expressions of optimism may be actionable under federal securities laws, to the extent that one of three implied factual assertions—that the statement is genuinely believed, that there is reasonable basis for that belief, and that the speaker is not aware of any undisclosed facts tending to seriously undermine the accuracy of the statement—is inaccurate. See generally Barnes and Bagley (1994), discussing the risks of litigation involved when companies speak and lamenting the resulting practical confusion.

103. There is, of course, a fine line here. Lacking direct evidence of mental state, showing the existence of undisclosed adverse information is the only practicable way of establishing a circumstantial case of lack of genuine optimism.

104. The bespeaks caution doctrine, which has a slightly older vintage than the corporate puffery doctrine, holds that forward-looking statements are not actionable (even if otherwise totally fraudulent) if they are accompanied by some sort of meaningful cautionary language that leads investors to realize that the predictions might not come to pass. See, for example, *In re Donald J. Trump Casino Securities Litigation* (1993), finding no securities violation where the bond prospectus adequately conveyed risks to investors. See generally Langevoort (1994), analyzing the bespeaks caution doctrine and its difficulties. The substance of my concern, at least as the doctrine is applied aggressively in fraud-on-the-market cases, is that most intelligent investors already know that most predictions will not precisely come to pass; they do not need to be told. But the fact that the forward-looking information is somewhat speculative does not mean that it is unreliable (indeed, intelligent investors are influenced regularly by management's estimates). This notwithstanding, Congress has effectively codified the bespeaks caution doctrine in its safe harbor for forward-looking information under the Private Securities Litigation Reform Act of 1995.

105. A few courts have gone so far as to suggest that forward-looking projections and estimates are inherently not actionable unless worded as a guarantee, a concept that leaves almost no room for finding such statements fraudulent even when plainly significant to investors. Few estimates are ever worded as guarantees. See Roussel (1998).

106. See Cox (1986), arguing that firm managers are selective in deciding when to issue a forecast and may choose to do so only when it will increase the firm's market value.

107. See Fried (1998), explaining how corporate insiders consistently earn excess returns trading in their own shares and how market participants use publicly available information about insiders' trades to improve their own investment decisions. Studies have long shown that management has some ability to outperform the market, and we need not assume that this is based simply on unlawful trading.

108. Obviously, much more may go into reliance on brokers as well. See generally Langevoort (1996a).

109. In this sense, his decision is consistent with the dicta in *Shaw* v. *Digital Equipment Corp.* (1996) that there should be no per se rule of general optimism; all

matters are somewhat contextual. See also Roussel (1998), arguing that context must be considered in applying the corporate puffery defense.

110. See, for example, Barnes and Bagley (1994), who recommend that companies reduce their litigation risk by exercising more control over the disclosure process and over their dealings with the analysts and the public, including restricting one-on-one conversations with analysts to a minimum.

111. See Bauman (1979), arguing that the SEC "should express its views on . . . disclosure issues through rules or guidelines, rather than to leave the answers entirely to the courts" (p. 990).

112. In general, I would support imposing on an issuer a duty to warn investors of changed circumstances with a carefully tailored privilege to conceal certain kinds of sensitive information and limits on fraud-on-the-market private liability exposure. See Langevoort (1997b); compare Oesterle (1998), proposing an alternative broader phrasing of the duty to disclose.

References

Restatement (Second) of Torts. §§ 529, 551(2)(b) (1981).

Restatement (Second) of Contracts. § 159 illus. B (1981).

Alexander, J. C. "Do the Merits Matter? A Study of Settlements in Securities Class Actions." *Stanford Law Review,* 1991, *43,* 497–598.

Arlen, J. H., and Carney, W. J. "Vicarious Liability for Fraud on Securities Markets: Theory and Evidence." *University of Illinois Law Review,* 1992, *1992,* 691–740.

Ayres, I. "Back to Basics: Regulating How Corporations Speak to the Market." *Virginia Law Review,* 1991, *77,* 945–999.

Backman v. *Polaroid Corp.* 910 F.2d 10 (1st Cir. 1990).

Banca Cremi S.A. v. *Alexander Brown and Sons, Inc.* 132 F.3d 1017, 1028–1029 (4th Cir. 1997).

Barnes, D. E., Jr., and Bagley, C. E. "Great Expectations: Risk Management Through Risk Disclosure." *Stanford Journal of Law, Business, and Finance,* 1994, *1.*

Barnett, R. E. "Rational Bargaining Theory and Contract: Default Rules, Hypothetical Consent, the Duty to Disclose, and Fraud." *Harvard Journal of Law and Public Policy,* 1992, *15,* 783–803.

Basic Inc. v. *Levinson.* 485 U.S. 224 (1988).

Baskin v. *Collins.* 806 S.W.2d 3, 5 (Ark. 1991).

Bauman, J. D. "Rule 10b-5 and the Corporation's Affirmative Duty to Disclose." *Georgia Law Journal,* 1979, *67,* 935, 990.

Berger v. *Security Pacific Information Systems, Inc.* 795 P.2d 1380 (Colo. Ct. App. 1990).

Birmingham, R. L. "The Duty to Disclose and the Prisoner's Dilemma: *Laidlaw* v. *Oregon.*" *William and Mary Law Review,* 1988, *29,* 239–283.

Brass v. *American Film Technologies, Inc..* 987 F.2d 142 (2d Cir. 1993).

Bronston v. *United States.* 409 U.S. 352, 361–362 (1973).

Brudney, V. "Insiders, Outsiders, and Informational Advantages Under the Federal Securities Laws." *Harvard Law Review,* 1979, *93,* 322–376.

Cara Corp. v. *Continental Bank.* 148 B.R. 760, 763 (Bankr. E.D. Pa. 1992).

Carleton, W. T., Chen, C. R., and Steiner, T. L. "Optimism Biases Among Brokerage and Non-Brokerage Firms' Equity Recommendations: Agency Costs in the Investment Industry." *Financial Management,* Spring 1998, 27, 17–30.

Chasins v. *Smith, Barney and Co.* 438 F.2d 1167, 1172 (2d Cir. 1970).

Chiarella v. *United States.* 445 U.S. 222, 228 (1980).

Cialdini, R. B. *Influence: The Psychology of Persuasion.* New York: Quill/William Morrow, 1993.

Cooper v. *Pickett.* 122 F.3d 1186, 1193–1194 (9th Cir. 1997).

Cox, J. D. "Insider Trading Regulation and the Production of Information: Theory and Evidence." *Washington University Law Quarterly,* 1986, *475,* 475–505.

Cox, J. D., Hillman, R. W., and Langevoort, D. C. *Securities Regulation: Cases and Materials* (2nd ed.). Aspen Law and Business Foundation Press, 1997.

Daniel, K., Hirshleifer, D., and Subrahmanyam, A. "Investor Psychology and Security Market Under- and Overreactions." *Journal of Finance,* 1998, *53,* 1839–1885.

Darby, M. R., and Karni, E. "Free Competition and the Optimal Amount of Fraud." *Journal of Law and Economics* 1973, *16,* 67–88.

DeBondt, W.F.M., and Thaler, R. H. "Do Security Analysts Overreact?" *American Economic Review,* May 1990, 80, 52–57.

DeLong, J. B. "The Survival of Noise Traders in Financial Markets." *Journal of Business,* 1991, *64,* 1–19.

DeMott, D. A. "Do You Have the Right to Remain Silent? Duties of Disclosure in Business Transactions." *Delaware Journal of Corporate Law,* 1994, *19,* 65–102.

DiFonzo, N., and Prashant Bordia, P. "Rumor and Prediction: Making Sense (But Losing Dollars) in the Stock Market." *Organizational Behavior and Human Decision Processes,* 1997, *71,* 329–353.

Easterbrook, F. H., and Fischel, D. R. *The Economic Structure of Corporate Law.* Cambridge, Mass.: Harvard University Press, 1991.

Eisenstadt v. *Centel Corp.* 113 F.3d 738, 741–745 (7th Cir. 1997).

Emery v. *American General Finance, Inc.* 71 F.3d 1343, 1347–1348 (7th Cir. 1995).

Evanowski v. *Bankworcester Corp.* 788 F. Supp. 611, 615 (D. Mass. 1991).

FDIC v. *W. R. Grace and Co.* 877 F.2d 614, 619 (7th Cir. 1989).

Fecht v. *Price Co.* 70 F.3d 1078, 1081 (9th Cir. 1995).

First Virginia Bankshares v. *Benson.* 559 F.2d 1307, 1314–1317 (5th Cir. 1977).

Fischel, D. R. "Insider Trading and Investment Analysts: An Economic Analysis of Dirks v. *Securities and Exchange Commission.*" *Hofstra Law Review,* 1984, *13,* 127–146.

Fisher, W. O. "The Analyst-Added Premium as a Defense in Open Market Securities Fraud Cases." *Business Lawyer,* 1997, *53,* 35–64.

Fried, J. M. "Reducing the Profitability of Corporate Insider Trading Through Pretrading Disclosure." *Southern California Law Review,* 1998, *71,* 303–392.

Gilovich, T. *How We Know What Isn't So.* New York: Free Press, 1991.

Glassman v. *Computervision Corp.* 90 F.3d 617, 632–34 (1st Cir. 1996).

Goffman, E. *Frame Analysis: An Essay on the Organization of Experience.* 1974.

Grandon v. *Merrill Lynch and Co.* 147 F.3d 184, 191 (2d Cir. 1998).

Greenfield v. *Heublein, Inc.* 742 F.2d 751, 758 (3d Cir. 1984).

Grundfest, J. A. "Disimplying Private Rights of Action Under the Federal Securities Laws: The Commission's Authority." *Harvard Law Review,* 1994, *107,* 961–1024.

Gulati, M. "When Corporate Managers Fear a Good Thing Is Coming to an End: The Case of Interim Nondisclosure." *UCLA Law Review,* 1999, *46,* 675–756.

Heit v. *Weitzen.* 402 F.2d 909 (2d Cir. 1968).

Holland, J. H., Holyoak, K. J., Nisbett, R. E., and Thagard, P. R. *Induction: Processes of Inference, Learning, and Discovery.* Cambridge, Mass.: MIT Press, 1986.

In re Ames Department Stores Stock Litigation. 991 F.2d 953, 958 (2d Cir. 1993).

In re Apple Computer Securities Litigation. 886 F.2d 1109 (9th Cir. 1989).

In re Burlington Coat Factory Securities Litigation. 114 F.3d 1410, 1432 (3d Cir. 1997).

In re Carter-Wallace Inc. Securities Litigation. 150 F.3d 153, 156–157 (2d Cir. 1998).

In re Discovery Zone Securities Litigation [1996–1997 Transfer Binder]. Fed. Sec. L. Rep. (CCH) ¶ 99,381, at 96,462–464 (N.D. Ill. 1996).

In re Donald J. Trump Casino Securities Litigation. 7 F.3d 357, 368–369 (3d Cir. 1993).

In re Fidelity/Micron Securities Litigation. 964 F. Supp. 539, 547–548 (D. Mass. 1997).

In re Lyondell Petrochemical Co. Securities Litigation. 984 F.2d 1050, 1052 (9th Cir. 1993).

In re Time Warner Inc. Securities Litigation. 9 F.3d 259, 266 (2d Cir. 1993).

In re Verifone Securities Litigation. 784 F. Supp. 1471, 1481 (N.D. Cal. 1992), aff'd, 11 F.3d 865 (9th Cir. 1993).

In re Wells Fargo Securities Litigation. 12 F.3d 922, 926 (9th Cir. 1993).

James, F., Jr., & Gray, O. S. "Misrepresentation—Part II." *Maryland Law Review,* 1977, *37,* 488, 523–526.

Junius Construction Co. v. Cohen. 178 N.E. 672, 674 (N.Y. 1931).

Kahan, M. "Securities Laws and the Social Costs of 'Inaccurate' Stock Prices." *Duke Law Journal,* 1992a, *41,* 977–1044.

Kahan, M. "Games, Lies and Securities Fraud." *New York University Law Review,* 1992b, *67,* 750–800.

Karmel, R. S. "Is the Shingle Theory Dead?" *Washington and Lee Law Review,* 1995, *52,* 1271–1297.

Katz, L. "All Deceptions Are Not Equal." *New York Times,* Aug. 19, 1998.

Keeton, R. E., Page, W., Dobbs, D. B., and Owen, D. G. *Prosser and Keeton on the Law of Torts* (5th ed.). 1984.

Kitch, E. W. "The Theory and Practice of Securities Disclosure." *Brooklyn Law Review,* 1995, *763,* 786–888.

Klausner, M. "Sociological Theory and the Behavior of Financial Markets." In P. A. Adler and P. Adler (eds.), *The Social Dynamics of Financial Markets.* Greenwich, Conn.: JAI Press, 1984.

Kraakman, R., Park, H., and Shavell, S. "When Are Shareholder Suits in Shareholder Interests?" *Georgia Law Journal,* 1994, *82,* 1733–1779.

Kronman, A. T. "Disclosure, Mistake, Information, and the Law of Contracts." *Journal of Legal Studies,* 1978.

Langevoort, D. C. "Investment Analysts and the Law of Insider Trading." *Virginia Law Review,* 1990, *76,* 1023–1054.

Langevoort, D. C. "Theories, Assumptions, and Securities Regulation: Market Efficiency Revisited." *University of Pennsylvania Law Review,* 1992, *140,* 851–920.

Langevoort, D. C. "Disclosures That 'Bespeak Caution.'" *Business Lawyer,* 1994, *49,* 1157–1175.

Langevoort, D. C. "Ego, Human Behavior, and Law." *Virginia Law Review,* 1995, *81,* 853–886.

Langevoort, D. C. "Selling Hope, Selling Risk: Some Lessons for Law from Behavioral Economics About Stockbrokers and Sophisticated Customers." *California Law Review,* 1996a, *84,* 627–701.

Langevoort, D. C. "Capping Damages for Open-Market Securities Fraud." *Arizona Law Review,* 1996b, *38,* 639–664.

Langevoort, D. C. "Organized Illusions: A Behavioral Theory of Why Corporations Mislead Stock Market Investors (and Cause Other Social Harms)." *University of Pennsylvania Law Review,* 1997a, *146,* 101–172.

Langevoort, D. C. "Towards More Effective Risk Disclosure for Technology-Enhanced Investing." *Washington University Law Quarterly,* 1997b, *75,* 753–777.

Langevoort, D. C. "What Was Kaye Scholer Thinking?" *Law and Social Inquiry,* 1998, *23,* 297–303.

Leone v. *Advest Inc.* 624 F. Supp. 297 (S.D.N.Y. 1985).

Lev, B., and de Villiers, M. "Stock Price Crashes and 10b-5 Damages: A Legal, Economic and Policy Analysis." *Stanford Law Review,* 1994, *47,* 7–37.

Levinson v. *Basic.* 786 F.2d 741 (6th Cir. 1986), rev'd, 485 U.S. 224 (1988).

Levmore, S. "Securities and Secrets: Insider Trading and the Law of Contracts." *Virginia Law Review,* 1982, *68,* 117–160.

Lewis, M. *The Money Culture.* New York: Norton, 1991.

Lieb v. *Merrill Lynch, Pierce, Fenner and Smith.* 461 F. Supp. 951, 953 (E.D. Mich. 1978).

Loss, L., and Seligman, J. *Securities Regulation* (3rd ed.). Aspen Law and Business, 1991.

Macey, J. R., and Miller, G. P. "Good Finance, Bad Economics: An Analysis of the Fraud-on-the-Market Theory." *Stanford Law Review*, 1990, *42*, 1059–1092.

Mahoney, P. G. "Precaution Costs and the Law of Fraud in Impersonal Markets." *Virginia Law Review*, 1992, *78*, 628–670.

Mahoney, P. G. "Mandatory Disclosure as a Solution to Agency Problems." *University of Chicago Law Review*, 1995a, *62*, 725–740.

Mahoney, P. G. "Is There a Cure for 'Excessive" Trading?'" *Virginia Law Review*, 1995b, *81*, 713–749.

McGann v. Ernst and Young. 102 F.3d 390, 397 (9th Cir. 1996).

Model Rules of Professional Conduct. 1983.

Nash v. Trustees of Boston University. 776 F. Supp. 73, 78–82 (D.R.I. 1990).

Nei v. Burley. 446 N.E.2d 674, 676 (Mass. 1983).

Note. "Living in a Material World: Corporate Disclosure of Midquarter Results." *Harvard Law Review*, 1997, *110*, 923–940.

O'Connor v. R. F. Lafferty and Co. 965 F.2d 893 (10th Cir. 1992).

Oesterle, D. A. "The Inexorable March Toward a Continuous Disclosure Requirement for Publicly Traded Corporations: 'Are We There Yet?'" *Cardozo Law Review*, 1998, *20*, 135–225.

O'Hare, J. "The Resurrection of the Dodo: The Unfortunate Reemergence of the Puffery Defense in Private Securities Fraud Actions." *Ohio State Law Journal*, 1998, *59*, 1697–1740.

Ollerman v. O'Rourke Co. 288 N.W.2d 95, 107 (Wis. 1980).

O'Shaughnessy, J. *Why People Buy.* New York: Oxford University Press, 1987.

Page, W., Dobbs, D. B., Keeton, R. E., and Owen, D. G. *Prosser and Keeton on the Law of Torts* (5th ed.). 1984.

Palmieri, N. W. "Good Faith Disclosures Required During Precontractual Negotiations." *Seton Hall Law Review*, 1993, *24*, 70–213.

Panzirer v. Wolf. 663 F.2d 365, 366 (2d Cir. 1981).

Pashley v. Pacific Electric Co. 153 P.2d 325, 330 (Cal. 1944).

Peerless Mills, Inc. v. AT&T. 527 F.2d 445, 449 (2d Cir. 1975).

Peters, G. M. "The Use of Lies in Negotiation." *Ohio State Law Journal*, 1986, *48*, 1–50.

Pfeffer, J., and Salancik, G. R. *The External Control of Organizations: A Resource Dependence Perspective.* New York: Harper & Row, 1978.

Phillips, R. P., and Miller, G. C. "Symposium on the Private Securities Litigation Reform Act of 1995." *Business Lawyer*, 1996, *51*, 1009–1070.

Posner, R. A. *Economic Analysis of Law* (4th ed.). Boston: Little, Brown, 1992.

Prentice, R. A., and Langmore, J. H. "Beware of Vaporware: Product Hype and the Securities Fraud Liability of High-Tech Companies." *Harvard Journal of Law and Technology*, 1994, *8*, 1–74.

Private Securities Litigation Reform Act of 1995. 15 U.S.C. sec. 78u-4. 1997. Supp. 1999.

Raab v. *General Physics Corp.* 4 F.3d 286 (4th Cir. 1993).

Randi W. v. *Muroc Joint Unified School District.* 929 P.2d 582 (1997).

Roeder v. *Alpha Industries.* 814 F.2d 22 (1st Cir. 1987).

Romano, R. "Empowering Investors: A Market Approach to Securities Regulation." *Yale Law Journal*, 1998, *107*, 2359–2430.

Rose, C. M. "Trust in the Mirror of Betrayal." *Boston University Law Review*, 1995, *75*, 531–558.

Rosenblum, R. H. "An Issuer's Duty Under Rule 10b-5 to Correct and Update Materially Misleading Statements." *Catholic University Law Review*, 1991, *40*, 289–330.

Ross v. *A. H. Robins Co.* 465 F. Supp. 904, 908 (S.D.N.Y. 1979).

Roussel, R. G. "Securities Fraud or Mere Puffery: Refinement of the Corporate Puffery Defense." *Vanderbilt Law Review*, 1998, *51*, 1049–1092.

Salancik, G. R., and Meindl, J. R. "Corporate Attributions as Strategic Illusions of Management Control." *Administrative Science Quarterly*, 1984, *29*, 238–254.

Schneider, C. W. "Duty to Update: Does a Snapshot Disclosure Require the Commencement of a Motion Picture?" *Insights*, Feb. 1989, pp. 3–6.

Schneider, C. W. "The Uncertain Duty to Update—Polaroid II Brings a Welcome Limitation." *Insights*, Oct. 1990.

Schneider, C. W., and Dubow, J. A. "Forward-Looking Information—Navigating in the Safe Harbor." *Business Law*, 1996, *51*, 2, 10.

Securities and Exchange Commission v. *Great American Industries, Inc.* 407 F.2d 453, 461 (2d Cir. 1968).

Securities and Exchange Commission v. *Texas Gulf Sulphur Co.* 401 F.2d 833, 864 (2d Cir. 1968).

Shavell, S. "Acquisition and Disclosure of Information Prior to Sale." *RAND Journal of Economics*, 1994, *25*, 20–36.

Shaw v. *Digital Equipment Corp.* 82 F.3d 1194 (1st Cir. 1996).

Shawmut Bank v. *Kress Association.* 33 F.3d 1477, 1485 (9th Cir. 1994).

Shell, G. R. "Opportunism and Trust in the Negotiation of Commercial Contracts: Toward a New Cause of Action." *Vanderbilt Law Review*, 1991, *4*, 221–282.

Simon, W. H. "The Kaye Scholer Affair: The Lawyer's Duty of Candor and the Bar's Temptations of Evasion and Apology." *Law and Social Inquiry*, 1998, *23*, 365–372.

Smith, R. "Conference Calls to Big Investors Often Leave Little Guys Hung Up." *Wall Street Journal*, June 21, 1995, p. C1.

Starkman v. *Marathon Oil Co.* 772 F.2d 231, 239–242 (6th Cir. 1985).

Staw, B. M., McKechnie, P. I., and Puffer, S. M. "The Justification of Organizational Performance." *Administrative Science Quarterly,* 1983, *28,* 582–600.

Stout, L. A. "The Unimportance of Being Efficient: An Economic Analysis of Stock Market Pricing and Securities Regulation." *Michigan Law Review,* 1988, *87,* 613–709.

Stout, L. A. "Are Stock Markets Costly Casinos? Disagreement, Market Failure, and Securities Regulation." *Virginia Law Review,* 1995, *81,* 611–712.

Stransky v. *Cummins Engine Co.* 51 F.3d 1329, 1332–1333 (7th Cir. 1995).

Strawn v. *Canuso.* 657 A.2d 420, 431 (N.J. 1995).

Strudler, A. "Moral Complexity in the Law of Nondisclosure." *UCLA Law Review,* 1997, *45,* 337–384.

Tetlock, P. E., Skitka, L., and Boettgar, R. "Social and Cognitive Strategies for Coping with Accountability: Conformity, Complexity and Bolstering." *Journal of Personality and Social Psychology,* 1989, *57,* 632–640.

Thompson, R. B. "'Simplicity and Certainty' in the Measure of Recovery Under Rule 10b-5." *Business Lawyer,* 1996, *51,* 1177–1201.

Turnbull v. *LaRose.* 702 P.2d 1331, 1334 (Alaska 1985).

United States v. *DeZarn.* 157 F.3d 1042, 1051 (6th Cir. 1998).

Vai v. *Bank of America National Trust and Savings Association.* 364 P.2d 247, 255 (Cal. 1961).

Vanyo, B. G., and Salceda, I. E. "Defending Securities Class Actions in an Era of Change." *Securities Litigation,* 1995, 77.

Varity Corp. v. *Howe.* 516 U.S. 489 (1996).

V.S.H. Realty Inc. v. *Texaco Inc.* 757 F.2d 411, 415 (1st Cir. 1985).

Watson v. *Avon Street Business Center, Inc.* 311 S.E.2d 795, 797–798 (Va. 1984).

Weiner v. *Quaker Oats Co.* 129 F.3d 310, 320–321 (3d Cir. 1997).

Weiss, E. J., and Beckerman, J. S. "Let the Money Do the Monitoring: How Institutional Investors Can Reduce Agency Costs in Securities Class Actions." *Yale Law Journal,* 1995, *104,* 2053–2127.

Westphal, J. D., and Zajac, E. J. "The Symbolic Management of Stockholders: Corporate Governance Reforms and Shareholder Reactions." *Administrative Science Quarterly,* 1998, *43,* 127–153.

White, J. J. "Machiavelli and the Bar: Ethical Limitations on Lying in Negotiation." *American Bar Foundation Research Journal,* 1980, *1980,* 926–938.

Wielgos v. *Commonwealth Edison Co.* 892 F.2d 509 (7th Cir. 1989).

Wirth v. *Commercial Resources Inc.* 630 P.2d 292, 297 (N.M. Ct. App. 1981).

Wonnell, C. T. "The Structure of a General Theory of Nondisclosure." *Case Western Reserve Law Review,* 1991, *41,* pp. 329–386.

Zimpel v. *Trawick.* 679 F. Supp. 1502 (W.D. Ark. 1988).

CHAPTER TWENTY-SEVEN

Mindfulness in the Law and Alternative Dispute Resolution

Scott R. Peppet

This essay explores whether mindfulness squares with partisanship. I must warn the reader at the outset that I will raise a potentially dizzying number of difficult questions in beginning to work through this topic, all in a very few pages. I do not provide, nor do I have, clear answers to some of these questions. My goal is to provoke, raise doubts, and begin to chart the way toward a theory of negotiation ethics, not to argue each point extensively. That will have to wait for another day.[1]

The essay is partly a response to Riskin (2002) and partly a coda. Riskin explores several of the ways that mindfulness might benefit lawyers, including reducing stress, increasing professional satisfaction, facilitating listening, and softening the lawyer's standard adversarial stance.[2] He briefly discusses its potential impact on negotiation, suggesting that mindfulness practice may make a negotiator more mentally agile and thus better able to manage both the tension between creating and distributing value and the choice between adversarial and problem-solving strategies.[3] Mindfulness, in short, will make the negotiator more free to choose how to negotiate.

This essay suggests the opposite. Mindfulness may lead to more deeply-held ethical commitments, which in turn may prevent some forms of partisanship that are required for certain negotiation strategies and tactics. Although mindfulness may not be the only path to such commitments, it is our topic here and I will attempt to show that introducing these practices to negotiators—lawyers and non-lawyers alike—may ultimately lead them to eschew adversarial negotiation strategies.[4] I certainly don't claim that this would be a bad thing, but it may, for some, conflict with their vision of the lawyer's role. My point is that the conflict is real, and that mindfulness may exacerbate, not resolve, it.

THE MINDFUL NEGOTIATOR

For brevity, I will largely assume that over time, a mindful person will become a more ethical person. This assumption is certainly open to challenge, and it deserves greater exploration than I can offer here. But I will take it as a given. Mindfulness offers a broader view of each experience than we normally adopt. It is a view that permits, even requires, careful weighing of one's immediate needs or wants against a more long-term and thoughtful consideration of one's interests. If each experience or interaction is seen in the context of one's life as a whole and against the background of one's self-realization instead of as a discrete transaction disconnected from one's personal development, the costs of ethically questionable behavior become more salient. Deception, for example, always risks spoiling a negotiation or one's relationship with the other side. From this broader perspective, however, deception also risks damaging one's integrity—turning you into (or beginning to turn you into) the sort of person that you don't want to be. Because that damage, in turn, may hinder further self-realization and growth, the mindful person will avoid such deceptive actions.[5] This can be the first step toward a more ethical life—taken initially out of self-interest and the desire to progress as a person.

If one accepts this argument, it raises an obvious question: just how far will increased awareness, attention, and focus go in terms of strengthening one's ethical commitments?[6] Riskin (2002) seems to agree that increased attention to ethics accompanies increased mindfulness. He notes that certain "positive states of mind"—such as loving-kindness, compassion, empathy, and equanimity—tend to "develop routinely in the course of extensive mindfulness meditation practice" (p. 65). And in the legal context he acknowledges the possibility that "a deeper understanding of one's own motives and a commitment to ethical decision-making might make it difficult for some lawyers to undertake certain activities that are widely—but not universally—considered essential for proper lawyering" (p. 64). Ultimately, however, Riskin doubts that mindfulness will so change a lawyer as to make the lawyer unable to pursue his client's interests as zealously as the client might hope. He concludes that it is "quite unlikely" that mindfulness will make lawyers so soft that they will be unwilling to "tear down a hostile witness in a trial, twist the facts, or otherwise push hard enough for their clients' positions" (p. 64). A mindful lawyer, the argument goes, can still be an adversarial lawyer—and, by implication, a mindful client can still be competitive and choose an adversarial approach to her negotiations.

I am less sure than Riskin seems to be about this reconciliation of mindfulness and partisanship.[7] One can imagine that the practices Riskin describes might have a far more significant impact on a person's ethical commitments, whether lawyer or non-lawyer, than he seems to admit. To explore this possibility, imagine that, at the extreme, a diligent mindfulness practitioner might eventually reach a state of complete dedication to an ethical life. I will call this person a "saint" because she adopts a more conscientious stance toward her relations with the world and others than most of us will ever achieve.[8] Our saint would also have to be sufficiently strong-willed to live up to her moral commitments. She must have developed herself to the point that the contingencies of her life—her history, attachments, psychology, and emotions—no longer lead her to act against these deeply held beliefs. She is so mindful as to be somewhat frightening.

What sort of ethical commitments would our saint adopt? For the sake of argument, I will assert that at the very least such a person would commit to both honesty and fairness, resolving neither to deceive nor to take advantage of other human beings[9] for her own ends[10] and to respect and take others' interests into account.[11] There is good reason to believe that a very mindful person would adopt such a saintly view of life. Even without turning extensively to religious doctrine, one can imagine that our saint would be consistently non-partisan when it came to her own and others' interests.[12] The saint would realize, as the philosopher Henry Sidgwick (1992) put it, that "the good of any one individual is of no more importance, from the point of view (if I may say so) of the Universe, than the good of any other" (p. 382). Thomas Nagel (1986) calls this an "objective" viewpoint: one that is removed from the individual's own interests.[13] It is a view most often associated with R. M. Hare (1963, 1981, 1984), who described such non-partisan principles as "universalizable." Hare argued that an ethical imperative must be universalizable in the sense that it recommends an action regardless of the perspective or contingencies of the actor.[14] If I think it is morally acceptable for me to torture you, I must also think it is acceptable for you to torture me (Hare, 1999). As I am unlikely to accept this, freedom to torture is a poor candidate for a moral imperative. This thinking ultimately leads us to a commitment to consider others' interests.[15] Somewhat like Kant, Hare (1999) explains that "if we are trying to universalize our maxims, we shall try to further the ends of other people on equal terms with ourselves, treating them as if they were our own ends" (p. 14).

Is there reason to believe that mindfulness will lead to this sort of moral perspective-taking? This is an empirical claim, and one that I can neither substantiate nor refute. But it is plausible, or at least plausible enough to deserve attention. Riskin (2002) notes that mindfulness training can help to loosen up a practitioner's attachment to self and ego.[16] As a practitioner looks deeper into the nature of his own and others' conditions, his own life, interests and position may become less primary and others' interests more salient. This, in turn, may permit more compassion, empathy and concern for others' well being. Mindfulness may, in short, allow him to "know" others' experiences or perspectives—know what it is like to be them, in their unique condition—in a way previously unavailable to him. (One cannot, of course, ever know another's experience in an ultimate sense or in the way that one knows the taste of broccoli. Although you might observe or reflect upon another person endlessly, you will never observe from the outside—in what it is like to be that person from the inside—out (Vendler, 1988; Nagel, 1979). But perhaps we don't need such perfect knowledge to ground moral commitments. One can approximate, and it seems reasonable that one's approximation, though never perfect, becomes more accurate to the extent that we can weaken the grip of our own partisan perspective.)

Assuming such perspective-taking occurs, will it lead to our saint's basic commitments to honesty and fairness? I acknowledge that this is a big leap, indeed the biggest leap in this essay. To say that moral imperatives are universalizable does not tell you the content of those imperatives. Arguing for (or even defining) honesty and fairness, however, is beyond my reach or ability here. I must simply assert that both are sufficiently fundamental, and sufficiently derivable from this sort of moral perspective-taking (or from other sorts of reasoning about morals), to attribute to our saint.[17]

To recap, our first proposition is that a more mindful person will likely become a more ethical person. Second, she will become more ethical in a particular way—that is, by committing to a less partisan, more universal perspective. In the negotiation context this change will likely lead her at least to commit (1) not to deceive or manipulate others, given that she would not want to be deceived or manipulated, and (2) to try to respect and take others' interests into account as she would expect others to take her interests into account.

Few of us, of course, are likely to achieve sainthood in the sense described here. I do not think, however, that this failure, if it is one, will be due to our rejecting these basic principles of honesty and fairness. I believe that most reflective people, including mindfulness practitioners, will arrive at these commitments. More likely, the failure will result from a lack of will, or, put differently, from an inability to realize consistently the principles because of our being rooted in an individual life, at a certain time, in a certain setting. The challenges of life are jarring; we do not always respond to them as we know we should.

Nevertheless, all of this suggests that perhaps Riskin understates the effect that mindfulness practice will have on the choice of negotiation strategies. Although Riskin (2002) suggests that mindfulness will better equip negotiators to apply either problem-solving or more adversarial strategies "moment to moment" (p. 55), a more likely effect, I think, is that mindful negotiators will abandon a truly competitive approach to negotiation. It will no longer be morally responsible to, as Riskin describes it, "mislead the other side," (p. 54) or perhaps even to ascribe to the basic tenets of what Riskin calls the "lawyer's standard philosophical map" (p. 13). Negotiators will not only have pragmatic reasons to search for integrative, value-creating solutions to a problem; they will have moral reasons as well.[18] They not only ought to problem-solve because it is good practical advice but also because it would be wrong not to.

This is true, I think, of both the saint and the more humble novice to mindfulness. Indeed, negotiation and strategic interaction may be a perfect testing ground for a mindfulness practitioner's new-found ethical aspirations. Moreover, negotiation presents these moral choices in a foreseeable and easily recognizable way. It is a salient context with obvious ethical import. Although a saint may practice discernment and equanimity regardless of situation, and may not need context to provide a warning, many more of us will welcome the reminder to be mindful of our behavior.

SOME EXAMPLES

Adversarial bargaining is common in legal negotiations. One study of civil litigation in New Jersey found that litigators thought that "positional" bargaining was used in 71 percent of the cases and problem-solving was used in approximately 16 percent (Heumann and Hyman, 1997). This suggests that a mindful negotiator committed to honesty and fairness—and thus to certain forms of problem-solving instead of adversarial bargaining—would be in a distinct minority. But what, exactly, would such a negotiator be required to forego to adhere to our basic commitments to honesty and fairness?

Many common "hard bargaining" tactics derive their power largely from deception.[19] Making an arbitrary and inflated demand, advocating an issue that one does not really care about in order to create a "bargaining chip," or making a threat that one does not intend to carry out are all intended to induce action by another person through distortion.[20] These tactics conflict with a basic moral commitment to honesty. Similarly, extreme variants of commitment tactics (Schelling, 1960), good cop/bad cop, or personal attacks may be suspect because of the underlying purpose of denigrating or circumventing the other person's interests in order to better satisfy one's own.

Certain positive legal permissions to bend the truth in negotiations may also seem less important in the face of a general moral commitment to honesty or fairness. The law of fraud, for example, distinguishes between misrepresentations of fact and misrepresentations of mere opinion. "Bluffing" and "puffing" are permissible; factual misrepresentations are not (Adler and Silverstein, 2000). Likewise, the American Bar Association's Model Rules of Professional Conduct (1999) permit certain sorts of misrepresentations in negotiation. Model Rule 4.1

states that a lawyer shall not knowingly make a false statement of material fact or law to a third person, nor fail to disclose a material fact to a third person when disclosure is necessary to avoid assisting a client's criminal or fraudulent act (subject to the constraints of Rule 1.6 governing client confidences). The Comment to Rule 4.1, however, permits certain forms of exaggeration and mis-representation—regarding "estimates of price or value placed on the subject of a transaction" or "a party's intentions as to an acceptable settlement of a claim." In short, it is acceptable for a lawyer to misrepresent a client's reservation price or intentions regarding what constitutes an acceptable settlement.

One might believe that a lawyer-negotiator is morally justified in telling such lies about reservation price even if a non-lawyer negotiator is not. And one could argue[21] about whether these legal distinctions align sufficiently with moral reasoning (Green, 2001). What "honesty" and "fairness" require is certainly intricate. Even without bringing these basic duties into such detailed focus, however, the point remains: becoming more mindful may restrict a negotiator's freedom to adopt what might otherwise be considered acceptable, even if somewhat "sharp," approaches to bargaining.

OBJECTIONS

I can imagine many objections to this brief argument. One is that arriving at ethical principles of this sort is a task in which we all engage already, or should, so long as we are reflective about how to live. Mindful awareness is not required for moral acuity—traditional practical reasoning about what morality requires will do the job. I actually agree with this argument, but I don't think that it detracts much from the discussion here. Increased awareness of self and circumstance may facilitate such reasoning, even if it is not necessary. And it may lead most mindfulness practitioners toward these ethical principles even if others could also arrive there independently.

A second objection is that our saint—or even any negotiator espousing the saint's ethic (though perhaps not living up to it consistently)—simply cannot be described accurately as "negotiating." Honest bargaining that takes all interests seriously is not really bargaining, it's something else, because deception, the argument goes, is inherent to negotiation.[22] James White (1980) has stated, for example, that "to conceal one's true position, to mislead an opponent about one's true settling point, is the essence of negotiation" (p. 926).[23] Walter Steele (1986) put a point on this argument with the following hypothetical:

> Consider the negotiating standards of two holy men, one a willing buyer and the other a willing seller. If their personal commitments to holiness prevented them from making the slightest misrepresentation or from engaging in any abuse of

their bargaining positions, how would the ultimate outcome of their negotiations differ from the outcome achieved by two lawyer negotiators? If deceit truly is inherent to negotiation, the outcome achieved by the holy men could not be defined as the product of a negotiation (pp. 1390–1391).[24]

Not everyone agrees with this characterization,[25] but it is certainly common. Perhaps the best example of this sort of thinking is, again, Model Rule 4.1's permission of misrepresentations about reservation price. According to the Rule's Comments, misleading statements of this sort are permitted because "under generally accepted conventions in negotiation, certain types of statements ordinarily are not taken as statements of material fact." Although the rules do not say so explicitly, this Comment seems to imply that barring all types of misrepresentation would demand too much—it would make negotiation as we normally understand it impossible.

I disagree with this view, both as expressed in Steele's hypothetical and in the Comment to Model Rule 4.1. Although many negotiators may deceive and manipulate, I see nothing that requires one to do so, nor do I think that one can be effective only by doing so. Negotiation requires parties to manage different and sometimes conflicting interests to determine whether a jointly-created outcome can be found that is more satisfying than any self-help alternative (see Lax and Sebenius, 1986). Two saints could honestly disclose their alternatives and reservation values, their interests and priorities, and still face a variety of challenging decisions regarding how best to maximize achievable joint gain and divide the pie.[26] Even for the enlightened there would likely be no easy answer as to whether to give more of the economic surplus in a transaction to the person who needed it more, wanted it more, or deserved it more. Two saints might disagree about how to classify a used car in the "blue book" scheme, or about when an employment agreement should vest an executive's stock options. I see no reason to redescribe their interaction over these matters as something other than negotiation merely because they chose to avoid dishonesty or manipulation.

I must make one caveat, however. One can imagine a person who becomes so universal in her views—so detached from the particulars of her individual position—that she no longer values her own interests at all. Her only interest becomes to serve others' interests. Although it is difficult to imagine how two such people could interact (wouldn't they merely circle each other endlessly, each trying to help the other?), I think the introduction of even one such person into what would otherwise be a negotiation does require redescription of the interaction as something other than bargaining. In this extreme circumstance there would not be two people with differing or conflicting interests; only one with interests and another with a desire to serve. There would be nothing to negotiate about—person A would express needs and person B would satisfy them to the best of B's ability.

Finally, one might object that lawyers have a duty to compete. If a lawyer refuses to do so because of ethical commitments that include consideration of an opponent's interests, then even if we cannot redescribe that lawyer's interactions as something other than negotiation, perhaps we should simply decide that the person can no longer be a lawyer. Robert Condlin (1992), for example, has written that lawyers "must use any legally available move or procedure helpful to a client's bargaining position. Among other things, this means that all forms of leverage must be exploited, inflated demands made, and private information obtained and used whenever any of these actions would advance the client's stated objectives" (p. 71). If negotiating lawyers will not play the game, they should be disqualified as players.

Although it opens yet another difficult line of argument, I think it unlikely that a saint, or even just a very reflective person, would decide, like Condlin, to prioritize client loyalty over the saint's already-discussed ethical commitments. As Riskin explains, mindfulness loosens one's attachments—one's loyalties. This is, again, what suggests that these practices might aid in adopting a more universal perspective on moral questions.[27] It also suggests, however, that a loyalty-driven ethic, peculiar to one's particular duties to a particular client, will be relatively unpersuasive to our saint as compared to the basic obligations to honesty and fairness.[28]

CONCLUSION

Luckily, however, I need not resolve these matters here. This discussion of role ends the essay exactly as I set out—illustrating the complexity of Riskin's introduction of mindfulness to legal negotiation. Although I have made many assumptions, my general point is simple. Increasing one's awareness has ethical consequences. One becomes, over time, a different sort of person. And that sort of person may no longer wish to engage in certain negotiation strategies. Rather than becoming more free, moment to moment, to choose a negotiation approach, a mindful negotiator may constrain himself, limiting his freedom of action in deference to his ethical commitments. And this, particularly for lawyers, may chafe against the lawyer's understanding—or others' understanding—of the lawyer's role.

Notes

1. I develop some of these ideas further in an article currently under development titled "Honesty and Fairness."

2. See also Keeva (1999), discussing the benefits of mindfulness for lawyers.

3. Riskin (2002) argues that mindfulness permits a negotiator to hold the negotiator's dilemma "in her awareness at virtually all points before and during a negotiation

and decide, moment to moment, whether and how to use or blend adversarial or problem-solving strategies and techniques" (p. 55).

4. I must leave a related, interesting, but unfortunately altogether too broad topic for treatment elsewhere, perhaps by others. This is the question of what ethical challenges lawyer-negotiators who are not interested in mindfulness may face if they negotiate on behalf of particularly ethical or mindful clients. I can see at least two such problems. One is that these lawyers are likely to distrust the clients' mindful states, believing perhaps that any altruism or collaboration clients say they desire will be short-lived. These lawyers may feel duty-bound to protect their clients' interests as the lawyers understand them, even while potentially dismissing their clients' expression of those interests. Second, lawyers may feel a need to protect their clients from information learned from the other side. Mnookin, Tulumello, and I (2001) have identified the agent's "assimilation problem"—that a principal may equate empathy with agreement and thus fear that the agent is beginning to identify too closely with the other side's perspective and interests. A lawyer negotiating on behalf of a mindful client faces the opposite problem. Assuming that the attorney interacts with the other side without the client present, the attorney will possess private information about the other side—for example, that the other side is deeply upset at the prospect of going to court and fears the emotional turmoil of litigation. A lawyer may fear that telling the client about the opponent's fear will lead the client to give in too readily. As a result, the lawyer may keep information from the client or even mislead the client about what the lawyer knows. See generally Lerman (1990) and Menkel-Meadow (1990).

5. For two very different but equally eloquent discussions of this increasing reluctance to act immorally, see Nozick (1981), pp. 505–525, discussing iterative self-improvement as a path to ethical principles, and Batchelor (1997): "Our deeds, words, and intentions create an ethical ambience that either supports or weakens resolve. If we behave in a way that harms either others or ourselves, the capacity to focus on the task [of mindful awakening] will be weakened" (pp. 45–48). Self-selection likely also creates a correlation between mindfulness and ethical strength. Those who become interested in mindfulness training may often be those who already reflect on their ethical duties and what constitutes a good life.

6. This is not a question reserved only for those interested in mindfulness but is instead a basic question in ethical theory. As Nozick (1989) has noted, the ability to focus attention is a fundamental component of our autonomy and a determinant of our character and makeup over time. See Nozick (1989): "What we presently focus upon is affected by what we are like, yet over the long run a person is molded by where his or her attention continually dwells" (p. 122).

7. To be fair, Riskin's article (2002) is not devoted to this topic, and thus it is hard to know what his considered opinion would be on the matter. I have tried to assemble his position on mindfulness, ethics, and the lawyer's role as best I can.

8. For the purposes of this essay I make no reference to religious canons regarding the qualifications for sainthood. The "saint" here is merely an extremely aware, moral person.

9. One can question whether such a commitment should be limited to human beings instead of all forms of sentient life, as have both serious ethicists and various religious figures. See, for example, Singer (1975, 1993). Because I focus here on negotiation, I will ignore the question of the ethical treatment of nonhuman life.

10. There are various justifications for deceit, such as to save a life or serve some other moral end. Here I refer to self-interested deceit designed merely to further one's own welfare. This does not do justice to the complexities of this topic but will have to do for now.

11. These various commitments are not necessarily connected. One might decide not to deceive or manipulate but not take the further step of affirmatively committing to take others' substantive interests into account. For our purposes here, however, I will assume that our saint adopts both sorts of principles.

12. See Nagel (1979): "Moral equality attempts to give equal weight, in essential respects, to each person's point of view. This might even be described as the mark of an enlightened ethic" (p. 112).

13. According to Nagel (1986), "A view or form of thought is more objective than another if it relies less on the specifics of the individual's makeup and position in the world, or on the character of the particular type of creature he is. . . . We may think of reality as a set of concentric spheres, progressively revealed as we detach gradually from the contingencies of the self" (p. 5). Rawls (1971) adopts a similar, though not identical, viewpoint when he reasons from behind his famous "veil of ignorance." Rawls writes, "Somehow we must nullify the effects of specific contingencies which put men at odds and tempt them to exploit social and natural circumstances to their own advantage" (p. 136). The legal system too rests on an ideal of "blind justice," impartial as between persons irrespective of their individual characteristics. See Sidgwick (1992), who discusses parallels between the universal point of view and this legal ideal. Indeed, there is an odd similarity here to what Dean Anthony Kronman (1993, p. 113) has called "that peculiar bifocality" that law students acquire through the case method in law school, which he describes as a "forcing ground for the moral imagination" because it requires the law student to "disengage himself from the sympathetic attachments he may have formed" and see things from multiple perspectives. Of course, not all (Kronman included) agree that law school serves as a place for moral development. See, for example, Sells (1994), who describes how the case method leads to a sort of "false individuality."

14. Hare (1963) writes, "All that is essential . . . is that B should disregard the fact that he plays the particular role in the situation which he does, without disregarding the inclinations which people have in situations of this sort. In other words, he must be prepared to give weight to A's inclinations and interests as if they were his own" (p. 94).

15. Negotiation scholars have long advocated taking others' interests into account. See generally Fisher, Ury, and Patton (1991). Such perspective taking permits creative problem solving and more efficient negotiation. My argument here, however, suggests that putting yourself in the other person's shoes may actually be a moral

imperative, not merely a pragmatic prescription. I hope to develop this idea more fully in forthcoming work.

16. Nozick (1989) has questioned whether meditative insight into the unreality of the self or ego is valid. He notes that "observational support for the no-self view is rooted within Buddhist meditative practice" but that "this practice also is guided by the doctrine itself—part of the practice consists in meditating on various pieces of the doctrine—so the reports of what gets observed are themselves to some degree a product of the theory already held, hence somewhat contaminated" (p. 1). This does not mean, as Nozick points out, that such insights are therefore incorrect, merely that they are not entirely dependable.

17. There is certainly disagreement about the role of lies and their justification. For an excellent treatment, see Simon (1999), arguing for a contextual approach to lying instead of a categorical one. For a useful discussion of manipulation and deception, see Scanlon (1998). Scanlon's contractualism is but one example of an approach that might lead to such commitments through rational analysis even without mindful insight or perspective taking. He argues that contractualism "gives us a direct reason to be concerned with other people's points of view: not because we might, for all we know, actually be them, or because we might occupy their position in some other possible world, but in order to find principles that they, as well as we, have reason to accept" (p. 191). The most well-known modern discussion of deception is Bok (1978), who argues that lies may be justified only as a last resort. For the most often discussed categorical bar on lying, see Kant (1991).

18. See generally Nozick (1981), who discusses whether cooperating, in the context of a prisoner's dilemma game, could qualify as a fundamental moral principle.

19. See Goodpaster (1996) (reviewing hard bargaining tactics); Gifford (1985) (same); and Peters (1987), discussing various tactics and ultimately condemning all forms of deception in bargaining.

20. One might even take the position that exaggerated arguments about the state of the law—arguments too abstracted from existing law to be justified—constitute lies. See Nagel (1999), discussing "the intriguing but distressing question of whether an individual who claims to be speaking like a lawyer ought to be understood to be lying" (p. 605).

21. See Strudler (1998), relying on Benjamin Constant's arguments that certain lies—particularly lies about reservation values—are morally permissible because telling the truth is required only when the recipient has a right to the truth, which a counterpart in negotiation may not. He concludes that "lies that sophisticated lawyers tell each other about their reservation prices in certain circumstances may not be wrong in any relevant way" (p. 1567).

22. See, for example, Raiffa (1982) ("Such posturing is part of the game"), and Hazard (1981).

23. White (1980) argues ultimately that certain forms of deception in negotiation are immoral, even if not illegal.

24. Steele (1986) goes on to say, "But if the results achieved by their methods are somehow better or fairer than the result achieved by lawyers, then perhaps the legal definition of negotiation should be changed" (p. 1391). I will return to this question about the lawyer's role below.

25. See Cohen (2001), who writes, "The act of negotiation does not relieve one of the moral duty to respect others"; Loder (1994); and Applbaum (1999), arguing against the notion that negotiation requires or legitimizes deception. Some have also argued that lawyers should
be fair in their negotiations, although this is a less common position. See Rubin (1975) and Schwartz (1978), who writes, "When acting in a nonadvocate capacity . . . a lawyer must . . . [refrain from] unfair, unconscionable, or unjust, though not unlawful, means . . . [or pursuing] unfair, unconscionable, or unjust, though not unlawful, ends" (p. 679).

26. The saints would still face, for example, the problem that there are sometimes trade-offs between "fair" division and efficiencies or value creation. See, for example, Brams and Taylor (1996, 1999) and Raiffa (1996).

27. See note 16 and the accompanying text.

28. See generally, for example, Rhode (2000), discussing the basic premises of partisanship and arguing that the most common justifications for the advocate's role "unravel at several key points"; Simon (1998a, 1998b); and Luban (1984, 1988).

References

Adler, R. S., and Silverstein, E. M. "When David Meets Goliath: Dealing with Power Differentials in Negotiations." *Harvard Negotiation Law Review*, 2000, *5*, 1–104.

Applbaum, A. I. *Ethics for Adversaries: The Morality of Roles in Public and Professional Life.* Princeton, N.J.: Princeton University Press, 1999.

Batchelor, S. *Buddhism Without Beliefs.* New York: Riverhead Books, 1997.

Bok, S. *Lying: Moral Choice in Public and Private Life.* New York: Pantheon Books, 1978.

Brams, S. J., and Taylor, A. D. *Fair Division: From Cake-Cutting to Dispute Resolution.* Cambridge; New York: Cambridge University Press, 1996.

Brams, S. J., and Taylor, A. D. *The Win-Win Solution: Guaranteeing Fair Shares to Everybody.* New York: Norton, 1999.

Cohen, J. R. "When People Are the Means: Negotiating with Respect." *Georgia Journal of Legal Ethics*, 2001, *14*, 739–802.

Condlin, R. J. "Bargaining in the Dark: The Normative Incoherence of Lawyer Dispute Bargaining Role." *Maryland Law Review*, 1992, *51*, 1–104.

Fisher, R., Ury, W., and Patton, B. *Getting to Yes: Negotiating Agreement Without Giving In* (2nd ed.). New York: Penguin Books, 1991.

Gifford, D. G. "A Context-Based Theory of Strategy Selection in Legal Negotiation." *Ohio State Law Journal*, 1985, *46*, 41–94.

Goodpaster, G. "A Primer on Competitive Bargaining." *Journal of Dispute Resolution,* 1996, *1996,* 325–377.

Green, S. P. "Lying, Misleading, and Falsely Denying: How Moral Concepts Inform the Law of Perjury, Fraud, and False Statements." *Hastings Law Journal,* 2001, *53,* 157–212.

Hare, R. M. *Freedom and Reason.* Oxford: Clarendon Press, 1963.

Hare, R. M. *Moral Thinking.* Oxford: Clarendon Press, 1981.

Hare, R. M. "Arguing About Rights." *Emory Law Journal,* 1984, *33,* 631–647.

Hazard, G. C., Jr. "The Lawyer's Obligation to Be Trustworthy When Dealing with Opposing Parties." *South Carolina Law Review,* 1981, *33,* 181–196.

Heumann, M., and Hyman, J. M. "Negotiation Methods and Litigation Settlement Methods in New Jersey: 'You Can't Always Get What You Want.'" *Ohio State Journal on Dispute Resolution,* 1997, *12,* 253–310.

Kant, I. *The Metaphysics of Morals* (M. Gregor, trans.). Cambridge: Cambridge University Press, 1991. (Originally published 1797.)

Keeva, S. *Transforming Practices: Finding Joy and Satisfaction in the Legal Life.* Chicago: Contemporary Books, 1999.

Kronman, A. T. *The Lost Lawyer.* London: Methuen, 1993.

Lax, D. A., and Sebenius, J. K. *The Manager as Negotiator.* New York: Free Press, and London: Collier Macmillan, 1986.

Lerman, L. G. "Lying to Clients." *University of Pennsylvania Law Review,* 1990, *138,* 659–760.

Loder, R. E. "Moral Truthseeking and the Virtuous Negotiator." *Georgetown Journal of Legal Ethics,* 1994, *8,* 45–102.

Luban, D. *The Good Lawyer: Lawyers' Roles and Lawyers' Ethics.* Totowa, N.J.: Rowman & Allanheld, 1984.

Luban, D. *Lawyers and Justice: An Ethical Study.* Princeton, N.J.: Princeton University Press, 1988.

Menkel-Meadow, C. "Lying to Clients for Economic Gain or Paternalistic Judgment: A Proposal for a Golden Rule of Candor." *University of Pennsylvania Law Review,* 1990, *138,* 761–783.

Mnookin, R. H., Peppet, S. R., and Tulumello, A. S. *Beyond Winning: Negotiating to Create Value in Deals and Disputes.* Cambridge, Mass.: Belknap Press of Harvard University Press, 2001.

Nagel, R. F. "Lies and Law." *Harvard Journal of Law* and *Public Policy,* 1999, *22,* 605–617.

Nagel, T. *Mortal Questions.* New York: Cambridge University Press, 1979.

Nagel, T. *The View from Nowhere.* New York: Oxford University Press, 1986.

Nozick, R. *Philosophical Explanations.* Oxford: Clarendon Press, 1981.

Nozick, R. *The Examined Life.* New York: Simon & Schuster, 1989.

Peters, G. M. "The Use of Lies in Negotiation." *Ohio State Law Journal,* 1987, *48,* 1–50.

Raiffa, H. *The Art and Science of Negotiation.* Cambridge, Mass.: Belknap Press of Harvard University Press, 1982.

Raiffa, H. *Lectures on Negotiation Analysis.* Cambridge Mass.: PON Books, 1996.

Rawls, J. *A Theory of Justice.* Cambridge, Mass.: Belknap Press of Harvard University Press, 1971.

Rhode, D. L. *In the Interests of Justice: Reforming the Legal Profession.* Oxford; New York: Oxford University Press, 2000.

Riskin, L. L. "The Contemplative Lawyer: On the Potential Contributions of Mindfulness Meditation to Law Students, Lawyers and Their Clients." *Harvard Negotiation Law Review,* 2002, *7,* 1–66.

Rubin, A. B. "A Causerie on Lawyers' Ethics in Negotiation." *Louisiana Law Review,* 1975, *35,* 577–593.

Scanlon, T. M. *What We Owe to Each Other.* Cambridge, Mass.: Belknap Press of Harvard University Press, 1998.

Schelling, T. C. "An Essay on Bargaining." In T. C. Schelling, *The Strategy of Conflict.* Cambridge, Mass.: Harvard University Press, 1960.

Schwartz, M. L. "The Professionalism and Accountability of Lawyers." *California Law Review,* 1978, *66,* 669–697.

Sells, B. *The Soul of the Law.* Rockport, Mass.: Element, 1994.

Sidgwick, H. *The Methods of Ethics* (7th ed.). 1992.

Simon, W. H. *The Practice of Justice: A Theory of Lawyers' Ethics.* Cambridge, Mass.: Harvard University Press, 1998a.

Simon, W. H. "'Thinking Like a Lawyer' About Ethical Questions." *Hofstra Law Review,* 1998b, *27,* xxx1–11.

Simon, W. H. "Virtuous Lying: A Critique of Quasi-Categorical Moralism." *Georgetown Journal of Legal Ethics,* 1999, *12,* 433–463.

Singer, P. *Animal Liberation.* New York: Avon Books, 1975.

Singer, P. *Practical Ethics.* Cambridge; New York: Cambridge University Press, 1993.

Steele, W. W. "Deceptive Negotiating and High-Toned Morality." *Vanderbilt Law Review,* 1986, *39,* 1387–1404.

Strudler, A. "Incommensurable Goods, Rightful Lies, and the Wrongness of Fraud." *University of Pennsylvania Law Review,* 1998, *146,* 1529–1567.

White, J. J. "Machiavelli and the Bar: Ethical Limitations on Lying in Negotiation." *American Bar Foundation Research Journal,* 1980, *1980,* 926–938.

Vendler, Z. "Changing Places?" In D. Seanor and N. Fotion (eds.), *Hare and Critics.* Oxford (Oxfordshire): Clarendon Press; and New York: Oxford University Press, 1988.

CHAPTER TWENTY-EIGHT

Protecting the Confidentiality of Settlement Negotiations

Wayne D. Brazil

DISCOVERABILITY VERSUS ADMISSIBILITY: IS THERE A "PRIVILEGE" FOR SETTLEMENT COMMUNICATIONS?

Attorneys must be careful to distinguish pretrial discoverability from admissibility at trial. Litigators cannot safely assume that statements made during settlement negotiations that would not be admitted at trial (by virtue of Rule 408, or Rule 403, or simply because they would be irrelevant) are also immune from discovery. Courts attempting to resolve the discoverability question must face issues and conduct analyses that are quite different from the issues and analyses relevant when ruling on the question of admissibility. Unfortunately for counsel, who would like to be able to predict the likelihood that settlement communications will remain confidential, the published opinions on discoverability of settlement negotiations do not reflect a consensus about basic issues in this area. As the paragraphs that follow make clear, some courts are sympathetic with the need to preserve confidentiality even as against discovery, while many others have ruled that settlement communications are discoverable despite the policies that inform Rule 408.

Whether or not communications made during settlement negotiations are discoverable may depend, in part, on whether courts will recognize a "privilege" for settlement communications under Rule 408 or federal common law. This question is important because the scope of discovery is defined as "any matter, not privileged, which is relevant to the subject matter involved in the pending action." It follows that if communications made in connection with settlement are privileged, they will fall outside the scope of discovery, even if they are relevant. While no appellate court in the federal system has addressed this question directly, several district court opinions express or imply views on this matter. The majority view seems to be that settlement communications are not "privileged" within the meaning of the rules that define the scope of discovery. The same question arises under analogous state statutes. As discussed below, the only appellate court in California that has addressed this question also has concluded that there is no generalizable "privilege" that shields settlement communications from discovery.

Support for the Existence of a Settlement Privilege

The case law support for the view that Rule 408, or its common-law antecedent, creates a privilege is relatively thin and appears to represent the minority view. At least one important opinion from a federal court of appeal prior to 1975, when the Rules of Evidence became effective, uses the word *"privileged"* when referring to settlement communications. This reference, however, appears almost casual, not the product of self-conscious analysis about the significance of the word *"privilege."*

More recently, Judge MacMahon of the United States District Court for the Southern District of New York appeared to endorse the notion that Federal Rule of Evidence 408 creates a "settlement privilege." This privilege would block discovery of communications related to settlement unless the party seeking the discovery can show clearly that Rule 408 would not bar admission of the communications at a subsequent trial. Unfortunately, the only reasoning the court offers in support of this conclusion is a cryptic suggestion that denying discovery of the product of earlier settlement negotiations is necessary "in order to safeguard the policy favoring settlements."

Two of the other opinions that support the argument that Rule 408 creates or reflects a privilege offer a little more by way of explanation but focus on the trial stage rather than on the discovery stage. *Kennon* v. *Slipstreamer, Inc.* presented the issue of whether or not a trial judge had committed reversible error when, in explaining to the jury why certain defendants were no longer present, he disclosed not only the fact that they had settled with the plaintiff but also the nominal amount for which they were released. In support of his dissenting view that the trial court had not committed reversible error, Circuit Judge Thornberry emphasized that Rule 408 "is rooted in the policy of promoting settlement by privileging settlements and settlement negotiations." When Judge Thornberry insisted that the rule "is based on the privilege rationale," however, his purpose was not to argue against the discoverability of such material, but to support his minority view that a party could effectively waive the operation of Rule 408 at time of trial by agreeing to the introduction of its own settlement offer or demand. Thus his dissenting opinion lends only oblique support to arguments that Rule 408 has created a generalized privilege for settlement negotiations that protects them from pretrial discovery.

Counsel will find a little more support for such an argument in the rationale that supports Senior District Judge Marovitz's conclusion in *Dunlop* v. *Board of Governors*. This case presented the issue of whether the court should strike an affidavit submitted in support of a motion for summary judgment because the affidavit contained accounts of positions the parties had taken in settlement negotiations. In explaining its decision to strike the affidavit, the court pointed out that the purpose of the rule is "to encourage settlement and compromise negotiations." The court then proceeded to argue that "it is only through such orderly and 'privileged' discourse regarding claims that this policy is most effectively served, and only when the privileges thereby received are strictly enforced will opposing counsel feel free to candidly and fully set forth their proposed compromises."

While these opinions in *Kennon* and *Dunlop* addressed issues raised at the trial stage, the rationale that supports them surely is not irrelevant to the question we face here, which is whether federal law, through Rule 408 or otherwise, creates a "privilege" that can offer settlement communications some protection from discovery. The root of the rationale in each opinion is identical: if the law wants to encourage settlement by encouraging frank negotiations, it is important to create an environment in which counsel and parties can be fairly confident that what they say as they negotiate, and the terms of any agreements they might reach, will not be used against them later. Arguably, the law will fail to create such an environment if settlement communications are discoverable simply on a showing that "the information sought appears reasonably calculated to lead to the discovery of admissible evidence."

A strong argument in favor of viewing Rule 408 as creating a privilege can be built from the principal purpose of this rule. Because its principal purpose is to encourage settlement by encouraging "freedom of communication w ith respect to compromise, even among lawyers," Rule 408 has something very important in common with traditionally recognized privileges. The principal reason the law cloaks communications between attorney and client with confidentiality, for example, is to encourage clients to "tell all" to their lawyers. The traditional privileges, in short, have been designed to open up lines of communication in certain settings in which full communication will serve important societal interests. The fact that Rule 408 is designed to serve a closely analogous function is a major argument in favor of viewing it as creating a privilege.

Support for the View That No Settlement Privilege Exists

The traditional privileges attach to communications between persons who have ongoing, supportive, interdependent, nonadversarial relationships (e.g., between priest and penitent, husband and wife, doctor and patient, lawyer and client). One purpose of the traditionally recognized privileges is to strengthen these relationships, relationships that society has an interest in fostering. Parties to settlement negotiations, in sharp contrast, are by definition adversaries. While in a small percentage of cases they may end up with ongoing relationships, society usually has no independent interest in nurturing close ties between adverse litigants, at least none that parallels the kind of societal interest that inspires the traditional privileges. Because no special relationship that society is committed to fostering is involved in most settlement negotiations, it can be argued that a key rationale supporting traditional privileges is inapplicable to the kinds of communications covered by Rule 408.

Additional arguments can be marshaled against the view that Rule 408 creates a privilege. One such argument is that the rule purports to apply only at the trial stage and offers no express protection against pretrial discovery of settlement communications. Another argument is that by its own terms, Rule 408 erects no barrier to admission at trial of settlement communications when the evidence is offered for any purpose other than "to prove liability for or invalidity of the claim or its amount." Thus the protection Rule 408 offers is much more limited than the protection offered by a privilege like the attorney-client privilege. The attorney-client privilege attaches automatically to certain kinds of communications and can be penetrated only on an extraordinary showing. Rule 408, however, does not come into play at all unless a party wants to introduce the settlement communication at trial for the only purpose that is forbidden by the rule. The rule alone is not a bar if the party who wants to introduce the evidence can proffer any one of the scores of other purposes that might make the evidence relevant. Since Rule 408 promises so much less, it cannot serve as the source of an expectation of privacy that is nearly as strong as the expectation created by the attorney-client privilege.

Another reason that might be cited by courts in declining to hold that Rule 408 creates a privilege lies in the fact that the legislative history of Rule 501 strongly suggests that Congress did not want the Federal Rules of Evidence to serve as a source of "privilege" law. As originally submitted by the Supreme Court to Congress, article V of the proposed Federal Rules of Evidence contained thirteen rules, nine of which defined specific nonconstitutional privileges that the federal courts would have been required to recognize. Another of these proposed thirteen rules announced that federal courts could recognize only those privileges identified in the proposed rules or in some other act of

Congress. Significantly, the prohibition against admission of settlement negotiations to prove liability was not in this package of privileges. It was set forth not in the article dealing with privileges, but in the article entitled "Relevancy and Its Limits," in which it is presently located. Thus, it would appear that the Advisory Committee and the Supreme Court did not consider the protection offered by Rule 408 a privilege. Moreover, Congress rejected the privilege rules as proposed by the Advisory Committee and the Court and substituted in their place what is now Rule 501, which essentially provides that privileges in federal question cases "shall be governed by the [evolving] principles of the common law." Thus, Congress in effect decided that the Federal Rules of Evidence should not be used to establish or to change the scope of privileges. Since Congress rejected the use of the Federal Rules for this purpose, it would seem difficult to argue that Rule 408 creates a privilege.

While they have not directly endorsed all the arguments described above, several federal courts have concluded that there is no generalized privilege that protects settlement communications from discovery. Before discussing opinions whose reasoning would appear to apply to cases of all kinds, it is important to discuss a Seventh Circuit opinion that deals with the special problems associated with settlement of class actions. In *In re General Motors Corp.*, the trial court had approved settlement as to a subclass of plaintiffs after refusing to permit lawyers for disgruntled class members to conduct discovery into how the negotiations were handled by other lawyers who purported to represent the interests of all members. The appellate court concluded that this refusal constituted an abuse of discretion and reversible error. The court pointed out that, before approving proposed class action settlements, district courts have a special responsibility to make meaningful inquiry into their fairness. If lawyers for class members who did not have an opportunity to participate in the negotiations challenge this fairness, meaningful review requires affording them an opportunity to discover "'the options considered and rejected, the topics discussed, the defendant's reaction to various proposals, and the amount of compromise necessary to obtain a settlement.'"

The court of appeals noted that there was "no convincing basis" for an argument that the conduct of these class action settlement negotiations "is protected from examination by some form of privilege." The court insisted that its ruling was consistent with the letter and spirit of Rule 408. It was consistent with the letter of that rule because, on its face, Rule 408 "only governs admissibility." It was consistent with the spirit of the rule, which seeks to promote settlement, because:

> participants in negotiations to settle class actions are aware that Rule 23(e) requires the trial court's approval of any settlement reached. Moreover, they are or should be aware that the court will inquire into the conduct of the negotiations. . . . To the

extent that such inquiry discourages settlements, it should only discourage those negotiated in circumstances so irregular as to cast substantial doubt on their fairness.

In other words, the Seventh Circuit panel concluded that participants in class action settlement negotiations had no reasonable expectation of privacy, at least as against other members of the class. Where there is no reasonable expectation of privacy, no privilege should attach.

Because no published opinion takes exception to the holding or reasoning of *In re General Motors Corp.*, counsel who participate in class action settlement negotiations should appreciate the substantial likelihood that their words and deeds in that context are both discoverable and admissible in a proceeding to assess the fairness of the proposed agreement or the adequacy of the representation of the class. Similar risks may attend any negotiations in which the court must approve the terms of a purported settlement.

In *Federal Trade Commission* v. *Standard Financial Management Corp,* a First Circuit panel held that the common-law right of access reaches financial statements submitted in confidence as part of a negotiated consent decree and that the parties resisting disclosure of these documents had failed to make the compelling showing that would be required to overcome this common-law right. The *Standard Financial* court accepted the premise that a common-law right of access attaches to all documents considered by a court "in the course of adjudicatory proceedings." The court then held that a judge's consideration of a proposed consent decree constitutes an "adjudicatory proceeding." According to the court, even when the proposed decree already has been hammered out through private settlement negotiations between a governmental agency and private parties, the trial court retains a responsibility to "make its own inquiry into the issue of reasonableness" before it can put its imprimatur on the decree as proposed. In the case at hand, the district court had relied on the confidential financial statements "in assessing the reasonableness of the order, i.e., in determining the litigants' substantive rights, and in performing its adjudicatory function. The common-law presumption of public access therefore attached to them." The court went on to hold that a party who attempts to overcome the common-law right of access must make a compelling showing and that the courts should prohibit public disclosure (in this case to a newspaper) only when the interests that would be served by sealing the documents clearly outweigh the policy and tradition that support the public right of access. In the case at hand, the First Circuit upheld the trial court's decision to unseal the financial documents even though they had been submitted to the governmental agency as part of settlement negotiations on the assumption that they would remain confidential. En route to its holding the court noted that the "appropriateness of making court files accessible is accentuated in cases where the government is a party: in such circumstances, the public's right to know what the executive branch is about coalesces with the concomitant right of the citizenry to appraise the judicial branch."

Two of the most important cases outside the class action environment that hold that settlement communications are not privileged from discovery involved the Freedom of Information Act (FOIA). Because the opinions in these cases obviously were influenced by the policies favoring disclosure that inform the FOIA, it may not be safe to assume that these courts would adopt the same posture in cases in which the target of the discovery is not the federal government and the FOIA is irrelevant. Neither court, however, limited its holding that Rule 408 does not create a generalized discovery privilege. Thus, on their face, these opinions apply across the board.

District Judge Hogan wrote the first of these two opinions in *Center for Auto Safety* v. *Department of Justice.* Because it has been cited with approval in subsequent opinions from other courts, the pertinent passage from this opinion warrants full reproduction here:

> Moreover, the argument that a "settlement negotiation" privilege is authorized under F.R.E. 408 is also misplaced. The cited rule limits a document's relevance at trial, not its disclosure for other purposes [citing 2 Weinstein's Evidence Par. 408 (1)]. The protection afforded by Rule 408 is far less broad than the DOJ [Department of Justice] asserts. While its intent is to foster settlement negotiations, the sole means chosen to effectuate that end is a limitation on their [sic] admission of evidence produced during settlement negotiations for the purpose of proving liability at trial, not the application of a broad discovery privilege. Otherwise parties would be unable to discover compromise offers which could be offered for a relevant purpose, i.e., proving bias or prejudice of a witness, opposing a claim of undue delay, proving an effort to obstruct a criminal investigation or prosecution, or enforcing a settlement agreement.

This interpretation of Rule 408 is arguably inconsistent with the Advisory Committee's note, which indicates that excluding evidence of settlement negotiations as irrelevant is not as "consistently impressive" as the rationale that focuses on the importance of promoting settlement by encouraging "freedom of communication with respect to compromise." The *Center for Auto Safety* passage in effect reverses the position taken by the Advisory Committee by slighting, or discrediting altogether, the privilege rationale for Rule 408 and restoring the pre–Rule 408 predominance of considerations of relevance. Moreover, the paragraph cited from Judge Weinstein's treatise lends no real support to this reversal because that paragraph only makes the obvious point—a point made in the text of Rule 408 as well—that a party cannot hide relevant facts simply by presenting them in a settlement discussion before they are requested in discovery, a principle that applies to all privileges.

While *Center for Auto Safety* is not faithful to the reordering of rationales for Rule 408 that is suggested by the Advisory Committee, the opinion is consistent with the structure of the rule itself. In fact, the reasoning in *Center for Auto Safety* exposes the central difficulty that arises from the kind of compromise between competing concerns that Rule 408 embodies. The compromise in the rule consists of the decision to make settlement communications inadmissible only for limited purposes—to prove liability for, the invalidity of, or the amount of damages from a claim—clearly leaving open the possibility that courts could admit this same kind of evidence for any of a large number of other purposes.

By leaving open the possibility that settlement communications could be admitted for any one of an almost limitless number of other purposes, the drafters of the rule in essence eviscerated the privilege rationale that they purported to find so "consistently impressive" and that they intended to make the principal underpinning of the newly formulated rule. The protection of Rule 408 virtually evaporates; there are so many conceivable purposes for which settlement communications might be admissible, and counsel easily can argue that they cannot determine whether there is some permissible purpose for which the communications might be admissible at trial unless they can discover their contents. The *Center for Auto Safety* opinion shows that the drafters constructed a rule that is unfaithful to its own rationale. To truly serve the privilege rationale, a rule would have to offer at least presumptive protection from both discovery and admissibility in most circumstances (perhaps analogous to the protection offered by the work product doctrine as it applies to material that does not reflect a lawyer's mental impressions or legal theories). By adopting the much more limited approach reflected in Rule 408, the drafters made results such as those reached in *Center for Auto Safety* virtually inevitable.

Several other reported opinions support the notion that there is no generalized "privilege" for settlement communications. In *NAACP Legal Defense and Educational Fund, Inc.* v. *Department of Justice,* for example, the court paraphrases part of the key passage from *Center for Auto Safety* to justify the conclusion that Rule 408 "was never intended to be a broad discovery privilege." Examples of opinions that reach the same conclusion on the privilege issue but do not rely on *Center for Auto Safety* include *Triax Co.* v. *United States* and *Manufacturing Systems, Inc.* v. *Computer Technology, Inc.* In an opinion issued just before Rule 408 became effective, Judge Charles Richey concluded that while settlement communications "are clearly not admissible at trial for a number of public policy reasons, such negotiations do not fall within the confines of the privileges recognized as common law."

Judge Selya's recent opinion in *Bennett* v. *La Pere* reflects the most aggressive assault on the notion that settlement communications should be at least presumptively privileged from discovery. The court addressed "whether a nonsettling defendant in a civil action may compel disclosure of an accord reached between the plaintiffs and (former) codefendants." The court first faced the question whether or not the remaining defendant could show that the settlement documents met the "liberal view of the standards of relevance applicable in discovery proceedings." The judge answered this question in the affirmative. Significantly, he pointed out that Rule 408 bars admission of such material only for limited, specified purposes, leaving open the possibility of admissibility for other purposes, and that there is "no satisfactory way for the [remaining defendant] to determine whether it can slip within the integument of the Rule 408 exception unless it gains discovery access to the settlement documents." The court confirmed the implication of this observation, noting that "in our adversary system" the only fair way to reach a conclusion about whether there might be a permissible use of the settlement documents at trial is to compel their disclosure in discovery.

Having thus concluded that it would be virtually impossible to block discovery of such material on grounds of irrelevance, the *Bennett* court asked whether there were any other considerations that "might militate against disclosure." In particular, it discussed whether some policy consideration reflected in Rule 408 should either bar discovery of the settlement materials or, short of creating an absolute bar, lead courts to require parties who seek discovery of such material to make some showing of justification or need beyond satisfying the liberal relevance standard of Rule 26(b). Rejecting the reasoning and conclusion in *Bottaro* v. *Hatton Associates,* the court held that nothing in Rule 408's language or purposes justifies a conclusion that it creates any special obstacles to discovery. In finding that the settlement documents in question were "not privileged" and were discoverable, the court relied not only on the fact that Rule 408 applies only to admissibility at trial, but also on his argument that compelling disclosure of the terms of a completed settlement could not adversely affect the policy goal of encouraging settlements. In making the latter argument the court asserted that the only fear that might inhibit settlement, and that Rule 408 attempts to assuage, is the fear that a pretrial settlement proposal would be used against the party who made it during a subsequent trial in the same case.

The one fear that the court in *Bennett* was willing to acknowledge is not the only fear that Rule 408 is designed to assuage, as the courts in *Bottaro* v. *Hatton Associates,* and *Weissman* v. *Fruchtman* recognize. The *Bennett* opinion misconstrues Rule 408 in part because it accepts an unrealistically narrow view of the several different ways that fear of disclosure could impair the settlement dynamic. If the only fear the drafters of Rule 408 wanted to combat was fear that the terms of a settlement proposal would be used against the party who made the proposal, they would have written the rule much more narrowly than they did. If combating this fear had been their only objective, the drafters certainly would not have extended the protections of the rule to evidence "of conduct or statements made in compromise negotiations." The Advisory Committee's note leaves no room to question the reason the drafters expanded the common-law doctrine through the rule to cover "admissions of fact" and other statements made during settlement discussions: the drafters believed that the "inevitable effect" of the narrower common-law approach had been "to inhibit freedom of communication with respect to compromise, even among lawyers." The rule was designed to encourage communication about a broad range of settlement-related matters, not just about offers or demands.

Common sense supports the drafters' broader vision. The *Bennett* court's approach would enable counsel to exchange only offers and demands and would reduce "negotiations" to irrational volleys of numbers. It is hard to understand how a law that encourages only the exchange of numbers, with no regard for the reasoning or the evidence that supports those numbers, could contribute much to fostering settlement. It takes no genius to see that a rule that offers some protection to lawyers who share the reasoning underlying their positions will contribute much more to the prospects for settlement than a rule that permits only mechanical and sterile exchanges of bottom lines. Moreover, adopting rules whose effect is to reduce the negotiation process to mere number swapping degrades our system in fact and in the eyes of litigants who are forced to use it.

The *Bennett* court also mistakenly assumed that the purposes of Rule 408 are fully satisfied once a settlement agreement has been reached by some or all of the parties to a particular action. What people say in negotiations to settle one lawsuit may well be relevant to other litigation in which they are involved or in which they fear they might become involved. I have hosted many settlement conferences during which parties have expressed concerns about related cases or parallel situations involving nonparties, or in which one party has been unwilling to settle unless it is assured that the terms will not be disclosed to others who might be encouraged to file new claims or hold out for more money in cases already docketed. It is naive not to recognize that lawyers and litigants are constantly concerned about how their statements or actions in one setting might come back to haunt them in other settings. If courts construe rules so as to increase the circumstances in which communications made during negotiations can be discovered or admitted into evidence, they create inhibiting forces that reinforce the instinct parties and lawyers already have to play their cards as close to their chests as possible.

A Test for Discoverability That Appropriately Reflects the Policy Objectives

For the reasons just described, I disagree strongly with the *Bennett* court's suggestion that it is appropriate to decide whether negotiation material is discoverable simply by using the same kind of analysis that courts would use for any other nonprivileged matter. Although it may be fair to say that Rule 408 does not create a privilege, the rule clearly reflects a significant federal policy in favor of promoting settlements by encouraging freedom of communication that is not implicated by most discovery requests. This policy would be seriously jeopardized if courts routinely permitted discovery of communications made in settlement discussions. Counsel seeking to protect settlement materials from discovery should argue vigorously that courts should order disclosure only after conducting a balancing analysis in which the federal policy of promoting settlement is given the full weight it deserves.

Case law supports this balancing approach. For example, in *Bottaro* v. *Hatton Associates,* the opinion Judge Selya attached in *Bennett,* the court declared, "Given the strong public policy of favoring settlements and the congressional intent to further that policy by insulating the bargaining table from unnecessary intrusions, we . . . require some particularized showing of a likelihood that admissible evidence will be generated by the dissemination of the terms of a settlement agreement."

In *Weissman* v. *Fruchtman,* the court quoted this passage from *Bottaro* with approval. The court relied on it to justify blocking a party's access to settlement materials when he could not make a clear showing that these materials would be admissible at trial or lead to discovery of admissible evidence. In effect, the *Bottaro* and *Weissman* courts reversed the presumption that the *Bennett* court indulged in favor of discovery. The *Bennett* court held that a party must have discovery access to settlement materials in order to determine whether they might be admissible on some theory that would not be barred by Rule 408. The *Bottaro* and *Weissman* courts, in contrast, insisted that because free discovery access to such materials would threaten the policy objectives of Rule 408, courts should protect these materials unless a party can make a persuasive showing that such materials are likely to be admissible or to lead to significant other evidence.

Groton v. *Connecticut Light & Power* further supports the approach endorsed by *Bottaro* and *Weissman.* In *Groton,* the court used a balancing test to determine whether to permit discovery that might interfere with ongoing settlement negotiations. The court made clear that it would prohibit discovery of this kind where the potential prejudice to the settling parties outweighed the need for disclosure.

Even without *Bottaro, Weissman,* and *Groton,* lawyers would be on solid ground in asking a court to conduct a balancing analysis before permitting discovery of confidential settlement communications. Federal courts conduct exactly this type of balancing analysis when a party seeks a protective order under Federal Rule of Civil Procedure 26(c). Rule 26(c) clearly contemplates the courts' making particularized judgments comparing the potential utility of requested information with the harm that might be done if the information were disclosed. Rule 26(c) also expressly empowers courts to enter orders that certain discovery not be conducted at all, or that "certain matters not be inquired into, or that the scope of the discovery be limited to certain matters," or that "trade secrets or other confidential research, development, or commercial information not be disclosed or be disclosed only in a designated way." Rule 26(c) obviously acknowledges that there will be circumstances in which the interests that support preserving the confidentiality of certain material will outweigh the interests that might be served by permitting discovery of this material.

Thus, even if federal courts refuse to hold that Rule 408 creates a "privilege," they should afford settlement material an extra level of protection from routine discovery by conducting a balancing analysis in which the federal policy reflected in Rule 408 is given the full weight it deserves. Courts should acknowledge that the public policies reflected in Rule 408 create a substantial presumption against discovery of settlement material. Moreover, courts should permit rebuttal of this presumption only after a strong showing that the competing interests clearly outweigh the interests and the policies favoring confidentiality and that the competing interests cannot be satisfied in some other, less intrusive manner.

The only authority in this subject area is from a California court and points, albeit somewhat unclearly, in the direction of *Bottaro* and its progeny. In *Covell* v. *Superior Court,* the appellate court considered section 1152 of the California Evidence Code, which served as a model for Federal Rule of Evidence 408 and affords the same kind of protection to settlement negotiations as the federal rule. The court concluded that the section does not create a privilege, relying entirely on one fact: section 1152 is not located in the division of the California Evidence Code that defines "privileges." While this reasoning is not profound, it may be sufficient.

The *Covell* court went on to hold, however, that the settlement material was not discoverable, even though it was not privileged, because the party seeking it had failed to show that it was "reasonably calculated to lead to the discovery of admissible evidence." Most significantly, the spirit in which the court reviewed the relevance arguments seems more demanding than one would normally expect at the discovery stage. The appellate court took the unusual step of finding that the trial court had abused its discretion when it ordered disclosure of the material. The appellate court's willingness to take this unusual step supports an inference that, under California law, judges will impose a more demanding standard for discovery of settlement material than they would for discovery of material that is unprotected by the kinds of public policies reflected in section 1152 of the California Evidence Code.

Settlements with Public Entities: Public Right of Access

Lawyers who represent public entities in settlement negotiations, or private parties who decide to enter a settlement agreement with a public entity, must be aware of the possibility that interested persons could use the Freedom of

Information Act (FOIA), or a state law equivalent like the California Public Records Act, to force disclosure of both the terms of a settlement agreement and other documents related to settlement negotiations. This section focuses primarily on the applicability of the FOIA to materials generated in connection with settlement negotiations conducted by agencies of the federal government. It also includes a discussion of the only major opinion from a California appellate court that addresses the applicability of California's Public Records Act to an effort by a third party to compel disclosure of the terms of a settlement entered by a local government with a tort claimant.

FOIA contains no exemption that explicitly mentions materials generated in connection with settlement negotiations. Because of this, and the general admonition that courts are to construe FOIA's exemptions narrowly and to resolve doubts in favor of disclosure, there are circumstances in which citizens can use FOIA to force governmental agencies to disclose documents generated in connection with settlements. The reported decisions suggest that documents related to settlement negotiations will be deemed exempt from FOIA if they have not been disclosed to or received from an adversary. These decisions also suggest, however, that documents disclosed to or received from an adversary during confidential settlement negotiations are vulnerable to an FOIA request, regardless of the nature of the interest that inspires the request.

Among the nine exemptions from FOIA, the one that seemed most promising to lawyers trying to preserve the confidentiality of settlement documents was number five, which covers "inter-agency or intra-agency memoranda or letters which would not be available by law to a party other than an agency in litigation with the agency." This exemption protects government-generated documents whose confidentiality the government has maintained and which satisfy the criteria for any clearly established privilege. For example, this exemption would prevent use of FOIA to compel disclosure of a document the government generated in connection with settlement negotiations if the document satisfied the criteria for the attorney-client privilege or the work product doctrine. Similarly, the fifth exemption applies to documents that would be protected from disclosure in civil litigation by the "deliberative process" privilege.

On several occasions government lawyers have tried unsuccessfully to persuade courts that there is a separate "settlement privilege" in civil litigation and that materials that would qualify for it also should fall within the protections of the fifth exemption. The seminal case is *County of Madison, New York v. United States Department of Justice.* In that opinion, Chief Judge Coffin, writing for a unanimous panel, ordered the government to disclose documents generated in connection with settlement negotiations in an earlier, related matter. The documents in question had either been sent by the party opponent to the government or by lawyers for the government to opposing counsel during the course of the negotiations. The appellate court refused to categorize these documents as "intra-agency" memoranda or letters.

The court also rejected an argument that FOIA empowers federal courts, under the guise of exercising equitable discretion, to decide whether considerations of "public policy" justify adding exemptions to FOIA for categories of documents not specifically exempted by Congress on the face of the statute. The court acknowledged the importance of the government's ability to resolve disputes by settlement and conceded that the government's ability to reach consensual agreements with adversaries in litigation would be impaired if parties knew that under FOIA, "written settlement communications will be available to anyone, irrespective of the merit of his or her need to know." The *County of Madison* panel felt constrained, nonetheless, to honor the letter and spirit of FOIA, which they emphasized "is not a withholding statute but a disclosure statute." The court ruled that the public policy favoring settlement simply cannot justify distorting FOIA's language and giving courts discretionary power to limit the statute's disclosure mandate by carving out an exemption that is not even intimated in that language. The effect of *County of Madison* is clear: exemption five will not protect documents related to settlement that were generated by or shared with a party opponent, even if both the government and its opponent intended all such documents to remain confidential.

Center for Auto Safety v. *Department of Justice* followed and in some measure extended the reasoning of *County of Madison.* The former case arose when the Center for Auto Safety attempted to use FOIA to force the Justice Department (DOJ) to disclose documents it had shared with or received from the "big four" American auto manufacturers during the course of negotiations to modify a consent decree entered in an antitrust action. In the end, the court rejected the Justice Department's arguments that these documents were exempt from disclosure under either exemption five or exemption seven of FOIA.

First, the court ruled that memoranda or letters exchanged by the government and the consent decree defendants could not be considered "intra-agency" documents within the meaning of exemption five. The court rejected the argument that entry of the original consent decree somehow converted the auto makers into the equivalent of independent contractors working with the government to ensure that the public interest was satisfied. Instead, the court insisted that the auto makers remained adverse parties and thus that communications between them and the DOJ could not be considered "intra-agency." This ruling applied even to drafts of consent decrees prepared by DOJ lawyers and accompanying memoranda, both of which included comments and notations that reflected, among other things, "the mental impressions and views of various agency personnel." Drawing on *Coastal States Gas Corp.* v. *Department of Energy,* Judge Hogan held that documents that might otherwise be protected can be swept within the scope of FOIA once they are shown to adversaries because in so doing the governmental agency can be deemed either to adopt the documents as its position on an issue or to use them "in its dealings with the public." The court articulated its holding clearly: "while these documents may at one time have been used for internal advisory purposes and would therefore be protected, when the DOJ elected to use them as tools in their negotiations with the public [the defendants] they lost their internal status, and their qualification for Exemption 5."

In a significant part of the opinion, the court held that even if the documents in question somehow could be deemed "intra-agency" they would not satisfy the second requirement of exemption five—that they would be protected by some privilege that would have protected them against an adverse party if the agency had been involved in litigation. Noting that there is a "presumption against recognizing new discovery privileges under Exemption 5," Judge Hogan concluded that "there is no clear congressional intent to include a settlement negotiation privilege within Exemption 5" and that Federal Rule of Evidence 408 neither acknowledged nor created any such privilege. According to the court, since there is no clearly established "settlement negotiation privilege," the mere use of documents in settlement negotiations does not mean that they "would not be available by law to a party . . . in litigation with the agency," as required by the second clause of exemption five.

In combination, *County of Madison* and *Center for Auto Safety* stand for this proposition: exemption five will not protect documents related to settlement unless they have *not* been shared with or received from an adverse party *and* they meet all the requirements of a clearly established discovery privilege. The *County of Madison* court did make a suggestion, however, to which government counsel should attend. Relying on *Federal Open Market Committee* v. *Merrill,* the court implied that FOIA could not be used to acquire these kinds of materials, even when shared with an adverse party, if counsel had persuaded a court to enter a protective order making the settlement negotiations and the documents related thereto confidential. Counsel practicing in the Second Circuit should be able to rely on this method of protecting confidentiality, but those practicing in the Third Circuit cannot assume that sealing orders will protect such material.

The *Center for Auto Safety* court disposed of the government's arguments under exemption 7A with comparable dispatch. Congress recently expanded this exemption but apparently not in ways that would eviscerate *County of Madison*'s reasoning or dislodge its conclusion. To qualify under exemption seven, even as amended, the documents must have been "compiled for law enforcement purposes" and satisfy at least one of six other criteria. The case law suggests that a document will not be deemed to have been generated "for law enforcement purposes" unless it was created in connection with an investigation that focused on "'specifically alleged illegal acts, illegal acts of particular identified officials, acts which if proved result in civil or criminal sanctions.'" Most documents generated in connection with efforts to settle civil litigation will not satisfy this requirement.

In 1984 and 1985 two federal district courts followed the lead of the *County of Madison* and *Center for Auto Safety* opinions in refusing to acknowledge a "settlement negotiation privilege" under exemption five and ordered governmental agencies to disclose terms of settlements or settlement-related documents that had been shared with an adversary. These two cases are *Norwood* v. *Federal Aviation Administration* and *NAACP Legal Defense and Educational Fund, Inc.* v. *United States Department of Justice.*

Norwood adds an important factor to the exemption five analysis. Pointing out that "the Supreme Court has held that 'final dispositions' of matters by an agency can never be exempt under exemption 5," *Norwood* announced that "the FAA [Federal Aviation Administration] cannot use exemption 5 to withhold production of the settlement agreements themselves, since the settlement agreements represent the final disposition of an agency case." Whether or not other courts will find this reasoning persuasive is difficult to predict, but counsel should be aware that exemption five might offer no protection at all to the final terms of settlement agreements.

The *Norwood* opinion discusses an additional exemption that might apply to some settlement documents. Exemption six covers "personnel and medical files and similar files the disclosure of which would constitute a clearly unwarranted invasion of personal privacy." In *Norwood,* a lawyer who represented 170 terminated air traffic controllers was using the FOIA in an effort to gain access to settlement agreements and related documents between the FAA and controllers reinstated after the nationwide strike in 1981. District Judge Horton declared that in order to qualify for exemption six the government would have to show three things: "(1) that the requested information is properly classified as a 'personnel,' 'medical,' or 'similar' file [and not simply put in a personnel file to shield it from the scope of FOIA]; (2) that the release of the information would violate substantial privacy interests of those involved; and (3) that the privacy interest is not outweighed by the public interest in disclosure." The court concluded that the removal letters and the settlement agreements had been properly classified as "personnel" matters, but that the government had failed to carry its burdens with respect to the remaining two requirements. In concluding that the documents had to be disclosed, the court made it clear that it would hold government counsel to demanding standards with respect to the second and third requirements, thus implying that it would be difficult to use exemption six to avoid disclosure of settlement documents.

Other exemptions to the FOIA might, in rare cases, protect documents related to settlement, but as far as I am aware only one of these other exemptions is the subject of a reported opinion in which a court ruled on an effort to discover materials related to settlement negotiations. In *Parker* v. *Equal Employment Opportunity Commission,* Judge Robinson, relying on exemption three, rejected an effort to use the FOIA to compel the Equal Employment Opportunity

Commission (EEOC) to disclose "all predetermination settlement agreements and conciliation agreements made in the Commission's Philadelphia Regional Office during March, 1974." Exemption three covers agency records that are "specifically exempted from disclosure by statute," as long as the statute in question meets specified criteria. The court held that these documents qualified for exemption three even though the statute that governs EEOC procedures does not mention these kinds of documents, and the statute would impose a duty of confidentiality only on negotiations that occur after the commission has found reasonable cause to believe that a charge of an unlawful employment practice is true. The significance of the latter point is that "predetermination settlements [agreements] are entered into after a charge is filed but before any determination of reasonable cause by the Commission." Despite these technical difficulties, both the district court and the appellate court were satisfied that Congress intended to place a cloak of confidentiality around all types of informal negotiations conducted by the commission and all of the agreements that such negotiations produced. Both courts concluded that Congress had elevated the public interest in fostering settlement of Equal Employment Opportunity Commission (EEOC) claims, by extending a promise of confidentiality, above the public interests generally reflected in the FOIA. Thus, both the predetermination settlements and the conciliation agreements are "specifically exempted from disclosure by statute" within the meaning of exemption three. No other reported opinion has interpreted this exemption with respect to settlement agreements.

The extent to which state law analogues to the FOIA might be used to force disclosure of settlement materials is not at all clear. In fact, only one reported opinion by a California appellate court even addresses this question. That opinion suggests that attorneys who negotiate settlements with or on behalf of public agencies in California cannot safely assume that the terms of the deals they strike will remain confidential. In *Register Division of Freedom Newspapers, Inc.* v. *County of Orange,* the appellate court affirmed a trial court's ruling that California's Public Records Act entitled a newspaper to access to virtually all of the documents related to a confidential settlement of a tort claim brought by a prison inmate against a county government. The court explicitly concluded that the public agency's promise to the plaintiff to maintain the confidentiality of the negotiations and of the terms of the agreement was insufficient to overcome the statutory mandate of public access to the records involved.

Holding that the terms of the settlement itself, as well as most related documents, had to be disclosed, the court of appeal made some sweeping pronouncements that seem to reflect little sympathy for the notion that confidentiality can be a key to the success of the settlement process. Among other things, the county defendant had argued that disclosure of settlement documents would encourage people to file frivolous claims and would compromise the public body's freedom to decide that it was in the taxpayer's best interests to offer a nuisance value settlement rather than incur the much greater expense of defending a case through trial and appeal. "Against this interest," responded the court:

> must be measured the public interest in finding out how decisions to spend public funds are formulated and in insuring governmental processes remain open and subject to public scrutiny. We find these considerations clearly outweigh any public interest served by conducting settlement of tort claims in secret, especially in light of the policies of disclosure and openness in governmental affairs fostered by both the CPRA [California Public Records Act] and Brown Act. While County's concern with the potential for escalating tort claims against it is genuine, opening up the County's settlement process to public scrutiny will, nevertheless, put prospective claimants on notice that only meritorious claims will ultimately be settled with public funds. This in turn will strengthen public confidence in the ability of governmental entities to efficiently administer the public purse.

In a footnote that apparently was intended to offer some reassurance to public bodies, the court added a potentially significant, but unclear, limitation on the implications of this paragraph: "Plaintiff does not claim, nor do we hold, every discussion regarding settlement of an actual or potential case against the county should be made public. We limit the scope of our holding to the actual discussion and actions of the claims settlement committee."

Because the *Register* court's analysis turned almost entirely on California statutes, the law that emerges from this lengthy opinion is binding only in California courts. Counsel working in other states must determine whether their states have statutes comparable to California's Public Records Act.

ALTERNATIVE METHODS OF ENHANCED PROTECTION OF SETTLEMENT NEGOTIATIONS

In light of the numerous threats to the confidentiality of settlement communications previously discussed, the following section presents a number of alternative approaches counsel can consider in order to protect settlement negotiations from disclosure. It discusses the use of protective orders or sealing orders, side agreements under seal, Federal Rule of Civil Procedure 68 and recently enacted state mediation statutes, and the enforceability of private contracts between settling parties to ensure confidentiality.

Protective or Sealing Orders

A protective or sealing order entered by a federal court apparently will prevent interested persons from being able to use FOIA to force disclosure of settlement agreements and related documents. The court in *Center for Auto Safety* stated, "In the antitrust decree modification context, the DOJ is in the position of petitioning the supervisory court for a protective order under [Federal Rule of Civil Procedure] 26(c) which would qualify as a *per se* discovery privilege and bar to disclosure under FOIA." Other authorities suggest that the protections from FOIA that are available through protective or sealing orders are not limited to antitrust or consent decree settings.

One technical, but apparently sufficient, reason that court orders can protect documents otherwise discoverable under FOIA is that this statute reaches only "agency" records, and courts generally do not consider themselves to be "agencies" within the meaning of the statute. Thus, settlement documents that become court documents are simply outside the purview of the FOIA.

The most explicit consideration of this issue occurred in the trial court and affirming appellate court opinions in *In re Franklin National Bank Securities Litigation,* and *Federal Deposit Insurance Corp. v. Ernst & Ernst.* These opinions resulted from an effort by the Public Interest Research Group (PIRG) to use FOIA to force disclosure of the terms of a settlement agreement between the Federal Deposit Insurance Corporation (FDIC), the trustee for the bankrupt Franklin National Bank, and its accountant, Ernst & Ernst. PIRG launched this effort some two years after District Judge Jack B. Weinstein had entered an order, at the parties' request, sealing the settlement documents and commanding the parties to maintain the confidentiality of the terms of the agreement. PIRG first presented its request for information about the settlement to the FDIC, invoking the FOIA. Relying on the court's order, the FDIC rejected the request. Thereafter, PIRG petitioned Judge Weinstein to vacate the order sealing the documents and compelling confidentiality.

The court rejected PIRG's argument that "a court's order to a federal agency to withhold agency records from the public is limited to the reasons for withholding permitted in the FOIA." Judge Weinstein reasoned that the goals of the FOIA are

> not necessarily defeated when an agency obtains protection from a court which is broader than the FOIA exemptions. The Act was intended to circumscribe the discretion of agencies rather than that of courts. In the context of this case it cannot be said that the FDIC manipulated this court in order to avoid the agency's obligations under the FOIA. Rather, the court properly issued a not unusual protective order in aid of its own jurisdiction.

In a subsequent section of the opinion, Judge Weinstein emphasized that it was not the FDIC, but private litigant Ernst & Ernst, that insisted on the confidentiality provision in the settlement agreement and the court order sanctioning it. The court might have been less confident about the implications of the FOIA for such a sealing order if the party who took the initiative and had the principal interest in seeking the order had been the federal agency that otherwise would have been constrained to disclose the terms of the agreement.

After rejecting the FOIA argument, the trial court considered the merits of PIRG's petition to modify the sealing order. It balanced the interests that would be served by disclosure against those that had been advanced by sealing the settlement documents initially and those that would be harmed by withdrawing the protection of confidentiality after the parties had relied on it for two years. This balancing analysis acknowledges that there might be some circumstances in which a court could be persuaded to "unseal" a settlement agreement. PIRG, however, failed to persuade the judge to exercise his discretion in favor of disclosure. In conducting its balancing analysis, the court emphasized how much time and resources were saved by the settlement of this massive case and the fact that one of the private parties absolutely refused to enter a settlement unless its terms were sealed. Thus, "without secrecy of the terms, a settlement would not have been consummated."

When Judge Weinstein turned to the interests that would be harmed by disclosure after the fact, he found substantial additional grounds for denying PIRG's request. He noted:

> The settlement agreement resulted in the payment of substantial amounts of money and induced substantial changes of position by many parties in reliance on the condition of secrecy. For the court to induce such acts and then to decline to support the parties in their reliance would work an injustice on these litigants and make future settlements predicated upon confidentiality less likely.

In sum, the trial court found that "the strong public policy favoring settlement of disputes, particularly in complicated cases, and the importance of the stability of judgments and settlements" outweighed the interests that would be advanced by disclosure.

On appeal, the Second Circuit upheld Judge Weinstein's refusal to modify the original sealing order "essentially for the reasons stated" in his opinion. The appellate panel agreed that courts could order agencies to withhold documents even when no FOIA exemption covered the material in question. More specifically, the Second Circuit held that "the FOIA does not apply to a court's order directing an agency not to reveal the terms of an agreement crucial to the settlement of an action." The higher court also emphasized that after "a confidentiality order has been entered and relied upon, it can only be modified if an 'extraordinary circumstance' or 'compelling need' warrants the requested modification."

A different panel of Second Circuit judges revisited this general subject three years later in *Palmieri* v. *State of New York*. The FOIA was not involved in *Palmieri*. Instead, the issue was simply what kind of showing was required to compel modification of existing protective orders that had covered both settlement negotiations between private parties and the terms of the settlement itself. What is particularly interesting about the *Palmieri* opinion is that it reflects considerable resistance to vacating such sealing orders even when the effort to penetrate the seal is being made by the Attorney General of the State of New York and a state grand jury for the purpose of developing evidence of possible criminal conduct arising out of the same circumstances that were the subject of the earlier settled civil antitrust action. Even in this situation, the Second Circuit held that the persons seeking to vacate the sealing order must satisfy a demanding standard by showing either that the original order was "improvidently granted" or that "extraordinary circumstances" or a "compelling need" justified the modification.

The appellate court went on to suggest that none of the required showings would be easy to make. For example, to establish that the sealing order had been improvidently granted, the state attorney general would be required to show that the issuing judge "reasonably should have recognized a substantial likelihood that the settlement would facilitate or further criminal activity." If the attorney general failed to carry this burden, the parties' reliance on the sealing orders, "as evidenced by their unwillingness to engage in settlement negotiations without the protections afforded, raises a presumption in favor of upholding those orders." Finally, the appellate panel pointed out that the attorney general's ability to make the required showing of a "compelling need" would be compromised, although not necessarily fatally, by the fact that the government and the grand jury had at their disposal "special investigatory powers not available to private litigants."

In sum, the tone of the *Palmieri* opinion is not hospitable to efforts to vacate orders that created the environment of secrecy that was essential to conducting settlement negotiations and concluding an agreement. Not surprisingly, the Second Circuit is not so inhospitable to such requests when targets of criminal investigations attempt to use sealing orders to prevent disclosure of corporate records that existed before litigation commenced, before any protective order was sought, and before settlement negotiations commenced.

A recent opinion by a divided panel of judges from the Third Circuit contrasts sharply with the Second Circuit opinions in *Palmieri* and *FDIC* v. *Ernst & Ernst*. As no governmental agency was involved in *Bank of America* v. *Hotel Rittenhouse Associates*, the party seeking disclosure of settlement documents could not rely on the FOIA. The two judges who formed the majority in *Hotel Rittenhouse*, however, focused on a doctrine that the Second Circuit opinions had ignored: the "common law right of access to judicial records and proceedings." In fact, the majority relied on this doctrine to overrule the district court's refusal to unseal settlement documents and other papers filed in a civil proceeding. In so doing, the court not only reversed the presumptions favoring sealing orders that are reflected in the Second Circuit opinions, but went much further by holding that the interests advanced by promising litigants that their settlement will remain confidential cannot outweigh, at least absent some extraordinary showing, the common-law right of public access to court documents. As the majority phrased it, "the generalized interest in encouraging settlements does not rise to the level of interests that we have recognized may outweigh the public's common law right of access." Thus the majority made it clear that "the presumption of access" that attaches to sealed court documents is very strong and that a party seeking to overcome this presumption, and thus to maintain the confidentiality of such sealed documents, bears a heavy burden indeed.

Because Judge Sloviter's opinion for the two-judge majority in *Hotel Rittenhouse* is so explosive in implications and so inconsistent with recent opinions from the Second Circuit, it is necessary to understand the context in which it arose. This context may expose a basis for distinguishing the case from situations more commonly arising in civil litigation. By looking carefully at the context, one also can develop practical suggestions for lawyers that should enable them to avoid the outcome reflected in the *Hotel Rittenhouse* case.

Two aspects of the background against which *Hotel Rittenhouse* was decided seem to have been most important to the court's decision: (1) the parties who entered the settlement decided to file the agreement, under seal, and thus to make it formally a record in the case; and (2) after filing the settlement agreement under seal, the parties began disputing its meaning and, most importantly, each filed motions petitioning the court to interpret and enforce the contract. The district court permitted the parties to conduct their enforcement litigation entirely under seal: their motions, cross-motions, responses and replies remained under wraps, even when the court entered a judgment compelling one of the parties to pay the other more than $38 million pursuant to the contract and ordered the marshal to sell the subject commercial property. In the meantime, the concrete subcontractor for the project was pressing an $800,000 claim for work done on the property. This contractor filed an action in state court charging that the two parties to the federal action had conspired to defraud him and that the sealing of the settlement action was one of the acts they committed in furtherance of their fraudulent scheme. The contractor's petition to unseal the settlement agreement and the subsequent motion papers led to the *Hotel Rittenhouse* opinion.

The court of appeals emphasized the fact that the parties had voluntarily elected to file their settlement in the district court and then had sought to use that court to achieve their private enforcement ends. Judge Sloviter noted that the parties had an alternative that probably would have enabled them to protect the confidentiality of their agreement. "It is likely," she wrote, "that had [the parties] chosen to settle and file a voluntary stipulation of dismissal, as provided in Rule 41(a)(1) of the Federal Rules of Civil Procedure, they would have been able to prevent public, and even [the cement subcontractor's], access to these papers." But the filing of the settlement documents, even under seal, made them part of the court record and, as such, "subject to the access accorded such records."

In distinguishing the Second Circuit's opinion in *Federal Deposit Insurance Corp.* v. *Ernst & Ernst,* Judge Sloviter emphasized two factors. The first, and apparently the more important, was that in the *Hotel Rittenhouse* case, unlike in *Ernst & Ernst,* "there were *motions* filed and *orders* entered that were kept secret, in direct contravention of the open access to judicial records that the common law protects." Driving the point home, the court declared that "having undertaken to utilize the judicial process to interpret the settlement and to enforce it, the parties are no longer entitled to invoke the confidentiality ordinarily accorded settlement agreements." Judge Sloviter also distinguished *Ernst & Ernst* by pointing out that it implicated interests of much greater public import and of a much larger number of people than did the *Hotel Rittenhouse* matter. But because the cases were dissimilar, the two judges who made up the majority in *Hotel Rittenhouse* refused to decide whether the kind of showing of particularized need to maintain confidentiality that had been made in *Ernst & Ernst* was sufficient to "override the strong presumption of access."

From the structure of the court's opinion in *Hotel Rittenhouse,* it appears that there are virtually no circumstances in which Judges Sloviter and Aldisert would uphold the confidentiality of settlement documents and related papers when such materials have been the subject of litigated motions, orders, and judgments. The odds that these two judges would vote to preserve confidentiality appear to be somewhat better—but still not good—when there has been no litigation about the terms of the agreement and thus when the only court document that would remain under wraps is the settlement contract itself.

The lesson to be learned from *Hotel Rittenhouse* should be clear: lawyers practicing in the Third Circuit must decide whether preserving the confidentiality of the terms of their clients' agreement is more important than improved ability to enforce its terms. If preserving confidentiality is the more important consideration, counsel in the Third Circuit should not file their agreement. Instead, they should file a stipulated dismissal and rely on a separate action, sounding in contract, for enforcement purposes.

Two additional points about the majority opinion in *Hotel Rittenhouse* remain to be made. The first arises from Judge Sloviter's emphasis that there might be two independent bases on which a party could seek disclosure of sealed settlement documents. The basis on which the majority ruled in *Hotel Rittenhouse* was the "common law right of access to judicial records and proceedings." This common-law right gave rise to the test used in the court's opinion: a balancing analysis in which the scales are heavily weighted in favor of disclosure. Thus, the party seeking to preserve confidentiality must overcome the "strong presumption" in favor of access.

The second point to note is that the majority intimated, but refused to formally decide, that the First Amendment might offer parties a separate, and independently sufficient, predicate for attacking the sealing of settlement documents. Moreover, Judges Sloviter and Aldisert suggested that the "test" to which the First Amendment might give rise in situations like this might be even more difficult for parties resisting disclosure to survive. That test apparently would parallel the "compelling state interest" test developed by the Supreme Court for analyzing statutes that restrict core political speech on the basis of its content. Vigorously applied, this test is virtually impossible to pass. The significance of all this is that the court intentionally left open the possibility that even if its reasoning under the common-law right of access were to be rejected at some point in the future by the Supreme Court, it would have another, even more powerful, doctrine to invoke to support the same conclusion.

Judge Sloviter's reasoning has at least two vulnerabilities that could be used by counsel in other jurisdictions to persuade their courts not to follow *Hotel Rittenhouse*. The first "soft spot" in Judge Sloviter's reasoning is her unpersuasive effort to distinguish the Supreme Court's opinion in *Seattle Times Co. v. Rhinehart*, in which the High Court held that the First Amendment did not prevent a district court from entering a protective order sealing certain discovery documents. The *Hotel Rittenhouse* court argued that discovery "is ordinarily conducted in private" and that the public somehow has a less powerful interest in access to discovery documents than to a settlement agreement that is filed under seal. In many courts, of course, discovery documents are routinely filed and accessible to the public. Moreover, a number of settlement agreements contain confidentiality clauses. As a general proposition, there may be a greater expectation of privacy with respect to the terms of settlement than there is with respect to discovery documents. For these reasons, Judge Sloviter's effort to distinguish *Seattle Times* remains unpersuasive.

The second problem with Judge Sloviter's opinion is her reliance on the "common law right of access." This is a controversial, ill-defined and unevenly supported doctrine, especially as it applies to civil litigation.

Lawyers searching for help in efforts to challenge the reasoning of *Hotel Rittenhouse* may look to the essentially contemporaneous opinion by the Supreme Court of Minnesota in *Minneapolis Star & Tribune Co. v. Schumacher*. Like *Hotel Rittenhouse*, *Schumacher* dealt with settlement documents that had become part of the record of a civil action and did not address unfiled settlement agreements. After considering the relevant precedents from the United States Supreme Court, the Supreme Court of Minnesota decided in *Schumacher* that "no First Amendment right of access exists" in settlement documents. In reaching this conclusion, the high court of Minnesota relied heavily on its perception that "historically, the majority of settlements entered into between parties have been private" and on its belief that allowing public access to settlement documents might jeopardize the important policy objective of encouraging consensual disposition of lawsuits.

The *Schumacher* court went on to acknowledge, however, that even though the First Amendment gives rise to no general right of access to settlement documents that are made a part of the record in civil actions, the common law creates a presumption in favor of such access that can be overcome only by showing "strong countervailing reasons why access [to the filed settlement documents] should be restricted." The court promptly softened the implications of this position, however, by (1) announcing that the standard of review for decisions by trial judges over whether to grant access to sealed settlement documents is abuse of discretion, and (2) holding that the trial judge had not abused his discretion in refusing to permit a newspaper to have access to "settlement and distribution papers" and transcripts of settlement hearings in five wrongful death actions against an airline that was being sued by other victims of the same accident. In affirming the trial judge's action, the Supreme Court noted that the "historical and philosophical privacy of settlement documents, along with the relevant facts and circumstances of this case, demonstrate that the privacy interests asserted by the litigants were strong enough to justify restricting access."

It is arguable that the effect of relying on the "historical and philosophical privacy of settlement documents" is to eviscerate the strong presumption in favor of access that the court purported to acknowledge. If the court permits the historical privacy of settlement to offset the presumption in favor of access, the "test" that emerges is an open balancing (that is, not weighted in favor of any outcome). And if the scales are not tipped at the outset significantly in favor of disclosure, trial courts will enjoy considerable discretion in deciding whether or not to permit access to sealed settlement documents. In *Schumacher,* the trial court was satisfied by a showing that if the settlement documents were made public the plaintiffs might be subjected to harassment, exploitation, and intrusions on their privacy. Neither the trial court nor the Minnesota Supreme Court ascribed much countervailing weight in the balancing process to the great public interest in the airline crash or to the pendency of other litigation arising out of the same incident. In fact, the Supreme Court used the level of public interest in the event and its aftermath to buttress its conclusion that disclosure of the terms of the settlements might lead to further intrusions on the privacy of the settling plaintiffs.

In spirit, *Schumacher* and *Hotel Rittenhouse* could not be more antithetical. The Minnesota Supreme Court seems to be more sympathetic than the Third Circuit with the goal of promoting settlement and with the argument that affording real protection to the privacy of settlement contracts is essential to that goal. By contrast, the Third Circuit ascribes more weight to the importance of public access to records that show how civil proceedings were closed. Which of the competing assumptions that underlie these two approaches is wisest is a question to which we have no empirical answer. Thus, the debate will continue at least until the Supreme Court of the United States enters the fray.

Side Agreements Under Seal

Janus Films, Inc. v. *Miller*, a recent Second Circuit opinion, exposes a different kind of risk that lawyers face when they file a side agreement under seal in connection with a consent judgment or a settlement judgment. *Janus Films* was a copyright infringement action that the parties purported to settle in open court on the second day of trial. The proposed settlement included a concession of liability by the defendant, an agreement that judgment would be entered "for statutory damages, attorney's fees, and costs in the total amount of $100,000," and "a separate, confidential agreement, to be placed under seal, regarding 'the terms and conditions of collection' of the judgment." The confidential side agreement permitted the defendant to satisfy the monetary aspect of the judgment by "payment of a sum considerably less than the $100,000 over an extended period of time." Despite the defendant's subsequent change of mind and attempt to avoid the commitment he had made in open court, the trial judge entered a judgment that described the $100,000 obligation and certain injunctive relief, but did not mention either the content or the existence of the side agreement.

The Second Circuit panel was not comfortable with the way the trial judge had handled the side agreement. Noting that it was dealing with an issue of first impression, the Court of Appeals distinguished between

> a judgment that concerns only the parties to the lawsuit being settled and a judgment likely to be of concern to others. The former, which might be called a "private judgment," is illustrated by a judgment that resolves the claims of all parties to a dispute involving a tort or a breach of contract. The latter, which might be called a "public judgment," is illustrated by the pending case, where a judgment resolves a dispute concerning a copyright that may be enforced against other members of the public besides the defendant in this litigation.

Because the case did not involve a "private judgment," the appellate panel declined to consider whether courts should permit parties in such actions to terminate their suit through entry of a consent judgment or a settlement judgment accompanied by a separate side agreement that is filed under seal.

With respect to "public judgments," however, the *Janus Films* court announced a new rule. Noting that "there is always the distinct risk that either party may seek to induce others to settle similar disputes on terms exactly like or at least similar to the terms of the judgment," the Second Circuit held that parties who terminate litigation by having the trial court enter a consent judgment or a settlement judgment should be required to disclose the content of any side agreements that are part of the arrangement that concludes the suit. This holding does not mean that parties cannot settle cases on confidential terms. As the *Janus Films* panel pointed out, litigants who have settled their dispute retain the option of forgoing entry of judgment, terminating the case by a stipulated dismissal, and "keeping confidential all aspects of their settlement." If terms of disposition are "likely to be asserted against other[s]," however, the parties may not "secure a judicial imprimatur for an obligation that [they have secretly] agreed means less than its terms state."

Federal Rule of Civil Procedure 68 and State Mediation Statutes

Attorneys who are especially concerned about preserving the confidentiality of offers or demands, or of statements made during negotiations, should consider proceeding under Federal Rule of Civil Procedure 68, or a state law analogue, like section 998 of the California Code of Civil Procedure, or turning to a "mediation" process that enjoys special state statutory protection.

The bar to admissibility that is articulated in Federal Rule of Civil Procedure 68, and in section 998 of the California Code of Civil Procedure, is virtually unqualified, in sharp contrast to the limited protection offered by Federal Rule of Evidence 408. Rule 68 flatly declares that evidence of an unaccepted offer that was made under the rule is "not admissible except in a proceeding to determine costs." The language of section 998 of the California Code of Civil Procedure is similarly sweeping: "If such offer is not accepted . . . it . . . cannot be given in evidence upon the trial." These prohibitions seem operative regardless of the purpose for which the evidence would be proffered at trial and thus avoid the limitations on the scope of Rule 408. Since neither Rule 68 nor section 998 purports to extend protection to evidence of "conduct or statements made in compromise negotiations," counsel cannot be sure to what extent these rules of procedure can be invoked to protect communications that accompany and explain protected offers. Moreover, by their express terms, these rules apply only to offers that are not accepted. It is unlikely that these rules would offer any protection in a case in which a person who was not a party to a settlement agreement is attempting to compel disclosure of settlement communications or terms.

As an alternative to simple two-party settlement negotiations, counsel could proceed with private mediations that are covered by recently enacted state confidentiality statutes with much greater confidence in the scope of the protection they afford. As one commentator has noted, recent "legislative enactments in several states have provided near-absolute protection for communications made in mediation, [thus greatly enhancing] the protection available to mediation under the traditional rules of evidence and contract." Some of the most populous states in the country, including California, New York, and Florida, have enacted such laws.

The California version of these statutes appears as section 1152.5 of the Evidence Code, which was added in 1985. Except for certain family law matters that are covered by other confidentiality provisions, this statute applies to any kind of civil dispute. When parties "agree to conduct and participate in a mediation for the purpose of compromising, settling, or resolving a civil dispute," and when, before the mediation begins, they agree in writing to invoke the protections of the statute after setting forth the provisions of the statute in their agreement, the law prohibits admitting evidence "of anything said or . . . any admission made in the course of the mediation" or any "document prepared for the purpose of, or in the course of, or pursuant to, the mediation."

The Law Revision Commission's comment to the 1985 addition makes clear that parties can waive their confidentiality rights under this section either by failing to object to a proffer at the time of trial or by mutual consent. The same comment points out that the purpose of this section is "to encourage this alternative to a judicial determination of the action" and that the justification for the confidentiality provision is the same as the justification for the much narrower provision contained in section 1152, which renders offers of compromise "inadmissible to prove . . . liability for the loss or damage or any part of it." The Law Revision Commission's comment emphasizes that instead of attempting to limit the applicability of the statute through a definition of the term *"mediation,"* the legislature decided that it would make the statutory protections available only when "the persons who will participate in the mediation (including the mediator) execute a written agreement before the mediation begins stating that Section 1152.5 of the Evidence Code applies to the mediation" and only when their agreement sets "out the full text of subdivisions (a) and (b) of Section 1152.5."

Thus, California practitioners who want to take advantage of the broad protections available through this statute should develop forms that recite all the relevant provisions of the statute and that expressly articulate the commitments to confidentiality that all parties and the mediator make. When they follow the proper procedure, California lawyers should be able to use this statute to fill virtually any gap left by section 1152 of the California Evidence Code, which applies only to "offers to compromise."

There is no reason to believe that because a dispute is already the subject of litigation the protections of section 1152.5 are rendered inaccessible. There is reason to believe, however, that this more generous section would not apply to negotiations between the parties that did not involve a neutral third party. While the new statute does not purport to define *"mediation,"* it clearly contemplates a process that involves the participation of a neutral person who must sign the confidentiality agreement. Counsel cannot simply change the label of direct settlement negotiations to "mediation" and assume that they will enjoy the protections of the new statute, but must involve a neutral person from the outset.

Before deciding to proceed under section 1152.5, counsel should consider the disadvantages that might derive from the breadth of its protections. As a commentator has pointed out concerning comparable statutes enacted in other states, proceeding under statutes that on their face bar use of evidence from mediations regardless of the purpose for which the evidence would be used could create extra difficulties for a party who subsequently seeks either (1) to enforce an agreement that resulted from the mediation or (2) to resist enforcement of an agreement that was the product of duress, fraud, mutual mistake, or overreaching. Similarly, the broad language of a statute like section 1152.5 could impair efforts to redress wrongs arising out of violation of some specific duty relating to the conduct of negotiations, such as the duty to bargain in good faith in labor disputes, or the duty of an insurance carrier to consider in good faith reasonable settlement proposals.

Apparently anticipating this problem, the Minnesota legislature explicitly provided that the promise of confidentiality that extends generally to communications made in connection with mediations does not apply when a party applies to a court "to have a mediated settlement agreement set aside or reformed." Even though they acted a year later than their counterparts in Minnesota, California legislators failed to add any such caveat or qualifier to the promise of confidentiality in section 1152.5. Thus, counsel cannot be sure how California courts will respond when a party attempts to use material or statements made in connection with a mediation to enforce or to defeat a mediated settlement agreement. Given this uncertainty, counsel must assess separately the needs and risks presented by each specific situation that calls for some effort to reach a settlement, then either (1) choose from the pre-existing procedures the one that best fits that situation or (2) attempt to create, through private contract, a mini-trial process that is specially tailored to meet the needs of the parties.

Private Caucus Settlement Conferences

A private caucus settlement conference hosted by a judge or magistrate offers two sources of protection for communications. In conferences structured on this model the parties have virtually no direct interaction. The person to whom they present the reasoning that supports their offers or demands, and to whom they divulge how far they might be willing to go in an effort to compromise differences, is the judge—not opposing counsel. Furthermore, the parties can ask the judge to keep secret the admissions or concessions about which they are most sensitive, or the most potentially damaging reasons for the positions they are taking. An opponent who does not learn these things cannot attempt to introduce them at trial.

The second source of protection for communications made during judicially hosted settlement conferences is the difficulty an opponent would have compelling a judge who had hosted such a conference to testify at trial about what a party said to her in confidence during the negotiations. There may be circumstances under which this kind of testimony could be compelled, but the judicial community is likely to require a compelling showing before permitting a party to penetrate this sensitive arena.

Using Private Contracts to Extend Protection

Another tool that counsel might consider using to increase protection for their settlement communications is a contract with the opposition designed explicitly for the purpose of guaranteeing confidentiality. In such a contract, the parties might commit themselves not to attempt to introduce at a trial on the merits, for any purpose, any statements made during settlement negotiations. Such a contract clearly would reach further than Rule 408 and erect a stone wall instead of a split rail fence between settlement negotiations and trial. Such contracts, of course, cannot bind parties who do not sign them and may have little effect on the capacity of a non-party to discover or introduce at trial the settlement communications covered by the contract.

Unfortunately, the enforceability of such contracts is not always clear. There is a risk, though probably small, that a federal judge would refuse to enforce such an agreement on the ground that it embodies a doctrine Congress refused to enact when it adopted the Federal Rules of Evidence. There also is a risk that a federal judge would view such a contract as invading a judicial prerogative—restricting the judge's power to make sure that all the evidence that will help the jury ascertain the truth is accessible. Clearly there is a substantial risk that a judge will refuse to honor such a contract if doing so would make it impossible to determine whether a subsequent settlement agreement should be enforced. To write such an agreement that purported to go this far would be unwise in most circumstances. Similarly, courts can be expected to penetrate any such agreement when it is necessary to determine whether the parties engaged in illegal conduct or set up a relationship that violated public policy.

Confidentiality contracts that threaten none of these more compelling public policies, however, may be enforceable, at least in instances when they are entered into by parties who are competent and represented by counsel, and between whom there are not dangerous differences in bargaining power. A California appellate court has upheld such a contract as it applied to a voluntary mediation.

Lawyers looking for creative ways to use contracts to increase protection for the confidentiality of settlement communications might find interesting a suggestion in *United States* v. *Cook*. In a footnote, a panel of Fifth Circuit judges indicated that they would be receptive to an argument that a party who promised—as part of a settlement contract in one case—not to use that settlement outside the action in which it was entered, should be estopped from introducing evidence from the settlement in a subsequent suit. Defendants in a criminal trial that the government launched after it had settled an earlier civil matter with them argued that "the government was estopped from using the injunction documents [a consent decree that resulted from a settlement agreement] because of the specific prohibition they contained against their use for any purpose other than 'the purpose of this action.'" Characterizing this argument as "persuasive," the *Cook* court went on to opine that in "simple equity, the government should not be allowed to induce or obtain a defendant's consent to settlement under specific terms, and later violate those terms." This comment suggests that counsel should consider adding clauses that explicitly limit the permissible uses of settlement material to their settlement contracts or to agreements that fix the rules for settlement negotiations.

The caveat that courts will not enforce such agreements if their purpose or effect violates public policy is reflected in the opinion of the California Court of Appeal in *Mary R. v. B.&R. Corp.* In that case, the court refused to enforce a term of a settlement agreement that purported to prohibit the plaintiff, the alleged victim of child molestation by a physician, from revealing information to regulatory authorities. While the facts of that case were unusual, the principle that emerges from it could apply in a wide range of more commonly occurring situations. In the securities area, for example, courts might well refuse to honor a contract, whether or not it led to a settlement agreement, in which the parties agreed that neither would share with the Securities and Exchange Commission or anyone else information about insider trading that it learned during settlement discussions. Similarly, parties should not expect courts to enforce agreements between competitors that purport to prohibit disclosure or admission at trial of communications whose purpose or effect was to promote anticompetitive activities, even if these communications occurred during settlement negotiations.

Moreover, courts that follow precedents developed in cases dealing with the enforceability of "stipulations" could find many different grounds on which to relieve a party of an apparent contractual commitment limiting the admissibility of communications made or acts committed during the course of settlement discussions. Courts may relieve a party from a stipulation because it was procured by fraud, because it was entered as a result of misrepresentation, mistake of fact, or excusable neglect, or because there has been such a substantial change in circumstances that binding the party to the stipulation would be unfair. The significance of these grounds for relief from a stipulation lies in the fact that they also are commonly presented bases for relief from a settlement agreement. As explained earlier, Rule 408 would not bar admission of communications made during settlement negotiations if the purpose for which they would be admitted is to prove that the settlement contract is unenforceable because it was procured by fraud, or was entered as a result of misrepresentation, mistake of fact, or excusable neglect. Thus a party might be able to use the same ground both to escape a contractual commitment not to disclose communications made during negotiations and to defeat the settlement agreement itself.

One additional warning is in order here. When the basis for subject matter jurisdiction in federal court is diversity of citizenship, there is a possibility that state law, rather than federal common law, will determine whether or not a contract that enlarges the protections of Rule 408—for example, by making communications during negotiations inadmissible for any purpose—is enforceable. Professors Wright and Graham suggest that courts deciding whether to enforce such contracts should consider doctrines developed in the law of procedure and doctrines developed in the substantive law of contract, arguing that procedural analysis should be based on federal common law in diversity cases, but that the substantive contract analysis should be based on the law of the relevant state. In *Blum* v. *Morgan Guaranty Trust Co.*, the Eleventh Circuit assumed, without conducting a detailed analysis under *Erie Railroad Co.* v. *Tompkins* and its progeny, that in a diversity case the enforceability of stipulations whose effect is to limit the admissibility of evidence is a question to be resolved under state law.

CONCLUSION

Despite commonly made assumptions, and the apparent promise of Federal Rule of Evidence 408, there are many circumstances in which many courts would permit both the discovery and the admission at trial of confidential settlement communications. Given the unpredictability of judicial rulings in this area, and the unforeseeability of events that could result in disclosure or admission at trial of settlement communications, good lawyers have no choice but to proceed with caution in this area. If confidentiality is their client's paramount concern, counsel should not rely on the rules of evidence for protection and should consider taking some of the extra precautions described in the latter sections of this article.

CHAPTER TWENTY-NINE

Settlements and the Erosion of the Public Realm

David Luban

A decade has passed since Owen Fiss published what is perhaps the best known paper on out-of-court settlements, the polemic "Against Settlement" (1984).[1] Proponents of settlements argue not only that they provide necessary relief from overcrowded dockets, but also that settlements are likely to achieve a higher quality of justice than adjudication. Though others have subsequently cast doubt on both of these claims,[2] Fiss was the first and boldest to argue that settlements are no cause for celebration—that, at best, they are "a capitulation to the conditions of mass society and should be neither encouraged nor praised" (p. 1075). His argument provoked immediate and largely negative reaction. However, despite its fame (or perhaps notoriety), "Against Settlement" has not been properly understood, and the vision underlying its arguments rarely has been made explicit. In part, this misunderstanding is because Fiss himself couches his arguments in somewhat misleading terms; in part, it is because the underlying vision is an uncommon one. The vision underlying Fiss's polemic is powerful and attractive, but it is not without its disturbing undercurrents. I also suspect—and this suspicion will be a large part of my argument—that, even on its own terms, Fiss's opposition to settlements may need to be rethought. My aim in this essay is thus both to revisit the arguments of "Against Settlement" and its critics and to ask some basic questions. Can anybody realistically continue to be against settlements? Is "for or against" really the issue at all, or has it become (was it always?) not whether to settle but when? What are the appropriate terms for evaluating a settlement? Is there a jurisprudence of settlements waiting to be invented?[3]

This essay proceeds as follows. I first analyze several arguments that may be offered on behalf of adjudication and against settlement. Some of these focus on the public goods created and public bads forestalled by adjudication, but the primary focus is on Fiss's more controversial and surprising argument that adjudication can in itself be a central part of our political life, because adjudication is how we articulate public values. Though I view these arguments sympathetically, my provisional conclusion is that imaginary legal systems in which no cases settle, like those in which all cases settle, would be thoroughly undesirable. Thus the question cannot be "for or against settlement?" but "how much settlement?" I next argue that even on Fiss's own terms, our rapidly expanding legal system cannot tolerate a greatly accelerated adjudication rate because of the confusion and bad law that would result. Thus, it seems likely that Fiss's arguments cannot support the conclusion that the practice of settlement should be dramatically curtailed. In Part III, I suggest that the settlement process can realize some of the values Fiss and I both find in adjudication. These include openness, legal justice, and the creation of public goods. Settlements can fulfill these values, at least in part, but only if they are crafted with this end in mind— and only if we are prepared to oppose settlements that defeat these values. Unfortunately, judges sometimes overlook this point and treat the settlement process as though it were the sacrosanct private business of the settling parties, in which outsiders simply should not meddle. I illustrate this point by considering at some length recent controversies over secret settlements, which I oppose. I conclude by briefly discussing two recent settlements, the asbestos settlement in *Georgine* v. *Amchem Products, Inc.* and the Justice Department's proposed antitrust settlement with Microsoft.

THE NORMATIVE VALUE OF ADJUDICATION

Learned Hand (1926) once wrote, "I must say that as a litigant I should dread a lawsuit beyond almost anything short of sickness and death" (p. 105). This is conventional wisdom. Lawsuits are expensive, terrifying, frustrating, infuriating, humiliating, time-consuming, perhaps all-consuming. Small wonder, then, that both judges and litigants prefer settlements, which are cheaper, quicker, less public, and less all-or-nothing than adjudications. In an aphorism recently cited by Samuel Gross and Kent Syverud (1991), a trial is a failed settlement. Though trials and judgments may sometimes be necessary, they are like surgeries: painful last resorts for otherwise incurable ailments, which are likely to place the patient in a weakened condition at least temporarily and almost certain to leave lasting scars. Pursuing this metaphor, settlements provide the noninvasive alternate therapy that, if successful, is invariably better than surgery.

Fiss's opposition to settlements arises because of his unexpected dissent from the conventional wisdom that trials signal pathologies—his belief that adjudication may be a sign of health rather than a drastic cure for disease. This view is counterintuitive and wildly unpopular in a culture in which lawyer-bashing has become a national hobby, lawsuits a lightning rod for talk show resentniks, and the civil justice system a cherished target of rage and demagoguery. Yet the arguments for adjudication are neither eccentric nor frivolous. The first group of arguments, which is less controversial and more familiar, is instrumental in nature. These arguments do not commend adjudication as a good in itself, but rather as a necessary condition for fulfilling other values that our culture accepts. The second argument, at once less familiar and more controversial, considers adjudication an intrinsic good, a process that is as much a sign of a healthy society as free elections.[4]

THE INSTRUMENTAL ARGUMENTS

Adjudication as a Public Good

In 1978, University of Chicago economist William M. Landes and then-lawprofessor Richard A. Posner wrote an article entitled "Adjudication as a Private Good" in which they consider our courts as though they were private vendors of a service—dispute resolution—in competition with other purveyors of the same service, such as commercial arbitrators. Landes and Posner argue that treating adjudication as a private good is perfectly coherent, and that economic competition could increase the efficiency of the judicial system. After all, litigants hiring their own judges would create an incentive for quick and cheap dispute resolution as well as for judicial fairness, because litigants would refuse to hire an inefficient or biased judge. If public courts couldn't compete, litigants would switch to alternative providers.

However, Landes and Posner continue, our court system not only resolves disputes, but also produces rules and precedents. Though private judges may well be efficient purveyors of dispute resolution, they are terribly inefficient producers of rules. Why would litigants who engage the services of a rent-a-judge want to pay extra for a reasoned opinion enunciating a rule that benefits only future litigants? Future litigants, after all, would receive the benefits of the rule for free.[5] Landes and Posner thus conclude that because the private market would systematically underproduce rules and precedents, the state should control the provision of judicial services.

The Landes-Posner objection to private adjudication is an objection to settlements as well, a point that Jules Coleman and Charles Silver (1986) have elaborated: settlements, like private adjudications, produce no rules or precedents binding on nonparties. Rules and precedents, in turn, have obvious importance for guiding future behavior and imposing order and certainty on a transactional world that would otherwise be in flux and chaos. Even those who favor settlement over adjudication generally rank order and certainty very high on the scale of legal values.[6] Indeed, one of Fiss's criticisms of the alternative dispute resolution (ADR) movement is that its proponents value peace over justice.[7] Settlements bring peace whereas adjudication, though perhaps more just, creates disruption. Regardless of whether Fiss is right that to be prosettlement is to value peace over justice, the present argument yields a surprising result: adjudication may often prove superior to settlement for securing peace because the former, unlike the latter, creates rules and precedents.

Economists define a public good as a beneficial product that cannot be provided to one consumer without making it available to all (or at least many others). The textbook example is a lighthouse: if one shipper erects a lighthouse, she cannot prevent other ships navigating the same waters from using it for free. The Landes/Posner/Coleman/Silver analysis shows that precedents and legal rules are public goods. Although the original litigants of the cases "purchase" the rules, future litigants use these rules without paying. This exemplifies a more general economic precept: absent public intervention, private economic actors often have inadequate incentives to produce public goods, because it is individually rational to be a free rider (Olson, 1971).

Civil adjudication can create other public goods besides rules and precedents. For example, it may develop the advocacy skills of litigating attorneys. Kevin McMunigal (1990) has noted that, as the number of civil trials declines,[8] litigators' advocacy skills tend to atrophy. Ironically, this degeneration may distort not only trials but the settlement process as well: litigators without adequate trial experience are less able to evaluate cases accurately and are more likely to settle out of fear of their own inadequacy. If McMunigal is correct, the attorney skills developed through trials are a public good that will lead to settlements that better reflect the value of a case.[9] McMunigal's argument presumably applies to the skills of trial judges as well: if a judge tries only a handful of cases each year, then crucial trial skills such as ruling on objections will atrophy.

The public-good character of attorney skills receives indirect acknowledgment in one provision of the legal profession's ethics codes. This is the prohibition on settlements containing terms in which an attorney agrees not to represent future clients in similar litigation.[10] The practice of "lawyer buyout" dates back at least half a century, and there is anecdotal evidence that it has persisted despite the bar's prohibition.[11] Lawyer buyout is an attempt by a party subject to repeated litigation to neutralize experienced, well-informed adversaries. It is a practice that privatizes a lawyer's skills and knowledge: they are traded in for a one-time bonus to the lawyer's current client, rather than being preserved as public goods. Yet it is clear that when a lawyer invests substantial time in some kind of specialized litigation, at the expense of the client who is paying the bills, the lawyer's expertise becomes a public good.

The ban on lawyer buyout is virtually the only piece of the ethics codes that recognizes that accumulated legal skills are a public good that should not be squandered on a single favorable settlement.[12] It strikingly contrasts with the ethics codes' more typical position that a lawyer who fails to maximize a client's outcome out of concern for future clients is guilty of a conflict of interest.[13] Lawyer buyout illustrates one dynamic by which the settlement process can undercut the creation of public goods.

To take another example, the discovery and publicizing of facts, which may subsequently be used by political actors, ordinary citizens, or other agents in the legal system (litigants as well as lawyers), is a public good created by adjudication. In a world of private settlements, such facts would most likely be underproduced.

Even the authority of courts may be conceptualized as a public good furthered by adjudication. Whenever disputants rely on the final and public judgment of a court to resolve their controversy, they enhance the courts' claim as an authoritative resolver of controversies. However, when disputants turn elsewhere for resolution—private arbitration, nonjudicial government agencies, or private bargaining—the salience of adjudication fades and the authority of courts weakens. Each litigant who proceeds to judgment and acquiesces in it thereby subsidizes a judicial authority that is available for future litigants.

Of course, this line of thought begs the question of whether judicial authority is a good at all, and it is this point that proponents of settlement, ADR, and private ordering are inclined to doubt. What Judith Resnik (1986) has called our "failing faith" in adjudication reflects growing public doubt about reposing authority in the courts rather than in alternative fora. On the other hand, authority has a reflexive character: the more authority adjudication by courts carries, the more authority it will earn, both because it casts a longer and more firmly contoured shadow on out-of-court negotiations, and because its authority inspires more litigants to use it, further enhancing its authority (adjudication becomes a coordination equilibrium).[14] My point here is not to defend the "failing faith," but simply to note conditionally that, *if* we regard adjudicatory authority as a good at all, it is a public good that adjudication advances and settlement undermines (unless the settlement has itself been brokered by the court).

Settlements and Public Bads

A second instrumental argument against settlement focuses not on the public goods it fails to create, but on the "public bads" it may inflict. The point is simple: two parties trying to apportion a loss are most likely to reach agreement if they can find a way to shift the burden to a third party who is not present at the bargaining table. For example, the parties to an environmental dispute may settle it through an agreement that a chemical company will dispose of waste at sites purchased in a remote community with no political clout. Similarly, a law firm may settle a malpractice claim with the Resolution Trust Corporation by agreeing not to contest liability provided that the settlement is within the firm's insurance limits, or a labor union and an employer may settle a controversy by passing the losses on to consumers (Luban, 1989). Adjudication may make such agreements impossible because the terms are no longer in the parties' hands, or because the public character of a trial makes it impossible for the parties to pass along their losses without scandal and protest.

THE INTRINSIC ARGUMENTS: ADJUDICATION AS AN ELABORATION OF PUBLIC VALUES

The first of the preceding arguments emphasized that adjudication, which produces rules and precedents, is instrumentally useful because these provide a normative framework for future transactions. However, legal rules and precedents are valuable not only as a source of certainty, but also as a reasoned elaboration and visible expression of public values. Law on this view amounts to what Hegel (1971) called "objective spirit"—the spirit of a political community manifested in a public and objective form.[15]

This view is, to say the least, out of step with contemporary American antipathy to government and foreign to the current conventional wisdom about the evils of litigation and litigiousness. We most often think of law as a network of constraints on private conduct, undoubtedly necessary given the refractoriness of human nature, but hardly desirable. Oliver Wendell Holmes wrote in *The Common Law* that the "cumbrous and expensive machinery [of the law] ought not to be set in motion unless some clear benefit is to be derived from disturbing the *status quo*. State interference is an evil, where it cannot be shown to be a good" (1963, p. 77). Viewed from this characteristically proprivate-sector standpoint, the idea of the law as a source of meaning and value for the community is undoubtedly strange.

It is less strange, of course, for constitutional lawyers, since the Bill of Rights seems to many people to represent our deepest public values. Moreover, the view is hardly a historical novelty: it is, after all, the driving spirit behind the Hebrew Bible. The Sinai Covenant, by which God established the Children of Israel as "His people" (Deuteronomy 29:13), centers around the giving and accepting of the law: "If you obey my voice and keep my covenant, you shall be my treasured possession out of all the peoples" (Exodus 19:5). The crucial sequence of events narrated in the Bible—enslavement by the Egyptians, liberation by the hand of God, wandering in the wilderness to educate the former slaves to the spirit of freedom, and finally the giving and accepting of the law, which was identical to creating the Israelites as a distinct nation—offers a paradigm of politics. As Michael Walzer (1985) observes:

Since late medieval or early modern times, there has existed in the West a characteristic way of thinking about political change, a pattern that we commonly
impose upon events, a story that we repeat to one another. The story has
roughly this form: oppression, liberation, social contract, political struggle, new
society (danger of restoration). We call the whole process *revolutionary*. . . .
This isn't a story told everywhere; it isn't a universal pattern; it belongs to
the West, . . . and its source, its original version, is the Exodus of Israel from
Egypt (p. 133).

Significantly, Walzer—who argues that the Exodus story has been a perpetual
inspiration for political revolutionaries—omits from his description of the pattern the feature that I most wish to stress: lawmaking. This feature belongs in
the sequence between "political struggle" and "new society." The sequence,
therefore, should be oppression, liberation, social contract, political struggle,
lawmaking, new society. Lawmaking is in one sense the antithesis of revolutionary politics, which is, no doubt, why Walzer overlooks it. Without lawmaking no new society will emerge, only a paramilitary rump government. In
this respect, Walzer's account is untrue to the actual genius of the Hebrew
Bible's implicit political theory, which revolves around the law. The Sabbath
prayers refer to the Torah as the Tree of Life, and indeed the law turned out to
be the condition of survival for Diaspora Jews—a source of collective life and
hardly a mere system of expectation enhancement and constraint on private initiative. Historian Paul Johnson (1987) accurately describes the Jewish identification of collective life with the preservation and elaboration of the law as a
"great enterprise in social metaphysics." He reflects: "Having lost the Kingdom
of Israel, the Jews turned the Torah into a fortress of the mind and spirit, in
which they could dwell in safety and even in content" (p. 149).

Of course, the Hebraic exaltation of law comprises only one strand of the
experience of law in America's religious culture. America is a Christian, not a
Jewish culture, and Christianity, unlike Judaism, is quite ambivalent about the
value of law. It is at its most antagonistic and antinomian in Galatians, where
St. Paul writes, "Christ redeemed us from the curse of the law" (3:13), and
again, "before faith came, we were imprisoned and guarded under the law until
faith would be revealed. Therefore the law was our disciplinarian until Christ
came, so that we might be justified by faith. But now that faith has come, we
are no longer under a custodian" (3:23–25). To Paul, the law is a source of con-
finement, not of life; the only law he honors is the law of love and not of the
courts: "For the whole law is summed up in a single commandment, 'You shall
love your neighbor as yourself'" (5:14).

Just as the Hebrew Bible inspires the view of the law as a constitutive aspect
of communal life, texts such as the letters of St. Paul inspire the call to resolve
disputes through reconciliation rather than legalism. These Christian scriptures
are *ur*-texts of the prosettlement, ADR, movement.[16] Yet Christianity is not
entirely hostile to the law, as the Sermon on the Mount makes clear: "Do not

think that I have come to abolish the law or the prophets; I have come not to abolish but to fulfill. For truly, I tell you, until heaven and earth pass away, not one letter, not one stroke of a letter, will pass from the law until all is accomplished" (Matthew 5:17–18). Thus at least one strand of Christianity accords with the Hebraic exaltation of the law, though perhaps not with the Hebraic identification of the Torah as the objective spirit of the community.

These theological reflections should remind us that the idea of law's constitutive as well as instrumental value is hardly a theorist's innovation. We may elaborate on this idea, an important one for Fiss's argument, by turning from theology to secular political theory, from Jerusalem to Athens.

Unfortunately, Fiss (1984) develops his argument in what appears to me a somewhat misleading way, one that allows readers to underestimate its strength. "Against Settlement" belongs to a series of articles in which Fiss distinguishes between two very different models of adjudication: adjudication as dispute resolution and adjudication as structural transformation (see Fiss, 1979, 1982a, 1985b). Dispute resolution, he explains, presupposes two neighbors of roughly equal capacity (perhaps the mythical Coasean farmer and rancher, or the cowboys and the farmers in *Oklahoma!*) quarreling in a state of nature and turning to a third party as an alternative to shooting irons (Fiss, 1984). It is our addiction to the dispute resolution picture, Fiss believes, that underlies the drive to settlement.

However, we do not live in the world portrayed by the dispute resolution model. Rather, our lives and fortunes are everywhere mediated by large, bureaucratic institutions—not only government bureaucracies, but corporations, HMOs, schools, and unions. When these institutions become oppressive, we need structural transformations and not stopgap dispute resolution, which falsely presupposes disputants of roughly equal bargaining power. In Fiss's view, adjudication as structural transformation—exemplified by the class action suit to desegregate a school district—is a more important paradigm of what adjudication means in the modern world (Fiss, 1979). Fiss, one should remember, is an expert on the injunctive process, particularly the civil rights injunction (Fiss, 1978; Fiss and Rendleman, 1984). Haunting his opposition to settlements is an unspoken question: *Where would we be if* Brown v. Board of Education *had settled quietly out of court?*

The problem with posing the argument this way is that it narrows and excessively marginalizes the constitutive role of adjudication. Class action lawsuits are rare and are becoming rarer.[17] Class actions for structural transformation injunctions are rarer still, not only because the federal judiciary has become hostile to such forms of judicial activism, but also because of the difficulties of financing such litigation.[18] More generally, in cases in which statutory attorneys' fees are unavailable, parties and attorneys will be overwhelmingly likely to monetize disputes rather than to seek other forms of relief. Plaintiffs need a *res* to compensate their attorneys, attorneys need a *res* to get paid by their clients, and defendants faced with the alternative of paying money or transforming their own structure will be very likely to opt for the less intrusive option of paying monetary damages.[19] Nowadays, the most important class actions, whose settlements most need examination, are mass torts, which remain a prominent part of the docket, rather than structural transformation suits.[20]

In response to the objection that structural transformation suits compose only a tiny part of the universe of litigation, Fiss (1984) argues that the importance of structural transformation suits more than compensates for their infrequency. He argues as well that even nonstructural transformation suits can have public significance. Yet I do not believe that he has fully explained the philosophical basis of that significance, and the declining salience of structural transformation suits makes his argument against settlements seem somewhat anachronistic.[21] As a result, he has been understood as focusing exclusively on public law litigation, rather than as aiming to call into question the meaningfulness of the public/private distinction. For this reason, the argument that follows is only partly Fissian in spirit, and hardly at all in detail. It aims to make explicit the implicit philosophical premises of Fiss's argument.

Let us first consider two "pure" accounts of the legitimacy of government and of the judicial role. The first, sympathetic with the Holmes passage quoted earlier and the dispute resolution picture, is the familiar view that human freedom is best realized in settings free from governmental interference—the "private realm," which ambiguously includes both intimate relationships (the private as the personal) and market transactions (the private as "the private sector"). On this view, because of government's inevitable tendency to invade and to interfere with privacy, the public sector is bound to prove an impediment to human freedom. Government is nevertheless necessary to solve certain otherwise intractable problems. It defends against external enemies and keeps the internal peace by punishing wrongdoers, protecting rights, and resolving disputes. In addition, government provides some public goods, such as highways or legal precedents.

Let us call this account the "problem-solving conception."[22] Its essential features are three: (1) it identifies "public" with "governmental" and "private" with "intimate or market relationships"; (2) it locates human freedom in the private sphere, and hence mistrusts governmental intervention; and (3) it understands the functions of government in wholly pragmatic terms, as interventions meant to solve problems within civil society that civil society cannot solve on its own. Thus, one can invoke this conception to defend the activist state, but that defense will be couched entirely in instrumental terms. The problem-solving conception is, I think it is safe to say, the dominant version of state legitimacy in contemporary America. Political discussion in today's Congress and mass media revolves largely around the question of whether government or private initiative is better able to solve our national problems. The idea that government might have some purpose other than competing with the private sector to build better mousetraps seems entirely absent from contemporary debates between liberals and conservatives, Democrats and Republicans.

At the other extreme lies what I shall call the "public-life conception," which derives from the political thought of the ancient world and has enjoyed a periodic revival from Machiavelli to Rousseau to contemporary civic republicans. The best known modern defender of the public-life conception is Hannah Arendt (1958). For the ancient Greeks, Arendt tells us, active participation in political life constituted the highest human good, the kind of fulfillment that distinguishes us from the beasts. Only political action in the "public space" can redeem our lives from the futility born of the knowledge that we will soon be gone from the world. Far from "the private sector" providing a temple of individual liberty, dwelling in it amounted in the ancient view to a kind of slavery. Freedom lies in the public realm.[23] Thus, although the public-life conception agrees with the problem-solving conception that "public" has to do with public affairs, the public-life conception locates freedom in the public sphere, not in market relationships or personal intimacy. Moreover, though adherents of the public-life conception do not deny that political action aims to solve problems, they insist that at bottom we engage in action for the sake of exercising our freedom.[24]

The public-life conception underlies contemporary civic republicans' approval of deliberative democracy, by which they mean the public use of reason and deliberation in making public decisions. Civic republicans have, moreover, a distinctive conception of reason, quite different from one they associate (fairly or not) with the problem-solving conception. Problem-solving reason essentially consists in being smart, in getting your sums right, in finding the best means to a given end. Deliberation, on the other hand, consists in being sage rather than smart, in building consensus around ideals rather than getting the right answer, and in discovering worthy ends in addition to efficient means.[25] In different words, the public-life conception contrasts reason-as-deliberation to reason-as-technical-ability.

The public-life and the problem-solving conceptions each offer justification for the legal system and the judicial function. The problem-solving conception of adjudication is broadly Hobbesian in character. Peacekeeping and coordination require governmental monopoly or near-monopoly on the use of violence and coercion. Justifying this monopoly, in turn, requires government to engage in the business of adjudicating disputes, because dispute resolution is effective only when the state's coercive power backs it up. In principle, of course, private arbitrators could carry out adjudication, with the state merely stepping in to enforce the result. However, because the losing party to the private arbitration could contest its legitimacy, the state would eventually have to readjudicate to decide whether to enforce the decision of the private arbitrator. The state inevitably would engage in the adjudication business somewhere down the line. The centralization of legal authority arises from the government's possession of the guns. Best of all, of course, is if it never has to use them, and the wisdom of the judge consists not in issuing the wisest orders, but in facilitating the quickest and most painless resolution of disputes. Rather than debating principles, the judge tries to wrestle the interests of the parties into alignment.

On the public-life conception, by contrast, the values realized in laws are a kind of public morality—objective spirit—and even ostensibly private disputes between apolitical citizens may have a public dimension engaging these values. Because the law is the visible residue of public action (shortly we shall see what this means), the law elevates private disputes into the public realm. Fiss (1982a) defines adjudication as "the process by which the values embodied in an authoritative legal text, such as the Constitution, are given concrete meaning and expression" (p. 46), and he adds that these "public values" are "the values that define a society and give it its identity and inner coherence" (p. 126).[26] As Fiss (1979) explains: "Courts exist to give meaning to our public values, not to resolve disputes" (p. 29). Adjudication, then, is necessary to define and redefine the conditions of the public space. Furthermore, in line with the public-life conception's view of public life as reasoned deliberation, Fiss insists that the unique genius of the courts is their twin requirements of independence and dialogue. Independence guarantees an impartial use of reason, and dialogue guarantees that courts must listen to all comers and reply with reasoned opinions.

If I am right, Fiss's view emerges out of the public-life conception. The difference between the public-life and problem-solving pictures is that for the public-life conception all adjudications are public in significance—they are political, inevitably embroiling the meaning and legitimacy of government. In Fiss's words: "Civil litigation is an institutional arrangement for using state power to bring a recalcitrant reality closer to our chosen ideals" (1984, p. 1089). For the problem-solving conception, by contrast, government gets involved only by unhappy necessity in the private ordering of human affairs. On this view, judicial involvement in a dispute is a necessary evil, whereas for the public-life conception it is an essential good.

Central to Fiss's view of adjudication is the idea that it "gives concrete meaning and expression" to the "values embodied in an authoritative legal text" (1982b, p. 121). I have also suggested that legal texts are the visible residue of political action. Let me relate these ideas to the point mentioned earlier in connection with Walzer that lawmaking occupies a central position in the cycles of politics.

Arendt (1968) argues that political action, as distinct from the activities by which we make a living or leave tangible monuments in the form of art and technology, is the most meaningful activity because it enables people to "show in deed and word, for better or worse, who they are and what they can do" (p. viii). One of Arendt's most important insights is that, at bottom, all politics is revolutionary politics. In politics, nothing is ever settled or final; every political victory will be denied or evaded by those who dislike it.[27] Spin doctors minister to the body politic, and in politics they are the only doctors there are. Arendt (1972) acutely observes that lying is natural in politics: the same faculty of imagination that allows human beings to envision something new, and thereby enter the realm of political action, allows us to dissemble what we know. Force and violence are likewise intrinsic to politics. If every political achievement begins to be denied and undone as soon as it has happened, those who particicipate in politics may be compelled to seek definitive victory through force of arms. It is in this sense that war is politics by other means.

Even apart from dishonesty, every political event is subject to the vagaries of different participants' interpretations and memories. These recollections are inevitably multiple, inconsistent, self-serving, and themselves political. The realm of political action, Arendt rightly argues, is the realm of human plurality;[28] the existence of many people and many peoples makes politics possible and inevitable. It likewise makes disagreement, misrepresentation, and contestation inevitable. If revolution means the undoing of political equilibrium, then all politics is revolutionary because the status quo is always up for grabs.

However, like Walzer (1985), Arendt's political theory strikingly and systematically neglects the law.[29] She should have said: *without law* all politics is revolutionary politics. Law is the necessary counterpoise to the exhilarating but also unbearable unsettledness of politics. As John Finnis (1980) observes, the basic technique by which law orders human affairs consists in "the treating of (usually datable) past acts . . . as giving, *now,* sufficient and exclusionary reason for acting in a way *then* 'provided for'" (p. 269). Where politics moves continuously, law moves in discrete steps: a statute or the enunciation of a legal rule by a court generates a provisional resting point—provisional, because political forces can repeal a statute or undo a legal rule, but a resting point nonetheless, because until that happens, codifying a decision in law or judicial precedent brings the political controversy to a close. Law is a means of channeling and controlling the primordial energy of politics by insisting that some political actions can achieve victories that last over time, that form resting points or new baselines in the never-ending whirlwind of human affairs (Luban, 1994a).

It is worth reflecting on the dynamics of lawmaking, which may be captured in a simple formula: contestation, compromise, codification. A political struggle—within a legislature, for example—results in a compromise. The parties agree on terms that give neither of them a decisive victory. They proceed to write their compromise in the form of laws, which contain qualifications that are concessions to the other side and formulas that are mutually acceptable because they are ambiguous, allowing all sides to save face.

Eventually, however, the strains of social life highlight the weak points in the law, the fault-lines in the compromise. Problem situations arise that the legislators either never contemplated or deliberately ignored in the process of compromise and codification. Many of these controversies end up in court. If they reach adjudication, the judge will readdress, elaborate, and explain what the legislators purposefully left unsettled. It is in this sense that adjudication is "the process by which the values embodied in an authoritative legal text . . . are given concrete meaning and expression" (Fiss, 1982a, p. 121).

Often, the judge's resolution of a legal problem—for example, choosing between two inconsistent but reasonable interpretations of statutory language— will unravel a past political compromise. Part of the judicial craft consists in unraveling as little as possible in addressing a case. Every judicial interpretation may let the political genie back out of the bottle, and so adjudication becomes a Janus-faced affair: when a judge enunciates a rule, she may be simultaneously settling a new political problem and reopening an old one. But that is no cause for regret: it is an essential part of the dynamics of a healthy polity.

In adjudication, the law—the residue of political action—receives elaboration and reasoned reconsideration in the light of subsequent cases and controversies that have revealed its weak points. This process is as much a part of political vitality as free elections and legislative debate. Adjudication provides occasions for law, and therefore the politics it codifies, to assume tangible form. Take away those occasions and an essential dimension of human experience, political action, will either be extinguished or else degenerate into interminable and unresolved conflict.[30]

At this point, the reader may object that the view presented here is completely perverse. Instead of treating adjudication as a social service that the state provides disputing parties to keep the peace, the public-life conception treats disputing parties as little more than convenient occasions for the law to work itself pure. This conception seemingly regards adjudication as a kind of spiritual exercise performed by the brooding omnipresence in the sky, the better to contemplate itself in its majesty. It makes people the tools of the law, rather than the other way around.

This objection would be well taken only if parties were forced to litigate. Because they are not, there is nothing wrong with using their resort to the courts as an occasion for improving the law. Parties still get their dispute adjudicated, as at least one of them requested. At the same time, however, the litigants serve as nerve endings registering the aches and pains of the body politic, which the court attempts to treat by refining the law. Using litigants as stimuli for refining the law is a legitimate public interest in the literal sense of the term: the public is interested in learning the practical implications of past political choices and the values they embody. The law is a self-portrait of our politics, and adjudication is at once the interpretation and the refinement of the portrait.

The standard objection to such accounts questions the propriety of judges telling us what our values mean. Without entering into the well traveled and muddy channels of debate over the countermajoritarian difficulty, a common-sense reply to the objection exists. The legitimacy for this enterprise of judicial interpretation is simply that an educated jurist, insulated from immediate political pressures, impartial between the litigants, and required to listen to both sides seems as good a candidate as any to give concrete meaning and expression to the values embodied in an authoritative legal text.[31]

Is the public-life conception of adjudication inconsistent with the case or controversy requirement of Article III? In the most famous of all attacks on judicial activism, James Bradley Thayer (1893) argued that, if judges were meant to be originative lawmakers, "they would not have been allowed merely . . . incidental and postponed control. They would have been let in . . . to a revision of the laws before they began to operate" (p. 136). But in fact, the case or controversy requirement is perfectly intelligible on the public-life conception. Absent a case or controversy, a "court of revision" would simply be guessing where the ambiguities in law stand in need of elaboration and interpretation. The case or controversy requirement functions not as an intrinsic devaluation of judicial power or authority, but as a filter ensuring that scarce judicial resources are expended only where needed.

What of cases in which no legal issue is at stake and the purpose of the trial is only to ascertain facts in dispute? Even here, there is often virtue to a public and authoritative determination of facts. The virtue is partly instrumental: a judicial finding of fact is a public good like a precedent, because it can play a role in subsequent litigation. But here, as in the case of adjudication of legal issues, an intrinsic public interest may be satisfied by a public and authoritative finding of fact. Consider the extraordinary importance that citizens of post-tyrannical regimes find in "truth commissions" that investigate past human rights abuses even when an amnesty removes the practical point of the investigation. On the view of adjudication elaborated here, trials are more low-key and routinized "truth commission" inquests.

Moreover, there is an obvious connection between truth and legal justice: if legal justice arises from applying law to facts, it presupposes accurate facts. To the extent that out-of-court settlements are based on bargaining power and negotiation skills, facts lose their importance to the outcome, and the outcome will resemble legal justice only coincidentally.[32]

At this point, we can see why Fiss finds nothing to celebrate in settlements. When a case settles, it does so on terms agreeable to its parties, but those terms are not necessarily illuminating to the law or to the public. Indeed, those terms may be harmful to the public. Instead of reasoned reconsideration of the law, we often find little more than a bare announcement of how much money changed hands (often accompanied by a disclaimer of actual liability)—unless the settlement is sealed, in which case we don't even find that out. It is true that settlement information has some precedential value: both plaintiffs' lawyers and defense lawyers share information about settlements to evaluate cases for future settlements. However, settlement information offers no reasons or reasoning, nothing to feed or provoke further argument. The relationship between settlements and judgments is like the relationship between a signal (such as a cry of unhappiness) and an explanation (such as a description of why I am unhappy). Both reveal information, but only the latter provides a basis for further conversation. A world without adjudication would be a world without public conversation about the strains of commitment that the law imposes.

Notes

1.   A LEXIS search reveals that Fiss's article has been cited in over two hundred law review articles. Understandably, given Fiss's polemical aim to denounce the received judicial wisdom that settlement is vastly preferable to adjudication, the article has appeared a bare half-dozen times in reported judicial opinions.

2. See Galanter and Cahill (1994), challenging the idea that settlements are intrinsically desirable, and Sarokin (1986), arguing that despite expediency, settlement may encourage future disputes and that judicial involvement in settlements compromises perception and function of courts.

3. This article complements and elaborates on two earlier efforts: Luban (1985), explaining fairness in negotiation, and Luban (1989), discussing criteria for determining justice of alternative dispute resolution (ADR).

   A point of terminology: we often use the words *litigate* and *litigation* to refer to trials, but because only a minority of cases are tried, this usage is careless. I will use *litigation* and its cognates to refer generically to the processes begun when a lawsuit is filed. In my parlance, then, a lawyer who settles a case has litigated it just as much as a lawyer who goes to trial. I will use the words *adjudicate* or *adjudication* to refer to trial, though this too is careless usage because many cases are resolved after some judicial decision (for example, a summary judgment or a ruling on a significant motion) that is not a full-dress trial.

4. I am extrapolating freely from Fiss's own writing, and only I am responsible for whatever stupidities emerge. Fiss does not raise arguments of the first, instrumental category, and the arguments of the second category that I draw from his work are stated here in a starker, more polarized form than in Fiss's essay. These reflections take the form of very free variations on a theme from Fiss.

5. This argument overlooks the possibility that the parties to the dispute might themselves be future litigants with an interest in creating precedent and regularity. This will not be true in many cases, however, so it is not too farfetched to neglect this effect.

6. Part of the attractiveness of settlement is that it ends disputes, and hence reestablishes order more quickly and less disruptively than adjudication.

7. I have argued, in sympathy with Fiss, for the priority of justice over peace. See Luban (1994a).

8. Yeazell (1994) has noted that in the half-century between the enactment of the Federal Rules of Civil Procedure and 1990, the rate of trials per filed civil cases dropped by four-fifths, from 19.9 percent of filings to 4.3 percent.

9. Whether enhanced attorney skills would lead to juster trials of course turns on one's faith in adversarial advocacy's producing right outcomes rather than obfuscation.

10. Rule 5.6(b) of the Model Rules of Professional Conduct (1983) prohibits settlements that restrict an attorney's right to practice, as does DR 2–108(B) of the Model Code of Professional Responsibility (1981).

11. See Brodeur (1985), describing lawyer buyout in early asbestos settlement; Cherniack (1986), describing lawyer buyout in the 1930s industrial accident; Mintz (1985), describing lawyer buyout in Dalkon Shield litigation; and Stern (1977), describing lawyer buyout in a 1970s class action and referring to it as "fairly standard practice." See also Galanter (1990).

12. It is possible to evade this rule. In their commentary on Model Rule 5.6(b), Hazard and Hodes (1994) point out that it is legal for a client who wishes to buy out the opposing lawyer to wait until the case is over and then retain that lawyer's services, ostensibly for future litigation on the same subject, but actually to conflict the lawyer out of future adverse representations.

    The evidence that the ABA *Code of Professional Responsibility* meant to prohibit lawyer buyout is unmistakable: the first draft of DR 2–108(B) specifically allowed a lawyer to "enter into an agreement not to accept any other representation arising out of a transaction or event embraced in the subject matter of controversy or suit thus settled," but this permission to engage in lawyer buyout was deleted in the final draft. For this legislative history, see American Bar Foundation (1979).

13. See, for example, Model Rules of Professional Conduct (1983): Rule 1.2(a), the attorney shall abide by the client's wishes and decisions; Rule 1.3, the attorney shall represent the client with reasonable diligence; and Rule 1.7(b), the conflict of interest provision. See also Model Code of Professional Responsibility (1981): EC 2–27, the attorney should represent the client despite the client's unpopularity or adverse reaction from the community; EC 2–28, the attorney should not decline representation to avoid conflict with judges, other attorneys, or others; EC 2–29, the appointed attorney shall not seek to avoid representing the client because of personal repugnance to the client or case; DR 5–101(A), except with full disclosure and consent, the attorney shall not accept a prospective client if the attorney's own interest might affect representation; DR 5–105(A), the attorney shall not accept a prospective client if representation would adversely affect a current client; and DR 7–101(A), zealous representation of client provision.

14. Robel (1993) argues that increasing the recourse of litigants to private justice undermines the authority of federal courts.

15. Hegel (1971) argues that "the constitution presupposes that consciousness of the collective spirit, and conversely that spirit presupposes the constitution: for the actual spirit only has a definite consciousness of its principles, in so far as it has them actually existent before it" (p. 268).

16. McThenia and Shaffer (1985) argue: "The religious tradition seeks not *resolution* (which connotes the sort of doctrinal integrity in the law that seems to us to be Fiss's highest priority) but reconciliation of brother to brother, sister to sister,

sister to brother, child to parent, neighbor to neighbor, buyer to seller, defendant to plaintiff, *and judge to both.*" See also Fiss (1985a), a rejoinder to McThenia and Shaffer.

17. The Administrative Office of the United States Courts began keeping data on the incidence of class actions in 1977 in its Annual Report. Between 1977 and 1990, the total annual number of civil filings in U.S. district courts increased by 67 percent, while the number of class actions decreased by 71 percent. In 1977, class actions represented 2.4 percent of the civil docket, whereas in 1990 they represented only .42 percent.

18. This is in part because the Supreme Court has made it increasingly difficult for civil rights attorneys to recover attorneys' fees. See, for example, *Evans* v. *Jeff D.*, 475 U.S. 717 (1986), holding that no violation of section 1988 results from negotiation of settlement in section 1983 action that excludes attorneys' fees; North *Carolina Department of Transportation* v. *Crest Street Community Council, Inc.* (1986), holding that the prevailing party in federal administrative proceeding under Title VI has no right to attorneys' fees under section 1988 when recovery is sought in federal action filed solely to recover such fees; *Webb* v. *Board of Education of Dyer County, Tennessee* (1985), holding that the prevailing party in section 1983 action was not automatically entitled to section 1988 attorneys' fees for services performed in connection with nonmandatory state administrative proceedings. See generally Silver (1989).

Between 1977 and 1990, the number of civil rights class actions decreased by 91 percent. Civil rights class actions include the paradigmatic structural reform cases. In 1977, civil rights class actions represented 1.4 percent of the civil docket, while in 1990 they represented only .08 percent.

19. The drive to monetize cases affects settlements as well as adjudication. Studies have shown that "where the claimant is represented by a lawyer who is paid a portion of the recovery, there is a tendency to avoid outcomes (such as reinstatement, agreement to desist, etc.) that do not create a fund of cash out of which the lawyer can be paid." Galanter and Cahill (1994), summarizing Kritzer (1987). See also McEwen and Maiman (1981), who observe that most mediated settlements in Maine small claims court focus on money to exclusion of other issues.

20. It is difficult to show quantitatively that mass torts have become more salient: quantitative data such as those included in the Annual Reports do not break out mass torts as a separate category. Their salience seems undeniable, however: recent years have witnessed headline-grabbing suits over such products as Agent Orange, Benedectin, silicone gel breast implants, asbestos, DES, and Dalkon Shields, and these have involved hundreds of thousands, perhaps millions, of plaintiff class members.

21. Fiss (1984) offers an additional argument that applies to lawsuits having nothing to do with structural transformation. He argues that the rush to settlement undermines justice because it permits cases to be decided by a contest of brute bargaining power. Disparities in wealth imply disparities in bargaining power. This is undoubtedly true, but there is little reason to believe that adjudication offers a

comparative advantage. Fiss counts on the judge to overcome wealth-based disparities in the "quality of presentation" at trial. However, wealthier parties can invest more resources in factual investigation and legal research, and these factors, rather than "quality of presentation," generally determine the outcome of a trial. Moreover, the expenses and delays involved in taking a case through trial can devour whatever benefit the poorer litigant receives from it. The all-or-nothing character of adjudication exposes poorer litigants to the risks and anxieties that motivated Hand's gloomy comparison of lawsuits with sickness and death. These risks and anxieties themselves amount to a kind of penalty for entering the courtroom, a penalty that may annul whatever gains in justice the courtroom provides.

22. I choose this term in partial echo of the subtitle of Menkel-Meadow's important article "Toward Another View of Legal Negotiation: The Structure of Problem Solving" (1984). Menkel-Meadow views successful negotiation as an effort to move beyond the bargaining positions of parties to their underlying needs in order to craft solutions that respond to the parties' problems. This view of the dispute resolution process informs Menkel-Meadow's support of ADR, which, when properly done, will aim to solve the disputants' underlying problems. I am generalizing this view of the role of the neutral party in ADR to an overall account of political legitimacy.

23. Arendt (1958) argues that "the distinction between private and public coincides with the opposition of necessity and freedom" (p. 73).

24. Arendt (1958) distinguishes between acting *in order to* accomplish a task and acting *for the sake of* the intrinsic meaningfulness of the activity. Arendt (1965) interpreted the American Revolution and the Constitution along the lines of the public-life conception, stressing that the founders possessed a notion of "public happiness" not far removed from the ancient conception of positive freedom, though—she believed—they were untrue to their own experience of politics and revolution when they situated the "pursuit of happiness" in the private rather than the public realm.

This is perhaps a good place for a caveat. It is tempting to view the problem-solving conception as "liberalism," and the public-life conception as something alien to the liberal tradition. But this view is untrue to the historical complexity of these ideas, to the fact that both conceptions have informed the liberal tradition. Thus, for example, a paradigmatic liberal such as Louis Brandeis derived his progressive hostility to big business as well as his classical-liberal hostility to big government from his view that small units of public and private enterprise are necessary to recapture the positive freedom of the Greek polis. See Strum (1984).

25. For a recent elaboration of this notion, see Kronman (1993), who terms this not "reason" but "practical wisdom."

26. This view is very similar to the theory advanced by Dworkin (1986).

27. Consider the fact that the 104th Congress, in which the majority party in the House of Representatives switched for the first time in forty years, almost immediately began reconsidering a crime bill that its predecessor had enacted after prolonged negotiations a year before.

28. In Arendt's words (1958), "Action, the only activity that goes on directly between men without the intermediary of things or matter, corresponds to the human condition of plurality, to the fact that men, not Man, live on the earth and inhabit the world. While all aspects of the human condition are somehow related to politics, this plurality is specifically *the* condition . . . of all political life" (p. 7).

29. Here and throughout the subsequent paragraphs I am indebted to Kahn (1995).

30. In Fiss's words (1984), "The purpose of adjudication . . . is not to maximize the ends of private parties, nor simply to secure the peace, but to explicate and give force to the values embodied in authoritative texts such as the Constitution and statutes: to interpret those values and to bring reality into accord with them."

31. This is not far from Fiss's answer in his 1979 article or in his 1982b article. I should add that I am not greatly troubled by the countermajoritarian difficulty. See Luban (1994b).

32. See Coleman and Silver (1986), who argue that settlements usually do not give parties what they deserve under law, and Luban (1989), who argues that bargaining based on threat advantage does not provide appropriate criteria for evaluating justice of settlements and that litigants find themselves enmeshed in the dilemma of compromise because of "all-or-nothing" character of litigation. I agree with Professor Menkel-Meadow (1995), however, that legal justice may not be the same as justice. Her point that settlements may be necessary to achieve justice, when justice and legal justice part ways, is a valid objection to the public-life conception.

References

American Bar Foundation. *Annotated Code of Professional Responsibility.* Chicago: American Bar Association, 1979.

Arendt, H. *The Human Condition.* Chicago: University of Chicago Press, 1958.

Arendt, H. *On Revolution.* New York: Viking Press, 1965.

Arendt, H. *Men in Dark Times.* New York: Harcourt, Brace & World, 1968.

Arendt, H. "Lying in Politics." In H. Arendt (ed.), *Crises of the Republic.* New York: Harcourt Brace Jovanovich, 1972.

Brodeur, P. *Outrageous Misconduct: The Asbestos Industry on Trial.* New York: Pantheon Books, 1985.

Cherniack, M. *The Hawk's Nest Incident: America's Worst Industrial Disaster.* New Haven, Conn.: Yale University Press, 1986.

Coleman, J., and Silver, C. "Justice in Settlements." *Social Philosophy and Policy,* 1986, *4*, 102.

Dworkin, R. *Law's Empire.* Cambridge, Mass.: Belknap Press of Harvard University Press, 1986.

Evans v. *Jeff D.* 475 U.S. 717 (1986).

Finnis, J. *Natural Law and Natural Rights.* Oxford: Clarendon Press; New York: Oxford University Press, 1980.

Fiss, O. M. *The Civil Rights Injunction*. Bloomington: Indiana University Press, 1978.

Fiss, O. M. "The Supreme Court 1978 Term—Foreword: The Forms of Justice." *Harvard Law Review*, 1979, *93*, 29.

Fiss, O. M. "The Social and Political Foundations of Adjudication." *Law and Human Behavior*, 1982a, *6*, 121–128.

Fiss, O. M. "Objectivity and Interpretation." *Stanford Law Review*, 1982b, *34*, 739–763.

Fiss, O. M. "Against Settlement." *Yale Law Journal*, 1984, *93*, 1073–1090.

Fiss, O. M. "Out of Eden." *Yale Law Journal*, 1985a, *94*, 1669–1673.

Fiss, O. M. "Two Models of Adjudication." In R. Goldwin and W. Schambra (eds.), *How Does the Constitution Secure Rights?* Washington, D.C.: American Enterprise Institute for Public Policy Research, 1985b.

Fiss, O. M., and Rendleman, D. *Injunctions* (2nd ed.). Nieola, N.Y.: Foundation Press, 1984.

Galanter, M. "A Note on Lawyer Buyout." Unpublished manuscript, 1990.

Galanter, M., and Cahill, M. "'Most Cases Settle': Judicial Promotion and Regulation of Settlements." *Stanford Law Review*, 1994, *46*, 1339–1391.

Gross, S. R., and Syverud, K. D. "Getting to No: A Study of Settlement Negotiations and the Selection of Cases for Trial." *Michigan Law Review*, 1991, *90*, 319–393.

Hand, L. *Lectures on Legal Topics*. 1926.

Hazard, G. C., Jr., and Hodes, W. W. *The Law of Lawyering: A Handbook on the Model Rules of Professional Conduct*. Englewood Clifs, N.J.: Prentice Hall Law & Business, 1994.

Hegel, G.W.F. *Hegel's Philosophy of Mind* (W. Wallace, trans.). Oxford: Clarendon Press, 1971.

Holmes, O. W., Jr. *The Common Law* (M. D. Howe, ed.). Boston: Little, Brown, 1963. (Originally published 1881.)

Johnson, P. *A History of the Jews*. New York: Harper & Row, 1987.

Kahn, P. *"Marbury* and Modernity." Unpublished manuscript, 1995.

Kritzer, H. M. "Fee Arrangements and Negotiation." *Law and Society Review*, 1987, *21*, 341–348.

Kronman, A. T. *The Lost Lawyer: Failing Ideals of the Legal Profession*. Cambridge, Mass.: Belknap Press of Harvard University Press, 1993.

Landes, W. M., and Posner, R. A. "Adjudication as a Private Good." *Journal of Legal Studies*, 1978, 235.

Luban, D. "Bargaining and Compromise: Recent Work on Negotiation and Informal Justice." *Philosophy and Public Affairs*, 1985, *14*, 397–416.

Luban, D. "The Quality of Justice." *Denver University Law Review*, 1989, *66*, 381–417.

Luban, D. *Legal Modernism*. Ann Arbor: University of Michigan Press, 1994a.

Luban, D. "Justice Holmes and the Metaphysics of Judicial Restraint." *Duke Law Journal*, 1994b, *44*, 449–523.

McEwen, C. A., and Maiman, R. J. "Small Claims Mediation in Maine: An Empirical Assessment." *Maine Law Review,* 1981, *33,* 237–268.

McMunigal, K. C. "The Costs of Settlement: The Impact of Scarcity of Adjudication on Litigating Lawyers." *UCLA Law Review,* 1990, *37,* 833–881.

McThenia, A. W., and Shaffer, T. "For Reconciliation." *Yale Law Journal,* 1985, *94,* 1660–1668.

Menkel-Meadow, C. "Toward Another View of Legal Negotiation: The Structure of Problem Solving." *UCLA Law Review,* 1984, *31,* 754–832.

Menkel-Meadow, C. "Whose Dispute Is It Anyway? A Philosophical and Democratic Defense of Settlement (in Some Cases)." *Georgetown Law Journal,* 1995, *83,* 133–148.

Mintz, M. *At Any Cost: Corporate Greed, Women, and the Dalkon Shield.* New York: Pantheon Books, 1985.

North Carolina Department of Transportation v. *Crest Street Community Council, Inc.* 479 U.S. 6 (1986).

Olson, M. *The Logic of Collective Action: Public Goods and the Theory of Groups* (Rev. ed.). Cambridge, Mass.: Harvard University Press, 1971.

Resnik, J. "Failing Faith: Adjudicatory Procedure in Decline." *University of Chicago Law Review,* 1986, *53,* 494–560.

Robel, L. K. "Private Justice and the Federal Bench." *Indiana Law Journal,* 1993, *8.* 891–906.

Sarokin, H. L. "Justice Rushed Is Justice Ruined." *Rutgers Law Review,* 1986, *38,* 431–438.

Silver, M. A. "Evening the Odds: The Case for Attorneys' Fee Awards for Administrative Resolution of Title VI and Title VII Disputes." *North Carolina Law Review,* 1989, *67,* 379–433.

Stern, M. *The Buffalo Creek Disaster.* New York: Vintage Books, 1977.

Strum, P. *Louis D. Brandeis: Justice for the People.* Cambridge, Mass.: Harvard University Press, 1984.

Thayer, J. B. "The Origin and Scope of the American Doctrine of Constitutional Law." *Harvard Law Review,* 1893, *7,* 129, 136.

Walzer, M. *Exodus and Revolution.* New York: Basic Books, 1985.

Webb v. *Board of Education of Dyer County, Tennessee.* 471 U.S. 234, 243 (1985).

Yeazell, S. C. "The Misunderstood Consequences of Modern Civil Process." *Wisconsin Law Review,* 1994, *1994,* 631–678.

CHAPTER THIRTY

Public Access to Private Settlements

Carrie Menkel-Meadow

Legal policy has long protected the confidentiality of negotiations designed to produce settlements. Yet a growing number of legal jurisdictions have been moving in the opposite direction—permitting, and in some cases mandating, disclosure of settlements.

The context is an ever-expanding movement to require the disclosure of settlements dealing with public health and safety, hazards, public officials, public bodies, or, most broadly, public issues. To that end, more and more states are passing new laws requiring disclosure of settlements, or revising their rules of procedure to modify common practices involving confidentiality of discovery, protective orders and sealing of litigation records. Inevitably, policies allowing public access to settlements where there is a public interest will clash with long-standing policies that encourage settlement by providing both an atmosphere for candid discussion and the protection of a confidential or sealed settlement.

WHO WANTS ACCESS?

A number of different interest groups, each with its own rationale, favor public disclosure of settlements. Public interest organizations seek both information about and disclosure of public harms, ranging from environmental problems, to products liability, to discrimination cases. Plaintiffs' lawyers want to share information in cases involving multiple injuries or potential harms and prevent the "first" plaintiff from securing a large settlement (in return for secrecy promises) at the expense of other injured victims. Elected and other public officials (including some judges and regulatory officials) believe that certain issues should almost always be aired in the public eye. The media seek to report disputes with public implications, ranging from alleged corruption of public or private officials to public health and safety, products liability, antitrust, patent infringements, and individual injuries.

Press attempts to intervene as interested third parties and gain access to discovery or settlement proceedings pose starkly the question of what is public and what is private as in *Cincinnati Gas & Electric Co.* v. *General Electric* (1988). Do disputes between private individuals or organizations become public at a particular stage in the litigation process, such as the time of filing a lawsuit, conducting discovery, arguing a motion, participating in a summary jury trial, or mandatory settlement conference? Of what relevance is the location of the proceeding. If the parties attend an early neutral evaluation conference at the court's request, for example, is that proceeding public even if it is held in a private law office (as is the case in the Northern District of California and a growing number of other federal jurisdictions)? Or, as some argue, is it the nature or subject matter of the dispute (public health and safety, hazards or injuries to the public, disputes involving public officials or agencies) that renders it ripe for public disclosure regardless of the timing or location of the proceeding?

HOW AND WHY IS PUBLIC ACCESS MANDATED?

Both the media and public interest groups have argued that a constitutional right to know, derived from the First Amendment and other common law principles, provides a public right of access to any dispute that uses public institutions or fora, such as the courts. Another rationale is that there should be exceptions to the usual presumptions in favor of confidentiality when the public may be affected. Such exceptions must apply, for example, in cases involving utility rate setting, hazardous waste sites, products liability, and class actions in securities or discrimination matters. The claims here are that the public has the right to know if products are defective and likely to hurt them or that they live near hazardous waste sites or that the cost of consuming resources may rise. Although styled as individual lawsuits, the claims go, these are issues that affect us all. Some people who favor access perceive the courts as another instrument of public legal regulation, even if the parties to a given case are simply seeking to resolve their private dispute.

Efforts to make public the conduct of litigation and negotiations have been applied to discovery (challenging protective orders) and settlements (challenging the sealing of specific settlements or whole court files). For the most part, courts have continued to protect some secrecy and confidentiality interests in both the discovery and settlement contexts. They also have preferred to retain a case-by-case approach to protecting the broad scope of discovery and encouraging cooperation in both information disclosure and the settlement of cases, as in *Seattle Times* v. *Rhinehart* (1984; see also Chapter Twenty-Eight, this volume).

When considering challenges to confidentiality, courts look to such factors as whether the common law treats a particular event as public (a trial is; a negotiation discussion is not) or whether particular documents are public records (discovery documents are rarely filed with the courts anymore), or whether there is some important public function (like monitoring of the judicial process) being served. But there are a variety of hybrid situations just waiting for litigation on issues of confidentiality. These may include early neutral evaluation procedures held in private law offices under the court's aegis or mandatory settlement conferences held in courtrooms or judges' chambers.

Case law favoring confidentiality is being challenged in a variety of ways. Some state legislatures have passed statutes mandating disclosure of information and settlements, such as Florida's Sunshine in Litigation Act. In other states, procedural rules have been modified to shift the burdens of presumption away from confidentiality in the seeking of protective orders or sealing of records. Texas, for example, in Rule 76a creates a presumption of openness applied to unfiled discovery documents and settlement agreements that "have a probable adverse effect on public health and safety."

Challenges to settlement agreements can come from disgruntled third parties, renegade parties, the media, and even *sua sponte* from the courts themselves. Some courts have allowed nonparties to an agreement to force disclosure of terms or to force disclosure of private side agreements to publicly entered court orders; examples are *Bank of America* v. *Hotel Rittenhouse Association* (1986) and *Janus Films, Inc.* v. *Miller* (1986). Courts differ greatly in the scrutiny applied to private settlements in our party-initiated litigation system. With class action settlements and desires to make a private settlement an order of the court for enforcement purposes, the imprimatur of the court is clear. In other cases, the role the court plays in facilitating a settlement in pretrial conferences or elsewhere is less clear.

As the movement for openness in litigation expands, we are likely to see legal challenges at every level of the system—legislative, judicial, and administrative—with all of the complexity and conflicting commands that such issues inevitably entail.

STATE LEGISLATION

One of the first state laws to provide for access to agreements is the 1990 Florida Sunshine in Litigation Act, which provides for the full disclosure of any agreement that has the purpose or effect of concealing a public hazard, defined as an "instrumentality . . . device, instrument, person, procedure, product . . . that has caused and is likely to cause injury." The act allows any "substantially affected person, including representatives of the news media," to contest an order, agreement, judgment, or contract that might violate the concealment section. The statute also provides for disclosure of any agreement that has the purpose and effect of concealing a settlement or resolution of any claim or action against the state or any duly constituted government body. There is some attempt to protect trade secrets, if they are not also public hazards.

Other states that have successfully passed similar legislation include Arkansas (preventing secret agreements with governmental agencies), Oregon (preventing secrecy in settlements with governmental agencies or officials "unless specific privacy interests of a private individual outweigh the public's interest in the terms of settlement"), and South Carolina (requiring disclosure of all settlements paid with public monies). In some cases, exceptions are made for trade secrets or other actions that would be protected by other statutes, such as state freedom of information acts.

A number of other states have introduced bills to mandate public disclosure of settlements in cases of environmental hazard, products liability, and financial fraud (California); public hazard; settlements made at the termination of public employment (Colorado); and similar public harms. Some states propose to void all agreements with nondisclosure clauses if they involve government agencies or public hazard (Michigan). Other states have proposed rule changes to the rules of procedure that govern sealing of records (Massachusetts and New York) and the granting of protection orders, often shifting presumptions away from confidentiality and protection toward open disclosure.

During the past few years, most efforts at the state and federal levels to open settlements to public scrutiny have failed (more than twenty states have considered and refused to pass such bills thus far). Often the proposal has involved costly lobbying efforts pitting public interest organizations and the plaintiffs' bar against business interests. Ironically, in some situations, it is the plaintiffs who seek secrecy in settlements and discovery efforts. Legislators are increasingly being caught up in complex efforts to draft for specific exceptions such as individual privacy, job terminations, and medical conditions.

WHAT'S NEXT?

The challenge facing legislatures and courts is how to balance the competing concerns. How can they make some matters accessible to the public when, for instance, there are significant public health, safety, and accountability issues at stake, without at the same time destroying our system's ability to serve parties who seek to resolve their disputes amicably and privately? To the extent that privacy remains one of the reasons lawsuits are settled, some disputants will depart the public courts altogether rather than have their settlement made public. That prospect, already evident in the use of private judging and other private alternative dispute resolution mechanisms, raises questions about the legitimacy of the judicial process. In other cases, settlements will be pushed forward in time, before litigation is instituted. That strategy would preserve secrecy, but with the possible effect of rushing a settlement before an optimal exchange of information.

Those who seek full and open disclosure must also consider what harm is done to "innocent" third parties in the course of discovery or settlement negotiations, and even the occasional harm done to those who benefit from settlements. At a jurisprudential level, those who seek full openness in all cases must justify the transformation of our civil system from a voluntary (at least for plaintiffs), party-initiated system to one that will become literally just another arm of state regulation.

Some assurances of confidentiality and secrecy are often needed to ensure the candor that is required to settle cases on the basis of party needs and interests that go beyond the legally relevant facts in cases and that might be damaging to the parties and others if released. These concerns motivate the many efforts to grant mediators and other third-party intervenors confidentiality, privilege, and immunity. It is ironic that in states like California, competing bills are currently pending to increase confidentiality protections for some mediators, while other proposals seek to open up to greater public scrutiny a wide variety of alternative dispute resolution mechanisms.

Out of these competing concerns, one thing is clear: it is unlikely that one simple rule can govern all situations. Some parties may prefer to leave decisions about confidentiality up to judicial discretion and let the common law system do what it does best: make judgments on a case-by-case basis. Others may aim to legislate with greater precision—where real public harm is demonstrated and revelations of litigation information or settlement are the only or best way to prevent harm.

To improve both the quality and quantity of satisfactory settlements to legal problems, many interests need to be considered and balanced. Complete openness will likely thwart the legal process as much as facilitate it, and bright-line rules about public fora and public issues will not always be easily drawn. We are likely to see a volatile period of legislative and judicial activity in this area. During this confusing period of conflicting legal mandates, consumers and providers of dispute resolution services should continue to draft individualized contract terms to meet the needs of their dispute. They also should be fully cognizant of the legal conditions and restrictions of the jurisdictions in which dispute resolution is being conducted.

References

Bank of America v. *Hotel Rittenhouse Association.* 800 F.2d 339 (3d Cir. 1986), cert. denied, 107 S. Ct. 921 (1987).

Cincinnati Gas & Electric Co. v. *General Electric.* 854 F.2d 900 (6th Cir. 1988).

Janus Films, Inc. v. *Miller.* 801 F.2d 578 (2d Cir. 1986).

Seattle Times v. *Rhinehart.* 467 U.S. 20 (1984).

CHAPTER THIRTY-ONE

Expanding the Ethical Obligations
of the Mediator

Mediator Accountability to Parties Not at the Table

Lawrence Susskind

To whom are mediators (i.e., professional neutrals) accountable? The answer, usually, is "to the parties" with whom they are working. In the parlance of dispute resolution theory, "the parties to a dispute must own the resolution." The case for adherence to this principle is typically framed in strategic terms. Agreements won't be implemented (i.e., they won't be durable) if the parties feel they were strong-armed into accepting something that didn't really meet their needs. They must feel that they (not the neutral) crafted the details of the agreement. They also have to accept the underlying principles that account for the allocation of gains and losses, or, presumably, they won't follow through on what they promised. Thus, mediators are supposed to keep their personal preferences to themselves and focus solely on what the parties at the table say they want and need.

Once the parties sign an agreement, of course, all kinds of obstacles can still emerge to undermine implementation: the context can shift (e.g., the parties' priorities can shift), new information can emerge that causes the parties to reconsider the logic of what they promised, leadership within the various "sides" can change, etc., but if the parties "feel ownership" of what was agreed, the argument goes, the chances of implementation are significantly enhanced. So, success in mediation is typically measured by the extent to which the parties feel their interests have been met.[1]

Mediators usually remind the parties, right before they ask them to initial an agreement, that once they sign, any failure to fulfill their commitments will undermine their reputations in the world at large. This can impose long-term costs on non-compliers, whatever reasons or explanations they may have for such behavior. So, neutrals are supposed to be accountable to the parties, not push their personal views or values, make sure all parties at the table feel ownership of whatever agreement emerges, and highlight the reputational consequences of not living up to negotiated agreements. In real life, however, that's not how it works. Mediators rarely remain indifferent to the terms of emerging agreements, they often argue for or against specific elements of an agreement (in their conversations with the parties) no matter how strongly one or more parties might feel, and they usually make the case for a "package agreement" not just on strategic grounds, but on moral or ethical grounds as well.

Some of the reasons for this disjuncture between theory and practice have to do with the difficulties involved in identifying the relevant stakeholders to a mediated negotiation. Who are the parties to whom the mediator is supposed to be accountable? Only those at the table? What about those whose interests are affected but, for a variety of reasons, are not present during the mediation? In a divorce mediation, the court can review (and reject) a mediated agreement on the grounds that it does not take adequate account of either the interests of one of the parties, the interests of the children, or relevant state law. The parties may "own" the agreement, and the mediator may have deferred to the parties' wishes, but that does not mean that the agreement is automatically acceptable. In such instances, the court may seek to protect one of the parties (who was bullied by the other into giving something away to which they were entitled), the interests of minors who were not at the table, or the interests of the state. So, implementability of a mediated agreement does not depend solely on meeting the interests of the parties at the table.

Even in mediations that are not reviewable in court, this is true. In public dispute mediation, where developers sit with angry neighbors and other interested parties, the product of a mediation can be rejected by other public agencies, legislative bodies, or even media-generated public dialogue (that leads to a referendum). It is not a question of how satisfied the parties at the table were, how accurately they represented the concerns of their "constituents," or how carefully the mediator avoided any effort to shape the substance of the agreement. Rather, since mediated agreements in such contexts are only an approximation of how competing public concerns ought to be balanced, interests beyond those represented at the table must be served or the agreement will be rendered inoperable. That stands the conventional wisdom about implementability hinging on ownership by the parties at the table on its head.

I want to offer several different justifications for holding mediators accountable to interests not at the table. Three, in particular, focus on what might be considered "doing the right thing" not for strategic purposes, but for ethical or moral reasons. The first is what I have dubbed "for reasons of precedent." While many of the circumstances surrounding each mediation are unique, most mediations concern a class of problems or controversies not unlike those that have occurred before and will certainly occur again. And, while one of the supposed advantages of mediation (over adjudication) is that the special circumstances in each situation can be addressed de novo, it is wrong to presume that the outcome of one mediation (whether formally recorded or not) has no impact on subsequent efforts to resolve similar disputes. In fact, I would argue that mediated agreements can have more impact on other informal settlements of similar cases than the results of litigation because the credibility and legitimacy of mediated agreements in which all sides have a chance to ensure that their interests are met are greater than court-imposed resolutions that may well have ignored the particularities of the case. So, mediated agreements set informal precedents. As such, mediators would do well to remind the parties at the table that what they work out will have an impact on others in similar situations.

Thus, mediators should urge the parties to do more than "meet their own interests well." Rather, they should encourage all parties to be sure that they set a positive precedent with regard to meeting the needs of those with similar interests in situations in other times and places. In the same way that a single "representative" in a mediation is supposed to "speak for" a larger "class" of stakeholders, concerns about precedent suggest that representatives may actually speak for a larger class of stakeholders—over time—who are not at the table and don't even know that they are being represented. Once this level of representation is acknowledged, it should be clear that mediators (and parties) have responsibilities that extend beyond the "presenting" situation.

The second reason that mediators should be concerned about the interests of parties not present at the table is what I call "the responsibilities of leadership." When mediation is used as a mechanism to distribute value, decide matters of public policy, or resolve contending claims, the parties should see themselves as leaders who have been tapped to solve difficult problems. They should be encouraged (the way any leader would be) to do the best they can in such situations. Doing their best obviously means avoiding waste, being as creative as possible, and taking account of all relevant information and competent technical advice. In short, it means not settling for a "second best" solution when a better option is within reach. Why does any leader in any situation try to do an excellent job? In part, because they want to be judged favorably by their peers and subordinates. But, also, in many situations, because they accept the responsibilities that leaders are presumed to accept (in exchange for the opportunity to play an important role in some kind of decision-making). I see this, in part, as consistent with accounts of the heroic acts of "everyday citizens" in the aftermath of the World Trade Center attack. Mediators owe it to the parties in any mediation to assist them in meeting the responsibilities that fall to them in the leadership roles they have assumed.

The third justification for mediators to play a more pro-active role in helping to shape "high quality" agreements and not just to go along with whatever the parties want, is the need to "publicize the benefits of mediation" and to educate people about the mediation alternatives that already exist. Every mediator has an obligation to the mediation profession to ensure that each mediation effort is as "successful" as possible. By this I mean that mediation should not only satisfy the interests of the parties at the table, but also seek to produce fairer, more efficient, more stable, and wiser results than would otherwise result from other ways of handling those disagreements.[2]

In the same way that lawyers are "officers of the court" and have certain obligations that extend beyond merely representing the interests of their clients, mediators, too, have a responsibility to help make the case for mediation by ensuring that the outcomes in each instance are as beneficial as possible to all relevant stakeholders. To do this, they may have to push the parties to go beyond the obvious solution. While outcomes unacceptable to the parties at the table cannot be imposed by a mediator, that still leaves a great deal of room for mediators to encourage parties to "maximize joint gains."

There are three moves that mediators (of all kinds) can make that would be consistent with these justifications. First, they can frame the purposes of mediation more broadly than they traditionally do. That is, they can acknowledge their responsibilities to all relevant stakeholders in every oral and written contract they make with their clients. Most mediators have written contracts with their clients most of the time. These usually spell out what is expected of both the mediator and the parties. A clause acknowledging the mediator's responsibility for helping all relevant parties pursue "the highest quality agreement possible" would, in my view, open up the dialogue on the scope of the mediator's responsibilities in the right way. Second, mediators ought to make explicit the fact that they intend to evaluate their own success in the broader terms I am prescribing. While this need not be spelled out in every contract, it seems to me appropriate for mediators to note in their marketing materials and in the reflections they publish about their practice that they have responsibilities that transcend the interests of the parties at the table.

Along these lines, I would urge the mediation profession to make explicit in the codes of ethics that are emerging, that "best practice," in fact, requires mediators to attend to (1) the precedent-setting nature of the agreements they produce, (2) the responsibilities of people in leadership roles to do all that they can to maximize joint gains for all relevant stakeholders, and (3) the reputation of the profession which requires mediators to seek the "highest quality" agreements possible.

Let me try to anticipate some of the criticisms likely to be leveled at these proposals. First, the "traditionalists" will say that mediators undermine their claim to neutrality (and thus, their professional identity) if they inject concerns beyond those expressed by the parties in a mediation process. I obviously disagree. I am not suggesting that mediators try to "represent" the interests of stakeholders who are not present; rather, I am suggesting that they draw the attention of the parties at the table to such concerns (and that they do so for something other than strategic reasons). This would not mean that the mediators are "taking sides." They could still claim that they are non-partisan with regard to the substance of the outcome. On the other hand, they would make it clear that they have a responsibility to ensure that the interests of all relevant stakeholders are given due consideration.

Second, the "relativists" will say that the quality of any mediated agreement is "in the eye of the beholder" and that there are no objective measures to indicate whether one agreement is, in fact, any better than another. So, my effort to argue on behalf of mediation that seeks to maximize joint gains is misconceived. My response is that they are right in one respect: there is no way to develop a single objective measure of the quality of a negotiated agreement. However, that does not negate the fact that agreements can generate greater or less gains for each side (as measured by those parties themselves). So, it would not be that difficult to rate various agreements with regard to the extent to which they maximize joint gains. Again, I am not suggesting that mediators should advocate a particular outcome in each mediation. Rather, I am urging that professional mediators take an "activist" role in seeking to generate as much value as possible for as many parties as possible by managing the consensus-building process with that end in mind.3

Finally, the "anti-professionals" will argue that it is wrong for mediators to act in ways designed specifically to enhance the reputation of their profession. They will point out, first, that a great deal of mediation is done by individuals with process management skills who are not professional mediators. These individuals would have no reason to act on behalf of the profession. That may be true. However, the profession is growing, and I cannot think of any other profession that would encourage its members to be indifferent to the way their actions shape public perception of, and the demand for, the services the profession provides. The anti-professionals will also assert that mediators seeking the "highest-quality" agreements are sure to short-change one or another party at the table in their efforts to tend to the interests of parties not directly represented; and that this would represent a bias. Again, I think this misconstrues what it would mean for a mediator to urge the participants in a mediation to make a self-conscious effort to maximize the fairness, efficiency, stability, and wisdom of any agreements they generate. As a profession, mediation should stand for something. Its practitioners should be willing to stand up and say that their job is to assist the parties in any dispute resolution effort in generating "the greatest good possible for the greatest number of stakeholders."

Notes

1. For more on strategies for evaluating mediation efforts, see Innes (1999).

2. For a more extended analysis of these criteria, see Susskind and Cruikshank (1987).

3. For an extended discussion of "activist mediation," see Forester and Stiftel (1989).

References

Forester, J., and Stitzel, D. "Beyond Neutrality: The Possibilities of Activist Mediation in Public Sector Conflicts." *Negotiation Journal, 5* (3), July 1989.

Innes, J. E. "Evaluating Consensus Building." In L. Susskind, S. McKearnan, and J. Thomas-Larmer (eds.), *The Consensus Building Handbook.* Thousand Oaks, Calif.: Sage, 1999.

Susskind, L., and Cruikshank, J. *Breaking the Impasse: Consensual Approaches to Resolving Public Disputes.* New York: Basic Books, 1987.

Susskind, L., and Field, P. *Dealing with an Angry Public.* New York: Free Press, 1996.

BIBLIOGRAPHY

Aaron, D. "Note: Ethics, Law Enforcement, and Fair Dealing: A Prosecutor's Duty to Disclose Nonevidentiary Information." *Fordham Law Review,* 1999, *67,* 3005.

Albin, C. "The Role of Fairness in Negotiation." *Negotiation Journal,* 1993, *9,* 223–244.

Anderson, D. E., Ansfield, M. E., and DePaulo, B. M. "Love's Best Habit: Deception in the Context of Relationships." In P. Philippot, R. S. Feldman, and E. J. Coats (eds.), *The Social Context of Nonverbal Behavior.* Cambridge: Cambridge University Press, 1999.

Anton, R. J. "Drawing the Line: An Exploratory Test of Ethical Behavior in Negotiations." *International Journal of Conflict Management,* 1990, *1,* 265–280.

Applbaum, A. I. "Professional Detachment: The Executioner of Paris." In *Ethics for Adversaries: The Morality of Roles in Public and Professional Life.* Princeton, N.J.: Princeton University Press, 1999.

Avruch, K. "Culture and Negotiation Pedagogy." *Negotiation Journal,* 2000, *16* (4), 339–346.

Axelrod, R. *The Evolution of Cooperation.* New York: Basic Books, 1984.

Bazerman, M., and Neale, M. *Negotiating Rationally.* New York: Free Press, 1993.

Bazerman, M. H., and Neale, M. A. "The Role of Fairness Considerations and Relationships in a Judgment Perspective of Negotiation." In K. J. Arrow, L. Ross, A. Tversky, and R. Wilson, *Barriers to Conflict Resolution.* New York: Norton, 1995.

Bell, D. A. *Ethical Ambition: Living a Life of Meaning and Worth.* New York: Blooms-bury, 2002.

Bellman, H. S. "Some Reflections on the Practice of Mediation." *Negotiation Journal* 1998, *14,* 205–210.

Bernard, P., and Garth, B. (eds.). *Dispute Resolution Ethics: A Comprehensive Guide.* Washington, D.C.: American Bar Association, 2002.

Blount, S. "Whoever Said That Markets Were Fair?" *Negotiation Journal,* 2000, *16,* 237–252.

Bok, S. *Lying: Moral Choices in Public and Private Life.* New York: Pantheon Books, 1978.

Boskey, J. B. "The Proper Role of the Mediator: Rational Assessment, Not Pressure." *Negotiation Journal,* 1994, *10,* 367.

Bowling, D., and Hoffman, D. "Bringing Peace into the Room: The Personal Qualities of the Mediator and Their Impact on the Mediation." *Negotiation Journal,* 2000, *16,* 5.

Brazil, W. "Protecting the Confidentiality of Settlement Negotiations." *Hastings Law Journal,* 1998, *39,* 955.

Burns, R. P. "Some Ethical Issues Surrounding Mediation." *Fordham Law Review,* 2001, *70,* 691.

Burr, A. M. "Ethics in Negotiation: Does Getting to Yes Require Candor?" *Dispute Resolution Journal,* 2001, *56,* 8–15.

Carr, A. Z. "Is Business Bluffing Ethical?" *Harvard Business Review,* Jan.–Feb. 1968.

Carson, T. L., Wokutch, R. E., and Murrmann, K. F. "Bluffing in Labor Negotiations: Legal and Ethical Issues." *Journal of Business Ethics,* 1982, *1,* 13.

Cialdini, R. B. "Interpersonal Influence: Being Ethical and Effective." In S. Oskamp and S. Spacapan (eds.), *Interpersonal Processes: The Claremont Symposium on Applied Social Psychology.* Thousand Oaks, Calif.: Sage, 1986.

Cohen, J. R. "The Ethics of Respect in Negotiation." *Negotiation Journal,* 2002, *18,* 115–119.

Condlin, R. "Cases on Both Sides: Patterns of Argument in Legal Dispute Negotiations." *Maryland Law Review,* 1986, *44,* 65–136.

Condlin, R. "Bargaining in the Dark: The Normative Incoherence of Lawyer Dispute Bargaining Role." *Maryland Law Review,* 1992, *51,* 1–104.

Costello, E. J. "ADR: Virtue or Vice." *Dispute Resolution Journal,* 1999, *54,* 62–70.

Crampton, P. C., and Dees, J. G. "Promoting Honesty in Negotiation: An Exercise in Practical Ethics." *Business Ethics Quarterly,* 1993, *3,* 359–394.

Craver, C. "Negotiation Ethics: How to Be Deceptive Without Being Dishonest/How to Be Assertive Without Being Offensive." *South Texas Law Review,* 1997, *38,* 713–734.

Davis, A. M. "An Interview with Mary Parker Follet." *Negotiation Journal,* 1989, *July,* 223–235.

Dees, G. J., and Cramton, P. C. "Shrewd Bargaining on the Moral Frontier: Toward a Theory of Morality in Practice." *Business Ethics Quarterly,* 1991, *1,* 135–167.

Dees, J. G., and Cramton, P. C. "Deception and Mutual Trust: A Reply to Strudler." *Business Ethics Quarterly,* 1995, *5,* 823–832.

DeMott, D. "Do You Have the Right to Remain Silent? Duties of Disclosure in Business Transactions." *Delaware Journal of Corporate Law,* 1994, 19, 65.

DePaulo, B. M., and others. "Lying in Everyday Life." *Journal of Personality and Social Psychology,* 1996, *70,* 979–995.

DePaulo, P. J., and DePaulo, B. M. "Can Deception by Salespersons and Customers Be Detected Through Nonverbal Behavioral Cues?" *Journal of Applied Social Psychology,* 1989, *19,* 1552–1577.

Dukes, F. "Public Conflict Resolution: A Transformative Approach." *Negotiation Journal,* 1993, *9,* 45–57.

Faure, G. O. "Negotiating in the Orient: Encounters in the Peshawar Bazaar, Pakistan." *Negotiation Journal,* 1991, *7,* 279–290.

Fisher, R. "Comment." *Journal of Legal Education,* 1984, *120.*

Fisher, R. "A Code of Negotiation Practices for Lawyers." *Negotiation Journal,* 1985, *1,* 105–110.

Fisher, R. "'Quick-Fix' Solutions Are Not the Answer." *Negotiation Journal,* 1992, *8,* 15.

Frank, J. D. "Hard Thoughts on the Gulf War." *Negotiation Journal,* 1992, *8,* 11–14.

Frank, R. H., Thomas Gilovich, T., and Regan, D. T. "Does Studying Economics Inhibit Cooperation?" *Journal of Economic Perspectives,* 1993, *7,* 159–171.

Frankel, T. "Regulation and Investors' Trust in the Securities Markets." *Brooklyn Law Review,* 2002, *68,* 439–448.

French, W., Hasslein, C., and van Es, R. "Constructivist Negotiation Ethics." *Journal of Business Ethics,* 2002, *39,* 83–90.

Freund, J. *Smart Negotiating: How to Make Good Deals in the Real World.* New York: Simon & Schuster, 1992.

Friedman, R. A., and Shapiro, D. L. "Deception and Mutual Gains Bargaining: Are They Mutually Exclusive?" *Negotiation Journal,* 1995, *11,* 243–253.

Gadlin, H. "Careful Maneuvers: Mediating Sexual Harassment." *Negotiation Journal,* 1991, *7,* 139–153.

Gadlin, H. "Conflict Resolution, Cultural Differences, and the Culture of Racism." *Negotiation Journal,* 1994, *10,* 33–47.

Gadlin, H., and Pino, E. W. "Neutrality: A Guide for the Organizational Ombudsperson." *Negotiation Journal,* 1997, *13,* 17–37.

Gibson, K., Thompson, L., and Bazerman, M. H. "Shortcomings of Neutrality in Mediation: Solutions Based on Rationality." *Negotiation Journal,* 1996, *2,* 69–80.

Guernsey, T. F. " Truthfulness in Negotiation." *University of Richmond Law Review,* 1982, *17,* 99–127.

Hartwell, S. "Understanding and Dealing with Deception in Legal Negotiation." *Ohio State Journal of Dispute Resolution,* 1991, *6,* 171–200.

Hazard, G. "The Lawyer's Obligation to Be Trustworthy When Dealing with Opposing Parties." *South Carolina Law Review,* 1981, *33,* 181–196.

Honeyman, C. "Bias and Mediators' Ethics." *Negotiation Journal,* 1986, *2,* 175–178.

Honeyman, C. "Two Out of Three." *Negotiation Journal,* 1995, *11,* 5–10.

Joy, P. A. "Making Ethics Opinions Meaningful: Toward More Effective Regulation of Lawyers' Conduct." *Georgetown Journal of Legal Ethics,* 2002, *15,* 313–396.

Kim, S. H., and Smith, R. H. "Revenge and Conflict Escalation." *Negotiation Journal,* 1993, *9,* 37–43.

Kolb, D. M., and Coolidge, G. G. "Her Place at the Table: A Consideration of Gender Issues in Negotiation." In J. W. Breslin and J. Z. Rubin (eds.), *Negotiation Theory and Practice.* Cambridge, Mass.: PON Books, 1991.

Kronzon, S., and Darley, J. "Is This Tactic Ethical? Biased Judgments of Ethics in Negotiation." *Basic and Applied Social Psychology,* 1999, *21,* 49–60.

Langevoort, D. "Half-Truths: Protecting Mistaken Inferences by Investors and Others." *Stanford Law Review,* 1999, *52,* 88–125.

Lax, D. A., and Sebenius, J. K. "Three Ethical Issues in Negotiation." *Negotiation Journal,* 1986, *2,* 363–370.

Lewicki, R. J., and Robinson, R. J. "Ethical and Unethical Bargaining Tactics: An Empirical Study." *Journal of Business Ethics,* 1998, *17,* 665–682.

Liebman, C. B. "Mediation as Parallel Seminars: Lessons from the Student Takeover of Columbia University's Hamilton Hall." *Negotiation Journal,* 2000, *16,* 157–181.

Loder, R. E. "Moral Truthseeking and the Virtuous Negotiator." *Georgetown Journal of Legal Ethics,* 1994, *8,* 45–102.

Lowenthal, G. "A General Theory of Negotiation: Process, Strategy and Behavior." *University of Kansas Law Review,* 1982, *31,* 69–114.

Lowenthal, G. "The Bar's Failure to Require Truthful Bargaining by Lawyers." *Georgetown Journal of Legal Ethics,* 1988, 411–447.

Luban, D. "Settlements and the Erosion of the Public Realm." *Georgetown Law Journal,* 1995, *83,* 2619–2662.

Lubet, S. "Notes on the Bedouin Horse Trade or 'Why Won't the Market Clear, Daddy?'" *Texas Law Review,* 1996, *74,* 1039–1057.

Marriott, H. E. "'Deviations' in an Intercultural Business Negotiation." In A. Firth (ed.), *The Discourse of Negotiation: Studies of Language in the Workplace.* New York: Pergamon Press, 1995.

Matz, D. E. "Mediator Pressure and Party Autonomy: Are They Consistent with Each Other?" *Negotiation Journal,* 1994, *10,* 359–365.

McEwen, C. A., and Milburn, T. W. "Explaining a Paradox of Mediation." *Negotiation Journal,* 1993, *9,* 23–36.

Meltsner, M. "The Jagged Line Between Mediation and Couples Therapy." *Negotiation Journal*, 1993, *9*, 261–269.

Meltsner, M., and Schrag, P. "Negotiating Tactics for Legal Services Lawyers." *Clearinghouse Review*, 1973, *7*, 259–262.

Meltsner, M., and Schrag, P. *Public Interest Advocacy: Materials for Clinical Legal Education.* New York: Little, Brown, 1974.

Menkel-Meadow, C. "Public Access to Private Settlements." *Alternatives*, 1993, *116*, 85.

Menkel-Meadow, C. "Whose Dispute Is It Anyway? A Philosophical and Democratic Defense of Settlement (in Some Cases)." *Georgetown Law Journal*, 1995, *83*, 2663–2696.

Menkel-Meadow, C. "Ethics Issues in Arbitration and Related Dispute Resolution Processes: What's Happening and What's Not." *University of Miami Law Review*, 2002, *56*, 949.

Menkel-Meadow, C. "Ethics, Morality, and Professional Responsibility in Negotiation." In P. Bernard and B. Garth (eds.), *Dispute Resolution Ethics: A Comprehensive Guide.* Washington, D.C.: ABA Press, 2002.

Menkel-Meadow, C. "The Lawyer as Consensus Builder: Ethics for a New Practice." *Tennessee Law Review*, 2002, *70*, 63–119.

Mnookin, R. H., Peppet, S. R., and Tulumello, A. S. *Beyond Winning,* Cambridge, Mass.: Belknap Press of Harvard University Press, 2000.

Mnookin R. and Susskind L. *Negotiating on Behalf of Others: Advice to Lawyers, Business Executives, Sports Agents, Diplomats, Politicians, and Everybody Else.* Thousand Oaks, Calif.: Sage, 1999.

Moldoveanu, M. C., and Stevenson, H. H. "Ethical Universals in Practice: An Analysis of Five Principles." *Journal of Socio-Economics*, 1998, *27*, 721–752.

Murray, J. S. "Negotiating United States Policy to Counter Terrorism." *Negotiation Journal*, 1990, *6*, 15–22.

Norton, E. H. "Bargaining and the Ethics of Process." *NYU Law Review, 1989, 64,* 494–539.

O'Connor, K., and Carnevale, P. "A Nasty but Effective Negotiation Strategy: Misrepresentation of Common-Value Issue." *Personality and Social Psychology Bulletin*, 1997, *23*, 504–515.

Pepper, S. "The Lawyer's Amoral Ethical Role: A Defense, a Problem, and Some Possibilities." *American Bar Foundation Research Journal*, 1986, *4*, 613–635.

Peppet, S. R. "Can Saints Negotiate? A Brief Introduction to the Problems of Perfect Ethics in Bargaining." *Harvard Negotiation Law Review*, 2002, *7*, 83–96.

Perschbacher, R. "Regulating Lawyers' Negotiations." *Arizona Law Review*, 1985, *27*, 75–138.

Peters, D. "The Uses of Lies in Negotiation." *Ohio State Law Journal*, 1987, *48*, 1.

Provis, C. "Ethics, Deception, and Labor Negotiation." *Journal of Business Ethics*, 2000, *28*, 145–158.

Raiffa, H. "Ethical and Moral Issues." In *The Art and Science of Negotiation.* Cambridge, Mass.: Belknap Press of Harvard University Press, 1982.

Raiffa, H. *Lectures on Negotiation Analysis: Presentation Masters.* Cambridge, Mass.: PON Books, 1996.

Raiffa, H., Richardson, J., and Metcalfe, D. *Negotiation Analysis: The Science and Art of Collaborative Decision Making.* Cambridge, Mass.: Belknap Press of Harvard University Press, 2002.

Regan, M. *Bankrupt in Milwaukee: The Story of a Wall Street Lawyer's Fall.* Ann Arbor: University of Michigan Press, 2004.

Reitz, H. J., Wall, J. A., Jr., and Love, M. S. "Ethics in Negotiation: Oil and Water or Good Lubrication?" *Business Horizons,* May–June 1998, 230–244.

Rose, C. "Trust in the Mirror of Betrayal." *Boston University Law Review,* 1995, *75,* 531–558.

Rosenberger, P. "Laissez-'Fair': An Argument for the Status Quo Ethical Constraints on Lawyers as Negotiators." *Ohio State Journal on Dispute Resolution,* 1998, *13,* 611.

Ross, L., and Stillinger, C. "Barriers to Conflict Resolution." *Negotiation Journal,* 1991, Oct., 389–404.

Rubin, A. "A Causerie on Lawyer's Ethics in Negotiation." *Louisiana Law Review,* 1975, *35,* 577–593.

Salem, P. E. "In Theory: A Critique of Western Conflict Resolution from a Non-Western Perspective." *Negotiation Journal,* 1994, *9,* 361.

Schoeny, M., and Warfield, W. "Reconnecting Systems Maintenance with Social Justice: A Critical Role for Conflict Resolution." *Negotiation Journal,* 2000, *16,* 253–268.

Schwartz, M. "The Professionalism and Accountability of Lawyers." *California Law Review,* 1978, *66,* 669–697.

Schweitzer, M. E., and Croson, R. "Curtailing Deception: The Impact of Direct Questions on Lies and Omissions." *International Journal of Conflict Management,* 1999, *10,* 225–248.

Sebenius, J. K. "On 'Offers That Can't Be Refused.'" *Negotiation Journal,* 1992, *8,* 49–57.

Shah-Kazemi, S. N. "Cross-Cultural Mediation: A Critical View of the Dynamics of Culture in Family Disputes." *International Journal of Law, Policy, and the Family,* 2000, *14,* 302–325.

Shapiro, D. L., and Bies, R. I. "Threats, Bluffs, and Disclaimers in Negotiations." *Organizational Behavior and Human Behavior Processes,* 1994, *60,* 14–35.

Shapiro, D. L., Sheppard, B. H., and Cheraskin, L. "Business on a Handshake." *Negotiation Journal,* 1992, *8,* 365–377.

Shell, G. R. "Chapter 11: Bargaining with the Devil Without Losing Your Soul: Ethics in Negotiation." *In Bargaining for Advantage.* New York: Penguin Books, 2000.

Smith, W. P. "Effectiveness of the Biased Mediator." *Negotiation Journal,* 1985, *1,* 363–372.

Spector, B. I. "Deciding to Negotiate with Villains." *Negotiation Journal,* 1999, *15,* 43–59.

Stanley, R. C. "A Professional Model of Ethics." *Loyola Law Review,* 2001, *47,* 773–796.

Steele, W. "Deceptive Negotiating and High Toned Morality." *Vanderbilt Law Review,* 1986, *39,* 1387–1404.

Stewart, T. A. "Whom Can You Trust? It's Not So Easy to Tell." *Fortune,* June 12, 2000.

Strudler, A. "On the Ethics of Deception in Negotiation." *Business Ethics Quarterly,* 1995, *5,* 805–822.

Strudler, A. "Moral Complexity in the Law of Non-Disclosure." *UCLA Law Review,* 1997, *45,* 337.

Susskind, L. E. "Confessions of a Public Dispute Mediator." *Negotiation Journal,* 2000, *16,* 129–132.

Tenbrunsel, A. E. "Misrepresentation and Expectations of Misrepresentation in an Ethical Dilemma: The Role of Incentives and Temptation." *Academy of Management Journal,* 1998, *41,* 330–339.

Touval, S. "The Context of Mediation." *Negotiation Journal,* 1985, *1,* 373–378.

Touval, S. "Ethical Dilemmas in International Mediation." *Negotiation Journal,* 1995, *11,* 333–337.

Ury, W. L. "Conflict Resolution Among the Bushmen: Lessons in Dispute Systems Design." *Negotiation Journal,* 1995, *11,* 379–389.

Volkema, R. "Ethicality in Negotiations: An Analysis of Perceptual Similarities and Differences Between Brazil and the United States." *Journal of Business Research,* 1999, *45,* 59–67.

Volkema, R. J., and Fleury, M.T.L. "Alternative Negotiating Conditions and the Choice of Negotiation Tactics: A Cross-Cultural Comparison." *Journal of Business Ethics,* 2002, *36,* 381–398.

Watkins, M., and Winters, K. "Interveners with Interests and Power." *Negotiation Journal,* 1997, *13,* 119–142.

Weiss, S. "Negotiating with Romans—Part 1." *Sloan Management Review,* 1994, *35,* 51–61.

Weiss, S. "Negotiating with Romans—Part 2." *Sloan Management Review,* 1994, *35,* 85–99.

Wendel, W. B. "Public Values and Professional Responsibility." *Notre Dame Law Review,* 1999, *75,* 1–123.

Wetlaufer, G. "The Ethics of Lying in Negotiation." *Iowa Law Review,* 1990, *75,* 1219.

Wetlaufer, G. "The Limits of Integrative Bargaining." *Georgetown Law Journal,* 1996, *85,* 369.

White, J. J. "Machiavelli and the Bar: Ethical Limitations on Lying in Negotiations." *American Bar Foundation Research Journal,* 1980, *4,* 926–938.

White, J. J. "The Pros and Cons of Getting to Yes." *Journal of Legal Education,* 1984, *34,* 115–124.

Wokutch, R. E., and Carson, T. L. "The Ethics and Profitability of Bluffing in Business." *Westminster Institute Review,* 1981, *1.*

THE CONTRIBUTORS

Arthur Isak Applbaum is Professor of Ethics and Public Policy at the Kennedy School of Government, Harvard University.

Sissela Bok is an Annenberg Visiting Fellow and a Distinguished Fellow at the Harvard Center for Population and Development Studies.

Wayne D. Brazil is U.S. Magistrate Judge in the U.S. District Court for the Northern District of California.

Albert Z. Carr (deceased) was Assistant to the Chairman of the War Production Board during World War II and later served on the White House staff and as a Special Consultant to President Truman.

Jonathan R. Cohen is Assistant Professor of Law at Levin College of Law, University of Florida.

Peter C. Cramton is Professor of Economics at the University of Maryland.

Rachel Croson is Associate Professor of Operations and Management at the Wharton School, University of Pennsylvania.

J. Gregory Dees is Miriam and Peter Haas Centennial Professor in Public Service, School of Business, Stanford University.

Roger Fisher is the Samuel Williston Professor of Law (Emeritus), Harvard Law School.

Robert H. Frank is Henrietta Johnson Louis Professor of Management, Johnson School, Cornell University.

James C. Freund is a former partner (now retired) at Skadden, Arps, Slate, Meagher, and Flom in New York City.

Thomas Gilovich is a Professor of Psychology at Cornell University.

Geoffrey C. Hazard, Jr. is Trustee Professor of Law at the University of Pennsylvania Law School.

Deborah M. Kolb is Professor of Management at the Simmons School of Management.

Donald C. Langevoort is Thomas Aquinas Reynolds Professor of Law, Georgetown University Law Center.

David A. Lax is a principal with Lax-Sebenius, LLC.

Roy J. Lewicki is Dean's Distinguished Teaching Professor and Professor of Management and Human Resources at Fischer College of Business, Ohio State University.

David Luban is Frederick J. Haas Professor of Law and Philosophy, Georgetown University Law Center.

Michael Meltsner is Visiting Professor of Law at Harvard Law School.

Carrie Menkel-Meadow is Professor of Law and Director of the Georgetown-Hewlett Program on Conflict Resolution and Legal Problem Solving at Georgetown University Law Center.

Eleanor Holmes Norton is the Washington, D.C., delegate to the U.S. Congress and Professor of Law at Georgetown University Law Center.

Scott R. Peppet is Associate Professor of Law, School of Law, University of Colorado.

Howard Raiffa is the Frank P. Ramsey Professor (Emeritus) of Managerial Economics at Harvard University.

Dennis T. Regan is a Professor of Psychology at Cornell University.

Robert J. Robinson is Barry and Virginia Weinman Distinguished Professor of Entrepreneurship and E-Business, College of Business, University of Hawaii.

Alvin B. Rubin (deceased) was formerly U.S. Circuit Court for the Fifth Circuit Judge.

Philip Schrag is Professor of Law at Georgetown University Law Center.

Murray L. Schwartz is David G. Price and Dalles P. Price Professor of Law Emeritus, University of California, Los Angeles.

Maurice E. Schweitzer is an Assistant Professor of Operations and Information Management at the Wharton School, University of Pennsylvania.

James K. Sebenius is the Gordon Donaldson Professor of Business Administration at the Harvard Business School.

G. Richard Shell is Thomas Gerrity Professor of Legal Studies and Management at the Wharton School, University of Pennsylvania.

Alan Strudler is an Associate Professor of Legal Studies and the Director of the Wharton Ethics Program at the Wharton School, University of Pennsylvania.

Lawrence Susskind is Ford Professor of Urban and Environmental Planning at the Massachusetts Institute of Technology.

Gerald B. Wetlaufer is Professor of Law at the College of Law, University of Iowa.

Michael Wheeler is the Class of 1952 Professor of Management Practice at the Harvard Business School.

James J. White is Robert A. Sullivan Professor of Law, University of Michigan Law School.

Judith Williams is a principal in The Shadow Negotiation, LLP.

NAME INDEX

SUBJECT INDEX

A

ABA Code of negotiation practices for lawyers: I: roles, 25; benefits of using, 23; II: goals, 25–26; III: good practices—general guidelines, 26–27; III: good practices—in pursuit of good outcome, 27–29; memo to new clients on negotiation approach, 24–25. *See also* Lawyers

ABA Code of Professional Responsibility: adoption of, 351; on advancement of client's interest, 24; comparing accountability of nonlawyer representative to, 341–343; contents/rules mandated by, 352–353; on disclosures by lawyer, 168; on fairness to other participants, 170; on false statements by lawyer, 168; on lawyer response to client misrepresentation, 169, 336; NY State Bar Association's addition to, 348n.17; proposed Rule 4.1(a) on client confidences, 169; regarding confidence and attorney-client privilege, 347n.15; "unlawful" as defined in, 346n.5. *See also* Legal profession

ABA Committee on Ethics, 357

ABA Model Rules of Professional Conduct: considering five cases under, 95–98; in context of truth and candor norms, 94–95; described, 61; introduction to, 102n.2; on lawyer's behavior during negotiations, 91–92; regarding mandatory disclosure, 98–101; regarding rules of representations, 420n.5; truth as defined by, 93–94. *See also* Ethical behavior

Accountability: comparing ABA Code of Professional Responsibility to nonadvocate lawyer, 341–343; of nonadvocate lawyer, 341–345

Adjudication: class action lawsuits, 493–494; comparing settlement to public good of, 488–490, 499–500; intrinsic arguments on public values elaborated by, 491–500; law reconsidered through, 498–500; normative value of, 487–488; problem-solving conception of, 494–496; public-life conception of, 495–496. *See also* Settlements

"Adjudication as a Private Good" (Landes and Posner), 488

ADR (alternative dispute resolution), 489

Adversarial bargaining, 444–445

Advocate's principles, 331–332

Affirmative disclosure duties: half-truth doctrine and, 402–403; requirements for, 295n.15

"Against Settlement" (Fiss), 486